RACE PROFILES
JUMPS 2010-2011

Dr Peter May

Raceform

Published in 2010 by Raceform
Compton, Newbury, Berkshire, RG20 6NL

Copyright © Peter May 2010

The right of Peter May to be identified as the author of this work has been asserted by him in accordance with the Copyright, Designs and Patents Act 1988.

All rights reserved. No part of this publication may be reproduced, stored in a retrieval system, or transmitted in any form or by any means, electronic, mechanical, photocopying, recording, or otherwise, without the prior written permission of the publishers.

A catalogue record for this book is available from the British Library.

ISBN 978-1-906820-54-1

Designed by Fiona Pike

Printed in the UK by Thomson Litho, Glasgow

Contents

Introduction 4

Race Profiles

Hurdle Races 7
- 3yo Hurdle Races — 7
- 4yo Hurdle Races — 13
- Novices' Hurdle Races (class 1..3) — 20
- Novices' Hurdle Races (class 4..6) — 29
- Maiden Hurdle Races — 38
- Claiming Hurdle Races — 47
- Selling Hurdle Races — 56
- Amateur Hurdle Races — 65
- Conditions Hurdle Races (class 1..3) — 74
- Conditions Hurdle Races (class 4..6) — 83
- Novices' Handicap Hurdle Races — 92
- Selling Handicap Hurdle Races — 101
- Handicap Hurdle Races (class 1..3) — 109
- Handicap Hurdle Races (class 4..6) — 118

Chases
- Novices' Chases (class 1..3) — 127
- Novices' Chases (class 4..6) — 136
- Maiden Chases — 145
- Claiming Chases — 154
- Amateur Chases — 163
- Conditions Chases (class 1..3) — 171
- Conditions Chases (class 4..6) — 180
- Novices' Handicap Chases — 189
- Selling Handicap Chases — 198
- Handicap Chases (class 1..3) — 207
- Handicap Chases (class 4..6) — 216
- Hunter Chases — 225

NH Flat Races 234

For each race classification the profile for all races is supplemented by profiles over the main distances, field size and days off the track.

Race Profiles

Introduction

The book is essentially a reference guide allowing readers to identify the most likely winner of each race based on the historical profiles of similar events.

Race Profiling

Unlike Form Study, race profiling does not attempt to quantify the ability of a horse. Instead it extracts the key characteristics of the race and uses these features to generate a profile of the most likely race winner. These profiles can have few or many attributes depending on the significance of the features and the depth of data supporting each one. Some races do not lend themselves to profiling and it is difficult to find a reliable profile for the likely winner. This may be due to a lack of historical data, on which to base the profile, or simply that the race is won by a wide range of horses without favouring a specific type. However many races have very exact profiles and are won on a regular basis by horses that exhibit a specific set of qualities.

The logic underlying the Race Profiling method concerns the dominance of horses with certain characteristics in specific races. Often races are won by a particular type of horse, with others having only a minimal chance. For instance, age is often a key factor. Jumps races are often won by the younger horses, however there are cases where a very narrow age range can be associated with a race. Under such circumstances the horses lying outside this range can be considered unlikely winners, and if one or more happens to be a short price, then it may be possible to return a good profit by not only backing the horses with positive traits, but by laying those animals possessing negative profiles.

Specific Race Profiles

Essentially there are two types of profile: a Specific Race Profile and a General Race Profile. The former is most commonly applied to the main races of the year in the form of five year- or ten year- trends. In order to generate a specific race profile the credentials of the recent winners of the race are examined and the key trends extracted.

Unfortunately this sample only constitutes a small proportion of the ever expanding pool of races run each season and an alternative approach is required for the other events. One Class 5 maiden hurdle race, for instance, is very much like another, so extracting the details for a particular maiden hurdle race run at Wincanton in November may not be that informative or reliable. However given the degree of similarity between these less prominent events it is possible to analyse all similar races to generate a profile of the likely winner based on a large sample of events. For instance when considering a 3 mile handicap hurdle race at Newbury it may be helpful to find the profile of the most likely winner of all long distance handicap hurdle races. And given the amount of data available, this could be further restricted to a similar field size, the same race class, or to races run on a similar surface or a similar track. Consequently a more general approach, as opposed to the specific ten-year trends, is more applicable to the majority of races run each season.

General Race Profiles

General race profiles, as the title suggests, are based on a wide range of races, as opposed to a single event. It is possible to create a two-mile handicap chase profile, for instance, based on all such races run in a specific country. Whilst this is a very general profile it can be further restricted by the main discriminating factors such as going, time of year, race class and track. Using these additional inputs the profile can be structured to provide the information required based on the largest possible sample of races. Consequently it becomes more robust than a single race profile and hence more reliable.

The main advantage of general race profiles is their applicability. Few races can be profiled in isolation, whereas general profiles will apply to the remaining majority. Furthermore, changing trends are more likely to be apparent from an analysis of several races as opposed to a single event. For instance, increased competitiveness in a specific sector of racing may reduce the proportion of events won by the favourite. When analysing a single race this may become obvious after a reasonable time period and number of races, but in a general profile it will be visible sooner, allowing the bettor to take advantage of the changing pattern and structure his/her bets accordingly.

This text presents a set of these general race profiles for all of the jump race classifications run in Great Britain and can be used to establish the key qualities a horse needs to possess in order to win a particular event.

Notation

In the main profile tables five columns of data are presented. The first, headed by "Prop" shows the proportion of races won by the horses in each of the categories; the next two columns show the number of winners and the number of runners. Column four, Wins%, is the overall win rate (winners divided by runners) expressed as a percentage. The "£" column shows the average profit at starting price to a level £1 stake on all runners in that category. For the *Other Factors* and *Trainer Analysis* sections just the number of wins, runners and average profit are displayed.

To qualify as a beaten favourite the horse had to be the sole market leader on its latest run in a jumps race; to be top-rated by the BHA the horse has to be clear of the other runners in the race based on this rating, joint-top-rated runners do not qualify. Class movement is determined by race class. So a horse moving from a class 4 race to a class 3 race would be considered, for this analysis, to be moving up in class. The *seven day winners* classification groups together all horses which won their latest jumps race within the last seven days.

In order to generate the profiles, only races from Great Britain run during the last five years have been used, however previous race performances in Ireland are included. Novice's hurdle races exclude races restricted to just three-year-olds and four-year-olds; Beginners' chases are included in the Novices' chase group.

Introduction

Race Classifications

Included in Race Title	Equivalent Race Profile Classification
3yo Hurdle	3yo Hurdle Races
4yo Hurdle	4yo Hurdle Races
Novices' Hurdle	Novices' Hurdle Races
Maiden Hurdle	Maiden Hurdle Races
Claiming Hurdle	Claiming Hurdle Races
Novices' Claiming Hurdle	Claiming Hurdle Races
Selling Hurdle	Selling Hurdle Races
Amateur Selling Hurdle	Selling Hurdle Races
Novices' Selling Hurdle	Selling Hurdle Races
Amateur Hurdle	Amateur Hurdle Races
Conditions Hurdle	Conditions Hurdle Races
Intermediate Conditions Hurdle	Conditions Hurdle Races
Handicap Hurdle	Handicap Hurdle Races
Intermediate Handicap Hurdle	Handicap Hurdle Races
Amateur Handicap Hurdle	Handicap Hurdle Races
Conditional Handicap Hurdle	Handicap Hurdle Races
Novices' Handicap Hurdle	Novices' Handicap Hurdle Races
Selling Handicap Hurdle	Selling Handicap Hurdle Races
Novices' Selling Handicap Hurdle	Selling Handicap Hurdle Races
Novices' Chase	Novices' Chase
Beginners' Chas	Novices' Chase
Maiden Chase	Maiden Chase
Claiming Chase	Claiming Chase
Novices' Claiming Chase	Claiming Chase
Amateur Chase	Amateur Chase
Conditions Chase	Conditions Chase
Handicap Chase	Handicap Chase
Amateur Handicap Chase	Handicap Chase
Intermediate Handicap Chase	Handicap Chase
Novices' Handicap Chase	Novices' Handicap Chase
Selling Handicap Chase	Selling Handicap Chase
Hunter Chase	Hunter Chase
Novices' Hunter Chase	Hunter Chase
National Hunt Flat Race	National Hunt Flat Race

3-Y.O Hurdle Races

3-Y.O Hurdle Races

Age	Prop	Win	Runs	Wins%	£
3yo	100%	402	4260	9.4%	-0.34

ANALYSIS BY BHB RATING

Age	Prop	Win	Runs	Wins%	£
150+	0%	0	0	0.0%	0.00
130..149	3%	11	22	50.0%	1.15
120..129	1%	6	47	12.8%	-0.57
110..119	2%	9	66	13.6%	-0.41
100..109	3%	11	73	15.1%	0.06
80..99	1%	4	92	4.3%	-0.80
60..79	0%	1	18	5.6%	4.61
..59	0%	0	2	0.0%	-1.00
Unrated	90%	360	3940	9.1%	-0.37

ANALYSIS BY WEIGHT CARRIED

Age	Prop	Win	Runs	Wins%	£
12-01+	0%	1	1	100.0%	0.40
11-8..12-00	2%	7	24	29.2%	-0.38
11-0..11-07	27%	107	569	18.8%	-0.23
10-8..10-13	54%	216	2338	9.2%	-0.38
10-0..10-07	16%	65	1219	5.3%	-0.40
..9-13	1%	6	109	5.5%	0.44

ANALYSIS BY DAYS SINCE LAST RUN

Age	Prop	Win	Runs	Wins%	£
1..7	5%	20	170	11.8%	-0.08
8..14	14%	58	627	9.3%	-0.49
15..28	27%	108	931	11.6%	-0.09
29..60	14%	57	501	11.4%	-0.20
61..100	3%	11	102	10.8%	-0.44
101+	0%	1	29	3.4%	-0.81
Unraced	37%	147	1900	7.7%	-0.47

ANALYSIS BY TODAY'S STARTING PRICE

Age	Prop	Win	Runs	Wins%	£
Odds On	17%	68	118	57.6%	-0.10
Ev-2/1	24%	96	259	37.1%	-0.03
9/4-4/1	21%	85	418	20.3%	-0.17
9/2-6/1	8%	31	287	10.8%	-0.33
13/2-10/1	15%	60	509	11.8%	0.08
11/1-16/1	9%	38	579	6.6%	-0.05
18/1-33/1	5%	20	750	2.7%	-0.27
40/1+	1%	4	1340	0.3%	-0.81

ANALYSIS BY STARTING PRICE LAST TIME

Age	Prop	Win	Runs	Wins%	£
Odds On	5%	20	69	29.0%	-0.37
Ev-2/1	10%	41	163	25.2%	-0.11
9/4-4/1	13%	54	265	20.4%	0.10
9/2-6/1	6%	25	171	14.6%	-0.27
13/2-10/1	9%	35	297	11.8%	0.01
11/1-16/1	9%	38	342	11.1%	-0.17
18/1-33/1	7%	27	421	6.4%	-0.43
40/1+	4%	15	632	2.4%	-0.42
Unraced	37%	147	1900	7.7%	-0.47

ANALYSIS BY DISTANCE BEATEN LAST TIME

Age	Prop	Win	Runs	Wins%	£
..-10 lgh	5%	22	68	32.4%	-0.22
-10..0	12%	47	217	21.7%	-0.17
0.1..2	8%	33	124	26.6%	0.05
2.1..5	8%	33	152	21.7%	0.03
5.1..10	7%	30	171	17.5%	-0.10
10.1..20	8%	31	337	9.2%	-0.07
20.0..30	4%	16	234	6.8%	-0.35
30.1+	7%	27	733	3.7%	-0.41
Not Compl	4%	16	324	4.9%	-0.32
Unraced	37%	147	1900	7.7%	-0.47

ANALYSIS BY SUCCESS RATE IN LAST 10 RUNS

Age	Prop	Win	Runs	Wins%	£
No Wins	62%	157	1919	8.2%	-0.26
1 Win	29%	75	335	22.4%	-0.22
2 Wins	5%	14	82	17.1%	-0.06
3 Wins	3%	7	15	46.7%	0.75
4 Wins	1%	2	6	33.3%	-0.57
5+ Wins	0%	0	3	0.0%	-1.00

ANALYSIS BY SUCCESS RATE IN LAST 3 RUNS

Age	Prop	Win	Runs	Wins%	£
No Wins	62%	158	1932	8.2%	-0.26
1 Win	30%	76	341	22.3%	-0.20
2 Wins	6%	16	76	21.1%	0.11
3 Wins	2%	5	11	45.5%	-0.24

ANALYSIS BY POSITION LAST TIME

Age	Prop	Win	Runs	Wins%	£
Won	17%	69	285	24.2%	-0.18
2nd or 3rd	27%	109	545	20.0%	-0.01
Unplaced	15%	61	1206	5.1%	-0.34
Fell,BD,UR	2%	9	132	6.8%	-0.17
Pulled Up	1%	5	176	2.8%	-0.47
Ref/RanOut	0%	2	10	20.0%	0.90
CO/SlipUp	0%	0	6	0.0%	-1.00
Unraced	37%	147	1900	7.7%	-0.47

OTHER FACTORS (WINS-RUNS, £)

Course Winner:	11-55	-£0.20
Distance Winner:	52-272	-£0.27
Going Winner:	35-157	-£0.28
Beaten Favourite:	32-128	£0.04
7-Day Winners:	7-15	£0.37
BHA Top Rated:	26-142	£0.37
Absolute Favourites:	148-376	-£0.15

TRAINERS (WINS-RUNS, £)

N A Twiston-Davies 6-37 £0.03; P A Blockley 7-31 £0.01.

Race Profiles

3-Y.O Hurdle Races: 2 to 5 runners

ANALYSIS BY AGE

Age	Prop	Win	Runs	Wins%	£
3yo	100%	19	92	20.7%	0.13

ANALYSIS BY BHB RATING

Age	Prop	Win	Runs	Wins%	£
150+	0%	0	0	0.0%	0.00
130..149	11%	2	2	100.0%	0.46
120..129	5%	1	4	25.0%	-0.70
110..119	5%	1	2	50.0%	3.00
100..109	11%	2	2	100.0%	10.37
80..99	0%	0	0	0.0%	0.00
60..79	0%	0	1	0.0%	-1.00
..59	0%	0	0	0.0%	0.00
Unrated	68%	13	81	16.0%	-0.15

ANALYSIS BY WEIGHT CARRIED

Age	Prop	Win	Runs	Wins%	£
12-01+	0%	0	0	0.0%	0.00
11-8..12-00	5%	1	1	100.0%	0.67
11-0..11-07	53%	10	34	29.4%	0.01
10-8..10-13	32%	6	35	17.1%	-0.14
10-0..10-07	11%	2	22	9.1%	0.73
..9-13	0%	0	0	0.0%	0.00

ANALYSIS BY DAYS SINCE LAST RUN

Age	Prop	Win	Runs	Wins%	£
1..7	0%	0	4	0.0%	-1.00
8..14	16%	3	14	21.4%	-0.19
15..28	58%	11	25	44.0%	2.16
29..60	16%	3	17	17.6%	-0.51
61..100	0%	0	0	0.0%	0.00
101+	0%	0	0	0.0%	0.00
Unraced	11%	2	32	6.3%	-0.83

ANALYSIS BY TODAY'S STARTING PRICE

Age	Prop	Win	Runs	Wins%	£
Odds On	42%	8	14	57.1%	-0.19
Ev-2/1	11%	2	11	18.2%	-0.57
9/4-4/1	11%	2	11	18.2%	-0.32
9/2-6/1	5%	1	7	14.3%	-0.21
13/2-10/1	16%	3	10	30.0%	1.40
11/1-16/1	11%	2	9	22.2%	2.33
18/1-33/1	5%	1	17	5.9%	0.24
40/1+	0%	0	13	0.0%	-1.00

ANALYSIS BY STARTING PRICE LAST TIME

Age	Prop	Win	Runs	Wins%	£
Odds On	11%	2	3	66.7%	0.12
Ev-2/1	16%	3	9	33.3%	-0.56
9/4-4/1	21%	4	9	44.4%	0.60
9/2-6/1	11%	2	4	50.0%	5.25
13/2-10/1	5%	1	7	14.3%	-0.75
11/1-16/1	16%	3	11	27.3%	0.48
18/1-33/1	5%	1	11	9.1%	0.91
40/1+	5%	1	6	16.7%	1.17
Unraced	11%	2	32	6.3%	-0.83

ANALYSIS BY DISTANCE BEATEN LAST TIME

Age	Prop	Win	Runs	Wins%	£
..-10 lgh	16%	3	7	42.9%	-0.23
-10..0	16%	3	9	33.3%	0.79
0.1..2	16%	3	6	50.0%	-0.16
2.1..5	11%	2	5	40.0%	2.20
5.1..10	11%	2	5	40.0%	-0.06
10.1..20	5%	1	5	20.0%	2.40
20.0..30	5%	1	4	25.0%	1.00
30.1+	5%	1	11	9.1%	0.91
Not Compl	5%	1	8	12.5%	-0.31
Unraced	11%	2	32	6.3%	-0.83

ANALYSIS BY SUCCESS RATE IN LAST 10 RUNS

Age	Prop	Win	Runs	Wins%	£
No Wins	35%	6	33	18.2%	0.61
1 Win	59%	10	23	43.5%	0.92
2 Wins	0%	0	3	0.0%	-1.00
3 Wins	0%	0	0	0.0%	0.00
4 Wins	6%	1	1	100.0%	0.25
5+ Wins	0%	0	0	0.0%	0.00

ANALYSIS BY SUCCESS RATE IN LAST 3 RUNS

Age	Prop	Win	Runs	Wins%	£
No Wins	35%	6	35	17.1%	0.52
1 Win	59%	10	22	45.5%	1.01
2 Wins	0%	0	2	0.0%	-1.00
3 Wins	6%	1	1	100.0%	0.25

ANALYSIS BY POSITION LAST TIME

Age	Prop	Win	Runs	Wins%	£
Won	32%	6	16	37.5%	0.34
2nd or 3rd	37%	7	17	41.2%	1.44
Unplaced	16%	3	19	15.8%	0.59
Fell,BD,UR	0%	0	5	0.0%	-1.00
Pulled Up	5%	1	3	33.3%	0.83
Ref/RanOut	0%	0	0	0.0%	0.00
CO/SlipUp	0%	0	0	0.0%	0.00
Unraced	11%	2	32	6.3%	-0.83

OTHER FACTORS (WINS-RUNS, £)

Course Winner:	1-2	£0.38
Distance Winner:	4-13	-£0.46
Going Winner:	2-10	-£0.60
Beaten Favourite:	3-4	£0.13
7-Day Winners:	0-2	-£1.00
BHA Top Rated:	3-3	£2.66
Absolute Favourites:	10-19	-£0.15

3-Y.O Hurdle Races

3-Y.O Hurdle Races: 6 to 10 runners

ANALYSIS BY AGE

Age	Prop	Win	Runs	Wins%	£
3yo	100%	181	1525	11.9%	-0.23

ANALYSIS BY BHB RATING

Age	Prop	Win	Runs	Wins%	£
150+	0%	0	0	0.0%	0.00
130..149	2%	4	11	36.4%	0.53
120..129	2%	3	20	15.0%	-0.71
110..119	2%	3	29	10.3%	-0.57
100..109	2%	4	32	12.5%	0.02
80..99	1%	1	28	3.6%	-0.88
60..79	1%	1	5	20.0%	19.20
..59	0%	0	2	0.0%	-1.00
Unrated	91%	165	1398	11.8%	-0.28

ANALYSIS BY WEIGHT CARRIED

Age	Prop	Win	Runs	Wins%	£
12-01+	1%	1	1	100.0%	0.40
11-8..12-00	2%	3	8	37.5%	-0.26
11-0..11-07	28%	51	259	19.7%	-0.15
10-8..10-13	55%	99	803	12.3%	-0.31
10-0..10-07	13%	23	419	5.5%	-0.35
..9-13	2%	4	35	11.4%	2.73

ANALYSIS BY DAYS SINCE LAST RUN

Age	Prop	Win	Runs	Wins%	£
1..7	5%	9	60	15.0%	0.04
8..14	14%	26	225	11.6%	-0.34
15..28	27%	48	333	14.4%	0.25
29..60	14%	26	198	13.1%	-0.38
61..100	2%	4	32	12.5%	-0.55
101+	0%	0	9	0.0%	-1.00
Unraced	38%	68	668	10.2%	-0.38

ANALYSIS BY TODAY'S STARTING PRICE

Age	Prop	Win	Runs	Wins%	£
Odds On	20%	36	66	54.5%	-0.14
Ev-2/1	28%	50	129	38.8%	0.01
9/4-4/1	22%	40	177	22.6%	-0.07
9/2-6/1	7%	13	123	10.6%	-0.35
13/2-10/1	9%	17	194	8.8%	-0.18
11/1-16/1	8%	14	217	6.5%	-0.07
18/1-33/1	5%	9	260	3.5%	-0.06
40/1+	1%	2	359	0.6%	-0.60

ANALYSIS BY STARTING PRICE LAST TIME

Age	Prop	Win	Runs	Wins%	£
Odds On	4%	8	36	22.2%	-0.49
Ev-2/1	9%	16	70	22.9%	-0.31
9/4-4/1	14%	26	105	24.8%	0.10
9/2-6/1	8%	14	67	20.9%	0.00
13/2-10/1	9%	16	116	13.8%	0.39
11/1-16/1	10%	19	116	16.4%	0.12
18/1-33/1	4%	7	147	4.8%	-0.62
40/1+	4%	7	200	3.5%	-0.15
Unraced	38%	68	668	10.2%	-0.38

ANALYSIS BY DISTANCE BEATEN LAST TIME

Age	Prop	Win	Runs	Wins%	£
..-10 lgh	6%	10	29	34.5%	-0.08
-10..0	12%	22	100	22.0%	-0.18
0.1..2	8%	14	44	31.8%	0.09
2.1..5	9%	17	59	28.8%	0.11
5.1..10	7%	12	63	19.0%	-0.23
10.1..20	5%	9	122	7.4%	-0.40
20.0..30	6%	10	86	11.6%	0.34
30.1+	5%	9	236	3.8%	-0.23
Not Compl	6%	10	118	8.5%	0.04
Unraced	38%	68	668	10.2%	-0.38

ANALYSIS BY SUCCESS RATE IN LAST 10 RUNS

Age	Prop	Win	Runs	Wins%	£
No Wins	60%	68	672	10.1%	-0.12
1 Win	31%	35	130	26.9%	-0.04
2 Wins	6%	7	43	16.3%	0.00
3 Wins	3%	3	6	50.0%	-0.05
4 Wins	0%	0	3	0.0%	-1.00
5+ Wins	0%	0	3	0.0%	-1.00

ANALYSIS BY SUCCESS RATE IN LAST 3 RUNS

Age	Prop	Win	Runs	Wins%	£
No Wins	61%	69	678	10.2%	-0.12
1 Win	30%	34	135	25.2%	-0.10
2 Wins	6%	7	36	19.4%	0.19
3 Wins	3%	3	8	37.5%	-0.29

ANALYSIS BY POSITION LAST TIME

Age	Prop	Win	Runs	Wins%	£
Won	18%	32	129	24.8%	-0.16
2nd or 3rd	28%	50	212	23.6%	0.06
Unplaced	12%	21	398	5.3%	-0.23
Fell,BD,UR	3%	5	46	10.9%	0.26
Pulled Up	2%	3	65	4.6%	-0.29
Ref/RanOut	1%	2	6	33.3%	2.17
CO/SlipUp	0%	0	1	0.0%	-1.00
Unraced	38%	68	668	10.2%	-0.38

OTHER FACTORS (WINS-RUNS, £)

Course Winner:	2-28	-£0.56
Distance Winner:	26-124	-£0.04
Going Winner:	18-69	-£0.32
Beaten Favourite:	13-58	-£0.36
7-Day Winners:	3-5	£1.51
BHA Top Rated:	8-61	£1.01
Absolute Favourites:	72-169	-£0.11

Race Profiles

3-Y.O Hurdle Races: 11 runners or more

ANALYSIS BY AGE

Age	Prop	Win	Runs	Wins%	£
3yo	100%	202	2643	7.6%	-0.43

ANALYSIS BY BHB RATING

Age	Prop	Win	Runs	Wins%	£
150+	0%	0	0	0.0%	0.00
130..149	2%	5	9	55.6%	2.06
120..129	1%	2	23	8.7%	-0.42
110..119	2%	5	35	14.3%	-0.46
100..109	2%	5	39	12.8%	-0.44
80..99	1%	3	64	4.7%	-0.77
60..79	0%	0	12	0.0%	-1.00
..59	0%	0	0	0.0%	0.00
Unrated	90%	182	2461	7.4%	-0.42

ANALYSIS BY WEIGHT CARRIED

Age	Prop	Win	Runs	Wins%	£
12-01+	0%	0	0	0.0%	0.00
11-8..12-00	1%	3	15	20.0%	-0.52
11-0..11-07	23%	46	276	16.7%	-0.33
10-8..10-13	55%	111	1500	7.4%	-0.42
10-0..10-07	20%	40	778	5.1%	-0.46
..9-13	1%	2	74	2.7%	-0.65

ANALYSIS BY DAYS SINCE LAST RUN

Age	Prop	Win	Runs	Wins%	£
1..7	5%	11	106	10.4%	-0.12
8..14	14%	29	388	7.5%	-0.58
15..28	24%	49	573	8.6%	-0.38
29..60	14%	28	286	9.8%	-0.06
61..100	3%	7	70	10.0%	-0.39
101+	0%	1	20	5.0%	-0.72
Unraced	38%	77	1200	6.4%	-0.51

ANALYSIS BY TODAY'S STARTING PRICE

Age	Prop	Win	Runs	Wins%	£
Odds On	12%	24	38	63.2%	0.00
Ev-2/1	22%	44	119	37.0%	-0.01
9/4-4/1	21%	43	230	18.7%	-0.24
9/2-6/1	8%	17	157	10.8%	-0.31
13/2-10/1	20%	40	305	13.1%	0.20
11/1-16/1	11%	22	353	6.2%	-0.10
18/1-33/1	5%	10	473	2.1%	-0.41
40/1+	1%	2	968	0.2%	-0.89

ANALYSIS BY STARTING PRICE LAST TIME

Age	Prop	Win	Runs	Wins%	£
Odds On	5%	10	30	33.3%	-0.28
Ev-2/1	11%	22	84	26.2%	0.11
9/4-4/1	12%	24	151	15.9%	0.07
9/2-6/1	4%	9	100	9.0%	-0.67
13/2-10/1	9%	18	174	10.3%	-0.21
11/1-16/1	8%	16	215	7.4%	-0.35
18/1-33/1	9%	19	263	7.2%	-0.38
40/1+	3%	7	426	1.6%	-0.57
Unraced	38%	77	1200	6.4%	-0.51

ANALYSIS BY DISTANCE BEATEN LAST TIME

Age	Prop	Win	Runs	Wins%	£
..-10 lgh	4%	9	32	28.1%	-0.35
-10..0	11%	22	108	20.4%	-0.23
0.1..2	8%	16	74	21.6%	0.04
2.1..5	7%	14	88	15.9%	-0.15
5.1..10	8%	16	103	15.5%	-0.03
10.1..20	10%	21	210	10.0%	0.07
20.0..30	2%	5	144	3.5%	-0.79
30.1+	8%	17	486	3.5%	-0.53
Not Compl	2%	5	198	2.5%	-0.53
Unraced	38%	77	1200	6.4%	-0.51

ANALYSIS BY SUCCESS RATE IN LAST 10 RUNS

Age	Prop	Win	Runs	Wins%	£
No Wins	66%	83	1214	6.8%	-0.36
1 Win	24%	30	182	16.5%	-0.49
2 Wins	6%	7	36	19.4%	-0.05
3 Wins	3%	4	9	44.4%	1.29
4 Wins	1%	1	2	50.0%	-0.32
5+ Wins	0%	0	0	0.0%	0.00

ANALYSIS BY SUCCESS RATE IN LAST 3 RUNS

Age	Prop	Win	Runs	Wins%	£
No Wins	66%	83	1219	6.8%	-0.36
1 Win	26%	32	184	17.4%	-0.42
2 Wins	7%	9	38	23.7%	0.08
3 Wins	1%	1	2	50.0%	-0.32

ANALYSIS BY POSITION LAST TIME

Age	Prop	Win	Runs	Wins%	£
Won	15%	31	140	22.1%	-0.26
2nd or 3rd	26%	52	316	16.5%	-0.14
Unplaced	18%	37	789	4.7%	-0.42
Fell,BD,UR	2%	4	81	4.9%	-0.36
Pulled Up	0%	1	108	0.9%	-0.62
Ref/RanOut	0%	0	4	0.0%	-1.00
CO/SlipUp	0%	0	5	0.0%	-1.00
Unraced	38%	77	1200	6.4%	-0.51

OTHER FACTORS (WINS-RUNS, £)

Course Winner:	8-25	£0.17
Distance Winner:	22-135	-£0.46
Going Winner:	15-78	-£0.20
Beaten Favourite:	16-66	£0.40
7-Day Winners:	4-8	£0.00
BHA Top Rated:	15-78	-£0.21
Absolute Favourites:	66-188	-£0.18

3-Y.O Hurdle Races

3-Y.O Hurdle Races: up to 7 days off the track

ANALYSIS BY AGE

Age	Prop	Win	Runs	Wins%	£
3yo	100%	167	2070	8.1%	-0.44

ANALYSIS BY BHB RATING

Age	Prop	Win	Runs	Wins%	£
150+	0%	0	0	0.0%	0.00
130..149	1%	1	2	50.0%	2.50
120..129	0%	0	0	0.0%	0.00
110..119	0%	0	4	0.0%	-1.00
100..109	0%	0	4	0.0%	-1.00
80..99	0%	0	1	0.0%	-1.00
60..79	0%	0	1	0.0%	-1.00
..59	0%	0	1	0.0%	-1.00
Unrated	99%	166	2057	8.1%	-0.44

ANALYSIS BY WEIGHT CARRIED

Age	Prop	Win	Runs	Wins%	£
12-01+	0%	0	0	0.0%	0.00
11-8..12-00	1%	2	4	50.0%	-0.32
11-0..11-07	8%	13	137	9.5%	-0.53
10-8..10-13	73%	122	1240	9.8%	-0.39
10-0..10-07	16%	26	637	4.1%	-0.54
..9-13	2%	4	52	7.7%	-0.30

ANALYSIS BY DAYS SINCE LAST RUN

Age	Prop	Win	Runs	Wins%	£
1..7	12%	20	170	11.8%	-0.08
8..14	0%	0	0	0.0%	0.00
15..28	0%	0	0	0.0%	0.00
29..60	0%	0	0	0.0%	0.00
61..100	0%	0	0	0.0%	0.00
101+	0%	0	0	0.0%	0.00
Unraced	88%	147	1900	7.7%	-0.47

ANALYSIS BY TODAY'S STARTING PRICE

Age	Prop	Win	Runs	Wins%	£
Odds On	14%	23	36	63.9%	-0.02
Ev-2/1	21%	35	101	34.7%	-0.09
9/4-4/1	23%	38	186	20.4%	-0.16
9/2-6/1	10%	16	134	11.9%	-0.25
13/2-10/1	16%	26	243	10.7%	-0.03
11/1-16/1	12%	20	295	6.8%	-0.04
18/1-33/1	5%	8	398	2.0%	-0.46
40/1+	1%	1	677	0.1%	-0.94

ANALYSIS BY STARTING PRICE LAST TIME

Age	Prop	Win	Runs	Wins%	£
Odds On	1%	2	4	50.0%	-0.32
Ev-2/1	1%	2	5	40.0%	1.35
9/4-4/1	2%	4	13	30.8%	-0.09
9/2-6/1	1%	2	8	25.0%	-0.34
13/2-10/1	2%	3	15	20.0%	1.50
11/1-16/1	2%	4	31	12.9%	-0.29
18/1-33/1	2%	3	34	8.8%	0.90
40/1+	0%	0	60	0.0%	-1.00
Unraced	88%	147	1900	7.7%	-0.47

ANALYSIS BY DISTANCE BEATEN LAST TIME

Age	Prop	Win	Runs	Wins%	£
..-10 lgh	2%	3	6	50.0%	1.06
-10..0	2%	4	9	44.4%	-0.08
0.1..2	1%	2	5	40.0%	1.45
2.1..5	2%	3	10	30.0%	0.10
5.1..10	0%	0	4	0.0%	-1.00
10.1..20	1%	2	19	10.5%	-0.61
20.0..30	1%	2	18	11.1%	1.10
30.1+	1%	2	58	3.4%	-0.59
Not Compl	1%	2	41	4.9%	0.05
Unraced	88%	147	1900	7.7%	-0.47

ANALYSIS BY SUCCESS RATE IN LAST 10 RUNS

Age	Prop	Win	Runs	Wins%	£
No Wins	65%	13	148	8.8%	-0.09
1 Win	25%	5	19	26.3%	-0.06
2 Wins	5%	1	2	50.0%	-0.32
3 Wins	0%	0	0	0.0%	0.00
4 Wins	5%	1	1	100.0%	0.36
5+ Wins	0%	0	0	0.0%	0.00

ANALYSIS BY SUCCESS RATE IN LAST 3 RUNS

Age	Prop	Win	Runs	Wins%	£
No Wins	65%	13	149	8.7%	-0.09
1 Win	25%	5	18	27.8%	-0.01
2 Wins	5%	1	2	50.0%	-0.32
3 Wins	5%	1	1	100.0%	0.36

ANALYSIS BY POSITION LAST TIME

Age	Prop	Win	Runs	Wins%	£
Won	4%	7	15	46.7%	0.37
2nd or 3rd	3%	5	18	27.8%	0.23
Unplaced	4%	6	96	6.3%	-0.27
Fell,BD,UR	1%	1	14	7.1%	-0.86
Pulled Up	1%	1	26	3.8%	0.58
Ref/RanOut	0%	0	1	0.0%	-1.00
CO/SlipUp	0%	0	0	0.0%	0.00
Unraced	88%	147	1900	7.7%	-0.47

OTHER FACTORS (WINS-RUNS, £)

Course Winner:	3-6	£1.43
Distance Winner:	5-14	£0.25
Going Winner:	4-9	£0.53
Beaten Favourite:	1-5	-£0.55
7-Day Winners:	7-15	£0.37
BHA Top Rated:	1-8	-£0.13
Absolute Favourites:	51-139	-£0.20

Race Profiles

3-Y.O Hurdle Races: 100+ days off the track

ANALYSIS BY AGE
Age	Prop	Win	Runs	Wins%	£
3yo	100%	1	32	3.1%	-0.83

ANALYSIS BY BHB RATING
Age	Prop	Win	Runs	Wins%	£
150+	0%	0	0	0.0%	0.00
130..149	0%	0	0	0.0%	0.00
120..129	0%	0	0	0.0%	0.00
110..119	0%	0	0	0.0%	0.00
100..109	0%	0	1	0.0%	-1.00
80..99	0%	0	1	0.0%	-1.00
60..79	0%	0	0	0.0%	0.00
..59	0%	0	0	0.0%	0.00
Unrated	100%	1	30	3.3%	-0.82

ANALYSIS BY WEIGHT CARRIED
Age	Prop	Win	Runs	Wins%	£
12-01+	0%	0	0	0.0%	0.00
11-8..12-00	0%	0	0	0.0%	0.00
11-0..11-07	0%	0	6	0.0%	-1.00
10-8..10-13	100%	1	17	5.9%	-0.68
10-0..10-07	0%	0	6	0.0%	-1.00
..9-13	0%	0	3	0.0%	-1.00

ANALYSIS BY DAYS SINCE LAST RUN
Age	Prop	Win	Runs	Wins%	£
1..7	0%	0	0	0.0%	0.00
8..14	0%	0	0	0.0%	0.00
15..28	0%	0	0	0.0%	0.00
29..60	0%	0	0	0.0%	0.00
61..100	0%	0	3	0.0%	-1.00
101+	100%	1	29	3.4%	-0.81
Unraced	0%	0	0	0.0%	0.00

ANALYSIS BY TODAY'S STARTING PRICE
Age	Prop	Win	Runs	Wins%	£
Odds On	0%	0	0	0.0%	0.00
Ev-2/1	0%	0	0	0.0%	0.00
9/4-4/1	0%	0	1	0.0%	-1.00
9/2-6/1	100%	1	1	100.0%	4.50
13/2-10/1	0%	0	3	0.0%	-1.00
11/1-16/1	0%	0	3	0.0%	-1.00
18/1-33/1	0%	0	7	0.0%	-1.00
40/1+	0%	0	17	0.0%	-1.00

ANALYSIS BY STARTING PRICE LAST TIME
Age	Prop	Win	Runs	Wins%	£
Odds On	0%	0	0	0.0%	0.00
Ev-2/1	0%	0	0	0.0%	0.00
9/4-4/1	0%	0	2	0.0%	-1.00
9/2-6/1	0%	0	3	0.0%	-1.00
13/2-10/1	0%	0	6	0.0%	-1.00
11/1-16/1	0%	0	4	0.0%	-1.00
18/1-33/1	100%	1	10	10.0%	-0.45
40/1+	0%	0	7	0.0%	-1.00
Unraced	0%	0	0	0.0%	0.00

ANALYSIS BY DISTANCE BEATEN LAST TIME
Age	Prop	Win	Runs	Wins%	£
..-10 lgh	0%	0	0	0.0%	0.00
-10..0	0%	0	3	0.0%	-1.00
0.1..2	0%	0	0	0.0%	0.00
2.1..5	0%	0	2	0.0%	-1.00
5.1..10	0%	0	0	0.0%	0.00
10.1..20	0%	0	0	0.0%	0.00
20.0..30	100%	1	1	100.0%	4.50
30.1+	0%	0	14	0.0%	-1.00
Not Compl	0%	0	12	0.0%	-1.00
Unraced	0%	0	0	0.0%	0.00

ANALYSIS BY SUCCESS RATE IN LAST 10 RUNS
Age	Prop	Win	Runs	Wins%	£
No Wins	100%	1	26	3.8%	-0.79
1 Win	0%	0	6	0.0%	-1.00
2 Wins	0%	0	0	0.0%	0.00
3 Wins	0%	0	0	0.0%	0.00
4 Wins	0%	0	0	0.0%	0.00
5+ Wins	0%	0	0	0.0%	0.00

ANALYSIS BY SUCCESS RATE IN LAST 3 RUNS
Age	Prop	Win	Runs	Wins%	£
No Wins	100%	1	27	3.7%	-0.80
1 Win	0%	0	5	0.0%	-1.00
2 Wins	0%	0	0	0.0%	0.00
3 Wins	0%	0	0	0.0%	0.00

ANALYSIS BY POSITION LAST TIME
Age	Prop	Win	Runs	Wins%	£
Won	0%	0	3	0.0%	-1.00
2nd or 3rd	0%	0	1	0.0%	-1.00
Unplaced	100%	1	16	6.3%	-0.66
Fell,BD,UR	0%	0	3	0.0%	-1.00
Pulled Up	0%	0	9	0.0%	-1.00
Ref/RanOut	0%	0	0	0.0%	0.00
CO/SlipUp	0%	0	0	0.0%	0.00
Unraced	0%	0	0	0.0%	0.00

OTHER FACTORS (WINS-RUNS, £)
Distance Winner:	0-2	-£1.00
Going Winner:	0-1	-£1.00

4-Y.O Hurdle Races

4-Y.O Hurdle Races

ANALYSIS BY AGE

Age	Prop	Win	Runs	Wins%	£
4yo	100%	207	2068	10.0%	-0.27

ANALYSIS BY BHB RATING

Age	Prop	Win	Runs	Wins%	£
150+	2%	5	7	71.4%	1.02
130..149	11%	23	114	20.2%	-0.05
120..129	9%	19	100	19.0%	-0.31
110..119	11%	22	133	16.5%	0.31
100..109	5%	11	93	11.8%	-0.46
80..99	3%	7	100	7.0%	0.35
60..79	0%	0	20	0.0%	-1.00
..59	0%	0	0	0.0%	0.00
Unrated	58%	121	1511	8.0%	-0.36

ANALYSIS BY WEIGHT CARRIED

Age	Prop	Win	Runs	Wins%	£
12-01+	0%	0	0	0.0%	0.00
11-8..12-00	9%	18	53	34.0%	0.35
11-0..11-07	42%	88	605	14.5%	-0.21
10-8..10-13	41%	86	965	8.9%	-0.12
10-0..10-07	8%	16	421	3.8%	-0.71
..9-13	0%	0	34	0.0%	-1.00

ANALYSIS BY DAYS SINCE LAST RUN

Age	Prop	Win	Runs	Wins%	£
1..7	2%	5	69	7.2%	-0.77
8..14	13%	27	269	10.0%	-0.31
15..28	29%	60	524	11.5%	0.02
29..60	30%	62	528	11.7%	-0.10
61..100	6%	13	158	8.2%	-0.45
101+	2%	4	100	4.0%	-0.92
Unraced	18%	37	430	8.6%	-0.50

ANALYSIS BY TODAY'S STARTING PRICE

Age	Prop	Win	Runs	Wins%	£
Odds On	21%	43	74	58.1%	-0.08
Ev-2/1	26%	54	152	35.5%	-0.09
9/4-4/1	22%	46	214	21.5%	-0.14
9/2-6/1	9%	19	112	17.0%	0.03
13/2-10/1	8%	17	217	7.8%	-0.26
11/1-16/1	6%	12	233	5.2%	-0.27
18/1-33/1	5%	11	366	3.0%	-0.25
40/1+	3%	6	710	0.8%	-0.42

ANALYSIS BY STARTING PRICE LAST TIME

Age	Prop	Win	Runs	Wins%	£
Odds On	7%	15	66	22.7%	0.09
Ev-2/1	17%	36	133	27.1%	-0.14
9/4-4/1	13%	28	182	15.4%	-0.44
9/2-6/1	5%	10	121	8.3%	-0.58
13/2-10/1	17%	35	198	17.7%	-0.15
11/1-16/1	5%	11	205	5.4%	-0.21
18/1-33/1	12%	25	274	9.1%	0.21
40/1+	5%	11	469	2.3%	-0.35
Unraced	18%	37	430	8.6%	-0.50

ANALYSIS BY DISTANCE BEATEN LAST TIME

Age	Prop	Win	Runs	Wins%	£
..-10 lgh	4%	9	38	23.7%	-0.45
-10..0	20%	41	189	21.7%	-0.04
0.1..2	6%	13	68	19.1%	-0.33
2.1..5	6%	12	69	17.4%	-0.44
5.1..10	15%	31	160	19.4%	-0.29
10.1..20	11%	23	231	10.0%	0.31
20.0..30	7%	15	192	7.8%	-0.47
30.1+	10%	20	512	3.9%	-0.17
Not Compl	3%	7	189	3.7%	-0.60
Unraced	18%	37	430	8.6%	-0.50

ANALYSIS BY SUCCESS RATE IN LAST 10 RUNS

Age	Prop	Win	Runs	Wins%	£
No Wins	44%	76	1156	6.6%	-0.24
1 Win	38%	65	328	19.8%	-0.01
2 Wins	11%	19	114	16.7%	-0.41
3 Wins	5%	8	32	25.0%	-0.39
4 Wins	1%	1	13	7.7%	-0.77
5+ Wins	1%	2	5	40.0%	0.70

ANALYSIS BY SUCCESS RATE IN LAST 3 RUNS

Age	Prop	Win	Runs	Wins%	£
No Wins	46%	79	1209	6.5%	-0.26
1 Win	41%	70	334	21.0%	0.06
2 Wins	11%	19	96	19.8%	-0.49
3 Wins	2%	3	9	33.3%	0.39

ANALYSIS BY POSITION LAST TIME

Age	Prop	Win	Runs	Wins%	£
Won	24%	50	226	22.1%	-0.11
2nd or 3rd	28%	58	321	18.1%	-0.10
Unplaced	27%	56	912	6.1%	-0.19
Fell,BD,UR	0%	1	71	1.4%	-0.91
Pulled Up	3%	6	116	5.2%	-0.40
Ref/RanOut	0%	0	2	0.0%	-1.00
CO/SlipUp	0%	0	0	0.0%	0.00
Unraced	18%	37	430	8.6%	-0.50

OTHER FACTORS (WINS-RUNS, £)

Course Winner:	15-69	£0.61
Distance Winner:	58-279	-£0.05
Going Winner:	38-166	-£0.10
Beaten Favourite:	29-105	-£0.01
7-Day Winners:	3-7	£0.36
BHA Top Rated:	45-156	£0.57
Absolute Favourites:	88-197	-£0.04

Race Profiles

4-Y.O Hurdle Races: 2m to 2m3f

ANALYSIS BY AGE

Age	Prop	Win	Runs	Wins%	£
4yo	100%	207	2068	10.0%	-0.27

ANALYSIS BY BHB RATING

Age	Prop	Win	Runs	Wins%	£
150+	2%	5	7	71.4%	1.02
130..149	11%	23	114	20.2%	-0.05
120..129	9%	19	100	19.0%	-0.31
110..119	11%	22	133	16.5%	0.31
100..109	5%	11	93	11.8%	-0.46
80..99	3%	7	100	7.0%	0.35
60..79	0%	0	20	0.0%	-1.00
..59	0%	0	0	0.0%	0.00
Unrated	58%	121	1511	8.0%	-0.36

ANALYSIS BY WEIGHT CARRIED

Age	Prop	Win	Runs	Wins%	£
12-01+	0%	0	0	0.0%	0.00
11-8..12-00	9%	18	53	34.0%	0.35
11-0..11-07	42%	88	605	14.5%	-0.21
10-8..10-13	41%	86	965	8.9%	-0.12
10-0..10-07	8%	16	421	3.8%	-0.71
..9-13	0%	0	34	0.0%	-1.00

ANALYSIS BY DAYS SINCE LAST RUN

Age	Prop	Win	Runs	Wins%	£
1..7	2%	5	69	7.2%	-0.77
8..14	13%	27	269	10.0%	-0.31
15..28	29%	60	524	11.5%	0.02
29..60	30%	62	528	11.7%	-0.10
61..100	6%	13	158	8.2%	-0.45
101+	2%	4	100	4.0%	-0.92
Unraced	18%	37	430	8.6%	-0.50

ANALYSIS BY TODAY'S STARTING PRICE

Age	Prop	Win	Runs	Wins%	£
Odds On	21%	43	74	58.1%	-0.08
Ev-2/1	26%	54	152	35.5%	-0.09
9/4-4/1	22%	46	214	21.5%	-0.14
9/2-6/1	17%	19	112	17.0%	0.03
13/2-10/1	8%	17	217	7.8%	-0.26
11/1-16/1	6%	12	233	5.2%	-0.27
18/1-33/1	5%	11	366	3.0%	-0.25
40/1+	3%	6	710	0.8%	-0.42

ANALYSIS BY STARTING PRICE LAST TIME

Age	Prop	Win	Runs	Wins%	£
Odds On	7%	15	66	22.7%	0.09
Ev-2/1	17%	36	133	27.1%	-0.14
9/4-4/1	13%	28	182	15.4%	-0.44
9/2-6/1	5%	10	121	8.3%	-0.58
13/2-10/1	17%	35	198	17.7%	-0.15
11/1-16/1	5%	11	205	5.4%	-0.21
18/1-33/1	12%	25	274	9.1%	0.21
40/1+	5%	11	469	2.3%	-0.35
Unraced	18%	37	430	8.6%	-0.50

ANALYSIS BY DISTANCE BEATEN LAST TIME

Age	Prop	Win	Runs	Wins%	£
..-10 lgh	4%	9	38	23.7%	-0.45
-10..0	20%	41	189	21.7%	-0.04
0.1..2	6%	13	68	19.1%	-0.33
2.1..5	6%	12	69	17.4%	-0.44
5.1..10	15%	31	160	19.4%	-0.29
10.1..20	11%	23	231	10.0%	0.31
20.0..30	7%	15	192	7.8%	-0.47
30.1+	10%	20	512	3.9%	-0.17
Not Compl	3%	7	189	3.7%	-0.60
Unraced	18%	37	430	8.6%	-0.50

ANALYSIS BY SUCCESS RATE IN LAST 10 RUNS

Age	Prop	Win	Runs	Wins%	£
No Wins	44%	76	1156	6.6%	-0.24
1 Win	38%	65	328	19.8%	-0.01
2 Wins	11%	19	114	16.7%	-0.41
3 Wins	5%	8	32	25.0%	-0.39
4 Wins	1%	1	13	7.7%	-0.77
5+ Wins	1%	2	5	40.0%	0.70

ANALYSIS BY SUCCESS RATE IN LAST 3 RUNS

Age	Prop	Win	Runs	Wins%	£
No Wins	46%	79	1209	6.5%	-0.26
1 Win	41%	70	334	21.0%	0.06
2 Wins	11%	19	96	19.8%	-0.49
3 Wins	2%	3	9	33.3%	0.39

ANALYSIS BY POSITION LAST TIME

Age	Prop	Win	Runs	Wins%	£
Won	24%	50	226	22.1%	-0.11
2nd or 3rd	28%	58	321	18.1%	-0.10
Unplaced	27%	56	912	6.1%	-0.19
Fell,BD,UR	0%	1	71	1.4%	-0.91
Pulled Up	3%	6	116	5.2%	-0.40
Ref/RanOut	0%	0	2	0.0%	-1.00
CO/SlipUp	0%	0	0	0.0%	0.00
Unraced	18%	37	430	8.6%	-0.50

OTHER FACTORS (WINS-RUNS, £)

Course Winner:	15-69	£0.61
Distance Winner:	58-279	-£0.05
Going Winner:	38-166	-£0.10
Beaten Favourite:	29-105	-£0.01
7-Day Winners:	3-7	£0.36
BHA Top Rated:	45-156	£0.57
Absolute Favourites:	88-197	-£0.04

4-Y.O Hurdle Races

4-Y.O Hurdle Races: 2 to 5 runners

ANALYSIS BY AGE

Age	Prop	Win	Runs	Wins%	£
4yo	100%	26	119	21.8%	-0.30

ANALYSIS BY BHB RATING

Age	Prop	Win	Runs	Wins%	£
150+	8%	2	2	100.0%	0.32
130..149	19%	5	20	25.0%	-0.49
120..129	19%	5	16	31.3%	-0.35
110..119	0%	0	12	0.0%	-1.00
100..109	0%	0	4	0.0%	-1.00
80..99	8%	2	9	22.2%	-0.28
60..79	0%	0	0	0.0%	0.00
..59	0%	0	0	0.0%	0.00
Unrated	46%	12	56	21.4%	-0.04

ANALYSIS BY WEIGHT CARRIED

Age	Prop	Win	Runs	Wins%	£
12-01+	0%	0	0	0.0%	0.00
11-8..12-00	12%	3	9	33.3%	0.06
11-0..11-07	50%	13	45	28.9%	-0.35
10-8..10-13	35%	9	52	17.3%	-0.17
10-0..10-07	4%	1	12	8.3%	-0.88
..9-13	0%	0	1	0.0%	-1.00

ANALYSIS BY DAYS SINCE LAST RUN

Age	Prop	Win	Runs	Wins%	£
1..7	0%	0	5	0.0%	-1.00
8..14	15%	4	15	26.7%	-0.33
15..28	19%	5	31	16.1%	-0.01
29..60	19%	5	26	19.2%	-0.55
61..100	8%	2	10	20.0%	-0.74
101+	12%	3	12	25.0%	-0.59
Unraced	27%	7	20	35.0%	0.17

Analysis By Today's Starting Price

Age	Prop	Win	Runs	Wins%	£
Odds On	54%	14	17	82.4%	0.26
Ev-2/1	19%	5	19	26.3%	-0.40
9/4-4/1	19%	5	21	23.8%	0.02
9/2-6/1	4%	1	7	14.3%	-0.14
13/2-10/1	0%	0	9	0.0%	-1.00
11/1-16/1	0%	0	14	0.0%	-1.00
18/1-33/1	4%	1	18	5.6%	0.28
40/1+	0%	0	14	0.0%	-1.00

ANALYSIS BY STARTING PRICE LAST TIME

Age	Prop	Win	Runs	Wins%	£
Odds On	8%	2	9	22.2%	-0.29
Ev-2/1	15%	4	14	28.6%	-0.57
9/4-4/1	15%	4	11	36.4%	-0.27
9/2-6/1	8%	2	10	20.0%	-0.42
13/2-10/1	12%	3	13	23.1%	-0.53
11/1-16/1	8%	2	17	11.8%	-0.83
18/1-33/1	0%	0	12	0.0%	-1.00
40/1+	8%	2	13	15.4%	0.91
Unraced	27%	7	20	35.0%	0.17

ANALYSIS BY DISTANCE BEATEN LAST TIME

Age	Prop	Win	Runs	Wins%	£
..-10 lgh	4%	1	3	33.3%	-0.49
-10..0	15%	4	15	26.7%	-0.42
0.1..2	8%	2	7	28.6%	-0.16
2.1..5	4%	1	7	14.3%	-0.73
5.1..10	8%	2	7	28.6%	-0.57
10.1..20	4%	1	11	9.1%	-0.87
20.0..30	15%	4	17	23.5%	-0.58
30.1+	12%	3	19	15.8%	-0.61
Not Compl	4%	1	13	7.7%	0.77
Unraced	27%	7	20	35.0%	0.17

ANALYSIS BY SUCCESS RATE IN LAST 10 RUNS

Age	Prop	Win	Runs	Wins%	£
No Wins	32%	6	39	15.4%	-0.11
1 Win	42%	8	38	21.1%	-0.59
2 Wins	11%	2	11	18.2%	-0.55
3 Wins	16%	3	7	42.9%	-0.36
4 Wins	0%	0	4	0.0%	-1.00
5+ Wins	0%	0	0	0.0%	0.00

ANALYSIS BY SUCCESS RATE IN LAST 3 RUNS

Age	Prop	Win	Runs	Wins%	£
No Wins	32%	6	48	12.5%	-0.27
1 Win	58%	11	42	26.2%	-0.46
2 Wins	11%	2	9	22.2%	-0.72
3 Wins	0%	0	0	0.0%	0.00

ANALYSIS BY POSITION LAST TIME

Age	Prop	Win	Runs	Wins%	£
Won	19%	5	18	27.8%	-0.43
2nd or 3rd	23%	6	24	25.0%	-0.47
Unplaced	27%	7	44	15.9%	-0.68
Fell,BD,UR	0%	0	4	0.0%	-1.00
Pulled Up	4%	1	9	11.1%	1.56
Ref/RanOut	0%	0	0	0.0%	0.00
CO/SlipUp	0%	0	0	0.0%	0.00
Unraced	27%	7	20	35.0%	0.17

OTHER FACTORS (WINS-RUNS, £)

Course Winner:	1-9	-£0.86
Distance Winner:	9-44	-£0.65
Going Winner:	6-24	-£0.42
Beaten Favourite:	5-14	-£0.08
7-Day Winners:	0-1	-£1.00
BHA Top Rated:	10-23	-£0.32
Absolute Favourites:	18-25	£0.21

Race Profiles

4-Y.O Hurdle Races: 6 to 10 runners

ANALYSIS BY AGE

Age	Prop	Win	Runs	Wins%	£
4yo	100%	94	758	12.4%	-0.19

ANALYSIS BY BHB RATING

Age	Prop	Win	Runs	Wins%	£
150+	0%	0	1	0.0%	-1.00
130..149	11%	10	27	37.0%	-0.11
120..129	13%	12	58	20.7%	-0.21
110..119	6%	6	55	10.9%	0.11
100..109	10%	9	44	20.5%	0.04
80..99	3%	3	42	7.1%	0.03
60..79	0%	0	7	0.0%	-1.00
..59	0%	0	0	0.0%	0.00
Unrated	57%	54	524	10.3%	-0.25

ANALYSIS BY WEIGHT CARRIED

Age	Prop	Win	Runs	Wins%	£
12-01+	0%	0	0	0.0%	0.00
11-8..12-00	10%	9	31	29.0%	-0.03
11-0..11-07	43%	40	198	20.2%	0.17
10-8..10-13	40%	38	387	9.8%	-0.27
10-0..10-07	7%	7	134	5.2%	-0.51
..9-13	0%	0	8	0.0%	-1.00

ANALYSIS BY DAYS SINCE LAST RUN

Age	Prop	Win	Runs	Wins%	£
1..7	5%	5	26	19.2%	-0.40
8..14	11%	10	99	10.1%	-0.61
15..28	29%	27	193	14.0%	-0.07
29..60	31%	29	193	15.0%	0.24
61..100	6%	6	60	10.0%	-0.41
101+	1%	1	34	2.9%	-0.91
Unraced	17%	16	153	10.5%	-0.35

ANALYSIS BY TODAY'S STARTING PRICE

Age	Prop	Win	Runs	Wins%	£
Odds On	16%	15	31	48.4%	-0.25
Ev-2/1	32%	30	82	36.6%	-0.06
9/4-4/1	27%	25	102	24.5%	-0.02
9/2-6/1	7%	7	47	14.9%	-0.12
13/2-10/1	6%	6	82	7.3%	-0.26
11/1-16/1	5%	5	95	5.3%	-0.17
18/1-33/1	5%	5	126	4.0%	0.02
40/1+	1%	1	193	0.5%	-0.48

ANALYSIS BY STARTING PRICE LAST TIME

Age	Prop	Win	Runs	Wins%	£
Odds On	7%	7	24	29.2%	-0.10
Ev-2/1	12%	11	45	24.4%	-0.44
9/4-4/1	14%	13	75	17.3%	-0.23
9/2-6/1	3%	3	41	7.3%	-0.80
13/2-10/1	24%	23	87	26.4%	0.42
11/1-16/1	4%	4	79	5.1%	0.49
18/1-33/1	13%	12	103	11.7%	-0.26
40/1+	5%	5	151	3.3%	-0.46
Unraced	17%	16	153	10.5%	-0.35

ANALYSIS BY DISTANCE BEATEN LAST TIME

Age	Prop	Win	Runs	Wins%	£
..-10 lgh	6%	6	15	40.0%	-0.10
-10..0	22%	21	85	24.7%	0.16
0.1..2	6%	6	26	23.1%	0.06
2.1..5	3%	3	22	13.6%	-0.65
5.1..10	18%	17	66	25.8%	0.06
10.1..20	11%	10	93	10.8%	-0.26
20.0..30	6%	6	79	7.6%	-0.28
30.1+	6%	6	157	3.8%	-0.02
Not Compl	3%	3	62	4.8%	-0.77
Unraced	17%	16	153	10.5%	-0.35

ANALYSIS BY SUCCESS RATE IN LAST 10 RUNS

Age	Prop	Win	Runs	Wins%	£
No Wins	41%	32	416	7.7%	-0.24
1 Win	42%	33	139	23.7%	0.17
2 Wins	13%	10	45	22.2%	-0.46
3 Wins	3%	2	3	66.7%	1.08
4 Wins	1%	1	2	50.0%	0.50
5+ Wins	0%	0	0	0.0%	0.00

ANALYSIS BY SUCCESS RATE IN LAST 3 RUNS

Age	Prop	Win	Runs	Wins%	£
No Wins	44%	34	434	7.8%	-0.27
1 Win	45%	35	133	26.3%	0.29
2 Wins	12%	9	38	23.7%	-0.45
3 Wins	0%	0	0	0.0%	0.00

ANALYSIS BY POSITION LAST TIME

Age	Prop	Win	Runs	Wins%	£
Won	29%	27	99	27.3%	0.13
2nd or 3rd	28%	26	122	21.3%	0.02
Unplaced	23%	22	322	6.8%	-0.19
Fell,BD,UR	1%	1	25	4.0%	-0.74
Pulled Up	2%	2	36	5.6%	-0.78
Ref/RanOut	0%	0	1	0.0%	-1.00
CO/SlipUp	0%	0	0	0.0%	0.00
Unraced	17%	16	153	10.5%	-0.35

OTHER FACTORS (WINS-RUNS, £)

Course Winner:	8-28	£1.46
Distance Winner:	29-113	£0.06
Going Winner:	15-61	-£0.25
Beaten Favourite:	9-40	-£0.42
7-Day Winners:	3-3	£2.17
BHA Top Rated:	14-62	-£0.32
Absolute Favourites:	38-88	-£0.05

4-Y.O Hurdle Races

4-Y.O Hurdle Races: 11 runners or more

ANALYSIS BY AGE

Age	Prop	Win	Runs	Wins%	£
4yo	99%	87	1191	7.3%	-0.31

ANALYSIS BY BHB RATING

Age	Prop	Win	Runs	Wins%	£
150+	3%	3	4	75.0%	1.88
130..149	9%	8	67	11.9%	0.11
120..129	2%	2	26	7.7%	-0.51
110..119	18%	16	66	24.2%	0.71
100..109	2%	2	45	4.4%	-0.89
80..99	2%	2	49	4.1%	0.73
60..79	0%	0	13	0.0%	-1.00
..59	0%	0	0	0.0%	0.00
Unrated	63%	55	931	5.9%	-0.43

ANALYSIS BY WEIGHT CARRIED

Age	Prop	Win	Runs	Wins%	£
12-01+	0%	0	0	0.0%	0.00
11-8..12-00	7%	6	13	46.2%	1.48
11-0..11-07	40%	35	362	9.7%	-0.41
10-8..10-13	44%	39	526	7.4%	0.00
10-0..10-07	9%	8	275	2.9%	-0.81
..9-13	0%	0	25	0.0%	-1.00

ANALYSIS BY DAYS SINCE LAST RUN

Age	Prop	Win	Runs	Wins%	£
1..7	0%	0	38	0.0%	-1.00
8..14	15%	13	155	8.4%	-0.12
15..28	32%	28	300	9.3%	0.08
29..60	32%	28	309	9.1%	-0.27
61..100	6%	5	88	5.7%	-0.44
101+	0%	0	54	0.0%	-1.00
Unraced	16%	14	257	5.4%	-0.63

ANALYSIS BY TODAY'S STARTING PRICE

Age	Prop	Win	Runs	Wins%	£
Odds On	16%	14	26	53.8%	-0.09
Ev-2/1	22%	19	51	37.3%	-0.02
9/4-4/1	18%	16	91	17.6%	-0.33
9/2-6/1	13%	11	58	19.0%	0.17
13/2-10/1	13%	11	126	8.7%	-0.21
11/1-16/1	8%	7	124	5.6%	-0.26
18/1-33/1	6%	5	222	2.3%	-0.45
40/1+	6%	5	503	1.0%	-0.38

ANALYSIS BY STARTING PRICE LAST TIME

Age	Prop	Win	Runs	Wins%	£
Odds On	7%	6	33	18.2%	0.34
Ev-2/1	24%	21	74	28.4%	0.12
9/4-4/1	13%	11	96	11.5%	-0.63
9/2-6/1	6%	5	70	7.1%	-0.47
13/2-10/1	10%	9	98	9.2%	-0.60
11/1-16/1	6%	5	109	4.6%	-0.63
18/1-33/1	15%	13	159	8.2%	0.61
40/1+	5%	4	305	1.3%	-0.35
Unraced	16%	14	257	5.4%	-0.63

ANALYSIS BY DISTANCE BEATEN LAST TIME

Age	Prop	Win	Runs	Wins%	£
..-10 lgh	2%	2	20	10.0%	-0.72
-10..0	18%	16	89	18.0%	-0.18
0.1..2	6%	5	35	14.3%	-0.65
2.1..5	9%	8	40	20.0%	-0.28
5.1..10	14%	12	87	13.8%	-0.54
10.1..20	14%	12	127	9.4%	0.83
20.0..30	6%	5	96	5.2%	-0.60
30.1+	13%	11	336	3.3%	-0.21
Not Compl	3%	3	114	2.6%	-0.66
Unraced	16%	14	257	5.4%	-0.63

ANALYSIS BY SUCCESS RATE IN LAST 10 RUNS

Age	Prop	Win	Runs	Wins%	£
No Wins	51%	38	701	5.4%	-0.24
1 Win	32%	24	151	15.9%	-0.03
2 Wins	9%	7	58	12.1%	-0.35
3 Wins	4%	3	22	13.6%	-0.59
4 Wins	0%	0	7	0.0%	-1.00
5+ Wins	3%	2	5	40.0%	0.70

ANALYSIS BY SUCCESS RATE IN LAST 3 RUNS

Age	Prop	Win	Runs	Wins%	£
No Wins	53%	39	727	5.4%	-0.26
1 Win	32%	24	159	15.1%	0.00
2 Wins	11%	8	49	16.3%	-0.47
3 Wins	4%	3	9	33.3%	0.39

ANALYSIS BY POSITION LAST TIME

Age	Prop	Win	Runs	Wins%	£
Won	20%	18	109	16.5%	-0.28
2nd or 3rd	30%	26	175	14.9%	-0.13
Unplaced	31%	27	546	4.9%	-0.15
Fell,BD,UR	0%	0	42	0.0%	-1.00
Pulled Up	3%	3	71	4.2%	-0.46
Ref/RanOut	0%	0	1	0.0%	-1.00
CO/SlipUp	0%	0	0	0.0%	0.00
Unraced	16%	14	257	5.4%	-0.63

OTHER FACTORS (WINS-RUNS, £)

Course Winner:	6-32	£0.28
Distance Winner:	20-122	£0.06
Going Winner:	17-81	£0.10
Beaten Favourite:	15-51	£0.34
7-Day Winners:	0-3	-£1.00
BHA Top Rated:	21-71	£1.64
Absolute Favourites:	32-84	-£0.11

Race Profiles

4-Y.O Hurdle Races: up to 7 days off the track

ANALYSIS BY AGE

Age	Prop	Win	Runs	Wins%	£
4yo	100%	42	498	8.4%	-0.53

ANALYSIS BY BHB RATING

Age	Prop	Win	Runs	Wins%	£
150+	0%	0	0	0.0%	0.00
130..149	2%	1	4	25.0%	0.00
120..129	0%	0	5	0.0%	-1.00
110..119	0%	0	3	0.0%	-1.00
100..109	2%	1	5	20.0%	-0.55
80..99	2%	1	7	14.3%	-0.54
60..79	0%	0	1	0.0%	-1.00
..59	0%	0	0	0.0%	0.00
Unrated	93%	39	474	8.2%	-0.53

ANALYSIS BY WEIGHT CARRIED

Age	Prop	Win	Runs	Wins%	£
12-01+	0%	0	0	0.0%	0.00
11-8..12-00	5%	2	7	28.6%	0.16
11-0..11-07	17%	7	66	10.6%	-0.65
10-8..10-13	69%	29	294	9.9%	-0.40
10-0..10-07	10%	4	123	3.3%	-0.80
..9-13	0%	0	9	0.0%	-1.00

ANALYSIS BY DAYS SINCE LAST RUN

Age	Prop	Win	Runs	Wins%	£
1..7	12%	5	69	7.2%	-0.77
8..14	0%	0	0	0.0%	0.00
15..28	0%	0	0	0.0%	0.00
29..60	0%	0	0	0.0%	0.00
61..100	0%	0	0	0.0%	0.00
101+	0%	0	0	0.0%	0.00
Unraced	88%	37	430	8.6%	-0.50

ANALYSIS BY TODAY'S STARTING PRICE

Age	Prop	Win	Runs	Wins%	£
Odds On	10%	4	10	40.0%	-0.28
Ev-2/1	21%	9	23	39.1%	-0.02
9/4-4/1	38%	16	46	34.8%	0.47
9/2-6/1	10%	4	24	16.7%	0.04
13/2-10/1	12%	5	36	13.9%	0.35
11/1-16/1	7%	3	57	5.3%	-0.30
18/1-33/1	2%	1	102	1.0%	-0.79
40/1+	0%	0	201	0.0%	-1.00

ANALYSIS BY STARTING PRICE LAST TIME

Age	Prop	Win	Runs	Wins%	£
Odds On	2%	1	3	33.3%	-0.25
Ev-2/1	0%	0	5	0.0%	-1.00
9/4-4/1	5%	2	8	25.0%	-0.03
9/2-6/1	2%	1	2	50.0%	-0.17
13/2-10/1	0%	0	10	0.0%	-1.00
11/1-16/1	0%	0	10	0.0%	-1.00
18/1-33/1	2%	1	8	12.5%	-0.50
40/1+	0%	0	23	0.0%	-1.00
Unraced	88%	37	430	8.6%	-0.50

ANALYSIS BY DISTANCE BEATEN LAST TIME

Age	Prop	Win	Runs	Wins%	£
..-10 lgh	2%	1	2	50.0%	0.13
-10..0	5%	2	5	40.0%	0.45
0.1..2	0%	0	0	0.0%	0.00
2.1..5	2%	1	5	20.0%	-0.67
5.1..10	2%	1	5	20.0%	-0.10
10.1..20	0%	0	8	0.0%	-1.00
20.0..30	0%	0	7	0.0%	-1.00
30.1+	0%	0	20	0.0%	-1.00
Not Compl	0%	0	17	0.0%	-1.00
Unraced	88%	37	430	8.6%	-0.50

ANALYSIS BY SUCCESS RATE IN LAST 10 RUNS

Age	Prop	Win	Runs	Wins%	£
No Wins	40%	2	50	4.0%	-0.88
1 Win	20%	1	9	11.1%	-0.64
2 Wins	0%	0	6	0.0%	-1.00
3 Wins	40%	2	3	66.7%	1.08
4 Wins	0%	0	1	0.0%	-1.00
5+ Wins	0%	0	0	0.0%	0.00

ANALYSIS BY SUCCESS RATE IN LAST 3 RUNS

Age	Prop	Win	Runs	Wins%	£
No Wins	40%	2	55	3.6%	-0.89
1 Win	40%	2	10	20.0%	-0.28
2 Wins	20%	1	4	25.0%	-0.44
3 Wins	0%	0	0	0.0%	0.00

ANALYSIS BY POSITION LAST TIME

Age	Prop	Win	Runs	Wins%	£
Won	7%	3	7	42.9%	0.36
2nd or 3rd	5%	2	8	25.0%	-0.23
Unplaced	0%	0	37	0.0%	-1.00
Fell,BD,UR	0%	0	9	0.0%	-1.00
Pulled Up	0%	0	8	0.0%	-1.00
Ref/RanOut	0%	0	0	0.0%	0.00
CO/SlipUp	0%	0	0	0.0%	0.00
Unraced	88%	37	430	8.6%	-0.50

OTHER FACTORS (WINS-RUNS, £)

Course Winner:	2-3	£1.08
Distance Winner:	1-10	-£0.60
Going Winner:	2-7	-£0.11
Beaten Favourite:	0-7	-£1.00
7-Day Winners:	3-7	£0.36
BHA Top Rated:	1-4	£0.00
Absolute Favourites:	10-29	-£0.20

4-Y.O Hurdle Races

4-Y.O Hurdle Races: 100+ days off the track

ANALYSIS BY AGE

Age	Prop	Win	Runs	Wins%	£
4yo	100%	4	102	3.9%	-0.92

ANALYSIS BY BHB RATING

Age	Prop	Win	Runs	Wins%	£
150+	25%	1	1	100.0%	0.11
130..149	25%	1	9	11.1%	-0.80
120..129	0%	0	8	0.0%	-1.00
110..119	0%	0	4	0.0%	-1.00
100..109	0%	0	3	0.0%	-1.00
80..99	0%	0	7	0.0%	-1.00
60..79	0%	0	3	0.0%	-1.00
..59	0%	0	0	0.0%	0.00
Unrated	50%	2	67	3.0%	-0.93

ANALYSIS BY WEIGHT CARRIED

Age	Prop	Win	Runs	Wins%	£
12-01+	0%	0	0	0.0%	0.00
11-8..12-00	0%	0	3	0.0%	-1.00
11-0..11-07	50%	2	29	6.9%	-0.86
10-8..10-13	50%	2	44	4.5%	-0.91
10-0..10-07	0%	0	23	0.0%	-1.00
..9-13	0%	0	3	0.0%	-1.00

ANALYSIS BY DAYS SINCE LAST RUN

Age	Prop	Win	Runs	Wins%	£
1..7	0%	0	0	0.0%	0.00
8..14	0%	0	0	0.0%	0.00
15..28	0%	0	0	0.0%	0.00
29..60	0%	0	0	0.0%	0.00
61..100	0%	0	2	0.0%	-1.00
101+	100%	4	100	4.0%	-0.92
Unraced	0%	0	0	0.0%	0.00

ANALYSIS BY TODAY'S STARTING PRICE

Age	Prop	Win	Runs	Wins%	£
Odds On	50%	2	3	66.7%	-0.02
Ev-2/1	50%	2	4	50.0%	0.25
9/4-4/1	0%	0	5	0.0%	-1.00
9/2-6/1	0%	0	3	0.0%	-1.00
13/2-10/1	0%	0	6	0.0%	-1.00
11/1-16/1	0%	0	11	0.0%	-1.00
18/1-33/1	0%	0	25	0.0%	-1.00
40/1+	0%	0	45	0.0%	-1.00

ANALYSIS BY STARTING PRICE LAST TIME

Age	Prop	Win	Runs	Wins%	£
Odds On	0%	0	4	0.0%	-1.00
Ev-2/1	25%	1	5	20.0%	-0.78
9/4-4/1	50%	2	11	18.2%	-0.56
9/2-6/1	0%	0	8	0.0%	-1.00
13/2-10/1	25%	1	14	7.1%	-0.86
11/1-16/1	0%	0	15	0.0%	-1.00
18/1-33/1	0%	0	19	0.0%	-1.00
40/1+	0%	0	26	0.0%	-1.00
Unraced	0%	0	0	0.0%	0.00

ANALYSIS BY DISTANCE BEATEN LAST TIME

Age	Prop	Win	Runs	Wins%	£
..-10 lgh	0%	0	2	0.0%	-1.00
-10..0	25%	1	6	16.7%	-0.81
0.1..2	0%	0	4	0.0%	-1.00
2.1..5	0%	0	0	0.0%	0.00
5.1..10	0%	0	12	0.0%	-1.00
10.1..20	25%	1	12	8.3%	-0.75
20.0..30	50%	2	16	12.5%	-0.76
30.1+	0%	0	36	0.0%	-1.00
Not Compl	0%	0	14	0.0%	-1.00
Unraced	0%	0	0	0.0%	0.00

ANALYSIS BY SUCCESS RATE IN LAST 10 RUNS

Age	Prop	Win	Runs	Wins%	£
No Wins	50%	2	72	2.8%	-0.93
1 Win	0%	0	9	0.0%	-1.00
2 Wins	0%	0	11	0.0%	-1.00
3 Wins	50%	2	5	40.0%	-0.41
4 Wins	0%	0	3	0.0%	-1.00
5+ Wins	0%	0	2	0.0%	-1.00

ANALYSIS BY SUCCESS RATE IN LAST 3 RUNS

Age	Prop	Win	Runs	Wins%	£
No Wins	50%	2	76	2.6%	-0.93
1 Win	25%	1	17	5.9%	-0.89
2 Wins	25%	1	9	11.1%	-0.88
3 Wins	0%	0	0	0.0%	0.00

ANALYSIS BY POSITION LAST TIME

Age	Prop	Win	Runs	Wins%	£
Won	25%	1	8	12.5%	-0.86
2nd or 3rd	50%	2	19	10.5%	-0.75
Unplaced	25%	1	61	1.6%	-0.97
Fell,BD,UR	0%	0	3	0.0%	-1.00
Pulled Up	0%	0	10	0.0%	-1.00
Ref/RanOut	0%	0	1	0.0%	-1.00
CO/SlipUp	0%	0	0	0.0%	0.00
Unraced	0%	0	0	0.0%	0.00

OTHER FACTORS (WINS-RUNS, £)

Course Winner:	0-7	-£1.00
Distance Winner:	2-24	-£0.88
Going Winner:	1-17	-£0.93
Beaten Favourite:	0-9	-£1.00
BHA Top Rated:	1-3	-£0.39
Absolute Favourites:	4-6	£0.32

Race Profiles

Novices' Hurdle Races (class 1..3)

ANALYSIS BY AGE

Age	Prop	Win	Runs	Wins%	£
3yo	0%	0	0	0.0%	0.00
4yo	23%	99	851	11.6%	-0.38
5yo	35%	151	1523	9.9%	-0.45
6yo	26%	112	1171	9.6%	-0.32
7yo	14%	59	567	10.4%	-0.39
8yo	2%	9	147	6.1%	-0.75
9yo	0%	1	37	2.7%	-0.91
10yo	0%	1	20	5.0%	-0.55
11yo	0%	0	9	0.0%	-1.00
12yo+	0%	0	6	0.0%	-1.00

ANALYSIS BY BHB RATING

Age	Prop	Win	Runs	Wins%	£
150+	2%	10	36	27.8%	-0.47
130..149	22%	94	468	20.1%	-0.02
120..129	14%	60	333	18.0%	-0.07
110..119	8%	34	261	13.0%	-0.43
100..109	3%	12	146	8.2%	-0.34
80..99	1%	3	119	2.5%	0.13
60..79	0%	0	69	0.0%	-1.00
..59	0%	0	2	0.0%	-1.00
Unrated	51%	219	2897	7.6%	-0.52

ANALYSIS BY WEIGHT CARRIED

Age	Prop	Win	Runs	Wins%	£
12-01+	0%	0	1	0.0%	-1.00
11-8..12-00	25%	109	410	26.6%	-0.11
11-0..11-07	51%	221	2188	10.1%	-0.40
10-8..10-13	19%	84	1171	7.2%	-0.41
10-0..10-07	4%	18	534	3.4%	-0.61
..9-13	0%	0	27	0.0%	-1.00

ANALYSIS BY DAYS SINCE LAST RUN

Age	Prop	Win	Runs	Wins%	£
1..7	2%	8	100	8.0%	-0.77
8..14	11%	47	486	9.7%	-0.55
15..28	34%	145	1297	11.2%	-0.40
29..60	31%	133	1112	12.0%	-0.16
61..100	7%	30	284	10.6%	-0.47
101+	12%	53	668	7.9%	-0.48
Unraced	4%	16	384	4.2%	-0.70

ANALYSIS BY TODAY'S STARTING PRICE

Age	Prop	Win	Runs	Wins%	£
Odds On	25%	109	180	60.6%	-0.05
Ev-2/1	21%	92	245	37.6%	-0.06
9/4-4/1	19%	82	423	19.4%	-0.23
9/2-6/1	10%	44	290	15.2%	-0.05
13/2-10/1	13%	56	489	11.5%	0.03
11/1-16/1	8%	33	488	6.8%	0.01
18/1-33/1	3%	11	681	1.6%	-0.60
40/1+	1%	5	1535	0.3%	-0.81

ANALYSIS BY STARTING PRICE LAST TIME

Age	Prop	Win	Runs	Wins%	£
Odds On	16%	68	289	23.5%	0.00
Ev-2/1	21%	90	401	22.4%	0.02
9/4-4/1	17%	75	537	14.0%	-0.20
9/2-6/1	9%	40	332	12.0%	-0.32
13/2-10/1	12%	53	491	10.8%	-0.49
11/1-16/1	10%	42	475	8.8%	-0.44
18/1-33/1	8%	33	577	5.7%	-0.46
40/1+	3%	15	845	1.8%	-0.68
Unraced	4%	16	384	4.2%	-0.70

ANALYSIS BY DISTANCE BEATEN LAST TIME

Age	Prop	Win	Runs	Wins%	£
..-10 lgh	10%	45	189	23.8%	0.17
-10..0	30%	130	676	19.2%	-0.12
0.1..2	14%	62	236	26.3%	0.19
2.1..5	9%	39	242	16.1%	-0.20
5.1..10	7%	29	323	9.0%	-0.50
10.1..20	9%	41	453	9.1%	-0.41
20.0..30	5%	22	393	5.6%	-0.31
30.1+	7%	31	1008	3.1%	-0.69
Not Compl	4%	17	427	4.0%	-0.66
Unraced	4%	16	384	4.2%	-0.70

ANALYSIS BY SUCCESS RATE IN LAST 10 RUNS

Age	Prop	Win	Runs	Wins%	£
No Wins	19%	77	2062	3.7%	-0.65
1 Win	34%	140	861	16.3%	-0.04
2 Wins	22%	93	538	17.3%	-0.23
3 Wins	15%	63	282	22.3%	0.15
4 Wins	7%	30	143	21.0%	-0.13
5+ Wins	3%	13	61	21.3%	-0.26

ANALYSIS BY SUCCESS RATE IN LAST 3 RUNS

Age	Prop	Win	Runs	Wins%	£
No Wins	26%	107	2311	4.6%	-0.56
1 Win	42%	174	1043	16.7%	-0.15
2 Wins	25%	104	495	21.0%	-0.13
3 Wins	7%	31	98	31.6%	0.14

ANALYSIS BY POSITION LAST TIME

Age	Prop	Win	Runs	Wins%	£
Won	41%	175	864	20.3%	-0.05
2nd or 3rd	31%	136	839	16.2%	-0.21
Unplaced	20%	88	1818	4.8%	-0.55
Fell,BD,UR	3%	12	136	8.8%	-0.20
Pulled Up	1%	4	277	1.4%	-0.87
Ref/RanOut	0%	0	9	0.0%	-1.00
CO/SlipUp	0%	1	4	25.0%	-0.69
Unraced	4%	16	384	4.2%	-0.70

OTHER FACTORS (WINS-RUNS, £)

Course Winner:	48-229	-£0.16
Distance Winner:	136-780	-£0.17
Going Winner:	148-775	-£0.10
Beaten Favourite:	62-305	-£0.03
7-Day Winners:	2-19	-£0.80
BHA Top Rated:	88-308	-£0.27
Absolute Favourites:	184-409	-£0.10

Novices' Hurdle Races (class 1..3)

Novices' Hurdle Races (class 1..3): 2m to 2m3f

ANALYSIS BY AGE

Age	Prop	Win	Runs	Wins%	£
3yo	0%	0	0	0.0%	0.00
4yo	36%	71	594	12.0%	-0.33
5yo	39%	77	765	10.1%	-0.40
6yo	17%	34	419	8.1%	-0.46
7yo	6%	12	185	6.5%	-0.66
8yo	1%	2	46	4.3%	-0.91
9yo	0%	0	10	0.0%	-1.00
10yo	1%	1	5	20.0%	0.80
11yo	0%	0	4	0.0%	-1.00
12yo+	0%	0	1	0.0%	-1.00

ANALYSIS BY BHB RATING

Age	Prop	Win	Runs	Wins%	£
150+	0%	0	5	0.0%	-1.00
130..149	19%	37	170	21.8%	-0.11
120..129	16%	31	144	21.5%	0.23
110..119	8%	16	111	14.4%	-0.50
100..109	3%	5	54	9.3%	0.11
80..99	1%	1	50	2.0%	-0.58
60..79	0%	0	26	0.0%	-1.00
..59	0%	0	0	0.0%	0.00
Unrated	54%	107	1469	7.3%	-0.53

ANALYSIS BY WEIGHT CARRIED

Age	Prop	Win	Runs	Wins%	£
12-01+	0%	0	0	0.0%	0.00
11-8..12-00	24%	48	174	27.6%	-0.07
11-0..11-07	48%	95	954	10.0%	-0.45
10-8..10-13	20%	40	593	6.7%	-0.48
10-0..10-07	7%	14	292	4.8%	-0.44
..9-13	0%	0	16	0.0%	-1.00

ANALYSIS BY DAYS SINCE LAST RUN

Age	Prop	Win	Runs	Wins%	£
1..7	3%	5	53	9.4%	-0.74
8..14	14%	27	259	10.4%	-0.52
15..28	38%	75	589	12.7%	-0.25
29..60	20%	40	420	9.5%	-0.37
61..100	6%	11	103	10.7%	-0.44
101+	13%	25	337	7.4%	-0.54
Unraced	7%	14	268	5.2%	-0.63

ANALYSIS BY TODAY'S STARTING PRICE

Age	Prop	Win	Runs	Wins%	£
Odds On	26%	51	90	56.7%	-0.09
Ev-2/1	22%	43	124	34.7%	-0.15
9/4-4/1	16%	32	180	17.8%	-0.26
9/2-6/1	11%	21	123	17.1%	0.05
13/2-10/1	13%	25	193	13.0%	0.16
11/1-16/1	10%	19	214	8.9%	0.31
18/1-33/1	2%	3	335	0.9%	-0.82
40/1+	2%	3	770	0.4%	-0.81

ANALYSIS BY STARTING PRICE LAST TIME

Age	Prop	Win	Runs	Wins%	£
Odds On	20%	39	142	27.5%	0.11
Ev-2/1	21%	41	182	22.5%	0.29
9/4-4/1	13%	26	224	11.6%	-0.46
9/2-6/1	8%	16	149	10.7%	-0.34
13/2-10/1	11%	22	210	10.5%	-0.38
11/1-16/1	9%	18	217	8.3%	-0.54
18/1-33/1	8%	16	266	6.0%	-0.49
40/1+	3%	5	371	1.3%	-0.79
Unraced	7%	14	268	5.2%	-0.63

ANALYSIS BY DISTANCE BEATEN LAST TIME

Age	Prop	Win	Runs	Wins%	£
..-10 lgh	12%	24	76	31.6%	0.32
-10..0	30%	60	291	20.6%	0.05
0.1..2	14%	27	103	26.2%	0.16
2.1..5	7%	13	93	14.0%	-0.02
5.1..10	7%	13	148	8.8%	-0.65
10.1..20	9%	17	197	8.6%	-0.64
20.0..30	6%	11	192	5.7%	-0.31
30.1+	5%	10	473	2.1%	-0.86
Not Compl	4%	8	188	4.3%	-0.36
Unraced	7%	14	268	5.2%	-0.63

ANALYSIS BY SUCCESS RATE IN LAST 10 RUNS

Age	Prop	Win	Runs	Wins%	£
No Wins	19%	35	1000	3.5%	-0.65
1 Win	34%	63	375	16.8%	-0.04
2 Wins	23%	42	216	19.4%	-0.23
3 Wins	14%	26	97	26.8%	0.16
4 Wins	8%	14	53	26.4%	0.02
5+ Wins	2%	3	20	15.0%	-0.20

ANALYSIS BY SUCCESS RATE IN LAST 3 RUNS

Age	Prop	Win	Runs	Wins%	£
No Wins	25%	45	1078	4.2%	-0.65
1 Win	42%	77	445	17.3%	-0.01
2 Wins	27%	49	204	24.0%	-0.03
3 Wins	7%	12	34	35.3%	0.18

ANALYSIS BY POSITION LAST TIME

Age	Prop	Win	Runs	Wins%	£
Won	43%	84	367	22.9%	0.11
2nd or 3rd	25%	50	334	15.0%	-0.31
Unplaced	21%	41	872	4.7%	-0.66
Fell,BD,UR	4%	7	64	10.9%	0.54
Pulled Up	1%	1	117	0.9%	-0.82
Ref/RanOut	0%	0	7	0.0%	-1.00
CO/SlipUp	0%	0	0	0.0%	0.00
Unraced	7%	14	268	5.2%	-0.63

OTHER FACTORS (WINS-RUNS, £)

Course Winner:	26-98	£0.13
Distance Winner:	93-526	-£0.17
Going Winner:	73-328	-£0.05
Beaten Favourite:	27-137	-£0.04
7-Day Winners:	2-10	-£0.62
BHA Top Rated:	40-134	-£0.19
Absolute Favourites:	83-186	-£0.12

Race Profiles

Novices' Hurdle Races (class 1..3): 2m4f to 2m7f

ANALYSIS BY AGE

Age	Prop	Win	Runs	Wins%	£
3yo	0%	0	0	0.0%	0.00
4yo	15%	27	246	11.0%	-0.47
5yo	38%	66	644	10.2%	-0.44
6yo	33%	58	539	10.8%	-0.39
7yo	11%	20	249	8.0%	-0.58
8yo	3%	5	55	9.1%	-0.68
9yo	0%	0	13	0.0%	-1.00
10yo	0%	0	6	0.0%	-1.00
11yo	0%	0	5	0.0%	-1.00
12yo+	0%	0	4	0.0%	-1.00

ANALYSIS BY BHB RATING

Age	Prop	Win	Runs	Wins%	£
150+	3%	6	12	50.0%	0.16
130..149	22%	38	176	21.6%	-0.12
120..129	10%	18	116	15.5%	-0.55
110..119	7%	12	113	10.6%	-0.41
100..109	3%	5	69	7.2%	-0.65
80..99	0%	0	43	0.0%	-1.00
60..79	0%	0	28	0.0%	-1.00
..59	0%	0	2	0.0%	-1.00
Unrated	55%	97	1202	8.1%	-0.48

ANALYSIS BY WEIGHT CARRIED

Age	Prop	Win	Runs	Wins%	£
12-01+	0%	0	0	0.0%	0.00
11-8..12-00	27%	47	168	28.0%	-0.11
11-0..11-07	51%	90	899	10.0%	-0.42
10-8..10-13	20%	36	486	7.4%	-0.51
10-0..10-07	2%	3	199	1.5%	-0.85
..9-13	0%	0	9	0.0%	-1.00

ANALYSIS BY DAYS SINCE LAST RUN

Age	Prop	Win	Runs	Wins%	£
1..7	1%	2	35	5.7%	-0.91
8..14	9%	15	177	8.5%	-0.63
15..28	27%	48	524	9.2%	-0.60
29..60	40%	70	496	14.1%	-0.19
61..100	7%	13	132	9.8%	-0.51
101+	15%	26	295	8.8%	-0.39
Unraced	1%	2	102	2.0%	-0.87

ANALYSIS BY TODAY'S STARTING PRICE

Age	Prop	Win	Runs	Wins%	£
Odds On	24%	42	69	60.9%	-0.05
Ev-2/1	23%	41	89	46.1%	0.19
9/4-4/1	22%	38	182	20.9%	-0.22
9/2-6/1	11%	19	125	15.2%	-0.04
13/2-10/1	11%	20	222	9.0%	-0.21
11/1-16/1	6%	10	211	4.7%	-0.27
18/1-33/1	3%	5	256	2.0%	-0.50
40/1+	1%	1	607	0.2%	-0.92

ANALYSIS BY STARTING PRICE LAST TIME

Age	Prop	Win	Runs	Wins%	£
Odds On	13%	22	100	22.0%	0.02
Ev-2/1	20%	36	152	23.7%	-0.33
9/4-4/1	22%	39	236	16.5%	0.00
9/2-6/1	10%	18	136	13.2%	-0.21
13/2-10/1	13%	22	201	10.9%	-0.59
11/1-16/1	10%	17	200	8.5%	-0.58
18/1-33/1	7%	13	248	5.2%	-0.46
40/1+	4%	7	386	1.8%	-0.79
Unraced	1%	2	102	2.0%	-0.87

ANALYSIS BY DISTANCE BEATEN LAST TIME

Age	Prop	Win	Runs	Wins%	£
..-10 lgh	10%	17	66	25.8%	0.38
-10..0	27%	47	267	17.6%	-0.28
0.1..2	14%	25	99	25.3%	-0.07
2.1..5	13%	22	110	20.0%	-0.23
5.1..10	8%	14	133	10.5%	-0.46
10.1..20	13%	22	210	10.5%	-0.14
20.0..30	3%	5	157	3.2%	-0.47
30.1+	8%	14	435	3.2%	-0.75
Not Compl	5%	8	182	4.4%	-0.87
Unraced	1%	2	102	2.0%	-0.87

ANALYSIS BY SUCCESS RATE IN LAST 10 RUNS

Age	Prop	Win	Runs	Wins%	£
No Wins	21%	36	887	4.1%	-0.64
1 Win	35%	61	390	15.6%	-0.25
2 Wins	21%	36	217	16.6%	-0.32
3 Wins	14%	24	104	23.1%	0.14
4 Wins	6%	11	42	26.2%	-0.24
5+ Wins	3%	6	19	31.6%	0.11

ANALYSIS BY SUCCESS RATE IN LAST 3 RUNS

Age	Prop	Win	Runs	Wins%	£
No Wins	28%	48	1012	4.7%	-0.58
1 Win	44%	76	432	17.6%	-0.23
2 Wins	21%	37	175	21.1%	-0.31
3 Wins	7%	13	40	32.5%	0.33

ANALYSIS BY POSITION LAST TIME

Age	Prop	Win	Runs	Wins%	£
Won	36%	64	333	19.2%	-0.15
2nd or 3rd	38%	67	373	18.0%	-0.18
Unplaced	20%	35	771	4.5%	-0.59
Fell,BD,UR	2%	4	61	6.6%	-0.86
Pulled Up	2%	3	117	2.6%	-0.88
Ref/RanOut	0%	0	1	0.0%	-1.00
CO/SlipUp	1%	1	3	33.3%	-0.58
Unraced	1%	2	102	2.0%	-0.87

OTHER FACTORS (WINS-RUNS, £)

Course Winner:	14-84	-£0.31
Distance Winner:	29-153	-£0.25
Going Winner:	53-291	-£0.30
Beaten Favourite:	28-128	-£0.16
7-Day Winners:	0-8	-£1.00
BHA Top Rated:	32-126	-£0.36
Absolute Favourites:	77-167	-£0.04

Novices' Hurdle Races (class 1..3)

Novices' Hurdle Races (class 1..3): 3m+

ANALYSIS BY AGE
Age	Prop	Win	Runs	Wins%	£
3yo	0%	0	0	0.0%	0.00
4yo	2%	1	11	9.1%	-0.78
5yo	14%	8	114	7.0%	-0.76
6yo	34%	20	213	9.4%	0.11
7yo	46%	27	133	20.3%	0.34
8yo	3%	2	46	4.3%	-0.67
9yo	2%	1	14	7.1%	-0.75
10yo	0%	0	9	0.0%	-1.00
11yo	0%	0	0	0.0%	0.00
12yo+	0%	0	1	0.0%	-1.00

ANALYSIS BY BHB RATING
Age	Prop	Win	Runs	Wins%	£
150+	7%	4	19	21.1%	-0.72
130..149	32%	19	122	15.6%	0.24
120..129	19%	11	73	15.1%	0.10
110..119	10%	6	37	16.2%	-0.28
100..109	3%	2	23	8.7%	-0.47
80..99	3%	2	26	7.7%	3.35
60..79	0%	0	15	0.0%	-1.00
..59	0%	0	0	0.0%	0.00
Unrated	25%	15	226	6.6%	-0.66

ANALYSIS BY WEIGHT CARRIED
Age	Prop	Win	Runs	Wins%	£
12-01+	0%	0	1	0.0%	-1.00
11-8..12-00	24%	14	68	20.6%	-0.21
11-0..11-07	61%	36	335	10.7%	-0.24
10-8..10-13	14%	8	92	8.7%	0.56
10-0..10-07	2%	1	43	2.3%	-0.74
..9-13	0%	0	2	0.0%	-1.00

ANALYSIS BY DAYS SINCE LAST RUN
Age	Prop	Win	Runs	Wins%	£
1..7	2%	1	12	8.3%	-0.50
8..14	8%	5	50	10.0%	-0.41
15..28	37%	22	184	12.0%	-0.30
29..60	39%	23	196	11.7%	0.34
61..100	10%	6	49	12.2%	-0.43
101+	3%	2	36	5.6%	-0.76
Unraced	0%	0	14	0.0%	-1.00

ANALYSIS BY TODAY'S STARTING PRICE
Age	Prop	Win	Runs	Wins%	£
Odds On	27%	16	21	76.2%	0.13
Ev-2/1	14%	8	32	25.0%	-0.41
9/4-4/1	20%	12	61	19.7%	-0.19
9/2-6/1	7%	4	42	9.5%	-0.39
13/2-10/1	19%	11	74	14.9%	0.43
11/1-16/1	7%	4	63	6.3%	-0.08
18/1-33/1	5%	3	90	3.3%	-0.10
40/1+	2%	1	158	0.6%	-0.36

ANALYSIS BY STARTING PRICE LAST TIME
Age	Prop	Win	Runs	Wins%	£
Odds On	12%	7	47	14.9%	-0.37
Ev-2/1	22%	13	67	19.4%	0.06
9/4-4/1	17%	10	77	13.0%	-0.09
9/2-6/1	10%	6	47	12.8%	-0.60
13/2-10/1	15%	9	80	11.3%	-0.52
11/1-16/1	12%	7	58	12.1%	0.43
18/1-33/1	7%	4	63	6.3%	-0.34
40/1+	5%	3	88	3.4%	0.26
Unraced	0%	0	14	0.0%	-1.00

ANALYSIS BY DISTANCE BEATEN LAST TIME
Age	Prop	Win	Runs	Wins%	£
..-10 lgh	7%	4	47	8.5%	-0.37
-10..0	39%	23	118	19.5%	-0.17
0.1..2	17%	10	34	29.4%	1.01
2.1..5	7%	4	39	10.3%	-0.53
5.1..10	3%	2	42	4.8%	-0.11
10.1..20	3%	2	46	4.3%	-0.65
20.0..30	10%	6	44	13.6%	0.22
30.1+	12%	7	100	7.0%	0.40
Not Compl	2%	1	57	1.8%	-0.96
Unraced	0%	0	14	0.0%	-1.00

ANALYSIS BY SUCCESS RATE IN LAST 10 RUNS
Age	Prop	Win	Runs	Wins%	£
No Wins	10%	6	175	3.4%	-0.74
1 Win	27%	16	96	16.7%	0.85
2 Wins	25%	15	105	14.3%	-0.07
3 Wins	22%	13	81	16.0%	0.17
4 Wins	8%	5	48	10.4%	-0.18
5+ Wins	7%	4	22	18.2%	-0.63

ANALYSIS BY SUCCESS RATE IN LAST 3 RUNS
Age	Prop	Win	Runs	Wins%	£
No Wins	24%	14	221	6.3%	-0.01
1 Win	36%	21	166	12.7%	-0.31
2 Wins	31%	18	116	15.5%	-0.02
3 Wins	10%	6	24	25.0%	-0.24

ANALYSIS BY POSITION LAST TIME
Age	Prop	Win	Runs	Wins%	£
Won	46%	27	164	16.5%	-0.22
2nd or 3rd	32%	19	132	14.4%	-0.08
Unplaced	20%	12	175	6.9%	0.21
Fell,BD,UR	2%	1	11	9.1%	-0.78
Pulled Up	0%	0	43	0.0%	-1.00
Ref/RanOut	0%	0	1	0.0%	-1.00
CO/SlipUp	0%	0	1	0.0%	-1.00
Unraced	0%	0	14	0.0%	-1.00

OTHER FACTORS (WINS-RUNS, £)
Course Winner:	8-47	-£0.47
Distance Winner:	14-101	£0.00
Going Winner:	22-156	£0.17
Beaten Favourite:	7-40	£0.46
7-Day Winners:	0-1	-£1.00
BHA Top Rated:	16-48	-£0.23
Absolute Favourites:	24-56	-£0.23

Race Profiles

Novices' Hurdle Races (class 1..3): 2 to 5 runners

ANALYSIS BY AGE

Age	Prop	Win	Runs	Wins%	£
3yo	0%	0	0	0.0%	0.00
4yo	21%	7	30	23.3%	-0.31
5yo	35%	12	56	21.4%	-0.25
6yo	21%	7	40	17.5%	-0.51
7yo	24%	8	25	32.0%	0.37
8yo	0%	0	5	0.0%	-1.00
9yo	0%	0	1	0.0%	-1.00
10yo	0%	0	2	0.0%	-1.00
11yo	0%	0	0	0.0%	0.00
12yo+	0%	0	0	0.0%	0.00

ANALYSIS BY BHB RATING

Age	Prop	Win	Runs	Wins%	£
150+	6%	2	4	50.0%	-0.38
130..149	21%	7	23	30.4%	-0.12
120..129	15%	5	21	23.8%	0.00
110..119	18%	6	17	35.3%	0.58
100..109	3%	1	4	25.0%	-0.70
80..99	0%	0	3	0.0%	-1.00
60..79	0%	0	2	0.0%	-1.00
..59	0%	0	0	0.0%	0.00
Unrated	38%	13	85	15.3%	-0.47

ANALYSIS BY WEIGHT CARRIED

Age	Prop	Win	Runs	Wins%	£
12-01+	0%	0	0	0.0%	0.00
11-8..12-00	44%	15	40	37.5%	-0.06
11-0..11-07	44%	15	81	18.5%	-0.17
10-8..10-13	9%	3	27	11.1%	-0.67
10-0..10-07	3%	1	11	9.1%	-0.75
..9-13	0%	0	0	0.0%	0.00

ANALYSIS BY DAYS SINCE LAST RUN

Age	Prop	Win	Runs	Wins%	£
1..7	3%	1	4	25.0%	0.38
8..14	21%	7	38	18.4%	-0.25
15..28	38%	13	48	27.1%	-0.15
29..60	26%	9	34	26.5%	-0.12
61..100	3%	1	7	14.3%	-0.21
101+	6%	2	22	9.1%	-0.81
Unraced	3%	1	6	16.7%	-0.70

ANALYSIS BY TODAY'S STARTING PRICE

Age	Prop	Win	Runs	Wins%	£
Odds On	41%	14	21	66.7%	0.00
Ev-2/1	21%	7	24	29.2%	-0.28
9/4-4/1	15%	5	26	19.2%	-0.30
9/2-6/1	15%	5	11	45.5%	1.64
13/2-10/1	6%	2	25	8.0%	-0.24
11/1-16/1	3%	1	10	10.0%	0.20
18/1-33/1	0%	0	21	0.0%	-1.00
40/1+	0%	0	21	0.0%	-1.00

ANALYSIS BY STARTING PRICE LAST TIME

Age	Prop	Win	Runs	Wins%	£
Odds On	15%	5	14	35.7%	0.42
Ev-2/1	12%	4	15	26.7%	-0.52
9/4-4/1	32%	11	37	29.7%	-0.11
9/2-6/1	12%	4	10	40.0%	0.39
13/2-10/1	15%	5	22	22.7%	-0.36
11/1-16/1	6%	2	17	11.8%	-0.21
18/1-33/1	6%	2	17	11.8%	-0.22
40/1+	0%	0	21	0.0%	-1.00
Unraced	3%	1	6	16.7%	-0.70

ANALYSIS BY DISTANCE BEATEN LAST TIME

Age	Prop	Win	Runs	Wins%	£
..-10 lgh	15%	5	10	50.0%	0.41
-10..0	26%	9	43	20.9%	-0.42
0.1..2	12%	4	11	36.4%	0.61
2.1..5	9%	3	7	42.9%	-0.14
5.1..10	6%	2	15	13.3%	-0.63
10.1..20	3%	1	13	7.7%	-0.81
20.0..30	9%	3	12	25.0%	0.61
30.1+	12%	4	27	14.8%	-0.36
Not Compl	6%	2	15	13.3%	-0.52
Unraced	3%	1	6	16.7%	-0.70

ANALYSIS BY SUCCESS RATE IN LAST 10 RUNS

Age	Prop	Win	Runs	Wins%	£
No Wins	3%	1	48	2.1%	-0.97
1 Win	45%	15	47	31.9%	0.20
2 Wins	24%	8	31	25.8%	-0.50
3 Wins	18%	6	17	35.3%	0.77
4 Wins	9%	3	9	33.3%	0.23
5+ Wins	0%	0	1	0.0%	-1.00

ANALYSIS BY SUCCESS RATE IN LAST 3 RUNS

Age	Prop	Win	Runs	Wins%	£
No Wins	12%	4	63	6.3%	-0.83
1 Win	61%	20	59	33.9%	0.15
2 Wins	24%	8	28	28.6%	0.24
3 Wins	3%	1	3	33.3%	-0.55

ANALYSIS BY POSITION LAST TIME

Age	Prop	Win	Runs	Wins%	£
Won	41%	14	53	26.4%	-0.26
2nd or 3rd	24%	8	35	22.9%	-0.28
Unplaced	26%	9	50	18.0%	-0.14
Fell,BD,UR	6%	2	7	28.6%	0.02
Pulled Up	0%	0	8	0.0%	-1.00
Ref/RanOut	0%	0	0	0.0%	0.00
CO/SlipUp	0%	0	0	0.0%	0.00
Unraced	3%	1	6	16.7%	-0.70

OTHER FACTORS (WINS-RUNS, £)

Course Winner:	4-11	-£0.43
Distance Winner:	12-46	-£0.11
Going Winner:	12-52	-£0.23
Beaten Favourite:	5-11	£0.80
7-Day Winners:	0-1	-£1.00
BHA Top Rated:	10-24	-£0.18
Absolute Favourites:	17-34	-£0.15

Novices' Hurdle Races (class 1..3)

Novices' Hurdle Races (class 1..3): 6 to 10 runners

ANALYSIS BY AGE

Age	Prop	Win	Runs	Wins%	£
3yo	0%	0	0	0.0%	0.00
4yo	20%	45	337	13.4%	-0.16
5yo	33%	74	644	11.5%	-0.46
6yo	27%	62	472	13.1%	-0.39
7yo	16%	36	220	16.4%	-0.14
8yo	4%	8	73	11.0%	-0.52
9yo	0%	1	27	3.7%	-0.87
10yo	0%	0	8	0.0%	-1.00
11yo	0%	0	5	0.0%	-1.00
12yo+	0%	0	5	0.0%	-1.00

ANALYSIS BY BHB RATING

Age	Prop	Win	Runs	Wins%	£
150+	3%	6	11	54.5%	0.06
130..149	22%	50	198	25.3%	0.00
120..129	17%	38	180	21.1%	0.06
110..119	9%	20	134	14.9%	-0.37
100..109	1%	3	61	4.9%	-0.83
80..99	1%	2	52	3.8%	-0.37
60..79	0%	0	36	0.0%	-1.00
..59	0%	0	1	0.0%	-1.00
Unrated	47%	107	1118	9.6%	-0.45

ANALYSIS BY WEIGHT CARRIED

Age	Prop	Win	Runs	Wins%	£
12-01+	0%	0	1	0.0%	-1.00
11-8..12-00	25%	56	231	24.2%	-0.19
11-0..11-07	54%	123	913	13.5%	-0.33
10-8..10-13	17%	39	435	9.0%	-0.39
10-0..10-07	4%	8	204	3.9%	-0.61
..9-13	0%	0	7	0.0%	-1.00

ANALYSIS BY DAYS SINCE LAST RUN

Age	Prop	Win	Runs	Wins%	£
1..7	3%	7	57	12.3%	-0.69
8..14	12%	28	203	13.8%	-0.35
15..28	37%	83	570	14.6%	-0.26
29..60	27%	61	444	13.7%	-0.33
61..100	8%	17	111	15.3%	-0.23
101+	12%	28	283	9.9%	-0.40
Unraced	1%	2	123	1.6%	-0.86

ANALYSIS BY TODAY'S STARTING PRICE

Age	Prop	Win	Runs	Wins%	£
Odds On	28%	63	102	61.8%	-0.03
Ev-2/1	23%	52	137	38.0%	-0.05
9/4-4/1	18%	40	226	17.7%	-0.28
9/2-6/1	12%	26	134	19.4%	0.22
13/2-10/1	11%	25	224	11.2%	0.01
11/1-16/1	7%	15	225	6.7%	0.01
18/1-33/1	2%	4	258	1.6%	-0.68
40/1+	0%	1	485	0.2%	-0.89

ANALYSIS BY STARTING PRICE LAST TIME

Age	Prop	Win	Runs	Wins%	£
Odds On	16%	36	130	27.7%	0.13
Ev-2/1	23%	53	204	26.0%	0.07
9/4-4/1	16%	36	226	15.9%	-0.14
9/2-6/1	9%	20	148	13.5%	-0.35
13/2-10/1	14%	32	220	14.5%	-0.35
11/1-16/1	8%	18	200	9.0%	-0.59
18/1-33/1	10%	22	243	9.1%	-0.18
40/1+	3%	7	297	2.4%	-0.85
Unraced	1%	2	123	1.6%	-0.86

ANALYSIS BY DISTANCE BEATEN LAST TIME

Age	Prop	Win	Runs	Wins%	£
..-10 lgh	9%	20	88	22.7%	-0.18
-10..0	32%	72	340	21.2%	-0.10
0.1..2	18%	40	117	34.2%	0.45
2.1..5	11%	24	111	21.6%	0.21
5.1..10	7%	15	126	11.9%	-0.42
10.1..20	7%	16	181	8.8%	-0.60
20.0..30	5%	12	161	7.5%	-0.33
30.1+	6%	14	369	3.8%	-0.75
Not Compl	5%	11	175	6.3%	-0.42
Unraced	1%	2	123	1.6%	-0.86

ANALYSIS BY SUCCESS RATE IN LAST 10 RUNS

Age	Prop	Win	Runs	Wins%	£
No Wins	18%	40	779	5.1%	-0.59
1 Win	30%	68	396	17.2%	-0.15
2 Wins	24%	53	266	19.9%	-0.17
3 Wins	17%	38	144	26.4%	0.04
4 Wins	8%	17	60	28.3%	0.24
5+ Wins	4%	8	23	34.8%	0.07

ANALYSIS BY SUCCESS RATE IN LAST 3 RUNS

Age	Prop	Win	Runs	Wins%	£
No Wins	26%	59	894	6.6%	-0.54
1 Win	38%	84	490	17.1%	-0.14
2 Wins	27%	61	235	26.0%	-0.06
3 Wins	9%	20	49	40.8%	0.51

ANALYSIS BY POSITION LAST TIME

Age	Prop	Win	Runs	Wins%	£
Won	41%	92	428	21.5%	-0.12
2nd or 3rd	36%	81	380	21.3%	-0.01
Unplaced	18%	40	685	5.8%	-0.60
Fell,BD,UR	4%	8	63	12.7%	0.46
Pulled Up	1%	2	103	1.9%	-0.92
Ref/RanOut	0%	0	6	0.0%	-1.00
CO/SlipUp	0%	1	3	33.3%	-0.58
Unraced	1%	2	123	1.6%	-0.86

OTHER FACTORS (WINS-RUNS, £)

Course Winner:	23-100	-£0.26
Distance Winner:	66-357	-£0.15
Going Winner:	83-388	-£0.17
Beaten Favourite:	36-138	£0.33
7-Day Winners:	2-14	-£0.73
BHA Top Rated:	48-167	-£0.37
Absolute Favourites:	100-216	-£0.12

Race Profiles

Novices' Hurdle Races (class 1..3): 11 runners or more

ANALYSIS BY AGE

Age	Prop	Win	Runs	Wins%	£
3yo	0%	0	0	0.0%	0.00
4yo	27%	47	484	9.7%	-0.53
5yo	38%	65	823	7.9%	-0.44
6yo	25%	43	659	6.5%	-0.26
7yo	9%	15	322	4.7%	-0.62
8yo	1%	1	69	1.4%	-0.97
9yo	0%	0	9	0.0%	-1.00
10yo	1%	1	10	10.0%	-0.10
11yo	0%	0	4	0.0%	-1.00
12yo+	0%	0	1	0.0%	-1.00

ANALYSIS BY BHB RATING

Age	Prop	Win	Runs	Wins%	£
150+	1%	2	21	9.5%	-0.76
130..149	22%	37	247	15.0%	-0.03
120..129	10%	17	132	12.9%	-0.27
110..119	5%	8	110	7.3%	-0.66
100..109	5%	8	81	9.9%	0.04
80..99	1%	1	64	1.6%	0.58
60..79	0%	0	31	0.0%	-1.00
..59	0%	0	1	0.0%	-1.00
Unrated	58%	99	1694	5.8%	-0.56

ANALYSIS BY WEIGHT CARRIED

Age	Prop	Win	Runs	Wins%	£
12-01+	0%	0	0	0.0%	0.00
11-8..12-00	22%	38	139	27.3%	0.00
11-0..11-07	48%	83	1194	7.0%	-0.47
10-8..10-13	24%	42	709	5.9%	-0.42
10-0..10-07	5%	9	319	2.8%	-0.61
..9-13	0%	0	20	0.0%	-1.00

ANALYSIS BY DAYS SINCE LAST RUN

Age	Prop	Win	Runs	Wins%	£
1..7	0%	0	39	0.0%	-1.00
8..14	7%	12	245	4.9%	-0.76
15..28	28%	49	679	7.2%	-0.53
29..60	37%	63	634	9.9%	-0.04
61..100	7%	12	166	7.2%	-0.65
101+	13%	23	363	6.3%	-0.53
Unraced	8%	13	255	5.1%	-0.63

ANALYSIS BY TODAY'S STARTING PRICE

Age	Prop	Win	Runs	Wins%	£
Odds On	19%	32	57	56.1%	-0.10
Ev-2/1	19%	33	84	39.3%	-0.02
9/4-4/1	22%	37	171	21.6%	-0.16
9/2-6/1	8%	13	145	9.0%	-0.43
13/2-10/1	17%	29	240	12.1%	0.08
11/1-16/1	10%	17	253	6.7%	0.00
18/1-33/1	4%	7	402	1.7%	-0.53
40/1+	2%	4	1029	0.4%	-0.76

ANALYSIS BY STARTING PRICE LAST TIME

Age	Prop	Win	Runs	Wins%	£
Odds On	16%	27	145	18.6%	-0.16
Ev-2/1	19%	33	182	18.1%	0.00
9/4-4/1	16%	28	274	10.2%	-0.26
9/2-6/1	9%	16	174	9.2%	-0.34
13/2-10/1	9%	16	249	6.4%	-0.63
11/1-16/1	13%	22	258	8.5%	-0.34
18/1-33/1	5%	9	317	2.8%	-0.68
40/1+	5%	8	527	1.5%	-0.58
Unraced	8%	13	255	5.1%	-0.63

ANALYSIS BY DISTANCE BEATEN LAST TIME

Age	Prop	Win	Runs	Wins%	£
..-10 lgh	12%	20	91	22.0%	0.48
-10..0	28%	49	293	16.7%	-0.09
0.1..2	10%	18	108	16.7%	-0.14
2.1..5	7%	12	124	9.7%	-0.56
5.1..10	7%	12	182	6.6%	-0.55
10.1..20	14%	24	259	9.3%	-0.26
20.0..30	4%	7	220	3.2%	-0.35
30.1+	8%	13	612	2.1%	-0.66
Not Compl	2%	4	237	1.7%	-0.84
Unraced	8%	13	255	5.1%	-0.63

ANALYSIS BY SUCCESS RATE IN LAST 10 RUNS

Age	Prop	Win	Runs	Wins%	£
No Wins	23%	36	1235	2.9%	-0.68
1 Win	36%	57	418	13.6%	0.04
2 Wins	20%	32	241	13.3%	-0.27
3 Wins	12%	19	121	15.7%	0.21
4 Wins	6%	10	74	13.5%	-0.47
5+ Wins	3%	5	37	13.5%	-0.44

ANALYSIS BY SUCCESS RATE IN LAST 3 RUNS

Age	Prop	Win	Runs	Wins%	£
No Wins	28%	44	1354	3.2%	-0.56
1 Win	44%	70	494	14.2%	-0.19
2 Wins	22%	35	232	15.1%	-0.24
3 Wins	6%	10	46	21.7%	-0.21

ANALYSIS BY POSITION LAST TIME

Age	Prop	Win	Runs	Wins%	£
Won	40%	69	383	18.0%	0.05
2nd or 3rd	27%	47	424	11.1%	-0.39
Unplaced	23%	39	1083	3.6%	-0.53
Fell,BD,UR	1%	2	66	3.0%	-0.85
Pulled Up	1%	2	166	1.2%	-0.84
Ref/RanOut	0%	0	3	0.0%	-1.00
CO/SlipUp	0%	0	1	0.0%	-1.00
Unraced	8%	13	255	5.1%	-0.63

OTHER FACTORS (WINS-RUNS, £)

Course Winner:	21-118	-£0.04
Distance Winner:	58-377	-£0.18
Going Winner:	53-335	£0.01
Beaten Favourite:	21-156	-£0.40
7-Day Winners:	0-4	-£1.00
BHA Top Rated:	30-117	-£0.14
Absolute Favourites:	67-159	-£0.08

Novices' Hurdle Races (class 1..3)

Novices' Hurdle Races (class 1..3): up to 7 days off the track

ANALYSIS BY AGE

Age	Prop	Win	Runs	Wins%	£
3yo	0%	0	0	0.0%	0.00
4yo	42%	10	157	6.4%	-0.64
5yo	46%	11	152	7.2%	-0.68
6yo	8%	2	98	2.0%	-0.74
7yo	4%	1	58	1.7%	-0.90
8yo	0%	0	16	0.0%	-1.00
9yo	0%	0	2	0.0%	-1.00
10yo	0%	0	0	0.0%	0.00
11yo	0%	0	0	0.0%	0.00
12yo+	0%	0	1	0.0%	-1.00

ANALYSIS BY BHB RATING

Age	Prop	Win	Runs	Wins%	£
150+	0%	0	0	0.0%	0.00
130..149	8%	2	11	18.2%	-0.60
120..129	13%	3	11	27.3%	-0.08
110..119	0%	0	8	0.0%	-1.00
100..109	0%	0	6	0.0%	-1.00
80..99	0%	0	10	0.0%	-1.00
60..79	0%	0	6	0.0%	-1.00
..59	0%	0	1	0.0%	-1.00
Unrated	79%	19	431	4.4%	-0.72

ANALYSIS BY WEIGHT CARRIED

Age	Prop	Win	Runs	Wins%	£
12-01+	0%	0	0	0.0%	0.00
11-8..12-00	13%	3	15	20.0%	-0.61
11-0..11-07	42%	10	219	4.6%	-0.73
10-8..10-13	42%	10	146	6.8%	-0.59
10-0..10-07	4%	1	100	1.0%	-0.88
..9-13	0%	0	4	0.0%	-1.00

ANALYSIS BY DAYS SINCE LAST RUN

Age	Prop	Win	Runs	Wins%	£
1..7	33%	8	100	8.0%	-0.77
8..14	0%	0	0	0.0%	0.00
15..28	0%	0	0	0.0%	0.00
29..60	0%	0	0	0.0%	0.00
61..100	0%	0	0	0.0%	0.00
101+	0%	0	0	0.0%	0.00
Unraced	67%	16	384	4.2%	-0.70

ANALYSIS BY TODAY'S STARTING PRICE

Age	Prop	Win	Runs	Wins%	£
Odds On	25%	6	11	54.5%	-0.06
Ev-2/1	21%	5	16	31.3%	-0.31
9/4-4/1	13%	3	26	11.5%	-0.55
9/2-6/1	13%	3	25	12.0%	-0.32
13/2-10/1	13%	3	47	6.4%	-0.41
11/1-16/1	17%	4	50	8.0%	0.18
18/1-33/1	0%	0	91	0.0%	-1.00
40/1+	0%	0	218	0.0%	-1.00

ANALYSIS BY STARTING PRICE LAST TIME

Age	Prop	Win	Runs	Wins%	£
Odds On	8%	2	10	20.0%	-0.28
Ev-2/1	4%	1	8	12.5%	-0.74
9/4-4/1	8%	2	9	22.2%	-0.54
9/2-6/1	4%	1	8	12.5%	-0.25
13/2-10/1	4%	1	10	10.0%	-0.86
11/1-16/1	4%	1	14	7.1%	-0.84
18/1-33/1	0%	0	12	0.0%	-1.00
40/1+	0%	0	29	0.0%	-1.00
Unraced	67%	16	384	4.2%	-0.70

ANALYSIS BY DISTANCE BEATEN LAST TIME

Age	Prop	Win	Runs	Wins%	£
..-10 lgh	4%	1	9	11.1%	-0.77
-10..0	4%	1	10	10.0%	-0.83
0.1..2	8%	2	2	100.0%	0.80
2.1..5	0%	0	3	0.0%	-1.00
5.1..10	4%	1	11	9.1%	-0.83
10.1..20	8%	2	8	25.0%	0.03
20.0..30	0%	0	6	0.0%	-1.00
30.1+	0%	0	29	0.0%	-1.00
Not Compl	4%	1	22	4.5%	-0.75
Unraced	67%	16	384	4.2%	-0.70

ANALYSIS BY SUCCESS RATE IN LAST 10 RUNS

Age	Prop	Win	Runs	Wins%	£
No Wins	13%	1	52	1.9%	-0.96
1 Win	25%	2	19	10.5%	-0.61
2 Wins	25%	2	13	15.4%	-0.41
3 Wins	25%	2	6	33.3%	-0.42
4 Wins	13%	1	7	14.3%	-0.68
5+ Wins	0%	0	3	0.0%	-1.00

ANALYSIS BY SUCCESS RATE IN LAST 3 RUNS

Age	Prop	Win	Runs	Wins%	£
No Wins	38%	3	62	4.8%	-0.90
1 Win	25%	2	21	9.5%	-0.67
2 Wins	38%	3	15	20.0%	-0.34
3 Wins	0%	0	2	0.0%	-1.00

ANALYSIS BY POSITION LAST TIME

Age	Prop	Win	Runs	Wins%	£
Won	8%	2	19	10.5%	-0.80
2nd or 3rd	17%	4	19	21.1%	-0.39
Unplaced	4%	1	40	2.5%	-0.94
Fell,BD,UR	4%	1	11	9.1%	-0.50
Pulled Up	0%	0	10	0.0%	-1.00
Ref/RanOut	0%	0	1	0.0%	-1.00
CO/SlipUp	0%	0	0	0.0%	0.00
Unraced	67%	16	384	4.2%	-0.70

OTHER FACTORS (WINS-RUNS, £)

Course Winner:	0-6	-£1.00
Distance Winner:	4-24	-£0.34
Going Winner:	4-24	-£0.69
Beaten Favourite:	1-6	-£0.08
7-Day Winners:	2-19	-£0.80
BHA Top Rated:	4-14	-£0.39
Absolute Favourites:	11-28	-£0.20

Race Profiles

Novices' Hurdle Races (class 1..3): 100+ days off the track

ANALYSIS BY AGE

Age	Prop	Win	Runs	Wins%	£
3yo	0%	0	0	0.0%	0.00
4yo	26%	14	120	11.7%	-0.44
5yo	35%	19	231	8.2%	-0.47
6yo	26%	14	182	7.7%	-0.37
7yo	9%	5	86	5.8%	-0.58
8yo	2%	1	32	3.1%	-0.93
9yo	2%	1	9	11.1%	-0.61
10yo	0%	0	8	0.0%	-1.00
11yo	0%	0	5	0.0%	-1.00
12yo+	0%	0	2	0.0%	-1.00

ANALYSIS BY BHB RATING

Age	Prop	Win	Runs	Wins%	£
150+	0%	0	0	0.0%	0.00
130..149	15%	8	21	38.1%	0.46
120..129	4%	2	20	10.0%	-0.17
110..119	4%	2	22	9.1%	-0.16
100..109	0%	0	23	0.0%	-1.00
80..99	2%	1	26	3.8%	-0.19
60..79	0%	0	14	0.0%	-1.00
..59	0%	0	0	0.0%	0.00
Unrated	76%	41	549	7.5%	-0.53

ANALYSIS BY WEIGHT CARRIED

Age	Prop	Win	Runs	Wins%	£
12-01+	0%	0	0	0.0%	0.00
11-8..12-00	7%	4	12	33.3%	-0.33
11-0..11-07	31%	17	242	7.0%	-0.56
10-8..10-13	52%	28	312	9.0%	-0.42
10-0..10-07	9%	5	107	4.7%	-0.53
..9-13	0%	0	2	0.0%	-1.00

ANALYSIS BY DAYS SINCE LAST RUN

Age	Prop	Win	Runs	Wins%	£
1..7	0%	0	0	0.0%	0.00
8..14	0%	0	0	0.0%	0.00
15..28	0%	0	0	0.0%	0.00
29..60	0%	0	0	0.0%	0.00
61..100	2%	1	7	14.3%	-0.75
101+	98%	53	668	7.9%	-0.48
Unraced	0%	0	0	0.0%	0.00

ANALYSIS BY TODAY'S STARTING PRICE

Age	Prop	Win	Runs	Wins%	£
Odds On	22%	12	17	70.6%	0.11
Ev-2/1	19%	10	22	45.5%	0.03
9/4-4/1	20%	11	46	23.9%	-0.02
9/2-6/1	13%	7	37	18.9%	0.14
13/2-10/1	7%	4	49	8.2%	-0.26
11/1-16/1	13%	7	71	9.9%	0.59
18/1-33/1	6%	3	126	2.4%	-0.46
40/1+	0%	0	307	0.0%	-1.00

ANALYSIS BY STARTING PRICE LAST TIME

Age	Prop	Win	Runs	Wins%	£
Odds On	17%	9	28	32.1%	0.77
Ev-2/1	17%	9	50	18.0%	-0.40
9/4-4/1	17%	9	69	13.0%	-0.36
9/2-6/1	13%	7	60	11.7%	0.07
13/2-10/1	13%	7	105	6.7%	-0.41
11/1-16/1	6%	3	93	3.2%	-0.90
18/1-33/1	17%	9	122	7.4%	-0.30
40/1+	2%	1	148	0.7%	-0.99
Unraced	0%	0	0	0.0%	0.00

ANALYSIS BY DISTANCE BEATEN LAST TIME

Age	Prop	Win	Runs	Wins%	£
..-10 lgh	6%	3	11	27.3%	0.90
-10..0	20%	11	63	17.5%	-0.32
0.1..2	9%	5	31	16.1%	-0.57
2.1..5	11%	6	37	16.2%	-0.16
5.1..10	6%	3	55	5.5%	-0.35
10.1..20	17%	9	87	10.3%	-0.24
20.0..30	11%	6	68	8.8%	-0.13
30.1+	11%	6	227	2.6%	-0.83
Not Compl	9%	5	96	5.2%	-0.60
Unraced	0%	0	0	0.0%	0.00

ANALYSIS BY SUCCESS RATE IN LAST 10 RUNS

Age	Prop	Win	Runs	Wins%	£
No Wins	39%	21	482	4.4%	-0.63
1 Win	31%	17	121	14.0%	-0.19
2 Wins	19%	10	42	23.8%	0.02
3 Wins	7%	4	20	20.0%	0.22
4 Wins	4%	2	7	28.6%	-0.45
5+ Wins	0%	0	3	0.0%	-1.00

ANALYSIS BY SUCCESS RATE IN LAST 3 RUNS

Age	Prop	Win	Runs	Wins%	£
No Wins	50%	27	517	5.2%	-0.59
1 Win	28%	15	116	12.9%	-0.38
2 Wins	19%	10	34	29.4%	0.51
3 Wins	4%	2	8	25.0%	0.34

ANALYSIS BY POSITION LAST TIME

Age	Prop	Win	Runs	Wins%	£
Won	26%	14	74	18.9%	-0.14
2nd or 3rd	22%	12	108	11.1%	-0.42
Unplaced	43%	23	397	5.8%	-0.54
Fell,BD,UR	2%	1	17	5.9%	-0.78
Pulled Up	7%	4	77	5.2%	-0.55
Ref/RanOut	0%	0	2	0.0%	-1.00
CO/SlipUp	0%	0	0	0.0%	0.00
Unraced	0%	0	0	0.0%	0.00

OTHER FACTORS (WINS-RUNS, £)

Course Winner:	3-18	-£0.38
Distance Winner:	11-65	-£0.37
Going Winner:	15-68	£0.01
Beaten Favourite:	9-50	-£0.06
BHA Top Rated:	6-31	-£0.63
Absolute Favourites:	24-42	£0.18

Novices' Hurdle Races (class 4..6)

ANALYSIS BY AGE

Age	Prop	Win	Runs	Wins%	£
3yo	0%	0	8	0.0%	-1.00
4yo	19%	373	4144	9.0%	-0.46
5yo	35%	672	7292	9.2%	-0.46
6yo	28%	545	5511	9.9%	-0.44
7yo	12%	221	2630	8.4%	-0.49
8yo	4%	79	913	8.7%	-0.54
9yo	1%	19	299	6.4%	-0.47
10yo	0%	6	114	5.3%	-0.67
11yo	0%	1	36	2.8%	-0.93
12yo+	0%	0	20	0.0%	-1.00

ANALYSIS BY BHB RATING

Age	Prop	Win	Runs	Wins%	£
150+	0%	0	0	0.0%	0.00
130..149	3%	54	119	45.4%	0.01
120..129	10%	190	565	33.6%	-0.17
110..119	17%	332	1116	29.7%	-0.01
100..109	10%	192	1160	16.6%	-0.25
80..99	4%	86	1130	7.6%	-0.33
60..79	0%	7	650	1.1%	-0.71
..59	0%	0	28	0.0%	-1.00
Unrated	55%	1055	16199	6.5%	-0.53

ANALYSIS BY WEIGHT CARRIED

Age	Prop	Win	Runs	Wins%	£
12-01+	0%	2	6	33.3%	-0.38
11-8..12-00	8%	155	526	29.5%	-0.13
11-0..11-07	41%	791	5499	14.4%	-0.30
10-8..10-13	40%	759	9718	7.8%	-0.49
10-0..10-07	11%	204	4876	4.2%	-0.61
..9-13	0%	5	342	1.5%	-0.85

ANALYSIS BY DAYS SINCE LAST RUN

Age	Prop	Win	Runs	Wins%	£
1..7	3%	57	588	9.7%	-0.65
8..14	15%	280	2655	10.5%	-0.47
15..28	30%	576	5473	10.5%	-0.47
29..60	22%	430	4278	10.1%	-0.45
61..100	6%	115	293	8.9%	-0.41
101+	17%	319	4314	7.4%	-0.41
Unraced	7%	139	2366	5.9%	-0.59

ANALYSIS BY TODAY'S STARTING PRICE

Age	Prop	Win	Runs	Wins%	£
Odds On	23%	448	726	61.7%	-0.03
Ev-2/1	26%	500	1303	38.4%	-0.04
9/4-4/1	23%	445	1866	23.8%	-0.05
9/2-6/1	8%	147	1115	13.2%	-0.19
13/2-10/1	9%	170	1913	8.9%	-0.20
11/1-16/1	5%	105	2165	4.8%	-0.29
18/1-33/1	4%	75	3479	2.2%	-0.44
40/1+	1%	26	8400	0.3%	-0.82

ANALYSIS BY STARTING PRICE LAST TIME

Age	Prop	Win	Runs	Wins%	£
Odds On	9%	168	390	43.1%	0.00
Ev-2/1	14%	259	912	28.4%	-0.17
9/4-4/1	19%	357	1718	20.8%	-0.18
9/2-6/1	11%	214	1218	17.6%	-0.16
13/2-10/1	15%	279	2162	12.9%	-0.25
11/1-16/1	11%	213	2398	8.9%	-0.38
18/1-33/1	9%	180	3447	5.2%	-0.46
40/1+	6%	107	6356	1.7%	-0.74
Unraced	7%	139	2366	5.9%	-0.59

ANALYSIS BY DISTANCE BEATEN LAST TIME

Age	Prop	Win	Runs	Wins%	£
..-10 lgh	6%	115	291	39.5%	-0.04
-10..0	20%	389	1355	28.7%	-0.12
0.1..2	9%	166	673	24.7%	-0.09
2.1..5	9%	163	781	20.9%	-0.17
5.1..10	11%	208	1206	17.2%	-0.26
10.1..20	15%	283	2408	11.8%	-0.22
20.0..30	8%	156	2160	7.2%	-0.43
30.1+	10%	187	6871	2.7%	-0.66
Not Compl	6%	110	2856	3.9%	-0.61
Unraced	7%	139	2366	5.9%	-0.59

ANALYSIS BY SUCCESS RATE IN LAST 10 RUNS

Age	Prop	Win	Runs	Wins%	£
No Wins	41%	723	14117	5.1%	-0.54
1 Win	39%	695	3336	20.8%	-0.20
2 Wins	15%	269	905	29.7%	-0.10
3 Wins	4%	72	196	36.7%	-0.04
4 Wins	1%	13	41	31.7%	-0.45
5+ Wins	0%	5	6	83.3%	0.81

ANALYSIS BY SUCCESS RATE IN LAST 3 RUNS

Age	Prop	Win	Runs	Wins%	£
No Wins	51%	903	15124	6.0%	-0.51
1 Win	39%	696	2983	23.3%	-0.22
2 Wins	9%	166	469	35.4%	-0.06
3 Wins	1%	12	25	48.0%	0.32

ANALYSIS BY POSITION LAST TIME

Age	Prop	Win	Runs	Wins%	£
Won	26%	504	1644	30.7%	-0.10
2nd or 3rd	31%	585	2985	19.6%	-0.16
Unplaced	30%	578	11137	5.2%	-0.54
Fell,BD,UR	3%	56	704	8.0%	-0.52
Pulled Up	3%	52	2069	2.5%	-0.64
Ref/RanOut	0%	2	43	4.7%	-0.56
CO/SlipUp	0%	0	19	0.0%	-1.00
Unraced	7%	139	2366	5.9%	-0.59

OTHER FACTORS (WINS-RUNS, £)

Course Winner:	188-734	-£0.19
Distance Winner:	384-1526	-£0.20
Going Winner:	407-1584	-£0.19
Beaten Favourite:	186-819	-£0.17
7-Day Winners:	20-41	£0.06
BHA Top Rated:	401-1404	-£0.13
Absolute Favourites:	865-1831	-£0.03

TRAINERS (WINS-RUNS, £)

M J Scudamore 4-30 £0.11; J I A Charlton 3-23 £0.04.

Race Profiles

Novices' Hurdle Races (class 4..6): 2m to 2m3f

ANALYSIS BY AGE

Age	Prop	Win	Runs	Wins%	£
3yo	0%	0	8	0.0%	-1.00
4yo	28%	269	2875	9.4%	-0.45
5yo	37%	355	4035	8.8%	-0.43
6yo	25%	241	2576	9.4%	-0.48
7yo	8%	76	1127	6.7%	-0.52
8yo	2%	19	323	5.9%	-0.77
9yo	0%	3	103	2.9%	-0.88
10yo	0%	1	39	2.6%	-0.94
11yo	0%	0	11	0.0%	-1.00
12yo+	0%	0	2	0.0%	-1.00

ANALYSIS BY BHB RATING

Age	Prop	Win	Runs	Wins%	£
150+	0%	0	0	0.0%	0.00
130..149	2%	20	44	45.5%	-0.14
120..129	9%	82	254	32.3%	-0.29
110..119	16%	154	496	31.0%	0.01
100..109	8%	80	514	15.6%	-0.25
80..99	4%	36	511	7.0%	-0.37
60..79	1%	5	273	1.8%	-0.50
..59	0%	0	17	0.0%	-1.00
Unrated	61%	587	8990	6.5%	-0.52

ANALYSIS BY WEIGHT CARRIED

Age	Prop	Win	Runs	Wins%	£
12-01+	0%	0	1	0.0%	-1.00
11-8..12-00	7%	65	246	26.4%	-0.30
11-0..11-07	42%	406	2972	13.7%	-0.27
10-8..10-13	38%	370	5057	7.3%	-0.53
10-0..10-07	12%	120	2632	4.6%	-0.58
..9-13	0%	3	191	1.6%	-0.90

ANALYSIS BY DAYS SINCE LAST RUN

Age	Prop	Win	Runs	Wins%	£
1..7	3%	26	321	8.1%	-0.75
8..14	14%	132	1362	9.7%	-0.42
15..28	29%	283	2737	10.3%	-0.43
29..60	21%	206	2169	9.5%	-0.49
61..100	5%	53	684	7.7%	-0.41
101+	17%	164	2233	7.3%	-0.40
Unraced	10%	100	1593	6.3%	-0.62

ANALYSIS BY TODAY'S STARTING PRICE

Age	Prop	Win	Runs	Wins%	£
Odds On	25%	244	385	63.4%	0.00
Ev-2/1	24%	234	616	38.0%	-0.05
9/4-4/1	22%	212	919	23.1%	-0.08
9/2-6/1	8%	78	559	14.0%	-0.13
13/2-10/1	9%	86	981	8.8%	-0.20
11/1-16/1	6%	56	1158	4.8%	-0.28
18/1-33/1	4%	39	1885	2.1%	-0.46
40/1+	2%	15	4596	0.3%	-0.80

ANALYSIS BY STARTING PRICE LAST TIME

Age	Prop	Win	Runs	Wins%	£
Odds On	8%	81	193	42.0%	-0.10
Ev-2/1	14%	139	472	29.4%	-0.15
9/4-4/1	17%	160	816	19.6%	-0.24
9/2-6/1	11%	108	589	18.3%	-0.17
13/2-10/1	14%	135	1095	12.3%	-0.28
11/1-16/1	10%	98	1223	8.0%	-0.37
18/1-33/1	9%	88	1796	4.9%	-0.41
40/1+	6%	55	3322	1.7%	-0.71
Unraced	10%	100	1593	6.3%	-0.62

ANALYSIS BY DISTANCE BEATEN LAST TIME

Age	Prop	Win	Runs	Wins%	£
..-10 lgh	5%	50	120	41.7%	-0.02
-10..0	20%	188	649	29.0%	-0.16
0.1..2	9%	89	327	27.2%	0.08
2.1..5	7%	69	388	17.8%	-0.31
5.1..10	11%	104	599	17.4%	-0.26
10.1..20	14%	138	1254	11.0%	-0.25
20.0..30	8%	74	1138	6.5%	-0.49
30.1+	11%	102	3638	2.8%	-0.60
Not Compl	5%	50	1393	3.6%	-0.60
Unraced	10%	100	1593	6.3%	-0.62

ANALYSIS BY SUCCESS RATE IN LAST 10 RUNS

Age	Prop	Win	Runs	Wins%	£
No Wins	44%	376	7415	5.1%	-0.52
1 Win	38%	331	1608	20.6%	-0.20
2 Wins	14%	118	387	30.5%	-0.16
3 Wins	4%	33	83	39.8%	-0.06
4 Wins	1%	5	12	41.7%	-0.43
5+ Wins	0%	1	1	100.0%	0.73

ANALYSIS BY SUCCESS RATE IN LAST 3 RUNS

Age	Prop	Win	Runs	Wins%	£
No Wins	51%	441	7847	5.6%	-0.50
1 Win	39%	338	1422	23.8%	-0.18
2 Wins	9%	81	226	35.8%	-0.19
3 Wins	0%	4	11	36.4%	-0.07

ANALYSIS BY POSITION LAST TIME

Age	Prop	Win	Runs	Wins%	£
Won	25%	238	770	30.9%	-0.14
2nd or 3rd	28%	266	1407	18.9%	-0.23
Unplaced	32%	310	5946	5.2%	-0.50
Fell,BD,UR	3%	25	374	6.7%	-0.64
Pulled Up	3%	25	982	2.5%	-0.57
Ref/RanOut	0%	0	20	0.0%	-1.00
CO/SlipUp	0%	0	7	0.0%	-1.00
Unraced	10%	100	1593	6.3%	-0.62

OTHER FACTORS (WINS-RUNS, £)

Course Winner:	87-335	-£0.28
Distance Winner:	242-991	-£0.18
Going Winner:	196-712	-£0.18
Beaten Favourite:	91-409	-£0.31
7-Day Winners:	9-20	£0.01
BHA Top Rated:	183-675	-£0.15
Absolute Favourites:	440-919	-£0.03

Novices' Hurdle Races (class 4..6)

Novices' Hurdle Races (class 4..6): 2m4f to 2m7f

ANALYSIS BY AGE

Age	Prop	Win	Runs	Wins%	£
3yo	0%	0	0	0.0%	0.00
4yo	13%	100	1189	8.4%	-0.51
5yo	35%	268	2819	9.5%	-0.50
6yo	32%	244	2338	10.4%	-0.40
7yo	13%	102	1144	8.9%	-0.52
8yo	5%	36	411	8.8%	-0.49
9yo	1%	9	123	7.3%	-0.58
10yo	0%	3	45	6.7%	-0.32
11yo	0%	1	15	6.7%	-0.82
12yo+	0%	0	10	0.0%	-1.00

ANALYSIS BY BHB RATING

Age	Prop	Win	Runs	Wins%	£
150+	0%	0	0	0.0%	0.00
130..149	3%	21	48	43.8%	-0.02
120..129	11%	81	231	35.1%	-0.12
110..119	19%	143	481	29.7%	-0.01
100..109	12%	93	487	19.1%	-0.17
80..99	5%	40	465	8.6%	-0.23
60..79	0%	1	284	0.4%	-0.86
..59	0%	0	8	0.0%	-1.00
Unrated	50%	384	6090	6.3%	-0.56

ANALYSIS BY WEIGHT CARRIED

Age	Prop	Win	Runs	Wins%	£
12-01+	0%	1	2	50.0%	-0.32
11-8..12-00	8%	61	196	31.1%	-0.02
11-0..11-07	41%	314	2025	15.5%	-0.32
10-8..10-13	41%	313	3890	8.0%	-0.51
10-0..10-07	9%	72	1861	3.9%	-0.62
..9-13	0%	2	120	1.7%	-0.72

ANALYSIS BY DAYS SINCE LAST RUN

Age	Prop	Win	Runs	Wins%	£
1..7	4%	27	220	12.3%	-0.51
8..14	15%	118	1027	11.5%	-0.48
15..28	30%	232	2231	10.4%	-0.53
29..60	23%	174	1673	10.4%	-0.39
61..100	7%	50	488	10.2%	-0.35
101+	17%	128	1793	7.1%	-0.49
Unraced	4%	34	662	5.1%	-0.54

ANALYSIS BY TODAY'S STARTING PRICE

Age	Prop	Win	Runs	Wins%	£
Odds On	21%	162	268	60.4%	-0.05
Ev-2/1	28%	215	555	38.7%	-0.03
9/4-4/1	25%	190	749	25.4%	0.02
9/2-6/1	7%	50	450	11.1%	-0.32
13/2-10/1	9%	67	761	8.8%	-0.20
11/1-16/1	6%	42	825	5.1%	-0.27
18/1-33/1	4%	30	1324	2.3%	-0.40
40/1+	1%	7	3162	0.2%	-0.88

ANALYSIS BY STARTING PRICE LAST TIME

Age	Prop	Win	Runs	Wins%	£
Odds On	9%	72	162	44.4%	0.09
Ev-2/1	12%	92	352	26.1%	-0.20
9/4-4/1	21%	157	732	21.4%	-0.12
9/2-6/1	11%	83	519	16.0%	-0.14
13/2-10/1	15%	115	873	13.2%	-0.33
11/1-16/1	12%	93	956	9.7%	-0.39
18/1-33/1	10%	74	1376	5.4%	-0.52
40/1+	6%	43	2462	1.7%	-0.77
Unraced	4%	34	662	5.1%	-0.54

ANALYSIS BY DISTANCE BEATEN LAST TIME

Age	Prop	Win	Runs	Wins%	£
..-10 lgh	6%	48	131	36.6%	-0.14
-10..0	21%	160	561	28.5%	-0.03
0.1..2	8%	63	279	22.6%	-0.22
2.1..5	10%	79	334	23.7%	-0.03
5.1..10	12%	91	526	17.3%	-0.27
10.1..20	15%	117	963	12.1%	-0.19
20.0..30	8%	59	865	6.8%	-0.51
30.1+	8%	63	2632	2.4%	-0.74
Not Compl	6%	49	1141	4.3%	-0.59
Unraced	4%	34	662	5.1%	-0.54

ANALYSIS BY SUCCESS RATE IN LAST 10 RUNS

Age	Prop	Win	Runs	Wins%	£
No Wins	39%	286	5529	5.2%	-0.58
1 Win	40%	290	1410	20.6%	-0.18
2 Wins	16%	120	391	30.7%	-0.09
3 Wins	4%	28	84	33.3%	-0.14
4 Wins	0%	2	14	14.3%	-0.64
5+ Wins	0%	3	4	75.0%	0.69

ANALYSIS BY SUCCESS RATE IN LAST 3 RUNS

Age	Prop	Win	Runs	Wins%	£
No Wins	51%	373	5966	6.3%	-0.53
1 Win	39%	286	1270	22.5%	-0.26
2 Wins	9%	65	186	34.9%	0.02
3 Wins	1%	5	10	50.0%	-0.02

ANALYSIS BY POSITION LAST TIME

Age	Prop	Win	Runs	Wins%	£
Won	27%	208	690	30.1%	-0.05
2nd or 3rd	34%	256	1301	19.7%	-0.10
Unplaced	28%	216	4306	5.0%	-0.62
Fell,BD,UR	3%	26	263	9.9%	-0.39
Pulled Up	3%	21	843	2.5%	-0.66
Ref/RanOut	0%	2	19	10.5%	-0.01
CO/SlipUp	0%	0	10	0.0%	-1.00
Unraced	4%	34	662	5.1%	-0.54

OTHER FACTORS (WINS-RUNS, £)

Course Winner:	72-305	-£0.14
Distance Winner:	109-422	-£0.28
Going Winner:	163-672	-£0.17
Beaten Favourite:	77-343	-£0.02
7-Day Winners:	11-19	£0.22
BHA Top Rated:	168-572	-£0.14
Absolute Favourites:	339-732	-£0.03

Race Profiles

Novices' Hurdle Races (class 4..6): 3m+

ANALYSIS BY AGE

Age	Prop	Win	Runs	Wins%	£
3yo	0%	0	0	0.0%	0.00
4yo	2%	4	80	5.0%	-0.38
5yo	26%	49	438	11.2%	-0.48
6yo	32%	60	597	10.1%	-0.48
7yo	23%	43	359	12.0%	-0.31
8yo	13%	24	179	13.4%	-0.23
9yo	4%	7	73	9.6%	0.30
10yo	1%	2	30	6.7%	-0.85
11yo	0%	0	10	0.0%	-1.00
12yo+	0%	0	8	0.0%	-1.00

ANALYSIS BY BHB RATING

Age	Prop	Win	Runs	Wins%	£
150+	0%	0	0	0.0%	0.00
130..149	7%	13	27	48.1%	0.30
120..129	14%	27	80	33.8%	0.09
110..119	19%	35	139	25.2%	-0.07
100..109	10%	19	159	11.9%	-0.54
80..99	5%	10	154	6.5%	-0.56
60..79	1%	1	93	1.1%	-0.89
..59	0%	0	3	0.0%	-1.00
Unrated	44%	84	1119	7.5%	-0.40

ANALYSIS BY WEIGHT CARRIED

Age	Prop	Win	Runs	Wins%	£
12-01+	1%	1	3	33.3%	-0.21
11-8..12-00	15%	29	84	34.5%	0.14
11-0..11-07	38%	71	502	14.1%	-0.44
10-8..10-13	40%	76	771	9.9%	-0.19
10-0..10-07	6%	12	383	3.1%	-0.81
..9-13	0%	0	31	0.0%	-1.00

ANALYSIS BY DAYS SINCE LAST RUN

Age	Prop	Win	Runs	Wins%	£
1..7	2%	4	47	8.5%	-0.69
8..14	16%	30	266	11.3%	-0.67
15..28	32%	61	505	12.1%	-0.35
29..60	26%	50	436	11.5%	-0.45
61..100	6%	12	121	9.9%	-0.63
101+	14%	27	288	9.4%	-0.02
Unraced	3%	5	111	4.5%	-0.35

ANALYSIS BY TODAY'S STARTING PRICE

Age	Prop	Win	Runs	Wins%	£
Odds On	22%	42	73	57.5%	-0.12
Ev-2/1	27%	51	132	38.6%	-0.04
9/4-4/1	23%	43	198	21.7%	-0.16
9/2-6/1	10%	19	106	17.9%	0.10
13/2-10/1	9%	17	171	9.9%	-0.12
11/1-16/1	4%	7	182	3.8%	-0.44
18/1-33/1	3%	6	270	2.2%	-0.46
40/1+	2%	4	642	0.6%	-0.69

ANALYSIS BY STARTING PRICE LAST TIME

Age	Prop	Win	Runs	Wins%	£
Odds On	8%	15	35	42.9%	0.19
Ev-2/1	15%	28	88	31.8%	-0.17
9/4-4/1	21%	40	170	23.5%	-0.13
9/2-6/1	12%	23	110	20.9%	-0.27
13/2-10/1	15%	29	194	14.9%	0.26
11/1-16/1	12%	22	219	10.0%	-0.44
18/1-33/1	10%	18	275	6.5%	-0.50
40/1+	5%	9	572	1.6%	-0.73
Unraced	3%	5	111	4.5%	-0.35

ANALYSIS BY DISTANCE BEATEN LAST TIME

Age	Prop	Win	Runs	Wins%	£
..-10 lgh	9%	17	40	42.5%	0.22
-10..0	22%	41	145	28.3%	-0.27
0.1..2	7%	14	67	20.9%	-0.38
2.1..5	8%	15	59	25.4%	0.00
5.1..10	7%	13	81	16.0%	-0.25
10.1..20	15%	28	191	14.7%	-0.16
20.0..30	12%	23	157	14.6%	0.41
30.1+	12%	22	601	3.7%	-0.63
Not Compl	6%	11	322	3.4%	-0.76
Unraced	3%	5	111	4.5%	-0.35

ANALYSIS BY SUCCESS RATE IN LAST 10 RUNS

Age	Prop	Win	Runs	Wins%	£
No Wins	33%	61	1173	5.2%	-0.50
1 Win	40%	74	318	23.3%	-0.28
2 Wins	17%	31	127	24.4%	0.04
3 Wins	6%	11	29	37.9%	0.30
4 Wins	3%	6	15	40.0%	-0.29
5+ Wins	1%	1	1	100.0%	1.38

ANALYSIS BY SUCCESS RATE IN LAST 3 RUNS

Age	Prop	Win	Runs	Wins%	£
No Wins	48%	89	1311	6.8%	-0.46
1 Win	39%	72	291	24.7%	-0.26
2 Wins	11%	20	57	35.1%	0.18
3 Wins	2%	3	4	75.0%	2.25

ANALYSIS BY POSITION LAST TIME

Age	Prop	Win	Runs	Wins%	£
Won	31%	58	184	31.5%	-0.16
2nd or 3rd	33%	63	277	22.7%	-0.09
Unplaced	28%	52	885	5.9%	-0.42
Fell,BD,UR	3%	5	67	7.5%	-0.41
Pulled Up	3%	6	244	2.5%	-0.84
Ref/RanOut	0%	0	4	0.0%	-1.00
CO/SlipUp	0%	0	2	0.0%	-1.00
Unraced	3%	5	111	4.5%	-0.35

OTHER FACTORS (WINS-RUNS, £)

Course Winner:	29-94	-£0.02
Distance Winner:	33-113	-£0.08
Going Winner:	48-200	-£0.26
Beaten Favourite:	18-67	-£0.12
7-Day Winners:	0-2	-£1.00
BHA Top Rated:	50-157	-£0.07
Absolute Favourites:	86-180	-£0.02

Novices' Hurdle Races (class 4..6)

Novices' Hurdle Races (class 4..6): 2 to 5 runners

ANALYSIS BY AGE
Age	Prop	Win	Runs	Wins%	£
3yo	0%	0	0	0.0%	0.00
4yo	19%	19	68	27.9%	-0.24
5yo	27%	28	147	19.0%	-0.06
6yo	29%	30	127	23.6%	0.05
7yo	13%	13	70	18.6%	0.01
8yo	8%	8	31	25.8%	-0.21
9yo	3%	3	13	23.1%	0.21
10yo	1%	1	4	25.0%	-0.74
11yo	0%	0	2	0.0%	-1.00
12yo+	0%	0	0	0.0%	0.00

ANALYSIS BY BHB RATING
Age	Prop	Win	Runs	Wins%	£
150+	0%	0	0	0.0%	0.00
130..149	5%	5	10	50.0%	-0.39
120..129	13%	13	28	46.4%	-0.05
110..119	23%	23	62	37.1%	0.02
100..109	20%	20	52	38.5%	0.52
80..99	4%	4	42	9.5%	-0.50
60..79	0%	0	16	0.0%	-1.00
..59	0%	0	0	0.0%	0.00
Unrated	36%	37	252	14.7%	-0.05

ANALYSIS BY WEIGHT CARRIED
Age	Prop	Win	Runs	Wins%	£
12-01+	0%	0	1	0.0%	-1.00
11-8..12-00	9%	9	29	31.0%	-0.23
11-0..11-07	47%	48	155	31.0%	-0.20
10-8..10-13	29%	30	179	16.8%	0.06
10-0..10-07	15%	15	95	15.8%	0.03
..9-13	0%	0	3	0.0%	-1.00

ANALYSIS BY DAYS SINCE LAST RUN
Age	Prop	Win	Runs	Wins%	£
1..7	6%	6	20	30.0%	-0.51
8..14	24%	24	87	27.6%	0.30
15..28	36%	37	125	29.6%	0.06
29..60	17%	17	85	20.0%	0.42
61..100	9%	9	40	22.5%	-0.17
101+	7%	7	76	9.2%	-0.78
Unraced	2%	2	29	6.9%	-0.71

ANALYSIS BY TODAY'S STARTING PRICE
Age	Prop	Win	Runs	Wins%	£
Odds On	45%	46	66	69.7%	0.04
Ev-2/1	21%	21	69	30.4%	-0.27
9/4-4/1	17%	17	75	22.7%	-0.09
9/2-6/1	7%	7	40	17.5%	0.06
13/2-10/1	7%	7	43	16.3%	0.52
11/1-16/1	0%	0	45	0.0%	-1.00
18/1-33/1	2%	2	64	3.1%	-0.11
40/1+	2%	2	60	3.3%	0.37

ANALYSIS BY STARTING PRICE LAST TIME
Age	Prop	Win	Runs	Wins%	£
Odds On	7%	7	17	41.2%	-0.17
Ev-2/1	17%	17	39	43.6%	-0.06
9/4-4/1	21%	21	48	43.8%	0.00
9/2-6/1	10%	10	26	38.5%	0.28
13/2-10/1	17%	17	69	24.6%	-0.28
11/1-16/1	17%	17	63	27.0%	0.75
18/1-33/1	4%	4	72	5.6%	-0.74
40/1+	7%	7	99	7.1%	0.17
Unraced	2%	2	29	6.9%	-0.71

ANALYSIS BY DISTANCE BEATEN LAST TIME
Age	Prop	Win	Runs	Wins%	£
..-10 lgh	11%	11	14	78.6%	0.31
-10..0	24%	24	61	39.3%	-0.11
0.1..2	10%	10	23	43.5%	-0.07
2.1..5	7%	7	27	25.9%	-0.54
5.1..10	11%	11	36	30.6%	-0.30
10.1..20	11%	11	56	19.6%	-0.47
20.0..30	5%	5	47	10.6%	-0.39
30.1+	14%	14	115	12.2%	0.46
Not Compl	7%	7	54	13.0%	0.25
Unraced	2%	2	29	6.9%	-0.71

ANALYSIS BY SUCCESS RATE IN LAST 10 RUNS
Age	Prop	Win	Runs	Wins%	£
No Wins	36%	36	271	13.3%	-0.04
1 Win	37%	37	102	36.3%	0.06
2 Wins	19%	19	43	44.2%	0.03
3 Wins	5%	5	14	35.7%	-0.40
4 Wins	3%	3	3	100.0%	1.07
5+ Wins	0%	0	0	0.0%	0.00

ANALYSIS BY SUCCESS RATE IN LAST 3 RUNS
Age	Prop	Win	Runs	Wins%	£
No Wins	47%	47	307	15.3%	-0.03
1 Win	44%	44	101	43.6%	0.09
2 Wins	8%	8	24	33.3%	-0.31
3 Wins	1%	1	1	100.0%	2.00

ANALYSIS BY POSITION LAST TIME
Age	Prop	Win	Runs	Wins%	£
Won	34%	35	76	46.1%	-0.04
2nd or 3rd	31%	32	91	35.2%	-0.21
Unplaced	25%	26	213	12.2%	0.00
Fell,BD,UR	2%	2	11	18.2%	0.32
Pulled Up	5%	5	40	12.5%	0.32
Ref/RanOut	0%	0	1	0.0%	-1.00
CO/SlipUp	0%	0	1	0.0%	-1.00
Unraced	2%	2	29	6.9%	-0.71

OTHER FACTORS (WINS-RUNS, £)
Course Winner:	11-32	-£0.04
Distance Winner:	21-60	-£0.16
Going Winner:	26-67	-£0.11
Beaten Favourite:	8-23	£0.05
7-Day Winners:	3-4	£0.20
BHA Top Rated:	30-72	-£0.07
Absolute Favourites:	60-100	£0.02

Race Profiles

Novices' Hurdle Races (class 4..6): 6 to 10 runners

ANALYSIS BY AGE

Age	Prop	Win	Runs	Wins%	£
3yo	0%	0	0	0.0%	0.00
4yo	17%	132	1184	11.1%	-0.37
5yo	35%	275	2094	13.1%	-0.39
6yo	28%	217	1773	12.2%	-0.43
7yo	13%	104	926	11.2%	-0.26
8yo	5%	35	340	10.3%	-0.50
9yo	1%	8	113	7.1%	-0.71
10yo	1%	4	36	11.1%	-0.71
11yo	0%	0	13	0.0%	-1.00
12yo+	0%	0	12	0.0%	-1.00

ANALYSIS BY BHB RATING

Age	Prop	Win	Runs	Wins%	£
150+	0%	0	0	0.0%	0.00
130..149	3%	25	46	54.3%	0.29
120..129	12%	91	236	38.6%	-0.11
110..119	20%	153	439	34.9%	0.01
100..109	9%	73	465	15.7%	-0.42
80..99	5%	39	437	8.9%	-0.27
60..79	1%	4	289	1.4%	-0.80
..59	0%	0	10	0.0%	-1.00
Unrated	50%	390	4569	8.5%	-0.44

ANALYSIS BY WEIGHT CARRIED

Age	Prop	Win	Runs	Wins%	£
12-01+	0%	1	2	50.0%	0.19
11-8..12-00	11%	84	227	37.0%	0.02
11-0..11-07	42%	329	1825	18.0%	-0.27
10-8..10-13	38%	296	2858	10.4%	-0.38
10-0..10-07	8%	62	1473	4.2%	-0.61
..9-13	0%	3	106	2.8%	-0.80

ANALYSIS BY DAYS SINCE LAST RUN

Age	Prop	Win	Runs	Wins%	£
1..7	3%	23	216	10.6%	-0.75
8..14	17%	132	923	14.3%	-0.39
15..28	31%	240	1789	13.4%	-0.45
29..60	21%	162	1270	12.8%	-0.40
61..100	7%	54	441	12.2%	-0.27
101+	14%	106	1250	8.5%	-0.36
Unraced	7%	58	602	9.6%	-0.28

ANALYSIS BY TODAY'S STARTING PRICE

Age	Prop	Win	Runs	Wins%	£
Odds On	29%	225	358	62.8%	-0.02
Ev-2/1	28%	215	554	38.8%	-0.02
9/4-4/1	21%	159	682	23.3%	-0.09
9/2-6/1	9%	58	380	15.3%	-0.07
13/2-10/1	7%	53	692	7.7%	-0.32
11/1-16/1	5%	35	704	5.0%	-0.27
18/1-33/1	3%	21	1107	1.9%	-0.49
40/1+	1%	9	2014	0.4%	-0.75

ANALYSIS BY STARTING PRICE LAST TIME

Age	Prop	Win	Runs	Wins%	£
Odds On	9%	69	138	50.0%	0.07
Ev-2/1	13%	101	305	33.1%	-0.13
9/4-4/1	20%	153	602	25.4%	-0.11
9/2-6/1	12%	92	405	22.7%	-0.07
13/2-10/1	15%	117	710	16.5%	-0.34
11/1-16/1	9%	73	751	9.7%	-0.58
18/1-33/1	9%	70	1069	6.5%	-0.47
40/1+	5%	42	1909	2.2%	-0.57
Unraced	7%	58	602	9.6%	-0.28

ANALYSIS BY DISTANCE BEATEN LAST TIME

Age	Prop	Win	Runs	Wins%	£
..-10 lgh	7%	56	118	47.5%	0.18
-10..0	22%	169	482	35.1%	-0.06
0.1..2	8%	62	224	27.7%	-0.25
2.1..5	9%	66	248	26.6%	-0.04
5.1..10	10%	81	393	20.6%	-0.20
10.1..20	13%	101	765	13.2%	-0.37
20.0..30	8%	65	663	9.8%	-0.39
30.1+	9%	71	2097	3.4%	-0.61
Not Compl	6%	46	899	5.1%	-0.48
Unraced	7%	58	602	9.6%	-0.28

ANALYSIS BY SUCCESS RATE IN LAST 10 RUNS

Age	Prop	Win	Runs	Wins%	£
No Wins	38%	270	4327	6.2%	-0.51
1 Win	42%	303	1147	26.4%	-0.11
2 Wins	15%	110	320	34.4%	-0.20
3 Wins	4%	30	78	38.5%	-0.05
4 Wins	0%	3	15	20.0%	-0.70
5+ Wins	0%	1	2	50.0%	-0.04

ANALYSIS BY SUCCESS RATE IN LAST 3 RUNS

Age	Prop	Win	Runs	Wins%	£
No Wins	48%	347	4683	7.4%	-0.48
1 Win	41%	293	1018	28.8%	-0.15
2 Wins	10%	71	177	40.1%	-0.10
3 Wins	1%	6	11	54.5%	0.39

ANALYSIS BY POSITION LAST TIME

Age	Prop	Win	Runs	Wins%	£
Won	29%	225	599	37.6%	-0.01
2nd or 3rd	29%	224	986	22.7%	-0.25
Unplaced	29%	222	3412	6.5%	-0.50
Fell,BD,UR	3%	24	228	10.5%	-0.58
Pulled Up	3%	20	639	3.1%	-0.45
Ref/RanOut	0%	2	17	11.8%	0.10
CO/SlipUp	0%	0	8	0.0%	-1.00
Unraced	7%	58	602	9.6%	-0.28

OTHER FACTORS (WINS-RUNS, £)

Course Winner:	82-277	-£0.23
Distance Winner:	162-503	-£0.11
Going Winner:	168-577	-£0.20
Beaten Favourite:	71-270	-£0.17
7-Day Winners:	11-19	£0.15
BHA Top Rated:	186-575	-£0.13
Absolute Favourites:	373-741	-£0.02

TRAINERS (WINS-RUNS, £)

C T Pogson 4-14 £0.06; N J Henderson 22-59 £0.01.

Novices' Hurdle Races (class 4..6)

Novices' Hurdle Races (class 4..6): 11 runners or more

ANALYSIS BY AGE
Age	Prop	Win	Runs	Wins%	£
3yo	0%	0	8	0.0%	-1.00
4yo	21%	222	2892	7.7%	-0.51
5yo	36%	369	5051	7.3%	-0.50
6yo	29%	298	3611	8.3%	-0.47
7yo	10%	104	1634	6.4%	-0.64
8yo	3%	36	542	6.6%	-0.58
9yo	1%	8	173	4.6%	-0.36
10yo	0%	1	74	1.4%	-0.65
11yo	0%	1	21	4.8%	-0.87
12yo+	0%	0	8	0.0%	-1.00

ANALYSIS BY BHB RATING
Age	Prop	Win	Runs	Wins%	£
150+	0%	0	0	0.0%	0.00
130..149	2%	24	63	38.1%	-0.13
120..129	8%	86	301	28.6%	-0.22
110..119	15%	156	615	25.4%	-0.02
100..109	10%	99	643	15.4%	-0.20
80..99	4%	43	651	6.6%	-0.37
60..79	0%	3	345	0.9%	-0.62
..59	0%	0	18	0.0%	-1.00
Unrated	60%	628	11378	5.5%	-0.57

ANALYSIS BY WEIGHT CARRIED
Age	Prop	Win	Runs	Wins%	£
12-01+	0%	1	3	33.3%	-0.55
11-8..12-00	6%	62	270	23.0%	-0.24
11-0..11-07	40%	414	3519	11.8%	-0.32
10-8..10-13	42%	433	6681	6.5%	-0.56
10-0..10-07	12%	127	3308	3.8%	-0.63
..9-13	0%	2	233	0.9%	-0.87

ANALYSIS BY DAYS SINCE LAST RUN
Age	Prop	Win	Runs	Wins%	£
1..7	3%	28	352	8.0%	-0.61
8..14	12%	124	1645	7.5%	-0.55
15..28	29%	299	3559	8.4%	-0.49
29..60	24%	251	2923	8.6%	-0.49
61..100	5%	52	812	6.4%	-0.50
101+	20%	206	2988	6.9%	-0.42
Unraced	8%	79	1735	4.6%	-0.70

ANALYSIS BY TODAY'S STARTING PRICE
Age	Prop	Win	Runs	Wins%	£
Odds On	17%	177	302	58.6%	-0.06
Ev-2/1	25%	264	680	38.8%	-0.03
9/4-4/1	26%	269	1109	24.3%	-0.02
9/2-6/1	8%	82	695	11.8%	-0.26
13/2-10/1	11%	110	1178	9.3%	-0.15
11/1-16/1	7%	70	1416	4.9%	-0.28
18/1-33/1	5%	52	2308	2.3%	-0.42
40/1+	1%	15	6326	0.2%	-0.86

ANALYSIS BY STARTING PRICE LAST TIME
Age	Prop	Win	Runs	Wins%	£
Odds On	9%	92	235	39.1%	-0.02
Ev-2/1	14%	141	568	24.8%	-0.20
9/4-4/1	18%	183	1068	17.1%	-0.23
9/2-6/1	11%	112	787	14.2%	-0.23
13/2-10/1	14%	145	1383	10.5%	-0.21
11/1-16/1	12%	123	1584	7.8%	-0.33
18/1-33/1	10%	106	2306	4.6%	-0.45
40/1+	6%	58	4348	1.3%	-0.83
Unraced	8%	79	1735	4.6%	-0.70

ANALYSIS BY DISTANCE BEATEN LAST TIME
Age	Prop	Win	Runs	Wins%	£
..-10 lgh	5%	48	159	30.2%	-0.23
-10..0	19%	196	812	24.1%	-0.15
0.1..2	9%	94	426	22.1%	-0.01
2.1..5	9%	90	506	17.8%	-0.21
5.1..10	11%	116	777	14.9%	-0.29
10.1..20	16%	171	1587	10.8%	-0.14
20.0..30	8%	86	1450	5.9%	-0.45
30.1+	10%	102	4659	2.2%	-0.71
Not Compl	5%	57	1903	3.0%	-0.70
Unraced	8%	79	1735	4.6%	-0.70

ANALYSIS BY SUCCESS RATE IN LAST 10 RUNS
Age	Prop	Win	Runs	Wins%	£
No Wins	43%	417	9519	4.4%	-0.57
1 Win	37%	355	2087	17.0%	-0.26
2 Wins	15%	140	542	25.8%	-0.05
3 Wins	4%	37	104	35.6%	0.01
4 Wins	1%	7	23	30.4%	-0.49
5+ Wins	0%	4	4	100.0%	1.24

ANALYSIS BY SUCCESS RATE IN LAST 3 RUNS
Age	Prop	Win	Runs	Wins%	£
No Wins	53%	509	10134	5.0%	-0.54
1 Win	37%	359	1864	19.3%	-0.28
2 Wins	9%	87	268	32.5%	-0.01
3 Wins	1%	5	13	38.5%	0.13

ANALYSIS BY POSITION LAST TIME
Age	Prop	Win	Runs	Wins%	£
Won	23%	244	969	25.2%	-0.17
2nd or 3rd	32%	329	1908	17.2%	-0.10
Unplaced	32%	330	7512	4.4%	-0.57
Fell,BD,UR	3%	30	465	6.5%	-0.52
Pulled Up	3%	27	1390	1.9%	-0.75
Ref/RanOut	0%	0	25	0.0%	-1.00
CO/SlipUp	0%	0	10	0.0%	-1.00
Unraced	8%	79	1735	4.6%	-0.70

OTHER FACTORS (WINS-RUNS, £)
Course Winner:	95-425	-£0.18
Distance Winner:	201-963	-£0.25
Going Winner:	213-940	-£0.18
Beaten Favourite:	107-526	-£0.19
7-Day Winners:	6-18	-£0.07
BHA Top Rated:	185-757	-£0.14
Absolute Favourites:	432-990	-£0.04

Race Profiles

Novices' Hurdle Races (class 4..6): up to 7 days off the track

ANALYSIS BY AGE

Age	Prop	Win	Runs	Wins%	£
3yo	0%	0	1	0.0%	-1.00
4yo	37%	72	947	7.6%	-0.40
5yo	31%	61	959	6.4%	-0.69
6yo	18%	36	551	6.5%	-0.78
7yo	9%	18	325	5.5%	-0.61
8yo	4%	8	124	6.5%	-0.62
9yo	1%	1	29	3.4%	-0.55
10yo	0%	0	14	0.0%	-1.00
11yo	0%	0	3	0.0%	-1.00
12yo+	0%	0	1	0.0%	-1.00

ANALYSIS BY BHB RATING

Age	Prop	Win	Runs	Wins%	£
150+	0%	0	0	0.0%	0.00
130..149	1%	2	3	66.7%	2.58
120..129	5%	9	18	50.0%	0.12
110..119	8%	16	32	50.0%	0.80
100..109	7%	13	47	27.7%	-0.25
80..99	3%	6	60	10.0%	-0.41
60..79	0%	0	34	0.0%	-1.00
..59	0%	0	1	0.0%	-1.00
Unrated	77%	150	2759	5.4%	-0.63

ANALYSIS BY WEIGHT CARRIED

Age	Prop	Win	Runs	Wins%	£
12-01+	0%	0	2	0.0%	-1.00
11-8..12-00	3%	6	14	42.9%	0.13
11-0..11-07	26%	50	539	9.3%	-0.55
10-8..10-13	53%	104	1527	6.8%	-0.56
10-0..10-07	18%	35	813	4.3%	-0.73
..9-13	1%	1	59	1.7%	-0.51

ANALYSIS BY DAYS SINCE LAST RUN

Age	Prop	Win	Runs	Wins%	£
1..7	29%	57	588	9.7%	-0.65
8..14	0%	0	0	0.0%	0.00
15..28	0%	0	0	0.0%	0.00
29..60	0%	0	0	0.0%	0.00
61..100	0%	0	0	0.0%	0.00
101+	0%	0	0	0.0%	0.00
Unraced	71%	139	2366	5.9%	-0.59

ANALYSIS BY TODAY'S STARTING PRICE

Age	Prop	Win	Runs	Wins%	£
Odds On	24%	48	64	75.0%	0.24
Ev-2/1	25%	49	93	52.7%	0.30
9/4-4/1	19%	38	164	23.2%	-0.07
9/2-6/1	8%	16	123	13.0%	-0.21
13/2-10/1	9%	17	249	6.8%	-0.40
11/1-16/1	8%	16	351	4.6%	-0.36
18/1-33/1	6%	11	553	2.0%	-0.44
40/1+	1%	1	1357	0.1%	-0.97

ANALYSIS BY STARTING PRICE LAST TIME

Age	Prop	Win	Runs	Wins%	£
Odds On	7%	13	19	68.4%	0.24
Ev-2/1	5%	10	21	47.6%	0.21
9/4-4/1	5%	9	31	29.0%	-0.41
9/2-6/1	3%	6	22	27.3%	0.52
13/2-10/1	6%	11	61	18.0%	-0.33
11/1-16/1	1%	2	53	3.8%	-0.86
18/1-33/1	3%	5	116	4.3%	-0.61
40/1+	1%	1	265	0.4%	-0.97
Unraced	71%	139	2366	5.9%	-0.59

ANALYSIS BY DISTANCE BEATEN LAST TIME

Age	Prop	Win	Runs	Wins%	£
..-10 lgh	4%	8	11	72.7%	0.17
-10..0	6%	12	31	38.7%	-0.02
0.1..2	4%	8	13	61.5%	0.32
2.1..5	3%	6	17	35.3%	0.64
5.1..10	3%	6	23	26.1%	-0.11
10.1..20	2%	4	58	6.9%	-0.84
20.0..30	2%	4	58	6.9%	-0.33
30.1+	2%	4	212	1.9%	-0.87
Not Compl	3%	5	165	3.0%	-0.89
Unraced	71%	139	2366	5.9%	-0.59

ANALYSIS BY SUCCESS RATE IN LAST 10 RUNS

Age	Prop	Win	Runs	Wins%	£
No Wins	37%	21	485	4.3%	-0.77
1 Win	30%	17	67	25.4%	-0.28
2 Wins	28%	16	28	57.1%	0.30
3 Wins	5%	3	7	42.9%	-0.30
4 Wins	0%	0	1	0.0%	-1.00
5+ Wins	0%	0	0	0.0%	0.00

ANALYSIS BY SUCCESS RATE IN LAST 3 RUNS

Age	Prop	Win	Runs	Wins%	£
No Wins	47%	27	509	5.3%	-0.75
1 Win	39%	22	63	34.9%	-0.02
2 Wins	14%	8	15	53.3%	0.07
3 Wins	0%	0	1	0.0%	-1.00

ANALYSIS BY POSITION LAST TIME

Age	Prop	Win	Runs	Wins%	£
Won	10%	20	41	48.8%	0.06
2nd or 3rd	11%	22	57	38.6%	0.25
Unplaced	5%	10	325	3.1%	-0.79
Fell,BD,UR	3%	5	64	7.8%	-0.71
Pulled Up	0%	0	94	0.0%	-1.00
Ref/RanOut	0%	0	5	0.0%	-1.00
CO/SlipUp	0%	0	2	0.0%	-1.00
Unraced	71%	139	2366	5.9%	-0.59

OTHER FACTORS (WINS-RUNS, £)

Course Winner:	8-16	£0.37
Distance Winner:	14-32	-£0.02
Going Winner:	22-44	£0.53
Beaten Favourite:	6-13	-£0.09
7-Day Winners:	20-41	£0.06
BHA Top Rated:	25-55	£0.55
Absolute Favourites:	85-148	£0.16

Novices' Hurdle Races (class 4..6)

Novices' Hurdle Races (class 4..6): 100+ days off the track

ANALYSIS BY AGE

Age	Prop	Win	Runs	Wins%	£
3yo	0%	0	0	0.0%	0.00
4yo	18%	57	644	8.9%	-0.39
5yo	40%	129	1463	8.8%	-0.32
6yo	25%	80	1135	7.0%	-0.45
7yo	11%	36	683	5.3%	-0.53
8yo	4%	13	256	5.1%	-0.63
9yo	1%	4	101	4.0%	-0.19
10yo	0%	1	33	3.0%	-0.21
11yo	0%	0	16	0.0%	-1.00
12yo+	0%	0	5	0.0%	-1.00

ANALYSIS BY BHB RATING

Age	Prop	Win	Runs	Wins%	£
150+	0%	0	0	0.0%	0.00
130..149	1%	4	8	50.0%	-0.14
120..129	4%	14	47	29.8%	-0.11
110..119	8%	26	108	24.1%	0.08
100..109	6%	19	146	13.0%	-0.24
80..99	3%	9	216	4.2%	-0.70
60..79	0%	0	182	0.0%	-1.00
..59	0%	0	9	0.0%	-1.00
Unrated	78%	248	3620	6.9%	-0.39

ANALYSIS BY WEIGHT CARRIED

Age	Prop	Win	Runs	Wins%	£
12-01+	0%	0	0	0.0%	0.00
11-8..12-00	3%	10	32	31.3%	0.64
11-0..11-07	21%	68	717	9.5%	-0.14
10-8..10-13	64%	204	2436	8.4%	-0.43
10-0..10-07	12%	37	1090	3.4%	-0.56
..9-13	0%	1	61	1.6%	-0.88

ANALYSIS BY DAYS SINCE LAST RUN

Age	Prop	Win	Runs	Wins%	£
1..7	0%	0	0	0.0%	0.00
8..14	0%	0	0	0.0%	0.00
15..28	0%	0	0	0.0%	0.00
29..60	0%	0	0	0.0%	0.00
61..100	0%	1	22	4.5%	-0.92
101+	100%	319	4314	7.4%	-0.41
Unraced	0%	0	0	0.0%	0.00

ANALYSIS BY TODAY'S STARTING PRICE

Age	Prop	Win	Runs	Wins%	£
Odds On	16%	52	77	67.5%	0.10
Ev-2/1	25%	81	200	40.5%	0.03
9/4-4/1	23%	72	297	24.2%	-0.03
9/2-6/1	7%	23	198	11.6%	-0.28
13/2-10/1	12%	38	377	10.1%	-0.09
11/1-16/1	8%	25	458	5.5%	-0.20
18/1-33/1	5%	17	801	2.1%	-0.51
40/1+	4%	12	1928	0.6%	-0.63

ANALYSIS BY STARTING PRICE LAST TIME

Age	Prop	Win	Runs	Wins%	£
Odds On	7%	22	69	31.9%	-0.13
Ev-2/1	11%	35	190	18.4%	-0.34
9/4-4/1	16%	50	406	12.3%	-0.28
9/2-6/1	12%	38	272	14.0%	-0.17
13/2-10/1	18%	58	566	10.2%	-0.12
11/1-16/1	16%	50	608	8.2%	-0.48
18/1-33/1	13%	42	838	5.0%	-0.32
40/1+	8%	25	1387	1.8%	-0.67
Unraced	0%	0	0	0.0%	0.00

ANALYSIS BY DISTANCE BEATEN LAST TIME

Age	Prop	Win	Runs	Wins%	£
..-10 lgh	4%	12	43	27.9%	-0.36
-10..0	18%	57	234	24.4%	-0.11
0.1..2	6%	20	135	14.8%	-0.17
2.1..5	7%	21	160	13.1%	-0.21
5.1..10	11%	35	281	12.5%	-0.22
10.1..20	18%	58	598	9.7%	-0.11
20.0..30	10%	32	468	6.8%	-0.33
30.1+	18%	58	1680	3.5%	-0.61
Not Compl	8%	27	737	3.7%	-0.54
Unraced	0%	0	0	0.0%	0.00

ANALYSIS BY SUCCESS RATE IN LAST 10 RUNS

Age	Prop	Win	Runs	Wins%	£
No Wins	51%	164	3536	4.6%	-0.45
1 Win	29%	92	606	15.2%	-0.34
2 Wins	18%	58	161	36.0%	0.16
3 Wins	2%	5	26	19.2%	-0.32
4 Wins	0%	1	7	14.3%	-0.83
5+ Wins	0%	0	0	0.0%	0.00

ANALYSIS BY SUCCESS RATE IN LAST 3 RUNS

Age	Prop	Win	Runs	Wins%	£
No Wins	59%	190	3708	5.1%	-0.45
1 Win	29%	93	537	17.3%	-0.29
2 Wins	12%	37	89	41.6%	0.17
3 Wins	0%	0	2	0.0%	-1.00

ANALYSIS BY POSITION LAST TIME

Age	Prop	Win	Runs	Wins%	£
Won	22%	69	275	25.1%	-0.14
2nd or 3rd	24%	78	598	13.0%	-0.16
Unplaced	46%	146	2742	5.3%	-0.47
Fell,BD,UR	3%	10	142	7.0%	-0.51
Pulled Up	5%	17	566	3.0%	-0.52
Ref/RanOut	0%	0	10	0.0%	-1.00
CO/SlipUp	0%	0	3	0.0%	-1.00
Unraced	0%	0	0	0.0%	0.00

OTHER FACTORS (WINS-RUNS, £)

Course Winner:	18-97	-£0.41
Distance Winner:	50-271	-£0.27
Going Winner:	52-233	-£0.15
Beaten Favourite:	33-214	-£0.15
BHA Top Rated:	41-186	-£0.17
Absolute Favourites:	131-269	£0.10

Race Profiles

Maiden Hurdle Races

ANALYSIS BY AGE

Age	Prop	Win	Runs	Wins%	£
3yo	0%	1	18	5.6%	-0.72
4yo	21%	179	2166	8.3%	-0.44
5yo	33%	279	3437	8.1%	-0.44
6yo	26%	219	2695	8.1%	-0.49
7yo	14%	116	1447	8.0%	-0.44
8yo	4%	36	513	7.0%	-0.53
9yo	0%	4	171	2.3%	-0.91
10yo	0%	4	54	7.4%	-0.56
11yo	0%	0	22	0.0%	-1.00
12yo+	0%	2	8	25.0%	1.09

ANALYSIS BY BHB RATING

Age	Prop	Win	Runs	Wins%	£
150+	0%	0	0	0.0%	0.00
130..149	0%	3	6	50.0%	-0.10
120..129	3%	21	60	35.0%	-0.15
110..119	10%	86	345	24.9%	-0.14
100..109	14%	120	575	20.9%	-0.01
80..99	9%	73	682	10.7%	-0.21
60..79	0%	3	348	0.9%	-0.94
..59	0%	0	13	0.0%	-1.00
Unrated	64%	534	8502	6.3%	-0.51

ANALYSIS BY WEIGHT CARRIED

Age	Prop	Win	Runs	Wins%	£
12-01+	0%	0	0	0.0%	0.00
11-8..12-00	0%	3	32	9.4%	-0.45
11-0..11-07	64%	538	5400	10.0%	-0.40
10-8..10-13	23%	197	3017	6.5%	-0.46
10-0..10-07	12%	97	2002	4.8%	-0.64
..9-13	1%	5	80	6.3%	-0.60

ANALYSIS BY DAYS SINCE LAST RUN

Age	Prop	Win	Runs	Wins%	£
1..7	2%	16	293	5.5%	-0.73
8..14	12%	98	1272	7.7%	-0.39
15..28	27%	227	2592	8.8%	-0.40
29..60	25%	207	2102	9.8%	-0.45
61..100	8%	63	718	8.8%	-0.41
101+	16%	132	2022	6.5%	-0.57
Unraced	12%	97	1532	6.3%	-0.50

ANALYSIS BY TODAY'S STARTING PRICE

Age	Prop	Win	Runs	Wins%	£
Odds On	14%	119	221	53.8%	-0.12
Ev-2/1	23%	197	499	39.5%	0.02
9/4-4/1	26%	217	954	22.7%	-0.07
9/2-6/1	10%	83	632	13.1%	-0.19
13/2-10/1	14%	114	1104	10.3%	-0.07
11/1-16/1	7%	59	1196	4.9%	-0.27
18/1-33/1	5%	41	1808	2.3%	-0.44
40/1+	1%	10	4117	0.2%	-0.85

ANALYSIS BY STARTING PRICE LAST TIME

Age	Prop	Win	Runs	Wins%	£
Odds On	3%	26	85	30.6%	-0.20
Ev-2/1	7%	60	279	21.5%	-0.32
9/4-4/1	17%	144	746	19.3%	-0.20
9/2-6/1	11%	92	559	16.5%	-0.10
13/2-10/1	18%	147	1068	13.8%	-0.21
11/1-16/1	13%	107	1189	9.0%	-0.36
18/1-33/1	13%	109	1837	5.9%	-0.51
40/1+	7%	58	3236	1.8%	-0.69
Unraced	12%	97	1532	6.3%	-0.50

ANALYSIS BY DISTANCE BEATEN LAST TIME

Age	Prop	Win	Runs	Wins%	£
..-10 lgh	0%	2	9	22.2%	-0.48
-10..0	2%	18	121	14.9%	-0.40
0.1..2	11%	96	380	25.3%	-0.05
2.1..5	13%	108	458	23.6%	-0.08
5.1..10	15%	125	703	17.8%	-0.23
10.1..20	19%	163	1234	13.2%	-0.08
20.0..30	8%	71	1064	6.7%	-0.50
30.1+	13%	105	3493	3.0%	-0.66
Not Compl	7%	55	1537	3.6%	-0.62
Unraced	12%	97	1532	6.3%	-0.50

ANALYSIS BY SUCCESS RATE IN LAST 10 RUNS

Age	Prop	Win	Runs	Wins%	£
No Wins	81%	603	8114	7.4%	-0.48
1 Win	15%	108	759	14.2%	-0.34
2 Wins	4%	29	116	25.0%	-0.12
3 Wins	0%	3	8	37.5%	-0.13
4 Wins	0%	0	2	0.0%	-1.00
5+ Wins	0%	0	0	0.0%	0.00

ANALYSIS BY SUCCESS RATE IN LAST 3 RUNS

Age	Prop	Win	Runs	Wins%	£
No Wins	90%	667	8470	7.9%	-0.47
1 Win	9%	65	485	13.4%	-0.33
2 Wins	1%	10	43	23.3%	-0.28
3 Wins	0%	1	1	100.0%	1.63

ANALYSIS BY POSITION LAST TIME

Age	Prop	Win	Runs	Wins%	£
Won	2%	20	129	15.5%	-0.40
2nd or 3rd	43%	357	1722	20.7%	-0.13
Unplaced	37%	311	5618	5.5%	-0.52
Fell,BD,UR	3%	22	375	5.9%	-0.53
Pulled Up	4%	30	1113	2.7%	-0.65
Ref/RanOut	0%	2	29	6.9%	-0.70
CO/SlipUp	0%	1	13	7.7%	-0.67
Unraced	12%	97	1532	6.3%	-0.50

OTHER FACTORS (WINS-RUNS, £)

Course Winner:	20-101	-£0.40
Distance Winner:	37-224	-£0.34
Going Winner:	40-249	-£0.49
Beaten Favourite:	91-410	-£0.23
BHA Top Rated:	132-528	-£0.06
Absolute Favourites:	326-797	-£0.05

Maiden Hurdle Races

Maiden Hurdle Races: 2m to 2m3f

ANALYSIS BY AGE
Age	Prop	Win	Runs	Wins%	£
3yo	0%	1	18	5.6%	-0.72
4yo	26%	114	1542	7.4%	-0.49
5yo	38%	165	1889	8.7%	-0.35
6yo	20%	88	1202	7.3%	-0.56
7yo	11%	49	560	8.8%	-0.31
8yo	3%	15	200	7.5%	-0.54
9yo	0%	1	46	2.2%	-0.91
10yo	0%	1	21	4.8%	-0.86
11yo	0%	0	7	0.0%	-1.00
12yo+	0%	0	3	0.0%	-1.00

ANALYSIS BY BHB RATING
Age	Prop	Win	Runs	Wins%	£
150+	0%	0	0	0.0%	0.00
130..149	0%	1	2	50.0%	-0.22
120..129	2%	10	29	34.5%	-0.11
110..119	8%	36	124	29.0%	-0.14
100..109	14%	62	265	23.4%	-0.06
80..99	5%	22	291	7.6%	-0.35
60..79	0%	1	114	0.9%	-0.93
..59	0%	0	6	0.0%	-1.00
Unrated	70%	302	4657	6.5%	-0.48

ANALYSIS BY WEIGHT CARRIED
Age	Prop	Win	Runs	Wins%	£
12-01+	0%	0	0	0.0%	0.00
11-8..12-00	1%	3	32	9.4%	-0.45
11-0..11-07	62%	271	2784	9.7%	-0.39
10-8..10-13	24%	106	1551	6.8%	-0.41
10-0..10-07	12%	53	1075	4.9%	-0.64
..9-13	0%	1	46	2.2%	-0.74

ANALYSIS BY DAYS SINCE LAST RUN
Age	Prop	Win	Runs	Wins%	£
1..7	2%	7	150	4.7%	-0.78
8..14	11%	47	690	6.8%	-0.35
15..28	24%	106	1268	8.4%	-0.33
29..60	25%	108	1008	10.7%	-0.47
61..100	7%	29	355	8.2%	-0.43
101+	16%	68	1001	6.8%	-0.60
Unraced	16%	69	1016	6.8%	-0.46

ANALYSIS BY TODAY'S STARTING PRICE
Age	Prop	Win	Runs	Wins%	£
Odds On	14%	61	122	50.0%	-0.18
Ev-2/1	26%	111	266	41.7%	0.07
9/4-4/1	23%	98	457	21.4%	-0.11
9/2-6/1	10%	43	330	13.0%	-0.18
13/2-10/1	13%	57	568	10.0%	-0.08
11/1-16/1	8%	35	636	5.5%	-0.18
18/1-33/1	6%	24	929	2.6%	-0.38
40/1+	1%	5	2180	0.2%	-0.84

ANALYSIS BY STARTING PRICE LAST TIME
Age	Prop	Win	Runs	Wins%	£
Odds On	4%	17	43	39.5%	0.06
Ev-2/1	8%	33	140	23.6%	-0.29
9/4-4/1	14%	60	369	16.3%	-0.27
9/2-6/1	11%	49	272	18.0%	0.01
13/2-10/1	16%	70	551	12.7%	-0.23
11/1-16/1	11%	48	563	8.5%	-0.35
18/1-33/1	14%	59	890	6.6%	-0.43
40/1+	7%	29	1644	1.8%	-0.70
Unraced	16%	69	1016	6.8%	-0.46

ANALYSIS BY DISTANCE BEATEN LAST TIME
Age	Prop	Win	Runs	Wins%	£
..-10 lgh	0%	1	5	20.0%	-0.67
-10..0	3%	12	69	17.4%	-0.37
0.1..2	11%	48	167	28.7%	-0.07
2.1..5	11%	49	232	21.1%	-0.10
5.1..10	14%	60	342	17.5%	-0.21
10.1..20	18%	80	615	13.0%	0.02
20.0..30	9%	39	551	7.1%	-0.48
30.1+	12%	52	1757	3.0%	-0.68
Not Compl	6%	24	734	3.3%	-0.57
Unraced	16%	69	1016	6.8%	-0.46

ANALYSIS BY SUCCESS RATE IN LAST 10 RUNS
Age	Prop	Win	Runs	Wins%	£
No Wins	81%	296	4038	7.3%	-0.47
1 Win	13%	49	367	13.4%	-0.29
2 Wins	5%	18	62	29.0%	-0.10
3 Wins	1%	2	4	50.0%	0.34
4 Wins	0%	0	1	0.0%	-1.00
5+ Wins	0%	0	0	0.0%	0.00

ANALYSIS BY SUCCESS RATE IN LAST 3 RUNS
Age	Prop	Win	Runs	Wins%	£
No Wins	88%	320	4192	7.6%	-0.47
1 Win	10%	36	254	14.2%	-0.20
2 Wins	2%	8	25	32.0%	0.01
3 Wins	0%	1	1	100.0%	1.63

ANALYSIS BY POSITION LAST TIME
Age	Prop	Win	Runs	Wins%	£
Won	3%	13	74	17.6%	-0.39
2nd or 3rd	38%	166	799	20.8%	-0.12
Unplaced	37%	162	2868	5.6%	-0.51
Fell,BD,UR	2%	10	194	5.2%	-0.63
Pulled Up	3%	13	518	2.5%	-0.55
Ref/RanOut	0%	1	14	7.1%	-0.50
CO/SlipUp	0%	0	5	0.0%	-1.00
Unraced	16%	69	1016	6.8%	-0.46

OTHER FACTORS (WINS-RUNS, £)
Course Winner:	11-49	-£0.30
Distance Winner:	37-223	-£0.04
Going Winner:	24-132	-£0.45
Beaten Favourite:	50-200	-£0.12
BHA Top Rated:	58-254	-£0.09
Absolute Favourites:	175-413	-£0.01

Race Profiles

Maiden Hurdle Races: 2m4f to 2m7f

ANALYSIS BY AGE

Age	Prop	Win	Runs	Wins%	£
3yo	0%	0	0	0.0%	0.00
4yo	19%	61	578	10.6%	-0.31
5yo	31%	101	1331	7.6%	-0.53
6yo	29%	96	1150	8.3%	-0.48
7yo	15%	50	666	7.5%	-0.47
8yo	4%	13	226	5.8%	-0.48
9yo	1%	2	92	2.2%	-0.91
10yo	1%	2	23	8.7%	-0.53
11yo	0%	0	10	0.0%	-1.00
12yo+	0%	1	1	100.0%	12.00

ANALYSIS BY BHB RATING

Age	Prop	Win	Runs	Wins%	£
150+	0%	0	0	0.0%	0.00
130..149	0%	1	2	50.0%	-0.40
120..129	2%	7	21	33.3%	-0.22
110..119	12%	38	162	23.5%	-0.14
100..109	13%	44	250	17.6%	-0.03
80..99	13%	42	296	14.2%	-0.02
60..79	0%	1	179	0.6%	-0.97
..59	0%	0	5	0.0%	-1.00
Unrated	59%	193	3162	6.1%	-0.55

ANALYSIS BY WEIGHT CARRIED

Age	Prop	Win	Runs	Wins%	£
12-01+	0%	0	0	0.0%	0.00
11-8..12-00	0%	0	0	0.0%	0.00
11-0..11-07	64%	209	2081	10.0%	-0.41
10-8..10-13	23%	76	1199	6.3%	-0.49
10-0..10-07	11%	37	769	4.8%	-0.65
..9-13	1%	4	28	14.3%	-0.28

ANALYSIS BY DAYS SINCE LAST RUN

Age	Prop	Win	Runs	Wins%	£
1..7	2%	7	122	5.7%	-0.70
8..14	12%	40	457	8.8%	-0.39
15..28	31%	102	1076	9.5%	-0.46
29..60	22%	72	873	8.2%	-0.49
61..100	9%	30	281	10.7%	-0.29
101+	16%	52	849	6.1%	-0.53
Unraced	7%	23	419	5.5%	-0.54

ANALYSIS BY TODAY'S STARTING PRICE

Age	Prop	Win	Runs	Wins%	£
Odds On	13%	43	74	58.1%	-0.06
Ev-2/1	22%	71	190	37.4%	-0.03
9/4-4/1	30%	97	404	24.0%	-0.03
9/2-6/1	10%	34	247	13.8%	-0.16
13/2-10/1	13%	43	434	9.9%	-0.12
11/1-16/1	6%	20	457	4.4%	-0.35
18/1-33/1	4%	14	713	2.0%	-0.46
40/1+	1%	4	1558	0.3%	-0.87

ANALYSIS BY STARTING PRICE LAST TIME

Age	Prop	Win	Runs	Wins%	£
Odds On	3%	9	37	24.3%	-0.38
Ev-2/1	6%	20	111	18.0%	-0.34
9/4-4/1	20%	64	312	20.5%	-0.20
9/2-6/1	10%	33	228	14.5%	-0.40
13/2-10/1	19%	62	421	14.7%	-0.17
11/1-16/1	14%	46	513	9.0%	-0.44
18/1-33/1	13%	41	760	5.4%	-0.58
40/1+	9%	28	1276	2.2%	-0.61
Unraced	7%	23	419	5.5%	-0.54

ANALYSIS BY DISTANCE BEATEN LAST TIME

Age	Prop	Win	Runs	Wins%	£
..-10 lgh	0%	0	3	0.0%	-1.00
-10..0	2%	6	49	12.2%	-0.40
0.1..2	13%	41	174	23.6%	0.10
2.1..5	15%	48	179	26.8%	-0.01
5.1..10	15%	50	300	16.7%	-0.28
10.1..20	21%	67	516	13.0%	-0.20
20.0..30	9%	28	417	6.7%	-0.47
30.1+	13%	42	1407	3.0%	-0.66
Not Compl	6%	21	613	3.4%	-0.67
Unraced	7%	23	419	5.5%	-0.54

ANALYSIS BY SUCCESS RATE IN LAST 10 RUNS

Age	Prop	Win	Runs	Wins%	£
No Wins	81%	246	3276	7.5%	-0.48
1 Win	16%	48	336	14.3%	-0.41
2 Wins	3%	8	43	18.6%	-0.28
3 Wins	0%	1	2	50.0%	-0.19
4 Wins	0%	0	1	0.0%	-1.00
5+ Wins	0%	0	0	0.0%	0.00

ANALYSIS BY SUCCESS RATE IN LAST 3 RUNS

Age	Prop	Win	Runs	Wins%	£
No Wins	92%	278	3440	8.1%	-0.47
1 Win	8%	23	201	11.4%	-0.52
2 Wins	1%	2	17	11.8%	-0.67
3 Wins	0%	0	0	0.0%	0.00

ANALYSIS BY POSITION LAST TIME

Age	Prop	Win	Runs	Wins%	£
Won	2%	6	51	11.8%	-0.43
2nd or 3rd	46%	150	741	20.2%	-0.14
Unplaced	39%	126	2256	5.6%	-0.53
Fell,BD,UR	2%	7	149	4.7%	-0.55
Pulled Up	4%	12	441	2.7%	-0.71
Ref/RanOut	0%	1	14	7.1%	-0.88
CO/SlipUp	0%	1	6	16.7%	-0.28
Unraced	7%	23	419	5.5%	-0.54

OTHER FACTORS (WINS-RUNS, £)

Course Winner:	8-47	-£0.53
Going Winner:	15-103	-£0.50
Beaten Favourite:	33-174	-£0.35
BHA Top Rated:	53-213	-£0.11
Absolute Favourites:	121-309	-£0.09

Maiden Hurdle Races

Maiden Hurdle Races: 3m+

ANALYSIS BY AGE

Age	Prop	Win	Runs	Wins%	£
3yo	0%	0	0	0.0%	0.00
4yo	5%	4	46	8.7%	-0.53
5yo	16%	13	217	6.0%	-0.61
6yo	44%	35	343	10.2%	-0.27
7yo	21%	17	221	7.7%	-0.66
8yo	10%	8	87	9.2%	-0.65
9yo	1%	1	33	3.0%	-0.92
10yo	1%	1	10	10.0%	0.00
11yo	0%	0	5	0.0%	-1.00
12yo+	1%	1	4	25.0%	-0.06

ANALYSIS BY BHB RATING

Age	Prop	Win	Runs	Wins%	£
150+	0%	0	0	0.0%	0.00
130..149	1%	1	2	50.0%	0.31
120..129	5%	4	10	40.0%	-0.10
110..119	15%	12	59	20.3%	-0.11
100..109	18%	14	60	23.3%	0.26
80..99	11%	9	95	9.5%	-0.39
60..79	1%	1	55	1.8%	-0.86
..59	0%	0	2	0.0%	-1.00
Unrated	49%	39	683	5.7%	-0.60

ANALYSIS BY WEIGHT CARRIED

Age	Prop	Win	Runs	Wins%	£
12-01+	0%	0	0	0.0%	0.00
11-8..12-00	0%	0	0	0.0%	0.00
11-0..11-07	73%	58	535	10.8%	-0.40
10-8..10-13	19%	15	267	5.6%	-0.63
10-0..10-07	9%	7	158	4.4%	-0.62
..9-13	0%	0	6	0.0%	-1.00

ANALYSIS BY DAYS SINCE LAST RUN

Age	Prop	Win	Runs	Wins%	£
1..7	3%	2	21	9.5%	-0.60
8..14	14%	11	125	8.8%	-0.66
15..28	24%	19	248	7.7%	-0.46
29..60	34%	27	221	12.2%	-0.22
61..100	5%	4	82	4.9%	-0.74
101+	15%	12	172	7.0%	-0.58
Unraced	6%	5	97	5.2%	-0.73

ANALYSIS BY TODAY'S STARTING PRICE

Age	Prop	Win	Runs	Wins%	£
Odds On	19%	15	25	60.0%	0.00
Ev-2/1	19%	15	43	34.9%	-0.09
9/4-4/1	28%	22	93	23.7%	-0.04
9/2-6/1	8%	6	55	10.9%	-0.29
13/2-10/1	18%	14	102	13.7%	0.18
11/1-16/1	5%	4	103	3.9%	-0.50
18/1-33/1	4%	3	166	1.8%	-0.62
40/1+	1%	1	379	0.3%	-0.87

ANALYSIS BY STARTING PRICE LAST TIME

Age	Prop	Win	Runs	Wins%	£
Odds On	0%	0	5	0.0%	-1.00
Ev-2/1	9%	7	28	25.0%	-0.42
9/4-4/1	25%	20	65	30.8%	0.26
9/2-6/1	13%	10	59	16.9%	0.58
13/2-10/1	19%	15	96	15.6%	-0.23
11/1-16/1	16%	13	113	11.5%	-0.03
18/1-33/1	11%	9	187	4.8%	-0.62
40/1+	1%	1	316	0.3%	-0.98
Unraced	6%	5	97	5.2%	-0.73

ANALYSIS BY DISTANCE BEATEN LAST TIME

Age	Prop	Win	Runs	Wins%	£
..-10 lgh	1%	1	1	100.0%	2.00
-10..0	0%	0	3	0.0%	-1.00
0.1..2	9%	7	39	17.9%	-0.63
2.1..5	14%	11	47	23.4%	-0.21
5.1..10	19%	15	61	24.6%	-0.08
10.1..20	20%	16	103	15.5%	-0.05
20.0..30	5%	4	96	4.2%	-0.75
30.1+	14%	11	329	3.3%	-0.55
Not Compl	13%	10	190	5.3%	-0.63
Unraced	6%	5	97	5.2%	-0.73

ANALYSIS BY SUCCESS RATE IN LAST 10 RUNS

Age	Prop	Win	Runs	Wins%	£
No Wins	81%	61	800	7.6%	-0.51
1 Win	15%	11	56	19.6%	-0.27
2 Wins	4%	3	11	27.3%	0.40
3 Wins	0%	0	2	0.0%	-1.00
4 Wins	0%	0	0	0.0%	0.00
5+ Wins	0%	0	0	0.0%	0.00

ANALYSIS BY SUCCESS RATE IN LAST 3 RUNS

Age	Prop	Win	Runs	Wins%	£
No Wins	92%	69	838	8.2%	-0.49
1 Win	8%	6	30	20.0%	-0.19
2 Wins	0%	0	1	0.0%	-1.00
3 Wins	0%	0	0	0.0%	0.00

ANALYSIS BY POSITION LAST TIME

Age	Prop	Win	Runs	Wins%	£
Won	1%	1	4	25.0%	-0.25
2nd or 3rd	51%	41	182	22.5%	-0.15
Unplaced	29%	23	494	4.7%	-0.55
Fell,BD,UR	6%	5	32	15.6%	0.13
Pulled Up	6%	5	154	3.2%	-0.78
Ref/RanOut	0%	0	1	0.0%	-1.00
CO/SlipUp	0%	0	2	0.0%	-1.00
Unraced	6%	5	97	5.2%	-0.73

OTHER FACTORS (WINS-RUNS, £)

Course Winner:	1-5	-£0.20
Distance Winner:	0-1	-£1.00
Going Winner:	1-14	-£0.71
Beaten Favourite:	8-36	-£0.23
BHA Top Rated:	21-61	£0.28
Absolute Favourites:	30-75	-£0.10

Race Profiles

Maiden Hurdle Races: 2 to 5 runners

ANALYSIS BY AGE

Age	Prop	Win	Runs	Wins%	£
3yo	0%	0	0	0.0%	0.00
4yo	0%	0	5	0.0%	-1.00
5yo	57%	4	15	26.7%	-0.37
6yo	14%	1	6	16.7%	-0.79
7yo	14%	1	4	25.0%	-0.54
8yo	14%	1	2	50.0%	3.50
9yo	0%	0	0	0.0%	0.00
10yo	0%	0	0	0.0%	0.00
11yo	0%	0	0	0.0%	0.00
12yo+	0%	0	0	0.0%	0.00

ANALYSIS BY BHB RATING

Age	Prop	Win	Runs	Wins%	£
150+	0%	0	0	0.0%	0.00
130..149	0%	0	0	0.0%	0.00
120..129	0%	0	0	0.0%	0.00
110..119	0%	0	2	0.0%	-1.00
100..109	43%	3	3	100.0%	0.82
80..99	14%	1	4	25.0%	-0.06
60..79	0%	0	3	0.0%	-1.00
..59	0%	0	0	0.0%	0.00
Unrated	43%	3	20	15.0%	-0.39

ANALYSIS BY WEIGHT CARRIED

Age	Prop	Win	Runs	Wins%	£
12-01+	0%	0	0	0.0%	0.00
11-8..12-00	0%	0	0	0.0%	0.00
11-0..11-07	86%	6	19	31.6%	-0.34
10-8..10-13	14%	1	6	16.7%	0.50
10-0..10-07	0%	0	7	0.0%	-1.00
..9-13	0%	0	0	0.0%	0.00

ANALYSIS BY DAYS SINCE LAST RUN

Age	Prop	Win	Runs	Wins%	£
1..7	0%	0	2	0.0%	-1.00
8..14	29%	2	6	33.3%	-0.46
15..28	14%	1	11	9.1%	-0.66
29..60	29%	2	4	50.0%	1.56
61..100	0%	0	2	0.0%	-1.00
101+	14%	1	3	33.3%	-0.27
Unraced	14%	1	4	25.0%	-0.50

ANALYSIS BY TODAY'S STARTING PRICE

Age	Prop	Win	Runs	Wins%	£
Odds On	43%	3	5	60.0%	-0.10
Ev-2/1	29%	2	4	50.0%	0.05
9/4-4/1	14%	1	5	20.0%	-0.25
9/2-6/1	0%	0	3	0.0%	-1.00
13/2-10/1	14%	1	5	20.0%	0.80
11/1-16/1	0%	0	3	0.0%	-1.00
18/1-33/1	0%	0	3	0.0%	-1.00
40/1+	0%	0	4	0.0%	-1.00

ANALYSIS BY STARTING PRICE LAST TIME

Age	Prop	Win	Runs	Wins%	£
Odds On	0%	0	0	0.0%	0.00
Ev-2/1	0%	0	0	0.0%	0.00
9/4-4/1	14%	1	2	50.0%	0.10
9/2-6/1	14%	1	4	25.0%	-0.64
13/2-10/1	14%	1	3	33.3%	-0.39
11/1-16/1	0%	0	2	0.0%	-1.00
18/1-33/1	14%	1	5	20.0%	-0.25
40/1+	29%	2	12	16.7%	-0.15
Unraced	14%	1	4	25.0%	-0.50

ANALYSIS BY DISTANCE BEATEN LAST TIME

Age	Prop	Win	Runs	Wins%	£
..-10 lgh	0%	0	0	0.0%	0.00
-10..0	0%	0	0	0.0%	0.00
0.1..2	14%	1	2	50.0%	-0.28
2.1..5	0%	0	0	0.0%	0.00
5.1..10	29%	2	5	40.0%	0.19
10.1..20	29%	2	4	50.0%	-0.23
20.0..30	0%	0	5	0.0%	-1.00
30.1+	0%	0	8	0.0%	-1.00
Not Compl	14%	1	4	25.0%	1.25
Unraced	14%	1	4	25.0%	-0.50

ANALYSIS BY SUCCESS RATE IN LAST 10 RUNS

Age	Prop	Win	Runs	Wins%	£
No Wins	83%	5	26	19.2%	-0.34
1 Win	17%	1	2	50.0%	0.10
2 Wins	0%	0	0	0.0%	0.00
3 Wins	0%	0	0	0.0%	0.00
4 Wins	0%	0	0	0.0%	0.00
5+ Wins	0%	0	0	0.0%	0.00

ANALYSIS BY SUCCESS RATE IN LAST 3 RUNS

Age	Prop	Win	Runs	Wins%	£
No Wins	100%	6	28	21.4%	-0.30
1 Win	0%	0	0	0.0%	0.00
2 Wins	0%	0	0	0.0%	0.00
3 Wins	0%	0	0	0.0%	0.00

ANALYSIS BY POSITION LAST TIME

Age	Prop	Win	Runs	Wins%	£
Won	0%	0	0	0.0%	0.00
2nd or 3rd	43%	3	6	50.0%	-0.09
Unplaced	29%	2	18	11.1%	-0.72
Fell,BD,UR	0%	0	2	0.0%	-1.00
Pulled Up	14%	1	2	50.0%	3.50
Ref/RanOut	0%	0	0	0.0%	0.00
CO/SlipUp	0%	0	0	0.0%	0.00
Unraced	14%	1	4	25.0%	-0.50

OTHER FACTORS (WINS-RUNS, £)

BHA Top Rated:	2-3	£0.21
Absolute Favourites:	4-7	-£0.07

Maiden Hurdle Races

Maiden Hurdle Races: 6 to 10 runners

ANALYSIS BY AGE

Age	Prop	Win	Runs	Wins%	£
3yo	0%	0	0	0.0%	0.00
4yo	20%	38	309	12.3%	-0.49
5yo	30%	56	514	10.9%	-0.31
6yo	26%	49	442	11.1%	-0.55
7yo	17%	33	238	13.9%	-0.16
8yo	4%	8	98	8.2%	-0.59
9yo	2%	3	38	7.9%	-0.69
10yo	1%	2	11	18.2%	0.18
11yo	0%	0	7	0.0%	-1.00
12yo+	0%	0	2	0.0%	-1.00

ANALYSIS BY BHB RATING

Age	Prop	Win	Runs	Wins%	£
150+	0%	0	0	0.0%	0.00
130..149	1%	2	3	66.7%	-0.08
120..129	4%	7	15	46.7%	-0.21
110..119	11%	20	74	27.0%	-0.19
100..109	16%	31	119	26.1%	-0.09
80..99	11%	21	157	13.4%	-0.09
60..79	1%	2	91	2.2%	-0.86
..59	0%	0	3	0.0%	-1.00
Unrated	56%	106	1197	8.9%	-0.47

ANALYSIS BY WEIGHT CARRIED

Age	Prop	Win	Runs	Wins%	£
12-01+	0%	0	0	0.0%	0.00
11-8..12-00	1%	1	4	25.0%	-0.50
11-0..11-07	62%	117	814	14.4%	-0.34
10-8..10-13	23%	44	494	8.9%	-0.41
10-0..10-07	14%	26	333	7.8%	-0.59
..9-13	1%	1	14	7.1%	-0.77

ANALYSIS BY DAYS SINCE LAST RUN

Age	Prop	Win	Runs	Wins%	£
1..7	2%	3	51	5.9%	-0.83
8..14	17%	32	239	13.4%	0.00
15..28	27%	51	421	12.1%	-0.49
29..60	26%	49	314	15.6%	-0.29
61..100	7%	13	114	11.4%	-0.56
101+	14%	27	309	8.7%	-0.48
Unraced	7%	14	211	6.6%	-0.64

ANALYSIS BY TODAY'S STARTING PRICE

Age	Prop	Win	Runs	Wins%	£
Odds On	24%	45	83	54.2%	-0.12
Ev-2/1	24%	45	113	39.8%	0.04
9/4-4/1	24%	46	188	24.5%	-0.01
9/2-6/1	10%	18	123	14.6%	-0.08
13/2-10/1	12%	23	203	11.3%	0.00
11/1-16/1	5%	9	210	4.3%	-0.37
18/1-33/1	1%	2	275	0.7%	-0.83
40/1+	1%	1	464	0.2%	-0.78

ANALYSIS BY STARTING PRICE LAST TIME

Age	Prop	Win	Runs	Wins%	£
Odds On	4%	7	17	41.2%	-0.07
Ev-2/1	7%	13	44	29.5%	-0.31
9/4-4/1	20%	38	131	29.0%	0.09
9/2-6/1	12%	22	110	20.0%	-0.20
13/2-10/1	20%	38	186	20.4%	-0.16
11/1-16/1	13%	25	192	13.0%	-0.26
18/1-33/1	12%	22	283	7.8%	-0.46
40/1+	5%	10	485	2.1%	-0.65
Unraced	7%	14	211	6.6%	-0.64

ANALYSIS BY DISTANCE BEATEN LAST TIME

Age	Prop	Win	Runs	Wins%	£
..-10 lgh	1%	2	3	66.7%	0.56
-10..0	2%	3	19	15.8%	-0.57
0.1..2	14%	27	68	39.7%	0.17
2.1..5	13%	24	77	31.2%	0.19
5.1..10	15%	28	117	23.9%	0.05
10.1..20	19%	36	189	19.0%	-0.11
20.0..30	11%	20	172	11.6%	-0.44
30.1+	11%	20	546	3.7%	-0.73
Not Compl	8%	15	257	5.8%	-0.29
Unraced	7%	14	211	6.6%	-0.64

ANALYSIS BY SUCCESS RATE IN LAST 10 RUNS

Age	Prop	Win	Runs	Wins%	£
No Wins	84%	147	1314	11.2%	-0.38
1 Win	13%	22	114	19.3%	-0.38
2 Wins	3%	5	18	27.8%	-0.48
3 Wins	1%	1	1	100.0%	1.75
4 Wins	0%	0	1	0.0%	-1.00
5+ Wins	0%	0	0	0.0%	0.00

ANALYSIS BY SUCCESS RATE IN LAST 3 RUNS

Age	Prop	Win	Runs	Wins%	£
No Wins	89%	156	1377	11.3%	-0.39
1 Win	9%	16	64	25.0%	-0.15
2 Wins	2%	3	7	42.9%	-0.13
3 Wins	0%	0	0	0.0%	0.00

ANALYSIS BY POSITION LAST TIME

Age	Prop	Win	Runs	Wins%	£
Won	3%	5	21	23.8%	-0.39
2nd or 3rd	47%	88	315	27.9%	0.01
Unplaced	35%	67	856	7.8%	-0.55
Fell,BD,UR	4%	7	59	11.9%	-0.51
Pulled Up	4%	7	192	3.6%	-0.21
Ref/RanOut	1%	1	3	33.3%	-0.44
CO/SlipUp	0%	0	2	0.0%	-1.00
Unraced	7%	14	211	6.6%	-0.64

OTHER FACTORS (WINS-RUNS, £)

Course Winner:	3-12	-£0.31
Distance Winner:	9-37	-£0.32
Going Winner:	10-41	-£0.38
Beaten Favourite:	23-70	£0.26
BHA Top Rated:	38-128	-£0.22
Absolute Favourites:	83-181	-£0.04

Race Profiles

Maiden Hurdle Races: 11 runners or more

ANALYSIS BY AGE

Age	Prop	Win	Runs	Wins%	£
3yo	0%	1	18	5.6%	-0.72
4yo	22%	141	1852	7.6%	-0.43
5yo	34%	219	2908	7.5%	-0.46
6yo	26%	169	2247	7.5%	-0.48
7yo	13%	82	1205	6.8%	-0.49
8yo	4%	27	413	6.5%	-0.54
9yo	0%	1	133	0.8%	-0.98
10yo	0%	2	43	4.7%	-0.75
11yo	0%	0	15	0.0%	-1.00
12yo+	0%	2	6	33.3%	1.79

ANALYSIS BY BHB RATING

Age	Prop	Win	Runs	Wins%	£
150+	0%	0	0	0.0%	0.00
130..149	0%	1	3	33.3%	-0.12
120..129	2%	14	45	31.1%	-0.12
110..119	10%	66	269	24.5%	-0.11
100..109	13%	86	453	19.0%	0.00
80..99	8%	51	521	9.8%	-0.25
60..79	0%	1	254	0.4%	-0.97
..59	0%	0	10	0.0%	-1.00
Unrated	66%	425	7285	5.8%	-0.52

ANALYSIS BY WEIGHT CARRIED

Age	Prop	Win	Runs	Wins%	£
12-01+	0%	0	0	0.0%	0.00
11-8..12-00	0%	2	28	7.1%	-0.44
11-0..11-07	64%	415	4567	9.1%	-0.41
10-8..10-13	24%	152	2517	6.0%	-0.47
10-0..10-07	11%	71	1662	4.3%	-0.65
..9-13	1%	4	66	6.1%	-0.56

ANALYSIS BY DAYS SINCE LAST RUN

Age	Prop	Win	Runs	Wins%	£
1..7	2%	13	240	5.4%	-0.71
8..14	10%	64	1027	6.2%	-0.48
15..28	27%	175	2160	8.1%	-0.38
29..60	24%	156	1784	8.7%	-0.49
61..100	8%	50	602	8.3%	-0.38
101+	16%	104	1710	6.1%	-0.59
Unraced	13%	82	1317	6.2%	-0.47

ANALYSIS BY TODAY'S STARTING PRICE

Age	Prop	Win	Runs	Wins%	£
Odds On	11%	71	133	53.4%	-0.12
Ev-2/1	23%	150	382	39.3%	0.01
9/4-4/1	26%	170	761	22.3%	-0.08
9/2-6/1	10%	65	506	12.8%	-0.21
13/2-10/1	14%	90	896	10.0%	-0.09
11/1-16/1	8%	50	983	5.1%	-0.25
18/1-33/1	6%	39	1530	2.5%	-0.36
40/1+	1%	9	3649	0.2%	-0.86

ANALYSIS BY STARTING PRICE LAST TIME

Age	Prop	Win	Runs	Wins%	£
Odds On	3%	19	68	27.9%	-0.23
Ev-2/1	7%	47	235	20.0%	-0.33
9/4-4/1	16%	105	613	17.1%	-0.26
9/2-6/1	11%	69	445	15.5%	-0.07
13/2-10/1	17%	108	879	12.3%	-0.22
11/1-16/1	13%	82	995	8.2%	-0.38
18/1-33/1	13%	86	1549	5.6%	-0.52
40/1+	7%	46	2739	1.7%	-0.70
Unraced	13%	82	1317	6.2%	-0.47

ANALYSIS BY DISTANCE BEATEN LAST TIME

Age	Prop	Win	Runs	Wins%	£
..-10 lgh	0%	0	6	0.0%	-1.00
-10..0	2%	15	102	14.7%	-0.37
0.1..2	11%	68	310	21.9%	-0.10
2.1..5	13%	84	381	22.0%	-0.13
5.1..10	15%	95	581	16.4%	-0.29
10.1..20	19%	125	1041	12.0%	-0.07
20.0..30	8%	51	887	5.7%	-0.51
30.1+	13%	85	2939	2.9%	-0.64
Not Compl	6%	39	1276	3.1%	-0.69
Unraced	13%	82	1317	6.2%	-0.47

ANALYSIS BY SUCCESS RATE IN LAST 10 RUNS

Age	Prop	Win	Runs	Wins%	£
No Wins	80%	451	6774	6.7%	-0.50
1 Win	15%	85	643	13.2%	-0.34
2 Wins	4%	24	98	24.5%	-0.05
3 Wins	0%	2	7	28.6%	-0.39
4 Wins	0%	0	1	0.0%	-1.00
5+ Wins	0%	0	0	0.0%	0.00

ANALYSIS BY SUCCESS RATE IN LAST 3 RUNS

Age	Prop	Win	Runs	Wins%	£
No Wins	90%	505	7065	7.1%	-0.48
1 Win	9%	49	421	11.6%	-0.36
2 Wins	1%	7	36	19.4%	-0.31
3 Wins	0%	1	1	100.0%	1.63

ANALYSIS BY POSITION LAST TIME

Age	Prop	Win	Runs	Wins%	£
Won	2%	15	108	13.9%	-0.40
2nd or 3rd	41%	266	1401	19.0%	-0.16
Unplaced	38%	242	4744	5.1%	-0.51
Fell,BD,UR	2%	15	314	4.8%	-0.53
Pulled Up	3%	22	919	2.4%	-0.74
Ref/RanOut	0%	1	26	3.8%	-0.73
CO/SlipUp	0%	1	11	9.1%	-0.61
Unraced	13%	82	1317	6.2%	-0.47

OTHER FACTORS (WINS-RUNS, £)

Course Winner:	17-89	-£0.41
Distance Winner:	28-187	-£0.35
Going Winner:	30-208	-£0.51
Beaten Favourite:	68-340	-£0.33
BHA Top Rated:	92-397	£0.00
Absolute Favourites:	239-609	-£0.05

Maiden Hurdle Races

Maiden Hurdle Races: up to 7 days off the track

ANALYSIS BY AGE

Age	Prop	Win	Runs	Wins%	£
3yo	0%	0	8	0.0%	-1.00
4yo	42%	48	601	8.0%	-0.40
5yo	31%	35	541	6.5%	-0.49
6yo	19%	22	342	6.4%	-0.52
7yo	5%	6	217	2.8%	-0.82
8yo	1%	1	83	1.2%	-0.90
9yo	0%	0	22	0.0%	-1.00
10yo	1%	1	10	10.0%	-0.70
11yo	0%	0	1	0.0%	-1.00
12yo+	0%	0	0	0.0%	0.00

ANALYSIS BY BHB RATING

Age	Prop	Win	Runs	Wins%	£
150+	0%	0	0	0.0%	0.00
130..149	0%	0	1	0.0%	-1.00
120..129	1%	1	2	50.0%	-0.33
110..119	2%	2	9	22.2%	0.44
100..109	4%	5	18	27.8%	0.21
80..99	4%	5	33	15.2%	-0.27
60..79	0%	0	16	0.0%	-1.00
..59	0%	0	1	0.0%	-1.00
Unrated	88%	100	1745	5.7%	-0.55

ANALYSIS BY WEIGHT CARRIED

Age	Prop	Win	Runs	Wins%	£
12-01+	0%	0	0	0.0%	0.00
11-8..12-00	0%	0	12	0.0%	-1.00
11-0..11-07	65%	73	900	8.1%	-0.41
10-8..10-13	27%	30	543	5.5%	-0.53
10-0..10-07	7%	8	351	2.3%	-0.88
..9-13	2%	2	19	10.5%	0.11

ANALYSIS BY DAYS SINCE LAST RUN

Age	Prop	Win	Runs	Wins%	£
1..7	14%	16	293	5.5%	-0.73
8..14	0%	0	0	0.0%	0.00
15..28	0%	0	0	0.0%	0.00
29..60	0%	0	0	0.0%	0.00
61..100	0%	0	0	0.0%	0.00
101+	0%	0	0	0.0%	0.00
Unraced	86%	97	1532	6.3%	-0.50

ANALYSIS BY TODAY'S STARTING PRICE

Age	Prop	Win	Runs	Wins%	£
Odds On	11%	12	20	60.0%	-0.01
Ev-2/1	23%	26	69	37.7%	0.00
9/4-4/1	25%	28	127	22.0%	-0.06
9/2-6/1	8%	9	95	9.5%	-0.42
13/2-10/1	15%	17	194	8.8%	-0.23
11/1-16/1	12%	13	225	5.8%	-0.09
18/1-33/1	5%	6	349	1.7%	-0.60
40/1+	2%	2	746	0.3%	-0.88

ANALYSIS BY STARTING PRICE LAST TIME

Age	Prop	Win	Runs	Wins%	£
Odds On	0%	0	0	0.0%	0.00
Ev-2/1	4%	4	7	57.1%	0.90
9/4-4/1	3%	3	11	27.3%	0.95
9/2-6/1	3%	3	18	16.7%	-0.22
13/2-10/1	3%	3	26	11.5%	-0.60
11/1-16/1	1%	1	33	3.0%	-0.83
18/1-33/1	2%	2	65	3.1%	-0.80
40/1+	0%	0	133	0.0%	-1.00
Unraced	86%	97	1532	6.3%	-0.50

ANALYSIS BY DISTANCE BEATEN LAST TIME

Age	Prop	Win	Runs	Wins%	£
..-10 lgh	0%	0	0	0.0%	0.00
-10..0	0%	0	0	0.0%	0.00
0.1..2	3%	3	8	37.5%	0.35
2.1..5	2%	2	9	22.2%	-0.22
5.1..10	3%	3	13	23.1%	-0.06
10.1..20	4%	4	30	13.3%	-0.33
20.0..30	2%	2	29	6.9%	-0.40
30.1+	1%	1	127	0.8%	-0.94
Not Compl	1%	1	77	1.3%	-0.97
Unraced	86%	97	1532	6.3%	-0.50

ANALYSIS BY SUCCESS RATE IN LAST 10 RUNS

Age	Prop	Win	Runs	Wins%	£
No Wins	100%	16	279	5.7%	-0.72
1 Win	0%	0	13	0.0%	-1.00
2 Wins	0%	0	1	0.0%	-1.00
3 Wins	0%	0	0	0.0%	0.00
4 Wins	0%	0	0	0.0%	0.00
5+ Wins	0%	0	0	0.0%	0.00

ANALYSIS BY SUCCESS RATE IN LAST 3 RUNS

Age	Prop	Win	Runs	Wins%	£
No Wins	100%	16	286	5.6%	-0.73
1 Win	0%	0	7	0.0%	-1.00
2 Wins	0%	0	0	0.0%	0.00
3 Wins	0%	0	0	0.0%	0.00

ANALYSIS BY POSITION LAST TIME

Age	Prop	Win	Runs	Wins%	£
Won	0%	0	0	0.0%	0.00
2nd or 3rd	8%	9	36	25.0%	-0.12
Unplaced	5%	6	180	3.3%	-0.76
Fell,BD,UR	1%	1	30	3.3%	-0.93
Pulled Up	0%	0	42	0.0%	-1.00
Ref/RanOut	0%	0	2	0.0%	-1.00
CO/SlipUp	0%	0	3	0.0%	-1.00
Unraced	86%	97	1532	6.3%	-0.50

OTHER FACTORS (WINS-RUNS, £)

Course Winner:	0-2	-£1.00
Distance Winner:	0-4	-£1.00
Going Winner:	0-4	-£1.00
Beaten Favourite:	3-6	£0.50
BHA Top Rated:	3-18	-£0.44
Absolute Favourites:	38-104	-£0.12

Race Profiles

Maiden Hurdle Races: 100+ days off the track

ANALYSIS BY AGE

Age	Prop	Win	Runs	Wins%	£
3yo	0%	0	0	0.0%	0.00
4yo	10%	13	261	5.0%	-0.46
5yo	38%	50	624	8.0%	-0.59
6yo	25%	33	560	5.9%	-0.70
7yo	17%	23	341	6.7%	-0.43
8yo	8%	11	147	7.5%	-0.37
9yo	1%	1	58	1.7%	-0.91
10yo	1%	1	24	4.2%	-0.58
11yo	0%	0	9	0.0%	-1.00
12yo+	0%	0	4	0.0%	-1.00

ANALYSIS BY BHB RATING

Age	Prop	Win	Runs	Wins%	£
150+	0%	0	0	0.0%	0.00
130..149	2%	3	3	100.0%	0.80
120..129	2%	3	10	30.0%	-0.21
110..119	9%	12	51	23.5%	-0.18
100..109	11%	14	83	16.9%	-0.22
80..99	8%	10	94	10.6%	0.26
60..79	0%	0	81	0.0%	-1.00
..59	0%	0	2	0.0%	-1.00
Unrated	68%	90	1704	5.3%	-0.63

ANALYSIS BY WEIGHT CARRIED

Age	Prop	Win	Runs	Wins%	£
12-01+	0%	0	0	0.0%	0.00
11-8..12-00	0%	0	7	0.0%	-1.00
11-0..11-07	75%	99	1095	9.0%	-0.48
10-8..10-13	20%	26	564	4.6%	-0.56
10-0..10-07	5%	7	350	2.0%	-0.84
..9-13	0%	0	12	0.0%	-1.00

ANALYSIS BY DAYS SINCE LAST RUN

Age	Prop	Win	Runs	Wins%	£
1..7	0%	0	0	0.0%	0.00
8..14	0%	0	0	0.0%	0.00
15..28	0%	0	0	0.0%	0.00
29..60	0%	0	0	0.0%	0.00
61..100	0%	0	6	0.0%	-1.00
101+	100%	132	2022	6.5%	-0.57
Unraced	0%	0	0	0.0%	0.00

ANALYSIS BY TODAY'S STARTING PRICE

Age	Prop	Win	Runs	Wins%	£
Odds On	15%	20	33	60.6%	0.01
Ev-2/1	16%	21	68	30.9%	-0.20
9/4-4/1	29%	38	159	23.9%	-0.04
9/2-6/1	8%	11	105	10.5%	-0.35
13/2-10/1	20%	27	191	14.1%	0.28
11/1-16/1	7%	9	212	4.2%	-0.33
18/1-33/1	4%	5	394	1.3%	-0.73
40/1+	1%	1	866	0.1%	-0.92

ANALYSIS BY STARTING PRICE LAST TIME

Age	Prop	Win	Runs	Wins%	£
Odds On	3%	4	21	19.0%	-0.56
Ev-2/1	8%	11	72	15.3%	-0.51
9/4-4/1	18%	24	193	12.4%	-0.42
9/2-6/1	14%	18	135	13.3%	-0.32
13/2-10/1	23%	31	289	10.7%	-0.18
11/1-16/1	12%	16	278	5.8%	-0.66
18/1-33/1	13%	17	385	4.4%	-0.64
40/1+	8%	11	655	1.7%	-0.77
Unraced	0%	0	0	0.0%	0.00

ANALYSIS BY DISTANCE BEATEN LAST TIME

Age	Prop	Win	Runs	Wins%	£
..-10 lgh	0%	0	4	0.0%	-1.00
-10..0	8%	11	77	14.3%	-0.50
0.1..2	10%	13	73	17.8%	-0.22
2.1..5	9%	12	70	17.1%	-0.12
5.1..10	9%	12	129	9.3%	-0.65
10.1..20	21%	28	254	11.0%	-0.32
20.0..30	11%	15	207	7.2%	-0.58
30.1+	20%	27	796	3.4%	-0.65
Not Compl	11%	14	418	3.3%	-0.69
Unraced	0%	0	0	0.0%	0.00

ANALYSIS BY SUCCESS RATE IN LAST 10 RUNS

Age	Prop	Win	Runs	Wins%	£
No Wins	78%	103	1770	5.8%	-0.57
1 Win	17%	23	220	10.5%	-0.59
2 Wins	3%	4	33	12.1%	-0.51
3 Wins	2%	2	5	40.0%	-0.15
4 Wins	0%	0	0	0.0%	0.00
5+ Wins	0%	0	0	0.0%	0.00

ANALYSIS BY SUCCESS RATE IN LAST 3 RUNS

Age	Prop	Win	Runs	Wins%	£
No Wins	86%	113	1838	6.1%	-0.57
1 Win	11%	15	169	8.9%	-0.65
2 Wins	2%	3	20	15.0%	-0.34
3 Wins	1%	1	1	100.0%	1.63

ANALYSIS BY POSITION LAST TIME

Age	Prop	Win	Runs	Wins%	£
Won	8%	11	82	13.4%	-0.53
2nd or 3rd	28%	37	286	12.9%	-0.42
Unplaced	53%	70	1248	5.6%	-0.57
Fell,BD,UR	2%	2	73	2.7%	-0.73
Pulled Up	8%	11	331	3.3%	-0.68
Ref/RanOut	1%	1	7	14.3%	-0.76
CO/SlipUp	0%	0	1	0.0%	-1.00
Unraced	0%	0	0	0.0%	0.00

OTHER FACTORS (WINS-RUNS, £)

Course Winner:	4-29	-£0.63
Distance Winner:	9-66	-£0.60
Going Winner:	8-85	-£0.72
Beaten Favourite:	15-102	-£0.29
BHA Top Rated:	19-81	-£0.19
Absolute Favourites:	49-123	-£0.03

Claiming Hurdle Races

ANALYSIS BY AGE

Age	Prop	Win	Runs	Wins%	£
3yo	0%	0	0	0.0%	0.00
4yo	4%	6	174	3.4%	-0.69
5yo	18%	24	244	9.8%	0.13
6yo	21%	28	259	10.8%	-0.38
7yo	18%	24	188	12.8%	-0.35
8yo	16%	21	193	10.9%	-0.30
9yo	7%	10	145	6.9%	-0.64
10yo	7%	9	95	9.5%	-0.61
11yo	6%	8	53	15.1%	-0.27
12yo+	3%	4	45	8.9%	-0.70

ANALYSIS BY BHB RATING

Age	Prop	Win	Runs	Wins%	£
150+	0%	0	0	0.0%	0.00
130..149	1%	2	4	50.0%	0.20
120..129	11%	15	44	34.1%	0.34
110..119	24%	32	145	22.1%	-0.07
100..109	27%	36	259	13.9%	-0.27
80..99	28%	38	417	9.1%	-0.32
60..79	1%	2	155	1.3%	-0.81
..59	0%	0	7	0.0%	-1.00
Unrated	7%	9	365	2.5%	-0.48

ANALYSIS BY WEIGHT CARRIED

Age	Prop	Win	Runs	Wins%	£
12-01+	0%	0	1	0.0%	-1.00
11-8..12-00	14%	19	110	17.3%	-0.33
11-0..11-07	36%	48	415	11.6%	-0.20
10-8..10-13	31%	42	463	9.1%	-0.31
10-0..10-07	19%	25	370	6.8%	-0.55
..9-13	0%	0	37	0.0%	-1.00

ANALYSIS BY DAYS SINCE LAST RUN

Age	Prop	Win	Runs	Wins%	£
1..7	4%	5	74	6.8%	-0.76
8..14	25%	34	263	12.9%	0.10
15..28	34%	46	399	11.5%	-0.35
29..60	20%	27	259	10.4%	-0.34
61..100	6%	8	101	7.9%	-0.39
101+	10%	14	242	5.8%	-0.61
Unraced	0%	0	58	0.0%	-1.00

ANALYSIS BY TODAY'S STARTING PRICE

Age	Prop	Win	Runs	Wins%	£
Odds On	6%	8	16	50.0%	-0.14
Ev-2/1	22%	30	91	33.0%	-0.16
9/4-4/1	33%	44	160	27.5%	0.10
9/2-6/1	16%	21	131	16.0%	0.02
13/2-10/1	11%	15	197	7.6%	-0.34
11/1-16/1	7%	10	170	5.9%	-0.16
18/1-33/1	4%	5	255	2.0%	-0.54
40/1+	1%	1	376	0.3%	-0.73

ANALYSIS BY STARTING PRICE LAST TIME

Age	Prop	Win	Runs	Wins%	£
Odds On	4%	6	13	46.2%	0.35
Ev-2/1	9%	12	49	24.5%	-0.25
9/4-4/1	11%	15	115	13.0%	-0.53
9/2-6/1	18%	24	128	18.8%	-0.12
13/2-10/1	22%	30	213	14.1%	0.01
11/1-16/1	14%	19	226	8.4%	-0.50
18/1-33/1	12%	16	272	5.9%	-0.51
40/1+	9%	12	322	3.7%	-0.35
Unraced	0%	0	58	0.0%	-1.00

ANALYSIS BY DISTANCE BEATEN LAST TIME

Age	Prop	Win	Runs	Wins%	£
..-10 lgh	5%	7	11	63.6%	0.66
-10..0	12%	16	84	19.0%	-0.19
0.1..2	4%	6	37	16.2%	-0.38
2.1..5	7%	10	49	20.4%	-0.13
5.1..10	8%	11	86	12.8%	-0.28
10.1..20	15%	20	181	11.0%	-0.31
20.0..30	14%	19	157	12.1%	-0.06
30.1+	19%	26	434	6.0%	-0.42
Not Compl	14%	19	299	6.4%	-0.49
Unraced	0%	0	58	0.0%	-1.00

ANALYSIS BY SUCCESS RATE IN LAST 10 RUNS

Age	Prop	Win	Runs	Wins%	£
No Wins	35%	47	757	6.2%	-0.35
1 Win	32%	43	330	13.0%	-0.34
2 Wins	22%	29	170	17.1%	-0.20
3 Wins	7%	10	67	14.9%	-0.58
4 Wins	4%	5	11	45.5%	0.15
5+ Wins	0%	0	3	0.0%	-1.00

ANALYSIS BY SUCCESS RATE IN LAST 3 RUNS

Age	Prop	Win	Runs	Wins%	£
No Wins	63%	84	1077	7.8%	-0.35
1 Win	33%	44	222	19.8%	-0.21
2 Wins	4%	6	39	15.4%	-0.62
3 Wins	0%	0	0	0.0%	0.00

ANALYSIS BY POSITION LAST TIME

Age	Prop	Win	Runs	Wins%	£
Won	17%	23	95	24.2%	-0.09
2nd or 3rd	23%	31	188	16.5%	-0.24
Unplaced	46%	61	756	8.1%	-0.33
Fell,BD,UR	3%	4	51	7.8%	-0.01
Pulled Up	11%	15	237	6.3%	-0.56
Ref/RanOut	0%	0	8	0.0%	-1.00
CO/SlipUp	0%	0	3	0.0%	-1.00
Unraced	0%	0	58	0.0%	-1.00

OTHER FACTORS (WINS-RUNS, £)

Course Winner:	25-168	-£0.19
Distance Winner:	49-329	-£0.34
Going Winner:	48-383	-£0.33
Beaten Favourite:	14-64	-£0.21
7-Day Winners:	4-12	£0.01
BHA Top Rated:	31-109	£0.00
Absolute Favourites:	45-125	-£0.02

Race Profiles

Claiming Hurdle Races: 2m to 2m3f

ANALYSIS BY AGE

Age	Prop	Win	Runs	Wins%	£
3yo	0%	0	0	0.0%	0.00
4yo	6%	5	144	3.5%	-0.77
5yo	20%	16	176	9.1%	-0.26
6yo	25%	20	174	11.5%	-0.35
7yo	17%	14	108	13.0%	-0.41
8yo	15%	12	105	11.4%	-0.42
9yo	7%	6	82	7.3%	-0.70
10yo	2%	2	40	5.0%	-0.82
11yo	6%	5	25	20.0%	-0.14
12yo+	1%	1	16	6.3%	-0.80

ANALYSIS BY BHB RATING

Age	Prop	Win	Runs	Wins%	£
150+	0%	0	0	0.0%	0.00
130..149	1%	1	1	100.0%	0.91
120..129	11%	9	25	36.0%	0.03
110..119	19%	15	65	23.1%	-0.05
100..109	27%	22	144	15.3%	-0.32
80..99	33%	27	256	10.5%	-0.28
60..79	0%	0	93	0.0%	-1.00
..59	0%	0	6	0.0%	-1.00
Unrated	9%	7	280	2.5%	-0.70

ANALYSIS BY WEIGHT CARRIED

Age	Prop	Win	Runs	Wins%	£
12-01+	0%	0	0	0.0%	0.00
11-8..12-00	17%	14	73	19.2%	-0.32
11-0..11-07	33%	27	246	11.0%	-0.30
10-8..10-13	27%	22	263	8.4%	-0.55
10-0..10-07	22%	18	261	6.9%	-0.56
..9-13	0%	0	27	0.0%	-1.00

ANALYSIS BY DAYS SINCE LAST RUN

Age	Prop	Win	Runs	Wins%	£
1..7	5%	4	48	8.3%	-0.73
8..14	22%	18	155	11.6%	-0.33
15..28	32%	26	231	11.3%	-0.42
29..60	23%	19	166	11.4%	-0.35
61..100	6%	5	65	7.7%	-0.51
101+	11%	9	154	5.8%	-0.58
Unraced	0%	0	51	0.0%	-1.00

ANALYSIS BY TODAY'S STARTING PRICE

Age	Prop	Win	Runs	Wins%	£
Odds On	6%	5	8	62.5%	0.10
Ev-2/1	26%	21	60	35.0%	-0.13
9/4-4/1	31%	25	92	27.2%	0.06
9/2-6/1	14%	11	76	14.5%	-0.08
13/2-10/1	14%	11	116	9.5%	-0.20
11/1-16/1	7%	6	96	6.3%	-0.14
18/1-33/1	2%	2	167	1.2%	-0.69
40/1+	0%	0	255	0.0%	-1.00

ANALYSIS BY STARTING PRICE LAST TIME

Age	Prop	Win	Runs	Wins%	£
Odds On	4%	3	7	42.9%	0.13
Ev-2/1	9%	7	31	22.6%	-0.30
9/4-4/1	12%	10	69	14.5%	-0.44
9/2-6/1	19%	15	78	19.2%	-0.12
13/2-10/1	22%	18	125	14.4%	-0.13
11/1-16/1	12%	10	132	7.6%	-0.53
18/1-33/1	15%	12	166	7.2%	-0.54
40/1+	7%	6	211	2.8%	-0.66
Unraced	0%	0	51	0.0%	-1.00

ANALYSIS BY DISTANCE BEATEN LAST TIME

Age	Prop	Win	Runs	Wins%	£
..-10 lgh	5%	4	7	57.1%	0.45
-10..0	11%	9	39	23.1%	-0.13
0.1..2	5%	4	31	12.9%	-0.64
2.1..5	7%	6	32	18.8%	-0.30
5.1..10	10%	8	55	14.5%	-0.06
10.1..20	15%	12	97	12.4%	-0.13
20.0..30	17%	14	99	14.1%	0.02
30.1+	17%	14	272	5.1%	-0.68
Not Compl	12%	10	187	5.3%	-0.71
Unraced	0%	0	51	0.0%	-1.00

ANALYSIS BY SUCCESS RATE IN LAST 10 RUNS

Age	Prop	Win	Runs	Wins%	£
No Wins	36%	29	512	5.7%	-0.56
1 Win	31%	25	174	14.4%	-0.21
2 Wins	22%	18	88	20.5%	-0.23
3 Wins	9%	7	40	17.5%	-0.56
4 Wins	2%	2	5	40.0%	0.03
5+ Wins	0%	0	0	0.0%	0.00

ANALYSIS BY SUCCESS RATE IN LAST 3 RUNS

Age	Prop	Win	Runs	Wins%	£
No Wins	67%	54	677	8.0%	-0.48
1 Win	30%	24	124	19.4%	-0.22
2 Wins	4%	3	18	16.7%	-0.68
3 Wins	0%	0	0	0.0%	0.00

ANALYSIS BY POSITION LAST TIME

Age	Prop	Win	Runs	Wins%	£
Won	16%	13	46	28.3%	-0.04
2nd or 3rd	23%	19	117	16.2%	-0.29
Unplaced	48%	39	469	8.3%	-0.42
Fell,BD,UR	2%	2	35	5.7%	-0.64
Pulled Up	10%	8	145	5.5%	-0.71
Ref/RanOut	0%	0	4	0.0%	-1.00
CO/SlipUp	0%	0	3	0.0%	-1.00
Unraced	0%	0	51	0.0%	-1.00

OTHER FACTORS (WINS-RUNS, £)

Course Winner:	9-83	-£0.61
Distance Winner:	32-206	-£0.41
Going Winner:	26-180	-£0.36
Beaten Favourite:	9-49	-£0.33
7-Day Winners:	3-8	-£0.05
BHA Top Rated:	19-66	-£0.01
Absolute Favourites:	31-77	£0.07

Claiming Hurdle Races

Claiming Hurdle Races: 2m4f to 2m7f

ANALYSIS BY AGE

Age	Prop	Win	Runs	Wins%	£
3yo	0%	0	0	0.0%	0.00
4yo	2%	1	29	3.4%	-0.28
5yo	15%	7	64	10.9%	1.15
6yo	13%	6	75	8.0%	-0.44
7yo	21%	10	73	13.7%	-0.20
8yo	19%	9	79	11.4%	-0.05
9yo	6%	3	52	5.8%	-0.51
10yo	13%	6	49	12.2%	-0.53
11yo	6%	3	26	11.5%	-0.33
12yo+	4%	2	23	8.7%	-0.79

ANALYSIS BY BHB RATING

Age	Prop	Win	Runs	Wins%	£
150+	0%	0	0	0.0%	0.00
130..149	2%	1	3	33.3%	-0.04
120..129	13%	6	18	33.3%	0.83
110..119	32%	15	75	20.0%	-0.10
100..109	26%	12	108	11.1%	-0.24
80..99	21%	10	143	7.0%	-0.35
60..79	2%	1	49	2.0%	-0.57
..59	0%	0	1	0.0%	-1.00
Unrated	4%	2	73	2.7%	0.44

ANALYSIS BY WEIGHT CARRIED

Age	Prop	Win	Runs	Wins%	£
12-01+	0%	0	1	0.0%	-1.00
11-8..12-00	11%	5	34	14.7%	-0.31
11-0..11-07	40%	19	157	12.1%	-0.03
10-8..10-13	36%	17	173	9.8%	0.05
10-0..10-07	13%	6	95	6.3%	-0.50
..9-13	0%	0	10	0.0%	-1.00

ANALYSIS BY DAYS SINCE LAST RUN

Age	Prop	Win	Runs	Wins%	£
1..7	2%	1	24	4.2%	-0.81
8..14	30%	14	102	13.7%	0.67
15..28	38%	18	141	12.8%	-0.16
29..60	17%	8	85	9.4%	-0.26
61..100	4%	2	33	6.1%	-0.33
101+	9%	4	79	5.1%	-0.66
Unraced	0%	0	6	0.0%	-1.00

ANALYSIS BY TODAY'S STARTING PRICE

Age	Prop	Win	Runs	Wins%	£
Odds On	6%	3	8	37.5%	-0.37
Ev-2/1	15%	7	24	29.2%	-0.22
9/4-4/1	38%	18	63	28.6%	0.19
9/2-6/1	17%	8	49	16.3%	0.04
13/2-10/1	6%	3	73	4.1%	-0.62
11/1-16/1	9%	4	64	6.3%	-0.06
18/1-33/1	6%	3	81	3.7%	-0.19
40/1+	2%	1	108	0.9%	-0.06

ANALYSIS BY STARTING PRICE LAST TIME

Age	Prop	Win	Runs	Wins%	£
Odds On	6%	3	6	50.0%	0.60
Ev-2/1	11%	5	18	27.8%	-0.16
9/4-4/1	9%	4	42	9.5%	-0.68
9/2-6/1	15%	7	47	14.9%	-0.20
13/2-10/1	26%	12	81	14.8%	0.30
11/1-16/1	15%	7	80	8.8%	-0.53
18/1-33/1	9%	4	92	4.3%	-0.38
40/1+	11%	5	98	5.1%	0.31
Unraced	0%	0	6	0.0%	-1.00

ANALYSIS BY DISTANCE BEATEN LAST TIME

Age	Prop	Win	Runs	Wins%	£
..-10 lgh	6%	3	4	75.0%	1.03
-10..0	15%	7	44	15.9%	-0.23
0.1..2	2%	1	5	20.0%	0.20
2.1..5	9%	4	17	23.5%	0.19
5.1..10	2%	1	26	3.8%	-0.81
10.1..20	17%	8	80	10.0%	-0.49
20.0..30	11%	5	54	9.3%	-0.14
30.1+	23%	11	138	8.0%	0.13
Not Compl	15%	7	96	7.3%	-0.08
Unraced	0%	0	6	0.0%	-1.00

ANALYSIS BY SUCCESS RATE IN LAST 10 RUNS

Age	Prop	Win	Runs	Wins%	£
No Wins	32%	15	212	7.1%	0.17
1 Win	36%	17	144	11.8%	-0.45
2 Wins	21%	10	75	13.3%	-0.16
3 Wins	4%	2	24	8.3%	-0.69
4 Wins	6%	3	6	50.0%	0.26
5+ Wins	0%	0	3	0.0%	-1.00

ANALYSIS BY SUCCESS RATE IN LAST 3 RUNS

Age	Prop	Win	Runs	Wins%	£
No Wins	57%	27	355	7.6%	-0.07
1 Win	36%	17	90	18.9%	-0.26
2 Wins	6%	3	19	15.8%	-0.51
3 Wins	0%	0	0	0.0%	0.00

ANALYSIS BY POSITION LAST TIME

Age	Prop	Win	Runs	Wins%	£
Won	21%	10	48	20.8%	-0.12
2nd or 3rd	21%	10	65	15.4%	-0.19
Unplaced	43%	20	255	7.8%	-0.13
Fell,BD,UR	4%	2	14	14.3%	1.71
Pulled Up	11%	5	78	6.4%	-0.36
Ref/RanOut	0%	0	4	0.0%	-1.00
CO/SlipUp	0%	0	0	0.0%	0.00
Unraced	0%	0	6	0.0%	-1.00

OTHER FACTORS (WINS-RUNS, £)

Course Winner:	16-81	£0.27
Distance Winner:	17-114	-£0.17
Going Winner:	20-182	-£0.27
Beaten Favourite:	5-15	£0.19
7-Day Winners:	1-4	£0.13
BHA Top Rated:	11-38	£0.09
Absolute Favourites:	12-42	-£0.20

Race Profiles

Claiming Hurdle Races: 3m+

ANALYSIS BY AGE

Age	Prop	Win	Runs	Wins%	£
3yo	0%	0	0	0.0%	0.00
4yo	0%	0	1	0.0%	-1.00
5yo	17%	1	4	25.0%	1.25
6yo	33%	2	10	20.0%	-0.38
7yo	0%	0	7	0.0%	-1.00
8yo	0%	0	9	0.0%	-1.00
9yo	17%	1	11	9.1%	-0.77
10yo	17%	1	6	16.7%	0.17
11yo	0%	0	2	0.0%	-1.00
12yo+	17%	1	6	16.7%	-0.08

ANALYSIS BY BHB RATING

Age	Prop	Win	Runs	Wins%	£
150+	0%	0	0	0.0%	0.00
130..149	0%	0	0	0.0%	0.00
120..129	0%	0	1	0.0%	-1.00
110..119	33%	2	5	40.0%	0.25
100..109	33%	2	7	28.6%	0.14
80..99	17%	1	18	5.6%	-0.61
60..79	17%	1	13	7.7%	-0.31
..59	0%	0	0	0.0%	0.00
Unrated	0%	0	12	0.0%	-1.00

ANALYSIS BY WEIGHT CARRIED

Age	Prop	Win	Runs	Wins%	£
12-01+	0%	0	0	0.0%	0.00
11-8..12-00	0%	0	3	0.0%	-1.00
11-0..11-07	33%	2	12	16.7%	-0.31
10-8..10-13	50%	3	27	11.1%	-0.31
10-0..10-07	17%	1	14	7.1%	-0.75
..9-13	0%	0	0	0.0%	0.00

ANALYSIS BY DAYS SINCE LAST RUN

Age	Prop	Win	Runs	Wins%	£
1..7	0%	0	2	0.0%	-1.00
8..14	33%	2	6	33.3%	1.42
15..28	33%	2	27	7.4%	-0.77
29..60	0%	0	8	0.0%	-1.00
61..100	17%	1	3	33.3%	1.33
101+	17%	1	9	11.1%	-0.72
Unraced	0%	0	1	0.0%	-1.00

ANALYSIS BY TODAY'S STARTING PRICE

Age	Prop	Win	Runs	Wins%	£
Odds On	0%	0	0	0.0%	0.00
Ev-2/1	33%	2	7	28.6%	-0.25
9/4-4/1	17%	1	5	20.0%	-0.30
9/2-6/1	33%	2	6	33.3%	1.08
13/2-10/1	17%	1	8	12.5%	0.13
11/1-16/1	0%	0	10	0.0%	-1.00
18/1-33/1	0%	0	7	0.0%	-1.00
40/1+	0%	0	13	0.0%	-1.00

ANALYSIS BY STARTING PRICE LAST TIME

Age	Prop	Win	Runs	Wins%	£
Odds On	0%	0	0	0.0%	0.00
Ev-2/1	0%	0	0	0.0%	0.00
9/4-4/1	17%	1	4	25.0%	-0.38
9/2-6/1	33%	2	3	66.7%	1.08
13/2-10/1	0%	0	7	0.0%	-1.00
11/1-16/1	33%	2	14	14.3%	-0.11
18/1-33/1	0%	0	14	0.0%	-1.00
40/1+	17%	1	13	7.7%	-0.31
Unraced	0%	0	1	0.0%	-1.00

ANALYSIS BY DISTANCE BEATEN LAST TIME

Age	Prop	Win	Runs	Wins%	£
..-10 lgh	0%	0	0	0.0%	0.00
-10..0	0%	0	1	0.0%	-1.00
0.1..2	17%	1	1	100.0%	4.50
2.1..5	0%	0	0	0.0%	0.00
5.1..10	33%	2	5	40.0%	0.05
10.1..20	0%	0	4	0.0%	-1.00
20.0..30	0%	0	4	0.0%	-1.00
30.1+	17%	1	24	4.2%	-0.63
Not Compl	33%	2	16	12.5%	-0.34
Unraced	0%	0	1	0.0%	-1.00

ANALYSIS BY SUCCESS RATE IN LAST 10 RUNS

Age	Prop	Win	Runs	Wins%	£
No Wins	50%	3	33	9.1%	-0.43
1 Win	17%	1	12	8.3%	-0.79
2 Wins	17%	1	7	14.3%	-0.21
3 Wins	17%	1	3	33.3%	0.17
4 Wins	0%	0	0	0.0%	0.00
5+ Wins	0%	0	0	0.0%	0.00

ANALYSIS BY SUCCESS RATE IN LAST 3 RUNS

Age	Prop	Win	Runs	Wins%	£
No Wins	50%	3	45	6.7%	-0.58
1 Win	50%	3	8	37.5%	0.44
2 Wins	0%	0	2	0.0%	-1.00
3 Wins	0%	0	0	0.0%	0.00

ANALYSIS BY POSITION LAST TIME

Age	Prop	Win	Runs	Wins%	£
Won	0%	0	1	0.0%	-1.00
2nd or 3rd	33%	2	6	33.3%	0.33
Unplaced	33%	2	32	6.3%	-0.63
Fell,BD,UR	0%	0	2	0.0%	-1.00
Pulled Up	33%	2	14	14.3%	-0.25
Ref/RanOut	0%	0	0	0.0%	0.00
CO/SlipUp	0%	0	0	0.0%	0.00
Unraced	0%	0	1	0.0%	-1.00

OTHER FACTORS (WINS-RUNS, £)

Course Winner:	0-4	-£1.00
Distance Winner:	0-9	-£1.00
Going Winner:	2-21	-£0.57
BHA Top Rated:	1-5	-£0.45
Absolute Favourites:	2-6	£0.04

Claiming Hurdle Races

Claiming Hurdle Races: 2 to 5 runners

ANALYSIS BY AGE

Age	Prop	Win	Runs	Wins%	£
3yo	0%	0	0	0.0%	0.00
4yo	0%	0	2	0.0%	-1.00
5yo	17%	1	4	25.0%	0.00
6yo	17%	1	4	25.0%	0.13
7yo	33%	2	7	28.6%	1.96
8yo	0%	0	3	0.0%	-1.00
9yo	17%	1	6	16.7%	-0.58
10yo	0%	0	1	0.0%	-1.00
11yo	0%	0	1	0.0%	-1.00
12yo+	17%	1	1	100.0%	1.00

ANALYSIS BY BHB RATING

Age	Prop	Win	Runs	Wins%	£
150+	0%	0	0	0.0%	0.00
130..149	0%	0	0	0.0%	0.00
120..129	17%	1	1	100.0%	2.75
110..119	17%	1	5	20.0%	-0.60
100..109	17%	1	7	14.3%	-0.64
80..99	50%	3	9	33.3%	1.83
60..79	0%	0	2	0.0%	-1.00
..59	0%	0	0	0.0%	0.00
Unrated	0%	0	5	0.0%	-1.00

ANALYSIS BY WEIGHT CARRIED

Age	Prop	Win	Runs	Wins%	£
12-01+	0%	0	0	0.0%	0.00
11-8..12-00	0%	0	1	0.0%	-1.00
11-0..11-07	50%	3	11	27.3%	-0.07
10-8..10-13	33%	2	11	18.2%	0.77
10-0..10-07	17%	1	6	16.7%	-0.33
..9-13	0%	0	0	0.0%	0.00

ANALYSIS BY DAYS SINCE LAST RUN

Age	Prop	Win	Runs	Wins%	£
1..7	17%	1	2	50.0%	0.88
8..14	17%	1	7	14.3%	1.43
15..28	17%	1	7	14.3%	-0.71
29..60	17%	1	7	14.3%	-0.43
61..100	0%	0	2	0.0%	-1.00
101+	33%	2	4	50.0%	0.75
Unraced	0%	0	0	0.0%	0.00

ANALYSIS BY TODAY'S STARTING PRICE

Age	Prop	Win	Runs	Wins%	£
Odds On	0%	0	0	0.0%	0.00
Ev-2/1	33%	2	10	20.0%	-0.55
9/4-4/1	50%	3	6	50.0%	1.04
9/2-6/1	0%	0	0	0.0%	0.00
13/2-10/1	0%	0	5	0.0%	-1.00
11/1-16/1	17%	1	5	20.0%	2.40
18/1-33/1	0%	0	1	0.0%	-1.00
40/1+	0%	0	2	0.0%	-1.00

ANALYSIS BY STARTING PRICE LAST TIME

Age	Prop	Win	Runs	Wins%	£
Odds On	17%	1	1	100.0%	2.75
Ev-2/1	0%	0	7	0.0%	-1.00
9/4-4/1	17%	1	3	33.3%	-0.17
9/2-6/1	17%	1	1	100.0%	3.00
13/2-10/1	17%	1	6	16.7%	1.83
11/1-16/1	33%	2	3	66.7%	1.17
18/1-33/1	0%	0	2	0.0%	-1.00
40/1+	0%	0	6	0.0%	-1.00
Unraced	0%	0	0	0.0%	0.00

ANALYSIS BY DISTANCE BEATEN LAST TIME

Age	Prop	Win	Runs	Wins%	£
..-10 lgh	0%	0	0	0.0%	0.00
-10..0	17%	1	4	25.0%	-0.06
0.1..2	0%	0	2	0.0%	-1.00
2.1..5	0%	0	2	0.0%	-1.00
5.1..10	17%	1	4	25.0%	-0.38
10.1..20	0%	0	2	0.0%	-1.00
20.0..30	17%	1	3	33.3%	0.33
30.1+	17%	1	8	12.5%	-0.75
Not Compl	33%	2	4	50.0%	4.38
Unraced	0%	0	0	0.0%	0.00

ANALYSIS BY SUCCESS RATE IN LAST 10 RUNS

Age	Prop	Win	Runs	Wins%	£
No Wins	17%	1	9	11.1%	0.89
1 Win	67%	4	10	40.0%	0.30
2 Wins	17%	1	7	14.3%	-0.46
3 Wins	0%	0	3	0.0%	-1.00
4 Wins	0%	0	0	0.0%	0.00
5+ Wins	0%	0	0	0.0%	0.00

ANALYSIS BY SUCCESS RATE IN LAST 3 RUNS

Age	Prop	Win	Runs	Wins%	£
No Wins	33%	2	19	10.5%	0.11
1 Win	67%	4	9	44.4%	0.42
2 Wins	0%	0	1	0.0%	-1.00
3 Wins	0%	0	0	0.0%	0.00

ANALYSIS BY POSITION LAST TIME

Age	Prop	Win	Runs	Wins%	£
Won	17%	1	4	25.0%	-0.06
2nd or 3rd	17%	1	6	16.7%	-0.58
Unplaced	33%	2	15	13.3%	-0.60
Fell,BD,UR	17%	1	1	100.0%	16.00
Pulled Up	17%	1	3	33.3%	0.50
Ref/RanOut	0%	0	0	0.0%	0.00
CO/SlipUp	0%	0	0	0.0%	0.00
Unraced	0%	0	0	0.0%	0.00

OTHER FACTORS (WINS-RUNS, £)

Course Winner:	2-7	-£0.07
Distance Winner:	2-12	£0.79
Going Winner:	1-10	-£0.55
Beaten Favourite:	0-4	-£1.00
7-Day Winners:	1-1	£2.75
BHA Top Rated:	3-6	£0.63
Absolute Favourites:	1-6	-£0.67

Race Profiles

Claiming Hurdle Races: 6 to 10 runners

ANALYSIS BY AGE

Age	Prop	Win	Runs	Wins%	£
3yo	0%	0	0	0.0%	0.00
4yo	6%	4	66	6.1%	-0.48
5yo	20%	13	82	15.9%	1.00
6yo	17%	11	107	10.3%	-0.54
7yo	15%	10	72	13.9%	-0.44
8yo	15%	10	84	11.9%	-0.13
9yo	5%	3	52	5.8%	-0.78
10yo	11%	7	55	12.7%	-0.45
11yo	9%	6	18	33.3%	0.69
12yo+	3%	2	19	10.5%	-0.68

ANALYSIS BY BHB RATING

Age	Prop	Win	Runs	Wins%	£
150+	0%	0	0	0.0%	0.00
130..149	2%	1	1	100.0%	0.91
120..129	14%	9	22	40.9%	0.16
110..119	21%	14	67	20.9%	-0.18
100..109	33%	22	119	18.5%	-0.12
80..99	23%	15	163	9.2%	-0.33
60..79	3%	2	58	3.4%	-0.48
..59	0%	0	2	0.0%	-1.00
Unrated	5%	3	123	2.4%	-0.08

ANALYSIS BY WEIGHT CARRIED

Age	Prop	Win	Runs	Wins%	£
12-01+	0%	0	0	0.0%	0.00
11-8..12-00	15%	10	42	23.8%	-0.25
11-0..11-07	30%	20	173	11.6%	-0.24
10-8..10-13	32%	21	169	12.4%	0.09
10-0..10-07	23%	15	152	9.9%	-0.40
..9-13	0%	0	19	0.0%	-1.00

ANALYSIS BY DAYS SINCE LAST RUN

Age	Prop	Win	Runs	Wins%	£
1..7	3%	2	34	5.9%	-0.89
8..14	29%	19	114	16.7%	0.53
15..28	35%	23	163	14.1%	-0.18
29..60	18%	12	95	12.6%	-0.39
61..100	8%	5	41	12.2%	-0.01
101+	8%	5	92	5.4%	-0.69
Unraced	0%	0	16	0.0%	-1.00

ANALYSIS BY TODAY'S STARTING PRICE

Age	Prop	Win	Runs	Wins%	£
Odds On	12%	8	15	53.3%	-0.08
Ev-2/1	23%	15	45	33.3%	-0.14
9/4-4/1	33%	22	81	27.2%	0.06
9/2-6/1	12%	8	53	15.1%	-0.03
13/2-10/1	12%	8	84	9.5%	-0.17
11/1-16/1	2%	1	72	1.4%	-0.83
18/1-33/1	5%	3	95	3.2%	-0.31
40/1+	2%	1	110	0.9%	-0.08

ANALYSIS BY STARTING PRICE LAST TIME

Age	Prop	Win	Runs	Wins%	£
Odds On	6%	4	7	57.1%	0.32
Ev-2/1	12%	8	23	34.8%	-0.07
9/4-4/1	8%	5	47	10.6%	-0.66
9/2-6/1	18%	12	64	18.8%	-0.37
13/2-10/1	20%	13	88	14.8%	0.07
11/1-16/1	14%	9	91	9.9%	-0.43
18/1-33/1	15%	10	110	9.1%	-0.31
40/1+	8%	5	109	4.6%	0.19
Unraced	0%	0	16	0.0%	-1.00

ANALYSIS BY DISTANCE BEATEN LAST TIME

Age	Prop	Win	Runs	Wins%	£
..-10 lgh	8%	5	8	62.5%	0.32
-10..0	14%	9	41	22.0%	-0.22
0.1..2	5%	3	16	18.8%	-0.33
2.1..5	11%	7	23	30.4%	0.27
5.1..10	3%	2	34	5.9%	-0.87
10.1..20	11%	7	71	9.9%	-0.57
20.0..30	14%	9	66	13.6%	-0.10
30.1+	27%	18	160	11.3%	0.29
Not Compl	9%	6	120	5.0%	-0.53
Unraced	0%	0	16	0.0%	-1.00

ANALYSIS BY SUCCESS RATE IN LAST 10 RUNS

Age	Prop	Win	Runs	Wins%	£
No Wins	32%	21	276	7.6%	-0.09
1 Win	30%	20	142	14.1%	-0.39
2 Wins	23%	15	76	19.7%	0.01
3 Wins	9%	6	33	18.2%	-0.55
4 Wins	6%	4	9	44.4%	0.09
5+ Wins	0%	0	3	0.0%	-1.00

ANALYSIS BY SUCCESS RATE IN LAST 3 RUNS

Age	Prop	Win	Runs	Wins%	£
No Wins	58%	38	421	9.0%	-0.19
1 Win	35%	23	96	24.0%	-0.11
2 Wins	8%	5	22	22.7%	-0.52
3 Wins	0%	0	0	0.0%	0.00

ANALYSIS BY POSITION LAST TIME

Age	Prop	Win	Runs	Wins%	£
Won	21%	14	49	28.6%	-0.13
2nd or 3rd	24%	16	85	18.8%	-0.25
Unplaced	45%	30	285	10.5%	-0.03
Fell,BD,UR	2%	1	20	5.0%	0.05
Pulled Up	8%	5	97	5.2%	-0.64
Ref/RanOut	0%	0	3	0.0%	-1.00
CO/SlipUp	0%	0	0	0.0%	0.00
Unraced	0%	0	16	0.0%	-1.00

OTHER FACTORS (WINS-RUNS, £)

Course Winner:	14-74	£0.13
Distance Winner:	28-146	-£0.17
Going Winner:	24-174	-£0.27
Beaten Favourite:	7-23	£0.05
7-Day Winners:	2-7	-£0.45
BHA Top Rated:	19-57	£0.07
Absolute Favourites:	24-61	-£0.01

Claiming Hurdle Races

Claiming Hurdle Races: 11 runners or more

ANALYSIS BY AGE

Age	Prop	Win	Runs	Wins%	£
3yo	0%	0	0	0.0%	0.00
4yo	3%	2	106	1.9%	-0.82
5yo	16%	10	158	6.3%	-0.31
6yo	26%	16	148	10.8%	-0.28
7yo	19%	12	109	11.0%	-0.44
8yo	18%	11	106	10.4%	-0.41
9yo	10%	6	87	6.9%	-0.56
10yo	3%	2	39	5.1%	-0.81
11yo	3%	2	34	5.9%	-0.76
12yo+	2%	1	25	4.0%	-0.78

ANALYSIS BY BHB RATING

Age	Prop	Win	Runs	Wins%	£
150+	0%	0	0	0.0%	0.00
130..149	2%	1	3	33.3%	-0.04
120..129	8%	5	21	23.8%	0.40
110..119	27%	17	73	23.3%	0.07
100..109	21%	13	133	9.8%	-0.39
80..99	32%	20	245	8.2%	-0.38
60..79	0%	0	95	0.0%	-1.00
..59	0%	0	5	0.0%	-1.00
Unrated	10%	6	237	2.5%	-0.68

ANALYSIS BY WEIGHT CARRIED

Age	Prop	Win	Runs	Wins%	£
12-01+	0%	0	1	0.0%	-1.00
11-8..12-00	15%	9	67	13.4%	-0.38
11-0..11-07	40%	25	231	10.8%	-0.17
10-8..10-13	31%	19	283	6.7%	-0.60
10-0..10-07	15%	9	212	4.2%	-0.67
..9-13	0%	0	18	0.0%	-1.00

ANALYSIS BY DAYS SINCE LAST RUN

Age	Prop	Win	Runs	Wins%	£
1..7	3%	2	38	5.3%	-0.74
8..14	23%	14	142	9.9%	-0.31
15..28	35%	22	229	9.6%	-0.46
29..60	23%	14	157	8.9%	-0.30
61..100	5%	3	58	5.2%	-0.65
101+	11%	7	146	4.8%	-0.60
Unraced	0%	0	42	0.0%	-1.00

ANALYSIS BY TODAY'S STARTING PRICE

Age	Prop	Win	Runs	Wins%	£
Odds On	0%	0	1	0.0%	-1.00
Ev-2/1	21%	13	36	36.1%	-0.09
9/4-4/1	31%	19	73	26.0%	0.08
9/2-6/1	21%	13	78	16.7%	0.05
13/2-10/1	11%	7	108	6.5%	-0.45
11/1-16/1	13%	8	93	8.6%	0.23
18/1-33/1	3%	2	159	1.3%	-0.67
40/1+	0%	0	264	0.0%	-1.00

ANALYSIS BY STARTING PRICE LAST TIME

Age	Prop	Win	Runs	Wins%	£
Odds On	2%	1	5	20.0%	-0.10
Ev-2/1	6%	4	19	21.1%	-0.18
9/4-4/1	15%	9	65	13.8%	-0.45
9/2-6/1	18%	11	63	17.5%	0.08
13/2-10/1	26%	16	119	13.4%	-0.13
11/1-16/1	13%	8	132	6.1%	-0.59
18/1-33/1	10%	6	160	3.8%	-0.64
40/1+	11%	7	207	3.4%	-0.62
Unraced	0%	0	42	0.0%	-1.00

ANALYSIS BY DISTANCE BEATEN LAST TIME

Age	Prop	Win	Runs	Wins%	£
..-10 lgh	3%	2	3	66.7%	1.58
-10..0	10%	6	39	15.4%	-0.18
0.1..2	5%	3	19	15.8%	-0.37
2.1..5	5%	3	24	12.5%	-0.44
5.1..10	13%	8	48	16.7%	0.14
10.1..20	21%	13	108	12.0%	-0.13
20.0..30	15%	9	88	10.2%	-0.04
30.1+	11%	7	266	2.6%	-0.84
Not Compl	18%	11	175	6.3%	-0.56
Unraced	0%	0	42	0.0%	-1.00

ANALYSIS BY SUCCESS RATE IN LAST 10 RUNS

Age	Prop	Win	Runs	Wins%	£
No Wins	40%	25	472	5.3%	-0.52
1 Win	31%	19	178	10.7%	-0.33
2 Wins	21%	13	87	14.9%	-0.36
3 Wins	6%	4	31	12.9%	-0.57
4 Wins	2%	1	2	50.0%	0.44
5+ Wins	0%	0	0	0.0%	0.00

ANALYSIS BY SUCCESS RATE IN LAST 3 RUNS

Age	Prop	Win	Runs	Wins%	£
No Wins	71%	44	637	6.9%	-0.47
1 Win	27%	17	117	14.5%	-0.34
2 Wins	2%	1	16	6.3%	-0.73
3 Wins	0%	0	0	0.0%	0.00

ANALYSIS BY POSITION LAST TIME

Age	Prop	Win	Runs	Wins%	£
Won	13%	8	42	19.0%	-0.05
2nd or 3rd	23%	14	97	14.4%	-0.20
Unplaced	47%	29	456	6.4%	-0.51
Fell,BD,UR	3%	2	30	6.7%	-0.58
Pulled Up	15%	9	137	6.6%	-0.54
Ref/RanOut	0%	0	5	0.0%	-1.00
CO/SlipUp	0%	0	3	0.0%	-1.00
Unraced	0%	0	42	0.0%	-1.00

OTHER FACTORS (WINS-RUNS, £)

Course Winner:	9-87	-£0.48
Distance Winner:	19-171	-£0.57
Going Winner:	23-199	-£0.38
Beaten Favourite:	7-37	-£0.28
7-Day Winners:	1-4	£0.13
BHA Top Rated:	9-46	-£0.16
Absolute Favourites:	20-58	£0.03

Race Profiles

Claiming Hurdle Races: up to 7 days off the track

ANALYSIS BY AGE

Age	Prop	Win	Runs	Wins%	£
3yo	0%	0	0	0.0%	0.00
4yo	0%	0	30	0.0%	-1.00
5yo	0%	0	23	0.0%	-1.00
6yo	20%	1	23	4.3%	-0.76
7yo	20%	1	21	4.8%	-0.82
8yo	40%	2	19	10.5%	-0.80
9yo	20%	1	11	9.1%	-0.59
10yo	0%	0	2	0.0%	-1.00
11yo	0%	0	2	0.0%	-1.00
12yo+	0%	0	1	0.0%	-1.00

ANALYSIS BY BHB RATING

Age	Prop	Win	Runs	Wins%	£
150+	0%	0	0	0.0%	0.00
130..149	20%	1	2	50.0%	-0.04
120..129	20%	1	6	16.7%	-0.38
110..119	20%	1	4	25.0%	0.13
100..109	20%	1	15	6.7%	-0.87
80..99	20%	1	24	4.2%	-0.77
60..79	0%	0	9	0.0%	-1.00
..59	0%	0	0	0.0%	0.00
Unrated	0%	0	72	0.0%	-1.00

ANALYSIS BY WEIGHT CARRIED

Age	Prop	Win	Runs	Wins%	£
12-01+	0%	0	1	0.0%	-1.00
11-8..12-00	0%	0	13	0.0%	-1.00
11-0..11-07	20%	1	38	2.6%	-0.90
10-8..10-13	40%	2	40	5.0%	-0.84
10-0..10-07	40%	2	34	5.9%	-0.78
..9-13	0%	0	6	0.0%	-1.00

ANALYSIS BY DAYS SINCE LAST RUN

Age	Prop	Win	Runs	Wins%	£
1..7	100%	5	74	6.8%	-0.76
8..14	0%	0	0	0.0%	0.00
15..28	0%	0	0	0.0%	0.00
29..60	0%	0	0	0.0%	0.00
61..100	0%	0	0	0.0%	0.00
101+	0%	0	0	0.0%	0.00
Unraced	0%	0	58	0.0%	-1.00

ANALYSIS BY TODAY'S STARTING PRICE

Age	Prop	Win	Runs	Wins%	£
Odds On	40%	2	3	66.7%	0.27
Ev-2/1	0%	0	6	0.0%	-1.00
9/4-4/1	40%	2	11	18.2%	-0.25
9/2-6/1	20%	1	10	10.0%	-0.45
13/2-10/1	0%	0	12	0.0%	-1.00
11/1-16/1	0%	0	15	0.0%	-1.00
18/1-33/1	0%	0	27	0.0%	-1.00
40/1+	0%	0	48	0.0%	-1.00

ANALYSIS BY STARTING PRICE LAST TIME

Age	Prop	Win	Runs	Wins%	£
Odds On	40%	2	3	66.7%	1.75
Ev-2/1	40%	2	4	50.0%	-0.04
9/4-4/1	0%	0	7	0.0%	-1.00
9/2-6/1	0%	0	10	0.0%	-1.00
13/2-10/1	20%	1	9	11.1%	-0.39
11/1-16/1	0%	0	15	0.0%	-1.00
18/1-33/1	0%	0	7	0.0%	-1.00
40/1+	0%	0	19	0.0%	-1.00
Unraced	0%	0	58	0.0%	-1.00

ANALYSIS BY DISTANCE BEATEN LAST TIME

Age	Prop	Win	Runs	Wins%	£
..-10 lgh	20%	1	1	100.0%	0.91
-10..0	60%	3	11	27.3%	-0.08
0.1..2	0%	0	4	0.0%	-1.00
2.1..5	20%	1	3	33.3%	0.83
5.1..10	0%	0	5	0.0%	-1.00
10.1..20	0%	0	7	0.0%	-1.00
20.0..30	0%	0	5	0.0%	-1.00
30.1+	0%	0	21	0.0%	-1.00
Not Compl	0%	0	17	0.0%	-1.00
Unraced	0%	0	58	0.0%	-1.00

ANALYSIS BY SUCCESS RATE IN LAST 10 RUNS

Age	Prop	Win	Runs	Wins%	£
No Wins	20%	1	41	2.4%	-0.87
1 Win	0%	0	16	0.0%	-1.00
2 Wins	60%	3	9	33.3%	0.13
3 Wins	0%	0	7	0.0%	-1.00
4 Wins	20%	1	1	100.0%	0.91
5+ Wins	0%	0	0	0.0%	0.00

ANALYSIS BY SUCCESS RATE IN LAST 3 RUNS

Age	Prop	Win	Runs	Wins%	£
No Wins	20%	1	55	1.8%	-0.90
1 Win	40%	2	13	15.4%	-0.37
2 Wins	40%	2	6	33.3%	-0.36
3 Wins	0%	0	0	0.0%	0.00

ANALYSIS BY POSITION LAST TIME

Age	Prop	Win	Runs	Wins%	£
Won	80%	4	12	33.3%	0.01
2nd or 3rd	0%	0	10	0.0%	-1.00
Unplaced	20%	1	35	2.9%	-0.84
Fell,BD,UR	0%	0	4	0.0%	-1.00
Pulled Up	0%	0	13	0.0%	-1.00
Ref/RanOut	0%	0	0	0.0%	0.00
CO/SlipUp	0%	0	0	0.0%	0.00
Unraced	0%	0	58	0.0%	-1.00

OTHER FACTORS (WINS-RUNS, £)

Course Winner:	1-5	-£0.10
Distance Winner:	2-20	-£0.81
Going Winner:	2-21	-£0.82
Beaten Favourite:	0-1	-£1.00
7-Day Winners:	4-12	£0.01
BHA Top Rated:	2-10	-£0.43
Absolute Favourites:	2-9	-£0.58

Claiming Hurdle Races

Claiming Hurdle Races: 100+ days off the track

ANALYSIS BY AGE

Age	Prop	Win	Runs	Wins%	£
3yo	0%	0	0	0.0%	0.00
4yo	0%	0	18	0.0%	-1.00
5yo	21%	3	43	7.0%	-0.40
6yo	29%	4	46	8.7%	-0.26
7yo	7%	1	24	4.2%	-0.77
8yo	21%	3	34	8.8%	-0.49
9yo	7%	1	29	3.4%	-0.91
10yo	7%	1	23	4.3%	-0.74
11yo	7%	1	14	7.1%	-0.85
12yo+	0%	0	13	0.0%	-1.00

ANALYSIS BY BHB RATING

Age	Prop	Win	Runs	Wins%	£
150+	0%	0	0	0.0%	0.00
130..149	7%	1	2	50.0%	0.44
120..129	7%	1	6	16.7%	-0.65
110..119	21%	3	30	10.0%	-0.37
100..109	43%	6	30	20.0%	0.53
80..99	14%	2	54	3.7%	-0.84
60..79	0%	0	27	0.0%	-1.00
..59	0%	0	4	0.0%	-1.00
Unrated	7%	1	91	1.1%	-0.84

ANALYSIS BY WEIGHT CARRIED

Age	Prop	Win	Runs	Wins%	£
12-01+	0%	0	0	0.0%	0.00
11-8..12-00	0%	0	14	0.0%	-1.00
11-0..11-07	43%	6	72	8.3%	-0.57
10-8..10-13	36%	5	88	5.7%	-0.53
10-0..10-07	21%	3	62	4.8%	-0.65
..9-13	0%	0	8	0.0%	-1.00

ANALYSIS BY DAYS SINCE LAST RUN

Age	Prop	Win	Runs	Wins%	£
1..7	0%	0	0	0.0%	0.00
8..14	0%	0	0	0.0%	0.00
15..28	0%	0	0	0.0%	0.00
29..60	0%	0	0	0.0%	0.00
61..100	0%	0	2	0.0%	-1.00
101+	100%	14	242	5.8%	-0.61
Unraced	0%	0	0	0.0%	0.00

ANALYSIS BY TODAY'S STARTING PRICE

Age	Prop	Win	Runs	Wins%	£
Odds On	0%	0	0	0.0%	0.00
Ev-2/1	21%	3	10	30.0%	-0.25
9/4-4/1	21%	3	18	16.7%	-0.25
9/2-6/1	21%	3	20	15.0%	-0.10
13/2-10/1	21%	3	28	10.7%	-0.05
11/1-16/1	14%	2	26	7.7%	0.08
18/1-33/1	0%	0	53	0.0%	-1.00
40/1+	0%	0	89	0.0%	-1.00

ANALYSIS BY STARTING PRICE LAST TIME

Age	Prop	Win	Runs	Wins%	£
Odds On	0%	0	1	0.0%	-1.00
Ev-2/1	0%	0	6	0.0%	-1.00
9/4-4/1	14%	2	23	8.7%	-0.65
9/2-6/1	14%	2	14	14.3%	0.21
13/2-10/1	43%	6	40	15.0%	-0.14
11/1-16/1	14%	2	51	3.9%	-0.75
18/1-33/1	7%	1	50	2.0%	-0.87
40/1+	7%	1	59	1.7%	-0.75
Unraced	0%	0	0	0.0%	0.00

ANALYSIS BY DISTANCE BEATEN LAST TIME

Age	Prop	Win	Runs	Wins%	£
..-10 lgh	0%	0	0	0.0%	0.00
-10..0	7%	1	5	20.0%	0.00
0.1..2	7%	1	5	20.0%	0.20
2.1..5	0%	0	2	0.0%	-1.00
5.1..10	21%	3	21	14.3%	-0.07
10.1..20	7%	1	25	4.0%	-0.74
20.0..30	21%	3	29	10.3%	-0.29
30.1+	29%	4	95	4.2%	-0.67
Not Compl	7%	1	62	1.6%	-0.93
Unraced	0%	0	0	0.0%	0.00

ANALYSIS BY SUCCESS RATE IN LAST 10 RUNS

Age	Prop	Win	Runs	Wins%	£
No Wins	21%	3	150	2.0%	-0.88
1 Win	64%	9	53	17.0%	0.25
2 Wins	7%	1	26	3.8%	-0.77
3 Wins	0%	0	12	0.0%	-1.00
4 Wins	7%	1	3	33.3%	-0.04
5+ Wins	0%	0	0	0.0%	0.00

ANALYSIS BY SUCCESS RATE IN LAST 3 RUNS

Age	Prop	Win	Runs	Wins%	£
No Wins	50%	7	204	3.4%	-0.72
1 Win	50%	7	39	17.9%	-0.05
2 Wins	0%	0	1	0.0%	-1.00
3 Wins	0%	0	0	0.0%	0.00

ANALYSIS BY POSITION LAST TIME

Age	Prop	Win	Runs	Wins%	£
Won	7%	1	5	20.0%	0.00
2nd or 3rd	29%	4	24	16.7%	0.27
Unplaced	57%	8	153	5.2%	-0.65
Fell,BD,UR	0%	0	8	0.0%	-1.00
Pulled Up	7%	1	52	1.9%	-0.91
Ref/RanOut	0%	0	1	0.0%	-1.00
CO/SlipUp	0%	0	1	0.0%	-1.00
Unraced	0%	0	0	0.0%	0.00

OTHER FACTORS (WINS-RUNS, £)

Course Winner:	4-31	-£0.15
Distance Winner:	3-56	-£0.70
Going Winner:	4-66	-£0.77
Beaten Favourite:	0-16	-£1.00
BHA Top Rated:	3-12	£0.22
Absolute Favourites:	3-10	-£0.10

Race Profiles

Selling Hurdle Races

ANALYSIS BY AGE

Age	Prop	Win	Runs	Wins%	£
3yo	2%	7	39	17.9%	0.60
4yo	13%	54	832	6.5%	-0.47
5yo	15%	66	941	7.0%	-0.58
6yo	24%	104	986	10.5%	-0.29
7yo	19%	80	778	10.3%	-0.12
8yo	11%	47	531	8.9%	-0.38
9yo	6%	27	269	10.0%	-0.48
10yo	4%	18	208	8.7%	-0.55
11yo	4%	17	134	12.7%	-0.17
12yo+	3%	12	107	11.2%	-0.16

ANALYSIS BY BHB RATING

Age	Prop	Win	Runs	Wins%	£
150+	0%	0	0	0.0%	0.00
130..149	0%	1	2	50.0%	0.13
120..129	3%	11	44	25.0%	-0.37
110..119	12%	52	209	24.9%	-0.15
100..109	25%	106	609	17.4%	-0.12
80..99	40%	173	1554	11.1%	-0.21
60..79	5%	23	813	2.8%	-0.40
..59	0%	0	30	0.0%	-1.00
Unrated	15%	66	1564	4.2%	-0.62

ANALYSIS BY WEIGHT CARRIED

Age	Prop	Win	Runs	Wins%	£
12-01+	0%	1	8	12.5%	-0.59
11-8..12-00	5%	21	133	15.8%	-0.16
11-0..11-07	31%	132	929	14.2%	-0.28
10-8..10-13	38%	165	2014	8.2%	-0.43
10-0..10-07	24%	104	1570	6.6%	-0.36
..9-13	2%	9	171	5.3%	-0.30

ANALYSIS BY DAYS SINCE LAST RUN

Age	Prop	Win	Runs	Wins%	£
1..7	9%	39	356	11.0%	-0.47
8..14	21%	89	933	9.5%	-0.43
15..28	30%	129	1247	10.3%	-0.34
29..60	20%	87	862	10.1%	-0.30
61..100	7%	31	335	9.3%	-0.28
101+	12%	50	841	5.9%	-0.37
Unraced	2%	7	251	2.8%	-0.44

ANALYSIS BY TODAY'S STARTING PRICE

Age	Prop	Win	Runs	Wins%	£
Odds On	7%	30	49	61.2%	0.02
Ev-2/1	23%	99	219	45.2%	0.16
9/4-4/1	27%	115	555	20.7%	-0.15
9/2-6/1	14%	61	452	13.5%	-0.15
13/2-10/1	16%	70	725	9.7%	-0.15
11/1-16/1	9%	37	701	5.3%	-0.24
18/1-33/1	3%	15	874	1.7%	-0.54
40/1+	1%	5	1250	0.4%	-0.73

ANALYSIS BY STARTING PRICE LAST TIME

Age	Prop	Win	Runs	Wins%	£
Odds On	1%	4	15	26.7%	-0.15
Ev-2/1	6%	27	119	22.7%	-0.19
9/4-4/1	15%	64	321	19.9%	-0.31
9/2-6/1	13%	58	354	16.4%	0.00
13/2-10/1	19%	80	696	11.5%	-0.32
11/1-16/1	20%	85	718	11.8%	-0.10
18/1-33/1	17%	73	1023	7.1%	-0.42
40/1+	8%	34	1328	2.6%	-0.61
Unraced	2%	7	251	2.8%	-0.44

ANALYSIS BY DISTANCE BEATEN LAST TIME

Age	Prop	Win	Runs	Wins%	£
..-10 lgh	1%	5	16	31.3%	-0.34
-10..0	6%	27	157	17.2%	-0.40
0.1..2	5%	23	124	18.5%	-0.30
2.1..5	7%	32	166	19.3%	-0.19
5.1..10	13%	57	285	20.0%	-0.03
10.1..20	16%	70	585	12.0%	-0.30
20.0..30	12%	53	544	9.7%	-0.31
30.1+	22%	96	1655	5.8%	-0.42
Not Compl	14%	62	1042	6.0%	-0.45
Unraced	2%	7	251	2.8%	-0.44

ANALYSIS BY SUCCESS RATE IN LAST 10 RUNS

Age	Prop	Win	Runs	Wins%	£
No Wins	52%	219	3164	6.9%	-0.44
1 Win	33%	139	1019	13.6%	-0.21
2 Wins	14%	58	313	18.5%	-0.05
3 Wins	2%	9	73	12.3%	-0.63
4 Wins	0%	0	5	0.0%	-1.00
5+ Wins	0%	0	0	0.0%	0.00

ANALYSIS BY SUCCESS RATE IN LAST 3 RUNS

Age	Prop	Win	Runs	Wins%	£
No Wins	79%	334	4042	8.3%	-0.37
1 Win	20%	84	492	17.1%	-0.28
2 Wins	2%	7	40	17.5%	-0.50
3 Wins	0%	0	0	0.0%	0.00

ANALYSIS BY POSITION LAST TIME

Age	Prop	Win	Runs	Wins%	£
Won	7%	32	173	18.5%	-0.40
2nd or 3rd	25%	108	603	17.9%	-0.21
Unplaced	52%	224	2760	8.1%	-0.33
Fell,BD,UR	4%	16	211	7.6%	-0.47
Pulled Up	10%	44	804	5.5%	-0.52
Ref/RanOut	0%	0	18	0.0%	-1.00
CO/SlipUp	0%	1	5	20.0%	-0.45
Unraced	2%	7	251	2.8%	-0.44

OTHER FACTORS (WINS-RUNS, £)

Course Winner:	61-397	-£0.11
Distance Winner:	114-793	-£0.25
Going Winner:	115-885	-£0.32
Beaten Favourite:	34-169	-£0.26
7-Day Winners:	7-22	-£0.22
BHA Top Rated:	82-352	-£0.16
Absolute Favourites:	151-396	£0.01

Selling Hurdle Races

Selling Hurdle Races: 2m to 2m3f

ANALYSIS BY AGE

Age	Prop	Win	Runs	Wins%	£
3yo	2%	7	39	17.9%	0.60
4yo	14%	40	680	5.9%	-0.48
5yo	18%	52	678	7.7%	-0.56
6yo	25%	71	695	10.2%	-0.30
7yo	19%	53	478	11.1%	-0.06
8yo	9%	25	306	8.2%	-0.56
9yo	7%	20	158	12.7%	-0.33
10yo	3%	10	111	9.0%	-0.50
11yo	2%	5	62	8.1%	-0.58
12yo+	1%	3	44	6.8%	-0.73

ANALYSIS BY BHB RATING

Age	Prop	Win	Runs	Wins%	£
150+	0%	0	0	0.0%	0.00
130..149	0%	1	2	50.0%	0.13
120..129	2%	5	18	27.8%	-0.28
110..119	11%	32	118	27.1%	-0.11
100..109	24%	69	375	18.4%	-0.10
80..99	38%	110	1031	10.7%	-0.34
60..79	5%	13	498	2.6%	-0.35
..59	0%	0	19	0.0%	-1.00
Unrated	20%	56	1190	4.7%	-0.56

ANALYSIS BY WEIGHT CARRIED

Age	Prop	Win	Runs	Wins%	£
12-01+	0%	0	3	0.0%	-1.00
11-8..12-00	4%	12	92	13.0%	-0.22
11-0..11-07	32%	92	635	14.5%	-0.31
10-8..10-13	38%	108	1340	8.1%	-0.46
10-0..10-07	24%	68	1056	6.4%	-0.36
..9-13	2%	6	125	4.8%	-0.39

ANALYSIS BY DAYS SINCE LAST RUN

Age	Prop	Win	Runs	Wins%	£
1..7	10%	28	233	12.0%	-0.48
8..14	18%	51	616	8.3%	-0.56
15..28	29%	83	818	10.1%	-0.36
29..60	19%	54	547	9.9%	-0.30
61..100	8%	24	240	10.0%	-0.22
101+	14%	39	584	6.7%	-0.39
Unraced	2%	7	213	3.3%	-0.34

ANALYSIS BY TODAY'S STARTING PRICE

Age	Prop	Win	Runs	Wins%	£
Odds On	7%	21	34	61.8%	0.06
Ev-2/1	25%	71	150	47.3%	0.21
9/4-4/1	26%	74	369	20.1%	-0.18
9/2-6/1	13%	36	285	12.6%	-0.21
13/2-10/1	17%	49	469	10.4%	-0.09
11/1-16/1	8%	24	457	5.3%	-0.24
18/1-33/1	2%	7	598	1.2%	-0.68
40/1+	1%	4	889	0.4%	-0.69

ANALYSIS BY STARTING PRICE LAST TIME

Age	Prop	Win	Runs	Wins%	£
Odds On	1%	3	12	25.0%	-0.06
Ev-2/1	7%	20	81	24.7%	-0.18
9/4-4/1	15%	42	198	21.2%	-0.23
9/2-6/1	11%	32	227	14.1%	-0.26
13/2-10/1	18%	52	440	11.8%	-0.33
11/1-16/1	20%	57	467	12.2%	-0.12
18/1-33/1	17%	49	679	7.2%	-0.39
40/1+	8%	24	934	2.6%	-0.64
Unraced	2%	7	213	3.3%	-0.34

ANALYSIS BY DISTANCE BEATEN LAST TIME

Age	Prop	Win	Runs	Wins%	£
..-10 lgh	1%	4	10	40.0%	-0.16
-10..0	8%	23	116	19.8%	-0.30
0.1..2	6%	16	79	20.3%	-0.25
2.1..5	6%	17	100	17.0%	-0.32
5.1..10	13%	36	196	18.4%	-0.06
10.1..20	18%	52	388	13.4%	-0.25
20.0..30	10%	30	354	8.5%	-0.46
30.1+	23%	67	1128	5.9%	-0.42
Not Compl	12%	34	667	5.1%	-0.53
Unraced	2%	7	213	3.3%	-0.34

ANALYSIS BY SUCCESS RATE IN LAST 10 RUNS

Age	Prop	Win	Runs	Wins%	£
No Wins	56%	156	2172	7.2%	-0.41
1 Win	30%	84	632	13.3%	-0.34
2 Wins	13%	35	193	18.1%	-0.25
3 Wins	1%	4	39	10.3%	-0.73
4 Wins	0%	0	2	0.0%	-1.00
5+ Wins	0%	0	0	0.0%	0.00

ANALYSIS BY SUCCESS RATE IN LAST 3 RUNS

Age	Prop	Win	Runs	Wins%	£
No Wins	79%	220	2697	8.2%	-0.40
1 Win	20%	56	315	17.8%	-0.30
2 Wins	1%	3	26	11.5%	-0.72
3 Wins	0%	0	0	0.0%	0.00

ANALYSIS BY POSITION LAST TIME

Age	Prop	Win	Runs	Wins%	£
Won	9%	27	126	21.4%	-0.29
2nd or 3rd	22%	64	370	17.3%	-0.22
Unplaced	54%	155	1879	8.2%	-0.35
Fell,BD,UR	2%	6	139	4.3%	-0.81
Pulled Up	9%	27	506	5.3%	-0.57
Ref/RanOut	0%	0	15	0.0%	-1.00
CO/SlipUp	0%	0	3	0.0%	-1.00
Unraced	2%	7	213	3.3%	-0.34

OTHER FACTORS (WINS-RUNS, £)

Course Winner:	35-252	-£0.19
Distance Winner:	76-571	-£0.32
Going Winner:	63-499	-£0.43
Beaten Favourite:	21-103	-£0.27
7-Day Winners:	7-15	£0.14
BHA Top Rated:	59-242	-£0.15
Absolute Favourites:	109-265	£0.09

Race Profiles

Selling Hurdle Races: 2m4f to 2m7f

ANALYSIS BY AGE

Age	Prop	Win	Runs	Wins%	£
3yo	0%	0	0	0.0%	0.00
4yo	10%	14	146	9.6%	-0.38
5yo	10%	13	249	5.2%	-0.66
6yo	22%	30	270	11.1%	-0.29
7yo	18%	25	284	8.8%	-0.20
8yo	15%	21	208	10.1%	-0.08
9yo	4%	6	96	6.3%	-0.70
10yo	6%	8	91	8.8%	-0.57
11yo	9%	12	66	18.2%	0.29
12yo+	5%	7	52	13.5%	-0.25

ANALYSIS BY BHB RATING

Age	Prop	Win	Runs	Wins%	£
150+	0%	0	0	0.0%	0.00
130..149	0%	0	0	0.0%	0.00
120..129	4%	6	22	27.3%	-0.34
110..119	13%	17	83	20.5%	-0.27
100..109	27%	37	221	16.7%	-0.09
80..99	42%	57	482	11.8%	0.00
60..79	7%	10	296	3.4%	-0.45
..59	0%	0	10	0.0%	-1.00
Unrated	7%	9	348	2.6%	-0.84

ANALYSIS BY WEIGHT CARRIED

Age	Prop	Win	Runs	Wins%	£
12-01+	1%	1	5	20.0%	-0.35
11-8..12-00	7%	9	41	22.0%	-0.03
11-0..11-07	29%	39	279	14.0%	-0.19
10-8..10-13	39%	53	614	8.6%	-0.37
10-0..10-07	24%	32	480	6.7%	-0.37
..9-13	1%	2	43	4.7%	-0.62

ANALYSIS BY DAYS SINCE LAST RUN

Age	Prop	Win	Runs	Wins%	£
1..7	8%	11	118	9.3%	-0.45
8..14	25%	34	279	12.2%	-0.19
15..28	31%	42	401	10.5%	-0.34
29..60	24%	32	298	10.7%	-0.27
61..100	5%	7	90	7.8%	-0.40
101+	7%	10	243	4.1%	-0.39
Unraced	0%	0	33	0.0%	-1.00

ANALYSIS BY TODAY'S STARTING PRICE

Age	Prop	Win	Runs	Wins%	£
Odds On	7%	9	14	64.3%	0.00
Ev-2/1	20%	27	64	42.2%	0.09
9/4-4/1	27%	37	176	21.0%	-0.14
9/2-6/1	18%	24	155	15.5%	-0.03
13/2-10/1	15%	21	234	9.0%	-0.19
11/1-16/1	7%	10	225	4.4%	-0.35
18/1-33/1	5%	7	255	2.7%	-0.27
40/1+	1%	1	339	0.3%	-0.80

ANALYSIS BY STARTING PRICE LAST TIME

Age	Prop	Win	Runs	Wins%	£
Odds On	1%	1	2	50.0%	-0.30
Ev-2/1	5%	7	34	20.6%	-0.12
9/4-4/1	15%	21	116	18.1%	-0.43
9/2-6/1	18%	24	115	20.9%	0.40
13/2-10/1	20%	27	231	11.7%	-0.25
11/1-16/1	18%	24	235	10.2%	-0.16
18/1-33/1	16%	22	324	6.8%	-0.50
40/1+	7%	10	372	2.7%	-0.50
Unraced	0%	0	33	0.0%	-1.00

ANALYSIS BY DISTANCE BEATEN LAST TIME

Age	Prop	Win	Runs	Wins%	£
..-10 lgh	1%	1	5	20.0%	-0.58
-10..0	2%	3	38	7.9%	-0.73
0.1..2	4%	6	40	15.0%	-0.44
2.1..5	11%	15	61	24.6%	0.09
5.1..10	14%	19	85	22.4%	-0.01
10.1..20	13%	18	187	9.6%	-0.35
20.0..30	16%	22	176	12.5%	-0.04
30.1+	20%	27	494	5.5%	-0.41
Not Compl	18%	25	343	7.3%	-0.39
Unraced	0%	0	33	0.0%	-1.00

ANALYSIS BY SUCCESS RATE IN LAST 10 RUNS

Age	Prop	Win	Runs	Wins%	£
No Wins	43%	58	927	6.3%	-0.51
1 Win	38%	51	359	14.2%	0.01
2 Wins	16%	22	109	20.2%	0.29
3 Wins	4%	5	31	16.1%	-0.46
4 Wins	0%	0	3	0.0%	-1.00
5+ Wins	0%	0	0	0.0%	0.00

ANALYSIS BY SUCCESS RATE IN LAST 3 RUNS

Age	Prop	Win	Runs	Wins%	£
No Wins	78%	106	1253	8.5%	-0.33
1 Win	19%	26	162	16.0%	-0.21
2 Wins	3%	4	14	28.6%	-0.10
3 Wins	0%	0	0	0.0%	0.00

ANALYSIS BY POSITION LAST TIME

Age	Prop	Win	Runs	Wins%	£
Won	3%	4	43	9.3%	-0.71
2nd or 3rd	31%	42	218	19.3%	-0.19
Unplaced	48%	65	825	7.9%	-0.30
Fell,BD,UR	5%	7	62	11.3%	-0.37
Pulled Up	13%	17	276	6.2%	-0.39
Ref/RanOut	0%	0	3	0.0%	-1.00
CO/SlipUp	1%	1	2	50.0%	0.38
Unraced	0%	0	33	0.0%	-1.00

OTHER FACTORS (WINS-RUNS, £)

Course Winner:	26-130	£0.13
Distance Winner:	36-210	-£0.07
Going Winner:	49-355	-£0.21
Beaten Favourite:	13-62	-£0.20
7-Day Winners:	0-6	-£1.00
BHA Top Rated:	20-103	-£0.25
Absolute Favourites:	40-122	-£0.13

Selling Hurdle Races

Selling Hurdle Races: 3m+

ANALYSIS BY AGE
Age	Prop	Win	Runs	Wins%	£
3yo	0%	0	0	0.0%	0.00
4yo	0%	0	6	0.0%	-1.00
5yo	10%	1	14	7.1%	-0.14
6yo	30%	3	21	14.3%	0.23
7yo	20%	2	16	12.5%	-0.45
8yo	10%	1	17	5.9%	-0.78
9yo	10%	1	15	6.7%	-0.67
10yo	0%	0	6	0.0%	-1.00
11yo	0%	0	6	0.0%	-1.00
12yo+	20%	2	11	18.2%	2.55

ANALYSIS BY BHB RATING
Age	Prop	Win	Runs	Wins%	£
150+	0%	0	0	0.0%	0.00
130..149	0%	0	0	0.0%	0.00
120..129	0%	0	4	0.0%	-1.00
110..119	30%	3	8	37.5%	0.58
100..109	0%	0	13	0.0%	-1.00
80..99	60%	6	41	14.6%	0.58
60..79	0%	0	19	0.0%	-1.00
..59	0%	0	1	0.0%	-1.00
Unrated	10%	1	26	3.8%	-0.35

ANALYSIS BY WEIGHT CARRIED
Age	Prop	Win	Runs	Wins%	£
12-01+	0%	0	0	0.0%	0.00
11-8..12-00	0%	0	0	0.0%	0.00
11-0..11-07	10%	1	15	6.7%	-0.84
10-8..10-13	40%	4	60	6.7%	-0.46
10-0..10-07	40%	4	34	11.8%	-0.01
..9-13	10%	1	3	33.3%	7.67

ANALYSIS BY DAYS SINCE LAST RUN
Age	Prop	Win	Runs	Wins%	£
1..7	0%	0	5	0.0%	-1.00
8..14	40%	4	38	10.5%	-0.11
15..28	40%	4	28	14.3%	0.15
29..60	10%	1	17	5.9%	-0.86
61..100	0%	0	5	0.0%	-1.00
101+	10%	1	14	7.1%	0.86
Unraced	0%	0	5	0.0%	-1.00

ANALYSIS BY TODAY'S STARTING PRICE
Age	Prop	Win	Runs	Wins%	£
Odds On	0%	0	1	0.0%	-1.00
Ev-2/1	10%	1	5	20.0%	-0.52
9/4-4/1	40%	4	10	40.0%	0.75
9/2-6/1	10%	1	12	8.3%	-0.46
13/2-10/1	0%	0	22	0.0%	-1.00
11/1-16/1	30%	3	19	15.8%	1.21
18/1-33/1	10%	1	21	4.8%	0.24
40/1+	0%	0	22	0.0%	-1.00

ANALYSIS BY STARTING PRICE LAST TIME
Age	Prop	Win	Runs	Wins%	£
Odds On	0%	0	1	0.0%	-1.00
Ev-2/1	0%	0	4	0.0%	-1.00
9/4-4/1	10%	1	7	14.3%	-0.46
9/2-6/1	20%	2	12	16.7%	1.08
13/2-10/1	10%	1	25	4.0%	-0.85
11/1-16/1	40%	4	16	25.0%	1.49
18/1-33/1	20%	2	20	10.0%	0.10
40/1+	0%	0	22	0.0%	-1.00
Unraced	0%	0	5	0.0%	-1.00

ANALYSIS BY DISTANCE BEATEN LAST TIME
Age	Prop	Win	Runs	Wins%	£
..-10 lgh	0%	0	1	0.0%	-1.00
-10..0	10%	1	3	33.3%	-0.21
0.1..2	10%	1	5	20.0%	0.00
2.1..5	0%	0	5	0.0%	-1.00
5.1..10	20%	2	4	50.0%	1.19
10.1..20	0%	0	10	0.0%	-1.00
20.0..30	10%	1	14	7.1%	-0.14
30.1+	20%	2	33	6.1%	-0.41
Not Compl	30%	3	32	9.4%	0.46
Unraced	0%	0	5	0.0%	-1.00

ANALYSIS BY SUCCESS RATE IN LAST 10 RUNS
Age	Prop	Win	Runs	Wins%	£
No Wins	50%	5	65	7.7%	-0.13
1 Win	40%	4	28	14.3%	-0.12
2 Wins	10%	1	11	9.1%	0.18
3 Wins	0%	0	3	0.0%	-1.00
4 Wins	0%	0	0	0.0%	0.00
5+ Wins	0%	0	0	0.0%	0.00

ANALYSIS BY SUCCESS RATE IN LAST 3 RUNS
Age	Prop	Win	Runs	Wins%	£
No Wins	80%	8	92	8.7%	-0.04
1 Win	20%	2	15	13.3%	-0.59
2 Wins	0%	0	0	0.0%	0.00
3 Wins	0%	0	0	0.0%	0.00

ANALYSIS BY POSITION LAST TIME
Age	Prop	Win	Runs	Wins%	£
Won	10%	1	4	25.0%	-0.41
2nd or 3rd	20%	2	15	13.3%	-0.33
Unplaced	40%	4	56	7.1%	-0.37
Fell,BD,UR	30%	3	10	30.0%	3.67
Pulled Up	0%	0	22	0.0%	-1.00
Ref/RanOut	0%	0	0	0.0%	0.00
CO/SlipUp	0%	0	0	0.0%	0.00
Unraced	0%	0	5	0.0%	-1.00

OTHER FACTORS (WINS-RUNS, £)
Course Winner:	0-15	-£1.00
Distance Winner:	2-12	-£0.26
Going Winner:	3-31	£0.13
Beaten Favourite:	0-4	-£1.00
7-Day Winners:	0-1	-£1.00
BHA Top Rated:	3-7	£0.80
Absolute Favourites:	2-9	-£0.18

Race Profiles

Selling Hurdle Races: 2 to 5 runners

ANALYSIS BY AGE

Age	Prop	Win	Runs	Wins%	£
3yo	0%	0	0	0.0%	0.00
4yo	14%	1	5	20.0%	-0.35
5yo	14%	1	4	25.0%	-0.50
6yo	14%	1	5	20.0%	-0.63
7yo	14%	1	7	14.3%	0.14
8yo	14%	1	6	16.7%	-0.25
9yo	14%	1	2	50.0%	0.00
10yo	14%	1	3	33.3%	-0.21
11yo	0%	0	1	0.0%	-1.00
12yo+	0%	0	2	0.0%	-1.00

ANALYSIS BY BHB RATING

Age	Prop	Win	Runs	Wins%	£
150+	0%	0	0	0.0%	0.00
130..149	0%	0	0	0.0%	0.00
120..129	0%	0	0	0.0%	0.00
110..119	0%	0	1	0.0%	-1.00
100..109	14%	1	5	20.0%	-0.60
80..99	57%	4	14	28.6%	0.01
60..79	0%	0	9	0.0%	-1.00
..59	0%	0	0	0.0%	0.00
Unrated	29%	2	6	33.3%	0.29

ANALYSIS BY WEIGHT CARRIED

Age	Prop	Win	Runs	Wins%	£
12-01+	0%	0	0	0.0%	0.00
11-8..12-00	0%	0	0	0.0%	0.00
11-0..11-07	71%	5	11	45.5%	0.67
10-8..10-13	14%	1	12	8.3%	-0.80
10-0..10-07	14%	1	12	8.3%	-0.73
..9-13	0%	0	0	0.0%	0.00

ANALYSIS BY DAYS SINCE LAST RUN

Age	Prop	Win	Runs	Wins%	£
1..7	0%	0	2	0.0%	-1.00
8..14	14%	1	7	14.3%	-0.36
15..28	43%	3	13	23.1%	-0.41
29..60	29%	2	5	40.0%	-0.23
61..100	14%	1	2	50.0%	3.00
101+	0%	0	4	0.0%	-1.00
Unraced	0%	0	2	0.0%	-1.00

ANALYSIS BY TODAY'S STARTING PRICE

Age	Prop	Win	Runs	Wins%	£
Odds On	14%	1	3	33.3%	-0.39
Ev-2/1	43%	3	4	75.0%	0.59
9/4-4/1	29%	2	10	20.0%	-0.23
9/2-6/1	0%	0	2	0.0%	-1.00
13/2-10/1	14%	1	4	25.0%	1.00
11/1-16/1	0%	0	7	0.0%	-1.00
18/1-33/1	0%	0	4	0.0%	-1.00
40/1+	0%	0	1	0.0%	-1.00

ANALYSIS BY STARTING PRICE LAST TIME

Age	Prop	Win	Runs	Wins%	£
Odds On	0%	0	0	0.0%	0.00
Ev-2/1	0%	0	2	0.0%	-1.00
9/4-4/1	14%	1	1	100.0%	2.25
9/2-6/1	29%	2	6	33.3%	-0.36
13/2-10/1	14%	1	9	11.1%	-0.74
11/1-16/1	14%	1	2	50.0%	0.00
18/1-33/1	29%	2	10	20.0%	0.25
40/1+	0%	0	3	0.0%	-1.00
Unraced	0%	0	2	0.0%	-1.00

ANALYSIS BY DISTANCE BEATEN LAST TIME

Age	Prop	Win	Runs	Wins%	£
..-10 lgh	0%	0	0	0.0%	0.00
-10..0	14%	1	2	50.0%	0.00
0.1..2	0%	0	0	0.0%	0.00
2.1..5	14%	1	2	50.0%	0.19
5.1..10	14%	1	4	25.0%	0.13
10.1..20	14%	1	4	25.0%	-0.50
20.0..30	14%	1	6	16.7%	-0.69
30.1+	14%	1	8	12.5%	-0.59
Not Compl	14%	1	7	14.3%	0.14
Unraced	0%	0	2	0.0%	-1.00

ANALYSIS BY SUCCESS RATE IN LAST 10 RUNS

Age	Prop	Win	Runs	Wins%	£
No Wins	57%	4	20	20.0%	-0.39
1 Win	29%	2	10	20.0%	-0.62
2 Wins	14%	1	3	33.3%	1.67
3 Wins	0%	0	0	0.0%	0.00
4 Wins	0%	0	0	0.0%	0.00
5+ Wins	0%	0	0	0.0%	0.00

ANALYSIS BY SUCCESS RATE IN LAST 3 RUNS

Age	Prop	Win	Runs	Wins%	£
No Wins	86%	6	26	23.1%	-0.16
1 Win	14%	1	7	14.3%	-0.71
2 Wins	0%	0	0	0.0%	0.00
3 Wins	0%	0	0	0.0%	0.00

ANALYSIS BY POSITION LAST TIME

Age	Prop	Win	Runs	Wins%	£
Won	14%	1	2	50.0%	0.00
2nd or 3rd	43%	3	9	33.3%	-0.17
Unplaced	29%	2	15	13.3%	-0.57
Fell,BD,UR	0%	0	3	0.0%	-1.00
Pulled Up	14%	1	4	25.0%	1.00
Ref/RanOut	0%	0	0	0.0%	0.00
CO/SlipUp	0%	0	0	0.0%	0.00
Unraced	0%	0	2	0.0%	-1.00

OTHER FACTORS (WINS-RUNS, £)

Course Winner:	2-4	£1.50
Distance Winner:	2-4	£1.50
Going Winner:	4-11	£0.29
Beaten Favourite:	0-3	-£1.00
BHA Top Rated:	0-5	-£1.00
Absolute Favourites:	4-7	£0.17

Selling Hurdle Races

Selling Hurdle Races: 6 to 10 runners

ANALYSIS BY AGE
Age	Prop	Win	Runs	Wins%	£
3yo	2%	4	22	18.2%	-0.60
4yo	13%	23	250	9.2%	-0.38
5yo	16%	28	304	9.2%	-0.52
6yo	22%	39	309	12.6%	-0.27
7yo	22%	39	245	15.9%	0.18
8yo	8%	14	142	9.9%	-0.58
9yo	5%	9	66	13.6%	-0.31
10yo	6%	10	59	16.9%	-0.32
11yo	2%	4	34	11.8%	-0.62
12yo+	3%	5	32	15.6%	-0.56

ANALYSIS BY BHB RATING
Age	Prop	Win	Runs	Wins%	£
150+	0%	0	0	0.0%	0.00
130..149	0%	0	0	0.0%	0.00
120..129	4%	7	24	29.2%	-0.42
110..119	16%	28	80	35.0%	0.11
100..109	23%	41	196	20.9%	-0.17
80..99	39%	68	488	13.9%	-0.09
60..79	5%	8	234	3.4%	-0.57
..59	0%	0	14	0.0%	-1.00
Unrated	13%	23	427	5.4%	-0.56

ANALYSIS BY WEIGHT CARRIED
Age	Prop	Win	Runs	Wins%	£
12-01+	0%	0	3	0.0%	-1.00
11-8..12-00	7%	12	55	21.8%	0.19
11-0..11-07	38%	66	323	20.4%	-0.06
10-8..10-13	31%	55	557	9.9%	-0.51
10-0..10-07	22%	38	471	8.1%	-0.30
..9-13	2%	4	54	7.4%	-0.48

ANALYSIS BY DAYS SINCE LAST RUN
Age	Prop	Win	Runs	Wins%	£
1..7	11%	19	127	15.0%	-0.17
8..14	19%	33	311	10.6%	-0.56
15..28	29%	50	364	13.7%	-0.38
29..60	17%	29	248	11.7%	-0.44
61..100	7%	13	85	15.3%	-0.06
101+	17%	29	268	10.8%	-0.04
Unraced	1%	2	60	3.3%	-0.13

ANALYSIS BY TODAY'S STARTING PRICE
Age	Prop	Win	Runs	Wins%	£
Odds On	11%	19	30	63.3%	0.03
Ev-2/1	27%	48	118	40.7%	0.05
9/4-4/1	29%	51	233	21.9%	-0.13
9/2-6/1	12%	21	149	14.1%	-0.14
13/2-10/1	13%	22	221	10.0%	-0.14
11/1-16/1	5%	9	213	4.2%	-0.38
18/1-33/1	2%	3	238	1.3%	-0.65
40/1+	1%	2	261	0.8%	-0.59

ANALYSIS BY STARTING PRICE LAST TIME
Age	Prop	Win	Runs	Wins%	£
Odds On	2%	3	10	30.0%	0.01
Ev-2/1	7%	13	46	28.3%	-0.04
9/4-4/1	19%	34	118	28.8%	-0.10
9/2-6/1	10%	17	101	16.8%	-0.21
13/2-10/1	19%	34	223	15.2%	-0.24
11/1-16/1	14%	25	199	12.6%	-0.43
18/1-33/1	18%	31	323	9.6%	-0.39
40/1+	9%	16	383	4.2%	-0.41
Unraced	1%	2	60	3.3%	-0.13

ANALYSIS BY DISTANCE BEATEN LAST TIME
Age	Prop	Win	Runs	Wins%	£
..-10 lgh	2%	4	9	44.4%	-0.14
-10..0	9%	15	68	22.1%	-0.27
0.1..2	3%	6	41	14.6%	-0.64
2.1..5	10%	18	58	31.0%	0.29
5.1..10	13%	22	86	25.6%	0.03
10.1..20	14%	24	152	15.8%	-0.31
20.0..30	12%	21	170	12.4%	-0.45
30.1+	23%	41	497	8.2%	-0.25
Not Compl	13%	22	322	6.8%	-0.56
Unraced	1%	2	60	3.3%	-0.13

ANALYSIS BY SUCCESS RATE IN LAST 10 RUNS
Age	Prop	Win	Runs	Wins%	£
No Wins	45%	78	932	8.4%	-0.47
1 Win	37%	64	333	19.2%	0.05
2 Wins	14%	25	115	21.7%	-0.26
3 Wins	3%	6	22	27.3%	-0.30
4 Wins	0%	0	1	0.0%	-1.00
5+ Wins	0%	0	0	0.0%	0.00

ANALYSIS BY SUCCESS RATE IN LAST 3 RUNS
Age	Prop	Win	Runs	Wins%	£
No Wins	73%	126	1208	10.4%	-0.35
1 Win	25%	43	182	23.6%	-0.19
2 Wins	2%	4	13	30.8%	-0.18
3 Wins	0%	0	0	0.0%	0.00

ANALYSIS BY POSITION LAST TIME
Age	Prop	Win	Runs	Wins%	£
Won	11%	19	77	24.7%	-0.25
2nd or 3rd	27%	48	204	23.5%	-0.13
Unplaced	48%	84	802	10.5%	-0.29
Fell,BD,UR	3%	5	60	8.3%	-0.69
Pulled Up	9%	16	252	6.3%	-0.53
Ref/RanOut	0%	0	5	0.0%	-1.00
CO/SlipUp	1%	1	3	33.3%	-0.08
Unraced	1%	2	60	3.3%	-0.13

OTHER FACTORS (WINS-RUNS, £)
Course Winner:	27-125	-£0.09
Distance Winner:	51-232	-£0.15
Going Winner:	53-265	-£0.15
Beaten Favourite:	16-60	£0.04
7-Day Winners:	4-15	-£0.48
BHA Top Rated:	40-153	-£0.20
Absolute Favourites:	63-161	-£0.08

Race Profiles

Selling Hurdle Races: 11 runners or more

ANALYSIS BY AGE

Age	Prop	Win	Runs	Wins%	£
3yo	1%	3	17	17.6%	2.15
4yo	12%	30	577	5.2%	-0.51
5yo	15%	37	633	5.8%	-0.60
6yo	26%	64	672	9.5%	-0.30
7yo	16%	40	526	7.6%	-0.26
8yo	13%	32	383	8.4%	-0.30
9yo	7%	17	201	8.5%	-0.54
10yo	3%	7	146	4.8%	-0.64
11yo	5%	13	99	13.1%	-0.01
12yo+	3%	7	73	9.6%	0.04

ANALYSIS BY BHB RATING

Age	Prop	Win	Runs	Wins%	£
150+	0%	0	0	0.0%	0.00
130..149	0%	1	2	50.0%	0.13
120..129	2%	4	20	20.0%	-0.32
110..119	10%	24	128	18.8%	-0.31
100..109	26%	64	408	15.7%	-0.08
80..99	40%	101	1052	9.6%	-0.27
60..79	6%	15	570	2.6%	-0.32
..59	0%	0	16	0.0%	-1.00
Unrated	16%	41	1131	3.6%	-0.65

ANALYSIS BY WEIGHT CARRIED

Age	Prop	Win	Runs	Wins%	£
12-01+	0%	1	5	20.0%	-0.35
11-8..12-00	4%	9	78	11.5%	-0.41
11-0..11-07	24%	61	595	10.3%	-0.42
10-8..10-13	44%	109	1445	7.5%	-0.40
10-0..10-07	26%	65	1087	6.0%	-0.38
..9-13	2%	5	117	4.3%	-0.22

ANALYSIS BY DAYS SINCE LAST RUN

Age	Prop	Win	Runs	Wins%	£
1..7	8%	20	227	8.8%	-0.64
8..14	22%	55	615	8.9%	-0.36
15..28	30%	76	870	8.7%	-0.32
29..60	22%	56	609	9.2%	-0.25
61..100	7%	17	248	6.9%	-0.38
101+	8%	21	569	3.7%	-0.52
Unraced	2%	5	189	2.6%	-0.53

ANALYSIS BY TODAY'S STARTING PRICE

Age	Prop	Win	Runs	Wins%	£
Odds On	4%	10	16	62.5%	0.08
Ev-2/1	19%	48	97	49.5%	0.28
9/4-4/1	25%	62	312	19.9%	-0.16
9/2-6/1	16%	40	301	13.3%	-0.15
13/2-10/1	19%	47	500	9.4%	-0.16
11/1-16/1	11%	28	481	5.8%	-0.16
18/1-33/1	5%	12	632	1.9%	-0.49
40/1+	1%	3	988	0.3%	-0.76

ANALYSIS BY STARTING PRICE LAST TIME

Age	Prop	Win	Runs	Wins%	£
Odds On	0%	1	5	20.0%	-0.47
Ev-2/1	6%	14	71	19.7%	-0.27
9/4-4/1	12%	29	202	14.4%	-0.45
9/2-6/1	16%	39	247	15.8%	0.10
13/2-10/1	18%	45	464	9.7%	-0.36
11/1-16/1	24%	59	517	11.4%	0.03
18/1-33/1	16%	40	690	5.8%	-0.44
40/1+	7%	18	942	1.9%	-0.69
Unraced	2%	5	189	2.6%	-0.53

ANALYSIS BY DISTANCE BEATEN LAST TIME

Age	Prop	Win	Runs	Wins%	£
..-10 lgh	0%	1	7	14.3%	-0.61
-10..0	4%	11	87	12.6%	-0.52
0.1..2	7%	17	83	20.5%	-0.14
2.1..5	5%	13	106	12.3%	-0.46
5.1..10	14%	34	195	17.4%	-0.05
10.1..20	18%	45	429	10.5%	-0.29
20.0..30	12%	31	368	8.4%	-0.24
30.1+	22%	54	1150	4.7%	-0.49
Not Compl	16%	39	713	5.5%	-0.41
Unraced	2%	5	189	2.6%	-0.53

ANALYSIS BY SUCCESS RATE IN LAST 10 RUNS

Age	Prop	Win	Runs	Wins%	£
No Wins	56%	137	2212	6.2%	-0.42
1 Win	30%	73	676	10.8%	-0.33
2 Wins	13%	32	195	16.4%	0.05
3 Wins	1%	3	51	5.9%	-0.76
4 Wins	0%	0	4	0.0%	-1.00
5+ Wins	0%	0	0	0.0%	0.00

ANALYSIS BY SUCCESS RATE IN LAST 3 RUNS

Age	Prop	Win	Runs	Wins%	£
No Wins	82%	202	2808	7.2%	-0.38
1 Win	16%	40	303	13.2%	-0.33
2 Wins	1%	3	27	11.1%	-0.66
3 Wins	0%	0	0	0.0%	0.00

ANALYSIS BY POSITION LAST TIME

Age	Prop	Win	Runs	Wins%	£
Won	5%	12	94	12.8%	-0.53
2nd or 3rd	23%	57	390	14.6%	-0.26
Unplaced	55%	138	1943	7.1%	-0.35
Fell,BD,UR	4%	11	148	7.4%	-0.37
Pulled Up	11%	27	548	4.9%	-0.53
Ref/RanOut	0%	0	13	0.0%	-1.00
CO/SlipUp	0%	0	2	0.0%	-1.00
Unraced	2%	5	189	2.6%	-0.53

OTHER FACTORS (WINS-RUNS, £)

Course Winner:	32-268	-£0.15
Distance Winner:	61-557	-£0.31
Going Winner:	58-609	-£0.41
Beaten Favourite:	18-106	-£0.41
7-Day Winners:	3-7	£0.32
BHA Top Rated:	42-194	-£0.11
Absolute Favourites:	84-228	£0.08

Selling Hurdle Races

Selling Hurdle Races: up to 7 days off the track

ANALYSIS BY AGE

Age	Prop	Win	Runs	Wins%	£
3yo	4%	2	11	18.2%	2.25
4yo	15%	7	168	4.2%	-0.75
5yo	11%	5	138	3.6%	-0.67
6yo	33%	15	113	13.3%	-0.14
7yo	17%	8	88	9.1%	-0.42
8yo	11%	5	40	12.5%	-0.32
9yo	9%	4	26	15.4%	0.14
10yo	0%	0	10	0.0%	-1.00
11yo	0%	0	9	0.0%	-1.00
12yo+	0%	0	4	0.0%	-1.00

ANALYSIS BY BHB RATING

Age	Prop	Win	Runs	Wins%	£
150+	0%	0	0	0.0%	0.00
130..149	0%	0	0	0.0%	0.00
120..129	2%	1	3	33.3%	-0.40
110..119	13%	6	24	25.0%	-0.35
100..109	15%	7	49	14.3%	-0.52
80..99	39%	18	131	13.7%	-0.19
60..79	4%	2	62	3.2%	-0.67
..59	0%	0	2	0.0%	-1.00
Unrated	26%	12	336	3.6%	-0.52

ANALYSIS BY WEIGHT CARRIED

Age	Prop	Win	Runs	Wins%	£
12-01+	0%	0	1	0.0%	-1.00
11-8..12-00	4%	2	9	22.2%	-0.38
11-0..11-07	28%	13	94	13.8%	-0.34
10-8..10-13	41%	19	252	7.5%	-0.45
10-0..10-07	24%	11	231	4.8%	-0.62
..9-13	2%	1	20	5.0%	0.70

ANALYSIS BY DAYS SINCE LAST RUN

Age	Prop	Win	Runs	Wins%	£
1..7	85%	39	356	11.0%	-0.47
8..14	0%	0	0	0.0%	0.00
15..28	0%	0	0	0.0%	0.00
29..60	0%	0	0	0.0%	0.00
61..100	0%	0	0	0.0%	0.00
101+	0%	0	0	0.0%	0.00
Unraced	15%	7	251	2.8%	-0.44

ANALYSIS BY TODAY'S STARTING PRICE

Age	Prop	Win	Runs	Wins%	£
Odds On	11%	5	9	55.6%	-0.01
Ev-2/1	24%	11	23	47.8%	0.22
9/4-4/1	24%	11	47	23.4%	-0.04
9/2-6/1	11%	5	46	10.9%	-0.37
13/2-10/1	15%	7	84	8.3%	-0.22
11/1-16/1	11%	5	84	6.0%	-0.08
18/1-33/1	2%	1	124	0.8%	-0.73
40/1+	2%	1	190	0.5%	-0.78

ANALYSIS BY STARTING PRICE LAST TIME

Age	Prop	Win	Runs	Wins%	£
Odds On	2%	1	4	25.0%	0.08
Ev-2/1	15%	7	19	36.8%	-0.05
9/4-4/1	7%	3	30	10.0%	-0.69
9/2-6/1	20%	9	31	29.0%	-0.02
13/2-10/1	9%	4	61	6.6%	-0.76
11/1-16/1	17%	8	54	14.8%	0.02
18/1-33/1	9%	4	74	5.4%	-0.73
40/1+	7%	3	83	3.6%	-0.57
Unraced	15%	7	251	2.8%	-0.44

ANALYSIS BY DISTANCE BEATEN LAST TIME

Age	Prop	Win	Runs	Wins%	£
..-10 lgh	4%	2	4	50.0%	0.15
-10..0	11%	5	18	27.8%	-0.30
0.1..2	4%	2	14	14.3%	-0.71
2.1..5	4%	2	11	18.2%	-0.36
5.1..10	17%	8	25	32.0%	0.45
10.1..20	13%	6	51	11.8%	-0.43
20.0..30	7%	3	51	5.9%	-0.67
30.1+	13%	6	103	5.8%	-0.65
Not Compl	11%	5	79	6.3%	-0.48
Unraced	15%	7	251	2.8%	-0.44

ANALYSIS BY SUCCESS RATE IN LAST 10 RUNS

Age	Prop	Win	Runs	Wins%	£
No Wins	46%	18	240	7.5%	-0.55
1 Win	36%	14	85	16.5%	-0.29
2 Wins	15%	6	25	24.0%	-0.32
3 Wins	3%	1	6	16.7%	-0.70
4 Wins	0%	0	0	0.0%	0.00
5+ Wins	0%	0	0	0.0%	0.00

ANALYSIS BY SUCCESS RATE IN LAST 3 RUNS

Age	Prop	Win	Runs	Wins%	£
No Wins	69%	27	312	8.7%	-0.53
1 Win	28%	11	41	26.8%	-0.03
2 Wins	3%	1	3	33.3%	-0.42
3 Wins	0%	0	0	0.0%	0.00

ANALYSIS BY POSITION LAST TIME

Age	Prop	Win	Runs	Wins%	£
Won	15%	7	22	31.8%	-0.22
2nd or 3rd	26%	12	61	19.7%	-0.22
Unplaced	33%	15	194	7.7%	-0.58
Fell,BD,UR	4%	2	21	9.5%	-0.42
Pulled Up	7%	3	54	5.6%	-0.47
Ref/RanOut	0%	0	2	0.0%	-1.00
CO/SlipUp	0%	0	2	0.0%	-1.00
Unraced	15%	7	251	2.8%	-0.44

OTHER FACTORS (WINS-RUNS, £)

Course Winner:	3-35	-£0.52
Distance Winner:	10-71	-£0.29
Going Winner:	9-75	-£0.56
Beaten Favourite:	5-20	-£0.19
7-Day Winners:	7-22	-£0.22
BHA Top Rated:	7-30	-£0.32
Absolute Favourites:	18-44	£0.04

Race Profiles

Selling Hurdle Races: 100+ days off the track

ANALYSIS BY AGE

Age	Prop	Win	Runs	Wins%	£
3yo	2%	1	2	50.0%	0.25
4yo	16%	8	91	8.8%	0.64
5yo	12%	6	138	4.3%	-0.73
6yo	20%	10	180	5.6%	-0.70
7yo	28%	14	160	8.8%	0.05
8yo	4%	2	100	2.0%	-0.79
9yo	6%	3	66	4.5%	-0.65
10yo	4%	2	47	4.3%	-0.82
11yo	4%	2	28	7.1%	0.29
12yo+	4%	2	35	5.7%	-0.16

ANALYSIS BY BHB RATING

Age	Prop	Win	Runs	Wins%	£
150+	0%	0	0	0.0%	0.00
130..149	0%	0	1	0.0%	-1.00
120..129	2%	1	6	16.7%	-0.42
110..119	14%	7	36	19.4%	-0.35
100..109	16%	8	68	11.8%	-0.10
80..99	30%	15	191	7.9%	0.01
60..79	8%	4	146	2.7%	-0.42
..59	0%	0	9	0.0%	-1.00
Unrated	30%	15	390	3.8%	-0.58

ANALYSIS BY WEIGHT CARRIED

Age	Prop	Win	Runs	Wins%	£
12-01+	2%	1	1	100.0%	2.25
11-8..12-00	4%	2	12	16.7%	1.59
11-0..11-07	28%	14	144	9.7%	-0.45
10-8..10-13	40%	20	378	5.3%	-0.42
10-0..10-07	24%	12	282	4.3%	-0.40
..9-13	2%	1	30	3.3%	-0.13

ANALYSIS BY DAYS SINCE LAST RUN

Age	Prop	Win	Runs	Wins%	£
1..7	0%	0	0	0.0%	0.00
8..14	0%	0	0	0.0%	0.00
15..28	0%	0	0	0.0%	0.00
29..60	0%	0	0	0.0%	0.00
61..100	0%	0	6	0.0%	-1.00
101+	100%	50	841	5.9%	-0.37
Unraced	0%	0	0	0.0%	0.00

ANALYSIS BY TODAY'S STARTING PRICE

Age	Prop	Win	Runs	Wins%	£
Odds On	4%	2	5	40.0%	-0.37
Ev-2/1	24%	12	25	48.0%	0.29
9/4-4/1	18%	9	63	14.3%	-0.42
9/2-6/1	14%	7	53	13.2%	-0.20
13/2-10/1	16%	8	106	7.5%	-0.34
11/1-16/1	10%	5	119	4.2%	-0.38
18/1-33/1	10%	5	191	2.6%	-0.28
40/1+	4%	2	285	0.7%	-0.53

ANALYSIS BY STARTING PRICE LAST TIME

Age	Prop	Win	Runs	Wins%	£
Odds On	0%	0	2	0.0%	-1.00
Ev-2/1	4%	2	21	9.5%	-0.45
9/4-4/1	14%	7	48	14.6%	-0.21
9/2-6/1	12%	6	57	10.5%	-0.21
13/2-10/1	24%	12	134	9.0%	-0.37
11/1-16/1	22%	11	138	8.0%	0.01
18/1-33/1	12%	6	186	3.2%	-0.70
40/1+	12%	6	261	2.3%	-0.40
Unraced	0%	0	0	0.0%	0.00

ANALYSIS BY DISTANCE BEATEN LAST TIME

Age	Prop	Win	Runs	Wins%	£
..-10 lgh	0%	0	0	0.0%	0.00
-10..0	2%	1	25	4.0%	-0.80
0.1..2	0%	0	10	0.0%	-1.00
2.1..5	6%	3	18	16.7%	-0.27
5.1..10	14%	7	41	17.1%	0.06
10.1..20	6%	3	92	3.3%	-0.91
20.0..30	12%	6	81	7.4%	-0.50
30.1+	32%	16	337	4.7%	-0.41
Not Compl	28%	14	243	5.8%	-0.09
Unraced	0%	0	0	0.0%	0.00

ANALYSIS BY SUCCESS RATE IN LAST 10 RUNS

Age	Prop	Win	Runs	Wins%	£
No Wins	56%	28	613	4.6%	-0.42
1 Win	36%	18	161	11.2%	0.01
2 Wins	6%	3	55	5.5%	-0.85
3 Wins	2%	1	16	6.3%	-0.80
4 Wins	0%	0	2	0.0%	-1.00
5+ Wins	0%	0	0	0.0%	0.00

ANALYSIS BY SUCCESS RATE IN LAST 3 RUNS

Age	Prop	Win	Runs	Wins%	£
No Wins	84%	42	752	5.6%	-0.35
1 Win	12%	6	86	7.0%	-0.59
2 Wins	4%	2	9	22.2%	-0.41
3 Wins	0%	0	0	0.0%	0.00

ANALYSIS BY POSITION LAST TIME

Age	Prop	Win	Runs	Wins%	£
Won	2%	1	25	4.0%	-0.80
2nd or 3rd	16%	8	67	11.9%	-0.36
Unplaced	56%	28	515	5.4%	-0.36
Fell,BD,UR	6%	3	43	7.0%	-0.21
Pulled Up	20%	10	193	5.2%	-0.38
Ref/RanOut	0%	0	4	0.0%	-1.00
CO/SlipUp	0%	0	0	0.0%	0.00
Unraced	0%	0	0	0.0%	0.00

OTHER FACTORS (WINS-RUNS, £)

Course Winner:	5-58	-£0.68
Distance Winner:	10-131	-£0.67
Going Winner:	7-150	-£0.67
Beaten Favourite:	1-28	-£0.70
BHA Top Rated:	10-45	-£0.24
Absolute Favourites:	13-39	-£0.14

Amateur Hurdle Races

ANALYSIS BY AGE

Age	Prop	Win	Runs	Wins%	£
3yo	0%	0	0	0.0%	0.00
4yo	9%	2	36	5.6%	-0.60
5yo	36%	8	69	11.6%	-0.71
6yo	18%	4	52	7.7%	-0.21
7yo	18%	4	35	11.4%	1.49
8yo	18%	4	18	22.2%	-0.41
9yo	0%	0	14	0.0%	-1.00
10yo	0%	0	5	0.0%	-1.00
11yo	0%	0	2	0.0%	-1.00
12yo+	0%	0	2	0.0%	-1.00

ANALYSIS BY BHB RATING

Age	Prop	Win	Runs	Wins%	£
150+	0%	0	0	0.0%	0.00
130..149	0%	0	4	0.0%	-1.00
120..129	9%	2	5	40.0%	6.12
110..119	27%	6	21	28.6%	-0.23
100..109	27%	6	21	28.6%	-0.28
80..99	5%	1	24	4.2%	0.42
60..79	0%	0	20	0.0%	-1.00
..59	0%	0	1	0.0%	-1.00
Unrated	32%	7	137	5.1%	-0.48

ANALYSIS BY WEIGHT CARRIED

Age	Prop	Win	Runs	Wins%	£
12-01+	0%	0	0	0.0%	0.00
11-8..12-00	9%	2	17	11.8%	1.26
11-0..11-07	45%	10	69	14.5%	-0.24
10-8..10-13	36%	8	100	8.0%	-0.39
10-0..10-07	9%	2	46	4.3%	-0.54
..9-13	0%	0	1	0.0%	-1.00

ANALYSIS BY DAYS SINCE LAST RUN

Age	Prop	Win	Runs	Wins%	£
1..7	9%	2	11	18.2%	-0.43
8..14	18%	4	39	10.3%	0.39
15..28	27%	6	59	10.2%	-0.73
29..60	23%	5	35	14.3%	0.54
61..100	5%	1	14	7.1%	-0.90
101+	14%	3	54	5.6%	-0.27
Unraced	5%	1	21	4.8%	-0.90

ANALYSIS BY TODAY'S STARTING PRICE

Age	Prop	Win	Runs	Wins%	£
Odds On	23%	5	8	62.5%	-0.03
Ev-2/1	36%	8	16	50.0%	0.19
9/4-4/1	14%	3	16	18.8%	-0.20
9/2-6/1	0%	0	15	0.0%	-1.00
13/2-10/1	9%	2	25	8.0%	-0.24
11/1-16/1	5%	1	33	3.0%	-0.64
18/1-33/1	14%	3	37	8.1%	1.76
40/1+	0%	0	83	0.0%	-1.00

ANALYSIS BY STARTING PRICE LAST TIME

Age	Prop	Win	Runs	Wins%	£
Odds On	23%	5	9	55.6%	0.08
Ev-2/1	18%	4	15	26.7%	-0.19
9/4-4/1	18%	4	24	16.7%	-0.21
9/2-6/1	9%	2	17	11.8%	1.59
13/2-10/1	14%	3	31	9.7%	-0.71
11/1-16/1	5%	1	30	3.3%	-0.70
18/1-33/1	5%	1	31	3.2%	0.10
40/1+	5%	1	55	1.8%	-0.38
Unraced	5%	1	21	4.8%	-0.90

ANALYSIS BY DISTANCE BEATEN LAST TIME

Age	Prop	Win	Runs	Wins%	£
..-10 lgh	9%	2	4	50.0%	7.91
-10..0	18%	4	19	21.1%	-0.50
0.1..2	5%	1	9	11.1%	-0.75
2.1..5	27%	6	11	54.5%	1.11
5.1..10	18%	4	26	15.4%	-0.32
10.1..20	9%	2	29	6.9%	0.59
20.0..30	5%	1	24	4.2%	-0.90
30.1+	5%	1	60	1.7%	-0.43
Not Compl	0%	0	30	0.0%	-1.00
Unraced	5%	1	21	4.8%	-0.90

ANALYSIS BY SUCCESS RATE IN LAST 10 RUNS

Age	Prop	Win	Runs	Wins%	£
No Wins	33%	7	150	4.7%	-0.52
1 Win	43%	9	36	25.0%	0.47
2 Wins	14%	3	14	21.4%	-0.46
3 Wins	5%	1	8	12.5%	-0.44
4 Wins	5%	1	4	25.0%	7.50
5+ Wins	0%	0	0	0.0%	0.00

ANALYSIS BY SUCCESS RATE IN LAST 3 RUNS

Age	Prop	Win	Runs	Wins%	£
No Wins	48%	10	166	6.0%	-0.31
1 Win	43%	9	39	23.1%	0.30
2 Wins	10%	2	7	28.6%	-0.17
3 Wins	0%	0	0	0.0%	0.00

ANALYSIS BY POSITION LAST TIME

Age	Prop	Win	Runs	Wins%	£
Won	27%	6	23	26.1%	0.96
2nd or 3rd	45%	10	53	18.9%	-0.36
Unplaced	23%	5	106	4.7%	-0.14
Fell,BD,UR	0%	0	10	0.0%	-1.00
Pulled Up	0%	0	20	0.0%	-1.00
Ref/RanOut	0%	0	0	0.0%	0.00
CO/SlipUp	0%	0	0	0.0%	0.00
Unraced	5%	1	21	4.8%	-0.90

OTHER FACTORS (WINS-RUNS, £)

Course Winner:	2-7	-£0.17
Distance Winner:	6-15	£0.11
Going Winner:	7-26	£0.82
Beaten Favourite:	5-14	-£0.17
BHA Top Rated:	10-20	£0.18
Absolute Favourites:	11-22	-£0.02

Race Profiles

Amateur Hurdle Races: 2m to 2m3f

ANALYSIS BY AGE

Age	Prop	Win	Runs	Wins%	£
3yo	0%	0	0	0.0%	0.00
4yo	11%	1	23	4.3%	-0.48
5yo	56%	5	32	15.6%	-0.65
6yo	22%	2	12	16.7%	-0.60
7yo	0%	0	12	0.0%	-1.00
8yo	11%	1	7	14.3%	-0.36
9yo	0%	0	2	0.0%	-1.00
10yo	0%	0	2	0.0%	-1.00
11yo	0%	0	0	0.0%	0.00
12yo+	0%	0	0	0.0%	0.00

ANALYSIS BY BHB RATING

Age	Prop	Win	Runs	Wins%	£
150+	0%	0	0	0.0%	0.00
130..149	0%	0	0	0.0%	0.00
120..129	11%	1	2	50.0%	-0.19
110..119	33%	3	11	27.3%	-0.07
100..109	22%	2	5	40.0%	-0.24
80..99	0%	0	8	0.0%	-1.00
60..79	0%	0	9	0.0%	-1.00
..59	0%	0	1	0.0%	-1.00
Unrated	33%	3	54	5.6%	-0.69

ANALYSIS BY WEIGHT CARRIED

Age	Prop	Win	Runs	Wins%	£
12-01+	0%	0	0	0.0%	0.00
11-8..12-00	11%	1	2	50.0%	1.25
11-0..11-07	44%	4	19	21.1%	-0.59
10-8..10-13	33%	3	43	7.0%	-0.81
10-0..10-07	11%	1	25	4.0%	-0.52
..9-13	0%	0	1	0.0%	-1.00

ANALYSIS BY DAYS SINCE LAST RUN

Age	Prop	Win	Runs	Wins%	£
1..7	0%	0	3	0.0%	-1.00
8..14	0%	0	15	0.0%	-1.00
15..28	22%	2	25	8.0%	-0.76
29..60	44%	4	15	26.7%	0.32
61..100	11%	1	5	20.0%	-0.71
101+	22%	2	21	9.5%	-0.75
Unraced	0%	0	6	0.0%	-1.00

ANALYSIS BY TODAY'S STARTING PRICE

Age	Prop	Win	Runs	Wins%	£
Odds On	44%	4	5	80.0%	0.29
Ev-2/1	22%	2	5	40.0%	0.05
9/4-4/1	22%	2	6	33.3%	0.47
9/2-6/1	0%	0	5	0.0%	-1.00
13/2-10/1	0%	0	10	0.0%	-1.00
11/1-16/1	11%	1	15	6.7%	-0.20
18/1-33/1	0%	0	14	0.0%	-1.00
40/1+	0%	0	30	0.0%	-1.00

ANALYSIS BY STARTING PRICE LAST TIME

Age	Prop	Win	Runs	Wins%	£
Odds On	44%	4	6	66.7%	0.41
Ev-2/1	22%	2	6	33.3%	-0.01
9/4-4/1	22%	2	7	28.6%	0.98
9/2-6/1	0%	0	4	0.0%	-1.00
13/2-10/1	11%	1	15	6.7%	-0.71
11/1-16/1	0%	0	9	0.0%	-1.00
18/1-33/1	0%	0	13	0.0%	-1.00
40/1+	0%	0	24	0.0%	-1.00
Unraced	0%	0	6	0.0%	-1.00

ANALYSIS BY DISTANCE BEATEN LAST TIME

Age	Prop	Win	Runs	Wins%	£
..-10 lgh	11%	1	2	50.0%	-0.19
-10..0	22%	2	5	40.0%	0.21
0.1..2	0%	0	2	0.0%	-1.00
2.1..5	44%	4	6	66.7%	0.77
5.1..10	11%	1	11	9.1%	-0.80
10.1..20	11%	1	12	8.3%	0.00
20.0..30	0%	0	12	0.0%	-1.00
30.1+	0%	0	26	0.0%	-1.00
Not Compl	0%	0	8	0.0%	-1.00
Unraced	0%	0	6	0.0%	-1.00

ANALYSIS BY SUCCESS RATE IN LAST 10 RUNS

Age	Prop	Win	Runs	Wins%	£
No Wins	22%	2	64	3.1%	-0.78
1 Win	67%	6	13	46.2%	0.09
2 Wins	0%	0	5	0.0%	-1.00
3 Wins	11%	1	2	50.0%	1.25
4 Wins	0%	0	0	0.0%	0.00
5+ Wins	0%	0	0	0.0%	0.00

ANALYSIS BY SUCCESS RATE IN LAST 3 RUNS

Age	Prop	Win	Runs	Wins%	£
No Wins	33%	3	69	4.3%	-0.74
1 Win	56%	5	12	41.7%	-0.18
2 Wins	11%	1	3	33.3%	0.50
3 Wins	0%	0	0	0.0%	0.00

ANALYSIS BY POSITION LAST TIME

Age	Prop	Win	Runs	Wins%	£
Won	33%	3	7	42.9%	0.10
2nd or 3rd	56%	5	25	20.0%	-0.49
Unplaced	11%	1	44	2.3%	-0.73
Fell,BD,UR	0%	0	2	0.0%	-1.00
Pulled Up	0%	0	6	0.0%	-1.00
Ref/RanOut	0%	0	0	0.0%	0.00
CO/SlipUp	0%	0	0	0.0%	0.00
Unraced	0%	0	6	0.0%	-1.00

OTHER FACTORS (WINS-RUNS, £)

Course Winner:	1-2	£1.25
Distance Winner:	3-5	£0.79
Going Winner:	3-7	£0.07
Beaten Favourite:	3-7	-£0.04
BHA Top Rated:	4-8	£0.14
Absolute Favourites:	5-9	-£0.03

Amateur Hurdle Races

Amateur Hurdle Races: 2m4f to 2m7f

ANALYSIS BY AGE

Age	Prop	Win	Runs	Wins%	£
3yo	0%	0	0	0.0%	0.00
4yo	13%	1	10	10.0%	-0.78
5yo	25%	2	19	10.5%	-0.65
6yo	13%	1	22	4.5%	-0.91
7yo	13%	1	8	12.5%	3.25
8yo	38%	3	7	42.9%	-0.14
9yo	0%	0	5	0.0%	-1.00
10yo	0%	0	1	0.0%	-1.00
11yo	0%	0	1	0.0%	-1.00
12yo+	0%	0	1	0.0%	-1.00

ANALYSIS BY BHB RATING

Age	Prop	Win	Runs	Wins%	£
150+	0%	0	0	0.0%	0.00
130..149	0%	0	0	0.0%	0.00
120..129	0%	0	0	0.0%	0.00
110..119	38%	3	4	75.0%	0.48
100..109	38%	3	9	33.3%	0.00
80..99	0%	0	9	0.0%	-1.00
60..79	0%	0	7	0.0%	-1.00
..59	0%	0	0	0.0%	0.00
Unrated	25%	2	45	4.4%	-0.20

ANALYSIS BY WEIGHT CARRIED

Age	Prop	Win	Runs	Wins%	£
12-01+	0%	0	0	0.0%	0.00
11-8..12-00	0%	0	1	0.0%	-1.00
11-0..11-07	63%	5	25	20.0%	0.70
10-8..10-15	38%	3	36	8.3%	-0.77
10-0..10-07	0%	0	12	0.0%	-1.00
..9-13	0%	0	0	0.0%	0.00

ANALYSIS BY DAYS SINCE LAST RUN

Age	Prop	Win	Runs	Wins%	£
1..7	25%	2	5	40.0%	0.25
8..14	13%	1	12	8.3%	-0.89
15..28	38%	3	15	20.0%	-0.51
29..60	0%	0	8	0.0%	-1.00
61..100	0%	0	6	0.0%	-1.00
101+	13%	1	16	6.3%	1.13
Unraced	13%	1	12	8.3%	-0.83

ANALYSIS BY TODAY'S STARTING PRICE

Age	Prop	Win	Runs	Wins%	£
Odds On	13%	1	1	100.0%	0.29
Ev-2/1	63%	5	9	55.6%	0.29
9/4-4/1	13%	1	7	14.3%	-0.43
9/2-6/1	0%	0	4	0.0%	-1.00
13/2-10/1	0%	0	7	0.0%	-1.00
11/1-16/1	0%	0	9	0.0%	-1.00
18/1-33/1	13%	1	12	8.3%	1.83
40/1+	0%	0	25	0.0%	-1.00

ANALYSIS BY STARTING PRICE LAST TIME

Age	Prop	Win	Runs	Wins%	£
Odds On	13%	1	2	50.0%	-0.35
Ev-2/1	25%	2	4	50.0%	0.56
9/4-4/1	25%	2	6	33.3%	-0.17
9/2-6/1	0%	0	6	0.0%	-1.00
13/2-10/1	13%	1	9	11.1%	-0.74
11/1-16/1	0%	0	10	0.0%	-1.00
18/1-33/1	0%	0	8	0.0%	-1.00
40/1+	13%	1	17	5.9%	1.00
Unraced	13%	1	12	8.3%	-0.83

ANALYSIS BY DISTANCE BEATEN LAST TIME

Age	Prop	Win	Runs	Wins%	£
..-10 lgh	0%	0	0	0.0%	0.00
-10..0	13%	1	5	20.0%	-0.74
0.1..2	13%	1	1	100.0%	1.25
2.1..5	13%	1	1	100.0%	1.63
5.1..10	25%	2	6	33.3%	0.06
10.1..20	0%	0	8	0.0%	-1.00
20.0..30	13%	1	9	11.1%	-0.74
30.1+	13%	1	21	4.8%	0.62
Not Compl	0%	0	11	0.0%	-1.00
Unraced	13%	1	12	8.3%	-0.83

ANALYSIS BY SUCCESS RATE IN LAST 10 RUNS

Age	Prop	Win	Runs	Wins%	£
No Wins	43%	3	47	6.4%	-0.17
1 Win	14%	1	9	11.1%	-0.74
2 Wins	43%	3	5	60.0%	0.51
3 Wins	0%	0	1	0.0%	-1.00
4 Wins	0%	0	0	0.0%	0.00
5+ Wins	0%	0	0	0.0%	0.00

ANALYSIS BY SUCCESS RATE IN LAST 3 RUNS

Age	Prop	Win	Runs	Wins%	£
No Wins	57%	4	50	8.0%	-0.14
1 Win	29%	2	11	18.2%	-0.58
2 Wins	14%	1	1	100.0%	0.29
3 Wins	0%	0	0	0.0%	0.00

ANALYSIS BY POSITION LAST TIME

Age	Prop	Win	Runs	Wins%	£
Won	13%	1	5	20.0%	-0.74
2nd or 3rd	50%	4	8	50.0%	0.41
Unplaced	25%	2	38	5.3%	-0.04
Fell,BD,UR	0%	0	4	0.0%	-1.00
Pulled Up	0%	0	7	0.0%	-1.00
Ref/RanOut	0%	0	0	0.0%	0.00
CO/SlipUp	0%	0	0	0.0%	0.00
Unraced	13%	1	12	8.3%	-0.83

OTHER FACTORS (WINS-RUNS, £)

Course Winner: 1-3 -£0.57
Distance Winner: 3-6 £0.28
Going Winner: 2-7 -£0.49
Beaten Favourite: 2-4 £0.22
BHA Top Rated: 5-8 £0.54
Absolute Favourites: 5-8 £0.32

Race Profiles

Amateur Hurdle Races: 3m+

ANALYSIS BY AGE

Age	Prop	Win	Runs	Wins%	£
3yo	0%	0	0	0.0%	0.00
4yo	0%	0	3	0.0%	-1.00
5yo	20%	1	18	5.6%	-0.88
6yo	20%	1	18	5.6%	0.89
7yo	60%	3	15	20.0%	2.53
8yo	0%	0	4	0.0%	-1.00
9yo	0%	0	7	0.0%	-1.00
10yo	0%	0	2	0.0%	-1.00
11yo	0%	0	1	0.0%	-1.00
12yo+	0%	0	1	0.0%	-1.00

ANALYSIS BY BHB RATING

Age	Prop	Win	Runs	Wins%	£
150+	0%	0	0	0.0%	0.00
130..149	0%	0	4	0.0%	-1.00
120..129	20%	1	3	33.3%	10.33
110..119	0%	0	6	0.0%	-1.00
100..109	20%	1	7	14.3%	-0.69
80..99	20%	1	7	14.3%	3.86
60..79	0%	0	4	0.0%	-1.00
..59	0%	0	0	0.0%	0.00
Unrated	40%	2	38	5.3%	-0.50

ANALYSIS BY WEIGHT CARRIED

Age	Prop	Win	Runs	Wins%	£
12-01+	0%	0	0	0.0%	0.00
11-8..12-00	20%	1	14	7.1%	1.43
11-0..11-07	20%	1	25	4.0%	-0.91
10-8..10-13	40%	2	21	9.5%	1.10
10-0..10-07	20%	1	9	11.1%	0.00
..9-13	0%	0	0	0.0%	0.00

ANALYSIS BY DAYS SINCE LAST RUN

Age	Prop	Win	Runs	Wins%	£
1..7	0%	0	3	0.0%	-1.00
8..14	60%	3	12	25.0%	3.42
15..28	20%	1	19	5.3%	-0.88
29..60	20%	1	12	8.3%	1.83
61..100	0%	0	3	0.0%	-1.00
101+	0%	0	17	0.0%	-1.00
Unraced	0%	0	3	0.0%	-1.00

ANALYSIS BY TODAY'S STARTING PRICE

Age	Prop	Win	Runs	Wins%	£
Odds On	0%	0	2	0.0%	-1.00
Ev-2/1	20%	1	2	50.0%	0.10
9/4-4/1	0%	0	3	0.0%	-1.00
9/2-6/1	0%	0	6	0.0%	-1.00
13/2-10/1	40%	2	8	25.0%	1.38
11/1-16/1	0%	0	9	0.0%	-1.00
18/1-33/1	40%	2	11	18.2%	5.18
40/1+	0%	0	28	0.0%	-1.00

ANALYSIS BY STARTING PRICE LAST TIME

Age	Prop	Win	Runs	Wins%	£
Odds On	0%	0	1	0.0%	-1.00
Ev-2/1	0%	0	5	0.0%	-1.00
9/4-4/1	0%	0	11	0.0%	-1.00
9/2-6/1	40%	2	7	28.6%	5.29
13/2-10/1	20%	1	7	14.3%	-0.69
11/1-16/1	20%	1	11	9.1%	-0.18
18/1-33/1	20%	1	10	10.0%	2.40
40/1+	0%	0	14	0.0%	-1.00
Unraced	0%	0	3	0.0%	-1.00

ANALYSIS BY DISTANCE BEATEN LAST TIME

Age	Prop	Win	Runs	Wins%	£
..-10 lgh	20%	1	2	50.0%	16.00
-10..0	20%	1	9	11.1%	-0.76
0.1..2	0%	0	6	0.0%	-1.00
2.1..5	20%	1	4	25.0%	1.50
5.1..10	20%	1	9	11.1%	0.00
10.1..20	20%	1	9	11.1%	2.78
20.0..30	0%	0	3	0.0%	-1.00
30.1+	0%	0	13	0.0%	-1.00
Not Compl	0%	0	11	0.0%	-1.00
Unraced	0%	0	3	0.0%	-1.00

ANALYSIS BY SUCCESS RATE IN LAST 10 RUNS

Age	Prop	Win	Runs	Wins%	£
No Wins	40%	2	39	5.1%	-0.51
1 Win	40%	2	14	14.3%	1.59
2 Wins	0%	0	4	0.0%	-1.00
3 Wins	0%	0	5	0.0%	-1.00
4 Wins	20%	1	4	25.0%	7.50
5+ Wins	0%	0	0	0.0%	0.00

ANALYSIS BY SUCCESS RATE IN LAST 3 RUNS

Age	Prop	Win	Runs	Wins%	£
No Wins	60%	3	47	6.4%	0.13
1 Win	40%	2	16	12.5%	1.26
2 Wins	0%	0	3	0.0%	-1.00
3 Wins	0%	0	0	0.0%	0.00

ANALYSIS BY POSITION LAST TIME

Age	Prop	Win	Runs	Wins%	£
Won	40%	2	11	18.2%	2.29
2nd or 3rd	20%	1	20	5.0%	-0.50
Unplaced	40%	2	24	8.3%	0.79
Fell,BD,UR	0%	0	4	0.0%	-1.00
Pulled Up	0%	0	7	0.0%	-1.00
Ref/RanOut	0%	0	0	0.0%	0.00
CO/SlipUp	0%	0	0	0.0%	0.00
Unraced	0%	0	3	0.0%	-1.00

OTHER FACTORS (WINS-RUNS, £)

Course Winner:	0-2	-£1.00
Distance Winner:	0-4	-£1.00
Going Winner:	2-12	£2.02
Beaten Favourite:	0-3	-£1.00
BHA Top Rated:	1-4	-£0.45
Absolute Favourites:	1-5	-£0.56

Amateur Hurdle Races

Amateur Hurdle Races: 2 to 5 runners

ANALYSIS BY AGE

Age	Prop	Win	Runs	Wins%	£
3yo	0%	0	0	0.0%	0.00
4yo	0%	0	1	0.0%	-1.00
5yo	50%	1	5	20.0%	-0.69
6yo	0%	0	2	0.0%	-1.00
7yo	0%	0	0	0.0%	0.00
8yo	50%	1	1	100.0%	1.38
9yo	0%	0	0	0.0%	0.00
10yo	0%	0	0	0.0%	0.00
11yo	0%	0	1	0.0%	-1.00
12yo+	0%	0	0	0.0%	0.00

ANALYSIS BY BHB RATING

Age	Prop	Win	Runs	Wins%	£
150+	0%	0	0	0.0%	0.00
130..149	0%	0	0	0.0%	0.00
120..129	0%	0	0	0.0%	0.00
110..119	0%	0	0	0.0%	0.00
100..109	100%	2	2	100.0%	0.97
80..99	0%	0	1	0.0%	-1.00
60..79	0%	0	0	0.0%	0.00
..59	0%	0	0	0.0%	0.00
Unrated	0%	0	7	0.0%	-1.00

ANALYSIS BY WEIGHT CARRIED

Age	Prop	Win	Runs	Wins%	£
12-01+	0%	0	0	0.0%	0.00
11-8..12-00	0%	0	0	0.0%	0.00
11-0..11-07	100%	2	6	33.3%	-0.34
10-8..10-13	0%	0	2	0.0%	-1.00
10-0..10-07	0%	0	2	0.0%	-1.00
..9-13	0%	0	0	0.0%	0.00

ANALYSIS BY DAYS SINCE LAST RUN

Age	Prop	Win	Runs	Wins%	£
1..7	0%	0	2	0.0%	-1.00
8..14	0%	0	2	0.0%	-1.00
15..28	50%	1	2	50.0%	0.19
29..60	50%	1	2	50.0%	-0.22
61..100	0%	0	2	0.0%	-1.00
101+	0%	0	0	0.0%	0.00
Unraced	0%	0	0	0.0%	0.00

ANALYSIS BY TODAY'S STARTING PRICE

Age	Prop	Win	Runs	Wins%	£
Odds On	50%	1	1	100.0%	0.57
Ev-2/1	50%	1	2	50.0%	0.19
9/4-4/1	0%	0	1	0.0%	-1.00
9/2-6/1	0%	0	1	0.0%	-1.00
13/2-10/1	0%	0	2	0.0%	-1.00
11/1-16/1	0%	0	1	0.0%	-1.00
18/1-33/1	0%	0	2	0.0%	-1.00
40/1+	0%	0	0	0.0%	0.00

ANALYSIS BY STARTING PRICE LAST TIME

Age	Prop	Win	Runs	Wins%	£
Odds On	50%	1	1	100.0%	0.57
Ev-2/1	0%	0	0	0.0%	0.00
9/4-4/1	0%	0	0	0.0%	0.00
9/2-6/1	0%	0	2	0.0%	-1.00
13/2-10/1	50%	1	4	25.0%	-0.41
11/1-16/1	0%	0	0	0.0%	0.00
18/1-33/1	0%	0	1	0.0%	-1.00
40/1+	0%	0	2	0.0%	-1.00
Unraced	0%	0	0	0.0%	0.00

ANALYSIS BY DISTANCE BEATEN LAST TIME

Age	Prop	Win	Runs	Wins%	£
..-10 lgh	0%	0	0	0.0%	0.00
-10..0	50%	1	2	50.0%	-0.22
0.1..2	0%	0	0	0.0%	0.00
2.1..5	0%	0	1	0.0%	-1.00
5.1..10	0%	0	0	0.0%	0.00
10.1..20	0%	0	1	0.0%	-1.00
20.0..30	50%	1	2	50.0%	0.19
30.1+	0%	0	3	0.0%	-1.00
Not Compl	0%	0	1	0.0%	-1.00
Unraced	0%	0	0	0.0%	0.00

ANALYSIS BY SUCCESS RATE IN LAST 10 RUNS

Age	Prop	Win	Runs	Wins%	£
No Wins	50%	1	8	12.5%	-0.70
1 Win	50%	1	2	50.0%	-0.22
2 Wins	0%	0	0	0.0%	0.00
3 Wins	0%	0	0	0.0%	0.00
4 Wins	0%	0	0	0.0%	0.00
5+ Wins	0%	0	0	0.0%	0.00

ANALYSIS BY SUCCESS RATE IN LAST 3 RUNS

Age	Prop	Win	Runs	Wins%	£
No Wins	50%	1	8	12.5%	-0.70
1 Win	50%	1	2	50.0%	-0.22
2 Wins	0%	0	0	0.0%	0.00
3 Wins	0%	0	0	0.0%	0.00

ANALYSIS BY POSITION LAST TIME

Age	Prop	Win	Runs	Wins%	£
Won	50%	1	2	50.0%	-0.22
2nd or 3rd	0%	0	2	0.0%	-1.00
Unplaced	50%	1	5	20.0%	-0.52
Fell,BD,UR	0%	0	1	0.0%	-1.00
Pulled Up	0%	0	0	0.0%	0.00
Ref/RanOut	0%	0	0	0.0%	0.00
CO/SlipUp	0%	0	0	0.0%	0.00
Unraced	0%	0	0	0.0%	0.00

OTHER FACTORS (WINS-RUNS, £)

Going Winner:	1-1	£0.57
BHA Top Rated:	2-2	£0.97
Absolute Favourites:	2-2	£0.97

Race Profiles

Amateur Hurdle Races: 6 to 10 runners

ANALYSIS BY AGE

Age	Prop	Win	Runs	Wins%	£
3yo	0%	0	0	0.0%	0.00
4yo	0%	0	14	0.0%	-1.00
5yo	55%	6	31	19.4%	-0.46
6yo	18%	2	21	9.5%	-0.76
7yo	9%	1	12	8.3%	1.83
8yo	18%	2	9	22.2%	-0.24
9yo	0%	0	4	0.0%	-1.00
10yo	0%	0	2	0.0%	-1.00
11yo	0%	0	0	0.0%	0.00
12yo+	0%	0	1	0.0%	-1.00

ANALYSIS BY BHB RATING

Age	Prop	Win	Runs	Wins%	£
150+	0%	0	0	0.0%	0.00
130..149	0%	0	0	0.0%	0.00
120..129	0%	0	1	0.0%	-1.00
110..119	36%	4	9	44.4%	0.41
100..109	36%	4	9	44.4%	0.23
80..99	0%	0	10	0.0%	-1.00
60..79	0%	0	9	0.0%	-1.00
..59	0%	0	1	0.0%	-1.00
Unrated	27%	3	55	5.5%	-0.29

ANALYSIS BY WEIGHT CARRIED

Age	Prop	Win	Runs	Wins%	£
12-01+	0%	0	0	0.0%	0.00
11-8..12-00	9%	1	3	33.3%	0.50
11-0..11-07	45%	5	26	19.2%	0.66
10-8..10-13	45%	5	47	10.6%	-0.68
10-0..10-07	0%	0	18	0.0%	-1.00
..9-13	0%	0	0	0.0%	0.00

ANALYSIS BY DAYS SINCE LAST RUN

Age	Prop	Win	Runs	Wins%	£
1..7	9%	1	4	25.0%	0.00
8..14	0%	0	15	0.0%	-1.00
15..28	36%	4	28	14.3%	-0.58
29..60	9%	1	13	7.7%	-0.67
61..100	9%	1	7	14.3%	-0.79
101+	27%	3	18	16.7%	1.18
Unraced	9%	1	9	11.1%	-0.78

ANALYSIS BY TODAY'S STARTING PRICE

Age	Prop	Win	Runs	Wins%	£
Odds On	9%	1	2	50.0%	-0.28
Ev-2/1	55%	6	12	50.0%	0.20
9/4-4/1	27%	3	10	30.0%	0.28
9/2-6/1	0%	0	7	0.0%	-1.00
13/2-10/1	0%	0	6	0.0%	-1.00
11/1-16/1	0%	0	14	0.0%	-1.00
18/1-33/1	9%	1	16	6.3%	1.13
40/1+	0%	0	27	0.0%	-1.00

ANALYSIS BY STARTING PRICE LAST TIME

Age	Prop	Win	Runs	Wins%	£
Odds On	18%	2	5	40.0%	0.05
Ev-2/1	27%	3	7	42.9%	0.42
9/4-4/1	18%	2	9	22.2%	-0.44
9/2-6/1	0%	0	5	0.0%	-1.00
13/2-10/1	18%	2	9	22.2%	-0.27
11/1-16/1	0%	0	10	0.0%	-1.00
18/1-33/1	0%	0	18	0.0%	-1.00
40/1+	9%	1	22	4.5%	0.55
Unraced	9%	1	9	11.1%	-0.78

ANALYSIS BY DISTANCE BEATEN LAST TIME

Age	Prop	Win	Runs	Wins%	£
..-10 lgh	0%	0	1	0.0%	-1.00
-10..0	18%	2	7	28.6%	-0.04
0.1..2	0%	0	1	0.0%	-1.00
2.1..5	36%	4	5	80.0%	1.28
5.1..10	27%	3	13	23.1%	-0.34
10.1..20	0%	0	10	0.0%	-1.00
20.0..30	0%	0	11	0.0%	-1.00
30.1+	9%	1	26	3.8%	0.31
Not Compl	0%	0	11	0.0%	-1.00
Unraced	9%	1	9	11.1%	-0.78

ANALYSIS BY SUCCESS RATE IN LAST 10 RUNS

Age	Prop	Win	Runs	Wins%	£
No Wins	20%	2	59	3.4%	-0.38
1 Win	60%	6	17	35.3%	-0.08
2 Wins	10%	1	6	16.7%	-0.33
3 Wins	10%	1	3	33.3%	0.50
4 Wins	0%	0	0	0.0%	0.00
5+ Wins	0%	0	0	0.0%	0.00

ANALYSIS BY SUCCESS RATE IN LAST 3 RUNS

Age	Prop	Win	Runs	Wins%	£
No Wins	40%	4	65	6.2%	-0.31
1 Win	50%	5	17	29.4%	-0.34
2 Wins	10%	1	3	33.3%	0.50
3 Wins	0%	0	0	0.0%	0.00

ANALYSIS BY POSITION LAST TIME

Age	Prop	Win	Runs	Wins%	£
Won	18%	2	8	25.0%	-0.16
2nd or 3rd	64%	7	21	33.3%	-0.05
Unplaced	9%	1	45	2.2%	-0.24
Fell,BD,UR	0%	0	2	0.0%	-1.00
Pulled Up	0%	0	9	0.0%	-1.00
Ref/RanOut	0%	0	0	0.0%	0.00
CO/SlipUp	0%	0	0	0.0%	0.00
Unraced	9%	1	9	11.1%	-0.78

OTHER FACTORS (WINS-RUNS, £)

Course Winner:	1-4	£0.13
Distance Winner:	5-9	£0.70
Going Winner:	2-8	-£0.18
Beaten Favourite:	4-8	£0.16
BHA Top Rated:	5-10	£0.45
Absolute Favourites:	5-11	-£0.04

Amateur Hurdle Races

Amateur Hurdle Races: 11 runners or more

ANALYSIS BY AGE

Age	Prop	Win	Runs	Wins%	£
3yo	0%	0	0	0.0%	0.00
4yo	22%	2	21	9.5%	-0.32
5yo	11%	1	33	3.0%	-0.95
6yo	22%	2	29	6.9%	0.24
7yo	33%	3	23	13.0%	1.30
8yo	11%	1	8	12.5%	-0.84
9yo	0%	0	10	0.0%	-1.00
10yo	0%	0	3	0.0%	-1.00
11yo	0%	0	1	0.0%	-1.00
12yo+	0%	0	1	0.0%	-1.00

ANALYSIS BY BHB RATING

Age	Prop	Win	Runs	Wins%	£
150+	0%	0	0	0.0%	0.00
130..149	0%	0	4	0.0%	-1.00
120..129	22%	2	4	50.0%	7.91
110..119	22%	2	12	16.7%	-0.71
100..109	0%	0	10	0.0%	-1.00
80..99	11%	1	13	7.7%	1.62
60..79	0%	0	11	0.0%	-1.00
..59	0%	0	0	0.0%	0.00
Unrated	44%	4	75	5.3%	-0.56

ANALYSIS BY WEIGHT CARRIED

Age	Prop	Win	Runs	Wins%	£
12-01+	0%	0	0	0.0%	0.00
11-8..12-00	11%	1	14	7.1%	1.43
11-0..11-07	33%	3	37	8.1%	-0.85
10-8..10-13	33%	3	51	5.9%	-0.11
10-0..10-07	22%	2	26	7.7%	-0.19
..9-13	0%	0	1	0.0%	-1.00

ANALYSIS BY DAYS SINCE LAST RUN

Age	Prop	Win	Runs	Wins%	£
1..7	11%	1	5	20.0%	-0.55
8..14	44%	4	22	18.2%	1.47
15..28	11%	1	29	3.4%	-0.94
29..60	33%	3	20	15.0%	1.39
61..100	0%	0	5	0.0%	-1.00
101+	0%	0	36	0.0%	-1.00
Unraced	0%	0	12	0.0%	-1.00

ANALYSIS BY TODAY'S STARTING PRICE

Age	Prop	Win	Runs	Wins%	£
Odds On	33%	3	5	60.0%	-0.05
Ev-2/1	11%	1	2	50.0%	0.13
9/4-4/1	0%	0	5	0.0%	-1.00
9/2-6/1	0%	0	7	0.0%	-1.00
13/2-10/1	22%	2	17	11.8%	0.12
11/1-16/1	11%	1	18	5.6%	-0.33
18/1-33/1	22%	2	19	10.5%	2.58
40/1+	0%	0	56	0.0%	-1.00

ANALYSIS BY STARTING PRICE LAST TIME

Age	Prop	Win	Runs	Wins%	£
Odds On	22%	2	3	66.7%	-0.03
Ev-2/1	11%	1	8	12.5%	-0.72
9/4-4/1	22%	2	15	13.3%	-0.08
9/2-6/1	22%	2	10	20.0%	3.40
13/2-10/1	0%	0	18	0.0%	-1.00
11/1-16/1	11%	1	20	5.0%	-0.55
18/1-33/1	11%	1	12	8.3%	1.83
40/1+	0%	0	31	0.0%	-1.00
Unraced	0%	0	12	0.0%	-1.00

ANALYSIS BY DISTANCE BEATEN LAST TIME

Age	Prop	Win	Runs	Wins%	£
..-10 lgh	22%	2	3	66.7%	10.87
-10..0	11%	1	10	10.0%	-0.87
0.1..2	11%	1	8	12.5%	-0.72
2.1..5	22%	2	5	40.0%	1.37
5.1..10	11%	1	13	7.7%	-0.31
10.1..20	22%	2	18	11.1%	1.56
20.0..30	0%	0	11	0.0%	-1.00
30.1+	0%	0	31	0.0%	-1.00
Not Compl	0%	0	18	0.0%	-1.00
Unraced	0%	0	12	0.0%	-1.00

ANALYSIS BY SUCCESS RATE IN LAST 10 RUNS

Age	Prop	Win	Runs	Wins%	£
No Wins	44%	4	83	4.8%	-0.60
1 Win	22%	2	17	11.8%	1.10
2 Wins	22%	2	8	25.0%	-0.56
3 Wins	0%	0	5	0.0%	-1.00
4 Wins	11%	1	4	25.0%	7.50
5+ Wins	0%	0	0	0.0%	0.00

ANALYSIS BY SUCCESS RATE IN LAST 3 RUNS

Age	Prop	Win	Runs	Wins%	£
No Wins	56%	5	93	5.4%	-0.28
1 Win	33%	3	20	15.0%	0.89
2 Wins	11%	1	4	25.0%	-0.68
3 Wins	0%	0	0	0.0%	0.00

ANALYSIS BY POSITION LAST TIME

Age	Prop	Win	Runs	Wins%	£
Won	33%	3	13	23.1%	1.84
2nd or 3rd	33%	3	30	10.0%	-0.53
Unplaced	33%	3	56	5.4%	-0.02
Fell,BD,UR	0%	0	7	0.0%	-1.00
Pulled Up	0%	0	11	0.0%	-1.00
Ref/RanOut	0%	0	0	0.0%	0.00
CO/SlipUp	0%	0	0	0.0%	0.00
Unraced	0%	0	12	0.0%	-1.00

OTHER FACTORS (WINS-RUNS, £)

Course Winner:	1-3	-£0.57
Distance Winner:	1-6	-£0.79
Going Winner:	4-17	£1.30
Beaten Favourite:	1-6	-£0.63
BHA Top Rated:	3-8	-£0.35
Absolute Favourites:	4-9	-£0.22

Race Profiles

Amateur Hurdle Races: up to 7 days off the track

ANALYSIS BY AGE

Age	Prop	Win	Runs	Wins%	£
3yo	0%	0	0	0.0%	0.00
4yo	33%	1	6	16.7%	-0.63
5yo	33%	1	12	8.3%	-0.67
6yo	33%	1	6	16.7%	-0.67
7yo	0%	0	6	0.0%	-1.00
8yo	0%	0	0	0.0%	0.00
9yo	0%	0	1	0.0%	-1.00
10yo	0%	0	1	0.0%	-1.00
11yo	0%	0	0	0.0%	0.00
12yo+	0%	0	0	0.0%	0.00

ANALYSIS BY BHB RATING

Age	Prop	Win	Runs	Wins%	£
150+	0%	0	0	0.0%	0.00
130..149	0%	0	1	0.0%	-1.00
120..129	0%	0	0	0.0%	0.00
110..119	33%	1	2	50.0%	0.13
100..109	33%	1	1	100.0%	3.00
80..99	0%	0	1	0.0%	-1.00
60..79	0%	0	1	0.0%	-1.00
..59	0%	0	0	0.0%	0.00
Unrated	33%	1	26	3.8%	-0.92

ANALYSIS BY WEIGHT CARRIED

Age	Prop	Win	Runs	Wins%	£
12-01+	0%	0	0	0.0%	0.00
11-8..12-00	0%	0	2	0.0%	-1.00
11-0..11-07	33%	1	8	12.5%	-0.72
10-8..10-13	67%	2	14	14.3%	-0.57
10-0..10-07	0%	0	7	0.0%	-1.00
..9-13	0%	0	1	0.0%	-1.00

ANALYSIS BY DAYS SINCE LAST RUN

Age	Prop	Win	Runs	Wins%	£
1..7	67%	2	11	18.2%	-0.43
8..14	0%	0	0	0.0%	0.00
15..28	0%	0	0	0.0%	0.00
29..60	0%	0	0	0.0%	0.00
61..100	0%	0	0	0.0%	0.00
101+	0%	0	0	0.0%	0.00
Unraced	33%	1	21	4.8%	-0.90

ANALYSIS BY TODAY'S STARTING PRICE

Age	Prop	Win	Runs	Wins%	£
Odds On	0%	0	0	0.0%	0.00
Ev-2/1	67%	2	4	50.0%	0.06
9/4-4/1	33%	1	1	100.0%	3.00
9/2-6/1	0%	0	4	0.0%	-1.00
13/2-10/1	0%	0	3	0.0%	-1.00
11/1-16/1	0%	0	1	0.0%	-1.00
18/1-33/1	0%	0	4	0.0%	-1.00
40/1+	0%	0	15	0.0%	-1.00

ANALYSIS BY STARTING PRICE LAST TIME

Age	Prop	Win	Runs	Wins%	£
Odds On	0%	0	1	0.0%	-1.00
Ev-2/1	67%	2	2	100.0%	2.13
9/4-4/1	0%	0	0	0.0%	0.00
9/2-6/1	0%	0	0	0.0%	0.00
13/2-10/1	0%	0	2	0.0%	-1.00
11/1-16/1	0%	0	0	0.0%	0.00
18/1-33/1	0%	0	3	0.0%	-1.00
40/1+	0%	0	3	0.0%	-1.00
Unraced	33%	1	21	4.8%	-0.90

ANALYSIS BY DISTANCE BEATEN LAST TIME

Age	Prop	Win	Runs	Wins%	£
..-10 lgh	0%	0	0	0.0%	0.00
-10..0	0%	0	0	0.0%	0.00
0.1..2	33%	1	1	100.0%	1.25
2.1..5	0%	0	0	0.0%	0.00
5.1..10	33%	1	3	33.3%	0.33
10.1..20	0%	0	1	0.0%	-1.00
20.0..30	0%	0	0	0.0%	0.00
30.1+	0%	0	4	0.0%	-1.00
Not Compl	0%	0	2	0.0%	-1.00
Unraced	33%	1	21	4.8%	-0.90

ANALYSIS BY SUCCESS RATE IN LAST 10 RUNS

Age	Prop	Win	Runs	Wins%	£
No Wins	0%	0	6	0.0%	-1.00
1 Win	0%	0	2	0.0%	-1.00
2 Wins	100%	2	2	100.0%	2.13
3 Wins	0%	0	1	0.0%	-1.00
4 Wins	0%	0	0	0.0%	0.00
5+ Wins	0%	0	0	0.0%	0.00

ANALYSIS BY SUCCESS RATE IN LAST 3 RUNS

Age	Prop	Win	Runs	Wins%	£
No Wins	50%	1	8	12.5%	-0.50
1 Win	50%	1	3	33.3%	-0.25
2 Wins	0%	0	0	0.0%	0.00
3 Wins	0%	0	0	0.0%	0.00

ANALYSIS BY POSITION LAST TIME

Age	Prop	Win	Runs	Wins%	£
Won	0%	0	0	0.0%	0.00
2nd or 3rd	67%	2	6	33.3%	0.04
Unplaced	0%	0	3	0.0%	-1.00
Fell,BD,UR	0%	0	2	0.0%	-1.00
Pulled Up	0%	0	0	0.0%	0.00
Ref/RanOut	0%	0	0	0.0%	0.00
CO/SlipUp	0%	0	0	0.0%	0.00
Unraced	33%	1	21	4.8%	-0.90

OTHER FACTORS (WINS-RUNS, £)

Distance Winner:1-1	£3.00	
Going Winner:	1-2	£0.13
Beaten Favourite:	1-2	£0.13
BHA Top Rated:	2-2	£2.13
Absolute Favourites:	2-4	£0.06

Amateur Hurdle Races

Amateur Hurdle Races: 100+ days off the track

ANALYSIS BY AGE

Age	Prop	Win	Runs	Wins%	£
3yo	0%	0	0	0.0%	0.00
4yo	0%	0	2	0.0%	-1.00
5yo	33%	1	18	5.6%	-0.88
6yo	33%	1	12	8.3%	-0.75
7yo	33%	1	8	12.5%	3.25
8yo	0%	0	6	0.0%	-1.00
9yo	0%	0	3	0.0%	-1.00
10yo	0%	0	4	0.0%	-1.00
11yo	0%	0	0	0.0%	0.00
12yo+	0%	0	1	0.0%	-1.00

ANALYSIS BY BHB RATING

Age	Prop	Win	Runs	Wins%	£
150+	0%	0	0	0.0%	0.00
130..149	0%	0	0	0.0%	0.00
120..129	0%	0	0	0.0%	0.00
110..119	0%	0	2	0.0%	-1.00
100..109	33%	1	4	25.0%	-0.44
80..99	0%	0	4	0.0%	-1.00
60..79	0%	0	8	0.0%	-1.00
..59	0%	0	0	0.0%	0.00
Unrated	67%	2	36	5.6%	0.03

ANALYSIS BY WEIGHT CARRIED

Age	Prop	Win	Runs	Wins%	£
12-01+	0%	0	0	0.0%	0.00
11-8..12-00	0%	0	1	0.0%	-1.00
11-0..11-07	67%	2	14	14.3%	1.64
10-8..10-13	33%	1	31	3.2%	-0.93
10-0..10-07	0%	0	8	0.0%	-1.00
..9-13	0%	0	0	0.0%	0.00

ANALYSIS BY DAYS SINCE LAST RUN

Age	Prop	Win	Runs	Wins%	£
1..7	0%	0	0	0.0%	0.00
8..14	0%	0	0	0.0%	0.00
15..28	0%	0	0	0.0%	0.00
29..60	0%	0	0	0.0%	0.00
61..100	0%	0	0	0.0%	0.00
101+	100%	3	54	5.6%	-0.27
Unraced	0%	0	0	0.0%	0.00

ANALYSIS BY TODAY'S STARTING PRICE

Age	Prop	Win	Runs	Wins%	£
Odds On	0%	0	1	0.0%	-1.00
Ev-2/1	67%	2	2	100.0%	1.63
9/4-4/1	0%	0	5	0.0%	-1.00
9/2-6/1	0%	0	2	0.0%	-1.00
13/2-10/1	0%	0	3	0.0%	-1.00
11/1-16/1	0%	0	4	0.0%	-1.00
18/1-33/1	33%	1	13	7.7%	1.62
40/1+	0%	0	24	0.0%	-1.00

ANALYSIS BY STARTING PRICE LAST TIME

Age	Prop	Win	Runs	Wins%	£
Odds On	67%	2	3	66.7%	0.75
Ev-2/1	0%	0	3	0.0%	-1.00
9/4-4/1	0%	0	5	0.0%	-1.00
9/2-6/1	0%	0	2	0.0%	-1.00
13/2-10/1	0%	0	8	0.0%	-1.00
11/1-16/1	0%	0	8	0.0%	-1.00
18/1-33/1	0%	0	8	0.0%	-1.00
40/1+	33%	1	17	5.9%	1.00
Unraced	0%	0	0	0.0%	0.00

ANALYSIS BY DISTANCE BEATEN LAST TIME

Age	Prop	Win	Runs	Wins%	£
..-10 lgh	0%	0	0	0.0%	0.00
-10..0	0%	0	3	0.0%	-1.00
0.1..2	0%	0	2	0.0%	-1.00
2.1..5	33%	1	1	100.0%	2.00
5.1..10	33%	1	8	12.5%	-0.72
10.1..20	0%	0	5	0.0%	-1.00
20.0..30	0%	0	6	0.0%	-1.00
30.1+	33%	1	21	4.8%	0.62
Not Compl	0%	0	8	0.0%	-1.00
Unraced	0%	0	0	0.0%	0.00

ANALYSIS BY SUCCESS RATE IN LAST 10 RUNS

Age	Prop	Win	Runs	Wins%	£
No Wins	33%	1	45	2.2%	-0.24
1 Win	67%	2	7	28.6%	-0.25
2 Wins	0%	0	0	0.0%	0.00
3 Wins	0%	0	2	0.0%	-1.00
4 Wins	0%	0	0	0.0%	0.00
5+ Wins	0%	0	0	0.0%	0.00

ANALYSIS BY SUCCESS RATE IN LAST 3 RUNS

Age	Prop	Win	Runs	Wins%	£
No Wins	33%	1	46	2.2%	-0.26
1 Win	67%	2	7	28.6%	-0.25
2 Wins	0%	0	1	0.0%	-1.00
3 Wins	0%	0	0	0.0%	0.00

ANALYSIS BY POSITION LAST TIME

Age	Prop	Win	Runs	Wins%	£
Won	0%	0	3	0.0%	-1.00
2nd or 3rd	67%	2	6	33.3%	-0.13
Unplaced	33%	1	37	2.7%	-0.08
Fell,BD,UR	0%	0	2	0.0%	-1.00
Pulled Up	0%	0	6	0.0%	-1.00
Ref/RanOut	0%	0	0	0.0%	0.00
CO/SlipUp	0%	0	0	0.0%	0.00
Unraced	0%	0	0	0.0%	0.00

OTHER FACTORS (WINS-RUNS, £)

Course Winner:	0-1	-£1.00
Distance Winner:	1-4	-£0.25
Going Winner:	0-2	-£1.00
Beaten Favourite:	2-7	-£0.25
BHA Top Rated:	0-1	-£1.00
Absolute Favourites:	1-4	-£0.44

Race Profiles

Conditions Hurdle Races (class 1..3)

ANALYSIS BY AGE

Age	Prop	Win	Runs	Wins%	£
3yo	0%	0	0	0.0%	0.00
4yo	9%	14	137	10.2%	-0.51
5yo	24%	36	254	14.2%	-0.08
6yo	32%	48	265	18.1%	0.04
7yo	15%	23	225	10.2%	-0.40
8yo	9%	14	149	9.4%	-0.63
9yo	6%	9	97	9.3%	-0.50
10yo	2%	3	45	6.7%	-0.09
11yo	1%	2	33	6.1%	-0.52
12yo+	1%	1	25	4.0%	-0.48

ANALYSIS BY BHB RATING

Age	Prop	Win	Runs	Wins%	£
150+	46%	69	437	15.8%	-0.30
130..149	26%	39	346	11.3%	-0.16
120..129	5%	7	61	11.5%	0.12
110..119	1%	2	52	3.8%	-0.67
100..109	1%	1	15	6.7%	-0.53
80..99	0%	0	20	0.0%	-1.00
60..79	0%	0	6	0.0%	-1.00
..59	0%	0	0	0.0%	0.00
Unrated	21%	32	293	10.9%	-0.33

ANALYSIS BY WEIGHT CARRIED

Age	Prop	Win	Runs	Wins%	£
12-01+	0%	0	0	0.0%	0.00
11-8..12-00	33%	50	333	15.0%	-0.31
11-0..11-07	59%	89	771	11.5%	-0.24
10-8..10-13	7%	11	86	12.8%	-0.18
10-0..10-07	0%	0	40	0.0%	-1.00
..9-13	0%	0	0	0.0%	0.00

ANALYSIS BY DAYS SINCE LAST RUN

Age	Prop	Win	Runs	Wins%	£
1..7	2%	3	35	8.6%	-0.76
8..14	9%	14	106	13.2%	-0.34
15..28	30%	45	391	11.5%	-0.27
29..60	29%	44	345	12.8%	-0.20
61..100	3%	5	76	6.6%	-0.77
101+	24%	36	222	16.2%	-0.07
Unraced	2%	3	55	5.5%	-0.59

ANALYSIS BY TODAY'S STARTING PRICE

Age	Prop	Win	Runs	Wins%	£
Odds On	21%	31	51	60.8%	-0.05
Ev-2/1	19%	29	88	33.0%	-0.15
9/4-4/1	22%	33	160	20.6%	-0.19
9/2-6/1	10%	15	102	14.7%	-0.08
13/2-10/1	15%	23	193	11.9%	0.09
11/1-16/1	9%	14	182	7.7%	0.11
18/1-33/1	3%	5	201	2.5%	-0.38
40/1+	0%	0	253	0.0%	-1.00

ANALYSIS BY STARTING PRICE LAST TIME

Age	Prop	Win	Runs	Wins%	£
Odds On	14%	21	84	25.0%	0.02
Ev-2/1	15%	22	114	19.3%	-0.03
9/4-4/1	17%	25	204	12.3%	-0.32
9/2-6/1	9%	14	115	12.2%	-0.45
13/2-10/1	18%	27	202	13.4%	-0.17
11/1-16/1	12%	18	192	9.4%	-0.36
18/1-33/1	9%	14	163	8.6%	-0.26
40/1+	4%	6	101	5.9%	-0.46
Unraced	2%	3	55	5.5%	-0.59

ANALYSIS BY DISTANCE BEATEN LAST TIME

Age	Prop	Win	Runs	Wins%	£
..-10 lgh	3%	4	31	12.9%	-0.26
-10..0	35%	52	243	21.4%	0.02
0.1..2	7%	11	89	12.4%	-0.23
2.1..5	12%	18	108	16.7%	-0.30
5.1..10	11%	16	122	13.1%	-0.45
10.1..20	13%	19	193	9.8%	-0.19
20.0..30	3%	5	107	4.7%	-0.62
30.1+	9%	13	177	7.3%	-0.38
Not Compl	6%	9	105	8.6%	-0.30
Unraced	2%	3	55	5.5%	-0.59

ANALYSIS BY SUCCESS RATE IN LAST 10 RUNS

Age	Prop	Win	Runs	Wins%	£
No Wins	6%	9	159	5.7%	-0.53
1 Win	16%	23	228	10.1%	-0.36
2 Wins	21%	31	252	12.3%	-0.21
3 Wins	22%	32	237	13.5%	-0.01
4 Wins	12%	18	151	11.9%	-0.50
5+ Wins	23%	34	148	23.0%	-0.10

ANALYSIS BY SUCCESS RATE IN LAST 3 RUNS

Age	Prop	Win	Runs	Wins%	£
No Wins	33%	49	532	9.2%	-0.35
1 Win	35%	52	430	12.1%	-0.22
2 Wins	23%	34	174	19.5%	-0.07
3 Wins	8%	12	39	30.8%	-0.41

ANALYSIS BY POSITION LAST TIME

Age	Prop	Win	Runs	Wins%	£
Won	37%	56	274	20.4%	-0.02
2nd or 3rd	29%	44	296	14.9%	-0.16
Unplaced	25%	38	500	7.6%	-0.46
Fell,BD,UR	5%	8	51	15.7%	0.35
Pulled Up	1%	1	53	1.9%	-0.92
Ref/RanOut	0%	0	0	0.0%	0.00
CO/SlipUp	0%	0	1	0.0%	-1.00
Unraced	2%	3	55	5.5%	-0.59

OTHER FACTORS (WINS-RUNS, £)

Course Winner:	51-339	-£0.20
Distance Winner:	92-673	-£0.25
Going Winner:	99-672	-£0.10
Beaten Favourite:	16-109	-£0.16
7-Day Winners:	2-9	-£0.51
BHA Top Rated:	39-113	-£0.04
Absolute Favourites:	61-137	-£0.05

Conditions Hurdle Races (class 1..3)

Conditions Hurdle Races (class 1..3): 2m to 2m3f

ANALYSIS BY AGE

Age	Prop	Win	Runs	Wins%	£
3yo	0%	0	0	0.0%	0.00
4yo	15%	10	96	10.4%	-0.47
5yo	31%	21	137	15.3%	-0.21
6yo	34%	23	111	20.7%	0.48
7yo	12%	8	79	10.1%	-0.17
8yo	3%	2	44	4.5%	-0.82
9yo	3%	2	32	6.3%	-0.68
10yo	1%	1	13	7.7%	1.00
11yo	1%	1	12	8.3%	-0.77
12yo+	0%	0	13	0.0%	-1.00

ANALYSIS BY BHB RATING

Age	Prop	Win	Runs	Wins%	£
150+	38%	26	154	16.9%	-0.10
130..149	25%	17	136	12.5%	-0.08
120..129	3%	2	24	8.3%	0.30
110..119	3%	2	26	7.7%	-0.35
100..109	1%	1	8	12.5%	-0.13
80..99	0%	0	11	0.0%	-1.00
60..79	0%	0	2	0.0%	-1.00
..59	0%	0	0	0.0%	0.00
Unrated	29%	20	176	11.4%	-0.34

ANALYSIS BY WEIGHT CARRIED

Age	Prop	Win	Runs	Wins%	£
12-01+	0%	0	0	0.0%	0.00
11-8..12-00	31%	21	142	14.8%	-0.22
11-0..11-07	62%	42	337	12.5%	-0.17
10-8..10-13	7%	5	41	12.2%	0.10
10-0..10-07	0%	0	17	0.0%	-1.00
..9-13	0%	0	0	0.0%	0.00

ANALYSIS BY DAYS SINCE LAST RUN

Age	Prop	Win	Runs	Wins%	£
1..7	4%	3	18	16.7%	-0.53
8..14	10%	7	57	12.3%	-0.45
15..28	26%	18	150	12.0%	-0.11
29..60	31%	21	138	15.2%	-0.05
61..100	1%	1	43	2.3%	-0.96
101+	24%	16	93	17.2%	0.27
Unraced	3%	2	38	5.3%	-0.68

ANALYSIS BY TODAY'S STARTING PRICE

Age	Prop	Win	Runs	Wins%	£
Odds On	24%	16	27	59.3%	-0.07
Ev-2/1	19%	13	42	31.0%	-0.23
9/4-4/1	19%	13	62	21.0%	-0.17
9/2-6/1	6%	4	38	10.5%	-0.33
13/2-10/1	18%	12	92	13.0%	0.18
11/1-16/1	9%	6	74	8.1%	0.19
18/1-33/1	6%	4	86	4.7%	0.21
40/1+	0%	0	116	0.0%	-1.00

ANALYSIS BY STARTING PRICE LAST TIME

Age	Prop	Win	Runs	Wins%	£
Odds On	18%	12	45	26.7%	0.37
Ev-2/1	15%	10	51	19.6%	0.29
9/4-4/1	10%	7	92	7.6%	-0.72
9/2-6/1	6%	4	31	12.9%	-0.60
13/2-10/1	18%	12	88	13.6%	-0.11
11/1-16/1	13%	9	75	12.0%	0.03
18/1-33/1	15%	10	72	13.9%	0.17
40/1+	3%	2	45	4.4%	-0.60
Unraced	3%	2	38	5.3%	-0.68

ANALYSIS BY DISTANCE BEATEN LAST TIME

Age	Prop	Win	Runs	Wins%	£
..-10 lgh	4%	3	15	20.0%	0.34
-10..0	31%	21	108	19.4%	0.13
0.1..2	6%	4	41	9.8%	-0.56
2.1..5	12%	8	42	19.0%	-0.34
5.1..10	13%	9	56	16.1%	-0.59
10.1..20	13%	9	76	11.8%	0.07
20.0..30	4%	3	49	6.1%	-0.36
30.1+	7%	5	65	7.7%	-0.29
Not Compl	6%	4	47	8.5%	0.14
Unraced	3%	2	38	5.3%	-0.68

ANALYSIS BY SUCCESS RATE IN LAST 10 RUNS

Age	Prop	Win	Runs	Wins%	£
No Wins	6%	4	91	4.4%	-0.71
1 Win	23%	15	108	13.9%	-0.14
2 Wins	26%	17	96	17.7%	0.24
3 Wins	20%	13	93	14.0%	0.00
4 Wins	9%	6	60	10.0%	-0.52
5+ Wins	17%	11	51	21.6%	0.22

ANALYSIS BY SUCCESS RATE IN LAST 3 RUNS

Age	Prop	Win	Runs	Wins%	£
No Wins	35%	23	222	10.4%	-0.38
1 Win	45%	30	198	15.2%	0.16
2 Wins	15%	10	64	15.6%	-0.23
3 Wins	5%	3	15	20.0%	-0.63

ANALYSIS BY POSITION LAST TIME

Age	Prop	Win	Runs	Wins%	£
Won	35%	24	123	19.5%	0.16
2nd or 3rd	28%	19	124	15.3%	-0.13
Unplaced	28%	19	205	9.3%	-0.42
Fell,BD,UR	6%	4	28	14.3%	0.91
Pulled Up	0%	0	19	0.0%	-1.00
Ref/RanOut	0%	0	0	0.0%	0.00
CO/SlipUp	0%	0	0	0.0%	0.00
Unraced	3%	2	38	5.3%	-0.68

OTHER FACTORS (WINS-RUNS, £)

Course Winner:	16-122	-£0.20
Distance Winner:	54-373	-£0.07
Going Winner:	42-263	£0.10
Beaten Favourite:	10-53	-£0.11
7-Day Winners:	2-6	-£0.26
BHA Top Rated:	16-49	-£0.03
Absolute Favourites:	29-62	-£0.06

Race Profiles

Conditions Hurdle Races (class 1..3): 2m4f to 2m7f

ANALYSIS BY AGE

Age	Prop	Win	Runs	Wins%	£
3yo	0%	0	0	0.0%	0.00
4yo	10%	4	36	11.1%	-0.53
5yo	23%	9	73	12.3%	-0.12
6yo	21%	8	67	11.9%	-0.53
7yo	15%	6	59	10.2%	-0.55
8yo	18%	7	35	20.0%	-0.08
9yo	8%	3	25	12.0%	-0.44
10yo	3%	1	8	12.5%	-0.50
11yo	0%	0	4	0.0%	-1.00
12yo+	3%	1	5	20.0%	1.60

ANALYSIS BY BHB RATING

Age	Prop	Win	Runs	Wins%	£
150+	41%	16	95	16.8%	-0.38
130..149	23%	9	86	10.5%	-0.38
120..129	13%	5	27	18.5%	0.37
110..119	0%	0	16	0.0%	-1.00
100..109	0%	0	4	0.0%	-1.00
80..99	0%	0	7	0.0%	-1.00
60..79	0%	0	3	0.0%	-1.00
..59	0%	0	0	0.0%	0.00
Unrated	23%	9	74	12.2%	-0.28

ANALYSIS BY WEIGHT CARRIED

Age	Prop	Win	Runs	Wins%	£
12-01+	0%	0	0	0.0%	0.00
11-8..12-00	26%	10	37	27.0%	0.22
11-0..11-07	62%	24	226	10.6%	-0.41
10-8..10-13	13%	5	29	17.2%	-0.21
10-0..10-07	0%	0	20	0.0%	-1.00
..9-13	0%	0	0	0.0%	0.00

ANALYSIS BY DAYS SINCE LAST RUN

Age	Prop	Win	Runs	Wins%	£
1..7	0%	0	5	0.0%	-1.00
8..14	13%	5	32	15.6%	-0.24
15..28	28%	11	99	11.1%	-0.33
29..60	23%	9	85	10.6%	-0.49
61..100	8%	3	14	21.4%	-0.02
101+	26%	10	63	15.9%	-0.30
Unraced	3%	1	14	7.1%	-0.29

ANALYSIS BY TODAY'S STARTING PRICE

Age	Prop	Win	Runs	Wins%	£
Odds On	15%	6	10	60.0%	-0.14
Ev-2/1	18%	7	25	28.0%	-0.22
9/4-4/1	28%	11	50	22.0%	-0.15
9/2-6/1	21%	8	30	26.7%	0.63
13/2-10/1	10%	4	45	8.9%	-0.20
11/1-16/1	5%	2	44	4.5%	-0.41
18/1-33/1	3%	1	42	2.4%	-0.50
40/1+	0%	0	66	0.0%	-1.00

ANALYSIS BY STARTING PRICE LAST TIME

Age	Prop	Win	Runs	Wins%	£
Odds On	5%	2	16	12.5%	-0.73
Ev-2/1	13%	5	30	16.7%	-0.47
9/4-4/1	23%	9	43	20.9%	0.17
9/2-6/1	13%	5	38	13.2%	-0.46
13/2-10/1	23%	9	48	18.8%	-0.02
11/1-16/1	15%	6	58	10.3%	-0.39
18/1-33/1	3%	1	38	2.6%	-0.66
40/1+	3%	1	27	3.7%	-0.78
Unraced	3%	1	14	7.1%	-0.29

ANALYSIS BY DISTANCE BEATEN LAST TIME

Age	Prop	Win	Runs	Wins%	£
..-10 lgh	3%	1	8	12.5%	-0.66
-10..0	36%	14	53	26.4%	0.11
0.1..2	5%	2	21	9.5%	-0.40
2.1..5	15%	6	28	21.4%	-0.28
5.1..10	13%	5	30	16.7%	0.07
10.1..20	8%	3	53	5.7%	-0.56
20.0..30	3%	1	28	3.6%	-0.77
30.1+	8%	3	46	6.5%	-0.50
Not Compl	8%	3	31	9.7%	-0.58
Unraced	3%	1	14	7.1%	-0.29

ANALYSIS BY SUCCESS RATE IN LAST 10 RUNS

Age	Prop	Win	Runs	Wins%	£
No Wins	5%	2	50	4.0%	-0.81
1 Win	13%	5	57	8.8%	-0.36
2 Wins	24%	9	64	14.1%	-0.23
3 Wins	26%	10	55	18.2%	0.16
4 Wins	18%	7	39	17.9%	-0.51
5+ Wins	13%	5	33	15.2%	-0.57

ANALYSIS BY SUCCESS RATE IN LAST 3 RUNS

Age	Prop	Win	Runs	Wins%	£
No Wins	26%	10	140	7.1%	-0.49
1 Win	32%	12	104	11.5%	-0.49
2 Wins	34%	13	42	31.0%	0.50
3 Wins	8%	3	12	25.0%	-0.52

ANALYSIS BY POSITION LAST TIME

Age	Prop	Win	Runs	Wins%	£
Won	38%	15	61	24.6%	0.01
2nd or 3rd	31%	12	72	16.7%	-0.17
Unplaced	21%	8	134	6.0%	-0.57
Fell,BD,UR	5%	2	12	16.7%	-0.29
Pulled Up	3%	1	18	5.6%	-0.75
Ref/RanOut	0%	0	0	0.0%	0.00
CO/SlipUp	0%	0	1	0.0%	-1.00
Unraced	3%	1	14	7.1%	-0.29

OTHER FACTORS (WINS-RUNS, £)

Course Winner:	15-62	£0.21
Distance Winner:	19-111	-£0.24
Going Winner:	24-151	-£0.07
Beaten Favourite:	1-27	-£0.87
BHA Top Rated:	11-30	£0.15
Absolute Favourites:	13-34	-£0.13

Conditions Hurdle Races (class 1..3)

Conditions Hurdle Races (class 1..3): 3m+

ANALYSIS BY AGE

Age	Prop	Win	Runs	Wins%	£
3yo	0%	0	0	0.0%	0.00
4yo	0%	0	5	0.0%	-1.00
5yo	14%	6	44	13.6%	0.39
6yo	40%	17	87	19.5%	-0.08
7yo	21%	9	87	10.3%	-0.50
8yo	12%	5	70	7.1%	-0.79
9yo	9%	4	40	10.0%	-0.40
10yo	2%	1	24	4.2%	-0.54
11yo	2%	1	17	5.9%	-0.24
12yo+	0%	0	7	0.0%	-1.00

ANALYSIS BY BHB RATING

Age	Prop	Win	Runs	Wins%	£
150+	63%	27	188	14.4%	-0.43
130..149	30%	13	124	10.5%	-0.10
120..129	0%	0	10	0.0%	-1.00
110..119	0%	0	10	0.0%	-1.00
100..109	0%	0	3	0.0%	-1.00
80..99	0%	0	2	0.0%	-1.00
60..79	0%	0	1	0.0%	-1.00
..59	0%	0	0	0.0%	0.00
Unrated	7%	3	43	7.0%	-0.36

ANALYSIS BY WEIGHT CARRIED

Age	Prop	Win	Runs	Wins%	£
12-01+	0%	0	0	0.0%	0.00
11-8..12-00	44%	19	154	12.3%	-0.53
11-0..11-07	53%	23	208	11.1%	-0.17
10-8..10-13	2%	1	16	6.3%	-0.84
10-0..10-07	0%	0	3	0.0%	-1.00
..9-13	0%	0	0	0.0%	0.00

ANALYSIS BY DAYS SINCE LAST RUN

Age	Prop	Win	Runs	Wins%	£
1..7	0%	0	12	0.0%	-1.00
8..14	5%	2	17	11.8%	-0.15
15..28	37%	16	142	11.3%	-0.41
29..60	33%	14	122	11.5%	-0.16
61..100	2%	1	19	5.3%	-0.90
101+	23%	10	66	15.2%	-0.34
Unraced	0%	0	3	0.0%	-1.00

ANALYSIS BY TODAY'S STARTING PRICE

Age	Prop	Win	Runs	Wins%	£
Odds On	21%	9	14	64.3%	0.06
Ev-2/1	21%	9	21	42.9%	0.10
9/4-4/1	21%	9	48	18.8%	-0.25
9/2-6/1	7%	3	34	8.8%	-0.44
13/2-10/1	16%	7	56	12.5%	0.18
11/1-16/1	14%	6	64	9.4%	0.38
18/1-33/1	0%	0	73	0.0%	-1.00
40/1+	0%	0	71	0.0%	-1.00

ANALYSIS BY STARTING PRICE LAST TIME

Age	Prop	Win	Runs	Wins%	£
Odds On	16%	7	23	30.4%	-0.12
Ev-2/1	16%	7	33	21.2%	-0.12
9/4-4/1	21%	9	69	13.0%	-0.10
9/2-6/1	12%	5	46	10.9%	-0.34
13/2-10/1	14%	6	66	9.1%	-0.36
11/1-16/1	7%	3	59	5.1%	-0.84
18/1-33/1	7%	3	53	5.7%	-0.57
40/1+	7%	3	29	10.3%	0.07
Unraced	0%	0	3	0.0%	-1.00

ANALYSIS BY DISTANCE BEATEN LAST TIME

Age	Prop	Win	Runs	Wins%	£
..-10 lgh	0%	0	8	0.0%	-1.00
-10..0	40%	17	82	20.7%	-0.20
0.1..2	12%	5	27	18.5%	0.40
2.1..5	9%	4	38	10.5%	-0.26
5.1..10	5%	2	36	5.6%	-0.65
10.1..20	16%	7	64	10.9%	-0.17
20.0..30	2%	1	30	3.3%	-0.90
30.1+	12%	5	66	7.6%	-0.39
Not Compl	5%	2	27	7.4%	-0.73
Unraced	0%	0	3	0.0%	-1.00

ANALYSIS BY SUCCESS RATE IN LAST 10 RUNS

Age	Prop	Win	Runs	Wins%	£
No Wins	7%	3	18	16.7%	1.17
1 Win	7%	3	63	4.8%	-0.74
2 Wins	12%	5	92	5.4%	-0.67
3 Wins	21%	9	89	10.1%	-0.13
4 Wins	12%	5	52	9.6%	-0.46
5+ Wins	42%	18	64	28.1%	-0.12

ANALYSIS BY SUCCESS RATE IN LAST 3 RUNS

Age	Prop	Win	Runs	Wins%	£
No Wins	37%	16	170	9.4%	-0.21
1 Win	23%	10	128	7.8%	-0.60
2 Wins	26%	11	68	16.2%	-0.28
3 Wins	14%	6	12	50.0%	-0.01

ANALYSIS BY POSITION LAST TIME

Age	Prop	Win	Runs	Wins%	£
Won	40%	17	90	18.9%	-0.27
2nd or 3rd	30%	13	100	13.0%	-0.18
Unplaced	26%	11	161	6.8%	-0.43
Fell,BD,UR	5%	2	11	18.2%	-0.34
Pulled Up	0%	0	16	0.0%	-1.00
Ref/RanOut	0%	0	0	0.0%	0.00
CO/SlipUp	0%	0	0	0.0%	0.00
Unraced	0%	0	3	0.0%	-1.00

OTHER FACTORS (WINS-RUNS, £)

Course Winner:	20-155	-£0.37
Distance Winner:	19-189	-£0.60
Going Winner:	33-258	-£0.31
Beaten Favourite:	5-29	£0.39
7-Day Winners:	0-3	-£1.00
BHA Top Rated:	12-34	-£0.22
Absolute Favourites:	19-41	£0.04

Race Profiles

Conditions Hurdle Races (class 1..3): 2 to 5 runners

ANALYSIS BY AGE

Age	Prop	Win	Runs	Wins%	£
3yo	0%	0	0	0.0%	0.00
4yo	9%	2	8	25.0%	-0.58
5yo	4%	1	18	5.6%	-0.86
6yo	39%	9	24	37.5%	-0.17
7yo	30%	7	25	28.0%	0.64
8yo	4%	1	7	14.3%	-0.21
9yo	9%	2	13	15.4%	-0.22
10yo	0%	0	2	0.0%	-1.00
11yo	4%	1	2	50.0%	0.38
12yo+	0%	0	2	0.0%	-1.00

ANALYSIS BY BHB RATING

Age	Prop	Win	Runs	Wins%	£
150+	52%	12	33	36.4%	0.12
130..149	35%	8	27	29.6%	0.04
120..129	0%	0	10	0.0%	-1.00
110..119	4%	1	8	12.5%	0.88
100..109	0%	0	5	0.0%	-1.00
80..99	0%	0	5	0.0%	-1.00
60..79	0%	0	2	0.0%	-1.00
..59	0%	0	0	0.0%	0.00
Unrated	9%	2	11	18.2%	-0.51

ANALYSIS BY WEIGHT CARRIED

Age	Prop	Win	Runs	Wins%	£
12-01+	0%	0	0	0.0%	0.00
11-8..12-00	61%	14	31	45.2%	0.44
11-0..11-07	26%	6	52	11.5%	-0.59
10-8..10-13	13%	3	13	23.1%	0.47
10-0..10-07	0%	0	5	0.0%	-1.00
..9-13	0%	0	0	0.0%	0.00

ANALYSIS BY DAYS SINCE LAST RUN

Age	Prop	Win	Runs	Wins%	£
1..7	4%	1	8	12.5%	-0.82
8..14	13%	3	18	16.7%	-0.26
15..28	17%	4	28	14.3%	-0.70
29..60	35%	8	24	33.3%	-0.19
61..100	0%	0	4	0.0%	-1.00
101+	30%	7	17	41.2%	1.51
Unraced	0%	0	2	0.0%	-1.00

ANALYSIS BY TODAY'S STARTING PRICE

Age	Prop	Win	Runs	Wins%	£
Odds On	39%	9	14	64.3%	-0.06
Ev-2/1	30%	7	20	35.0%	-0.06
9/4-4/1	13%	3	16	18.8%	-0.27
9/2-6/1	4%	1	5	20.0%	0.10
13/2-10/1	4%	1	13	7.7%	-0.38
11/1-16/1	9%	2	10	20.0%	1.80
18/1-33/1	0%	0	10	0.0%	-1.00
40/1+	0%	0	13	0.0%	-1.00

ANALYSIS BY STARTING PRICE LAST TIME

Age	Prop	Win	Runs	Wins%	£
Odds On	13%	3	7	42.9%	-0.19
Ev-2/1	22%	5	11	45.5%	-0.22
9/4-4/1	13%	3	12	25.0%	-0.46
9/2-6/1	4%	1	7	14.3%	-0.81
13/2-10/1	17%	4	14	28.6%	0.04
11/1-16/1	13%	3	17	17.6%	0.53
18/1-33/1	17%	4	18	22.2%	0.26
40/1+	0%	0	13	0.0%	-1.00
Unraced	0%	0	2	0.0%	-1.00

ANALYSIS BY DISTANCE BEATEN LAST TIME

Age	Prop	Win	Runs	Wins%	£
..-10 lgh	9%	2	4	50.0%	-0.22
-10..0	22%	5	21	23.8%	-0.54
0.1..2	9%	2	6	33.3%	-0.52
2.1..5	9%	2	8	25.0%	-0.40
5.1..10	22%	5	14	35.7%	0.13
10.1..20	9%	2	14	14.3%	-0.61
20.0..30	0%	0	10	0.0%	-1.00
30.1+	17%	4	13	30.8%	2.12
Not Compl	4%	1	9	11.1%	-0.68
Unraced	0%	0	2	0.0%	-1.00

ANALYSIS BY SUCCESS RATE IN LAST 10 RUNS

Age	Prop	Win	Runs	Wins%	£
No Wins	0%	0	11	0.0%	-1.00
1 Win	22%	5	20	25.0%	-0.09
2 Wins	17%	4	26	15.4%	-0.53
3 Wins	17%	4	19	21.1%	0.34
4 Wins	17%	4	15	26.7%	0.28
5+ Wins	26%	6	8	75.0%	0.26

ANALYSIS BY SUCCESS RATE IN LAST 3 RUNS

Age	Prop	Win	Runs	Wins%	£
No Wins	35%	8	42	19.0%	-0.32
1 Win	22%	5	36	13.9%	-0.61
2 Wins	35%	8	18	44.4%	1.19
3 Wins	9%	2	3	66.7%	0.01

ANALYSIS BY POSITION LAST TIME

Age	Prop	Win	Runs	Wins%	£
Won	30%	7	25	28.0%	-0.49
2nd or 3rd	26%	6	19	31.6%	-0.36
Unplaced	39%	9	46	19.6%	0.25
Fell,BD,UR	4%	1	5	20.0%	-0.42
Pulled Up	0%	0	4	0.0%	-1.00
Ref/RanOut	0%	0	0	0.0%	0.00
CO/SlipUp	0%	0	0	0.0%	0.00
Unraced	0%	0	2	0.0%	-1.00

OTHER FACTORS (WINS-RUNS, £)

Course Winner:	6-27	-£0.32
Distance Winner:	14-55	-£0.05
Going Winner:	16-53	£0.27
Beaten Favourite:	3-5	£0.40
7-Day Winners:	1-1	£0.44
BHA Top Rated:	11-21	-£0.10
Absolute Favourites:	13-22	£0.05

Conditions Hurdle Races (class 1..3)

Conditions Hurdle Races (class 1..3): 6 to 10 runners

ANALYSIS BY AGE

Age	Prop	Win	Runs	Wins%	£
3yo	0%	0	0	0.0%	0.00
4yo	10%	10	101	9.9%	-0.47
5yo	27%	28	172	16.3%	-0.07
6yo	29%	30	161	18.6%	0.14
7yo	14%	14	127	11.0%	-0.37
8yo	11%	11	98	11.2%	-0.59
9yo	5%	5	58	8.6%	-0.65
10yo	3%	3	26	11.5%	0.58
11yo	1%	1	20	5.0%	-0.35
12yo+	1%	1	16	6.3%	-0.19

ANALYSIS BY BHB RATING

Age	Prop	Win	Runs	Wins%	£
150+	42%	43	239	18.0%	-0.26
130..149	28%	29	241	12.0%	-0.02
120..129	6%	6	35	17.1%	0.35
110..119	1%	1	38	2.6%	-0.95
100..109	1%	1	9	11.1%	-0.22
80..99	0%	0	14	0.0%	-1.00
60..79	0%	0	4	0.0%	-1.00
..59	0%	0	0	0.0%	0.00
Unrated	22%	23	199	11.6%	-0.32

ANALYSIS BY WEIGHT CARRIED

Age	Prop	Win	Runs	Wins%	£
12-01+	0%	0	0	0.0%	0.00
11-8..12-00	24%	25	144	17.4%	-0.29
11-0..11-07	69%	71	541	13.1%	-0.16
10-8..10-13	7%	7	65	10.8%	-0.27
10-0..10-07	0%	0	29	0.0%	-1.00
..9-13	0%	0	0	0.0%	0.00

ANALYSIS BY DAYS SINCE LAST RUN

Age	Prop	Win	Runs	Wins%	£
1..7	2%	2	23	8.7%	-0.70
8..14	11%	11	80	13.8%	-0.29
15..28	32%	33	259	12.7%	-0.26
29..60	24%	25	183	13.7%	-0.04
61..100	4%	4	32	12.5%	-0.51
101+	25%	26	165	15.8%	-0.13
Unraced	2%	2	37	5.4%	-0.61

ANALYSIS BY TODAY'S STARTING PRICE

Age	Prop	Win	Runs	Wins%	£
Odds On	20%	21	35	60.0%	-0.04
Ev-2/1	17%	17	54	31.5%	-0.21
9/4-4/1	26%	27	122	22.1%	-0.12
9/2-6/1	9%	9	76	11.8%	-0.28
13/2-10/1	17%	17	131	13.0%	0.19
11/1-16/1	9%	9	116	7.8%	0.11
18/1-33/1	3%	3	114	2.6%	-0.29
40/1+	0%	0	131	0.0%	-1.00

ANALYSIS BY STARTING PRICE LAST TIME

Age	Prop	Win	Runs	Wins%	£
Odds On	13%	13	43	30.2%	0.06
Ev-2/1	11%	11	71	15.5%	-0.31
9/4-4/1	17%	17	126	13.5%	-0.37
9/2-6/1	11%	11	81	13.6%	-0.35
13/2-10/1	19%	20	127	15.7%	0.07
11/1-16/1	13%	13	121	10.7%	-0.38
18/1-33/1	10%	10	104	9.6%	-0.06
40/1+	6%	6	69	8.7%	-0.20
Unraced	2%	2	37	5.4%	-0.61

ANALYSIS BY DISTANCE BEATEN LAST TIME

Age	Prop	Win	Runs	Wins%	£
..-10 lgh	2%	2	19	10.5%	0.04
-10..0	35%	36	149	24.2%	0.06
0.1..2	6%	6	51	11.8%	-0.25
2.1..5	12%	12	65	18.5%	-0.22
5.1..10	11%	11	85	12.9%	-0.39
10.1..20	13%	13	123	10.6%	-0.23
20.0..30	5%	5	61	8.2%	-0.33
30.1+	9%	9	120	7.5%	-0.43
Not Compl	7%	7	69	10.1%	-0.03
Unraced	2%	2	37	5.4%	-0.61

ANALYSIS BY SUCCESS RATE IN LAST 10 RUNS

Age	Prop	Win	Runs	Wins%	£
No Wins	8%	8	103	7.8%	-0.34
1 Win	16%	16	163	9.8%	-0.29
2 Wins	25%	25	167	15.0%	0.00
3 Wins	21%	21	141	14.9%	-0.16
4 Wins	12%	12	85	14.1%	-0.40
5+ Wins	19%	19	83	22.9%	-0.17

ANALYSIS BY SUCCESS RATE IN LAST 3 RUNS

Age	Prop	Win	Runs	Wins%	£
No Wins	34%	34	339	10.0%	-0.27
1 Win	42%	42	283	14.8%	-0.07
2 Wins	16%	16	96	16.7%	-0.37
3 Wins	9%	9	24	37.5%	-0.24

ANALYSIS BY POSITION LAST TIME

Age	Prop	Win	Runs	Wins%	£
Won	37%	38	168	22.6%	0.06
2nd or 3rd	29%	30	187	16.0%	-0.11
Unplaced	25%	26	318	8.2%	-0.44
Fell,BD,UR	6%	6	36	16.7%	0.74
Pulled Up	1%	1	32	3.1%	-0.86
Ref/RanOut	0%	0	0	0.0%	0.00
CO/SlipUp	0%	0	1	0.0%	-1.00
Unraced	2%	2	37	5.4%	-0.61

OTHER FACTORS (WINS-RUNS, £)

Course Winner:	35-194	-£0.04
Distance Winner:	64-436	-£0.20
Going Winner:	66-418	-£0.05
Beaten Favourite:	9-70	-£0.64
7-Day Winners:	1-7	-£0.57
BHA Top Rated:	25-73	£0.13
Absolute Favourites:	40-91	-£0.08

Race Profiles

Conditions Hurdle Races (class 1..3): 11 runners or more

ANALYSIS BY AGE

Age	Prop	Win	Runs	Wins%	£
3yo	0%	0	0	0.0%	0.00
4yo	8%	2	28	7.1%	-0.63
5yo	29%	7	64	10.9%	0.11
6yo	38%	9	80	11.3%	-0.10
7yo	8%	2	73	2.7%	-0.80
8yo	8%	2	44	4.5%	-0.80
9yo	8%	2	26	7.7%	-0.33
10yo	0%	0	17	0.0%	-1.00
11yo	0%	0	11	0.0%	-1.00
12yo+	0%	0	7	0.0%	-1.00

ANALYSIS BY BHB RATING

Age	Prop	Win	Runs	Wins%	£
150+	58%	14	165	8.5%	-0.44
130..149	8%	2	78	2.6%	-0.69
120..129	4%	1	16	6.3%	0.31
110..119	0%	0	6	0.0%	-1.00
100..109	0%	0	1	0.0%	-1.00
80..99	0%	0	1	0.0%	-1.00
60..79	0%	0	0	0.0%	0.00
..59	0%	0	0	0.0%	0.00
Unrated	29%	7	83	8.4%	-0.31

ANALYSIS BY WEIGHT CARRIED

Age	Prop	Win	Runs	Wins%	£
12-01+	0%	0	0	0.0%	0.00
11-8..12-00	46%	11	158	7.0%	-0.48
11-0..11-07	50%	12	178	6.7%	-0.39
10-8..10-13	4%	1	8	12.5%	-0.56
10-0..10-07	0%	0	6	0.0%	-1.00
..9-13	0%	0	0	0.0%	0.00

ANALYSIS BY DAYS SINCE LAST RUN

Age	Prop	Win	Runs	Wins%	£
1..7	0%	0	4	0.0%	-1.00
8..14	0%	0	8	0.0%	-1.00
15..28	33%	8	104	7.7%	-0.19
29..60	46%	11	138	8.0%	-0.40
61..100	4%	1	40	2.5%	-0.95
101+	13%	3	40	7.5%	-0.54
Unraced	4%	1	16	6.3%	-0.50

ANALYSIS BY TODAY'S STARTING PRICE

Age	Prop	Win	Runs	Wins%	£
Odds On	4%	1	2	50.0%	-0.08
Ev-2/1	21%	5	14	35.7%	-0.03
9/4-4/1	13%	3	22	13.6%	-0.49
9/2-6/1	21%	5	21	23.8%	0.57
13/2-10/1	21%	5	49	10.2%	-0.06
11/1-16/1	13%	3	56	5.4%	-0.20
18/1-33/1	8%	2	77	2.6%	-0.43
40/1+	0%	0	109	0.0%	-1.00

ANALYSIS BY STARTING PRICE LAST TIME

Age	Prop	Win	Runs	Wins%	£
Odds On	21%	5	34	14.7%	0.02
Ev-2/1	25%	6	32	18.8%	0.64
9/4-4/1	21%	5	66	7.6%	-0.22
9/2-6/1	8%	2	27	7.4%	-0.65
13/2-10/1	13%	3	61	4.9%	-0.72
11/1-16/1	8%	2	54	3.7%	-0.61
18/1-33/1	0%	0	41	0.0%	-1.00
40/1+	0%	0	19	0.0%	-1.00
Unraced	4%	1	16	6.3%	-0.50

ANALYSIS BY DISTANCE BEATEN LAST TIME

Age	Prop	Win	Runs	Wins%	£
..-10 lgh	0%	0	8	0.0%	-1.00
-10..0	46%	11	73	15.1%	0.08
0.1..2	13%	3	32	9.4%	-0.16
2.1..5	17%	4	35	11.4%	-0.42
5.1..10	0%	0	23	0.0%	-1.00
10.1..20	17%	4	56	7.1%	0.02
20..30	0%	0	36	0.0%	-1.00
30.1+	0%	0	44	0.0%	-1.00
Not Compl	4%	1	27	3.7%	-0.87
Unraced	4%	1	16	6.3%	-0.50

ANALYSIS BY SUCCESS RATE IN LAST 10 RUNS

Age	Prop	Win	Runs	Wins%	£
No Wins	4%	1	45	2.2%	-0.84
1 Win	9%	2	45	4.4%	-0.74
2 Wins	9%	2	59	3.4%	-0.68
3 Wins	30%	7	77	9.1%	0.17
4 Wins	9%	2	51	3.9%	-0.90
5+ Wins	39%	9	57	15.8%	-0.05

ANALYSIS BY SUCCESS RATE IN LAST 3 RUNS

Age	Prop	Win	Runs	Wins%	£
No Wins	30%	7	151	4.6%	-0.55
1 Win	22%	5	111	4.5%	-0.50
2 Wins	43%	10	60	16.7%	0.03
3 Wins	4%	1	12	8.3%	-0.85

ANALYSIS BY POSITION LAST TIME

Age	Prop	Win	Runs	Wins%	£
Won	46%	11	81	13.6%	-0.03
2nd or 3rd	33%	8	90	8.9%	-0.22
Unplaced	13%	3	136	2.2%	-0.75
Fell,BD,UR	4%	1	10	10.0%	-0.65
Pulled Up	0%	0	17	0.0%	-1.00
Ref/RanOut	0%	0	0	0.0%	0.00
CO/SlipUp	0%	0	0	0.0%	0.00
Unraced	4%	1	16	6.3%	-0.50

OTHER FACTORS (WINS-RUNS, £)

Course Winner:	10-118	-£0.45
Distance Winner:	14-182	-£0.42
Going Winner:	17-201	-£0.28
Beaten Favourite:	4-34	£0.73
7-Day Winners:	0-1	-£1.00
BHA Top Rated:	3-19	-£0.62
Absolute Favourites:	8-24	-£0.04

Conditions Hurdle Races (class 1..3)

Conditions Hurdle Races (class 1..3): up to 7 days off the track

ANALYSIS BY AGE

Age	Prop	Win	Runs	Wins%	£
3yo	0%	0	0	0.0%	0.00
4yo	0%	0	29	0.0%	-1.00
5yo	50%	3	19	15.8%	-0.19
6yo	50%	3	17	17.6%	-0.09
7yo	0%	0	9	0.0%	-1.00
8yo	0%	0	7	0.0%	-1.00
9yo	0%	0	4	0.0%	-1.00
10yo	0%	0	3	0.0%	-1.00
11yo	0%	0	2	0.0%	-1.00
12yo+	0%	0	0	0.0%	0.00

ANALYSIS BY BHB RATING

Age	Prop	Win	Runs	Wins%	£
150+	17%	1	15	6.7%	-0.73
130..149	33%	2	13	15.4%	-0.66
120..129	0%	0	4	0.0%	-1.00
110..119	0%	0	5	0.0%	-1.00
100..109	0%	0	2	0.0%	-1.00
80..99	0%	0	1	0.0%	-1.00
60..79	0%	0	1	0.0%	-1.00
..59	0%	0	0	0.0%	0.00
Unrated	50%	3	49	6.1%	-0.54

ANALYSIS BY WEIGHT CARRIED

Age	Prop	Win	Runs	Wins%	£
12-01+	0%	0	0	0.0%	0.00
11-8..12-00	33%	2	14	14.3%	-0.68
11-0..11-07	67%	4	64	6.3%	-0.59
10-8..10-13	0%	0	9	0.0%	-1.00
10-0..10-07	0%	0	3	0.0%	-1.00
..9-13	0%	0	0	0.0%	0.00

ANALYSIS BY DAYS SINCE LAST RUN

Age	Prop	Win	Runs	Wins%	£
1..7	50%	3	35	8.6%	-0.76
8..14	0%	0	0	0.0%	0.00
15..28	0%	0	0	0.0%	0.00
29..60	0%	0	0	0.0%	0.00
61..100	0%	0	0	0.0%	0.00
101+	0%	0	0	0.0%	0.00
Unraced	50%	3	55	5.5%	-0.59

ANALYSIS BY TODAY'S STARTING PRICE

Age	Prop	Win	Runs	Wins%	£
Odds On	17%	1	1	100.0%	0.44
Ev-2/1	17%	1	5	20.0%	-0.40
9/4-4/1	33%	2	9	22.2%	-0.07
9/2-6/1	0%	0	1	0.0%	-1.00
13/2-10/1	33%	2	16	12.5%	0.13
11/1-16/1	0%	0	13	0.0%	-1.00
18/1-33/1	0%	0	14	0.0%	-1.00
40/1+	0%	0	31	0.0%	-1.00

ANALYSIS BY STARTING PRICE LAST TIME

Age	Prop	Win	Runs	Wins%	£
Odds On	17%	1	1	100.0%	0.44
Ev-2/1	0%	0	1	0.0%	-1.00
9/4-4/1	17%	1	5	20.0%	-0.40
9/2-6/1	0%	0	7	0.0%	-1.00
13/2-10/1	0%	0	5	0.0%	-1.00
11/1-16/1	17%	1	4	25.0%	0.00
18/1-33/1	0%	0	8	0.0%	-1.00
40/1+	0%	0	4	0.0%	-1.00
Unraced	50%	3	55	5.5%	-0.59

ANALYSIS BY DISTANCE BEATEN LAST TIME

Age	Prop	Win	Runs	Wins%	£
..-10 lgh	17%	1	2	50.0%	-0.28
-10..0	17%	1	7	14.3%	-0.57
0.1..2	0%	0	2	0.0%	-1.00
2.1..5	0%	0	6	0.0%	-1.00
5.1..10	0%	0	2	0.0%	-1.00
10.1..20	17%	1	4	25.0%	0.00
20.0..30	0%	0	1	0.0%	-1.00
30.1+	0%	0	7	0.0%	-1.00
Not Compl	0%	0	4	0.0%	-1.00
Unraced	50%	3	55	5.5%	-0.59

ANALYSIS BY SUCCESS RATE IN LAST 10 RUNS

Age	Prop	Win	Runs	Wins%	£
No Wins	0%	0	7	0.0%	-1.00
1 Win	33%	1	7	14.3%	-0.43
2 Wins	0%	0	5	0.0%	-1.00
3 Wins	33%	1	11	9.1%	-0.73
4 Wins	0%	0	2	0.0%	-1.00
5+ Wins	33%	1	3	33.3%	-0.52

ANALYSIS BY SUCCESS RATE IN LAST 3 RUNS

Age	Prop	Win	Runs	Wins%	£
No Wins	33%	1	20	5.0%	-0.80
1 Win	33%	1	9	11.1%	-0.67
2 Wins	33%	1	4	25.0%	-0.64
3 Wins	0%	0	2	0.0%	-1.00

ANALYSIS BY POSITION LAST TIME

Age	Prop	Win	Runs	Wins%	£
Won	33%	2	9	22.2%	-0.51
2nd or 3rd	0%	0	7	0.0%	-1.00
Unplaced	17%	1	15	6.7%	-0.73
Fell,BD,UR	0%	0	4	0.0%	-1.00
Pulled Up	0%	0	0	0.0%	0.00
Ref/RanOut	0%	0	0	0.0%	0.00
CO/SlipUp	0%	0	0	0.0%	0.00
Unraced	50%	3	55	5.5%	-0.59

OTHER FACTORS (WINS-RUNS, £)

Course Winner:	1-12	-£0.88
Distance Winner:	2-22	-£0.68
Going Winner:	2-20	-£0.78
Beaten Favourite:	0-2	-£1.00
7-Day Winners:	2-9	-£0.51
BHA Top Rated:	2-3	£0.81
Absolute Favourites:	2-3	£0.48

Race Profiles

Conditions Hurdle Races (class 1..3): 100+ days off the track

ANALYSIS BY AGE

Age	Prop	Win	Runs	Wins%	£
3yo	0%	0	0	0.0%	0.00
4yo	8%	3	21	14.3%	0.35
5yo	22%	8	49	16.3%	-0.47
6yo	17%	6	44	13.6%	-0.53
7yo	19%	7	39	17.9%	0.31
8yo	14%	5	23	21.7%	-0.08
9yo	8%	3	22	13.6%	-0.43
10yo	6%	2	10	20.0%	2.00
11yo	6%	2	9	22.2%	0.75
12yo+	0%	0	5	0.0%	-1.00

ANALYSIS BY BHB RATING

Age	Prop	Win	Runs	Wins%	£
150+	44%	16	59	27.1%	-0.18
130..149	19%	7	62	11.3%	0.13
120..129	3%	1	11	9.1%	-0.80
110..119	3%	1	13	7.7%	0.15
100..109	0%	0	0	0.0%	0.00
80..99	0%	0	4	0.0%	-1.00
60..79	0%	0	1	0.0%	-1.00
..59	0%	0	0	0.0%	0.00
Unrated	31%	11	72	15.3%	-0.03

ANALYSIS BY WEIGHT CARRIED

Age	Prop	Win	Runs	Wins%	£
12-01+	0%	0	0	0.0%	0.00
11-8..12-00	31%	11	54	20.4%	-0.37
11-0..11-07	61%	22	143	15.4%	-0.03
10-8..10-13	8%	3	17	17.6%	0.90
10-0..10-07	0%	0	8	0.0%	-1.00
..9-13	0%	0	0	0.0%	0.00

ANALYSIS BY DAYS SINCE LAST RUN

Age	Prop	Win	Runs	Wins%	£
1..7	0%	0	0	0.0%	0.00
8..14	0%	0	0	0.0%	0.00
15..28	0%	0	0	0.0%	0.00
29..60	0%	0	0	0.0%	0.00
61..100	0%	0	0	0.0%	0.00
101+	100%	36	222	16.2%	-0.07
Unraced	0%	0	0	0.0%	0.00

ANALYSIS BY TODAY'S STARTING PRICE

Age	Prop	Win	Runs	Wins%	£
Odds On	14%	5	9	55.6%	-0.10
Ev-2/1	31%	11	20	55.0%	0.38
9/4-4/1	22%	8	38	21.1%	-0.19
9/2-6/1	8%	3	20	15.0%	-0.13
13/2-10/1	8%	3	31	9.7%	-0.15
11/1-16/1	14%	5	33	15.2%	1.09
18/1-33/1	3%	1	33	3.0%	-0.21
40/1+	0%	0	38	0.0%	-1.00

ANALYSIS BY STARTING PRICE LAST TIME

Age	Prop	Win	Runs	Wins%	£
Odds On	14%	5	16	31.3%	-0.40
Ev-2/1	11%	4	21	19.0%	-0.55
9/4-4/1	17%	6	40	15.0%	-0.44
9/2-6/1	6%	2	17	11.8%	-0.31
13/2-10/1	19%	7	36	19.4%	-0.22
11/1-16/1	14%	5	37	13.5%	0.09
18/1-33/1	14%	5	41	12.2%	0.49
40/1+	6%	2	14	14.3%	0.64
Unraced	0%	0	0	0.0%	0.00

ANALYSIS BY DISTANCE BEATEN LAST TIME

Age	Prop	Win	Runs	Wins%	£
..-10 lgh	0%	0	6	0.0%	-1.00
-10..0	28%	10	39	25.6%	-0.12
0.1..2	6%	2	11	18.2%	-0.55
2.1..5	8%	3	19	15.8%	-0.56
5.1..10	17%	6	21	28.6%	-0.04
10.1..20	14%	5	39	12.8%	-0.23
20.0..30	3%	1	20	5.0%	-0.86
30.1+	17%	6	46	13.0%	0.33
Not Compl	8%	3	21	14.3%	1.09
Unraced	0%	0	0	0.0%	0.00

ANALYSIS BY SUCCESS RATE IN LAST 10 RUNS

Age	Prop	Win	Runs	Wins%	£
No Wins	8%	3	34	8.8%	-0.07
1 Win	14%	5	51	9.8%	-0.15
2 Wins	17%	6	42	14.3%	-0.22
3 Wins	33%	12	47	25.5%	0.22
4 Wins	11%	4	23	17.4%	0.21
5+ Wins	17%	6	25	24.0%	-0.47

ANALYSIS BY SUCCESS RATE IN LAST 3 RUNS

Age	Prop	Win	Runs	Wins%	£
No Wins	39%	14	98	14.3%	0.08
1 Win	31%	11	81	13.6%	-0.40
2 Wins	19%	7	38	18.4%	0.08
3 Wins	11%	4	5	80.0%	1.00

ANALYSIS BY POSITION LAST TIME

Age	Prop	Win	Runs	Wins%	£
Won	28%	10	45	22.2%	-0.24
2nd or 3rd	28%	10	49	20.4%	-0.44
Unplaced	36%	13	107	12.1%	-0.07
Fell,BD,UR	8%	3	12	25.0%	2.66
Pulled Up	0%	0	9	0.0%	-1.00
Ref/RanOut	0%	0	0	0.0%	0.00
CO/SlipUp	0%	0	0	0.0%	0.00
Unraced	0%	0	0	0.0%	0.00

OTHER FACTORS (WINS-RUNS, £)

Course Winner:	13-57	£0.10
Distance Winner:	23-109	£0.13
Going Winner:	21-113	£0.14
Beaten Favourite:	4-27	-£0.63
BHA Top Rated:	8-17	£0.13
Absolute Favourites:	16-29	£0.25

Conditions Hurdle Races (class 4..6)

ANALYSIS BY AGE

Age	Prop	Win	Runs	Wins%	£
3yo	0%	0	0	0.0%	0.00
4yo	16%	5	50	10.0%	-0.29
5yo	22%	7	71	9.9%	-0.49
6yo	28%	9	61	14.8%	-0.44
7yo	25%	8	53	15.1%	0.16
8yo	9%	3	25	12.0%	-0.45
9yo	0%	0	19	0.0%	-1.00
10yo	0%	0	11	0.0%	-1.00
11yo	0%	0	7	0.0%	-1.00
12yo+	0%	0	1	0.0%	-1.00

ANALYSIS BY BHB RATING

Age	Prop	Win	Runs	Wins%	£
150+	3%	1	5	20.0%	-0.60
130..149	3%	1	2	50.0%	-0.19
120..129	9%	3	8	37.5%	0.47
110..119	13%	4	19	21.1%	-0.45
100..109	13%	4	16	25.0%	0.26
80..99	41%	13	134	9.7%	-0.25
60..79	0%	0	28	0.0%	-1.00
..59	0%	0	2	0.0%	-1.00
Unrated	19%	6	84	7.1%	-0.58

ANALYSIS BY WEIGHT CARRIED

Age	Prop	Win	Runs	Wins%	£
12-01+	0%	0	0	0.0%	0.00
11-8..12-00	9%	3	10	30.0%	-0.34
11-0..11-07	53%	17	100	17.0%	-0.19
10-8..10-13	28%	9	118	7.6%	-0.37
10-0..10-07	9%	3	67	4.5%	-0.71
..9-13	0%	0	3	0.0%	-1.00

ANALYSIS BY DAYS SINCE LAST RUN

Age	Prop	Win	Runs	Wins%	£
1..7	9%	3	21	14.3%	-0.31
8..14	22%	7	34	20.6%	0.48
15..28	38%	12	85	14.1%	-0.20
29..60	16%	5	68	7.4%	-0.55
61..100	6%	2	27	7.4%	-0.66
101+	9%	3	52	5.8%	-0.84
Unraced	0%	0	11	0.0%	-1.00

ANALYSIS BY TODAY'S STARTING PRICE

Age	Prop	Win	Runs	Wins%	£
Odds On	16%	5	13	38.5%	-0.43
Ev-2/1	28%	9	15	60.0%	0.52
9/4-4/1	13%	4	29	13.8%	-0.42
9/2-6/1	13%	4	30	13.3%	-0.13
13/2-10/1	22%	7	46	15.2%	0.23
11/1-16/1	6%	2	34	5.9%	-0.24
18/1-33/1	3%	1	48	2.1%	-0.46
40/1+	0%	0	83	0.0%	-1.00

ANALYSIS BY STARTING PRICE LAST TIME

Age	Prop	Win	Runs	Wins%	£
Odds On	9%	3	5	60.0%	0.04
Ev-2/1	9%	3	12	25.0%	-0.44
9/4-4/1	19%	6	21	28.6%	0.28
9/2-6/1	9%	3	23	13.0%	-0.11
13/2-10/1	19%	6	32	18.8%	0.05
11/1-16/1	13%	4	50	8.0%	-0.44
18/1-33/1	19%	6	62	9.7%	-0.44
40/1+	3%	1	82	1.2%	-0.68
Unraced	0%	0	11	0.0%	-1.00

ANALYSIS BY DISTANCE BEATEN LAST TIME

Age	Prop	Win	Runs	Wins%	£
..-10 lgh	6%	2	4	50.0%	1.09
-10..0	19%	6	14	42.9%	1.12
0.1..2	0%	0	8	0.0%	-1.00
2.1..5	9%	3	15	20.0%	-0.21
5.1..10	9%	3	18	16.7%	0.00
10.1..20	9%	3	42	7.1%	-0.68
20.0..30	13%	4	27	14.8%	0.91
30.1+	19%	6	91	6.6%	-0.70
Not Compl	16%	5	68	7.4%	-0.68
Unraced	0%	0	11	0.0%	-1.00

ANALYSIS BY SUCCESS RATE IN LAST 10 RUNS

Age	Prop	Win	Runs	Wins%	£
No Wins	38%	12	183	6.6%	-0.48
1 Win	31%	10	70	14.3%	-0.15
2 Wins	16%	5	20	25.0%	-0.12
3 Wins	3%	1	7	14.3%	-0.81
4 Wins	9%	3	4	75.0%	0.23
5+ Wins	3%	1	3	33.3%	0.33

ANALYSIS BY SUCCESS RATE IN LAST 3 RUNS

Age	Prop	Win	Runs	Wins%	£
No Wins	63%	20	235	8.5%	-0.45
1 Win	25%	8	42	19.0%	0.08
2 Wins	9%	3	9	33.3%	-0.27
3 Wins	3%	1	1	100.0%	0.36

ANALYSIS BY POSITION LAST TIME

Age	Prop	Win	Runs	Wins%	£
Won	25%	8	18	44.4%	1.11
2nd or 3rd	9%	3	37	8.1%	-0.68
Unplaced	50%	16	165	9.7%	-0.33
Fell,BD,UR	6%	2	16	12.5%	-0.80
Pulled Up	3%	1	47	2.1%	-0.83
Ref/RanOut	6%	2	4	50.0%	1.59
CO/SlipUp	0%	0	0	0.0%	0.00
Unraced	0%	0	11	0.0%	-1.00

OTHER FACTORS (WINS-RUNS, £)

Course Winner:	6-26	-£0.14
Distance Winner:	10-45	-£0.19
Going Winner:	7-50	-£0.39
Beaten Favourite:	4-10	£0.57
7-Day Winners:	1-2	£0.25
BHA Top Rated:	7-31	-£0.57
Absolute Favourites:	12-30	-£0.18

Race Profiles

Conditions Hurdle Races (class 4..6): 2m to 2m3f

ANALYSIS BY AGE

Age	Prop	Win	Runs	Wins%	£
3yo	0%	0	0	0.0%	0.00
4yo	19%	4	41	9.8%	-0.21
5yo	29%	6	57	10.5%	-0.41
6yo	24%	5	36	13.9%	-0.44
7yo	14%	3	39	7.7%	-0.38
8yo	14%	3	11	27.3%	0.26
9yo	0%	0	9	0.0%	-1.00
10yo	0%	0	5	0.0%	-1.00
11yo	0%	0	2	0.0%	-1.00
12yo+	0%	0	0	0.0%	0.00

ANALYSIS BY BHB RATING

Age	Prop	Win	Runs	Wins%	£
150+	5%	1	5	20.0%	-0.60
130..149	5%	1	2	50.0%	-0.19
120..129	14%	3	6	50.0%	0.97
110..119	5%	1	8	12.5%	-0.75
100..109	10%	2	11	18.2%	-0.13
80..99	43%	9	85	10.6%	-0.17
60..79	0%	0	18	0.0%	-1.00
..59	0%	0	2	0.0%	-1.00
Unrated	19%	4	63	6.3%	-0.58

ANALYSIS BY WEIGHT CARRIED

Age	Prop	Win	Runs	Wins%	£
12-01+	0%	0	0	0.0%	0.00
11-8..12-00	5%	1	5	20.0%	-0.50
11-0..11-07	57%	12	53	22.6%	0.09
10-8..10-13	29%	6	88	6.8%	-0.40
10-0..10-07	10%	2	51	3.9%	-0.78
..9-13	0%	0	3	0.0%	-1.00

ANALYSIS BY DAYS SINCE LAST RUN

Age	Prop	Win	Runs	Wins%	£
1..7	14%	3	15	20.0%	-0.03
8..14	19%	4	22	18.2%	0.29
15..28	33%	7	48	14.6%	-0.05
29..60	19%	4	47	8.5%	-0.53
61..100	10%	2	22	9.1%	-0.59
101+	5%	1	35	2.9%	-0.89
Unraced	0%	0	11	0.0%	-1.00

ANALYSIS BY TODAY'S STARTING PRICE

Age	Prop	Win	Runs	Wins%	£
Odds On	19%	4	10	40.0%	-0.42
Ev-2/1	19%	4	4	100.0%	1.38
9/4-4/1	19%	4	22	18.2%	-0.24
9/2-6/1	10%	2	22	9.1%	-0.41
13/2-10/1	24%	5	33	15.2%	0.21
11/1-16/1	5%	1	21	4.8%	-0.38
18/1-33/1	5%	1	31	3.2%	-0.16
40/1+	0%	0	57	0.0%	-1.00

ANALYSIS BY STARTING PRICE LAST TIME

Age	Prop	Win	Runs	Wins%	£
Odds On	10%	2	3	66.7%	0.21
Ev-2/1	10%	2	9	22.2%	-0.49
9/4-4/1	10%	2	9	22.2%	-0.50
9/2-6/1	5%	1	11	9.1%	-0.59
13/2-10/1	24%	5	22	22.7%	0.41
11/1-16/1	14%	3	36	8.3%	-0.39
18/1-33/1	24%	5	40	12.5%	-0.30
40/1+	5%	1	59	1.7%	-0.56
Unraced	0%	0	11	0.0%	-1.00

ANALYSIS BY DISTANCE BEATEN LAST TIME

Age	Prop	Win	Runs	Wins%	£
..-10 lgh	5%	1	2	50.0%	-0.32
-10..0	14%	3	7	42.9%	1.50
0.1..2	0%	0	6	0.0%	-1.00
2.1..5	10%	2	7	28.6%	0.29
5.1..10	10%	2	12	16.7%	0.25
10.1..20	10%	2	32	6.3%	-0.66
20.0..30	14%	3	20	15.0%	0.93
30.1+	24%	5	63	7.9%	-0.67
Not Compl	14%	3	40	7.5%	-0.73
Unraced	0%	0	11	0.0%	-1.00

ANALYSIS BY SUCCESS RATE IN LAST 10 RUNS

Age	Prop	Win	Runs	Wins%	£
No Wins	43%	9	130	6.9%	-0.42
1 Win	24%	5	40	12.5%	-0.31
2 Wins	14%	3	10	30.0%	0.21
3 Wins	5%	1	3	33.3%	-0.57
4 Wins	10%	2	3	66.7%	0.12
5+ Wins	5%	1	3	33.3%	0.33

ANALYSIS BY SUCCESS RATE IN LAST 3 RUNS

Age	Prop	Win	Runs	Wins%	£
No Wins	67%	14	159	8.8%	-0.42
1 Win	24%	5	24	20.8%	0.16
2 Wins	5%	1	5	20.0%	-0.60
3 Wins	5%	1	1	100.0%	0.36

ANALYSIS BY POSITION LAST TIME

Age	Prop	Win	Runs	Wins%	£
Won	19%	4	9	44.4%	1.10
2nd or 3rd	10%	2	25	8.0%	-0.64
Unplaced	57%	12	116	10.3%	-0.26
Fell,BD,UR	10%	2	8	25.0%	-0.60
Pulled Up	0%	0	28	0.0%	-1.00
Ref/RanOut	5%	1	3	33.3%	1.50
CO/SlipUp	0%	0	0	0.0%	0.00
Unraced	0%	0	11	0.0%	-1.00

OTHER FACTORS (WINS-RUNS, £)

Course Winner:	4-13	-£0.05
Distance Winner:	7-31	-£0.16
Going Winner:	6-31	-£0.06
Beaten Favourite:	2-4	£0.22
7-Day Winners:	1-1	£1.50
BHA Top Rated:	5-22	-£0.64
Absolute Favourites:	8-19	-£0.18

Conditions Hurdle Races (class 4..6)

Conditions Hurdle Races (class 4..6): 2m4f to 2m7f

ANALYSIS BY AGE
Age	Prop	Win	Runs	Wins%	£
3yo	0%	0	0	0.0%	0.00
4yo	20%	1	7	14.3%	-0.57
5yo	20%	1	7	14.3%	-0.59
6yo	20%	1	11	9.1%	-0.86
7yo	40%	2	5	40.0%	2.80
8yo	0%	0	7	0.0%	-1.00
9yo	0%	0	5	0.0%	-1.00
10yo	0%	0	4	0.0%	-1.00
11yo	0%	0	3	0.0%	-1.00
12yo+	0%	0	0	0.0%	0.00

ANALYSIS BY BHB RATING
Age	Prop	Win	Runs	Wins%	£
150+	0%	0	0	0.0%	0.00
130..149	0%	0	0	0.0%	0.00
120..129	0%	0	0	0.0%	0.00
110..119	20%	1	2	50.0%	0.50
100..109	0%	0	1	0.0%	-1.00
80..99	60%	3	30	10.0%	-0.27
60..79	0%	0	4	0.0%	-1.00
..59	0%	0	0	0.0%	0.00
Unrated	20%	1	12	8.3%	-0.87

ANALYSIS BY WEIGHT CARRIED
Age	Prop	Win	Runs	Wins%	£
12-01+	0%	0	0	0.0%	0.00
11-8..12-00	20%	1	3	33.3%	-0.48
11-0..11-07	40%	2	21	9.5%	-0.72
10-8..10-13	40%	2	17	11.8%	0.12
10-0..10-07	0%	0	8	0.0%	-1.00
..9-13	0%	0	0	0.0%	0.00

ANALYSIS BY DAYS SINCE LAST RUN
Age	Prop	Win	Runs	Wins%	£
1..7	0%	0	3	0.0%	-1.00
8..14	60%	3	7	42.9%	2.13
15..28	0%	0	18	0.0%	-1.00
29..60	0%	0	8	0.0%	-1.00
61..100	0%	0	2	0.0%	-1.00
101+	40%	2	11	18.2%	-0.58
Unraced	0%	0	0	0.0%	0.00

ANALYSIS BY TODAY'S STARTING PRICE
Age	Prop	Win	Runs	Wins%	£
Odds On	20%	1	2	50.0%	-0.22
Ev-2/1	40%	2	4	50.0%	0.47
9/4-4/1	0%	0	2	0.0%	-1.00
9/2-6/1	20%	1	4	25.0%	0.50
13/2-10/1	0%	0	8	0.0%	-1.00
11/1-16/1	20%	1	7	14.3%	0.86
18/1-33/1	0%	0	7	0.0%	-1.00
40/1+	0%	0	15	0.0%	-1.00

ANALYSIS BY STARTING PRICE LAST TIME
Age	Prop	Win	Runs	Wins%	£
Odds On	20%	1	1	100.0%	0.57
Ev-2/1	0%	0	2	0.0%	-1.00
9/4-4/1	20%	1	4	25.0%	-0.25
9/2-6/1	40%	2	7	28.6%	1.27
13/2-10/1	0%	0	5	0.0%	-1.00
11/1-16/1	20%	1	7	14.3%	-0.14
18/1-33/1	0%	0	13	0.0%	-1.00
40/1+	0%	0	10	0.0%	-1.00
Unraced	0%	0	0	0.0%	0.00

ANALYSIS BY DISTANCE BEATEN LAST TIME
Age	Prop	Win	Runs	Wins%	£
..-10 lgh	0%	0	0	0.0%	0.00
-10..0	20%	1	4	25.0%	-0.61
0.1..2	0%	0	2	0.0%	-1.00
2.1..5	20%	1	3	33.3%	-0.04
5.1..10	20%	1	4	25.0%	-0.25
10.1..20	0%	0	4	0.0%	-1.00
20.0..30	20%	1	6	16.7%	1.17
30.1+	20%	1	11	9.1%	-0.45
Not Compl	0%	0	15	0.0%	-1.00
Unraced	0%	0	0	0.0%	0.00

ANALYSIS BY SUCCESS RATE IN LAST 10 RUNS
Age	Prop	Win	Runs	Wins%	£
No Wins	40%	2	30	6.7%	-0.47
1 Win	20%	1	13	7.7%	-0.54
2 Wins	20%	1	4	25.0%	-0.25
3 Wins	0%	0	1	0.0%	-1.00
4 Wins	20%	1	1	100.0%	0.57
5+ Wins	0%	0	0	0.0%	0.00

ANALYSIS BY SUCCESS RATE IN LAST 3 RUNS
Age	Prop	Win	Runs	Wins%	£
No Wins	60%	3	42	7.1%	-0.48
1 Win	0%	0	4	0.0%	-1.00
2 Wins	40%	2	3	66.7%	0.52
3 Wins	0%	0	0	0.0%	0.00

ANALYSIS BY POSITION LAST TIME
Age	Prop	Win	Runs	Wins%	£
Won	20%	1	4	25.0%	-0.61
2nd or 3rd	20%	1	6	16.7%	-0.52
Unplaced	60%	3	24	12.5%	-0.08
Fell,BD,UR	0%	0	5	0.0%	-1.00
Pulled Up	0%	0	10	0.0%	-1.00
Ref/RanOut	0%	0	0	0.0%	0.00
CO/SlipUp	0%	0	0	0.0%	0.00
Unraced	0%	0	0	0.0%	0.00

OTHER FACTORS (WINS-RUNS, £)
Course Winner:	1-5	-£0.40
Distance Winner:	2-6	£0.26
Going Winner:	1-10	-£0.84
Beaten Favourite:	0-1	-£1.00
7-Day Winners:	0-1	-£1.00
BHA Top Rated:	1-4	-£0.25
Absolute Favourites:	2-5	-£0.11

Race Profiles

Conditions Hurdle Races (class 4..6): 3m+

ANALYSIS BY AGE

Age	Prop	Win	Runs	Wins%	£
3yo	0%	0	0	0.0%	0.00
4yo	0%	0	2	0.0%	-1.00
5yo	0%	0	7	0.0%	-1.00
6yo	50%	3	14	21.4%	-0.12
7yo	50%	3	9	33.3%	1.07
8yo	0%	0	7	0.0%	-1.00
9yo	0%	0	5	0.0%	-1.00
10yo	0%	0	2	0.0%	-1.00
11yo	0%	0	2	0.0%	-1.00
12yo+	0%	0	1	0.0%	-1.00

ANALYSIS BY BHB RATING

Age	Prop	Win	Runs	Wins%	£
150+	0%	0	0	0.0%	0.00
130..149	0%	0	0	0.0%	0.00
120..129	0%	0	2	0.0%	-1.00
110..119	33%	2	9	22.2%	-0.40
100..109	33%	2	4	50.0%	1.65
80..99	17%	1	19	5.3%	-0.58
60..79	0%	0	6	0.0%	-1.00
..59	0%	0	0	0.0%	0.00
Unrated	17%	1	9	11.1%	-0.22

ANALYSIS BY WEIGHT CARRIED

Age	Prop	Win	Runs	Wins%	£
12-01+	0%	0	0	0.0%	0.00
11-8..12-00	17%	1	2	50.0%	0.25
11-0..11-07	50%	3	26	11.5%	-0.34
10-8..10-13	17%	1	13	7.7%	-0.78
10-0..10-07	17%	1	8	12.5%	0.06
..9-13	0%	0	0	0.0%	0.00

ANALYSIS BY DAYS SINCE LAST RUN

Age	Prop	Win	Runs	Wins%	£
1..7	0%	0	3	0.0%	-1.00
8..14	0%	0	5	0.0%	-1.00
15..28	83%	5	19	26.3%	0.18
29..60	17%	1	13	7.7%	-0.35
61..100	0%	0	3	0.0%	-1.00
101+	0%	0	6	0.0%	-1.00
Unraced	0%	0	0	0.0%	0.00

ANALYSIS BY TODAY'S STARTING PRICE

Age	Prop	Win	Runs	Wins%	£
Odds On	0%	0	1	0.0%	-1.00
Ev-2/1	50%	3	7	42.9%	0.07
9/4-4/1	0%	0	5	0.0%	-1.00
9/2-6/1	17%	1	4	25.0%	0.75
13/2-10/1	33%	2	5	40.0%	2.30
11/1-16/1	0%	0	6	0.0%	-1.00
18/1-33/1	0%	0	10	0.0%	-1.00
40/1+	0%	0	11	0.0%	-1.00

ANALYSIS BY STARTING PRICE LAST TIME

Age	Prop	Win	Runs	Wins%	£
Odds On	0%	0	1	0.0%	-1.00
Ev-2/1	17%	1	1	100.0%	1.10
9/4-4/1	50%	3	8	37.5%	1.42
9/2-6/1	0%	0	5	0.0%	-1.00
13/2-10/1	17%	1	5	20.0%	-0.50
11/1-16/1	0%	0	7	0.0%	-1.00
18/1-33/1	17%	1	9	11.1%	-0.22
40/1+	0%	0	13	0.0%	-1.00
Unraced	0%	0	0	0.0%	0.00

ANALYSIS BY DISTANCE BEATEN LAST TIME

Age	Prop	Win	Runs	Wins%	£
..-10 lgh	17%	1	2	50.0%	2.50
-10..0	33%	2	3	66.7%	2.53
0.1..2	0%	0	0	0.0%	0.00
2.1..5	0%	0	5	0.0%	-1.00
5.1..10	0%	0	2	0.0%	-1.00
10.1..20	17%	1	6	16.7%	-0.58
20.0..30	0%	0	1	0.0%	-1.00
30.1+	0%	0	17	0.0%	-1.00
Not Compl	33%	2	13	15.4%	-0.16
Unraced	0%	0	0	0.0%	0.00

ANALYSIS BY SUCCESS RATE IN LAST 10 RUNS

Age	Prop	Win	Runs	Wins%	£
No Wins	17%	1	23	4.3%	-0.87
1 Win	67%	4	17	23.5%	0.51
2 Wins	17%	1	6	16.7%	-0.58
3 Wins	0%	0	3	0.0%	-1.00
4 Wins	0%	0	0	0.0%	0.00
5+ Wins	0%	0	0	0.0%	0.00

ANALYSIS BY SUCCESS RATE IN LAST 3 RUNS

Age	Prop	Win	Runs	Wins%	£
No Wins	50%	3	34	8.8%	-0.61
1 Win	50%	3	14	21.4%	0.26
2 Wins	0%	0	1	0.0%	-1.00
3 Wins	0%	0	0	0.0%	0.00

ANALYSIS BY POSITION LAST TIME

Age	Prop	Win	Runs	Wins%	£
Won	50%	3	5	60.0%	2.52
2nd or 3rd	0%	0	6	0.0%	-1.00
Unplaced	17%	1	25	4.0%	-0.90
Fell,BD,UR	0%	0	3	0.0%	-1.00
Pulled Up	17%	1	9	11.1%	-0.11
Ref/RanOut	17%	1	1	100.0%	1.88
CO/SlipUp	0%	0	0	0.0%	0.00
Unraced	0%	0	0	0.0%	0.00

OTHER FACTORS (WINS-RUNS, £)

Course Winner:	1-8	-£0.13
Distance Winner:	1-8	-£0.69
Going Winner:	0-9	-£1.00
Beaten Favourite:	2-5	£1.18
BHA Top Rated:	1-5	-£0.50
Absolute Favourites:	2-6	-£0.23

Conditions Hurdle Races (class 4..6)

Conditions Hurdle Races (class 4..6): 2 to 5 runners

ANALYSIS BY AGE
Age	Prop	Win	Runs	Wins%	£
3yo	0%	0	0	0.0%	0.00
4yo	33%	1	4	25.0%	-0.50
5yo	0%	0	2	0.0%	-1.00
6yo	33%	1	5	20.0%	-0.42
7yo	0%	0	2	0.0%	-1.00
8yo	33%	1	1	100.0%	0.36
9yo	0%	0	1	0.0%	-1.00
10yo	0%	0	0	0.0%	0.00
11yo	0%	0	0	0.0%	0.00
12yo+	0%	0	0	0.0%	0.00

ANALYSIS BY BHB RATING
Age	Prop	Win	Runs	Wins%	£
150+	33%	1	5	20.0%	-0.60
130..149	0%	0	0	0.0%	0.00
120..129	0%	0	0	0.0%	0.00
110..119	33%	1	2	50.0%	0.44
100..109	0%	0	1	0.0%	-1.00
80..99	33%	1	4	25.0%	-0.66
60..79	0%	0	2	0.0%	-1.00
..59	0%	0	0	0.0%	0.00
Unrated	0%	0	1	0.0%	-1.00

ANALYSIS BY WEIGHT CARRIED
Age	Prop	Win	Runs	Wins%	£
12-01+	0%	0	0	0.0%	0.00
11-8..12-00	0%	0	1	0.0%	-1.00
11-0..11-07	67%	2	6	33.3%	-0.44
10-8..10-13	33%	1	5	20.0%	-0.42
10-0..10-07	0%	0	3	0.0%	-1.00
..9-13	0%	0	0	0.0%	0.00

ANALYSIS BY DAYS SINCE LAST RUN
Age	Prop	Win	Runs	Wins%	£
1..7	0%	0	0	0.0%	0.00
8..14	33%	1	2	50.0%	-0.32
15..28	67%	2	6	33.3%	-0.19
29..60	0%	0	5	0.0%	-1.00
61..100	0%	0	0	0.0%	0.00
101+	0%	0	2	0.0%	-1.00
Unraced	0%	0	0	0.0%	0.00

ANALYSIS BY TODAY'S STARTING PRICE
Age	Prop	Win	Runs	Wins%	£
Odds On	33%	1	1	100.0%	0.36
Ev-2/1	67%	2	3	66.7%	0.63
9/4-4/1	0%	0	1	0.0%	-1.00
9/2-6/1	0%	0	3	0.0%	-1.00
13/2-10/1	0%	0	2	0.0%	-1.00
11/1-16/1	0%	0	2	0.0%	-1.00
18/1-33/1	0%	0	2	0.0%	-1.00
40/1+	0%	0	1	0.0%	-1.00

ANALYSIS BY STARTING PRICE LAST TIME
Age	Prop	Win	Runs	Wins%	£
Odds On	33%	1	1	100.0%	1.00
Ev-2/1	33%	1	5	20.0%	-0.73
9/4-4/1	33%	1	1	100.0%	1.88
9/2-6/1	0%	0	1	0.0%	-1.00
13/2-10/1	0%	0	1	0.0%	-1.00
11/1-16/1	0%	0	2	0.0%	-1.00
18/1-33/1	0%	0	1	0.0%	-1.00
40/1+	0%	0	3	0.0%	-1.00
Unraced	0%	0	0	0.0%	0.00

ANALYSIS BY DISTANCE BEATEN LAST TIME
Age	Prop	Win	Runs	Wins%	£
..-10 lgh	33%	1	1	100.0%	0.36
-10..0	33%	1	2	50.0%	0.36
0.1..2	0%	0	1	0.0%	-1.00
2.1..5	0%	0	0	0.0%	0.00
5.1..10	0%	0	2	0.0%	-1.00
10.1..20	0%	0	1	0.0%	-1.00
20.0..30	0%	0	0	0.0%	0.00
30.1+	0%	0	6	0.0%	-1.00
Not Compl	33%	1	2	50.0%	0.44
Unraced	0%	0	0	0.0%	0.00

ANALYSIS BY SUCCESS RATE IN LAST 10 RUNS
Age	Prop	Win	Runs	Wins%	£
No Wins	33%	1	6	16.7%	-0.52
1 Win	0%	0	3	0.0%	-1.00
2 Wins	0%	0	1	0.0%	-1.00
3 Wins	0%	0	1	0.0%	-1.00
4 Wins	67%	2	2	100.0%	0.68
5+ Wins	0%	0	2	0.0%	-1.00

ANALYSIS BY SUCCESS RATE IN LAST 3 RUNS
Age	Prop	Win	Runs	Wins%	£
No Wins	33%	1	6	16.7%	-0.52
1 Win	0%	0	5	0.0%	-1.00
2 Wins	33%	1	3	33.3%	-0.33
3 Wins	33%	1	1	100.0%	0.36

ANALYSIS BY POSITION LAST TIME
Age	Prop	Win	Runs	Wins%	£
Won	67%	2	3	66.7%	0.12
2nd or 3rd	0%	0	0	0.0%	-1.00
Unplaced	0%	0	7	0.0%	-1.00
Fell,BD,UR	0%	0	0	0.0%	0.00
Pulled Up	0%	0	1	0.0%	-1.00
Ref/RanOut	33%	1	1	100.0%	1.88
CO/SlipUp	0%	0	0	0.0%	0.00
Unraced	0%	0	0	0.0%	0.00

OTHER FACTORS (WINS-RUNS, £)
Course Winner:	2-4	-£0.16
Distance Winner:	2-7	-£0.52
Going Winner:	0-3	-£1.00
Beaten Favourite:	1-1	£1.88
BHA Top Rated:	1-1	£0.36
Absolute Favourites:	2-3	£0.12

Race Profiles

Conditions Hurdle Races (class 4..6): 6 to 10 runners

ANALYSIS BY AGE

Age	Prop	Win	Runs	Wins%	£
3yo	0%	0	0	0.0%	0.00
4yo	22%	4	23	17.4%	0.46
5yo	22%	4	38	10.5%	-0.28
6yo	33%	6	33	18.2%	-0.34
7yo	17%	3	26	11.5%	-0.44
8yo	6%	1	10	10.0%	-0.25
9yo	0%	0	11	0.0%	-1.00
10yo	0%	0	4	0.0%	-1.00
11yo	0%	0	1	0.0%	-1.00
12yo+	0%	0	0	0.0%	0.00

ANALYSIS BY BHB RATING

Age	Prop	Win	Runs	Wins%	£
150+	0%	0	0	0.0%	0.00
130..149	0%	0	0	0.0%	0.00
120..129	17%	3	7	42.9%	0.69
110..119	17%	3	15	20.0%	-0.50
100..109	22%	4	12	33.3%	0.68
80..99	28%	5	57	8.8%	-0.13
60..79	0%	0	12	0.0%	-1.00
..59	0%	0	0	0.0%	0.00
Unrated	17%	3	43	7.0%	-0.63

ANALYSIS BY WEIGHT CARRIED

Age	Prop	Win	Runs	Wins%	£
12-01+	0%	0	0	0.0%	0.00
11-8..12-00	17%	3	6	50.0%	0.09
11-0..11-07	56%	10	56	17.9%	-0.16
10-8..10-13	17%	3	48	6.3%	-0.27
10-0..10-07	11%	2	34	5.9%	-0.51
..9-13	0%	0	2	0.0%	-1.00

ANALYSIS BY DAYS SINCE LAST RUN

Age	Prop	Win	Runs	Wins%	£
1..7	6%	1	9	11.1%	-0.72
8..14	11%	2	16	12.5%	-0.32
15..28	39%	7	41	17.1%	0.20
29..60	22%	4	31	12.9%	-0.15
61..100	6%	1	13	7.7%	-0.42
101+	17%	3	29	10.3%	-0.70
Unraced	0%	0	7	0.0%	-1.00

ANALYSIS BY TODAY'S STARTING PRICE

Age	Prop	Win	Runs	Wins%	£
Odds On	17%	3	7	42.9%	-0.37
Ev-2/1	33%	6	9	66.7%	0.66
9/4-4/1	6%	1	21	4.8%	-0.81
9/2-6/1	6%	1	11	9.1%	-0.36
13/2-10/1	33%	6	27	22.2%	0.80
11/1-16/1	0%	0	14	0.0%	-1.00
18/1-33/1	6%	1	21	4.8%	0.24
40/1+	0%	0	36	0.0%	-1.00

ANALYSIS BY STARTING PRICE LAST TIME

Age	Prop	Win	Runs	Wins%	£
Odds On	6%	1	2	50.0%	-0.22
Ev-2/1	6%	1	5	20.0%	-0.58
9/4-4/1	22%	4	15	26.7%	0.07
9/2-6/1	6%	1	9	11.1%	-0.68
13/2-10/1	22%	4	15	26.7%	0.04
11/1-16/1	6%	1	23	4.3%	-0.61
18/1-33/1	28%	5	30	16.7%	0.06
40/1+	6%	1	40	2.5%	-0.35
Unraced	0%	0	7	0.0%	-1.00

ANALYSIS BY DISTANCE BEATEN LAST TIME

Age	Prop	Win	Runs	Wins%	£
..-10 lgh	6%	1	1	100.0%	6.00
-10..0	22%	4	8	50.0%	0.83
0.1..2	0%	0	3	0.0%	-1.00
2.1..5	11%	2	5	40.0%	-0.02
5.1..10	11%	2	12	16.7%	0.00
10.1..20	11%	2	24	8.3%	-0.56
20.0..30	11%	2	14	14.3%	1.43
30.1+	17%	3	38	7.9%	-0.66
Not Compl	11%	2	34	5.9%	-0.73
Unraced	0%	0	7	0.0%	-1.00

ANALYSIS BY SUCCESS RATE IN LAST 10 RUNS

Age	Prop	Win	Runs	Wins%	£
No Wins	28%	5	85	5.9%	-0.38
1 Win	33%	6	34	17.6%	-0.14
2 Wins	22%	4	14	28.6%	0.14
3 Wins	6%	1	3	33.3%	-0.57
4 Wins	6%	1	2	50.0%	-0.22
5+ Wins	6%	1	1	100.0%	3.00

ANALYSIS BY SUCCESS RATE IN LAST 3 RUNS

Age	Prop	Win	Runs	Wins%	£
No Wins	56%	10	110	9.1%	-0.35
1 Win	33%	6	23	26.1%	0.28
2 Wins	11%	2	6	33.3%	-0.24
3 Wins	0%	0	0	0.0%	0.00

ANALYSIS BY POSITION LAST TIME

Age	Prop	Win	Runs	Wins%	£
Won	28%	5	9	55.6%	1.41
2nd or 3rd	11%	2	14	14.3%	-0.65
Unplaced	50%	9	82	11.0%	-0.15
Fell,BD,UR	6%	1	10	10.0%	-0.84
Pulled Up	0%	0	22	0.0%	-1.00
Ref/RanOut	6%	1	2	50.0%	2.75
CO/SlipUp	0%	0	0	0.0%	0.00
Unraced	0%	0	7	0.0%	-1.00

OTHER FACTORS (WINS-RUNS, £)

Course Winner:	3-11	£0.27
Distance Winner:	6-24	-£0.01
Going Winner:	3-23	-£0.65
Beaten Favourite:	0-4	-£1.00
7-Day Winners:	1-1	£1.50
BHA Top Rated:	5-18	-£0.42
Absolute Favourites:	8-16	£0.03

Conditions Hurdle Races (class 4..6)

Conditions Hurdle Races (class 4..6): 11 runners or more

ANALYSIS BY AGE

Age	Prop	Win	Runs	Wins%	£
3yo	0%	0	0	0.0%	0.00
4yo	0%	0	23	0.0%	-1.00
5yo	27%	3	31	9.7%	-0.71
6yo	18%	2	23	8.7%	-0.60
7yo	45%	5	25	20.0%	0.88
8yo	9%	1	14	7.1%	-0.64
9yo	0%	0	7	0.0%	-1.00
10yo	0%	0	7	0.0%	-1.00
11yo	0%	0	6	0.0%	-1.00
12yo+	0%	0	1	0.0%	-1.00

ANALYSIS BY BHB RATING

Age	Prop	Win	Runs	Wins%	£
150+	0%	0	0	0.0%	0.00
130..149	9%	1	2	50.0%	-0.19
120..129	0%	0	1	0.0%	-1.00
110..119	0%	0	2	0.0%	-1.00
100..109	0%	0	3	0.0%	-1.00
80..99	64%	7	73	9.6%	-0.32
60..79	0%	0	14	0.0%	-1.00
..59	0%	0	2	0.0%	-1.00
Unrated	27%	3	40	7.5%	-0.52

ANALYSIS BY WEIGHT CARRIED

Age	Prop	Win	Runs	Wins%	£
12-01+	0%	0	0	0.0%	0.00
11-8..12-00	0%	0	3	0.0%	-1.00
11-0..11-07	45%	5	38	13.2%	-0.19
10-8..10-13	45%	5	65	7.7%	-0.44
10-0..10-07	9%	1	30	3.3%	-0.89
..9-13	0%	0	1	0.0%	-1.00

ANALYSIS BY DAYS SINCE LAST RUN

Age	Prop	Win	Runs	Wins%	£
1..7	18%	2	12	16.7%	0.00
8..14	36%	4	16	25.0%	1.38
15..28	27%	3	38	7.9%	-0.63
29..60	9%	1	32	3.1%	-0.86
61..100	9%	1	14	7.1%	-0.88
101+	0%	0	21	0.0%	-1.00
Unraced	0%	0	4	0.0%	-1.00

ANALYSIS BY TODAY'S STARTING PRICE

Age	Prop	Win	Runs	Wins%	£
Odds On	9%	1	5	20.0%	-0.68
Ev-2/1	9%	1	3	33.3%	0.00
9/4-4/1	27%	3	7	42.9%	0.82
9/2-6/1	27%	3	16	18.8%	0.19
13/2-10/1	9%	1	17	5.9%	-0.53
11/1-16/1	18%	2	18	11.1%	0.44
18/1-33/1	0%	0	25	0.0%	-1.00
40/1+	0%	0	46	0.0%	-1.00

ANALYSIS BY STARTING PRICE LAST TIME

Age	Prop	Win	Runs	Wins%	£
Odds On	9%	1	2	50.0%	-0.19
Ev-2/1	9%	1	2	50.0%	0.63
9/4-4/1	9%	1	5	20.0%	0.60
9/2-6/1	18%	2	13	15.4%	0.35
13/2-10/1	18%	2	16	12.5%	0.13
11/1-16/1	27%	3	25	12.0%	-0.24
18/1-33/1	9%	1	31	3.2%	-0.90
40/1+	0%	0	39	0.0%	-1.00
Unraced	0%	0	4	0.0%	-1.00

ANALYSIS BY DISTANCE BEATEN LAST TIME

Age	Prop	Win	Runs	Wins%	£
..-10 lgh	0%	0	2	0.0%	-1.00
-10..0	9%	1	4	25.0%	2.25
0.1..2	0%	0	4	0.0%	-1.00
2.1..5	9%	1	10	10.0%	-0.30
5.1..10	9%	1	4	25.0%	0.50
10.1..20	9%	1	17	5.9%	-0.82
20.0..30	18%	2	13	15.4%	0.35
30.1+	27%	3	47	6.4%	-0.70
Not Compl	18%	2	32	6.3%	-0.70
Unraced	0%	0	4	0.0%	-1.00

ANALYSIS BY SUCCESS RATE IN LAST 10 RUNS

Age	Prop	Win	Runs	Wins%	£
No Wins	55%	6	92	6.5%	-0.58
1 Win	36%	4	33	12.1%	-0.09
2 Wins	9%	1	5	20.0%	-0.68
3 Wins	0%	0	3	0.0%	-1.00
4 Wins	0%	0	0	0.0%	0.00
5+ Wins	0%	0	0	0.0%	0.00

ANALYSIS BY SUCCESS RATE IN LAST 3 RUNS

Age	Prop	Win	Runs	Wins%	£
No Wins	82%	9	119	7.6%	-0.54
1 Win	18%	2	14	14.3%	0.14
2 Wins	0%	0	0	0.0%	0.00
3 Wins	0%	0	0	0.0%	0.00

ANALYSIS BY POSITION LAST TIME

Age	Prop	Win	Runs	Wins%	£
Won	9%	1	6	16.7%	1.17
2nd or 3rd	9%	1	20	5.0%	-0.65
Unplaced	64%	7	76	9.2%	-0.46
Fell,BD,UR	9%	1	6	16.7%	-0.73
Pulled Up	9%	1	24	4.2%	-0.67
Ref/RanOut	0%	0	1	0.0%	-1.00
CO/SlipUp	0%	0	0	0.0%	0.00
Unraced	0%	0	4	0.0%	-1.00

OTHER FACTORS (WINS-RUNS, £)

Course Winner:	1-11	-£0.55
Distance Winner:	2-14	-£0.36
Going Winner:	4-24	-£0.06
Beaten Favourite:	3-5	£1.57
7-Day Winners:	0-1	-£1.00
BHA Top Rated:	1-12	-£0.86
Absolute Favourites:	2-11	-£0.56

Race Profiles

Conditions Hurdle Races (class 4..6): up to 7 days off the track

ANALYSIS BY AGE

Age	Prop	Win	Runs	Wins%	£
3yo	0%	0	0	0.0%	0.00
4yo	33%	1	10	10.0%	-0.75
5yo	0%	0	10	0.0%	-1.00
6yo	0%	0	2	0.0%	-1.00
7yo	33%	1	5	20.0%	0.40
8yo	33%	1	2	50.0%	1.50
9yo	0%	0	1	0.0%	-1.00
10yo	0%	0	2	0.0%	-1.00
11yo	0%	0	0	0.0%	0.00
12yo+	0%	0	0	0.0%	0.00

ANALYSIS BY BHB RATING

Age	Prop	Win	Runs	Wins%	£
150+	0%	0	0	0.0%	0.00
130..149	0%	0	0	0.0%	0.00
120..129	33%	1	2	50.0%	0.25
110..119	0%	0	2	0.0%	-1.00
100..109	0%	0	0	0.0%	0.00
80..99	67%	2	12	16.7%	0.00
60..79	0%	0	2	0.0%	-1.00
..59	0%	0	0	0.0%	0.00
Unrated	0%	0	14	0.0%	-1.00

ANALYSIS BY WEIGHT CARRIED

Age	Prop	Win	Runs	Wins%	£
12-01+	0%	0	0	0.0%	0.00
11-8..12-00	33%	1	2	50.0%	0.25
11-0..11-07	33%	1	6	16.7%	-0.17
10-8..10-13	33%	1	14	7.1%	-0.50
10-0..10-07	0%	0	8	0.0%	-1.00
..9-13	0%	0	2	0.0%	-1.00

ANALYSIS BY DAYS SINCE LAST RUN

Age	Prop	Win	Runs	Wins%	£
1..7	100%	3	21	14.3%	-0.31
8..14	0%	0	0	0.0%	0.00
15..28	0%	0	0	0.0%	0.00
29..60	0%	0	0	0.0%	0.00
61..100	0%	0	0	0.0%	0.00
101+	0%	0	0	0.0%	0.00
Unraced	0%	0	11	0.0%	-1.00

ANALYSIS BY TODAY'S STARTING PRICE

Age	Prop	Win	Runs	Wins%	£
Odds On	0%	0	0	0.0%	0.00
Ev-2/1	33%	1	2	50.0%	0.25
9/4-4/1	33%	1	3	33.3%	0.67
9/2-6/1	33%	1	4	25.0%	0.75
13/2-10/1	0%	0	3	0.0%	-1.00
11/1-16/1	0%	0	3	0.0%	-1.00
18/1-33/1	0%	0	8	0.0%	-1.00
40/1+	0%	0	9	0.0%	-1.00

ANALYSIS BY STARTING PRICE LAST TIME

Age	Prop	Win	Runs	Wins%	£
Odds On	0%	0	0	0.0%	0.00
Ev-2/1	0%	0	0	0.0%	0.00
9/4-4/1	33%	1	3	33.3%	-0.17
9/2-6/1	0%	0	2	0.0%	-1.00
13/2-10/1	33%	1	5	20.0%	0.00
11/1-16/1	33%	1	2	50.0%	2.50
18/1-33/1	0%	0	3	0.0%	-1.00
40/1+	0%	0	6	0.0%	-1.00
Unraced	0%	0	11	0.0%	-1.00

ANALYSIS BY DISTANCE BEATEN LAST TIME

Age	Prop	Win	Runs	Wins%	£
..-10 lgh	0%	0	0	0.0%	0.00
-10..0	33%	1	2	50.0%	0.25
0.1..2	0%	0	1	0.0%	-1.00
2.1..5	33%	1	2	50.0%	2.50
5.1..10	0%	0	0	0.0%	0.00
10.1..20	0%	0	5	0.0%	-1.00
20.0..30	0%	0	0	0.0%	0.00
30.1+	33%	1	7	14.3%	-0.29
Not Compl	0%	0	4	0.0%	-1.00
Unraced	0%	0	11	0.0%	-1.00

ANALYSIS BY SUCCESS RATE IN LAST 10 RUNS

Age	Prop	Win	Runs	Wins%	£
No Wins	67%	2	14	14.3%	-0.14
1 Win	0%	0	5	0.0%	-1.00
2 Wins	33%	1	2	50.0%	0.25
3 Wins	0%	0	0	0.0%	0.00
4 Wins	0%	0	0	0.0%	0.00
5+ Wins	0%	0	0	0.0%	0.00

ANALYSIS BY SUCCESS RATE IN LAST 3 RUNS

Age	Prop	Win	Runs	Wins%	£
No Wins	67%	2	17	11.8%	-0.29
1 Win	33%	1	4	25.0%	-0.38
2 Wins	0%	0	0	0.0%	0.00
3 Wins	0%	0	0	0.0%	0.00

ANALYSIS BY POSITION LAST TIME

Age	Prop	Win	Runs	Wins%	£
Won	33%	1	2	50.0%	0.25
2nd or 3rd	33%	1	3	33.3%	1.33
Unplaced	33%	1	12	8.3%	-0.58
Fell,BD,UR	0%	0	0	0.0%	0.00
Pulled Up	0%	0	4	0.0%	-1.00
Ref/RanOut	0%	0	0	0.0%	0.00
CO/SlipUp	0%	0	0	0.0%	0.00
Unraced	0%	0	11	0.0%	-1.00

OTHER FACTORS (WINS-RUNS, £)

Course Winner:	1-3	£0.67
Distance Winner:	1-2	£0.25
Going Winner:	2-7	£0.07
Beaten Favourite:	0-1	-£1.00
7-Day Winners:	1-2	£0.25
BHA Top Rated:	0-1	-£1.00
Absolute Favourites:	1-2	£0.25

Conditions Hurdle Races (class 4..6)

Conditions Hurdle Races (class 4..6): 100+ days off the track

ANALYSIS BY AGE

Age	Prop	Win	Runs	Wins%	£
3yo	0%	0	0	0.0%	0.00
4yo	33%	1	6	16.7%	-0.50
5yo	0%	0	15	0.0%	-1.00
6yo	33%	1	8	12.5%	-0.80
7yo	33%	1	9	11.1%	-0.56
8yo	0%	0	4	0.0%	-1.00
9yo	0%	0	6	0.0%	-1.00
10yo	0%	0	2	0.0%	-1.00
11yo	0%	0	2	0.0%	-1.00
12yo+	0%	0	0	0.0%	0.00

ANALYSIS BY BHB RATING

Age	Prop	Win	Runs	Wins%	£
150+	0%	0	1	0.0%	-1.00
130..149	0%	0	0	0.0%	0.00
120..129	0%	0	0	0.0%	0.00
110..119	33%	1	2	50.0%	0.50
100..109	0%	0	3	0.0%	-1.00
80..99	33%	1	24	4.2%	-0.83
60..79	0%	0	7	0.0%	-1.00
..59	0%	0	1	0.0%	-1.00
Unrated	33%	1	14	7.1%	-0.89

ANALYSIS BY WEIGHT CARRIED

Age	Prop	Win	Runs	Wins%	£
12-01+	0%	0	0	0.0%	0.00
11-8..12-00	33%	1	1	100.0%	0.57
11-0..11-07	67%	2	19	10.5%	-0.63
10-8..10-13	0%	0	24	0.0%	-1.00
10-0..10-07	0%	0	8	0.0%	-1.00
..9-13	0%	0	0	0.0%	0.00

ANALYSIS BY DAYS SINCE LAST RUN

Age	Prop	Win	Runs	Wins%	£
1..7	0%	0	0	0.0%	0.00
8..14	0%	0	0	0.0%	0.00
15..28	0%	0	0	0.0%	0.00
29..60	0%	0	0	0.0%	0.00
61..100	0%	0	0	0.0%	0.00
101+	100%	3	52	5.8%	-0.84
Unraced	0%	0	0	0.0%	0.00

ANALYSIS BY TODAY'S STARTING PRICE

Age	Prop	Win	Runs	Wins%	£
Odds On	33%	1	3	33.3%	-0.48
Ev-2/1	33%	1	2	50.0%	0.50
9/4-4/1	33%	1	8	12.5%	-0.50
9/2-6/1	0%	0	2	0.0%	-1.00
13/2-10/1	0%	0	7	0.0%	-1.00
11/1-16/1	0%	0	7	0.0%	-1.00
18/1-33/1	0%	0	4	0.0%	-1.00
40/1+	0%	0	19	0.0%	-1.00

ANALYSIS BY STARTING PRICE LAST TIME

Age	Prop	Win	Runs	Wins%	£
Odds On	33%	1	1	100.0%	0.57
Ev-2/1	0%	0	3	0.0%	-1.00
9/4-4/1	33%	1	5	20.0%	-0.40
9/2-6/1	0%	0	2	0.0%	-1.00
13/2-10/1	33%	1	7	14.3%	-0.43
11/1-16/1	0%	0	7	0.0%	-1.00
18/1-33/1	0%	0	10	0.0%	-1.00
40/1+	0%	0	17	0.0%	-1.00
Unraced	0%	0	0	0.0%	0.00

ANALYSIS BY DISTANCE BEATEN LAST TIME

Age	Prop	Win	Runs	Wins%	£
..-10 lgh	0%	0	0	0.0%	0.00
-10..0	33%	1	3	33.3%	-0.48
0.1..2	0%	0	0	0.0%	0.00
2.1..5	0%	0	0	0.0%	0.00
5.1..10	33%	1	5	20.0%	-0.40
10.1..20	0%	0	8	0.0%	-1.00
20.0..30	0%	0	6	0.0%	-1.00
30.1+	33%	1	21	4.8%	-0.81
Not Compl	0%	0	9	0.0%	-1.00
Unraced	0%	0	0	0.0%	0.00

ANALYSIS BY SUCCESS RATE IN LAST 10 RUNS

Age	Prop	Win	Runs	Wins%	£
No Wins	0%	0	38	0.0%	-1.00
1 Win	0%	0	7	0.0%	-1.00
2 Wins	33%	1	4	25.0%	-0.25
3 Wins	0%	0	1	0.0%	-1.00
4 Wins	33%	1	1	100.0%	0.57
5+ Wins	33%	1	1	100.0%	3.00

ANALYSIS BY SUCCESS RATE IN LAST 3 RUNS

Age	Prop	Win	Runs	Wins%	£
No Wins	33%	1	44	2.3%	-0.91
1 Win	0%	0	6	0.0%	-1.00
2 Wins	67%	2	2	100.0%	1.28
3 Wins	0%	0	0	0.0%	0.00

ANALYSIS BY POSITION LAST TIME

Age	Prop	Win	Runs	Wins%	£
Won	33%	1	3	33.3%	-0.48
2nd or 3rd	0%	0	6	0.0%	-1.00
Unplaced	67%	2	34	5.9%	-0.79
Fell,BD,UR	0%	0	5	0.0%	-1.00
Pulled Up	0%	0	4	0.0%	-1.00
Ref/RanOut	0%	0	0	0.0%	0.00
CO/SlipUp	0%	0	0	0.0%	0.00
Unraced	0%	0	0	0.0%	0.00

OTHER FACTORS (WINS-RUNS, £)

Course Winner:	2-5	£0.40
Distance Winner:	1-7	-£0.78
Going Winner:	2-9	-£0.38
Beaten Favourite:	0-1	-£1.00
BHA Top Rated:	1-4	-£0.25
Absolute Favourites:	1-6	-£0.74

Race Profiles

Novices' Handicap Hurdle Races

ANALYSIS BY AGE

Age	Prop	Win	Runs	Wins%	£
3yo	1%	4	74	5.4%	-0.65
4yo	10%	67	1037	6.5%	-0.39
5yo	31%	207	2254	9.2%	-0.20
6yo	31%	208	2221	9.4%	-0.11
7yo	16%	108	1404	7.7%	-0.35
8yo	7%	49	684	7.2%	-0.14
9yo	4%	24	285	8.4%	-0.11
10yo	1%	4	95	4.2%	-0.59
11yo	0%	3	33	9.1%	-0.56
12yo+	0%	2	24	8.3%	0.96

ANALYSIS BY BHB RATING

Age	Prop	Win	Runs	Wins%	£
130..149	0%	1	24	4.2%	-0.67
120..129	3%	20	169	11.8%	-0.09
110..119	6%	41	569	7.2%	-0.42
100..109	22%	146	1491	9.8%	-0.22
80..99	56%	379	4667	8.1%	-0.24
60..79	13%	87	1163	7.5%	-0.08
..59	0%	0	2	0.0%	-1.00
Unrated	0%	2	26	7.7%	-0.70

ANALYSIS BY WEIGHT CARRIED

Age	Prop	Win	Runs	Wins%	£
12-01+	0%	0	4	0.0%	-1.00
11-8..12-00	19%	131	1269	10.3%	-0.25
11-0..11-07	39%	266	2945	9.0%	-0.23
10-8..10-13	20%	132	1732	7.6%	-0.30
10-0..10-07	16%	111	1613	6.9%	-0.12
..9-13	5%	36	548	6.6%	-0.15

ANALYSIS BY DAYS SINCE LAST RUN

Age	Prop	Win	Runs	Wins%	£
1..7	6%	43	352	12.2%	-0.17
8..14	17%	112	1304	8.6%	-0.28
15..28	29%	195	2480	7.9%	-0.30
29..60	24%	162	1986	8.2%	-0.16
61..100	8%	52	594	8.8%	0.04
101+	16%	110	1382	8.0%	-0.23
Unraced	0%	2	13	15.4%	0.12

ANALYSIS BY TODAY'S STARTING PRICE

Age	Prop	Win	Runs	Wins%	£
Odds On	4%	24	38	63.2%	0.05
Ev-2/1	9%	63	188	33.5%	-0.12
9/4-4/1	23%	154	784	19.6%	-0.14
9/2-6/1	15%	101	816	12.4%	-0.23
13/2-10/1	24%	160	1728	9.3%	-0.17
11/1-16/1	17%	113	1766	6.4%	-0.07
18/1-33/1	8%	51	1843	2.8%	-0.32
40/1+	1%	10	948	1.1%	-0.48

ANALYSIS BY STARTING PRICE LAST TIME

Age	Prop	Win	Runs	Wins%	£
Odds On	2%	13	89	14.6%	-0.43
Ev-2/1	7%	50	290	17.2%	-0.17
9/4-4/1	17%	113	928	12.2%	-0.25
9/2-6/1	12%	78	763	10.2%	-0.35
13/2-10/1	19%	129	1466	8.8%	-0.18
11/1-16/1	19%	128	1483	8.6%	-0.11
18/1-33/1	14%	96	1627	5.9%	-0.30
40/1+	10%	67	1452	4.6%	-0.21
Unraced	0%	2	13	15.4%	0.12

ANALYSIS BY DISTANCE BEATEN LAST TIME

Age	Prop	Win	Runs	Wins%	£
..-10 lgh	2%	16	80	20.0%	-0.33
-10..0	13%	91	677	13.4%	-0.28
0.1..2	5%	37	340	10.9%	-0.31
2.1..5	8%	53	506	10.5%	-0.37
5.1..10	11%	74	735	10.1%	-0.28
10.1..20	17%	112	1293	8.7%	-0.19
20.0..30	12%	79	1033	7.6%	-0.14
30.1+	21%	144	2337	6.2%	-0.16
Not Compl	10%	68	1097	6.2%	-0.30
Unraced	0%	2	13	15.4%	0.12

ANALYSIS BY SUCCESS RATE IN LAST 10 RUNS

Age	Prop	Win	Runs	Wins%	£
No Wins	60%	402	5720	7.0%	-0.24
1 Win	27%	181	1694	10.7%	-0.17
2 Wins	11%	72	536	13.4%	-0.16
3 Wins	2%	12	109	11.0%	-0.44
4 Wins	1%	6	32	18.8%	-0.43
5+ Wins	0%	1	7	14.3%	-0.66

ANALYSIS BY SUCCESS RATE IN LAST 3 RUNS

Age	Prop	Win	Runs	Wins%	£
No Wins	71%	477	6522	7.3%	-0.22
1 Win	23%	156	1330	11.7%	-0.21
2 Wins	6%	39	235	16.6%	-0.36
3 Wins	0%	2	11	18.2%	-0.56

ANALYSIS BY POSITION LAST TIME

Age	Prop	Win	Runs	Wins%	£
Won	16%	107	757	14.1%	-0.28
2nd or 3rd	25%	170	1659	10.2%	-0.29
Unplaced	49%	330	4592	7.2%	-0.17
Fell,BD,UR	3%	19	287	6.6%	-0.45
Pulled Up	7%	45	779	5.8%	-0.27
Ref/RanOut	0%	2	18	11.1%	0.56
CO/SlipUp	0%	1	6	16.7%	-0.17
Unraced	0%	2	13	15.4%	0.12

OTHER FACTORS (WINS-RUNS, £)

Course Winner:	38-332	-£0.34
Distance Winner:	87-836	-£0.29
Going Winner:	114-911	-£0.15
Beaten Favourite:	65-459	-£0.25
7-Day Winners:	22-81	-£0.18
BHA Top Rated:	0-1	-£1.00
Absolute Favourites:	155-602	-£0.17

TRAINERS (WINS-RUNS, £) E W Tuer 4-12 £1.58; Jennie Candlish 3-22 £0.84; T R George 13-79 £0.22; N J Henderson 17-96 £0.17; A W Carroll 6-67 £0.18; J S Smith 4-13 £0.87; J W Mullins 9-71 £0.16; Heather Dalton 4-30 £0.37; J Howard Johnson 4-41 £0.27; P J Hobbs 22-122 £0.09; James Moffatt 3-38 £0.26; P C Haslam 6-33 £0.30; T D Walford 3-17 £0.59; C T Pogson 3-21 £0.45; Mrs P Sly 3-20 £0.45; M D Hammond 3-13 £0.58; R Ford 5-24 £0.27; M G Quinlan 3-13 £0.48; Jim Best 6-19 £0.22; Andrew Turnell 3-20 £0.19.

Novices' Handicap Hurdle Races

Novices' Handicap Hurdle Races: 2m to 2m3f

ANALYSIS BY AGE

Age	Prop	Win	Runs	Wins%	£
3yo	1%	3	37	8.1%	-0.39
4yo	13%	36	627	5.7%	-0.52
5yo	34%	98	1090	9.0%	-0.23
6yo	33%	94	868	10.8%	0.21
7yo	11%	31	502	6.2%	-0.43
8yo	7%	20	251	8.0%	-0.13
9yo	2%	5	83	6.0%	-0.35
10yo	0%	0	20	0.0%	-1.00
11yo	0%	1	13	7.7%	-0.85
12yo+	0%	0	4	0.0%	-1.00

ANALYSIS BY BHB RATING

Age	Prop	Win	Runs	Wins%	£
150+	0%	0	0	0.0%	0.00
130..149	0%	0	5	0.0%	-1.00
120..129	1%	4	39	10.3%	-0.65
110..119	6%	18	215	8.4%	-0.24
100..109	22%	64	671	9.5%	-0.20
80..99	58%	166	2087	8.0%	-0.24
60..79	12%	34	451	7.5%	0.03
..59	0%	0	1	0.0%	-1.00
Unrated	1%	2	26	7.7%	-0.70

ANALYSIS BY WEIGHT CARRIED

Age	Prop	Win	Runs	Wins%	£
12-01+	0%	0	2	0.0%	-1.00
11-8..12-00	20%	59	552	10.7%	-0.28
11-0..11-07	38%	110	1306	8.4%	-0.25
10-8..10-13	19%	55	763	7.2%	-0.31
10-0..10-07	17%	48	677	7.1%	0.01
..9-13	6%	16	195	8.2%	-0.08

ANALYSIS BY DAYS SINCE LAST RUN

Age	Prop	Win	Runs	Wins%	£
1..7	7%	20	147	13.6%	0.21
8..14	16%	46	530	8.7%	-0.33
15..28	32%	91	1056	8.6%	-0.19
29..60	27%	77	902	8.5%	-0.13
61..100	7%	21	264	8.0%	0.05
101+	11%	32	587	5.5%	-0.46
Unraced	0%	1	9	11.1%	0.11

ANALYSIS BY TODAY'S STARTING PRICE

Age	Prop	Win	Runs	Wins%	£
Odds On	5%	13	21	61.9%	0.00
Ev-2/1	10%	30	87	34.5%	-0.04
9/4-4/1	20%	59	314	18.8%	-0.16
9/2-6/1	14%	39	360	10.8%	-0.32
13/2-10/1	24%	70	710	9.9%	-0.13
11/1-16/1	17%	49	765	6.4%	-0.08
18/1-33/1	8%	22	813	2.7%	-0.32
40/1+	2%	6	425	1.4%	-0.33

ANALYSIS BY STARTING PRICE LAST TIME

Age	Prop	Win	Runs	Wins%	£
Odds On	1%	4	32	12.5%	-0.78
Ev-2/1	8%	22	107	20.6%	-0.01
9/4-4/1	19%	54	409	13.2%	-0.20
9/2-6/1	10%	30	298	10.1%	-0.32
13/2-10/1	17%	48	622	7.7%	-0.30
11/1-16/1	20%	57	644	8.9%	-0.08
18/1-33/1	14%	40	718	5.6%	-0.20
40/1+	11%	32	656	4.9%	-0.20
Unraced	0%	1	9	11.1%	0.11

ANALYSIS BY DISTANCE BEATEN LAST TIME

Age	Prop	Win	Runs	Wins%	£
..-10 lgh	2%	6	27	22.2%	-0.41
-10..0	15%	42	277	15.2%	-0.15
0.1..2	8%	22	151	14.6%	-0.05
2.1..5	8%	22	226	9.7%	-0.37
5.1..10	12%	35	327	10.7%	-0.16
10.1..20	18%	51	600	8.5%	-0.13
20.0..30	11%	33	451	7.3%	-0.05
30.1+	20%	58	1015	5.7%	-0.28
Not Compl	6%	18	412	4.4%	-0.33
Unraced	0%	1	9	11.1%	0.11

ANALYSIS BY SUCCESS RATE IN LAST 10 RUNS

Age	Prop	Win	Runs	Wins%	£
No Wins	64%	184	2559	7.2%	-0.20
1 Win	25%	73	714	10.2%	-0.24
2 Wins	9%	27	175	15.4%	0.00
3 Wins	0%	1	34	2.9%	-0.92
4 Wins	0%	1	3	33.3%	-0.36
5+ Wins	0%	1	1	100.0%	1.38

ANALYSIS BY SUCCESS RATE IN LAST 3 RUNS

Age	Prop	Win	Runs	Wins%	£
No Wins	73%	210	2864	7.3%	-0.19
1 Win	22%	63	543	11.6%	-0.25
2 Wins	5%	13	75	17.3%	-0.33
3 Wins	0%	1	4	25.0%	-0.41

ANALYSIS BY POSITION LAST TIME

Age	Prop	Win	Runs	Wins%	£
Won	17%	48	304	15.8%	-0.17
2nd or 3rd	27%	78	679	11.5%	-0.17
Unplaced	50%	143	2094	6.8%	-0.20
Fell,BD,UR	2%	7	112	6.3%	-0.44
Pulled Up	3%	9	285	3.2%	-0.32
Ref/RanOut	0%	1	9	11.1%	0.44
CO/SlipUp	0%	1	3	33.3%	0.67
Unraced	0%	1	9	11.1%	0.11

OTHER FACTORS (WINS-RUNS, £)

Course Winner:	17-141	-£0.26
Distance Winner:	46-448	-£0.26
Going Winner:	42-340	-£0.22
Beaten Favourite:	24-183	-£0.36
7-Day Winners:	12-41	-£0.08
BHA Top Rated:	0-1	-£1.00
Absolute Favourites:	68-260	-£0.17

Race Profiles

Novices' Handicap Hurdle Races: 2m4f to 2m7f

ANALYSIS BY AGE

Age	Prop	Win	Runs	Wins%	£
3yo	0%	1	37	2.7%	-0.90
4yo	8%	22	340	6.5%	-0.23
5yo	31%	89	939	9.5%	-0.11
6yo	29%	83	1006	8.3%	-0.31
7yo	19%	53	635	8.3%	-0.30
8yo	7%	19	300	6.3%	-0.24
9yo	5%	14	128	10.9%	0.14
10yo	1%	3	51	5.9%	-0.45
11yo	0%	1	11	9.1%	-0.41
12yo+	0%	1	14	7.1%	0.50

ANALYSIS BY BHB RATING

Age	Prop	Win	Runs	Wins%	£
150+	0%	0	0	0.0%	0.00
130..149	0%	1	18	5.6%	-0.56
120..129	4%	11	101	10.9%	-0.20
110..119	6%	18	254	7.1%	-0.43
100..109	22%	64	641	10.0%	-0.22
80..99	54%	154	1933	8.0%	-0.23
60..79	13%	38	514	7.4%	-0.13
..59	0%	0	0	0.0%	0.00
Unrated	0%	0	0	0.0%	0.00

ANALYSIS BY WEIGHT CARRIED

Age	Prop	Win	Runs	Wins%	£
12-01+	0%	0	0	0.0%	0.00
11-8..12-00	19%	55	534	10.3%	-0.23
11-0..11-07	40%	114	1211	9.4%	-0.16
10-8..10-13	20%	58	729	8.0%	-0.28
10-0..10-07	15%	43	719	6.0%	-0.32
..9-13	6%	16	268	6.0%	-0.12

ANALYSIS BY DAYS SINCE LAST RUN

Age	Prop	Win	Runs	Wins%	£
1..7	6%	17	154	11.0%	-0.59
8..14	17%	50	585	8.5%	-0.17
15..28	28%	81	1042	7.8%	-0.36
29..60	19%	55	786	7.0%	-0.23
61..100	7%	21	252	8.3%	0.05
101+	21%	61	638	9.6%	-0.09
Unraced	0%	1	4	25.0%	0.13

ANALYSIS BY TODAY'S STARTING PRICE

Age	Prop	Win	Runs	Wins%	£
Odds On	3%	9	15	60.0%	0.01
Ev-2/1	8%	23	76	30.3%	-0.26
9/4-4/1	23%	66	343	19.2%	-0.16
9/2-6/1	14%	40	319	12.5%	-0.23
13/2-10/1	25%	71	771	9.2%	-0.17
11/1-16/1	19%	53	745	7.1%	0.06
18/1-33/1	7%	21	764	2.7%	-0.36
40/1+	1%	3	428	0.7%	-0.64

ANALYSIS BY STARTING PRICE LAST TIME

Age	Prop	Win	Runs	Wins%	£
Odds On	3%	9	49	18.4%	-0.10
Ev-2/1	8%	22	143	15.4%	-0.22
9/4-4/1	15%	42	388	10.8%	-0.26
9/2-6/1	12%	34	350	9.7%	-0.39
13/2-10/1	19%	55	617	8.9%	-0.20
11/1-16/1	20%	56	627	8.9%	-0.02
18/1-33/1	14%	40	694	5.8%	-0.39
40/1+	9%	27	589	4.6%	-0.18
Unraced	0%	1	4	25.0%	0.13

ANALYSIS BY DISTANCE BEATEN LAST TIME

Age	Prop	Win	Runs	Wins%	£
..-10 lgh	3%	8	44	18.2%	-0.29
-10..0	12%	33	290	11.4%	-0.35
0.1..2	3%	8	137	5.8%	-0.65
2.1..5	8%	23	201	11.4%	-0.33
5.1..10	10%	30	292	10.3%	-0.28
10.1..20	16%	47	537	8.8%	-0.22
20.0..30	12%	35	440	8.0%	-0.15
30.1+	21%	61	1005	6.1%	-0.14
Not Compl	14%	40	511	7.8%	-0.22
Unraced	0%	1	4	25.0%	0.13

ANALYSIS BY SUCCESS RATE IN LAST 10 RUNS

Age	Prop	Win	Runs	Wins%	£
No Wins	58%	166	2381	7.0%	-0.25
1 Win	28%	79	729	10.8%	-0.10
2 Wins	10%	28	264	10.6%	-0.40
3 Wins	3%	9	56	16.1%	-0.04
4 Wins	1%	3	21	14.3%	-0.49
5+ Wins	0%	0	6	0.0%	-1.00

ANALYSIS BY SUCCESS RATE IN LAST 3 RUNS

Age	Prop	Win	Runs	Wins%	£
No Wins	71%	202	2752	7.3%	-0.23
1 Win	23%	66	583	11.3%	-0.21
2 Wins	6%	17	117	14.5%	-0.39
3 Wins	0%	0	5	0.0%	-1.00

ANALYSIS BY POSITION LAST TIME

Age	Prop	Win	Runs	Wins%	£
Won	14%	41	334	12.3%	-0.34
2nd or 3rd	22%	63	685	9.2%	-0.38
Unplaced	50%	142	1930	7.4%	-0.16
Fell,BD,UR	4%	12	136	8.8%	-0.30
Pulled Up	9%	26	363	7.2%	-0.23
Ref/RanOut	0%	1	7	14.3%	1.14
CO/SlipUp	0%	0	2	0.0%	-1.00
Unraced	0%	1	4	25.0%	0.13

OTHER FACTORS (WINS-RUNS, £)

Course Winner:	13-143	-£0.46
Distance Winner:	30-290	-£0.27
Going Winner:	48-417	-£0.25
Beaten Favourite:	27-205	-£0.28
7-Day Winners:	7-29	-£0.33
Absolute Favourites:	59-253	-£0.27

Novices' Handicap Hurdle Races

Novices' Handicap Hurdle Races: 3m+

ANALYSIS BY AGE
Age	Prop	Win	Runs	Wins%	£
3yo	0%	0	0	0.0%	0.00
4yo	9%	9	70	12.9%	0.01
5yo	20%	20	225	8.9%	-0.38
6yo	30%	31	347	8.9%	-0.32
7yo	24%	24	267	9.0%	-0.31
8yo	10%	10	133	7.5%	0.06
9yo	5%	5	74	6.8%	-0.29
10yo	1%	1	24	4.2%	-0.54
11yo	1%	1	9	11.1%	-0.33
12yo+	1%	1	6	16.7%	3.33

ANALYSIS BY BHB RATING
Age	Prop	Win	Runs	Wins%	£
150+	0%	0	0	0.0%	0.00
130..149	0%	0	1	0.0%	-1.00
120..129	5%	5	29	17.2%	1.07
110..119	5%	5	100	5.0%	-0.76
100..109	18%	18	179	10.1%	-0.29
80..99	58%	59	647	9.1%	-0.24
60..79	15%	15	198	7.6%	-0.17
..59	0%	0	1	0.0%	-1.00
Unrated	0%	0	0	0.0%	0.00

ANALYSIS BY WEIGHT CARRIED
Age	Prop	Win	Runs	Wins%	£
12-01+	0%	0	2	0.0%	-1.00
11-8..12-00	17%	17	183	9.3%	-0.25
11-0..11-07	41%	42	428	9.8%	-0.37
10-8..10-13	19%	19	240	7.9%	-0.31
10-0..10-07	20%	20	217	9.2%	0.11
..9-13	4%	4	85	4.7%	-0.38

ANALYSIS BY DAYS SINCE LAST RUN
Age	Prop	Win	Runs	Wins%	£
1..7	6%	6	51	11.8%	0.00
8..14	16%	16	189	8.5%	-0.51
15..28	23%	23	382	6.0%	-0.45
29..60	29%	30	298	10.1%	-0.10
61..100	10%	10	78	12.8%	-0.01
101+	17%	17	157	10.8%	0.06
Unraced	0%	0	0	0.0%	0.00

ANALYSIS BY TODAY'S STARTING PRICE
Age	Prop	Win	Runs	Wins%	£
Odds On	2%	2	2	100.0%	0.82
Ev-2/1	10%	10	25	40.0%	0.01
9/4-4/1	28%	29	127	22.8%	-0.03
9/2-6/1	22%	22	137	16.1%	0.00
13/2-10/1	19%	19	247	7.7%	-0.33
11/1-16/1	11%	11	256	4.3%	-0.40
18/1-33/1	8%	8	266	3.0%	-0.22
40/1+	1%	1	95	1.1%	-0.46

ANALYSIS BY STARTING PRICE LAST TIME
Age	Prop	Win	Runs	Wins%	£
Odds On	0%	0	8	0.0%	-1.00
Ev-2/1	6%	6	40	15.0%	-0.40
9/4-4/1	17%	17	131	13.0%	-0.37
9/2-6/1	14%	14	115	12.2%	-0.28
13/2-10/1	25%	26	227	11.5%	0.21
11/1-16/1	15%	15	212	7.1%	-0.47
18/1-33/1	16%	16	215	7.4%	-0.33
40/1+	8%	8	207	3.9%	-0.30
Unraced	0%	0	0	0.0%	0.00

ANALYSIS BY DISTANCE BEATEN LAST TIME
Age	Prop	Win	Runs	Wins%	£
..-10 lgh	2%	2	9	22.2%	-0.29
-10..0	16%	16	110	14.5%	-0.40
0.1..2	7%	7	52	13.5%	-0.16
2.1..5	8%	8	79	10.1%	-0.43
5.1..10	9%	9	116	7.8%	-0.60
10.1..20	14%	14	156	9.0%	-0.29
20.0..30	11%	11	142	7.7%	-0.41
30.1+	25%	25	317	7.9%	0.17
Not Compl	10%	10	174	5.7%	-0.46
Unraced	0%	0	0	0.0%	0.00

ANALYSIS BY SUCCESS RATE IN LAST 10 RUNS
Age	Prop	Win	Runs	Wins%	£
No Wins	51%	52	780	6.7%	-0.32
1 Win	28%	29	251	11.6%	-0.16
2 Wins	17%	17	97	17.5%	0.19
3 Wins	2%	2	19	10.5%	-0.78
4 Wins	2%	2	8	25.0%	-0.29
5+ Wins	0%	0	0	0.0%	0.00

ANALYSIS BY SUCCESS RATE IN LAST 3 RUNS
Age	Prop	Win	Runs	Wins%	£
No Wins	64%	65	906	7.2%	-0.29
1 Win	26%	27	204	13.2%	-0.06
2 Wins	9%	9	43	20.9%	-0.32
3 Wins	1%	1	2	50.0%	0.25

ANALYSIS BY POSITION LAST TIME
Age	Prop	Win	Runs	Wins%	£
Won	18%	18	119	15.1%	-0.39
2nd or 3rd	28%	29	295	9.8%	-0.38
Unplaced	44%	45	568	7.9%	-0.09
Fell,BD,UR	0%	0	39	0.0%	-1.00
Pulled Up	10%	10	131	7.6%	-0.28
Ref/RanOut	0%	0	2	0.0%	-1.00
CO/SlipUp	0%	0	1	0.0%	-1.00
Unraced	0%	0	0	0.0%	0.00

OTHER FACTORS (WINS-RUNS, £)
Course Winner:	8-48	-£0.18
Distance Winner:	11-98	-£0.48
Going Winner:	24-154	£0.28
Beaten Favourite:	14-71	£0.14
7-Day Winners:	3-11	-£0.20
Absolute Favourites:	28-89	£0.13

Race Profiles

Novices' Handicap Hurdle Races: 2 to 5 runners

ANALYSIS BY AGE

Age	Prop	Win	Runs	Wins%	£
3yo	0%	0	0	0.0%	0.00
4yo	0%	0	9	0.0%	-1.00
5yo	33%	4	13	30.8%	-0.15
6yo	50%	6	17	35.3%	-0.13
7yo	8%	1	8	12.5%	-0.31
8yo	0%	0	3	0.0%	-1.00
9yo	0%	0	1	0.0%	-1.00
10yo	0%	0	0	0.0%	0.00
11yo	8%	1	1	100.0%	0.91
12yo+	0%	0	0	0.0%	0.00

ANALYSIS BY BHB RATING

Age	Prop	Win	Runs	Wins%	£
150+	0%	0	0	0.0%	0.00
130..149	0%	0	0	0.0%	0.00
120..129	8%	1	7	14.3%	-0.64
110..119	17%	2	6	33.3%	-0.28
100..109	42%	5	13	38.5%	0.13
80..99	25%	3	22	13.6%	-0.54
60..79	8%	1	4	25.0%	-0.57
..59	0%	0	0	0.0%	0.00
Unrated	0%	0	0	0.0%	0.00

ANALYSIS BY WEIGHT CARRIED

Age	Prop	Win	Runs	Wins%	£
12-01+	0%	0	0	0.0%	0.00
11-8..12-00	42%	5	14	35.7%	0.10
11-0..11-07	25%	3	17	17.6%	-0.56
10-8..10-13	8%	1	7	14.3%	-0.73
10-0..10-07	17%	2	9	22.2%	-0.25
..9-13	8%	1	5	20.0%	-0.65

ANALYSIS BY DAYS SINCE LAST RUN

Age	Prop	Win	Runs	Wins%	£
1..7	8%	1	6	16.7%	-0.79
8..14	25%	3	12	25.0%	-0.01
15..28	25%	3	11	27.3%	-0.18
29..60	25%	3	13	23.1%	-0.48
61..100	0%	0	0	0.0%	0.00
101+	17%	2	10	20.0%	-0.56
Unraced	0%	0	0	0.0%	0.00

ANALYSIS BY TODAY'S STARTING PRICE

Age	Prop	Win	Runs	Wins%	£
Odds On	50%	6	6	100.0%	0.72
Ev-2/1	25%	3	10	30.0%	-0.25
9/4-4/1	8%	1	12	8.3%	-0.63
9/2-6/1	17%	2	7	28.6%	0.57
13/2-10/1	0%	0	10	0.0%	-1.00
11/1-16/1	0%	0	1	0.0%	-1.00
18/1-33/1	0%	0	5	0.0%	-1.00
40/1+	0%	0	1	0.0%	-1.00

ANALYSIS BY STARTING PRICE LAST TIME

Age	Prop	Win	Runs	Wins%	£
Odds On	8%	1	1	100.0%	0.25
Ev-2/1	17%	2	5	40.0%	0.60
9/4-4/1	17%	2	9	22.2%	-0.60
9/2-6/1	25%	3	9	33.3%	-0.03
13/2-10/1	17%	2	10	20.0%	-0.64
11/1-16/1	17%	2	11	18.2%	-0.26
18/1-33/1	0%	0	5	0.0%	-1.00
40/1+	0%	0	2	0.0%	-1.00
Unraced	0%	0	0	0.0%	0.00

ANALYSIS BY DISTANCE BEATEN LAST TIME

Age	Prop	Win	Runs	Wins%	£
..-10 lgh	8%	1	5	20.0%	-0.75
-10..0	33%	4	5	80.0%	1.12
0.1..2	0%	0	3	0.0%	-1.00
2.1..5	8%	1	6	16.7%	-0.68
5.1..10	8%	1	7	14.3%	-0.66
10.1..20	8%	1	8	12.5%	-0.31
20.0..30	0%	0	4	0.0%	-1.00
30.1+	25%	3	10	30.0%	-0.09
Not Compl	8%	1	4	25.0%	-0.34
Unraced	0%	0	0	0.0%	0.00

ANALYSIS BY SUCCESS RATE IN LAST 10 RUNS

Age	Prop	Win	Runs	Wins%	£
No Wins	42%	5	28	17.9%	-0.40
1 Win	17%	2	9	22.2%	-0.21
2 Wins	33%	4	12	33.3%	-0.44
3 Wins	8%	1	3	33.3%	-0.17
4 Wins	0%	0	0	0.0%	0.00
5+ Wins	0%	0	0	0.0%	0.00

ANALYSIS BY SUCCESS RATE IN LAST 3 RUNS

Age	Prop	Win	Runs	Wins%	£
No Wins	58%	7	35	20.0%	-0.39
1 Win	17%	2	12	16.7%	-0.47
2 Wins	17%	2	4	50.0%	-0.27
3 Wins	8%	1	1	100.0%	1.50

ANALYSIS BY POSITION LAST TIME

Age	Prop	Win	Runs	Wins%	£
Won	42%	5	10	50.0%	0.18
2nd or 3rd	8%	1	11	9.1%	-0.83
Unplaced	42%	5	27	18.5%	-0.37
Fell,BD,UR	0%	0	2	0.0%	-1.00
Pulled Up	8%	1	2	50.0%	0.31
Ref/RanOut	0%	0	0	0.0%	0.00
CO/SlipUp	0%	0	0	0.0%	0.00
Unraced	0%	0	0	0.0%	0.00

OTHER FACTORS (WINS-RUNS, £)

Course Winner:	1-4	-£0.38
Distance Winner:	1-8	-£0.69
Going Winner:	2-6	£0.07
Beaten Favourite:	2-4	£0.97
7-Day Winners:	1-3	-£0.58
Absolute Favourites:	9-12	£0.48

Novices' Handicap Hurdle Races

Novices' Handicap Hurdle Races: 6 to 10 runners

ANALYSIS BY AGE

Age	Prop	Win	Runs	Wins%	£
3yo	0%	1	24	4.2%	-0.81
4yo	13%	27	241	11.2%	-0.35
5yo	31%	66	472	14.0%	0.01
6yo	25%	53	480	11.0%	-0.15
7yo	21%	44	322	13.7%	0.02
8yo	4%	8	140	5.7%	-0.55
9yo	4%	8	69	11.6%	0.24
10yo	0%	1	24	4.2%	-0.77
11yo	0%	1	10	10.0%	-0.35
12yo+	1%	2	7	28.6%	5.71

ANALYSIS BY BHB RATING

Age	Prop	Win	Runs	Wins%	£
150+	0%	0	0	0.0%	0.00
130..149	0%	0	3	0.0%	-1.00
120..129	4%	9	32	28.1%	1.38
110..119	4%	9	112	8.0%	-0.59
100..109	20%	42	339	12.4%	-0.27
80..99	57%	120	1009	11.9%	-0.13
60..79	14%	30	287	10.5%	0.15
..59	0%	0	1	0.0%	-1.00
Unrated	0%	1	6	16.7%	-0.54

ANALYSIS BY WEIGHT CARRIED

Age	Prop	Win	Runs	Wins%	£
12-01+	0%	0	1	0.0%	-1.00
11-8..12-00	22%	47	301	15.6%	-0.07
11-0..11-07	34%	72	576	12.5%	-0.12
10-8..10-13	20%	42	353	11.9%	-0.06
10-0..10-07	18%	37	404	9.2%	-0.16
..9-13	6%	13	154	8.4%	-0.18

ANALYSIS BY DAYS SINCE LAST RUN

Age	Prop	Win	Runs	Wins%	£
1..7	9%	20	103	19.4%	-0.08
8..14	17%	35	340	10.3%	-0.47
15..28	31%	65	544	11.9%	-0.08
29..60	18%	39	395	9.9%	-0.15
61..100	7%	14	129	10.9%	0.00
101+	18%	37	275	13.5%	0.24
Unraced	0%	1	3	33.3%	0.50

ANALYSIS BY TODAY'S STARTING PRICE

Age	Prop	Win	Runs	Wins%	£
Odds On	7%	14	21	66.7%	0.07
Ev-2/1	12%	25	90	27.8%	-0.28
9/4-4/1	32%	68	309	22.0%	-0.05
9/2-6/1	14%	30	248	12.1%	-0.26
13/2-10/1	18%	38	413	9.2%	-0.20
11/1-16/1	10%	22	311	7.1%	0.04
18/1-33/1	7%	14	285	4.9%	0.29
40/1+	0%	0	112	0.0%	-1.00

ANALYSIS BY STARTING PRICE LAST TIME

Age	Prop	Win	Runs	Wins%	£
Odds On	3%	6	18	33.3%	0.00
Ev-2/1	7%	14	65	21.5%	-0.23
9/4-4/1	17%	35	212	16.5%	-0.17
9/2-6/1	13%	27	187	14.4%	-0.15
13/2-10/1	18%	39	320	12.2%	-0.09
11/1-16/1	17%	35	321	10.9%	-0.22
18/1-33/1	14%	29	349	8.3%	-0.22
40/1+	12%	25	314	8.0%	0.15
Unraced	0%	1	3	33.3%	0.50

ANALYSIS BY DISTANCE BEATEN LAST TIME

Age	Prop	Win	Runs	Wins%	£
..-10 lgh	5%	10	15	66.7%	0.86
-10..0	15%	31	153	20.3%	-0.31
0.1..2	5%	11	72	15.3%	0.00
2.1..5	9%	18	113	15.9%	-0.29
5.1..10	8%	16	171	9.4%	-0.42
10.1..20	16%	33	300	11.0%	-0.23
20.0..30	12%	25	239	10.5%	-0.12
30.1+	19%	41	479	8.6%	0.04
Not Compl	12%	25	244	10.2%	0.03
Unraced	0%	1	3	33.3%	0.50

ANALYSIS BY SUCCESS RATE IN LAST 10 RUNS

Age	Prop	Win	Runs	Wins%	£
No Wins	60%	125	1257	9.9%	-0.13
1 Win	25%	52	368	14.1%	-0.10
2 Wins	13%	27	135	20.0%	0.00
3 Wins	1%	3	18	16.7%	-0.48
4 Wins	1%	3	6	50.0%	-0.07
5+ Wins	0%	0	2	0.0%	-1.00

ANALYSIS BY SUCCESS RATE IN LAST 3 RUNS

Age	Prop	Win	Runs	Wins%	£
No Wins	68%	143	1441	9.9%	-0.13
1 Win	22%	46	276	16.7%	-0.09
2 Wins	10%	21	68	30.9%	0.03
3 Wins	0%	0	1	0.0%	-1.00

ANALYSIS BY POSITION LAST TIME

Age	Prop	Win	Runs	Wins%	£
Won	19%	41	168	24.4%	-0.20
2nd or 3rd	27%	56	380	14.7%	-0.22
Unplaced	42%	89	995	8.9%	-0.09
Fell,BD,UR	2%	5	57	8.8%	-0.60
Pulled Up	9%	19	182	10.4%	0.22
Ref/RanOut	0%	0	3	0.0%	-1.00
CO/SlipUp	0%	0	1	0.0%	-1.00
Unraced	0%	1	3	33.3%	0.50

OTHER FACTORS (WINS-RUNS, £)

Course Winner:	18-103	-£0.23
Distance Winner:	32-174	£0.11
Going Winner:	41-206	£0.27
Beaten Favourite:	16-103	-£0.22
7-Day Winners:	10-19	£0.34
BHA Top Rated:	0-1	-£1.00
Absolute Favourites:	52-188	-£0.25

Race Profiles

Novices' Handicap Hurdle Races: 11 runners or more

ANALYSIS BY AGE

Age	Prop	Win	Runs	Wins%	£
3yo	1%	3	50	6.0%	-0.56
4yo	9%	40	787	5.1%	-0.39
5yo	30%	137	1769	7.7%	-0.25
6yo	33%	149	1724	8.6%	-0.10
7yo	14%	63	1074	5.9%	-0.46
8yo	9%	41	541	7.6%	-0.03
9yo	4%	16	215	7.4%	-0.22
10yo	1%	3	71	4.2%	-0.53
11yo	0%	1	22	4.5%	-0.73
12yo+	0%	0	17	0.0%	-1.00

ANALYSIS BY BHB RATING

Age	Prop	Win	Runs	Wins%	£
130..149	0%	1	21	4.8%	-0.62
120..129	2%	10	130	7.7%	-0.42
110..119	7%	30	451	6.7%	-0.38
100..109	22%	99	1139	8.7%	-0.21
80..99	57%	256	3636	7.0%	-0.26
60..79	12%	56	872	6.4%	-0.15
..59	0%	0	1	0.0%	-1.00
Unrated	0%	1	20	5.0%	-0.75

ANALYSIS BY WEIGHT CARRIED

Age	Prop	Win	Runs	Wins%	£
12-01+	0%	0	3	0.0%	-1.00
11-8..12-00	17%	79	954	8.3%	-0.32
11-0..11-07	42%	191	2352	8.1%	-0.25
10-8..10-13	20%	89	1372	6.5%	-0.36
10-0..10-07	16%	72	1200	6.0%	-0.11
..9-13	5%	22	389	5.7%	-0.12

ANALYSIS BY DAYS SINCE LAST RUN

Age	Prop	Win	Runs	Wins%	£
1..7	5%	22	243	9.1%	-0.19
8..14	16%	74	952	7.8%	-0.22
15..28	28%	127	1925	6.6%	-0.37
29..60	26%	120	1578	7.6%	-0.16
61..100	8%	38	465	8.2%	0.05
101+	16%	71	1097	6.5%	-0.35
Unraced	0%	1	10	10.0%	0.00

ANALYSIS BY TODAY'S STARTING PRICE

Age	Prop	Win	Runs	Wins%	£
Odds On	1%	4	11	36.4%	-0.36
Ev-2/1	8%	35	88	39.8%	0.05
9/4-4/1	19%	85	463	18.4%	-0.19
9/2-6/1	15%	69	561	12.3%	-0.23
13/2-10/1	27%	122	1305	9.3%	-0.16
11/1-16/1	20%	91	1454	6.3%	-0.09
18/1-33/1	8%	37	1553	2.4%	-0.43
40/1+	2%	10	835	1.2%	-0.41

ANALYSIS BY STARTING PRICE LAST TIME

Age	Prop	Win	Runs	Wins%	£
Odds On	1%	6	70	8.6%	-0.55
Ev-2/1	8%	34	220	15.5%	-0.17
9/4-4/1	17%	76	707	10.7%	-0.27
9/2-6/1	11%	48	567	8.5%	-0.41
13/2-10/1	19%	88	1136	7.7%	-0.20
11/1-16/1	20%	91	1151	7.9%	-0.08
18/1-33/1	15%	67	1273	5.3%	-0.32
40/1+	9%	42	1136	3.7%	-0.31
Unraced	0%	1	10	10.0%	0.00

ANALYSIS BY DISTANCE BEATEN LAST TIME

Age	Prop	Win	Runs	Wins%	£
..-10 lgh	1%	5	60	8.3%	-0.59
-10..0	12%	56	519	10.8%	-0.28
0.1..2	6%	26	265	9.8%	-0.39
2.1..5	8%	34	387	8.8%	-0.38
5.1..10	13%	57	557	10.2%	-0.23
10.1..20	17%	78	985	7.9%	-0.18
20.0..30	12%	54	790	6.8%	-0.14
30.1+	22%	100	1848	5.4%	-0.21
Not Compl	9%	42	849	4.9%	-0.40
Unraced	0%	1	10	10.0%	0.00

ANALYSIS BY SUCCESS RATE IN LAST 10 RUNS

Age	Prop	Win	Runs	Wins%	£
No Wins	60%	272	4435	6.1%	-0.27
1 Win	28%	127	1317	9.6%	-0.19
2 Wins	9%	41	389	10.5%	-0.21
3 Wins	2%	8	88	9.1%	-0.44
4 Wins	1%	3	26	11.5%	-0.51
5+ Wins	0%	1	5	20.0%	-0.52

ANALYSIS BY SUCCESS RATE IN LAST 3 RUNS

Age	Prop	Win	Runs	Wins%	£
No Wins	72%	327	5046	6.5%	-0.25
1 Win	24%	108	1042	10.4%	-0.23
2 Wins	4%	16	163	9.8%	-0.52
3 Wins	0%	1	9	11.1%	-0.74

ANALYSIS BY POSITION LAST TIME

Age	Prop	Win	Runs	Wins%	£
Won	13%	61	579	10.5%	-0.31
2nd or 3rd	25%	113	1268	8.9%	-0.31
Unplaced	52%	236	3570	6.6%	-0.19
Fell,BD,UR	3%	14	228	6.1%	-0.41
Pulled Up	6%	25	595	4.2%	-0.42
Ref/RanOut	0%	2	15	13.3%	0.87
CO/SlipUp	0%	1	5	20.0%	0.00
Unraced	0%	1	10	10.0%	0.00

OTHER FACTORS (WINS-RUNS, £)

Course Winner:	19-225	-£0.39
Distance Winner:	54-654	-£0.39
Going Winner:	71-699	-£0.27
Beaten Favourite:	47-352	-£0.27
7-Day Winners:	11-59	-£0.33
Absolute Favourites:	94-402	-£0.15

TRAINERS (WINS-RUNS, £)

R Ford 4-19 £0.49; Mrs E Slack 3-19 £0.42; T R George 9-66 £0.12; P F Nicholls 6-33 £0.22; Jim Best 5-16 £0.36; M Sheppard 3-45 £0.12; A J Martin 3-11 £0.46; Mrs K Walton 3-22 £0.23; N A Twiston-Davies 10-69 £0.05; A M Hales 4-32 £0.08.

Novices' Handicap Hurdle Races

Novices' Handicap Hurdle Races: up to 7 days off the track

ANALYSIS BY AGE
Age	Prop	Win	Runs	Wins%	£
3yo	2%	1	7	14.3%	-0.46
4yo	11%	5	58	8.6%	-0.52
5yo	24%	11	95	11.6%	-0.31
6yo	27%	12	81	14.8%	0.25
7yo	22%	10	66	15.2%	0.25
8yo	7%	3	32	9.4%	-0.60
9yo	7%	3	21	14.3%	-0.36
10yo	0%	0	3	0.0%	-1.00
11yo	0%	0	2	0.0%	-1.00
12yo+	0%	0	0	0.0%	0.00

ANALYSIS BY BHB RATING
Age	Prop	Win	Runs	Wins%	£
150+	0%	0	0	0.0%	0.00
130..149	0%	0	0	0.0%	0.00
120..129	4%	2	6	33.3%	0.21
110..119	7%	3	25	12.0%	-0.58
100..109	24%	11	58	19.0%	-0.24
80..99	56%	25	210	11.9%	-0.27
60..79	9%	4	62	6.5%	0.50
..59	0%	0	0	0.0%	0.00
Unrated	0%	0	4	0.0%	-1.00

ANALYSIS BY WEIGHT CARRIED
Age	Prop	Win	Runs	Wins%	£
12-01+	0%	0	2	0.0%	-1.00
11-8..12-00	20%	9	49	18.4%	-0.48
11-0..11-07	36%	16	116	13.8%	-0.34
10-8..10-13	20%	9	90	10.0%	-0.13
10-0..10-07	22%	10	74	13.5%	0.64
..9-13	2%	1	34	2.9%	-0.81

ANALYSIS BY DAYS SINCE LAST RUN
Age	Prop	Win	Runs	Wins%	£
1..7	96%	43	352	12.2%	-0.17
8..14	0%	0	0	0.0%	0.00
15..28	0%	0	0	0.0%	0.00
29..60	0%	0	0	0.0%	0.00
61..100	0%	0	0	0.0%	0.00
101+	0%	0	0	0.0%	0.00
Unraced	4%	2	13	15.4%	0.12

ANALYSIS BY TODAY'S STARTING PRICE
Age	Prop	Win	Runs	Wins%	£
Odds On	18%	8	14	57.1%	-0.11
Ev-2/1	22%	10	31	32.3%	-0.19
9/4-4/1	33%	15	55	27.3%	0.13
9/2-6/1	9%	4	43	9.3%	-0.40
13/2-10/1	4%	2	57	3.5%	-0.69
11/1-16/1	7%	3	66	4.5%	-0.32
18/1-33/1	4%	2	58	3.4%	0.17
40/1+	2%	1	41	2.4%	0.24

ANALYSIS BY STARTING PRICE LAST TIME
Age	Prop	Win	Runs	Wins%	£
Odds On	9%	4	5	80.0%	0.19
Ev-2/1	13%	6	19	31.6%	-0.08
9/4-4/1	27%	12	41	29.3%	0.27
9/2-6/1	16%	7	48	14.6%	-0.26
13/2-10/1	13%	6	52	11.5%	0.34
11/1-16/1	7%	3	71	4.2%	-0.80
18/1-33/1	9%	4	62	6.5%	0.03
40/1+	2%	1	54	1.9%	-0.37
Unraced	4%	2	13	15.4%	0.12

ANALYSIS BY DISTANCE BEATEN LAST TIME
Age	Prop	Win	Runs	Wins%	£
..-10 lgh	9%	4	13	30.8%	-0.10
-10..0	40%	18	69	26.1%	-0.21
0.1..2	7%	3	18	16.7%	-0.18
2.1..5	11%	5	28	17.9%	-0.23
5.1..10	7%	3	34	8.8%	-0.28
10.1..20	7%	3	44	6.8%	-0.70
20.0..30	2%	1	40	2.5%	-0.63
30.1+	7%	3	66	4.5%	0.26
Not Compl	7%	3	40	7.5%	0.37
Unraced	4%	2	13	15.4%	0.12

ANALYSIS BY SUCCESS RATE IN LAST 10 RUNS
Age	Prop	Win	Runs	Wins%	£
No Wins	37%	16	196	8.2%	0.04
1 Win	28%	12	105	11.4%	-0.62
2 Wins	33%	14	40	35.0%	0.11
3 Wins	2%	1	8	12.5%	-0.44
4 Wins	0%	0	3	0.0%	-1.00
5+ Wins	0%	0	0	0.0%	0.00

ANALYSIS BY SUCCESS RATE IN LAST 3 RUNS
Age	Prop	Win	Runs	Wins%	£
No Wins	40%	17	237	7.2%	-0.11
1 Win	35%	15	91	16.5%	-0.45
2 Wins	26%	11	24	45.8%	0.32
3 Wins	0%	0	0	0.0%	0.00

ANALYSIS BY POSITION LAST TIME
Age	Prop	Win	Runs	Wins%	£
Won	49%	22	81	27.2%	-0.18
2nd or 3rd	29%	13	74	17.6%	-0.06
Unplaced	11%	5	157	3.2%	-0.35
Fell,BD,UR	4%	2	12	16.7%	-0.68
Pulled Up	2%	1	26	3.8%	0.96
Ref/RanOut	0%	0	1	0.0%	-1.00
CO/SlipUp	0%	0	1	0.0%	-1.00
Unraced	4%	2	13	15.4%	0.12

OTHER FACTORS (WINS-RUNS, £)
Course Winner:	4-20	-£0.30
Distance Winner:	9-60	-£0.47
Going Winner:	18-75	£0.18
Beaten Favourite:	4-11	£0.03
7-Day Winners:	22-81	-£0.18
Absolute Favourites:	23-69	-£0.17

Race Profiles

Novices' Handicap Hurdle Races: 100+ days off the track

ANALYSIS BY AGE

Age	Prop	Win	Runs	Wins%	£
3yo	0%	0	0	0.0%	0.00
4yo	11%	12	155	7.7%	-0.37
5yo	32%	35	342	10.2%	0.04
6yo	24%	26	368	7.1%	-0.41
7yo	16%	18	260	6.9%	-0.38
8yo	11%	12	160	7.5%	-0.25
9yo	4%	4	69	5.8%	-0.08
10yo	2%	2	22	9.1%	-0.16
11yo	0%	0	7	0.0%	-1.00
12yo+	1%	1	9	11.1%	1.89

ANALYSIS BY BHB RATING

Age	Prop	Win	Runs	Wins%	£
150+	0%	0	0	0.0%	0.00
130..149	0%	0	1	0.0%	-1.00
120..129	2%	2	10	20.0%	2.35
110..119	5%	5	57	8.8%	-0.26
100..109	22%	24	222	10.8%	0.07
80..99	50%	55	836	6.6%	-0.43
60..79	22%	24	261	9.2%	0.02
..59	0%	0	1	0.0%	-1.00
Unrated	0%	0	4	0.0%	-1.00

ANALYSIS BY WEIGHT CARRIED

Age	Prop	Win	Runs	Wins%	£
12-01+	0%	0	0	0.0%	0.00
11-8..12-00	18%	20	211	9.5%	-0.35
11-0..11-07	35%	38	497	7.6%	-0.31
10-8..10-13	17%	19	304	6.3%	-0.27
10-0..10-07	25%	27	287	9.4%	-0.02
..9-13	5%	6	93	6.5%	-0.14

ANALYSIS BY DAYS SINCE LAST RUN

Age	Prop	Win	Runs	Wins%	£
1..7	0%	0	0	0.0%	0.00
8..14	0%	0	0	0.0%	0.00
15..28	0%	0	0	0.0%	0.00
29..60	0%	0	0	0.0%	0.00
61..100	0%	0	10	0.0%	-1.00
101+	100%	110	1382	8.0%	-0.23
Unraced	0%	0	0	0.0%	0.00

ANALYSIS BY TODAY'S STARTING PRICE

Age	Prop	Win	Runs	Wins%	£
Odds On	4%	4	4	100.0%	0.78
Ev-2/1	9%	10	23	43.5%	0.19
9/4-4/1	23%	25	108	23.1%	-0.01
9/2-6/1	12%	13	107	12.1%	-0.26
13/2-10/1	23%	25	251	10.0%	-0.10
11/1-16/1	19%	21	288	7.3%	0.07
18/1-33/1	10%	11	367	3.0%	-0.28
40/1+	1%	1	244	0.4%	-0.83

ANALYSIS BY STARTING PRICE LAST TIME

Age	Prop	Win	Runs	Wins%	£
Odds On	1%	1	9	11.1%	-0.44
Ev-2/1	5%	5	46	10.9%	-0.51
9/4-4/1	15%	17	149	11.4%	-0.07
9/2-6/1	7%	8	121	6.6%	-0.52
13/2-10/1	22%	24	245	9.8%	0.05
11/1-16/1	19%	21	260	8.1%	-0.08
18/1-33/1	16%	18	288	6.3%	-0.43
40/1+	15%	16	274	5.8%	-0.37
Unraced	0%	0	0	0.0%	0.00

ANALYSIS BY DISTANCE BEATEN LAST TIME

Age	Prop	Win	Runs	Wins%	£
..-10 lgh	2%	2	5	40.0%	0.25
-10..0	3%	3	33	9.1%	-0.70
0.1..2	3%	3	37	8.1%	-0.34
2.1..5	3%	3	44	6.8%	-0.47
5.1..10	5%	6	91	6.6%	-0.43
10.1..20	11%	12	172	7.0%	-0.22
20.0..30	15%	17	184	9.2%	-0.23
30.1+	44%	48	534	9.0%	0.00
Not Compl	15%	16	292	5.5%	-0.54
Unraced	0%	0	0	0.0%	0.00

ANALYSIS BY SUCCESS RATE IN LAST 10 RUNS

Age	Prop	Win	Runs	Wins%	£
No Wins	70%	77	1141	6.7%	-0.32
1 Win	16%	18	180	10.0%	0.05
2 Wins	8%	9	55	16.4%	0.47
3 Wins	3%	3	11	27.3%	-0.25
4 Wins	3%	3	4	75.0%	0.85
5+ Wins	0%	0	1	0.0%	-1.00

ANALYSIS BY SUCCESS RATE IN LAST 3 RUNS

Age	Prop	Win	Runs	Wins%	£
No Wins	85%	93	1256	7.4%	-0.26
1 Win	9%	10	112	8.9%	-0.13
2 Wins	6%	7	24	29.2%	0.38
3 Wins	0%	0	0	0.0%	0.00

ANALYSIS BY POSITION LAST TIME

Age	Prop	Win	Runs	Wins%	£
Won	5%	5	38	13.2%	-0.57
2nd or 3rd	18%	20	184	10.9%	-0.12
Unplaced	63%	69	879	7.8%	-0.15
Fell,BD,UR	1%	1	52	1.9%	-0.89
Pulled Up	14%	15	233	6.4%	-0.45
Ref/RanOut	0%	0	6	0.0%	-1.00
CO/SlipUp	0%	0	0	0.0%	0.00
Unraced	0%	0	0	0.0%	0.00

OTHER FACTORS (WINS-RUNS, £)

Course Winner:	3-33	-£0.24
Distance Winner:	8-70	£0.17
Going Winner:	15-101	£0.26
Beaten Favourite:	10-89	-£0.36
Absolute Favourites:	22-75	-£0.10

Selling Handicap Hurdle Races

Selling Handicap Hurdle Races

ANALYSIS BY AGE

Age	Prop	Win	Runs	Wins%	£
3yo	0%	0	9	0.0%	-1.00
4yo	6%	19	414	4.6%	-0.50
5yo	15%	45	621	7.2%	-0.29
6yo	23%	68	668	10.2%	-0.06
7yo	17%	50	580	8.6%	-0.19
8yo	15%	46	576	8.0%	-0.31
9yo	6%	17	364	4.7%	-0.56
10yo	7%	20	267	7.5%	-0.06
11yo	5%	14	147	9.5%	-0.18
12yo+	6%	18	148	12.2%	0.83

ANALYSIS BY BHB RATING

Age	Prop	Win	Runs	Wins%	£
150+	0%	0	0	0.0%	0.00
130..149	0%	0	0	0.0%	0.00
120..129	0%	0	0	0.0%	0.00
110..119	0%	0	0	0.0%	0.00
100..109	0%	1	11	9.1%	1.36
80..99	56%	167	1927	8.7%	-0.31
60..79	43%	129	1852	7.0%	-0.15
..59	0%	0	4	0.0%	-1.00
Unrated	0%	0	0	0.0%	0.00

ANALYSIS BY WEIGHT CARRIED

Age	Prop	Win	Runs	Wins%	£
12-01+	0%	0	1	0.0%	-1.00
11-8..12-00	18%	53	443	12.0%	-0.16
11-0..11-07	36%	106	1293	8.2%	-0.32
10-8..10-13	23%	68	885	7.7%	-0.15
10-0..10-07	16%	48	840	5.7%	-0.26
..9-13	7%	22	332	6.6%	-0.05

ANALYSIS BY DAYS SINCE LAST RUN

Age	Prop	Win	Runs	Wins%	£
1..7	10%	30	280	10.7%	-0.09
8..14	18%	53	699	7.6%	-0.44
15..28	32%	94	1169	8.0%	-0.24
29..60	23%	67	786	8.5%	0.01
61..100	7%	22	265	8.3%	0.07
101+	10%	31	595	5.2%	-0.46
Unraced	0%	0	0	0.0%	0.00

ANALYSIS BY TODAY'S STARTING PRICE

Age	Prop	Win	Runs	Wins%	£
Odds On	0%	1	3	33.3%	-0.39
Ev-2/1	5%	14	34	41.2%	0.05
9/4-4/1	20%	60	296	20.3%	-0.13
9/2-6/1	25%	73	442	16.5%	0.03
13/2-10/1	27%	79	917	8.6%	-0.23
11/1-16/1	14%	43	849	5.1%	-0.28
18/1-33/1	7%	21	868	2.4%	-0.35
40/1+	2%	6	385	1.6%	-0.20

ANALYSIS BY STARTING PRICE LAST TIME

Age	Prop	Win	Runs	Wins%	£
Odds On	0%	0	3	0.0%	-1.00
Ev-2/1	1%	3	19	15.8%	-0.34
9/4-4/1	10%	29	199	14.6%	-0.06
9/2-6/1	12%	35	294	11.9%	-0.19
13/2-10/1	24%	70	659	10.6%	-0.27
11/1-16/1	22%	65	777	8.4%	-0.13
18/1-33/1	20%	59	941	6.3%	-0.16
40/1+	12%	36	902	4.0%	-0.38
Unraced	0%	0	0	0.0%	0.00

ANALYSIS BY DISTANCE BEATEN LAST TIME

Age	Prop	Win	Runs	Wins%	£
..-10 lgh	1%	3	15	20.0%	-0.42
-10..0	5%	14	72	19.4%	0.23
0.1..2	5%	15	96	15.6%	-0.05
2.1..5	6%	19	128	14.8%	0.06
5.1..10	12%	36	248	14.5%	0.02
10.1..20	20%	58	557	10.4%	-0.16
20.0..30	14%	43	509	8.4%	0.02
30.1+	27%	80	1382	5.8%	-0.32
Not Compl	10%	29	787	3.7%	-0.44
Unraced	0%	0	0	0.0%	0.00

ANALYSIS BY SUCCESS RATE IN LAST 10 RUNS

Age	Prop	Win	Runs	Wins%	£
No Wins	66%	197	2861	6.9%	-0.24
1 Win	27%	79	771	10.2%	-0.17
2 Wins	6%	19	147	12.9%	-0.16
3 Wins	1%	2	15	13.3%	-0.30
4 Wins	0%	0	0	0.0%	0.00
5+ Wins	0%	0	0	0.0%	0.00

ANALYSIS BY SUCCESS RATE IN LAST 3 RUNS

Age	Prop	Win	Runs	Wins%	£
No Wins	89%	263	3537	7.4%	-0.23
1 Win	11%	33	250	13.2%	-0.20
2 Wins	0%	1	7	14.3%	-0.74
3 Wins	0%	0	0	0.0%	0.00

ANALYSIS BY POSITION LAST TIME

Age	Prop	Win	Runs	Wins%	£
Won	6%	17	87	19.5%	0.11
2nd or 3rd	23%	69	482	14.3%	0.02
Unplaced	61%	182	2441	7.5%	-0.22
Fell,BD,UR	3%	10	165	6.1%	0.17
Pulled Up	6%	19	604	3.1%	-0.59
Ref/RanOut	0%	0	13	0.0%	-1.00
CO/SlipUp	0%	0	2	0.0%	-1.00
Unraced	0%	0	0	0.0%	0.00

OTHER FACTORS (WINS-RUNS, £)

Course Winner:	45-335	£0.23
Distance Winner:	68-637	-£0.07
Going Winner:	59-707	-£0.23
Beaten Favourite:	9-106	-£0.61
7-Day Winners:	5-13	£0.36
Absolute Favourites:	57-254	-£0.09

Race Profiles

Selling Handicap Hurdle Races: 2m to 2m3f

ANALYSIS BY AGE

Age	Prop	Win	Runs	Wins%	£
3yo	0%	0	9	0.0%	-1.00
4yo	7%	13	302	4.3%	-0.59
5yo	16%	28	414	6.8%	-0.28
6yo	26%	45	396	11.4%	0.04
7yo	19%	34	341	10.0%	0.02
8yo	12%	21	329	6.4%	-0.37
9yo	8%	14	197	7.1%	-0.31
10yo	5%	8	124	6.5%	0.10
11yo	2%	4	65	6.2%	-0.53
12yo+	5%	8	67	11.9%	0.48

ANALYSIS BY BHB RATING

Age	Prop	Win	Runs	Wins%	£
150+	0%	0	0	0.0%	0.00
130..149	0%	0	0	0.0%	0.00
120..129	0%	0	0	0.0%	0.00
110..119	0%	0	0	0.0%	0.00
100..109	0%	0	0	0.0%	0.00
80..99	54%	95	1114	8.5%	-0.31
60..79	46%	80	1128	7.1%	-0.10
..59	0%	0	2	0.0%	-1.00
Unrated	0%	0	0	0.0%	0.00

ANALYSIS BY WEIGHT CARRIED

Age	Prop	Win	Runs	Wins%	£
12-01+	0%	0	1	0.0%	-1.00
11-8..12-00	19%	34	259	13.1%	-0.20
11-0..11-07	33%	58	761	7.6%	-0.32
10-8..10-13	22%	38	537	7.1%	-0.16
10-0..10-07	19%	33	494	6.7%	-0.07
..9-13	7%	12	192	6.3%	-0.18

ANALYSIS BY DAYS SINCE LAST RUN

Age	Prop	Win	Runs	Wins%	£
1..7	11%	20	182	11.0%	-0.14
8..14	19%	33	400	8.3%	-0.38
15..28	29%	50	692	7.2%	-0.32
29..60	25%	44	462	9.5%	0.32
61..100	7%	12	148	8.1%	0.03
101+	9%	16	360	4.4%	-0.58
Unraced	0%	0	0	0.0%	0.00

ANALYSIS BY TODAY'S STARTING PRICE

Age	Prop	Win	Runs	Wins%	£
Odds On	0%	0	2	0.0%	-1.00
Ev-2/1	6%	11	22	50.0%	0.29
9/4-4/1	20%	35	171	20.5%	-0.13
9/2-6/1	24%	42	257	16.3%	0.02
13/2-10/1	26%	45	539	8.3%	-0.26
11/1-16/1	13%	23	510	4.5%	-0.34
18/1-33/1	9%	15	521	2.9%	-0.23
40/1+	2%	4	222	1.8%	-0.03

ANALYSIS BY STARTING PRICE LAST TIME

Age	Prop	Win	Runs	Wins%	£
Odds On	0%	0	3	0.0%	-1.00
Ev-2/1	1%	2	10	20.0%	-0.13
9/4-4/1	9%	16	120	13.3%	-0.41
9/2-6/1	12%	21	164	12.8%	-0.04
13/2-10/1	22%	38	370	10.3%	-0.31
11/1-16/1	20%	35	460	7.6%	-0.14
18/1-33/1	22%	39	570	6.8%	-0.12
40/1+	14%	24	547	4.4%	-0.27
Unraced	0%	0	0	0.0%	0.00

ANALYSIS BY DISTANCE BEATEN LAST TIME

Age	Prop	Win	Runs	Wins%	£
..-10 lgh	1%	2	7	28.6%	-0.30
-10..0	5%	9	41	22.0%	0.34
0.1..2	3%	6	51	11.8%	-0.45
2.1..5	6%	11	72	15.3%	-0.07
5.1..10	15%	26	148	17.6%	0.30
10.1..20	17%	30	329	9.1%	-0.31
20.0..30	15%	27	312	8.7%	-0.06
30.1+	27%	48	806	6.0%	-0.24
Not Compl	9%	16	478	3.3%	-0.36
Unraced	0%	0	0	0.0%	0.00

ANALYSIS BY SUCCESS RATE IN LAST 10 RUNS

Age	Prop	Win	Runs	Wins%	£
No Wins	65%	114	1761	6.5%	-0.26
1 Win	27%	47	404	11.6%	-0.03
2 Wins	7%	13	72	18.1%	0.32
3 Wins	1%	1	7	14.3%	-0.29
4 Wins	0%	0	0	0.0%	0.00
5+ Wins	0%	0	0	0.0%	0.00

ANALYSIS BY SUCCESS RATE IN LAST 3 RUNS

Age	Prop	Win	Runs	Wins%	£
No Wins	86%	151	2113	7.1%	-0.22
1 Win	14%	24	128	18.8%	0.08
2 Wins	0%	0	3	0.0%	-1.00
3 Wins	0%	0	0	0.0%	0.00

ANALYSIS BY POSITION LAST TIME

Age	Prop	Win	Runs	Wins%	£
Won	6%	11	48	22.9%	0.25
2nd or 3rd	23%	40	259	15.4%	0.12
Unplaced	62%	108	1460	7.4%	-0.22
Fell,BD,UR	3%	5	104	4.8%	0.20
Pulled Up	6%	11	363	3.0%	-0.50
Ref/RanOut	0%	0	8	0.0%	-1.00
CO/SlipUp	0%	0	2	0.0%	-1.00
Unraced	0%	0	0	0.0%	0.00

OTHER FACTORS (WINS-RUNS, £)

Course Winner:	23-164	£0.07
Distance Winner:	44-387	-£0.08
Going Winner:	31-368	-£0.22
Beaten Favourite:	7-71	-£0.55
7-Day Winners:	4-9	£0.76
Absolute Favourites:	32-151	-£0.20

Selling Handicap Hurdle Races

Selling Handicap Hurdle Races: 2m4f to 2m7f

ANALYSIS BY AGE

Age	Prop	Win	Runs	Wins%	£
3yo	0%	0	0	0.0%	0.00
4yo	6%	6	102	5.9%	-0.21
5yo	13%	14	186	7.5%	-0.32
6yo	20%	22	258	8.5%	-0.19
7yo	12%	13	207	6.3%	-0.51
8yo	21%	23	221	10.4%	-0.20
9yo	3%	3	148	2.0%	-0.83
10yo	10%	11	129	8.5%	-0.19
11yo	7%	8	68	11.8%	0.06
12yo+	8%	9	65	13.8%	1.24

ANALYSIS BY BHB RATING

Age	Prop	Win	Runs	Wins%	£
150+	0%	0	0	0.0%	0.00
130..149	0%	0	0	0.0%	0.00
120..129	0%	0	0	0.0%	0.00
110..119	0%	0	0	0.0%	0.00
100..109	1%	1	11	9.1%	1.36
80..99	56%	61	723	8.4%	-0.33
60..79	43%	47	648	7.3%	-0.18
..59	0%	0	2	0.0%	-1.00
Unrated	0%	0	0	0.0%	0.00

ANALYSIS BY WEIGHT CARRIED

Age	Prop	Win	Runs	Wins%	£
12-01+	0%	0	0	0.0%	0.00
11-8..12-00	16%	17	167	10.2%	-0.12
11-0..11-07	38%	41	480	8.5%	-0.34
10-8..10-13	25%	27	316	8.5%	-0.17
10-0..10-07	13%	14	301	4.7%	-0.48
..9-13	9%	10	120	8.3%	0.31

ANALYSIS BY DAYS SINCE LAST RUN

Age	Prop	Win	Runs	Wins%	£
1..7	8%	9	92	9.8%	-0.01
8..14	15%	16	262	6.1%	-0.56
15..28	35%	38	422	9.0%	-0.11
29..60	20%	22	286	7.7%	-0.37
61..100	9%	10	113	8.8%	0.17
101+	13%	14	209	6.7%	-0.30
Unraced	0%	0	0	0.0%	0.00

ANALYSIS BY TODAY'S STARTING PRICE

Age	Prop	Win	Runs	Wins%	£
Odds On	1%	1	1	100.0%	0.83
Ev-2/1	3%	3	12	25.0%	-0.37
9/4-4/1	20%	22	115	19.1%	-0.17
9/2-6/1	26%	28	157	17.8%	0.11
13/2-10/1	26%	28	333	8.4%	-0.23
11/1-16/1	18%	20	306	6.5%	-0.09
18/1-33/1	5%	5	318	1.6%	-0.57
40/1+	2%	2	142	1.4%	-0.35

ANALYSIS BY STARTING PRICE LAST TIME

Age	Prop	Win	Runs	Wins%	£
Odds On	0%	0	0	0.0%	0.00
Ev-2/1	0%	0	8	0.0%	-1.00
9/4-4/1	11%	12	71	16.9%	0.51
9/2-6/1	12%	13	115	11.3%	-0.33
13/2-10/1	28%	31	266	11.7%	-0.18
11/1-16/1	23%	25	283	8.8%	-0.14
18/1-33/1	16%	17	331	5.1%	-0.26
40/1+	10%	11	310	3.5%	-0.52
Unraced	0%	0	0	0.0%	0.00

ANALYSIS BY DISTANCE BEATEN LAST TIME

Age	Prop	Win	Runs	Wins%	£
..-10 lgh	0%	0	6	0.0%	-1.00
-10..0	3%	3	28	10.7%	-0.42
0.1..2	7%	8	39	20.5%	0.43
2.1..5	7%	8	51	15.7%	0.34
5.1..10	8%	9	89	10.1%	-0.36
10.1..20	20%	22	204	10.8%	-0.03
20.0..30	13%	14	182	7.7%	0.04
30.1+	29%	32	519	6.2%	-0.38
Not Compl	12%	13	266	4.9%	-0.49
Unraced	0%	0	0	0.0%	0.00

ANALYSIS BY SUCCESS RATE IN LAST 10 RUNS

Age	Prop	Win	Runs	Wins%	£
No Wins	69%	75	984	7.6%	-0.19
1 Win	27%	29	326	8.9%	-0.32
2 Wins	4%	4	67	6.0%	-0.76
3 Wins	1%	1	7	14.3%	-0.21
4 Wins	0%	0	0	0.0%	0.00
5+ Wins	0%	0	0	0.0%	0.00

ANALYSIS BY SUCCESS RATE IN LAST 3 RUNS

Age	Prop	Win	Runs	Wins%	£
No Wins	94%	103	1274	8.1%	-0.21
1 Win	5%	5	106	4.7%	-0.69
2 Wins	1%	1	4	25.0%	-0.54
3 Wins	0%	0	0	0.0%	0.00

ANALYSIS BY POSITION LAST TIME

Age	Prop	Win	Runs	Wins%	£
Won	3%	3	34	8.8%	-0.52
2nd or 3rd	25%	27	202	13.4%	-0.09
Unplaced	61%	66	884	7.5%	-0.20
Fell,BD,UR	5%	5	48	10.4%	0.42
Pulled Up	7%	8	212	3.8%	-0.68
Ref/RanOut	0%	0	4	0.0%	-1.00
CO/SlipUp	0%	0	0	0.0%	0.00
Unraced	0%	0	0	0.0%	0.00

OTHER FACTORS (WINS-RUNS, £)

Course Winner:	20-150	£0.36
Distance Winner:	23-231	-£0.08
Going Winner:	22-301	-£0.35
Beaten Favourite:	2-33	-£0.70
7-Day Winners:	1-4	-£0.54
Absolute Favourites:	21-91	-£0.02

Race Profiles

Selling Handicap Hurdle Races: 3m+

ANALYSIS BY AGE

Age	Prop	Win	Runs	Wins%	£
3yo	0%	0	0	0.0%	0.00
4yo	0%	0	10	0.0%	-1.00
5yo	23%	3	21	14.3%	-0.25
6yo	8%	1	14	7.1%	-0.50
7yo	23%	3	32	9.4%	-0.30
8yo	15%	2	26	7.7%	-0.52
9yo	0%	0	19	0.0%	-1.00
10yo	8%	1	14	7.1%	-0.36
11yo	15%	2	14	14.3%	0.29
12yo+	8%	1	16	6.3%	0.63

ANALYSIS BY BHB RATING

Age	Prop	Win	Runs	Wins%	£
150+	0%	0	0	0.0%	0.00
130..149	0%	0	0	0.0%	0.00
120..129	0%	0	0	0.0%	0.00
110..119	0%	0	0	0.0%	0.00
100..109	0%	0	0	0.0%	0.00
80..99	85%	11	90	12.2%	-0.11
60..79	15%	2	76	2.6%	-0.59
..59	0%	0	0	0.0%	0.00
Unrated	0%	0	0	0.0%	0.00

ANALYSIS BY WEIGHT CARRIED

Age	Prop	Win	Runs	Wins%	£
12-01+	0%	0	0	0.0%	0.00
11-8..12-00	15%	2	17	11.8%	0.06
11-0..11-07	54%	7	52	13.5%	-0.07
10-8..10-13	23%	3	32	9.4%	0.23
10-0..10-07	8%	1	45	2.2%	-0.89
..9-13	0%	0	20	0.0%	-1.00

ANALYSIS BY DAYS SINCE LAST RUN

Age	Prop	Win	Runs	Wins%	£
1..7	8%	1	6	16.7%	0.33
8..14	31%	4	37	10.8%	-0.11
15..28	46%	6	55	10.9%	-0.30
29..60	8%	1	38	2.6%	-0.87
61..100	0%	0	4	0.0%	-1.00
101+	8%	1	26	3.8%	0.00
Unraced	0%	0	0	0.0%	0.00

ANALYSIS BY TODAY'S STARTING PRICE

Age	Prop	Win	Runs	Wins%	£
Odds On	0%	0	0	0.0%	0.00
Ev-2/1	0%	0	0	0.0%	0.00
9/4-4/1	23%	3	10	30.0%	0.33
9/2-6/1	23%	3	28	10.7%	-0.27
13/2-10/1	46%	6	45	13.3%	0.13
11/1-16/1	0%	0	33	0.0%	-1.00
18/1-33/1	8%	1	29	3.4%	-0.10
40/1+	0%	0	21	0.0%	-1.00

ANALYSIS BY STARTING PRICE LAST TIME

Age	Prop	Win	Runs	Wins%	£
Odds On	0%	0	0	0.0%	0.00
Ev-2/1	8%	1	1	100.0%	2.75
9/4-4/1	8%	1	8	12.5%	0.13
9/2-6/1	8%	1	15	6.7%	-0.70
13/2-10/1	8%	1	23	4.3%	-0.70
11/1-16/1	38%	5	34	14.7%	0.10
18/1-33/1	23%	3	40	7.5%	0.03
40/1+	8%	1	45	2.2%	-0.82
Unraced	0%	0	0	0.0%	0.00

ANALYSIS BY DISTANCE BEATEN LAST TIME

Age	Prop	Win	Runs	Wins%	£
..-10 lgh	8%	1	2	50.0%	0.88
-10..0	15%	2	3	66.7%	4.67
0.1..2	8%	1	6	16.7%	0.33
2.1..5	0%	0	5	0.0%	-1.00
5.1..10	8%	1	11	9.1%	-0.59
10.1..20	46%	6	24	25.0%	0.81
20.0..30	15%	2	15	13.3%	1.27
30.1+	0%	0	57	0.0%	-1.00
Not Compl	0%	0	43	0.0%	-1.00
Unraced	0%	0	0	0.0%	0.00

ANALYSIS BY SUCCESS RATE IN LAST 10 RUNS

Age	Prop	Win	Runs	Wins%	£
No Wins	62%	8	116	6.9%	-0.36
1 Win	23%	3	41	7.3%	-0.41
2 Wins	15%	2	8	25.0%	0.59
3 Wins	0%	0	1	0.0%	-1.00
4 Wins	0%	0	0	0.0%	0.00
5+ Wins	0%	0	0	0.0%	0.00

ANALYSIS BY SUCCESS RATE IN LAST 3 RUNS

Age	Prop	Win	Runs	Wins%	£
No Wins	69%	9	150	6.0%	-0.46
1 Win	31%	4	16	25.0%	0.86
2 Wins	0%	0	0	0.0%	0.00
3 Wins	0%	0	0	0.0%	0.00

ANALYSIS BY POSITION LAST TIME

Age	Prop	Win	Runs	Wins%	£
Won	23%	3	5	60.0%	3.15
2nd or 3rd	15%	2	21	9.5%	-0.29
Unplaced	62%	8	97	8.2%	-0.23
Fell,BD,UR	0%	0	13	0.0%	-1.00
Pulled Up	0%	0	29	0.0%	-1.00
Ref/RanOut	0%	0	1	0.0%	-1.00
CO/SlipUp	0%	0	0	0.0%	0.00
Unraced	0%	0	0	0.0%	0.00

OTHER FACTORS (WINS-RUNS, £)

Course Winner:	2-21	£0.57
Distance Winner:	1-19	£0.37
Going Winner:	6-38	£0.56
Beaten Favourite:	0-2	-£1.00
Absolute Favourites:	4-12	£0.77

Selling Handicap Hurdle Races

Selling Handicap Hurdle Races: 6 to 10 runners

ANALYSIS BY AGE

Age	Prop	Win	Runs	Wins%	£
3yo	0%	0	0	0.0%	0.00
4yo	9%	7	85	8.2%	-0.48
5yo	15%	12	107	11.2%	-0.18
6yo	22%	17	134	12.7%	-0.29
7yo	19%	15	109	13.8%	-0.17
8yo	13%	10	105	9.5%	-0.22
9yo	6%	5	52	9.6%	-0.39
10yo	5%	4	61	6.6%	-0.71
11yo	5%	4	26	15.4%	0.10
12yo+	6%	5	21	23.8%	1.31

ANALYSIS BY BHB RATING

Age	Prop	Win	Runs	Wins%	£
150+	0%	0	0	0.0%	0.00
130..149	0%	0	0	0.0%	0.00
120..129	0%	0	0	0.0%	0.00
110..119	0%	0	0	0.0%	0.00
100..109	0%	0	2	0.0%	-1.00
80..99	56%	44	368	12.0%	-0.27
60..79	44%	35	329	10.6%	-0.22
..59	0%	0	1	0.0%	-1.00
Unrated	0%	0	0	0.0%	0.00

ANALYSIS BY WEIGHT CARRIED

Age	Prop	Win	Runs	Wins%	£
12-01+	0%	0	1	0.0%	-1.00
11-8..12-00	14%	11	90	12.2%	-0.25
11-0..11-07	39%	31	244	12.7%	-0.27
10-8..10-13	24%	19	148	12.8%	0.00
10-0..10-07	16%	13	153	8.5%	-0.39
..9-13	6%	5	64	7.8%	-0.38

ANALYSIS BY DAYS SINCE LAST RUN

Age	Prop	Win	Runs	Wins%	£
1..7	11%	9	57	15.8%	-0.10
8..14	28%	22	153	14.4%	0.07
15..28	35%	28	200	14.0%	-0.15
29..60	14%	11	134	8.2%	-0.37
61..100	5%	4	54	7.4%	-0.41
101+	6%	5	102	4.9%	-0.76
Unraced	0%	0	0	0.0%	0.00

ANALYSIS BY TODAY'S STARTING PRICE

Age	Prop	Win	Runs	Wins%	£
Odds On	1%	1	2	50.0%	-0.08
Ev-2/1	6%	5	17	29.4%	-0.22
9/4-4/1	34%	27	133	20.3%	-0.15
9/2-6/1	25%	20	111	18.0%	0.12
13/2-10/1	25%	20	185	10.8%	-0.06
11/1-16/1	5%	4	114	3.5%	-0.51
18/1-33/1	3%	2	107	1.9%	-0.58
40/1+	0%	0	31	0.0%	-1.00

ANALYSIS BY STARTING PRICE LAST TIME

Age	Prop	Win	Runs	Wins%	£
Odds On	0%	0	1	0.0%	-1.00
Ev-2/1	1%	1	6	16.7%	-0.38
9/4-4/1	18%	14	59	23.7%	0.04
9/2-6/1	15%	12	65	18.5%	0.15
13/2-10/1	27%	21	128	16.4%	-0.07
11/1-16/1	16%	13	129	10.1%	-0.14
18/1-33/1	13%	10	148	6.8%	-0.49
40/1+	10%	8	164	4.9%	-0.51
Unraced	0%	0	0	0.0%	0.00

ANALYSIS BY DISTANCE BEATEN LAST TIME

Age	Prop	Win	Runs	Wins%	£
..-10 lgh	1%	1	4	25.0%	-0.06
-10..0	4%	3	15	20.0%	-0.28
0.1..2	1%	1	20	5.0%	-0.78
2.1..5	8%	6	29	20.7%	0.11
5.1..10	13%	10	49	20.4%	-0.11
10.1..20	27%	21	110	19.1%	0.24
20.0..30	13%	10	95	10.5%	-0.07
30.1+	24%	19	248	7.7%	-0.42
Not Compl	10%	8	130	6.2%	-0.51
Unraced	0%	0	0	0.0%	0.00

ANALYSIS BY SUCCESS RATE IN LAST 10 RUNS

Age	Prop	Win	Runs	Wins%	£
No Wins	66%	52	522	10.0%	-0.30
1 Win	28%	22	144	15.3%	-0.03
2 Wins	5%	4	30	13.3%	-0.40
3 Wins	1%	1	4	25.0%	0.25
4 Wins	0%	0	0	0.0%	0.00
5+ Wins	0%	0	0	0.0%	0.00

ANALYSIS BY SUCCESS RATE IN LAST 3 RUNS

Age	Prop	Win	Runs	Wins%	£
No Wins	92%	73	645	11.3%	-0.22
1 Win	6%	5	52	9.6%	-0.60
2 Wins	1%	1	3	33.3%	-0.39
3 Wins	0%	0	0	0.0%	0.00

ANALYSIS BY POSITION LAST TIME

Age	Prop	Win	Runs	Wins%	£
Won	5%	4	19	21.1%	-0.23
2nd or 3rd	23%	18	109	16.5%	-0.20
Unplaced	62%	49	443	11.1%	-0.18
Fell,BD,UR	5%	4	28	14.3%	0.21
Pulled Up	5%	4	97	4.1%	-0.70
Ref/RanOut	0%	0	3	0.0%	-1.00
CO/SlipUp	0%	0	1	0.0%	-1.00
Unraced	0%	0	0	0.0%	0.00

OTHER FACTORS (WINS-RUNS, £)

Course Winner:	11-61	-£0.01
Distance Winner:	16-102	-£0.11
Going Winner:	15-120	-£0.14
Beaten Favourite:	4-34	-£0.56
7-Day Winners:	1-2	-£0.08
Absolute Favourites:	16-71	-£0.22

Race Profiles

Selling Handicap Hurdle Races: 11 runners or more

ANALYSIS BY AGE

Age	Prop	Win	Runs	Wins%	£
3yo	0%	0	9	0.0%	-1.00
4yo	6%	12	329	3.6%	-0.51
5yo	15%	33	514	6.4%	-0.32
6yo	24%	51	533	9.6%	0.00
7yo	16%	35	470	7.4%	-0.19
8yo	17%	36	469	7.7%	-0.33
9yo	6%	12	312	3.8%	-0.59
10yo	7%	16	206	7.8%	0.13
11yo	4%	9	120	7.5%	-0.29
12yo+	6%	13	127	10.2%	0.75

ANALYSIS BY BHB RATING

Age	Prop	Win	Runs	Wins%	£
150+	0%	0	0	0.0%	0.00
130..149	0%	0	0	0.0%	0.00
120..129	0%	0	0	0.0%	0.00
110..119	0%	0	0	0.0%	0.00
100..109	0%	1	9	11.1%	1.89
80..99	56%	122	1557	7.8%	-0.32
60..79	43%	94	1520	6.2%	-0.13
..59	0%	0	3	0.0%	-1.00
Unrated	0%	0	0	0.0%	0.00

ANALYSIS BY WEIGHT CARRIED

Age	Prop	Win	Runs	Wins%	£
12-01+	0%	0	0	0.0%	0.00
11-8..12-00	19%	41	352	11.6%	-0.15
11-0..11-07	35%	75	1048	7.2%	-0.33
10-8..10-13	23%	49	736	6.7%	-0.18
10-0..10-07	16%	35	685	5.1%	-0.23
..9-13	8%	17	268	6.3%	0.03

ANALYSIS BY DAYS SINCE LAST RUN

Age	Prop	Win	Runs	Wins%	£
1..7	10%	21	222	9.5%	-0.08
8..14	14%	31	546	5.7%	-0.58
15..28	30%	66	968	6.8%	-0.26
29..60	26%	56	651	8.6%	0.09
61..100	8%	18	211	8.5%	0.20
101+	12%	25	491	5.1%	-0.41
Unraced	0%	0	0	0.0%	0.00

ANALYSIS BY TODAY'S STARTING PRICE

Age	Prop	Win	Runs	Wins%	£
Odds On	0%	0	1	0.0%	-1.00
Ev-2/1	4%	9	16	56.3%	0.41
9/4-4/1	15%	33	161	20.5%	-0.11
9/2-6/1	24%	52	330	15.8%	-0.02
13/2-10/1	27%	59	732	8.1%	-0.27
11/1-16/1	18%	39	734	5.3%	-0.24
18/1-33/1	9%	19	761	2.5%	-0.32
40/1+	3%	6	354	1.7%	-0.13

ANALYSIS BY STARTING PRICE LAST TIME

Age	Prop	Win	Runs	Wins%	£
Odds On	0%	0	2	0.0%	-1.00
Ev-2/1	1%	2	13	15.4%	-0.33
9/4-4/1	7%	15	140	10.7%	-0.10
9/2-6/1	11%	23	229	10.0%	-0.28
13/2-10/1	23%	49	531	9.2%	-0.32
11/1-16/1	24%	52	648	8.0%	-0.13
18/1-33/1	23%	49	790	6.2%	-0.10
40/1+	12%	27	736	3.7%	-0.36
Unraced	0%	0	0	0.0%	0.00

ANALYSIS BY DISTANCE BEATEN LAST TIME

Age	Prop	Win	Runs	Wins%	£
..-10 lgh	1%	2	11	18.2%	-0.56
-10..0	5%	11	57	19.3%	0.36
0.1..2	6%	14	76	18.4%	0.15
2.1..5	6%	13	99	13.1%	0.04
5.1..10	12%	26	199	13.1%	0.05
10.1..20	17%	37	447	8.3%	-0.26
20.0..30	15%	33	413	8.0%	0.04
30.1+	28%	61	1131	5.4%	-0.30
Not Compl	9%	20	656	3.0%	-0.44
Unraced	0%	0	0	0.0%	0.00

ANALYSIS BY SUCCESS RATE IN LAST 10 RUNS

Age	Prop	Win	Runs	Wins%	£
No Wins	67%	145	2335	6.2%	-0.23
1 Win	26%	56	626	8.9%	-0.21
2 Wins	7%	15	117	12.8%	-0.10
3 Wins	0%	1	11	9.1%	-0.50
4 Wins	0%	0	0	0.0%	0.00
5+ Wins	0%	0	0	0.0%	0.00

ANALYSIS BY SUCCESS RATE IN LAST 3 RUNS

Age	Prop	Win	Runs	Wins%	£
No Wins	87%	189	2887	6.5%	-0.23
1 Win	13%	28	198	14.1%	-0.09
2 Wins	0%	0	4	0.0%	-1.00
3 Wins	0%	0	0	0.0%	0.00

ANALYSIS BY POSITION LAST TIME

Age	Prop	Win	Runs	Wins%	£
Won	6%	13	68	19.1%	0.21
2nd or 3rd	24%	51	373	13.7%	0.08
Unplaced	61%	133	1994	6.7%	-0.22
Fell,BD,UR	3%	6	137	4.4%	0.16
Pulled Up	6%	14	506	2.8%	-0.58
Ref/RanOut	0%	0	10	0.0%	-1.00
CO/SlipUp	0%	0	1	0.0%	-1.00
Unraced	0%	0	0	0.0%	0.00

OTHER FACTORS (WINS-RUNS, £)

Course Winner:	34-274	£0.28
Distance Winner:	52-535	-£0.06
Going Winner:	44-587	-£0.25
Beaten Favourite:	5-72	-£0.63
7-Day Winners:	4-11	£0.44
Absolute Favourites:	41-182	-£0.03

Selling Handicap Hurdle Races

Selling Handicap Hurdle Races: up to 7 days off the track

ANALYSIS BY AGE

Age	Prop	Win	Runs	Wins%	£
3yo	0%	0	0	0.0%	0.00
4yo	10%	3	40	7.5%	-0.51
5yo	7%	2	33	6.1%	-0.75
6yo	20%	6	61	9.8%	-0.16
7yo	20%	6	45	13.3%	0.38
8yo	7%	2	36	5.6%	-0.62
9yo	3%	1	25	4.0%	-0.78
10yo	10%	3	23	13.0%	-0.26
11yo	10%	3	7	42.9%	2.00
12yo+	13%	4	10	40.0%	4.80

ANALYSIS BY BHB RATING

Age	Prop	Win	Runs	Wins%	£
150+	0%	0	0	0.0%	0.00
130..149	0%	0	0	0.0%	0.00
120..129	0%	0	0	0.0%	0.00
110..119	0%	0	0	0.0%	0.00
100..109	0%	0	3	0.0%	-1.00
80..99	70%	21	145	14.5%	-0.14
60..79	30%	9	132	6.8%	0.00
..59	0%	0	0	0.0%	0.00
Unrated	0%	0	0	0.0%	0.00

ANALYSIS BY WEIGHT CARRIED

Age	Prop	Win	Runs	Wins%	£
12-01+	0%	0	0	0.0%	0.00
11-8..12-00	23%	7	36	19.4%	0.29
11-0..11-07	33%	10	95	10.5%	-0.42
10-8..10-13	17%	5	53	9.4%	-0.40
10-0..10-07	13%	4	64	6.3%	-0.17
..9-13	13%	4	32	12.5%	1.19

ANALYSIS BY DAYS SINCE LAST RUN

Age	Prop	Win	Runs	Wins%	£
1..7	100%	30	280	10.7%	-0.09
8..14	0%	0	0	0.0%	0.00
15..28	0%	0	0	0.0%	0.00
29..60	0%	0	0	0.0%	0.00
61..100	0%	0	0	0.0%	0.00
101+	0%	0	0	0.0%	0.00
Unraced	0%	0	0	0.0%	0.00

ANALYSIS BY TODAY'S STARTING PRICE

Age	Prop	Win	Runs	Wins%	£
Odds On	3%	1	1	100.0%	0.83
Ev-2/1	10%	3	6	50.0%	0.29
9/4-4/1	13%	4	31	12.9%	-0.47
9/2-6/1	40%	12	43	27.9%	0.69
13/2-10/1	20%	6	65	9.2%	-0.19
11/1-16/1	7%	2	46	4.3%	-0.35
18/1-33/1	3%	1	52	1.9%	-0.35
40/1+	3%	1	36	2.8%	0.14

ANALYSIS BY STARTING PRICE LAST TIME

Age	Prop	Win	Runs	Wins%	£
Odds On	0%	0	0	0.0%	0.00
Ev-2/1	0%	0	1	0.0%	-1.00
9/4-4/1	13%	4	18	22.2%	-0.13
9/2-6/1	10%	3	25	12.0%	-0.32
13/2-10/1	27%	8	53	15.1%	-0.18
11/1-16/1	20%	6	51	11.8%	0.16
18/1-33/1	20%	6	69	8.7%	-0.38
40/1+	10%	3	63	4.8%	0.23
Unraced	0%	0	0	0.0%	0.00

ANALYSIS BY DISTANCE BEATEN LAST TIME

Age	Prop	Win	Runs	Wins%	£
..-10 lgh	3%	1	3	33.3%	-0.04
-10..0	13%	4	10	40.0%	0.48
0.1..2	3%	1	5	20.0%	1.00
2.1..5	10%	3	16	18.8%	-0.08
5.1..10	20%	6	30	20.0%	0.12
10.1..20	20%	6	39	15.4%	0.06
20.0..30	17%	5	49	10.2%	0.21
30.1+	3%	1	81	1.2%	-0.90
Not Compl	10%	3	47	6.4%	0.51
Unraced	0%	0	0	0.0%	0.00

ANALYSIS BY SUCCESS RATE IN LAST 10 RUNS

Age	Prop	Win	Runs	Wins%	£
No Wins	60%	18	203	8.9%	-0.02
1 Win	27%	8	63	12.7%	-0.39
2 Wins	13%	4	13	30.8%	0.37
3 Wins	0%	0	1	0.0%	-1.00
4 Wins	0%	0	0	0.0%	0.00
5+ Wins	0%	0	0	0.0%	0.00

ANALYSIS BY SUCCESS RATE IN LAST 3 RUNS

Age	Prop	Win	Runs	Wins%	£
No Wins	77%	23	252	9.1%	-0.09
1 Win	20%	6	27	22.2%	-0.04
2 Wins	3%	1	1	100.0%	0.83
3 Wins	0%	0	0	0.0%	0.00

ANALYSIS BY POSITION LAST TIME

Age	Prop	Win	Runs	Wins%	£
Won	17%	5	13	38.5%	0.36
2nd or 3rd	33%	10	43	23.3%	0.25
Unplaced	40%	12	177	6.8%	-0.36
Fell,BD,UR	7%	2	19	10.5%	0.58
Pulled Up	3%	1	27	3.7%	0.52
Ref/RanOut	0%	0	1	0.0%	-1.00
CO/SlipUp	0%	0	0	0.0%	0.00
Unraced	0%	0	0	0.0%	0.00

OTHER FACTORS (WINS-RUNS, £)

Course Winner:	9-28	£2.08
Distance Winner:	9-58	£0.41
Going Winner:	11-66	£0.40
Beaten Favourite:	0-3	-£1.00
7-Day Winners:	5-13	£0.36
Absolute Favourites:	8-29	-£0.10

Race Profiles

Selling Handicap Hurdle Races: 100+ days off the track

ANALYSIS BY AGE

Age	Prop	Win	Runs	Wins%	£
3yo	0%	0	1	0.0%	-1.00
4yo	6%	2	40	5.0%	0.00
5yo	6%	2	95	2.1%	-0.60
6yo	26%	8	71	11.3%	0.05
7yo	19%	6	98	6.1%	-0.62
8yo	29%	9	115	7.8%	-0.24
9yo	3%	1	73	1.4%	-0.94
10yo	0%	0	46	0.0%	-1.00
11yo	6%	2	28	7.1%	-0.46
12yo+	3%	1	32	3.1%	-0.19

ANALYSIS BY BHB RATING

Age	Prop	Win	Runs	Wins%	£
150+	0%	0	0	0.0%	0.00
130..149	0%	0	0	0.0%	0.00
120..129	0%	0	0	0.0%	0.00
110..119	0%	0	0	0.0%	0.00
100..109	3%	1	1	100.0%	25.00
80..99	39%	12	300	4.0%	-0.71
60..79	58%	18	298	6.0%	-0.30
..59	0%	0	0	0.0%	0.00
Unrated	0%	0	0	0.0%	0.00

ANALYSIS BY WEIGHT CARRIED

Age	Prop	Win	Runs	Wins%	£
12-01+	0%	0	0	0.0%	0.00
11-8..12-00	23%	7	87	8.0%	-0.40
11-0..11-07	26%	8	195	4.1%	-0.65
10-8..10-13	32%	10	129	7.8%	0.00
10-0..10-07	13%	4	132	3.0%	-0.79
..9-13	6%	2	56	3.6%	-0.18

ANALYSIS BY DAYS SINCE LAST RUN

Age	Prop	Win	Runs	Wins%	£
1..7	0%	0	0	0.0%	0.00
8..14	0%	0	0	0.0%	0.00
15..28	0%	0	0	0.0%	0.00
29..60	0%	0	0	0.0%	0.00
61..100	0%	0	4	0.0%	-1.00
101+	100%	31	595	5.2%	-0.46
Unraced	0%	0	0	0.0%	0.00

ANALYSIS BY TODAY'S STARTING PRICE

Age	Prop	Win	Runs	Wins%	£
Odds On	0%	0	0	0.0%	0.00
Ev-2/1	10%	3	6	50.0%	0.10
9/4-4/1	26%	8	36	22.2%	-0.09
9/2-6/1	10%	3	32	9.4%	-0.39
13/2-10/1	23%	7	137	5.1%	-0.53
11/1-16/1	16%	5	144	3.5%	-0.50
18/1-33/1	16%	5	165	3.0%	-0.22
40/1+	0%	0	79	0.0%	-1.00

ANALYSIS BY STARTING PRICE LAST TIME

Age	Prop	Win	Runs	Wins%	£
Odds On	0%	0	3	0.0%	-1.00
Ev-2/1	3%	1	5	20.0%	-0.55
9/4-4/1	13%	4	29	13.8%	1.19
9/2-6/1	10%	3	40	7.5%	-0.30
13/2-10/1	19%	6	106	5.7%	-0.69
11/1-16/1	13%	4	134	3.0%	-0.84
18/1-33/1	23%	7	148	4.7%	-0.41
40/1+	19%	6	134	4.5%	-0.35
Unraced	0%	0	0	0.0%	0.00

ANALYSIS BY DISTANCE BEATEN LAST TIME

Age	Prop	Win	Runs	Wins%	£
..-10 lgh	0%	0	3	0.0%	-1.00
-10..0	3%	1	17	5.9%	-0.12
0.1..2	0%	0	11	0.0%	-1.00
2.1..5	3%	1	17	5.9%	-0.76
5.1..10	6%	2	19	10.5%	-0.70
10.1..20	13%	4	66	6.1%	-0.72
20.0..30	26%	8	68	11.8%	0.54
30.1+	35%	11	236	4.7%	-0.46
Not Compl	13%	4	162	2.5%	-0.70
Unraced	0%	0	0	0.0%	0.00

ANALYSIS BY SUCCESS RATE IN LAST 10 RUNS

Age	Prop	Win	Runs	Wins%	£
No Wins	81%	25	447	5.6%	-0.38
1 Win	19%	6	132	4.5%	-0.66
2 Wins	0%	0	19	0.0%	-1.00
3 Wins	0%	0	1	0.0%	-1.00
4 Wins	0%	0	0	0.0%	0.00
5+ Wins	0%	0	0	0.0%	0.00

ANALYSIS BY SUCCESS RATE IN LAST 3 RUNS

Age	Prop	Win	Runs	Wins%	£
No Wins	94%	29	553	5.2%	-0.45
1 Win	6%	2	45	4.4%	-0.62
2 Wins	0%	0	1	0.0%	-1.00
3 Wins	0%	0	0	0.0%	0.00

ANALYSIS BY POSITION LAST TIME

Age	Prop	Win	Runs	Wins%	£
Won	3%	1	20	5.0%	-0.25
2nd or 3rd	13%	4	60	6.7%	-0.52
Unplaced	71%	22	360	6.1%	-0.36
Fell,BD,UR	6%	2	24	8.3%	0.50
Pulled Up	6%	2	134	1.5%	-0.91
Ref/RanOut	0%	0	1	0.0%	-1.00
CO/SlipUp	0%	0	0	0.0%	0.00
Unraced	0%	0	0	0.0%	0.00

OTHER FACTORS (WINS-RUNS, £)

Course Winner:	3-63	-£0.33
Distance Winner:	4-94	-£0.47
Going Winner:	5-106	-£0.46
Beaten Favourite:	1-16	-£0.86
Absolute Favourites:	9-34	-£0.10

Handicap Hurdle Races (class 1..3)

ANALYSIS BY AGE

Age	Prop	Win	Runs	Wins%	£
3yo	0%	1	9	11.1%	0.06
4yo	7%	81	876	9.2%	-0.26
5yo	24%	281	2684	10.5%	-0.14
6yo	25%	290	3131	9.3%	-0.25
7yo	21%	238	2631	9.0%	-0.19
8yo	13%	149	1838	8.1%	-0.20
9yo	5%	60	1062	5.6%	-0.22
10yo	3%	32	569	5.6%	-0.31
11yo	1%	12	277	4.3%	-0.49
12yo+	0%	3	140	2.1%	-0.75

ANALYSIS BY BHB RATING

Age	Prop	Win	Runs	Wins%	£
150+	1%	10	97	10.3%	0.27
130..149	14%	156	2333	6.7%	-0.30
120..129	28%	316	3610	8.8%	-0.24
110..119	37%	424	4262	9.9%	-0.13
100..109	17%	194	2257	8.6%	-0.24
80..99	4%	47	658	7.1%	-0.39

ANALYSIS BY WEIGHT CARRIED

Age	Prop	Win	Runs	Wins%	£
12-01+	0%	2	3	66.7%	1.04
11-8..12-00	17%	196	1856	10.6%	-0.20
11-0..11-07	35%	406	4181	9.7%	-0.16
10-8..10-13	20%	230	3098	7.4%	-0.34
10-0..10-07	21%	246	3173	7.8%	-0.18
..9-13	6%	67	906	7.4%	-0.24

ANALYSIS BY DAYS SINCE LAST RUN

Age	Prop	Win	Runs	Wins%	£
1..7	6%	65	507	12.8%	-0.07
8..14	15%	173	1843	9.4%	-0.20
15..28	30%	346	4092	8.5%	-0.24
29..60	25%	290	3171	9.1%	-0.17
61..100	7%	76	925	8.2%	-0.16
101+	17%	197	2640	7.5%	-0.30
Unraced	0%	0	39	0.0%	-1.00

ANALYSIS BY TODAY'S STARTING PRICE

Age	Prop	Win	Runs	Wins%	£
Odds On	2%	23	46	50.0%	-0.12
Ev-2/1	9%	103	303	34.0%	-0.09
9/4-4/1	23%	260	1373	18.9%	-0.20
9/2-6/1	20%	231	1468	15.7%	-0.02
13/2-10/1	23%	266	2875	9.3%	-0.16
11/1-16/1	14%	166	2989	5.6%	-0.20
18/1-33/1	7%	85	2842	3.0%	-0.28
40/1+	1%	13	1321	1.0%	-0.53

ANALYSIS BY STARTING PRICE LAST TIME

Age	Prop	Win	Runs	Wins%	£
Odds On	3%	40	320	12.5%	-0.24
Ev-2/1	9%	99	744	13.3%	-0.09
9/4-4/1	18%	209	1900	11.0%	-0.20
9/2-6/1	14%	155	1590	9.7%	-0.26
13/2-10/1	23%	261	2823	9.2%	-0.16
11/1-16/1	18%	210	2612	8.0%	-0.16
18/1-33/1	11%	128	2244	5.7%	-0.33
40/1+	4%	45	945	4.8%	-0.33
Unraced	0%	0	39	0.0%	-1.00

ANALYSIS BY DISTANCE BEATEN LAST TIME

Age	Prop	Win	Runs	Wins%	£
..-10 lgh	3%	38	292	13.0%	-0.38
-10..0	20%	234	1913	12.2%	-0.17
0.1..2	8%	91	900	10.1%	-0.27
2.1..5	9%	103	981	10.5%	-0.16
5.1..10	12%	142	1426	10.0%	-0.15
10.1..20	16%	183	2122	8.6%	-0.25
20.0..30	8%	92	1349	6.8%	-0.28
30.1+	13%	154	2529	6.1%	-0.22
Not Compl	10%	110	1666	6.6%	-0.20
Unraced	0%	0	39	0.0%	-1.00

ANALYSIS BY SUCCESS RATE IN LAST 10 RUNS

Age	Prop	Win	Runs	Wins%	£
No Wins	15%	170	2065	8.2%	-0.21
1 Win	32%	370	4454	8.3%	-0.21
2 Wins	29%	328	3945	8.3%	-0.23
3 Wins	16%	187	1889	9.9%	-0.18
4 Wins	5%	54	607	8.9%	-0.36
5+ Wins	3%	38	218	17.4%	0.03

ANALYSIS BY SUCCESS RATE IN LAST 3 RUNS

Age	Prop	Win	Runs	Wins%	£
No Wins	48%	554	7417	7.5%	-0.23
1 Win	37%	428	4464	9.6%	-0.21
2 Wins	12%	143	1157	12.4%	-0.18
3 Wins	2%	22	140	15.7%	-0.35

ANALYSIS BY POSITION LAST TIME

Age	Prop	Win	Runs	Wins%	£
Won	24%	273	2209	12.4%	-0.20
2nd or 3rd	25%	286	2935	9.7%	-0.28
Unplaced	42%	480	6378	7.5%	-0.20
Fell,BD,UR	4%	48	598	8.0%	-0.23
Pulled Up	5%	57	1024	5.6%	-0.24
Ref/RanOut	0%	2	26	7.7%	0.81
CO/SlipUp	0%	1	8	12.5%	-0.06
Unraced	0%	0	39	0.0%	-1.00

OTHER FACTORS (WINS-RUNS, £)

Course Winner:	239-2301	-£0.07
Distance Winner:	515-5872	-£0.23
Going Winner:	580-6419	-£0.20
Beaten Favourite:	110-956	-£0.19
7-Day Winners:	28-140	-£0.18
Absolute Favourites:	240-1012	-£0.20

TRAINERS (WINS-RUNS, £)

J S Goldie 7-57 £0.26; A C Whillans 3-23 £0.63; J T Stimpson 3-17 £0.85; J A B Old 5-38 £0.32; Mrs K Walton 3-27 £0.44; James Moffatt 4-51 £0.22; D W Whillans 3-32 £0.33; N B King 5-59 £0.17; C E Longsdon 7-52 £0.18; A W Carroll 10-108 £0.08; C Grant 6-65 £0.11; D Carroll 3-26 £0.27; C J Mann 19-146 £0.04; Mrs S J Smith 15-168 £0.03; Ferdy Murphy 20-161 £0.02; A Fleming 3-12 £0.25; N J Gifford 5-57 £0.05; D Burchell 4-52 £0.04; Dr R D P Newland 9-86 £0.02.

Race Profiles

Handicap Hurdle Races (class 1..3): 2m to 2m3f

ANALYSIS BY AGE

Age	Prop	Win	Runs	Wins%	£
3yo	0%	0	7	0.0%	-1.00
4yo	11%	56	551	10.2%	-0.25
5yo	28%	137	1362	10.1%	-0.19
6yo	24%	119	1340	8.9%	-0.28
7yo	18%	90	1033	8.7%	-0.20
8yo	11%	55	607	9.1%	-0.10
9yo	3%	17	322	5.3%	-0.36
10yo	2%	10	164	6.1%	-0.47
11yo	1%	4	72	5.6%	-0.45
12yo+	0%	2	30	6.7%	-0.17

ANALYSIS BY BHB RATING

Age	Prop	Win	Runs	Wins%	£
150+	0%	2	35	5.7%	-0.72
130..149	13%	62	838	7.4%	-0.25
120..129	31%	150	1530	9.8%	-0.16
110..119	35%	173	1825	9.5%	-0.22
100..109	17%	85	975	8.7%	-0.27
80..99	4%	18	285	6.3%	-0.48
60..79	0%	0	0	0.0%	0.00
..59	0%	0	0	0.0%	0.00
Unrated	0%	0	0	0.0%	0.00

ANALYSIS BY WEIGHT CARRIED

Age	Prop	Win	Runs	Wins%	£
12-01+	0%	1	2	50.0%	0.88
11-8..12-00	19%	93	763	12.2%	-0.16
11-0..11-07	38%	186	1706	10.9%	-0.07
10-8..10-13	16%	80	1340	6.0%	-0.53
10-0..10-07	20%	100	1357	7.4%	-0.23
..9-13	6%	30	320	9.4%	-0.03

ANALYSIS BY DAYS SINCE LAST RUN

Age	Prop	Win	Runs	Wins%	£
1..7	5%	26	230	11.3%	-0.17
8..14	14%	71	805	8.8%	-0.24
15..28	30%	149	1609	9.3%	-0.19
29..60	23%	114	1280	8.9%	-0.24
61..100	7%	34	399	8.5%	-0.31
101+	20%	96	1146	8.4%	-0.25
Unraced	0%	0	19	0.0%	-1.00

ANALYSIS BY TODAY'S STARTING PRICE

Age	Prop	Win	Runs	Wins%	£
Odds On	3%	13	24	54.2%	-0.06
Ev-2/1	11%	56	150	37.3%	0.00
9/4-4/1	23%	111	594	18.7%	-0.22
9/2-6/1	21%	102	636	16.0%	-0.01
13/2-10/1	20%	98	1135	8.6%	-0.23
11/1-16/1	15%	72	1253	5.7%	-0.19
18/1-33/1	7%	32	1145	2.8%	-0.33
40/1+	1%	6	551	1.1%	-0.47

ANALYSIS BY STARTING PRICE LAST TIME

Age	Prop	Win	Runs	Wins%	£
Odds On	4%	18	153	11.8%	-0.47
Ev-2/1	12%	58	334	17.4%	0.30
9/4-4/1	17%	84	827	10.2%	-0.30
9/2-6/1	11%	56	643	8.7%	-0.41
13/2-10/1	21%	105	1121	9.4%	-0.21
11/1-16/1	19%	93	1069	8.7%	-0.08
18/1-33/1	10%	51	902	5.7%	-0.38
40/1+	5%	25	420	6.0%	-0.24
Unraced	0%	0	19	0.0%	-1.00

ANALYSIS BY DISTANCE BEATEN LAST TIME

Age	Prop	Win	Runs	Wins%	£
..-10 lgh	2%	12	106	11.3%	-0.55
-10..0	21%	102	829	12.3%	-0.21
0.1..2	9%	44	375	11.7%	-0.07
2.1..5	9%	46	448	10.3%	-0.31
5.1..10	13%	64	648	9.9%	-0.12
10.1..20	18%	89	927	9.6%	-0.14
20.0..30	8%	37	556	6.7%	-0.33
30.1+	13%	65	1024	6.3%	-0.21
Not Compl	6%	31	556	5.6%	-0.45
Unraced	0%	0	19	0.0%	-1.00

ANALYSIS BY SUCCESS RATE IN LAST 10 RUNS

Age	Prop	Win	Runs	Wins%	£
No Wins	14%	69	835	8.3%	-0.31
1 Win	36%	174	1964	8.9%	-0.22
2 Wins	28%	135	1661	8.1%	-0.26
3 Wins	16%	78	754	10.3%	-0.13
4 Wins	4%	19	189	10.1%	-0.35
5+ Wins	3%	15	66	22.7%	0.59

ANALYSIS BY SUCCESS RATE IN LAST 3 RUNS

Age	Prop	Win	Runs	Wins%	£
No Wins	48%	235	3052	7.7%	-0.26
1 Win	38%	186	1890	9.8%	-0.17
2 Wins	12%	59	473	12.5%	-0.30
3 Wins	2%	10	54	18.5%	-0.19

ANALYSIS BY POSITION LAST TIME

Age	Prop	Win	Runs	Wins%	£
Won	23%	114	935	12.2%	-0.25
2nd or 3rd	26%	127	1228	10.3%	-0.18
Unplaced	45%	220	2754	8.0%	-0.19
Fell,BD,UR	3%	13	210	6.2%	-0.62
Pulled Up	3%	16	327	4.9%	-0.41
Ref/RanOut	0%	0	12	0.0%	-1.00
CO/SlipUp	0%	0	3	0.0%	-1.00
Unraced	0%	0	19	0.0%	-1.00

OTHER FACTORS (WINS-RUNS, £)

Course Winner:	101-938	-£0.15
Distance Winner:	291-3265	-£0.24
Going Winner:	259-2524	-£0.11
Beaten Favourite:	47-413	-£0.15
7-Day Winners:	13-62	-£0.17
Absolute Favourites:	121-440	-£0.11

Handicap Hurdle Races (class 1..3)

Handicap Hurdle Races (class 1..3): 2m4f to 2m7f

ANALYSIS BY AGE

Age	Prop	Win	Runs	Wins%	£
3yo	0%	1	2	50.0%	3.75
4yo	5%	23	274	8.4%	-0.24
5yo	23%	97	969	10.0%	-0.16
6yo	27%	113	1183	9.6%	-0.17
7yo	22%	92	994	9.3%	-0.17
8yo	13%	53	699	7.6%	-0.23
9yo	6%	25	405	6.2%	-0.29
10yo	2%	10	231	4.3%	-0.39
11yo	1%	5	120	4.2%	-0.59
12yo+	0%	1	54	1.9%	-0.81

ANALYSIS BY BHB RATING

Age	Prop	Win	Runs	Wins%	£
150+	1%	3	30	10.0%	-0.25
130..149	13%	53	834	6.4%	-0.36
120..129	26%	110	1331	8.3%	-0.25
110..119	41%	171	1681	10.2%	-0.05
100..109	16%	68	839	8.1%	-0.29
80..99	4%	15	216	6.9%	-0.43
60..79	0%	0	0	0.0%	0.00
..59	0%	0	0	0.0%	0.00
Unrated	0%	0	0	0.0%	0.00

ANALYSIS BY WEIGHT CARRIED

Age	Prop	Win	Runs	Wins%	£
12-01+	0%	0	0	0.0%	0.00
11-8..12-00	15%	62	714	8.7%	-0.29
11-0..11-07	36%	152	1645	9.2%	-0.21
10-8..10-13	24%	102	1113	9.2%	-0.17
10-0..10-07	19%	81	1116	7.3%	-0.19
..9-13	5%	23	343	6.7%	-0.33

ANALYSIS BY DAYS SINCE LAST RUN

Age	Prop	Win	Runs	Wins%	£
1..7	5%	22	173	12.7%	0.06
8..14	16%	67	666	10.1%	-0.18
15..28	28%	116	1530	7.6%	-0.33
29..60	27%	115	1200	9.6%	-0.11
61..100	6%	27	339	8.0%	-0.08
101+	17%	73	1009	7.2%	-0.28
Unraced	0%	0	14	0.0%	-1.00

ANALYSIS BY TODAY'S STARTING PRICE

Age	Prop	Win	Runs	Wins%	£
Odds On	2%	7	13	53.8%	-0.06
Ev-2/1	6%	26	94	27.7%	-0.25
9/4-4/1	23%	97	515	18.8%	-0.19
9/2-6/1	18%	74	531	13.9%	-0.13
13/2-10/1	26%	111	1119	9.9%	-0.10
11/1-16/1	16%	69	1084	6.4%	-0.09
18/1-33/1	8%	32	1079	3.0%	-0.32
40/1+	1%	4	496	0.8%	-0.65

ANALYSIS BY STARTING PRICE LAST TIME

Age	Prop	Win	Runs	Wins%	£
Odds On	4%	15	121	12.4%	-0.10
Ev-2/1	6%	27	280	9.6%	-0.38
9/4-4/1	20%	82	704	11.6%	-0.07
9/2-6/1	14%	57	604	9.4%	-0.25
13/2-10/1	25%	106	1062	10.0%	0.03
11/1-16/1	18%	74	981	7.5%	-0.28
18/1-33/1	11%	48	829	5.8%	-0.38
40/1+	3%	11	336	3.3%	-0.52
Unraced	0%	0	14	0.0%	-1.00

ANALYSIS BY DISTANCE BEATEN LAST TIME

Age	Prop	Win	Runs	Wins%	£
..-10 lgh	3%	14	119	11.8%	-0.31
-10..0	19%	80	713	11.2%	-0.22
0.1..2	7%	30	331	9.1%	-0.35
2.1..5	8%	34	347	9.8%	-0.15
5.1..10	12%	51	502	10.2%	-0.12
10.1..20	15%	62	799	7.8%	-0.37
20.0..30	8%	35	503	7.0%	-0.32
30.1+	14%	59	939	6.3%	-0.21
Not Compl	13%	55	664	8.3%	0.04
Unraced	0%	0	14	0.0%	-1.00

ANALYSIS BY SUCCESS RATE IN LAST 10 RUNS

Age	Prop	Win	Runs	Wins%	£
No Wins	16%	68	769	8.8%	-0.13
1 Win	30%	128	1610	8.0%	-0.22
2 Wins	29%	121	1480	8.2%	-0.22
3 Wins	16%	67	700	9.6%	-0.22
4 Wins	6%	26	267	9.7%	-0.30
5+ Wins	2%	10	91	11.0%	-0.47

ANALYSIS BY SUCCESS RATE IN LAST 3 RUNS

Age	Prop	Win	Runs	Wins%	£
No Wins	52%	217	2747	7.9%	-0.17
1 Win	36%	151	1684	9.0%	-0.28
2 Wins	11%	47	431	10.9%	-0.15
3 Wins	1%	5	55	9.1%	-0.77

ANALYSIS BY POSITION LAST TIME

Age	Prop	Win	Runs	Wins%	£
Won	23%	95	835	11.4%	-0.23
2nd or 3rd	25%	103	1096	9.4%	-0.30
Unplaced	40%	167	2325	7.2%	-0.24
Fell,BD,UR	5%	22	235	9.4%	0.13
Pulled Up	7%	31	416	7.5%	-0.05
Ref/RanOut	0%	1	8	12.5%	1.63
CO/SlipUp	0%	1	2	50.0%	2.75
Unraced	0%	0	14	0.0%	-1.00

OTHER FACTORS (WINS-RUNS, £)

Course Winner:	90-875	£0.03
Distance Winner:	148-1629	-£0.20
Going Winner:	192-2385	-£0.30
Beaten Favourite:	39-356	-£0.24
7-Day Winners:	8-55	-£0.28
Absolute Favourites:	69-365	-£0.35

Race Profiles

Handicap Hurdle Races (class 1..3): 3m+

ANALYSIS BY AGE

Age	Prop	Win	Runs	Wins%	£
3yo	0%	0	0	0.0%	0.00
4yo	1%	2	51	3.9%	-0.50
5yo	20%	47	353	13.3%	0.12
6yo	24%	58	608	9.5%	-0.33
7yo	24%	56	604	9.3%	-0.22
8yo	17%	41	532	7.7%	-0.26
9yo	8%	18	335	5.4%	-0.02
10yo	5%	12	174	6.9%	-0.06
11yo	1%	3	85	3.5%	-0.38
12yo+	0%	0	56	0.0%	-1.00

ANALYSIS BY BHB RATING

Age	Prop	Win	Runs	Wins%	£
150+	2%	5	32	15.6%	1.83
130..149	17%	41	661	6.2%	-0.29
120..129	24%	56	749	7.5%	-0.40
110..119	34%	80	756	10.6%	-0.09
100..109	17%	41	443	9.3%	-0.06
80..99	6%	14	157	8.9%	-0.17
60..79	0%	0	0	0.0%	0.00
..59	0%	0	0	0.0%	0.00
Unrated	0%	0	0	0.0%	0.00

ANALYSIS BY WEIGHT CARRIED

Age	Prop	Win	Runs	Wins%	£
12-01+	0%	1	1	100.0%	1.38
11-8..12-00	17%	41	379	10.8%	-0.12
11-0..11-07	29%	68	830	8.2%	-0.26
10-8..10-13	20%	48	645	7.4%	-0.23
10-0..10-07	27%	65	700	9.3%	-0.07
..9-13	6%	14	243	5.8%	-0.40

ANALYSIS BY DAYS SINCE LAST RUN

Age	Prop	Win	Runs	Wins%	£
1..7	7%	17	104	16.3%	-0.08
8..14	15%	35	372	9.4%	-0.12
15..28	34%	81	953	8.5%	-0.20
29..60	26%	61	691	8.8%	-0.13
61..100	6%	15	187	8.0%	0.03
101+	12%	28	485	5.8%	-0.46
Unraced	0%	0	6	0.0%	-1.00

ANALYSIS BY TODAY'S STARTING PRICE

Age	Prop	Win	Runs	Wins%	£
Odds On	1%	3	9	33.3%	-0.36
Ev-2/1	9%	21	59	35.6%	-0.04
9/4-4/1	22%	52	264	19.7%	-0.17
9/2-6/1	23%	55	301	18.3%	0.14
13/2-10/1	24%	57	621	9.2%	-0.15
11/1-16/1	11%	25	652	3.8%	-0.42
18/1-33/1	9%	21	618	3.4%	-0.09
40/1+	1%	3	274	1.1%	-0.44

ANALYSIS BY STARTING PRICE LAST TIME

Age	Prop	Win	Runs	Wins%	£
Odds On	3%	7	46	15.2%	0.16
Ev-2/1	6%	14	130	10.8%	-0.47
9/4-4/1	18%	43	369	11.7%	-0.23
9/2-6/1	18%	42	343	12.2%	0.01
13/2-10/1	21%	50	640	7.8%	-0.37
11/1-16/1	18%	43	562	7.7%	-0.09
18/1-33/1	12%	29	513	5.7%	-0.17
40/1+	4%	9	189	4.8%	-0.19
Unraced	0%	0	6	0.0%	-1.00

ANALYSIS BY DISTANCE BEATEN LAST TIME

Age	Prop	Win	Runs	Wins%	£
..-10 lgh	5%	12	67	17.9%	-0.24
-10..0	22%	52	371	14.0%	0.01
0.1..2	7%	17	194	8.8%	-0.53
2.1..5	10%	23	186	12.4%	0.20
5.1..10	11%	27	276	9.8%	-0.28
10.1..20	14%	32	396	8.1%	-0.24
20.0..30	8%	20	290	6.9%	-0.15
30.1+	13%	30	566	5.3%	-0.24
Not Compl	10%	24	446	5.4%	-0.26
Unraced	0%	0	6	0.0%	-1.00

ANALYSIS BY SUCCESS RATE IN LAST 10 RUNS

Age	Prop	Win	Runs	Wins%	£
No Wins	14%	33	461	7.2%	-0.16
1 Win	29%	68	880	7.7%	-0.18
2 Wins	30%	72	804	9.0%	-0.20
3 Wins	18%	42	435	9.7%	-0.19
4 Wins	4%	9	151	6.0%	-0.49
5+ Wins	5%	13	61	21.3%	0.18

ANALYSIS BY SUCCESS RATE IN LAST 3 RUNS

Age	Prop	Win	Runs	Wins%	£
No Wins	43%	102	1618	6.3%	-0.26
1 Win	38%	91	890	10.2%	-0.14
2 Wins	16%	37	253	14.6%	-0.01
3 Wins	3%	7	31	22.6%	0.10

ANALYSIS BY POSITION LAST TIME

Age	Prop	Win	Runs	Wins%	£
Won	27%	64	439	14.6%	-0.03
2nd or 3rd	24%	56	611	9.2%	-0.44
Unplaced	39%	93	1299	7.2%	-0.12
Fell,BD,UR	5%	13	153	8.5%	-0.23
Pulled Up	4%	10	281	3.6%	-0.34
Ref/RanOut	0%	1	6	16.7%	3.33
CO/SlipUp	0%	0	3	0.0%	-1.00
Unraced	0%	0	6	0.0%	-1.00

OTHER FACTORS (WINS-RUNS, £)

Course Winner:	48-488	-£0.10
Distance Winner:	76-978	-£0.23
Going Winner:	129-1510	-£0.19
Beaten Favourite:	24-187	-£0.22
7-Day Winners:	7-23	£0.04
Absolute Favourites:	50-207	-£0.14

Handicap Hurdle Races (class 1..3)

Handicap Hurdle Races (class 1..3): 2 to 5 runners

ANALYSIS BY AGE

Age	Prop	Win	Runs	Wins%	£
3yo	0%	0	0	0.0%	0.00
4yo	12%	4	7	57.1%	1.11
5yo	9%	3	31	9.7%	-0.56
6yo	26%	9	35	25.7%	0.11
7yo	21%	7	30	23.3%	-0.28
8yo	15%	5	25	20.0%	-0.30
9yo	6%	2	20	10.0%	-0.25
10yo	6%	2	4	50.0%	1.06
11yo	6%	2	7	28.6%	0.95
12yo+	0%	0	1	0.0%	-1.00

ANALYSIS BY BHB RATING

Age	Prop	Win	Runs	Wins%	£
150+	0%	0	2	0.0%	-1.00
130..149	6%	2	11	18.2%	-0.45
120..129	26%	9	39	23.1%	-0.22
110..119	32%	11	54	20.4%	-0.02
100..109	26%	9	42	21.4%	-0.12
80..99	9%	3	12	25.0%	0.40
60..79	0%	0	0	0.0%	0.00
..59	0%	0	0	0.0%	0.00
Unrated	0%	0	0	0.0%	0.00

ANALYSIS BY WEIGHT CARRIED

Age	Prop	Win	Runs	Wins%	£
12-01+	0%	0	0	0.0%	0.00
11-8..12-00	21%	7	40	17.5%	-0.37
11-0..11-07	32%	11	47	23.4%	-0.23
10-8..10-13	15%	5	27	18.5%	0.37
10-0..10-07	29%	10	42	23.8%	0.01
..9-13	3%	1	4	25.0%	-0.47

ANALYSIS BY DAYS SINCE LAST RUN

Age	Prop	Win	Runs	Wins%	£
1..7	3%	1	8	12.5%	-0.31
8..14	29%	10	33	30.3%	0.28
15..28	35%	12	58	20.7%	-0.36
29..60	18%	6	27	22.2%	0.09
61..100	3%	1	7	14.3%	0.71
101+	12%	4	27	14.8%	-0.37
Unraced	0%	0	0	0.0%	0.00

ANALYSIS BY TODAY'S STARTING PRICE

Age	Prop	Win	Runs	Wins%	£
Odds On	12%	4	5	80.0%	0.38
Ev-2/1	32%	11	33	33.3%	-0.16
9/4-4/1	35%	12	58	20.7%	-0.14
9/2-6/1	9%	3	23	13.0%	-0.22
13/2-10/1	9%	3	24	12.5%	0.21
11/1-16/1	3%	1	10	10.0%	0.20
18/1-33/1	0%	0	5	0.0%	-1.00
40/1+	0%	0	2	0.0%	-1.00

ANALYSIS BY STARTING PRICE LAST TIME

Age	Prop	Win	Runs	Wins%	£
Odds On	3%	1	5	20.0%	-0.20
Ev-2/1	9%	3	11	27.3%	-0.36
9/4-4/1	21%	7	24	29.2%	0.11
9/2-6/1	9%	3	23	13.0%	-0.63
13/2-10/1	26%	9	36	25.0%	0.14
11/1-16/1	15%	5	29	17.2%	-0.03
18/1-33/1	6%	2	17	11.8%	-0.51
40/1+	12%	4	15	26.7%	0.32
Unraced	0%	0	0	0.0%	0.00

ANALYSIS BY DISTANCE BEATEN LAST TIME

Age	Prop	Win	Runs	Wins%	£
..-10 lgh	3%	1	3	33.3%	0.67
-10..0	15%	5	22	22.7%	-0.35
0.1..2	3%	1	7	14.3%	-0.59
2.1..5	15%	5	19	26.3%	-0.26
5.1..10	12%	4	17	23.5%	-0.06
10.1..20	21%	7	30	23.3%	-0.19
20.0..30	9%	3	16	18.8%	0.78
30.1+	12%	4	25	16.0%	-0.17
Not Compl	12%	4	21	19.0%	-0.15
Unraced	0%	0	0	0.0%	0.00

ANALYSIS BY SUCCESS RATE IN LAST 10 RUNS

Age	Prop	Win	Runs	Wins%	£
No Wins	32%	11	32	34.4%	0.60
1 Win	18%	6	56	10.7%	-0.33
2 Wins	21%	7	39	17.9%	-0.48
3 Wins	18%	6	24	25.0%	-0.02
4 Wins	6%	2	5	40.0%	0.05
5+ Wins	6%	2	4	50.0%	0.37

ANALYSIS BY SUCCESS RATE IN LAST 3 RUNS

Age	Prop	Win	Runs	Wins%	£
No Wins	44%	15	83	18.1%	-0.16
1 Win	32%	11	60	18.3%	-0.16
2 Wins	24%	8	17	47.1%	0.35
3 Wins	0%	0	0	0.0%	0.00

ANALYSIS BY POSITION LAST TIME

Age	Prop	Win	Runs	Wins%	£
Won	18%	6	25	24.0%	-0.23
2nd or 3rd	29%	10	44	22.7%	-0.39
Unplaced	41%	14	70	20.0%	0.14
Fell,BD,UR	6%	2	9	22.2%	-0.19
Pulled Up	6%	2	10	20.0%	0.05
Ref/RanOut	0%	0	1	0.0%	-1.00
CO/SlipUp	0%	0	1	0.0%	-1.00
Unraced	0%	0	0	0.0%	0.00

OTHER FACTORS (WINS-RUNS, £)

Course Winner:	9-34	-£0.12
Distance Winner:	20-84	£0.04
Going Winner:	19-72	£0.03
Beaten Favourite:	5-13	£0.09
7-Day Winners:	0-1	-£1.00
Absolute Favourites:	13-31	-£0.07

Race Profiles

Handicap Hurdle Races (class 1..3): 6 to 10 runners

ANALYSIS BY AGE

Age	Prop	Win	Runs	Wins%	£
3yo	0%	1	4	25.0%	1.38
4yo	8%	38	307	12.4%	-0.24
5yo	23%	113	792	14.3%	-0.14
6yo	25%	121	912	13.3%	-0.14
7yo	22%	106	861	12.3%	-0.11
8yo	14%	67	606	11.1%	-0.02
9yo	4%	22	316	7.0%	-0.41
10yo	3%	16	173	9.2%	0.04
11yo	1%	5	82	6.1%	-0.28
12yo+	0%	2	45	4.4%	-0.44

ANALYSIS BY BHB RATING

Age	Prop	Win	Runs	Wins%	£
150+	1%	4	24	16.7%	-0.07
130..149	11%	52	382	13.6%	-0.10
120..129	25%	123	1035	11.9%	-0.17
110..119	40%	198	1567	12.6%	-0.07
100..109	18%	88	828	10.6%	-0.20
80..99	5%	26	262	9.9%	-0.32

ANALYSIS BY WEIGHT CARRIED

Age	Prop	Win	Runs	Wins%	£
12-01+	0%	2	3	66.7%	1.04
11-8..12-00	19%	94	683	13.8%	-0.13
11-0..11-07	36%	179	1303	13.7%	-0.07
10-8..10-13	19%	95	903	10.5%	-0.23
10-0..10-07	18%	89	900	9.9%	-0.16
..9-13	7%	32	306	10.5%	-0.13

ANALYSIS BY DAYS SINCE LAST RUN

Age	Prop	Win	Runs	Wins%	£
1..7	8%	39	179	21.8%	0.56
8..14	16%	79	623	12.7%	-0.16
15..28	28%	138	1265	10.9%	-0.33
29..60	25%	122	916	13.3%	-0.01
61..100	6%	28	257	10.9%	-0.21
101+	17%	85	845	10.1%	-0.09
Unraced	0%	0	13	0.0%	-1.00

ANALYSIS BY TODAY'S STARTING PRICE

Age	Prop	Win	Runs	Wins%	£
Odds On	3%	15	29	51.7%	-0.08
Ev-2/1	11%	56	170	32.9%	-0.13
9/4-4/1	30%	149	776	19.2%	-0.20
9/2-6/1	20%	100	661	15.1%	-0.05
13/2-10/1	22%	106	1008	10.5%	-0.06
11/1-16/1	9%	44	763	5.8%	-0.17
18/1-33/1	4%	19	531	3.6%	-0.17
40/1+	0%	2	160	1.3%	-0.49

ANALYSIS BY STARTING PRICE LAST TIME

Age	Prop	Win	Runs	Wins%	£
Odds On	2%	12	93	12.9%	-0.35
Ev-2/1	9%	42	241	17.4%	-0.04
9/4-4/1	17%	85	605	14.0%	-0.15
9/2-6/1	15%	74	526	14.1%	-0.15
13/2-10/1	24%	117	879	13.3%	0.00
11/1-16/1	18%	90	815	11.0%	-0.14
18/1-33/1	11%	54	680	7.9%	-0.24
40/1+	3%	17	246	6.9%	-0.29
Unraced	0%	0	13	0.0%	-1.00

ANALYSIS BY DISTANCE BEATEN LAST TIME

Age	Prop	Win	Runs	Wins%	£
..-10 lgh	4%	18	89	20.2%	-0.14
-10..0	20%	99	587	16.9%	-0.15
0.1..2	8%	40	264	15.2%	-0.16
2.1..5	7%	32	285	11.2%	-0.36
5.1..10	11%	55	433	12.7%	-0.16
10.1..20	16%	80	657	12.2%	-0.13
20.0..30	9%	44	427	10.3%	-0.12
30.1+	14%	71	804	8.8%	-0.19
Not Compl	11%	52	539	9.6%	0.07
Unraced	0%	0	13	0.0%	-1.00

ANALYSIS BY SUCCESS RATE IN LAST 10 RUNS

Age	Prop	Win	Runs	Wins%	£
No Wins	16%	79	674	11.7%	-0.03
1 Win	34%	169	1447	11.7%	-0.16
2 Wins	28%	138	1196	11.5%	-0.16
3 Wins	15%	75	546	13.7%	-0.07
4 Wins	3%	17	165	10.3%	-0.53
5+ Wins	3%	13	57	22.8%	0.22

ANALYSIS BY SUCCESS RATE IN LAST 3 RUNS

Age	Prop	Win	Runs	Wins%	£
No Wins	50%	247	2358	10.5%	-0.15
1 Win	38%	186	1387	13.4%	-0.13
2 Wins	10%	48	302	15.9%	-0.11
3 Wins	2%	10	38	26.3%	-0.07

ANALYSIS BY POSITION LAST TIME

Age	Prop	Win	Runs	Wins%	£
Won	24%	118	677	17.4%	-0.14
2nd or 3rd	24%	118	897	13.2%	-0.20
Unplaced	42%	204	1974	10.3%	-0.16
Fell,BD,UR	5%	24	190	12.6%	0.11
Pulled Up	5%	26	329	7.9%	0.03
Ref/RanOut	0%	1	13	7.7%	0.62
CO/SlipUp	0%	0	5	0.0%	-1.00
Unraced	0%	0	13	0.0%	-1.00

OTHER FACTORS (WINS-RUNS, £)

Course Winner:	94-797	-£0.15
Distance Winner:	217-1833	-£0.14
Going Winner:	241-1948	-£0.14
Beaten Favourite:	41-318	-£0.25
7-Day Winners:	16-48	£0.18
Absolute Favourites:	113-436	-£0.22

TRAINERS (WINS-RUNS, £)

L Lungo 3-25 £0.20; V R A Dartnall 5-22 £0.22; K Bishop 3-11 £0.41; R C Guest 3-20 £0.18; A W Carroll 4-37 £0.08; M A Barnes 5-23 £0.07.

Handicap Hurdle Races (class 1..3)

Handicap Hurdle Races (class 1..3): 11 runners or more

ANALYSIS BY AGE

Age	Prop	Win	Runs	Wins%	£
3yo	0%	0	5	0.0%	-1.00
4yo	6%	39	562	6.9%	-0.29
5yo	27%	165	1861	8.9%	-0.13
6yo	26%	160	2184	7.3%	-0.30
7yo	20%	125	1740	7.2%	-0.23
8yo	12%	77	1207	6.4%	-0.28
9yo	6%	36	726	5.0%	-0.14
10yo	2%	14	392	3.6%	-0.48
11yo	1%	5	188	2.7%	-0.63
12yo+	0%	1	94	1.1%	-0.89

ANALYSIS BY BHB RATING

Age	Prop	Win	Runs	Wins%	£
150+	1%	6	71	8.5%	0.42
130..149	16%	102	1940	5.3%	-0.34
120..129	30%	184	2536	7.3%	-0.27
110..119	35%	215	2641	8.1%	-0.17
100..109	16%	97	1387	7.0%	-0.26
80..99	3%	18	384	4.7%	-0.46
60..79	0%	0	0	0.0%	0.00
..59	0%	0	0	0.0%	0.00
Unrated	0%	0	0	0.0%	0.00

ANALYSIS BY WEIGHT CARRIED

Age	Prop	Win	Runs	Wins%	£
12-01+	0%	0	0	0.0%	0.00
11-8..12-00	15%	95	1133	8.4%	-0.24
11-0..11-07	35%	216	2831	7.6%	-0.21
10-8..10-13	21%	130	2168	6.0%	-0.39
10-0..10-07	24%	147	2231	6.6%	-0.19
..9-13	5%	34	596	5.7%	-0.30

ANALYSIS BY DAYS SINCE LAST RUN

Age	Prop	Win	Runs	Wins%	£
1..7	4%	25	320	7.8%	-0.42
8..14	14%	84	1187	7.1%	-0.23
15..28	32%	196	2769	7.1%	-0.20
29..60	26%	162	2228	7.3%	-0.23
61..100	8%	47	661	7.1%	-0.14
101+	17%	108	1768	6.1%	-0.40
Unraced	0%	0	26	0.0%	-1.00

ANALYSIS BY TODAY'S STARTING PRICE

Age	Prop	Win	Runs	Wins%	£
Odds On	1%	4	12	33.3%	-0.42
Ev-2/1	6%	36	100	36.0%	0.02
9/4-4/1	16%	99	539	18.4%	-0.21
9/2-6/1	21%	128	784	16.3%	0.01
13/2-10/1	25%	157	1843	8.5%	-0.22
11/1-16/1	19%	121	2216	5.5%	-0.22
18/1-33/1	11%	66	2306	2.9%	-0.30
40/1+	2%	11	1159	0.9%	-0.54

ANALYSIS BY STARTING PRICE LAST TIME

Age	Prop	Win	Runs	Wins%	£
Odds On	4%	27	222	12.2%	-0.19
Ev-2/1	9%	54	492	11.0%	-0.12
9/4-4/1	19%	117	1271	9.2%	-0.24
9/2-6/1	13%	78	1041	7.5%	-0.30
13/2-10/1	22%	135	1908	7.1%	-0.24
11/1-16/1	18%	115	1768	6.5%	-0.17
18/1-33/1	12%	72	1547	4.7%	-0.37
40/1+	4%	24	684	3.5%	-0.36
Unraced	0%	0	26	0.0%	-1.00

ANALYSIS BY DISTANCE BEATEN LAST TIME

Age	Prop	Win	Runs	Wins%	£
..-10 lgh	3%	19	200	9.5%	-0.51
-10..0	21%	130	1304	10.0%	-0.18
0.1..2	8%	50	629	7.9%	-0.32
2.1..5	11%	66	677	9.7%	-0.07
5.1..10	13%	83	976	8.5%	-0.14
10.1..20	15%	96	1435	6.7%	-0.31
20.0..30	7%	45	906	5.0%	-0.38
30.1+	13%	79	1700	4.6%	-0.23
Not Compl	9%	54	1106	4.9%	-0.34
Unraced	0%	0	26	0.0%	-1.00

ANALYSIS BY SUCCESS RATE IN LAST 10 RUNS

Age	Prop	Win	Runs	Wins%	£
No Wins	13%	80	1359	5.9%	-0.32
1 Win	31%	195	2951	6.6%	-0.24
2 Wins	29%	183	2710	6.8%	-0.26
3 Wins	17%	106	1319	8.0%	-0.22
4 Wins	6%	35	437	8.0%	-0.30
5+ Wins	4%	23	157	14.6%	-0.04

ANALYSIS BY SUCCESS RATE IN LAST 3 RUNS

Age	Prop	Win	Runs	Wins%	£
No Wins	47%	292	4976	5.9%	-0.27
1 Win	37%	231	3017	7.7%	-0.24
2 Wins	14%	87	838	10.4%	-0.22
3 Wins	2%	12	102	11.8%	-0.46

ANALYSIS BY POSITION LAST TIME

Age	Prop	Win	Runs	Wins%	£
Won	24%	149	1507	9.9%	-0.23
2nd or 3rd	25%	158	1994	7.9%	-0.31
Unplaced	42%	262	4334	6.0%	-0.22
Fell,BD,UR	4%	22	399	5.5%	-0.39
Pulled Up	5%	29	685	4.2%	-0.37
Ref/RanOut	0%	1	12	8.3%	1.17
CO/SlipUp	0%	1	2	50.0%	2.75
Unraced	0%	0	26	0.0%	-1.00

OTHER FACTORS (WINS-RUNS, £)

Course Winner:	136-1470	-£0.03
Distance Winner:	278-3955	-£0.27
Going Winner:	320-4399	-£0.23
Beaten Favourite:	64-625	-£0.17
7-Day Winners:	12-91	-£0.36
Absolute Favourites:	114-545	-£0.20

Race Profiles

Handicap Hurdle Races (class 1..3): up to 7 days off the track

ANALYSIS BY AGE

Age	Prop	Win	Runs	Wins%	£
3yo	0%	0	1	0.0%	-1.00
4yo	6%	4	49	8.2%	-0.65
5yo	23%	15	125	12.0%	-0.34
6yo	23%	15	121	12.4%	-0.19
7yo	12%	8	89	9.0%	-0.30
8yo	25%	16	74	21.6%	0.90
9yo	5%	3	44	6.8%	-0.51
10yo	5%	3	26	11.5%	0.33
11yo	2%	1	10	10.0%	0.30
12yo+	0%	0	7	0.0%	-1.00

ANALYSIS BY BHB RATING

Age	Prop	Win	Runs	Wins%	£
150+	0%	0	4	0.0%	-1.00
130..149	6%	4	82	4.9%	-0.69
120..129	23%	15	134	11.2%	-0.30
110..119	28%	18	160	11.3%	-0.15
100..109	32%	21	126	16.7%	0.43
80..99	11%	7	40	17.5%	-0.15
60..79	0%	0	0	0.0%	0.00
..59	0%	0	0	0.0%	0.00
Unrated	0%	0	0	0.0%	0.00

ANALYSIS BY WEIGHT CARRIED

Age	Prop	Win	Runs	Wins%	£
12-01+	2%	1	1	100.0%	2.75
11-8..12-00	3%	2	49	4.1%	-0.76
11-0..11-07	32%	21	136	15.4%	-0.18
10-8..10-13	23%	15	129	11.6%	-0.33
10-0..10-07	25%	16	175	9.1%	0.03
..9-13	15%	10	56	17.9%	0.37

ANALYSIS BY DAYS SINCE LAST RUN

Age	Prop	Win	Runs	Wins%	£
1..7	100%	65	507	12.8%	-0.07
8..14	0%	0	0	0.0%	0.00
15..28	0%	0	0	0.0%	0.00
29..60	0%	0	0	0.0%	0.00
61..100	0%	0	0	0.0%	0.00
101+	0%	0	0	0.0%	0.00
Unraced	0%	0	39	0.0%	-1.00

ANALYSIS BY TODAY'S STARTING PRICE

Age	Prop	Win	Runs	Wins%	£
Odds On	9%	6	11	54.5%	-0.03
Ev-2/1	17%	11	27	40.7%	0.05
9/4-4/1	23%	15	91	16.5%	-0.33
9/2-6/1	15%	10	66	15.2%	-0.11
13/2-10/1	18%	12	94	12.8%	0.10
11/1-16/1	8%	5	101	5.0%	-0.34
18/1-33/1	9%	6	107	5.6%	0.32
40/1+	0%	0	49	0.0%	-1.00

ANALYSIS BY STARTING PRICE LAST TIME

Age	Prop	Win	Runs	Wins%	£
Odds On	3%	2	6	33.3%	0.04
Ev-2/1	11%	7	28	25.0%	-0.26
9/4-4/1	22%	14	85	16.5%	-0.37
9/2-6/1	12%	8	55	14.5%	-0.25
13/2-10/1	23%	15	113	13.3%	-0.10
11/1-16/1	15%	10	99	10.1%	0.47
18/1-33/1	8%	5	84	6.0%	-0.37
40/1+	6%	4	37	10.8%	0.28
Unraced	0%	0	39	0.0%	-1.00

ANALYSIS BY DISTANCE BEATEN LAST TIME

Age	Prop	Win	Runs	Wins%	£
..-10 lgh	17%	11	36	30.6%	-0.01
-10..0	26%	17	103	16.5%	-0.23
0.1..2	11%	7	43	16.3%	-0.09
2.1..5	9%	6	33	18.2%	0.11
5.1..10	8%	5	52	9.6%	0.01
10.1..20	8%	5	74	6.8%	-0.31
20.0..30	6%	4	46	8.7%	0.12
30.1+	3%	2	56	3.6%	-0.25
Not Compl	12%	8	64	12.5%	0.28
Unraced	0%	0	39	0.0%	-1.00

ANALYSIS BY SUCCESS RATE IN LAST 10 RUNS

Age	Prop	Win	Runs	Wins%	£
No Wins	18%	12	94	12.8%	0.38
1 Win	28%	18	154	11.7%	-0.37
2 Wins	32%	21	159	13.2%	0.11
3 Wins	15%	10	63	15.9%	-0.31
4 Wins	5%	3	28	10.7%	-0.29
5+ Wins	2%	1	9	11.1%	-0.56

ANALYSIS BY SUCCESS RATE IN LAST 3 RUNS

Age	Prop	Win	Runs	Wins%	£
No Wins	35%	23	256	9.0%	-0.07
1 Win	49%	32	196	16.3%	-0.02
2 Wins	12%	8	48	16.7%	-0.26
3 Wins	3%	2	7	28.6%	-0.38

ANALYSIS BY POSITION LAST TIME

Age	Prop	Win	Runs	Wins%	£
Won	43%	28	140	20.0%	-0.18
2nd or 3rd	26%	17	121	14.0%	-0.03
Unplaced	18%	12	182	6.6%	-0.15
Fell,BD,UR	8%	5	32	15.6%	0.53
Pulled Up	3%	2	26	7.7%	-0.54
Ref/RanOut	2%	1	5	20.0%	3.20
CO/SlipUp	0%	0	1	0.0%	-1.00
Unraced	0%	0	39	0.0%	-1.00

OTHER FACTORS (WINS-RUNS, £)

Course Winner:	15-89	£0.16
Distance Winner:	33-244	-£0.01
Going Winner:	38-284	£0.02
Beaten Favourite:	3-19	-£0.61
7-Day Winners:	28-140	-£0.18
Absolute Favourites:	25-79	-£0.10

Handicap Hurdle Races (class 1..3)

Handicap Hurdle Races (class 1..3): 100+ days off the track

ANALYSIS BY AGE

Age	Prop	Win	Runs	Wins%	£
3yo	0%	0	1	0.0%	-1.00
4yo	5%	10	185	5.4%	-0.61
5yo	26%	51	509	10.0%	-0.18
6yo	26%	52	581	9.0%	-0.31
7yo	20%	40	528	7.6%	-0.26
8yo	14%	27	395	6.8%	-0.08
9yo	6%	11	231	4.8%	-0.51
10yo	3%	6	131	4.6%	-0.36
11yo	1%	1	59	1.7%	-0.61
12yo+	1%	1	29	3.4%	-0.66

ANALYSIS BY BHB RATING

Age	Prop	Win	Runs	Wins%	£
150+	2%	3	23	13.0%	0.34
130..149	16%	31	469	6.6%	-0.54
120..129	29%	58	756	7.7%	-0.24
110..119	41%	81	871	9.3%	-0.09
100..109	12%	23	407	5.7%	-0.46
80..99	2%	3	123	2.4%	-0.57
60..79	0%	0	0	0.0%	0.00
..59	0%	0	0	0.0%	0.00
Unrated	0%	0	0	0.0%	0.00

ANALYSIS BY WEIGHT CARRIED

Age	Prop	Win	Runs	Wins%	£
12-01+	0%	0	0	0.0%	0.00
11-8..12-00	22%	44	464	9.5%	-0.41
11-0..11-07	41%	82	862	9.5%	-0.11
10-8..10-13	15%	30	585	5.1%	-0.45
10-0..10-07	19%	38	573	6.6%	-0.23
..9-13	3%	5	165	3.0%	-0.54

ANALYSIS BY DAYS SINCE LAST RUN

Age	Prop	Win	Runs	Wins%	£
1..7	0%	0	0	0.0%	0.00
8..14	0%	0	0	0.0%	0.00
15..28	0%	0	0	0.0%	0.00
29..60	0%	0	0	0.0%	0.00
61..100	1%	2	9	22.2%	2.61
101+	99%	197	2640	7.5%	-0.30
Unraced	0%	0	0	0.0%	0.00

ANALYSIS BY TODAY'S STARTING PRICE

Age	Prop	Win	Runs	Wins%	£
Odds On	2%	3	6	50.0%	-0.10
Ev-2/1	11%	21	53	39.6%	0.07
9/4-4/1	16%	31	211	14.7%	-0.43
9/2-6/1	21%	42	252	16.7%	0.01
13/2-10/1	28%	55	524	10.5%	-0.05
11/1-16/1	12%	24	596	4.0%	-0.43
18/1-33/1	11%	21	666	3.2%	-0.21
40/1+	1%	2	341	0.6%	-0.76

ANALYSIS BY STARTING PRICE LAST TIME

Age	Prop	Win	Runs	Wins%	£
Odds On	6%	12	102	11.8%	-0.13
Ev-2/1	13%	25	197	12.7%	0.05
9/4-4/1	19%	37	432	8.6%	-0.24
9/2-6/1	11%	22	337	6.5%	-0.52
13/2-10/1	19%	38	547	6.9%	-0.27
11/1-16/1	18%	35	459	7.6%	-0.19
18/1-33/1	11%	21	426	4.9%	-0.46
40/1+	5%	9	149	6.0%	-0.35
Unraced	0%	0	0	0.0%	0.00

ANALYSIS BY DISTANCE BEATEN LAST TIME

Age	Prop	Win	Runs	Wins%	£
..-10 lgh	2%	3	56	5.4%	-0.63
-10..0	15%	30	347	8.6%	-0.28
0.1..2	6%	12	132	9.1%	-0.28
2.1..5	9%	17	158	10.8%	-0.17
5.1..10	7%	14	233	6.0%	-0.36
10.1..20	17%	34	366	9.3%	-0.12
20.0..30	11%	22	297	7.4%	-0.41
30.1+	18%	35	618	5.7%	-0.43
Not Compl	16%	32	442	7.2%	-0.14
Unraced	0%	0	0	0.0%	0.00

ANALYSIS BY SUCCESS RATE IN LAST 10 RUNS

Age	Prop	Win	Runs	Wins%	£
No Wins	12%	23	323	7.1%	-0.21
1 Win	28%	56	887	6.3%	-0.35
2 Wins	29%	58	818	7.1%	-0.34
3 Wins	19%	37	425	8.7%	-0.20
4 Wins	6%	11	128	8.6%	-0.37
5+ Wins	7%	14	68	20.6%	0.30

ANALYSIS BY SUCCESS RATE IN LAST 3 RUNS

Age	Prop	Win	Runs	Wins%	£
No Wins	45%	89	1312	6.8%	-0.26
1 Win	39%	77	1028	7.5%	-0.33
2 Wins	14%	28	273	10.3%	-0.24
3 Wins	3%	5	36	13.9%	-0.57

ANALYSIS BY POSITION LAST TIME

Age	Prop	Win	Runs	Wins%	£
Won	17%	33	404	8.2%	-0.33
2nd or 3rd	24%	47	498	9.4%	-0.23
Unplaced	45%	89	1309	6.8%	-0.33
Fell,BD,UR	7%	13	146	8.9%	-0.35
Pulled Up	9%	17	289	5.9%	-0.13
Ref/RanOut	0%	0	0	0.0%	-1.00
CO/SlipUp	0%	0	0	0.0%	0.00
Unraced	0%	0	0	0.0%	0.00

OTHER FACTORS (WINS-RUNS, £)

Course Winner:	36-474	-£0.36
Distance Winner:	95-1239	-£0.32
Going Winner:	103-1281	-£0.24
Beaten Favourite:	23-254	-£0.45
Absolute Favourites:	39-163	-£0.23

Race Profiles

Handicap Hurdle Races (class 4..6)

ANALYSIS BY AGE

Age	Prop	Win	Runs	Wins%	£
3yo	0%	4	31	12.9%	1.45
4yo	8%	144	1691	8.5%	-0.31
5yo	20%	388	3909	9.9%	-0.13
6yo	25%	482	5070	9.5%	-0.19
7yo	20%	375	4430	8.5%	-0.28
8yo	13%	244	3112	7.8%	-0.32
9yo	7%	141	1979	7.1%	-0.24
10yo	4%	78	1183	6.6%	-0.15
11yo	1%	28	609	4.6%	-0.40
12yo+	1%	12	384	3.1%	-0.62

ANALYSIS BY BHB RATING

Age	Prop	Win	Runs	Wins%	£
130..149	0%	0	1	0.0%	-1.00
120..129	1%	11	104	10.6%	-0.45
110..119	10%	184	1684	10.9%	-0.17
100..109	29%	541	5740	9.4%	-0.20
80..99	54%	1031	12506	8.2%	-0.25
60..79	7%	129	2356	5.5%	-0.32
..59	0%	0	3	0.0%	-1.00
Unrated	0%	0	4	0.0%	-1.00

ANALYSIS BY WEIGHT CARRIED

Age	Prop	Win	Runs	Wins%	£
12-01+	0%	5	16	31.3%	0.23
11-8..12-00	19%	358	3463	10.3%	-0.21
11-0..11-07	40%	759	8424	9.0%	-0.21
10-8..10-13	21%	391	4828	8.1%	-0.24
10-0..10-07	16%	303	4147	7.3%	-0.26
..9-13	4%	80	1520	5.3%	-0.43

ANALYSIS BY DAYS SINCE LAST RUN

Age	Prop	Win	Runs	Wins%	£
1..7	8%	151	1052	14.4%	-0.18
8..14	18%	349	3679	9.5%	-0.22
15..28	31%	580	6808	8.5%	-0.24
29..60	21%	394	4959	7.9%	-0.19
61..100	7%	127	1606	7.9%	-0.10
101+	15%	293	4264	6.9%	-0.26
Unraced	0%	2	30	6.7%	-0.52

ANALYSIS BY TODAY'S STARTING PRICE

Age	Prop	Win	Runs	Wins%	£
Odds On	2%	38	86	44.2%	-0.24
Ev-2/1	10%	190	508	37.4%	-0.02
9/4-4/1	26%	498	2251	22.1%	-0.06
9/2-6/1	17%	324	2369	13.7%	-0.15
13/2-10/1	22%	424	4760	8.9%	-0.19
11/1-16/1	14%	269	4872	5.5%	-0.21
18/1-33/1	7%	129	5065	2.5%	-0.34
40/1+	1%	24	2487	1.0%	-0.46

ANALYSIS BY STARTING PRICE LAST TIME

Age	Prop	Win	Runs	Wins%	£
Odds On	2%	29	145	20.0%	-0.14
Ev-2/1	6%	112	594	18.9%	-0.15
9/4-4/1	16%	310	2326	13.3%	-0.21
9/2-6/1	13%	246	2286	10.8%	-0.27
13/2-10/1	23%	437	4579	9.5%	-0.21
11/1-16/1	18%	334	4519	7.4%	-0.31
18/1-33/1	15%	290	4805	6.0%	-0.23
40/1+	7%	136	3114	4.4%	-0.20
Unraced	0%	2	30	6.7%	-0.52

ANALYSIS BY DISTANCE BEATEN LAST TIME

Age	Prop	Win	Runs	Wins%	£
..-10 lgh	3%	53	231	22.9%	0.17
-10..0	15%	276	1667	16.6%	-0.17
0.1..2	7%	131	937	14.0%	-0.24
2.1..5	9%	170	1223	13.9%	-0.13
5.1..10	10%	199	1887	10.5%	-0.22
10.1..20	16%	310	3566	8.7%	-0.30
20.0..30	11%	216	2758	7.8%	-0.16
30.1+	18%	343	6438	5.3%	-0.27
Not Compl	10%	196	3661	5.4%	-0.28
Unraced	0%	2	30	6.7%	-0.52

ANALYSIS BY SUCCESS RATE IN LAST 10 RUNS

Age	Prop	Win	Runs	Wins%	£
No Wins	40%	754	11029	6.8%	-0.26
1 Win	37%	702	7460	9.4%	-0.22
2 Wins	16%	301	2875	10.5%	-0.21
3 Wins	5%	103	782	13.2%	-0.21
4 Wins	1%	22	185	11.9%	-0.32
5+ Wins	1%	12	37	32.4%	0.46

ANALYSIS BY SUCCESS RATE IN LAST 3 RUNS

Age	Prop	Win	Runs	Wins%	£
No Wins	66%	1257	17496	7.2%	-0.25
1 Win	28%	530	4296	12.3%	-0.21
2 Wins	5%	101	545	18.5%	-0.18
3 Wins	0%	6	31	19.4%	-0.51

ANALYSIS BY POSITION LAST TIME

Age	Prop	Win	Runs	Wins%	£
Won	17%	329	1899	17.3%	-0.13
2nd or 3rd	27%	516	4033	12.8%	-0.15
Unplaced	45%	855	12799	6.7%	-0.27
Fell,BD,UR	3%	66	981	6.7%	-0.24
Pulled Up	6%	122	2569	4.7%	-0.28
Ref/RanOut	0%	3	69	4.3%	-0.75
CO/SlipUp	0%	3	18	16.7%	-0.21
Unraced	0%	2	30	6.7%	-0.52

OTHER FACTORS (WINS-RUNS, £)

Course Winner:	306-3087	-£0.21
Distance Winner:	542-5644	-£0.24
Going Winner:	596-6417	-£0.26
Beaten Favourite:	164-1147	-£0.21
7-Day Winners:	70-216	£0.09
Absolute Favourites:	464-1689	-£0.08

TRAINERS (WINS-RUNS, £)

R Dickin 9-93 £0.35; Andrew Turnell 11-63 £0.50; Miss J S Davis 4-61 £0.46; J S Goldie 12-75 £0.37; A W Carroll 22-186 £0.15; P G Murphy 7-39 £0.63; P D Evans 9-50 £0.45; R Johnson 5-88 £0.25; D McCain 7-42 £0.47; K A Morgan 4-42 £0.46; Mrs Marjorie Fife 3-36 £0.54; Mrs A M Thorpe 36-218 £0.08; A Parker 3-42 £0.40; Mrs A E Brooks 6-58 £0.29; J J Quinn 10-47 £0.34; D A Rees 3-39 £0.38; Miss C Dyson 3-32 £0.45; Miss P Robson 6-20 £0.71; N Wilson 7-43 £0.33.

Handicap Hurdle Races (class 4..6)

Handicap Hurdle Races (class 4..6): 2m to 2m3f

ANALYSIS BY AGE

Age	Prop	Win	Runs	Wins%	£
3yo	0%	3	21	14.3%	2.10
4yo	12%	88	993	8.9%	-0.37
5yo	23%	176	1808	9.7%	-0.17
6yo	25%	190	1955	9.7%	-0.18
7yo	19%	139	1579	8.8%	-0.26
8yo	11%	86	1036	8.3%	-0.20
9yo	5%	37	638	5.8%	-0.41
10yo	3%	21	350	6.0%	-0.18
11yo	1%	7	176	4.0%	-0.68
12yo+	0%	2	100	2.0%	-0.51

ANALYSIS BY BHB RATING

Age	Prop	Win	Runs	Wins%	£
130..149	0%	0	1	0.0%	-1.00
120..129	1%	4	30	13.3%	-0.09
110..119	9%	68	648	10.5%	-0.27
100..109	29%	217	2284	9.5%	-0.20
80..99	54%	407	4878	8.3%	-0.29
60..79	7%	53	812	6.5%	-0.09
..59	0%	0	2	0.0%	-1.00
Unrated	0%	0	1	0.0%	-1.00

ANALYSIS BY WEIGHT CARRIED

Age	Prop	Win	Runs	Wins%	£
12-01+	0%	2	5	40.0%	0.28
11-8..12-00	16%	123	1302	9.4%	-0.30
11-0..11-07	39%	294	3234	9.1%	-0.25
10-8..10-13	21%	160	1850	8.6%	-0.23
10-0..10-07	18%	136	1660	8.2%	-0.19
..9-13	5%	34	605	5.6%	-0.29

ANALYSIS BY DAYS SINCE LAST RUN

Age	Prop	Win	Runs	Wins%	£
1..7	8%	59	417	14.1%	-0.17
8..14	18%	134	1428	9.4%	-0.30
15..28	30%	227	2505	9.1%	-0.18
29..60	21%	154	1784	8.6%	-0.27
61..100	7%	50	657	7.6%	-0.19
101+	17%	124	1849	6.7%	-0.30
Unraced	0%	1	16	6.3%	-0.72

ANALYSIS BY TODAY'S STARTING PRICE

Age	Prop	Win	Runs	Wins%	£
Odds On	2%	15	34	44.1%	-0.23
Ev-2/1	10%	72	202	35.6%	-0.07
9/4-4/1	30%	226	966	23.4%	0.00
9/2-6/1	15%	113	883	12.8%	-0.21
13/2-10/1	22%	167	1818	9.2%	-0.15
11/1-16/1	13%	98	1877	5.2%	-0.25
18/1-33/1	7%	51	1914	2.7%	-0.32
40/1+	1%	7	962	0.7%	-0.58

ANALYSIS BY STARTING PRICE LAST TIME

Age	Prop	Win	Runs	Wins%	£
Odds On	1%	7	56	12.5%	-0.49
Ev-2/1	6%	47	235	20.0%	-0.13
9/4-4/1	16%	121	909	13.3%	-0.20
9/2-6/1	14%	103	904	11.4%	-0.33
13/2-10/1	23%	172	1714	10.0%	-0.17
11/1-16/1	17%	127	1716	7.4%	-0.30
18/1-33/1	15%	113	1850	6.1%	-0.27
40/1+	8%	58	1256	4.6%	-0.21
Unraced	0%	1	16	6.3%	-0.72

ANALYSIS BY DISTANCE BEATEN LAST TIME

Age	Prop	Win	Runs	Wins%	£
..-10 lgh	2%	14	73	19.2%	-0.02
-10..0	15%	110	650	16.9%	-0.15
0.1..2	7%	52	337	15.4%	-0.23
2.1..5	10%	73	502	14.5%	-0.05
5.1..10	10%	74	761	9.7%	-0.20
10.1..20	16%	122	1452	8.4%	-0.37
20.0..30	12%	89	1086	8.2%	-0.16
30.1+	17%	130	2471	5.3%	-0.32
Not Compl	11%	84	1308	6.4%	-0.20
Unraced	0%	1	16	6.3%	-0.72

ANALYSIS BY SUCCESS RATE IN LAST 10 RUNS

Age	Prop	Win	Runs	Wins%	£
No Wins	42%	312	4348	7.2%	-0.26
1 Win	38%	287	2917	9.8%	-0.21
2 Wins	14%	106	1034	10.3%	-0.28
3 Wins	5%	35	287	12.2%	-0.23
4 Wins	1%	4	48	8.3%	-0.48
5+ Wins	1%	4	6	66.7%	1.98

ANALYSIS BY SUCCESS RATE IN LAST 3 RUNS

Age	Prop	Win	Runs	Wins%	£
No Wins	68%	506	6753	7.5%	-0.24
1 Win	27%	201	1684	11.9%	-0.27
2 Wins	5%	40	198	20.2%	-0.12
3 Wins	0%	1	5	20.0%	-0.65

ANALYSIS BY POSITION LAST TIME

Age	Prop	Win	Runs	Wins%	£
Won	17%	124	723	17.2%	-0.14
2nd or 3rd	26%	192	1493	12.9%	-0.18
Unplaced	47%	349	5129	6.8%	-0.29
Fell,BD,UR	4%	27	384	7.0%	-0.39
Pulled Up	7%	53	877	6.0%	-0.11
Ref/RanOut	0%	1	26	3.8%	-0.67
CO/SlipUp	0%	2	8	25.0%	-0.03
Unraced	0%	1	16	6.3%	-0.72

OTHER FACTORS (WINS-RUNS, £)

Course Winner:	118-1115	-£0.19
Distance Winner:	260-2804	-£0.29
Going Winner:	214-2242	-£0.27
Beaten Favourite:	58-451	-£0.30
7-Day Winners:	27-87	-£0.11
Absolute Favourites:	177-665	-£0.12

TRAINERS (WINS-RUNS, £)

Miss Rebecca Curtis 3-11 £1.13; W S Coltherd 4-26 £0.44; Noel T Chance 3-17 £0.56; R Ford 4-14 £0.65; M Scudamore 3-32 £0.28; R Curtis 4-24 £0.38; C Grant 3-21 £0.40; N G Richards 11-67 £0.12; Andrew Turnell 5-39 £0.20; W Amos 4-22 £0.04; T R George 5-25 £0.29; B Ellison 6-25 £0.21; P C Haslam 5-40 £0.07; J J Quinn 5-28 £0.08; P F Nicholls 4-17 £0.10; M J Scudamore 3-18 £0.08; M Keighley 3-32 £0.02; D W Whillans 4-35 £0.01; P D Evans 3-23 £0.02.

Race Profiles

Handicap Hurdle Races (class 4..6): 2m4f to 2m7f

ANALYSIS BY AGE

Age	Prop	Win	Runs	Wins%	£
3yo	0%	1	10	10.0%	0.10
4yo	6%	41	561	7.3%	-0.30
5yo	19%	143	1491	9.6%	-0.15
6yo	29%	215	2051	10.5%	-0.11
7yo	19%	137	1798	7.6%	-0.36
8yo	13%	95	1299	7.3%	-0.43
9yo	8%	62	799	7.8%	-0.05
10yo	3%	22	423	5.2%	-0.46
11yo	2%	15	234	6.4%	0.01
12yo+	1%	6	153	3.9%	-0.52

ANALYSIS BY BHB RATING

Age	Prop	Win	Runs	Wins%	£
120..129	1%	4	51	7.8%	-0.60
110..119	12%	86	697	12.3%	-0.07
100..109	30%	218	2424	9.0%	-0.23
80..99	52%	384	4799	8.0%	-0.25
60..79	6%	45	844	5.3%	-0.32
..59	0%	0	1	0.0%	-1.00
Unrated	0%	0	3	0.0%	-1.00

ANALYSIS BY WEIGHT CARRIED

Age	Prop	Win	Runs	Wins%	£
12-01+	0%	1	8	12.5%	-0.13
11-8..12-00	21%	153	1415	10.8%	-0.17
11-0..11-07	41%	300	3407	8.8%	-0.22
10-8..10-13	20%	148	1883	7.9%	-0.28
10-0..10-07	14%	106	1533	6.9%	-0.23
..9-13	4%	29	573	5.1%	-0.49

ANALYSIS BY DAYS SINCE LAST RUN

Age	Prop	Win	Runs	Wins%	£
1..7	8%	62	392	15.8%	-0.21
8..14	17%	128	1371	9.3%	-0.32
15..28	31%	227	2756	8.2%	-0.26
29..60	20%	149	1969	7.6%	-0.28
61..100	7%	52	624	8.3%	0.01
101+	16%	118	1695	7.0%	-0.20
Unraced	0%	1	12	8.3%	-0.17

ANALYSIS BY TODAY'S STARTING PRICE

Age	Prop	Win	Runs	Wins%	£
Odds On	2%	12	33	36.4%	-0.38
Ev-2/1	11%	80	198	40.4%	0.06
9/4-4/1	24%	174	828	21.0%	-0.13
9/2-6/1	18%	132	943	14.0%	-0.14
13/2-10/1	23%	171	1916	8.9%	-0.19
11/1-16/1	15%	111	1905	5.8%	-0.16
18/1-33/1	6%	46	2062	2.2%	-0.43
40/1+	1%	11	934	1.2%	-0.36

ANALYSIS BY STARTING PRICE LAST TIME

Age	Prop	Win	Runs	Wins%	£
Odds On	2%	16	61	26.2%	0.29
Ev-2/1	6%	44	239	18.4%	-0.10
9/4-4/1	16%	115	907	12.7%	-0.29
9/2-6/1	12%	91	881	10.3%	-0.21
13/2-10/1	24%	176	1827	9.6%	-0.21
11/1-16/1	19%	138	1843	7.5%	-0.30
18/1-33/1	15%	107	1864	5.7%	-0.30
40/1+	7%	49	1185	4.1%	-0.17
Unraced	0%	1	12	8.3%	-0.17

ANALYSIS BY DISTANCE BEATEN LAST TIME

Age	Prop	Win	Runs	Wins%	£
..-10 lgh	3%	25	107	23.4%	0.27
-10..0	14%	101	642	15.7%	-0.21
0.1..2	7%	49	372	13.2%	-0.26
2.1..5	9%	64	469	13.6%	-0.21
5.1..10	11%	81	733	11.1%	-0.24
10.1..20	17%	124	1387	8.9%	-0.27
20.0..30	13%	93	1096	8.5%	-0.13
30.1+	18%	134	2543	5.3%	-0.26
Not Compl	9%	65	1458	4.5%	-0.34
Unraced	0%	1	12	8.3%	-0.17

ANALYSIS BY SUCCESS RATE IN LAST 10 RUNS

Age	Prop	Win	Runs	Wins%	£
No Wins	38%	280	4196	6.7%	-0.30
1 Win	37%	275	2946	9.3%	-0.20
2 Wins	17%	123	1236	10.0%	-0.16
3 Wins	6%	42	326	12.9%	-0.23
4 Wins	2%	13	89	14.6%	-0.10
5+ Wins	0%	3	14	21.4%	0.18

ANALYSIS BY SUCCESS RATE IN LAST 3 RUNS

Age	Prop	Win	Runs	Wins%	£
No Wins	66%	486	6863	7.1%	-0.26
1 Win	29%	213	1708	12.5%	-0.17
2 Wins	5%	36	222	16.2%	-0.22
3 Wins	0%	1	14	7.1%	-0.84

ANALYSIS BY POSITION LAST TIME

Age	Prop	Win	Runs	Wins%	£
Won	17%	126	750	16.8%	-0.14
2nd or 3rd	29%	214	1614	13.3%	-0.11
Unplaced	45%	331	4990	6.6%	-0.27
Fell,BD,UR	3%	19	361	5.3%	-0.28
Pulled Up	6%	45	1057	4.3%	-0.34
Ref/RanOut	0%	1	29	3.4%	-0.85
CO/SlipUp	0%	0	6	0.0%	-1.00
Unraced	0%	1	12	8.3%	-0.17

OTHER FACTORS (WINS-RUNS, £)

Course Winner:	121-1265	-£0.17
Distance Winner:	196-1931	-£0.13
Going Winner:	240-2669	-£0.28
Beaten Favourite:	67-441	-£0.21
7-Day Winners:	28-92	£0.11
Absolute Favourites:	191-664	-£0.03

TRAINERS (WINS-RUNS, £)

B I Case 5-34 £0.51; R Dickin 4-32 £0.54; D E Pipe 17-109 £0.16; Mrs A M Thorpe 15-79 £0.19; Mrs L Wadham 4-22 £0.64; J J Quinn 4-16 £0.81; Mrs P Robeson 4-23 £0.52; H D Daly 6-24 £0.44; A M Hales 6-34 £0.31; Miss T Jackson 3-17 £0.56; Mrs A Hamilton 3-12 £0.75; C L Tizzard 4-25 £0.34; A B Haynes 4-17 £0.47; D E Cantillon 3-14 £0.55; N J Hawke 6-79 £0.09; R H Alner 7-31 £0.20; D W P Arbuthnot 3-14 £0.41; Miss P Robson 4-12 £0.48; R Nixon 4-36 £0.16; M F Harris 9-85 £0.07.

Handicap Hurdle Races (class 4..6)

Handicap Hurdle Races (class 4..6): 3m+

ANALYSIS BY AGE

Age	Prop	Win	Runs	Wins%	£
3yo	0%	0	0	0.0%	0.00
4yo	4%	15	137	10.9%	0.16
5yo	17%	69	610	11.3%	0.09
6yo	19%	77	1064	7.2%	-0.38
7yo	24%	99	1053	9.4%	-0.16
8yo	15%	63	777	8.1%	-0.31
9yo	10%	42	542	7.7%	-0.33
10yo	9%	35	410	8.5%	0.19
11yo	1%	6	199	3.0%	-0.64
12yo+	1%	4	131	3.1%	-0.81

ANALYSIS BY BHB RATING

Age	Prop	Win	Runs	Wins%	£
150+	0%	0	0	0.0%	0.00
130..149	0%	0	0	0.0%	0.00
120..129	1%	3	23	13.0%	-0.57
110..119	7%	30	339	8.8%	-0.19
100..109	26%	106	1032	10.3%	-0.11
80..99	59%	240	2829	8.5%	-0.17
60..79	8%	31	700	4.4%	-0.57
..59	0%	0	0	0.0%	0.00
Unrated	0%	0	0	0.0%	0.00

ANALYSIS BY WEIGHT CARRIED

Age	Prop	Win	Runs	Wins%	£
12-01+	0%	2	3	66.7%	1.08
11-8..12-00	20%	82	746	11.0%	-0.12
11-0..11-07	40%	165	1783	9.3%	-0.11
10-8..10-13	20%	83	1095	7.6%	-0.17
10-0..10-07	15%	61	954	6.4%	-0.42
..9-13	4%	17	342	5.0%	-0.58

ANALYSIS BY DAYS SINCE LAST RUN

Age	Prop	Win	Runs	Wins%	£
1..7	7%	30	243	12.3%	-0.15
8..14	21%	87	880	9.9%	0.06
15..28	31%	126	1547	8.1%	-0.32
29..60	22%	91	1206	7.5%	-0.26
61..100	6%	25	325	7.7%	-0.11
101+	12%	51	720	7.1%	-0.31
Unraced	0%	0	2	0.0%	-1.00

ANALYSIS BY TODAY'S STARTING PRICE

Age	Prop	Win	Runs	Wins%	£
Odds On	3%	11	19	57.9%	-0.02
Ev-2/1	9%	38	108	35.2%	-0.07
9/4-4/1	24%	98	457	21.4%	-0.08
9/2-6/1	19%	79	543	14.5%	-0.10
13/2-10/1	21%	86	1026	8.4%	-0.24
11/1-16/1	15%	60	1090	5.5%	-0.20
18/1-33/1	8%	32	1089	2.9%	-0.22
40/1+	1%	6	591	1.0%	-0.42

ANALYSIS BY STARTING PRICE LAST TIME

Age	Prop	Win	Runs	Wins%	£
Odds On	1%	6	28	21.4%	-0.35
Ev-2/1	5%	21	120	17.5%	-0.29
9/4-4/1	18%	74	510	14.5%	-0.10
9/2-6/1	13%	52	501	10.4%	-0.25
13/2-10/1	22%	89	1038	8.6%	-0.29
11/1-16/1	17%	69	960	7.2%	-0.33
18/1-33/1	17%	70	1091	6.4%	-0.06
40/1+	7%	29	673	4.3%	-0.23
Unraced	0%	0	2	0.0%	-1.00

ANALYSIS BY DISTANCE BEATEN LAST TIME

Age	Prop	Win	Runs	Wins%	£
..-10 lgh	3%	14	51	27.5%	0.21
-10..0	16%	65	375	17.3%	-0.14
0.1..2	7%	30	228	13.2%	-0.22
2.1..5	8%	33	252	13.1%	-0.13
5.1..10	11%	44	393	11.2%	-0.22
10.1..20	16%	64	727	8.8%	-0.23
20.0..30	8%	34	576	5.9%	-0.19
30.1+	19%	79	1424	5.5%	-0.22
Not Compl	11%	47	895	5.3%	-0.29
Unraced	0%	0	2	0.0%	-1.00

ANALYSIS BY SUCCESS RATE IN LAST 10 RUNS

Age	Prop	Win	Runs	Wins%	£
No Wins	40%	162	2485	6.5%	-0.21
1 Win	34%	140	1597	8.8%	-0.25
2 Wins	18%	72	605	11.9%	-0.17
3 Wins	6%	26	169	15.4%	-0.12
4 Wins	1%	5	48	10.4%	-0.58
5+ Wins	1%	5	17	29.4%	0.15

ANALYSIS BY SUCCESS RATE IN LAST 3 RUNS

Age	Prop	Win	Runs	Wins%	£
No Wins	65%	265	3880	6.8%	-0.23
1 Win	28%	116	904	12.8%	-0.17
2 Wins	6%	25	125	20.0%	-0.18
3 Wins	1%	4	12	33.3%	-0.07

ANALYSIS BY POSITION LAST TIME

Age	Prop	Win	Runs	Wins%	£
Won	19%	79	426	18.5%	-0.10
2nd or 3rd	27%	110	926	11.9%	-0.19
Unplaced	43%	175	2680	6.5%	-0.22
Fell,BD,UR	5%	20	236	8.5%	0.08
Pulled Up	6%	24	635	3.8%	-0.43
Ref/RanOut	0%	1	14	7.1%	-0.68
CO/SlipUp	0%	1	4	25.0%	0.63
Unraced	0%	0	2	0.0%	-1.00

OTHER FACTORS (WINS-RUNS, £)

Course Winner:	67-707	-£0.31
Distance Winner:	86-909	-£0.32
Going Winner:	142-1506	-£0.20
Beaten Favourite:	39-255	-£0.06
7-Day Winners:	15-37	£0.53
Absolute Favourites:	96-360	-£0.09

TRAINERS (WINS-RUNS, £)

P Bowen 11-76 £0.04; A B Haynes 3-19 £0.13; R Lee 3-19 £0.05; M F Harris 3-23 £0.01.

Race Profiles

Handicap Hurdle Races (class 4..6): 2 to 5 runners

ANALYSIS BY AGE

Age	Prop	Win	Runs	Wins%	£
3yo	0%	0	0	0.0%	0.00
4yo	11%	4	18	22.2%	-0.42
5yo	21%	8	32	25.0%	0.11
6yo	29%	11	44	25.0%	-0.01
7yo	18%	7	39	17.9%	-0.38
8yo	0%	0	16	0.0%	-1.00
9yo	16%	6	13	46.2%	0.66
10yo	3%	1	10	10.0%	-0.78
11yo	0%	0	4	0.0%	-1.00
12yo+	3%	1	5	20.0%	-0.55

ANALYSIS BY BHB RATING

Age	Prop	Win	Runs	Wins%	£
150+	0%	0	0	0.0%	0.00
130..149	0%	0	0	0.0%	0.00
120..129	3%	1	1	100.0%	1.88
110..119	16%	6	19	31.6%	-0.01
100..109	29%	11	64	17.2%	-0.31
80..99	47%	18	82	22.0%	-0.18
60..79	5%	2	15	13.3%	-0.59
..59	0%	0	0	0.0%	0.00
Unrated	0%	0	0	0.0%	0.00

ANALYSIS BY WEIGHT CARRIED

Age	Prop	Win	Runs	Wins%	£
12-01+	0%	0	2	0.0%	-1.00
11-8..12-00	34%	13	42	31.0%	-0.02
11-0..11-07	37%	14	72	19.4%	-0.26
10-8..10-13	21%	8	33	24.2%	-0.02
10-0..10-07	8%	3	25	12.0%	-0.50
..9-13	0%	0	7	0.0%	-1.00

ANALYSIS BY DAYS SINCE LAST RUN

Age	Prop	Win	Runs	Wins%	£
1..7	18%	7	17	41.2%	0.05
8..14	21%	8	47	17.0%	-0.18
15..28	29%	11	57	19.3%	-0.38
29..60	16%	6	27	22.2%	-0.21
61..100	3%	1	5	20.0%	0.00
101+	13%	5	27	18.5%	-0.21
Unraced	0%	0	1	0.0%	-1.00

ANALYSIS BY TODAY'S STARTING PRICE

Age	Prop	Win	Runs	Wins%	£
Odds On	11%	4	10	40.0%	-0.32
Ev-2/1	47%	18	37	48.6%	0.20
9/4-4/1	21%	8	45	17.8%	-0.28
9/2-6/1	13%	5	24	20.8%	0.25
13/2-10/1	8%	3	35	8.6%	-0.26
11/1-16/1	0%	0	19	0.0%	-1.00
18/1-33/1	0%	0	9	0.0%	-1.00
40/1+	0%	0	2	0.0%	-1.00

ANALYSIS BY STARTING PRICE LAST TIME

Age	Prop	Win	Runs	Wins%	£
Odds On	5%	2	3	66.7%	2.67
Ev-2/1	5%	2	8	25.0%	-0.50
9/4-4/1	13%	5	27	18.5%	-0.55
9/2-6/1	16%	6	21	28.6%	-0.20
13/2-10/1	21%	8	43	18.6%	-0.24
11/1-16/1	26%	10	33	30.3%	0.39
18/1-33/1	11%	4	25	16.0%	-0.45
40/1+	3%	1	20	5.0%	-0.82
Unraced	0%	0	1	0.0%	-1.00

ANALYSIS BY DISTANCE BEATEN LAST TIME

Age	Prop	Win	Runs	Wins%	£
..-10 lgh	8%	3	6	50.0%	0.00
-10..0	16%	6	20	30.0%	0.08
0.1..2	13%	5	13	38.5%	-0.19
2.1..5	5%	2	13	15.4%	-0.08
5.1..10	5%	2	16	12.5%	-0.27
10.1..20	16%	6	27	22.2%	-0.03
20.0..30	3%	1	18	5.6%	-0.76
30.1+	26%	10	40	25.0%	-0.01
Not Compl	8%	3	27	11.1%	-0.73
Unraced	0%	0	1	0.0%	-1.00

ANALYSIS BY SUCCESS RATE IN LAST 10 RUNS

Age	Prop	Win	Runs	Wins%	£
No Wins	29%	11	73	15.1%	-0.35
1 Win	42%	16	72	22.2%	-0.28
2 Wins	16%	6	21	28.6%	0.11
3 Wins	8%	3	10	30.0%	-0.17
4 Wins	3%	1	3	33.3%	1.17
5+ Wins	3%	1	1	100.0%	0.73

ANALYSIS BY SUCCESS RATE IN LAST 3 RUNS

Age	Prop	Win	Runs	Wins%	£
No Wins	63%	24	129	18.6%	-0.23
1 Win	24%	9	43	20.9%	-0.42
2 Wins	11%	4	7	57.1%	0.88
3 Wins	3%	1	1	100.0%	0.73

ANALYSIS BY POSITION LAST TIME

Age	Prop	Win	Runs	Wins%	£
Won	24%	9	26	34.6%	0.06
2nd or 3rd	21%	8	37	21.6%	-0.32
Unplaced	47%	18	90	20.0%	-0.12
Fell,BD,UR	5%	2	9	22.2%	-0.43
Pulled Up	3%	1	17	5.9%	-0.87
Ref/RanOut	0%	0	1	0.0%	-1.00
CO/SlipUp	0%	0	0	0.0%	0.00
Unraced	0%	0	1	0.0%	-1.00

OTHER FACTORS (WINS-RUNS, £)

Course Winner:	9-28	-£0.01
Distance Winner:	18-66	-£0.24
Going Winner:	11-44	-£0.34
Beaten Favourite:	2-13	-£0.11
7-Day Winners:	2-7	-£0.51
Absolute Favourites:	19-37	£0.15

Handicap Hurdle Races (class 4..6)

Handicap Hurdle Races (class 4..6): 6 to 10 runners

ANALYSIS BY AGE

Age	Prop	Win	Runs	Wins%	£
3yo	0%	1	6	16.7%	0.83
4yo	8%	51	450	11.3%	-0.22
5yo	19%	132	1002	13.2%	-0.08
6yo	25%	170	1259	13.5%	-0.09
7yo	21%	141	1197	11.8%	-0.26
8yo	13%	91	782	11.6%	-0.15
9yo	7%	47	528	8.9%	-0.35
10yo	4%	29	293	9.9%	-0.02
11yo	2%	13	158	8.2%	-0.37
12yo+	1%	5	83	6.0%	-0.32

ANALYSIS BY BHB RATING

Age	Prop	Win	Runs	Wins%	£
120..129	1%	7	64	10.9%	-0.47
110..119	11%	78	545	14.3%	0.01
100..109	32%	218	1792	12.2%	-0.18
80..99	51%	345	2941	11.7%	-0.20
60..79	5%	32	413	7.7%	-0.15
..59	0%	0	1	0.0%	-1.00
Unrated	0%	0	2	0.0%	-1.00

ANALYSIS BY WEIGHT CARRIED

Age	Prop	Win	Runs	Wins%	£
12-01+	0%	0	2	0.0%	-1.00
11-8..12-00	14%	130	945	13.8%	-0.19
11-0..11-07	37%	250	2032	12.3%	-0.15
10-8..10-13	22%	147	1179	12.5%	-0.11
10-0..10-07	17%	115	1102	10.4%	-0.17
..9-13	6%	38	498	7.6%	-0.37

ANALYSIS BY DAYS SINCE LAST RUN

Age	Prop	Win	Runs	Wins%	£
1..7	9%	62	332	18.7%	0.03
8..14	22%	148	1022	14.5%	-0.09
15..28	30%	207	1816	11.4%	-0.18
29..60	19%	127	1148	11.1%	-0.23
61..100	7%	46	375	12.3%	0.09
101+	13%	90	1059	8.5%	-0.32
Unraced	0%	0	6	0.0%	-1.00

ANALYSIS BY TODAY'S STARTING PRICE

Age	Prop	Win	Runs	Wins%	£
Odds On	3%	21	38	55.3%	-0.07
Ev-2/1	14%	92	246	37.4%	-0.03
9/4-4/1	36%	242	1077	22.5%	-0.06
9/2-6/1	17%	117	879	13.3%	-0.17
13/2-10/1	17%	117	1341	8.7%	-0.20
11/1-16/1	9%	64	1078	5.9%	-0.14
18/1-33/1	4%	25	848	2.9%	-0.29
40/1+	0%	2	251	0.8%	-0.39

ANALYSIS BY STARTING PRICE LAST TIME

Age	Prop	Win	Runs	Wins%	£
Odds On	1%	9	34	26.5%	-0.28
Ev-2/1	7%	50	193	25.9%	0.00
9/4-4/1	15%	101	700	14.4%	-0.30
9/2-6/1	12%	83	651	12.7%	-0.35
13/2-10/1	23%	159	1226	13.0%	-0.17
11/1-16/1	18%	123	1152	10.7%	-0.23
18/1-33/1	16%	112	1141	9.8%	0.00
40/1+	6%	43	655	6.6%	-0.10
Unraced	0%	0	6	0.0%	-1.00

ANALYSIS BY DISTANCE BEATEN LAST TIME

Age	Prop	Win	Runs	Wins%	£
..-10 lgh	3%	18	69	26.1%	0.04
-10..0	17%	118	541	21.8%	-0.07
0.1..2	7%	46	268	17.2%	-0.16
2.1..5	10%	67	344	19.5%	0.04
5.1..10	12%	79	537	14.7%	-0.13
10.1..20	15%	104	912	11.4%	-0.27
20.0..30	11%	73	698	10.5%	-0.06
30.1+	16%	106	1501	7.1%	-0.20
Not Compl	10%	69	882	7.8%	-0.29
Unraced	0%	0	6	0.0%	-1.00

ANALYSIS BY SUCCESS RATE IN LAST 10 RUNS

Age	Prop	Win	Runs	Wins%	£
No Wins	36%	243	2501	9.7%	-0.17
1 Win	37%	253	2010	12.6%	-0.19
2 Wins	18%	125	917	13.6%	-0.16
3 Wins	7%	45	248	18.1%	-0.16
4 Wins	1%	10	61	16.4%	0.01
5+ Wins	1%	4	15	26.7%	0.33

ANALYSIS BY SUCCESS RATE IN LAST 3 RUNS

Age	Prop	Win	Runs	Wins%	£
No Wins	61%	418	4245	9.8%	-0.18
1 Win	32%	220	1298	16.9%	-0.10
2 Wins	6%	39	195	20.0%	-0.32
3 Wins	0%	3	14	21.4%	-0.53

ANALYSIS BY POSITION LAST TIME

Age	Prop	Win	Runs	Wins%	£
Won	20%	137	611	22.4%	-0.05
2nd or 3rd	28%	189	1123	16.8%	0.01
Unplaced	42%	286	3141	9.1%	-0.22
Fell,BD,UR	4%	24	248	9.7%	-0.28
Pulled Up	6%	39	602	6.5%	-0.32
Ref/RanOut	0%	3	21	14.3%	-0.17
CO/SlipUp	0%	2	6	33.3%	0.29
Unraced	0%	0	6	0.0%	-1.00

OTHER FACTORS (WINS-RUNS, £)

Course Winner:	123-955	-£0.19
Distance Winner:	203-1595	-£0.19
Going Winner:	228-1815	-£0.22
Beaten Favourite:	54-308	-£0.30
7-Day Winners:	29-77	£0.18
Absolute Favourites:	193-599	-£0.02

TRAINERS (WINS-RUNS, £)

N Wilson 4-20 £0.63; R Rowe 4-19 £0.60; D W Whillans 3-17 £0.56; M E Sowersby 4-24 £0.40; J Mackie 7-33 £0.22; J S Wainwright 3-20 £0.35; N P Mulholland 4-19 £0.32; Jim Best 15-49 £0.12; R A Fahey 5-16 £0.36; V R A Dartnall 5-18 £0.31; Mrs E Slack 5-27 £0.20; P Monteith 8-43 £0.10; Mrs D A Hamer 3-16 £0.25; Mrs K Waldron 3-12 £0.29; R H Alner 6-26 £0.13; J S Goldie 4-23 £0.13; Gordon Elliott 6-13 £0.18; A M Hales 3-22 £0.09; Mrs K Walton 3-18 £0.11; T R George 5-16 £0.09.

Race Profiles

Handicap Hurdle Races (class 4..6): 11 runners or more

ANALYSIS BY AGE

Age	Prop	Win	Runs	Wins%	£
3yo	0%	3	25	12.0%	1.60
4yo	8%	89	1223	7.3%	-0.34
5yo	21%	248	2875	8.6%	-0.14
6yo	26%	301	3767	8.0%	-0.23
7yo	19%	227	3194	7.1%	-0.28
8yo	13%	153	2314	6.6%	-0.37
9yo	7%	88	1438	6.1%	-0.21
10yo	4%	48	880	5.5%	-0.19
11yo	1%	15	447	3.4%	-0.41
12yo+	1%	6	296	2.0%	-0.70

ANALYSIS BY BHB RATING

Age	Prop	Win	Runs	Wins%	£
130..149	0%	0	1	0.0%	-1.00
120..129	0%	3	39	7.7%	-0.47
110..119	8%	100	1120	8.9%	-0.26
100..109	26%	312	3884	8.0%	-0.20
80..99	57%	668	9483	7.0%	-0.26
60..79	8%	95	1928	4.9%	-0.35
..59	0%	0	2	0.0%	-1.00
Unrated	0%	0	2	0.0%	-1.00

ANALYSIS BY WEIGHT CARRIED

Age	Prop	Win	Runs	Wins%	£
12-01+	0%	5	12	41.7%	0.64
11-8..12-00	18%	215	2476	8.7%	-0.22
11-0..11-07	42%	495	6320	7.8%	-0.22
10-8..10-13	20%	236	3616	6.5%	-0.28
10-0..10-07	16%	185	3020	6.1%	-0.29
..9-13	4%	42	1015	4.1%	-0.46

ANALYSIS BY DAYS SINCE LAST RUN

Age	Prop	Win	Runs	Wins%	£
1..7	7%	82	703	11.7%	-0.28
8..14	16%	193	2610	7.4%	-0.28
15..28	31%	362	4935	7.3%	-0.26
29..60	22%	261	3784	6.9%	-0.29
61..100	7%	80	1226	6.5%	-0.16
101+	17%	198	3178	6.2%	-0.24
Unraced	0%	2	23	8.7%	-0.37

ANALYSIS BY TODAY'S STARTING PRICE

Age	Prop	Win	Runs	Wins%	£
Odds On	1%	13	38	34.2%	-0.39
Ev-2/1	7%	80	225	35.6%	-0.05
9/4-4/1	21%	248	1129	22.0%	-0.06
9/2-6/1	17%	202	1466	13.8%	-0.15
13/2-10/1	26%	304	3384	9.0%	-0.18
11/1-16/1	17%	205	3775	5.4%	-0.22
18/1-33/1	9%	104	4208	2.5%	-0.35
40/1+	2%	22	2234	1.0%	-0.47

ANALYSIS BY STARTING PRICE LAST TIME

Age	Prop	Win	Runs	Wins%	£
Odds On	2%	18	108	16.7%	-0.17
Ev-2/1	5%	60	393	15.3%	-0.22
9/4-4/1	17%	204	1599	12.8%	-0.17
9/2-6/1	13%	157	1614	9.7%	-0.23
13/2-10/1	23%	270	3310	8.2%	-0.23
11/1-16/1	17%	201	3334	6.0%	-0.34
18/1-33/1	15%	174	3639	4.8%	-0.31
40/1+	8%	92	2439	3.8%	-0.22
Unraced	0%	2	23	8.7%	-0.37

ANALYSIS BY DISTANCE BEATEN LAST TIME

Age	Prop	Win	Runs	Wins%	£
..-10 lgh	3%	32	156	20.5%	0.23
-10..0	13%	152	1106	13.7%	-0.23
0.1..2	7%	80	656	12.2%	-0.27
2.1..5	9%	101	866	11.7%	-0.20
5.1..10	10%	118	1334	8.8%	-0.25
10.1..20	17%	200	2627	7.6%	-0.31
20.0..30	12%	142	2042	7.0%	-0.19
30.1+	19%	227	4897	4.6%	-0.29
Not Compl	11%	124	2752	4.5%	-0.27
Unraced	0%	2	23	8.7%	-0.37

ANALYSIS BY SUCCESS RATE IN LAST 10 RUNS

Age	Prop	Win	Runs	Wins%	£
No Wins	43%	500	8455	5.9%	-0.29
1 Win	37%	433	5378	8.1%	-0.22
2 Wins	14%	170	1937	8.8%	-0.24
3 Wins	5%	55	524	10.5%	-0.23
4 Wins	1%	11	121	9.1%	-0.53
5+ Wins	1%	7	21	33.3%	0.53

ANALYSIS BY SUCCESS RATE IN LAST 3 RUNS

Age	Prop	Win	Runs	Wins%	£
No Wins	69%	815	13122	6.2%	-0.27
1 Win	26%	301	2955	10.2%	-0.25
2 Wins	5%	58	343	16.9%	-0.12
3 Wins	0%	2	16	12.5%	-0.57

ANALYSIS BY POSITION LAST TIME

Age	Prop	Win	Runs	Wins%	£
Won	16%	183	1262	14.5%	-0.17
2nd or 3rd	27%	319	2873	11.1%	-0.21
Unplaced	47%	551	9568	5.8%	-0.28
Fell,BD,UR	3%	40	724	5.5%	-0.22
Pulled Up	7%	82	1950	4.2%	-0.27
Ref/RanOut	0%	0	47	0.0%	-1.00
CO/SlipUp	0%	1	12	8.3%	-0.46
Unraced	0%	2	23	8.7%	-0.37

OTHER FACTORS (WINS-RUNS, £)

Course Winner:	174-2104	-£0.23
Distance Winner:	321-3983	-£0.26
Going Winner:	357-4558	-£0.27
Beaten Favourite:	108-826	-£0.18
7-Day Winners:	39-132	£0.07
Absolute Favourites:	252-1053	-£0.12

TRAINERS (WINS-RUNS, £)

J J Quinn 8-28 £0.94; Miss J S Davis 3-46 £0.57; Mrs S J Smith 22-168 £0.15; J S Goldie 8-52 £0.48; Jean-Rene Auvray 3-22 £1.09; J J Lambe 9-53 £0.44; D Burchell 5-81 £0.28; Miss C Dyson 3-26 £0.79; P Butler 3-51 £0.33; C Grant 7-49 £0.34; Miss Kariana Key 3-19 £0.87; N G Richards 20-145 £0.11; Mrs Caroline Keevil 3-19 £0.82; C C Bealby 5-55 £0.26; T R George 10-68 £0.18; Miss P Robson 4-15 £0.77; D McCain 3-24 £0.42; Mrs A Hamilton 3-13 £0.77; Mrs S Gardner 5-41 £0.24; B Ellison 6-25 £0.39.

Handicap Hurdle Races (class 4..6)

Handicap Hurdle Races (class 4..6): up to 7 days off the track

ANALYSIS BY AGE

Age	Prop	Win	Runs	Wins%	£
3yo	0%	0	1	0.0%	-1.00
4yo	7%	10	87	11.5%	-0.59
5yo	20%	30	182	16.5%	-0.08
6yo	25%	39	249	15.7%	-0.12
7yo	27%	41	198	20.7%	0.06
8yo	12%	19	139	13.7%	0.01
9yo	6%	9	106	8.5%	-0.53
10yo	2%	3	62	4.8%	-0.40
11yo	1%	1	37	2.7%	-0.88
12yo+	1%	1	21	4.8%	-0.38

ANALYSIS BY BHB RATING

Age	Prop	Win	Runs	Wins%	£
150+	0%	0	0	0.0%	0.00
130..149	0%	0	0	0.0%	0.00
120..129	1%	1	4	25.0%	0.08
110..119	6%	9	58	15.5%	-0.53
100..109	22%	33	243	13.6%	-0.28
80..99	62%	95	644	14.8%	-0.07
60..79	10%	15	133	11.3%	-0.47
..59	0%	0	0	0.0%	0.00
Unrated	0%	0	0	0.0%	0.00

ANALYSIS BY WEIGHT CARRIED

Age	Prop	Win	Runs	Wins%	£
12-01+	1%	2	6	33.3%	0.06
11-8..12-00	14%	21	134	15.7%	-0.32
11-0..11-07	36%	55	373	14.7%	-0.25
10-8..10-13	25%	38	254	15.0%	0.13
10-0..10-07	17%	26	221	11.8%	-0.33
..9-13	7%	11	94	11.7%	-0.28

ANALYSIS BY DAYS SINCE LAST RUN

Age	Prop	Win	Runs	Wins%	£
1..7	99%	151	1052	14.4%	-0.18
8..14	0%	0	0	0.0%	0.00
15..28	0%	0	0	0.0%	0.00
29..60	0%	0	0	0.0%	0.00
61..100	0%	0	0	0.0%	0.00
101+	0%	0	0	0.0%	0.00
Unraced	1%	2	30	6.7%	-0.52

ANALYSIS BY TODAY'S STARTING PRICE

Age	Prop	Win	Runs	Wins%	£
Odds On	10%	16	31	51.6%	-0.16
Ev-2/1	28%	43	98	43.9%	0.12
9/4-4/1	27%	42	172	24.4%	-0.02
9/2-6/1	10%	16	118	13.6%	-0.16
13/2-10/1	14%	22	202	10.9%	0.01
11/1-16/1	6%	9	158	5.7%	-0.16
18/1-33/1	3%	5	197	2.5%	-0.30
40/1+	0%	0	106	0.0%	-1.00

ANALYSIS BY STARTING PRICE LAST TIME

Age	Prop	Win	Runs	Wins%	£
Odds On	2%	3	10	30.0%	-0.53
Ev-2/1	10%	15	43	34.9%	-0.16
9/4-4/1	21%	32	130	24.6%	-0.06
9/2-6/1	19%	29	118	24.6%	0.21
13/2-10/1	20%	30	232	12.9%	-0.18
11/1-16/1	15%	23	190	12.1%	-0.13
18/1-33/1	8%	13	203	6.4%	-0.28
40/1+	4%	6	126	4.8%	-0.56
Unraced	1%	2	30	6.7%	-0.52

ANALYSIS BY DISTANCE BEATEN LAST TIME

Age	Prop	Win	Runs	Wins%	£
..-10 lgh	12%	19	55	34.5%	-0.03
-10..0	33%	51	161	31.7%	0.13
0.1..2	8%	12	61	19.7%	-0.14
2.1..5	10%	15	83	18.1%	-0.22
5.1..10	10%	15	99	15.2%	-0.07
10.1..20	10%	16	138	11.6%	0.09
20.0..30	5%	7	96	7.3%	-0.39
30.1+	5%	8	192	4.2%	-0.48
Not Compl	5%	8	167	4.8%	-0.34
Unraced	1%	2	30	6.7%	-0.52

ANALYSIS BY SUCCESS RATE IN LAST 10 RUNS

Age	Prop	Win	Runs	Wins%	£
No Wins	27%	41	477	8.6%	-0.23
1 Win	38%	58	365	15.9%	-0.25
2 Wins	30%	45	161	28.0%	0.27
3 Wins	3%	5	37	13.5%	-0.57
4 Wins	1%	1	11	9.1%	-0.80
5+ Wins	1%	1	1	100.0%	1.10

ANALYSIS BY SUCCESS RATE IN LAST 3 RUNS

Age	Prop	Win	Runs	Wins%	£
No Wins	42%	64	730	8.8%	-0.28
1 Win	44%	67	264	25.4%	0.02
2 Wins	13%	19	55	34.5%	0.14
3 Wins	1%	1	3	33.3%	-0.57

ANALYSIS BY POSITION LAST TIME

Age	Prop	Win	Runs	Wins%	£
Won	46%	70	216	32.4%	0.09
2nd or 3rd	26%	40	224	17.9%	-0.14
Unplaced	22%	33	446	7.4%	-0.27
Fell,BD,UR	2%	3	55	5.5%	-0.44
Pulled Up	3%	5	102	4.9%	-0.23
Ref/RanOut	0%	0	9	0.0%	-1.00
CO/SlipUp	0%	0	0	0.0%	0.00
Unraced	1%	2	30	6.7%	-0.52

OTHER FACTORS (WINS-RUNS, £)

Course Winner:	29-164	-£0.13
Distance Winner:	55-312	-£0.20
Going Winner:	60-377	-£0.26
Beaten Favourite:	10-45	-£0.31
7-Day Winners:	70-216	£0.09
Absolute Favourites:	73-206	-£0.05

Race Profiles

Handicap Hurdle Races (class 4..6): 100+ days off the track

ANALYSIS BY AGE

Age	Prop	Win	Runs	Wins%	£
3yo	0%	0	2	0.0%	-1.00
4yo	8%	23	273	8.4%	-0.21
5yo	17%	51	669	7.6%	-0.35
6yo	26%	77	915	8.4%	-0.21
7yo	19%	57	877	6.5%	-0.23
8yo	16%	47	671	7.0%	-0.17
9yo	8%	23	448	5.1%	-0.36
10yo	3%	9	227	4.0%	-0.54
11yo	1%	3	118	2.5%	-0.33
12yo+	1%	3	80	3.8%	-0.13

ANALYSIS BY BHB RATING

Age	Prop	Win	Runs	Wins%	£
150+	0%	0	0	0.0%	0.00
130..149	0%	0	1	0.0%	-1.00
120..129	1%	4	36	11.1%	-0.37
110..119	12%	36	386	9.3%	-0.08
100..109	30%	87	1122	7.8%	-0.22
80..99	46%	136	2256	6.0%	-0.35
60..79	10%	30	475	6.3%	-0.13
..59	0%	0	2	0.0%	-1.00
Unrated	0%	0	2	0.0%	-1.00

ANALYSIS BY WEIGHT CARRIED

Age	Prop	Win	Runs	Wins%	£
12-01+	0%	0	0	0.0%	0.00
11-8..12-00	25%	72	705	10.2%	-0.06
11-0..11-07	39%	114	1625	7.0%	-0.29
10-8..10-13	16%	46	883	5.2%	-0.35
10-0..10-07	16%	48	785	6.1%	-0.21
..9-13	4%	13	282	4.6%	-0.55

ANALYSIS BY DAYS SINCE LAST RUN

Age	Prop	Win	Runs	Wins%	£
1..7	0%	0	0	0.0%	0.00
8..14	0%	0	0	0.0%	0.00
15..28	0%	0	0	0.0%	0.00
29..60	0%	0	0	0.0%	0.00
61..100	0%	0	16	0.0%	-1.00
101+	100%	293	4264	6.9%	-0.26
Unraced	0%	0	0	0.0%	0.00

ANALYSIS BY TODAY'S STARTING PRICE

Age	Prop	Win	Runs	Wins%	£
Odds On	1%	2	7	28.6%	-0.45
Ev-2/1	5%	15	55	27.3%	-0.26
9/4-4/1	26%	75	315	23.8%	0.02
9/2-6/1	13%	37	328	11.3%	-0.32
13/2-10/1	24%	70	755	9.3%	-0.15
11/1-16/1	19%	55	964	5.7%	-0.18
18/1-33/1	12%	35	1197	2.9%	-0.24
40/1+	1%	4	659	0.6%	-0.67

ANALYSIS BY STARTING PRICE LAST TIME

Age	Prop	Win	Runs	Wins%	£
Odds On	2%	7	50	14.0%	-0.25
Ev-2/1	6%	17	142	12.0%	-0.13
9/4-4/1	17%	50	484	10.3%	-0.17
9/2-6/1	14%	42	449	9.4%	-0.20
13/2-10/1	21%	62	865	7.2%	-0.29
11/1-16/1	18%	52	894	5.8%	-0.36
18/1-33/1	16%	46	847	5.4%	-0.20
40/1+	6%	17	549	3.1%	-0.35
Unraced	0%	0	0	0.0%	0.00

ANALYSIS BY DISTANCE BEATEN LAST TIME

Age	Prop	Win	Runs	Wins%	£
..-10 lgh	2%	6	32	18.8%	1.18
-10..0	8%	24	232	10.3%	-0.34
0.1..2	5%	14	127	11.0%	-0.17
2.1..5	4%	12	154	7.8%	-0.34
5.1..10	8%	23	289	8.0%	-0.26
10.1..20	15%	45	594	7.6%	-0.37
20.0..30	15%	43	517	8.3%	-0.29
30.1+	27%	80	1432	5.6%	-0.21
Not Compl	16%	46	903	5.1%	-0.31
Unraced	0%	0	0	0.0%	0.00

ANALYSIS BY SUCCESS RATE IN LAST 10 RUNS

Age	Prop	Win	Runs	Wins%	£
No Wins	37%	107	1971	5.4%	-0.35
1 Win	39%	114	1470	7.8%	-0.19
2 Wins	17%	50	607	8.2%	-0.16
3 Wins	6%	17	176	9.7%	-0.30
4 Wins	1%	2	45	4.4%	-0.58
5+ Wins	1%	3	11	27.3%	0.70

ANALYSIS BY SUCCESS RATE IN LAST 3 RUNS

Age	Prop	Win	Runs	Wins%	£
No Wins	70%	204	3265	6.2%	-0.27
1 Win	25%	74	888	8.3%	-0.24
2 Wins	5%	14	116	12.1%	-0.39
3 Wins	0%	1	11	9.1%	-0.80

ANALYSIS BY POSITION LAST TIME

Age	Prop	Win	Runs	Wins%	£
Won	10%	30	263	11.4%	-0.16
2nd or 3rd	19%	56	581	9.6%	-0.28
Unplaced	55%	162	2547	6.4%	-0.25
Fell,BD,UR	4%	11	195	5.6%	-0.66
Pulled Up	11%	33	680	4.9%	-0.22
Ref/RanOut	0%	0	11	0.0%	-1.00
CO/SlipUp	0%	1	3	33.3%	1.17
Unraced	0%	0	0	0.0%	0.00

OTHER FACTORS (WINS-RUNS, £)

Course Winner:	42-566	-£0.24
Distance Winner:	78-1076	-£0.28
Going Winner:	80-1183	-£0.34
Beaten Favourite:	33-277	-£0.13
Absolute Favourites:	54-218	-£0.10

Novices' Chases (class 1..3)

ANALYSIS BY AGE

Age	Prop	Win	Runs	Wins%	£
3yo	0%	0	0	0.0%	0.00
4yo	4%	32	117	27.4%	-0.19
5yo	16%	114	573	19.9%	-0.23
6yo	30%	218	1171	18.6%	-0.24
7yo	31%	223	1230	18.1%	-0.28
8yo	12%	89	690	12.9%	-0.48
9yo	5%	36	352	10.2%	-0.59
10yo	2%	13	122	10.7%	-0.28
11yo	0%	2	46	4.3%	-0.83
12yo+	0%	0	13	0.0%	-1.00

ANALYSIS BY BHB RATING

Age	Prop	Win	Runs	Wins%	£
150+	2%	17	69	24.6%	0.05
130..149	22%	161	638	25.2%	-0.21
120..129	15%	110	496	22.2%	-0.04
110..119	8%	60	421	14.3%	-0.31
100..109	1%	7	171	4.1%	-0.66
80..99	1%	5	240	2.1%	-0.77
60..79	0%	1	138	0.7%	-0.81
..59	0%	0	20	0.0%	-1.00
Unrated	50%	366	2121	17.3%	-0.33

ANALYSIS BY WEIGHT CARRIED

Age	Prop	Win	Runs	Wins%	£
12-01+	0%	1	1	100.0%	0.62
11-8..12-00	17%	127	472	26.9%	-0.21
11-0..11-07	58%	425	2322	18.3%	-0.25
10-8..10-13	18%	129	1094	11.8%	-0.47
10-0..10-07	6%	42	409	10.3%	-0.49
..9-13	0%	3	16	18.8%	-0.37

ANALYSIS BY DAYS SINCE LAST RUN

Age	Prop	Win	Runs	Wins%	£
1..7	2%	17	162	10.5%	-0.66
8..14	11%	80	617	13.0%	-0.51
15..28	35%	257	1410	18.2%	-0.29
29..60	24%	176	1015	17.3%	-0.38
61..100	6%	43	269	16.0%	-0.22
101+	19%	141	756	18.7%	-0.23
Unraced	2%	13	85	15.3%	0.47

ANALYSIS BY TODAY'S STARTING PRICE

Age	Prop	Win	Runs	Wins%	£
Odds On	32%	236	344	68.6%	0.08
Ev-2/1	24%	177	490	36.1%	-0.09
9/4-4/1	27%	197	820	24.0%	-0.03
9/2-6/1	5%	39	387	10.1%	-0.37
13/2-10/1	6%	43	547	7.9%	-0.29
11/1-16/1	4%	28	456	6.1%	-0.12
18/1-33/1	1%	5	488	1.0%	-0.74
40/1+	0%	2	782	0.3%	-0.83

ANALYSIS BY STARTING PRICE LAST TIME

Age	Prop	Win	Runs	Wins%	£
Odds On	17%	122	333	31.9%	-0.02
Ev-2/1	17%	126	469	26.9%	-0.18
9/4-4/1	24%	171	798	21.4%	-0.22
9/2-6/1	10%	76	426	17.8%	-0.33
13/2-10/1	13%	97	645	15.0%	-0.36
11/1-16/1	9%	69	534	12.9%	-0.34
18/1-33/1	5%	38	481	7.9%	-0.55
40/1+	2%	15	493	3.0%	-0.73
Unraced	2%	13	85	15.3%	0.47

ANALYSIS BY DISTANCE BEATEN LAST TIME

Age	Prop	Win	Runs	Wins%	£
..-10 lgh	14%	100	299	33.4%	0.02
-10..0	23%	168	713	23.6%	-0.25
0.1..2	9%	63	230	27.4%	-0.16
2.1..5	8%	60	258	23.3%	-0.01
5.1..10	9%	68	309	22.0%	-0.17
10.1..20	10%	70	495	14.1%	-0.45
20.0..30	6%	44	362	12.2%	-0.46
30.1+	10%	74	836	8.9%	-0.51
Not Compl	9%	67	727	9.2%	-0.51
Unraced	2%	13	85	15.3%	0.47

ANALYSIS BY SUCCESS RATE IN LAST 10 RUNS

Age	Prop	Win	Runs	Wins%	£
No Wins	5%	38	965	3.9%	-0.66
1 Win	18%	130	953	13.6%	-0.36
2 Wins	26%	185	920	20.1%	-0.26
3 Wins	24%	172	716	24.0%	-0.14
4 Wins	15%	105	391	26.9%	-0.21
5+ Wins	12%	84	284	29.6%	-0.16

ANALYSIS BY SUCCESS RATE IN LAST 3 RUNS

Age	Prop	Win	Runs	Wins%	£
No Wins	28%	201	2072	9.7%	-0.49
1 Win	47%	336	1532	21.9%	-0.22
2 Wins	21%	148	532	27.8%	-0.16
3 Wins	4%	29	93	31.2%	-0.16

ANALYSIS BY POSITION LAST TIME

Age	Prop	Win	Runs	Wins%	£
Won	37%	268	1011	26.5%	-0.17
2nd or 3rd	30%	217	1113	19.5%	-0.26
Unplaced	22%	162	1378	11.8%	-0.44
Fell,BD,UR	4%	32	286	11.2%	-0.55
Pulled Up	4%	32	429	7.5%	-0.50
Ref/RanOut	0%	2	8	25.0%	-0.28
CO/SlipUp	0%	1	4	25.0%	0.75
Unraced	2%	13	85	15.3%	0.47

OTHER FACTORS (WINS-RUNS, £)

Course Winner:	180-685	-£0.22
Distance Winner:	370-1722	-£0.31
Going Winner:	443-2020	-£0.26
Beaten Favourite:	96-356	-£0.07
7-Day Winners:	9-29	£0.20
BHA Top Rated:	159-551	-£0.15
Absolute Favourites:	365-688	£0.03

Race Profiles

Novices' Chases (class 1..3): 2m to 2m3f

ANALYSIS BY AGE
Age	Prop	Win	Runs	Wins%	£
3yo	0%	0	0	0.0%	0.00
4yo	9%	24	81	29.6%	-0.18
5yo	23%	58	296	19.6%	-0.34
6yo	30%	75	426	17.6%	-0.20
7yo	24%	60	365	16.4%	-0.22
8yo	12%	30	197	15.2%	-0.30
9yo	2%	5	89	5.6%	-0.82
10yo	1%	2	34	5.9%	-0.87
11yo	0%	0	8	0.0%	-1.00
12yo+	0%	0	3	0.0%	-1.00

ANALYSIS BY BHB RATING
Age	Prop	Win	Runs	Wins%	£
150+	3%	7	26	26.9%	0.21
130..149	18%	45	198	22.7%	-0.30
120..129	11%	28	147	19.0%	-0.20
110..119	7%	18	124	14.5%	-0.42
100..109	0%	1	60	1.7%	-0.87
80..99	1%	2	76	2.6%	-0.46
60..79	0%	0	39	0.0%	-1.00
..59	0%	0	3	0.0%	-1.00
Unrated	60%	153	826	18.5%	-0.23

ANALYSIS BY WEIGHT CARRIED
Age	Prop	Win	Runs	Wins%	£
12-01+	0%	0	0	0.0%	0.00
11-8..12-00	16%	41	142	28.9%	-0.20
11-0..11-07	62%	157	871	18.0%	-0.19
10-8..10-13	13%	33	327	10.1%	-0.63
10-0..10-07	9%	23	151	15.2%	-0.31
..9-13	0%	0	8	0.0%	-1.00

ANALYSIS BY DAYS SINCE LAST RUN
Age	Prop	Win	Runs	Wins%	£
1..7	2%	4	53	7.5%	-0.76
8..14	9%	23	224	10.3%	-0.60
15..28	31%	80	469	17.1%	-0.36
29..60	24%	62	348	17.8%	-0.39
61..100	6%	14	82	17.1%	-0.39
101+	25%	64	293	21.8%	0.01
Unraced	3%	7	30	23.3%	1.78

ANALYSIS BY TODAY'S STARTING PRICE
Age	Prop	Win	Runs	Wins%	£
Odds On	35%	88	127	69.3%	0.08
Ev-2/1	24%	62	174	35.6%	-0.11
9/4-4/1	27%	68	265	25.7%	0.01
9/2-6/1	5%	12	124	9.7%	-0.38
13/2-10/1	4%	11	189	5.8%	-0.48
11/1-16/1	4%	10	147	6.8%	0.02
18/1-33/1	0%	1	197	0.5%	-0.87
40/1+	1%	2	276	0.7%	-0.51

ANALYSIS BY STARTING PRICE LAST TIME
Age	Prop	Win	Runs	Wins%	£
Odds On	19%	48	163	29.4%	0.05
Ev-2/1	20%	51	178	28.7%	-0.19
9/4-4/1	22%	55	262	21.0%	-0.22
9/2-6/1	8%	20	141	14.2%	-0.47
13/2-10/1	14%	36	218	16.5%	-0.23
11/1-16/1	8%	21	178	11.8%	-0.62
18/1-33/1	4%	9	168	5.4%	-0.80
40/1+	3%	7	161	4.3%	-0.41
Unraced	3%	7	30	23.3%	1.78

ANALYSIS BY DISTANCE BEATEN LAST TIME
Age	Prop	Win	Runs	Wins%	£
..-10 lgh	13%	32	94	34.0%	-0.12
-10..0	22%	56	258	21.7%	-0.34
0.1..2	9%	23	81	28.4%	0.10
2.1..5	9%	23	89	25.8%	0.07
5.1..10	10%	25	108	23.1%	-0.28
10.1..20	7%	19	180	10.6%	-0.60
20.0..30	7%	19	142	13.4%	-0.33
30.1+	11%	29	288	10.1%	-0.58
Not Compl	8%	21	229	9.2%	-0.30
Unraced	3%	7	30	23.3%	1.78

ANALYSIS BY SUCCESS RATE IN LAST 10 RUNS
Age	Prop	Win	Runs	Wins%	£
No Wins	6%	15	301	5.0%	-0.41
1 Win	16%	40	332	12.0%	-0.53
2 Wins	28%	70	363	19.3%	-0.30
3 Wins	24%	60	234	25.6%	-0.12
4 Wins	16%	39	144	27.1%	-0.30
5+ Wins	9%	23	95	24.2%	-0.28

ANALYSIS BY SUCCESS RATE IN LAST 3 RUNS
Age	Prop	Win	Runs	Wins%	£
No Wins	29%	72	741	9.7%	-0.46
1 Win	47%	115	508	22.6%	-0.25
2 Wins	20%	50	186	26.9%	-0.22
3 Wins	4%	10	34	29.4%	-0.10

ANALYSIS BY POSITION LAST TIME
Age	Prop	Win	Runs	Wins%	£
Won	35%	88	352	25.0%	-0.28
2nd or 3rd	30%	75	378	19.8%	-0.24
Unplaced	25%	63	510	12.4%	-0.48
Fell,BD,UR	5%	12	100	12.0%	-0.36
Pulled Up	3%	8	122	6.6%	-0.23
Ref/RanOut	0%	1	4	25.0%	-0.50
CO/SlipUp	0%	0	3	0.0%	-1.00
Unraced	3%	7	30	23.3%	1.78

OTHER FACTORS (WINS-RUNS, £)
Course Winner:	55-218	-£0.27
Distance Winner:	169-850	-£0.36
Going Winner:	153-738	-£0.33
Beaten Favourite:	38-134	£0.17
7-Day Winners:	3-9	£0.05
BHA Top Rated:	49-180	-£0.12
Absolute Favourites:	133-241	£0.06

Novices' Chases (class 1..3)

Novices' Chases (class 1..3): 2m4f to 2m7f

ANALYSIS BY AGE
Age	Prop	Win	Runs	Wins%	£
3yo	0%	0	0	0.0%	0.00
4yo	2%	6	31	19.4%	-0.29
5yo	15%	39	180	21.7%	-0.23
6yo	30%	81	443	18.3%	-0.35
7yo	32%	85	473	18.0%	-0.36
8yo	13%	34	248	13.7%	-0.51
9yo	6%	16	138	11.6%	-0.41
10yo	2%	6	56	10.7%	-0.15
11yo	0%	1	21	4.8%	-0.83
12yo+	0%	0	6	0.0%	-1.00

ANALYSIS BY BHB RATING
Age	Prop	Win	Runs	Wins%	£
150+	1%	3	14	21.4%	-0.33
130..149	24%	65	195	33.3%	-0.06
120..129	16%	44	206	21.4%	-0.16
110..119	10%	28	204	13.7%	-0.27
100..109	1%	3	66	4.5%	-0.55
80..99	0%	1	104	1.0%	-0.95
60..79	0%	1	73	1.4%	-0.64
..59	0%	0	7	0.0%	-1.00
Unrated	46%	123	727	16.9%	-0.41

ANALYSIS BY WEIGHT CARRIED
Age	Prop	Win	Runs	Wins%	£
12-01+	0%	0	0	0.0%	0.00
11-8..12-00	17%	45	158	28.5%	-0.23
11-0..11-07	60%	161	835	19.3%	-0.29
10-8..10-13	18%	47	435	10.8%	-0.48
10-0..10-07	5%	13	164	7.9%	-0.62
..9-13	1%	2	4	50.0%	0.59

ANALYSIS BY DAYS SINCE LAST RUN
Age	Prop	Win	Runs	Wins%	£
1..7	3%	7	63	11.1%	-0.63
8..14	13%	34	217	15.7%	-0.48
15..28	37%	98	509	19.3%	-0.27
29..60	21%	57	379	15.0%	-0.54
61..100	7%	20	107	18.7%	0.02
101+	18%	49	297	16.5%	-0.32
Unraced	1%	3	24	12.5%	-0.35

ANALYSIS BY TODAY'S STARTING PRICE
Age	Prop	Win	Runs	Wins%	£
Odds On	33%	89	125	71.2%	0.11
Ev-2/1	24%	64	177	36.2%	-0.09
9/4-4/1	28%	74	318	23.3%	-0.06
9/2-6/1	5%	13	134	9.7%	-0.42
13/2-10/1	7%	18	194	9.3%	-0.16
11/1-16/1	3%	8	176	4.5%	-0.40
18/1-33/1	1%	2	171	1.2%	-0.65
40/1+	0%	0	301	0.0%	-1.00

ANALYSIS BY STARTING PRICE LAST TIME
Age	Prop	Win	Runs	Wins%	£
Odds On	15%	41	109	37.6%	-0.07
Ev-2/1	16%	42	153	27.5%	-0.29
9/4-4/1	25%	66	302	21.9%	-0.28
9/2-6/1	10%	28	154	18.2%	-0.23
13/2-10/1	15%	40	240	16.7%	-0.36
11/1-16/1	10%	28	208	13.5%	-0.21
18/1-33/1	6%	15	190	7.9%	-0.46
40/1+	2%	5	216	2.3%	-0.90
Unraced	1%	3	24	12.5%	-0.35

ANALYSIS BY DISTANCE BEATEN LAST TIME
Age	Prop	Win	Runs	Wins%	£
..-10 lgh	14%	37	105	35.2%	0.12
-10..0	22%	60	246	24.4%	-0.31
0.1..2	11%	29	88	33.0%	-0.22
2.1..5	7%	18	82	22.0%	0.04
5.1..10	9%	25	113	22.1%	-0.19
10.1..20	10%	28	187	15.0%	-0.41
20.0..30	4%	12	132	9.1%	-0.68
30.1+	10%	28	338	8.3%	-0.45
Not Compl	10%	28	281	10.0%	-0.58
Unraced	1%	3	24	12.5%	-0.35

ANALYSIS BY SUCCESS RATE IN LAST 10 RUNS
Age	Prop	Win	Runs	Wins%	£
No Wins	3%	9	402	2.2%	-0.76
1 Win	20%	54	380	14.2%	-0.34
2 Wins	26%	68	340	20.0%	-0.23
3 Wins	25%	67	247	27.1%	-0.12
4 Wins	12%	31	119	26.1%	-0.36
5+ Wins	14%	36	84	42.9%	0.01

ANALYSIS BY SUCCESS RATE IN LAST 3 RUNS
Age	Prop	Win	Runs	Wins%	£
No Wins	29%	77	804	9.6%	-0.51
1 Win	48%	128	574	22.3%	-0.23
2 Wins	19%	50	171	29.2%	-0.25
3 Wins	4%	10	23	43.5%	-0.05

ANALYSIS BY POSITION LAST TIME
Age	Prop	Win	Runs	Wins%	£
Won	36%	97	351	27.6%	-0.18
2nd or 3rd	31%	82	412	19.9%	-0.31
Unplaced	22%	58	528	11.0%	-0.43
Fell,BD,UR	4%	11	108	10.2%	-0.69
Pulled Up	6%	15	171	8.8%	-0.56
Ref/RanOut	0%	1	1	100.0%	2.75
CO/SlipUp	0%	1	1	100.0%	6.00
Unraced	1%	3	24	12.5%	-0.35

OTHER FACTORS (WINS-RUNS, £)
Course Winner:	71-258	-£0.22
Distance Winner:	123-508	-£0.25
Going Winner:	167-708	-£0.27
Beaten Favourite:	31-114	-£0.28
7-Day Winners:	1-10	£0.00
BHA Top Rated:	61-212	-£0.25
Absolute Favourites:	135-250	£0.02

Race Profiles

Novices' Chases (class 1..3): 3m+

ANALYSIS BY AGE

Age	Prop	Win	Runs	Wins%	£
3yo	0%	0	0	0.0%	0.00
4yo	1%	2	5	40.0%	0.23
5yo	8%	17	97	17.5%	0.09
6yo	30%	62	302	20.5%	-0.14
7yo	38%	78	392	19.9%	-0.24
8yo	12%	25	245	10.2%	-0.60
9yo	7%	15	125	12.0%	-0.64
10yo	2%	5	32	15.6%	0.11
11yo	0%	1	17	5.9%	-0.74
12yo+	0%	0	4	0.0%	-1.00

ANALYSIS BY BHB RATING

Age	Prop	Win	Runs	Wins%	£
150+	3%	7	29	24.1%	0.08
130..149	25%	51	245	20.8%	-0.25
120..129	19%	38	143	26.6%	0.30
110..119	7%	14	93	15.1%	-0.25
100..109	1%	3	45	6.7%	-0.57
80..99	1%	2	60	3.3%	-0.84
60..79	0%	0	26	0.0%	-1.00
..59	0%	0	10	0.0%	-1.00
Unrated	44%	90	568	15.8%	-0.38

ANALYSIS BY WEIGHT CARRIED

Age	Prop	Win	Runs	Wins%	£
12-01+	0%	1	1	100.0%	0.62
11-8..12-00	20%	41	172	23.8%	-0.20
11-0..11-07	52%	107	616	17.4%	-0.29
10-8..10-13	24%	49	332	14.8%	-0.31
10-0..10-07	3%	6	94	6.4%	-0.56
..9-13	0%	1	4	25.0%	-0.06

ANALYSIS BY DAYS SINCE LAST RUN

Age	Prop	Win	Runs	Wins%	£
1..7	3%	6	46	13.0%	-0.59
8..14	11%	23	176	13.1%	-0.44
15..28	39%	79	432	18.3%	-0.23
29..60	28%	57	288	19.8%	-0.14
61..100	4%	9	80	11.3%	-0.38
101+	14%	28	166	16.9%	-0.50
Unraced	1%	3	31	9.7%	-0.16

ANALYSIS BY TODAY'S STARTING PRICE

Age	Prop	Win	Runs	Wins%	£
Odds On	29%	59	92	64.1%	0.03
Ev-2/1	25%	51	139	36.7%	-0.07
9/4-4/1	27%	55	237	23.2%	-0.05
9/2-6/1	7%	14	129	10.9%	-0.33
13/2-10/1	7%	14	164	8.5%	-0.22
11/1-16/1	5%	10	133	7.5%	0.10
18/1-33/1	1%	2	120	1.7%	-0.65
40/1+	0%	0	205	0.0%	-1.00

ANALYSIS BY STARTING PRICE LAST TIME

Age	Prop	Win	Runs	Wins%	£
Odds On	16%	33	111	29.7%	-0.08
Ev-2/1	16%	33	138	23.9%	-0.06
9/4-4/1	24%	50	234	21.4%	-0.14
9/2-6/1	14%	28	131	21.4%	-0.31
13/2-10/1	10%	21	187	11.2%	-0.54
11/1-16/1	10%	20	148	13.5%	-0.19
18/1-33/1	7%	14	123	11.4%	-0.34
40/1+	1%	3	116	2.6%	-0.88
Unraced	1%	3	31	9.7%	-0.16

ANALYSIS BY DISTANCE BEATEN LAST TIME

Age	Prop	Win	Runs	Wins%	£
..-10 lgh	15%	31	100	31.0%	0.05
-10..0	25%	52	209	24.9%	-0.08
0.1..2	5%	11	61	18.0%	-0.42
2.1..5	9%	19	87	21.8%	-0.14
5.1..10	9%	18	88	20.5%	-0.01
10.1..20	11%	23	128	18.0%	-0.28
20.0..30	6%	13	88	14.8%	-0.35
30.1+	8%	17	210	8.1%	-0.49
Not Compl	9%	18	217	8.3%	-0.66
Unraced	1%	3	31	9.7%	-0.16

ANALYSIS BY SUCCESS RATE IN LAST 10 RUNS

Age	Prop	Win	Runs	Wins%	£
No Wins	7%	14	262	5.3%	-0.79
1 Win	18%	36	241	14.9%	-0.17
2 Wins	23%	47	217	21.7%	-0.25
3 Wins	22%	45	235	19.1%	-0.19
4 Wins	17%	35	128	27.3%	0.04
5+ Wins	12%	25	105	23.8%	-0.20

ANALYSIS BY SUCCESS RATE IN LAST 3 RUNS

Age	Prop	Win	Runs	Wins%	£
No Wins	26%	52	527	9.9%	-0.50
1 Win	46%	93	450	20.7%	-0.19
2 Wins	24%	48	175	27.4%	0.00
3 Wins	4%	9	36	25.0%	-0.28

ANALYSIS BY POSITION LAST TIME

Age	Prop	Win	Runs	Wins%	£
Won	40%	83	308	26.9%	-0.03
2nd or 3rd	29%	60	323	18.6%	-0.23
Unplaced	20%	41	340	12.1%	-0.39
Fell,BD,UR	4%	9	78	11.5%	-0.60
Pulled Up	4%	9	136	6.6%	-0.68
Ref/RanOut	0%	0	3	0.0%	-1.00
CO/SlipUp	0%	0	0	0.0%	0.00
Unraced	1%	3	31	9.7%	-0.16

OTHER FACTORS (WINS-RUNS, £)

Course Winner:	54-209	-£0.18
Distance Winner:	78-364	-£0.27
Going Winner:	123-574	-£0.18
Beaten Favourite:	27-108	-£0.16
7-Day Winners:	5-10	£0.52
BHA Top Rated:	49-159	-£0.05
Absolute Favourites:	97-197	-£0.01

Novices' Chases (class 1..3)

Novices' Chases (class 1..3): 2 to 5 runners

ANALYSIS BY AGE
Age	Prop	Win	Runs	Wins%	£
3yo	0%	0	0	0.0%	0.00
4yo	4%	16	46	34.8%	-0.19
5yo	19%	72	246	29.3%	-0.10
6yo	26%	99	427	23.2%	-0.26
7yo	30%	113	445	25.4%	-0.05
8yo	12%	46	265	17.4%	-0.46
9yo	6%	21	133	15.8%	-0.54
10yo	2%	6	45	13.3%	-0.50
11yo	0%	1	15	6.7%	-0.70
12yo+	0%	0	6	0.0%	-1.00

ANALYSIS BY BHB RATING
Age	Prop	Win	Runs	Wins%	£
150+	2%	6	17	35.3%	-0.33
130..149	28%	104	301	34.6%	-0.09
120..129	16%	58	214	27.1%	-0.06
110..119	7%	26	153	17.0%	-0.34
100..109	1%	4	59	6.8%	-0.45
80..99	1%	2	84	2.4%	-0.88
60..79	0%	0	48	0.0%	-1.00
..59	0%	0	9	0.0%	-1.00
Unrated	47%	174	743	23.4%	-0.20

ANALYSIS BY WEIGHT CARRIED
Age	Prop	Win	Runs	Wins%	£
12-01+	0%	0	0	0.0%	0.00
11-8..12-00	20%	74	243	30.5%	-0.17
11-0..11-07	60%	223	892	25.0%	-0.14
10-8..10-13	16%	58	349	16.6%	-0.44
10-0..10-07	5%	18	140	12.9%	-0.58
..9-13	0%	1	4	25.0%	-0.28

ANALYSIS BY DAYS SINCE LAST RUN
Age	Prop	Win	Runs	Wins%	£
1..7	2%	8	77	10.4%	-0.71
8..14	14%	51	266	19.2%	-0.39
15..28	35%	132	533	24.8%	-0.22
29..60	26%	97	400	24.3%	-0.31
61..100	6%	23	103	22.3%	0.00
101+	16%	58	221	26.2%	0.09
Unraced	1%	5	28	17.9%	-0.61

ANALYSIS BY TODAY'S STARTING PRICE
Age	Prop	Win	Runs	Wins%	£
Odds On	43%	162	235	68.9%	0.06
Ev-2/1	25%	92	263	35.0%	-0.13
9/4-4/1	22%	83	348	23.9%	-0.05
9/2-6/1	3%	11	141	7.8%	-0.52
13/2-10/1	5%	17	172	9.9%	-0.13
11/1-16/1	2%	7	137	5.1%	-0.27
18/1-33/1	0%	1	150	0.7%	-0.77
40/1+	0%	1	182	0.5%	-0.63

ANALYSIS BY STARTING PRICE LAST TIME
Age	Prop	Win	Runs	Wins%	£
Odds On	16%	59	158	37.3%	-0.05
Ev-2/1	20%	73	203	36.0%	-0.14
9/4-4/1	25%	92	329	28.0%	-0.12
9/2-6/1	12%	46	174	26.4%	-0.26
13/2-10/1	12%	44	212	20.8%	-0.30
11/1-16/1	8%	31	192	16.1%	-0.17
18/1-33/1	4%	16	178	9.0%	-0.63
40/1+	2%	8	154	5.2%	-0.34
Unraced	1%	5	28	17.9%	-0.61

ANALYSIS BY DISTANCE BEATEN LAST TIME
Age	Prop	Win	Runs	Wins%	£
..-10 lgh	13%	50	138	36.2%	0.00
-10..0	25%	95	295	32.2%	-0.20
0.1..2	8%	31	87	35.6%	-0.15
2.1..5	7%	28	101	27.7%	-0.06
5.1..10	9%	32	107	29.9%	-0.26
10.1..20	10%	39	189	20.6%	-0.21
20.0..30	6%	23	138	16.7%	-0.48
30.1+	9%	35	291	12.0%	-0.41
Not Compl	10%	36	254	14.2%	-0.21
Unraced	1%	5	28	17.9%	-0.61

ANALYSIS BY SUCCESS RATE IN LAST 10 RUNS
Age	Prop	Win	Runs	Wins%	£
No Wins	5%	20	313	6.4%	-0.48
1 Win	17%	64	353	18.1%	-0.27
2 Wins	27%	101	372	27.2%	-0.07
3 Wins	23%	85	286	29.7%	-0.21
4 Wins	17%	61	174	35.1%	-0.13
5+ Wins	10%	38	102	37.3%	-0.27

ANALYSIS BY SUCCESS RATE IN LAST 3 RUNS
Age	Prop	Win	Runs	Wins%	£
No Wins	26%	96	719	13.4%	-0.38
1 Win	51%	189	634	29.8%	-0.10
2 Wins	20%	73	211	34.6%	-0.16
3 Wins	3%	11	36	30.6%	-0.43

ANALYSIS BY POSITION LAST TIME
Age	Prop	Win	Runs	Wins%	£
Won	39%	145	433	33.5%	-0.13
2nd or 3rd	31%	116	451	25.7%	-0.19
Unplaced	19%	72	462	15.6%	-0.41
Fell,BD,UR	5%	19	113	16.8%	-0.43
Pulled Up	4%	16	137	11.7%	-0.02
Ref/RanOut	0%	1	3	33.3%	-0.33
CO/SlipUp	0%	0	1	0.0%	-1.00
Unraced	1%	5	28	17.9%	-0.61

OTHER FACTORS (WINS-RUNS, £)
Course Winner:	107-278	£0.04
Distance Winner:	189-670	-£0.24
Going Winner:	223-772	-£0.19
Beaten Favourite:	54-137	£0.23
7-Day Winners:	4-16	-£0.19
BHA Top Rated:	109-278	£0.07
Absolute Favourites:	210-361	£0.01

Race Profiles

Novices' Chases (class 1..3): 6 to 10 runners

ANALYSIS BY AGE
Age	Prop	Win	Runs	Wins%	£
3yo	0%	0	0	0.0%	0.00
4yo	5%	15	65	23.1%	-0.23
5yo	12%	38	293	13.0%	-0.36
6yo	34%	112	667	16.8%	-0.21
7yo	31%	102	693	14.7%	-0.39
8yo	12%	40	371	10.8%	-0.49
9yo	4%	14	187	7.5%	-0.59
10yo	2%	7	69	10.1%	-0.06
11yo	0%	1	29	3.4%	-0.88
12yo+	0%	0	6	0.0%	-1.00

ANALYSIS BY BHB RATING
Age	Prop	Win	Runs	Wins%	£
150+	2%	6	31	19.4%	-0.01
130..149	16%	54	262	20.6%	-0.20
120..129	16%	51	267	19.1%	0.01
110..119	10%	34	255	13.3%	-0.25
100..109	1%	3	103	2.9%	-0.76
80..99	1%	3	149	2.0%	-0.69
60..79	0%	1	84	1.2%	-0.69
..59	0%	0	10	0.0%	-1.00
Unrated	54%	177	1219	14.5%	-0.40

ANALYSIS BY WEIGHT CARRIED
Age	Prop	Win	Runs	Wins%	£
12-01+	0%	1	1	100.0%	0.62
11-8..12-00	16%	51	222	23.0%	-0.26
11-0..11-07	57%	186	1218	15.3%	-0.27
10-8..10-13	21%	68	682	10.0%	-0.48
10-0..10-07	6%	21	245	8.6%	-0.55
..9-13	1%	2	12	16.7%	-0.40

ANALYSIS BY DAYS SINCE LAST RUN
Age	Prop	Win	Runs	Wins%	£
1..7	2%	8	78	10.3%	-0.60
8..14	9%	28	333	8.4%	-0.60
15..28	36%	118	782	15.1%	-0.30
29..60	22%	73	527	13.9%	-0.39
61..100	5%	18	133	13.5%	-0.31
101+	23%	77	479	16.1%	-0.36
Unraced	2%	7	48	14.6%	0.94

ANALYSIS BY TODAY'S STARTING PRICE
Age	Prop	Win	Runs	Wins%	£
Odds On	22%	73	108	67.6%	0.10
Ev-2/1	24%	80	214	37.4%	-0.04
9/4-4/1	33%	107	447	23.9%	-0.03
9/2-6/1	8%	26	223	11.7%	-0.28
13/2-10/1	6%	19	315	6.0%	-0.43
11/1-16/1	6%	20	275	7.3%	0.04
18/1-33/1	1%	3	276	1.1%	-0.74
40/1+	0%	1	522	0.2%	-0.87

ANALYSIS BY STARTING PRICE LAST TIME
Age	Prop	Win	Runs	Wins%	£
Odds On	18%	58	189	30.7%	0.00
Ev-2/1	15%	50	220	22.7%	-0.11
9/4-4/1	22%	74	419	17.7%	-0.24
9/2-6/1	9%	28	224	12.5%	-0.37
13/2-10/1	16%	51	383	13.3%	-0.35
11/1-16/1	10%	33	308	10.7%	-0.47
18/1-33/1	6%	21	270	7.8%	-0.48
40/1+	2%	7	319	2.2%	-0.90
Unraced	2%	7	48	14.6%	0.94

ANALYSIS BY DISTANCE BEATEN LAST TIME
Age	Prop	Win	Runs	Wins%	£
..-10 lgh	14%	45	131	34.4%	0.06
-10..0	20%	66	359	18.4%	-0.27
0.1..2	9%	29	119	24.4%	-0.11
2.1..5	9%	31	138	22.5%	0.10
5.1..10	11%	35	188	18.6%	-0.10
10.1..20	9%	29	281	10.3%	-0.58
20.0..30	6%	20	201	10.0%	-0.43
30.1+	11%	36	491	7.3%	-0.56
Not Compl	9%	31	424	7.3%	-0.64
Unraced	2%	7	48	14.6%	0.94

ANALYSIS BY SUCCESS RATE IN LAST 10 RUNS
Age	Prop	Win	Runs	Wins%	£
No Wins	5%	16	603	2.7%	-0.75
1 Win	20%	66	560	11.8%	-0.38
2 Wins	25%	81	495	16.4%	-0.37
3 Wins	25%	82	363	22.6%	-0.01
4 Wins	12%	39	175	22.3%	-0.22
5+ Wins	12%	38	136	27.9%	-0.08

ANALYSIS BY SUCCESS RATE IN LAST 3 RUNS
Age	Prop	Win	Runs	Wins%	£
No Wins	30%	98	1240	7.9%	-0.55
1 Win	44%	142	798	17.8%	-0.26
2 Wins	21%	68	255	26.7%	-0.05
3 Wins	4%	14	39	35.9%	-0.04

ANALYSIS BY POSITION LAST TIME
Age	Prop	Win	Runs	Wins%	£
Won	34%	111	489	22.7%	-0.18
2nd or 3rd	29%	95	584	16.3%	-0.28
Unplaced	26%	85	835	10.2%	-0.45
Fell,BD,UR	4%	13	153	8.5%	-0.58
Pulled Up	5%	16	263	6.1%	-0.70
Ref/RanOut	0%	1	5	20.0%	-0.25
CO/SlipUp	0%	1	3	33.3%	1.33
Unraced	2%	7	48	14.6%	0.94

OTHER FACTORS (WINS-RUNS, £)
Course Winner:	65-356	-£0.41
Distance Winner:	168-898	-£0.31
Going Winner:	205-1084	-£0.26
Beaten Favourite:	41-190	-£0.19
7-Day Winners:	5-13	£0.68
BHA Top Rated:	45-253	-£0.42
Absolute Favourites:	146-305	£0.02

Novices' Chases (class 1..3)

Novices' Chases (class 1..3): 11 runners or more

ANALYSIS BY AGE

Age	Prop	Win	Runs	Wins%	£
3yo	0%	0	0	0.0%	0.00
4yo	4%	1	6	16.7%	0.25
5yo	17%	4	34	11.8%	-0.11
6yo	29%	7	77	9.1%	-0.36
7yo	33%	8	92	8.7%	-0.59
8yo	13%	3	54	5.6%	-0.57
9yo	4%	1	32	3.1%	-0.84
10yo	0%	0	8	0.0%	-1.00
11yo	0%	0	2	0.0%	-1.00
12yo+	0%	0	1	0.0%	-1.00

ANALYSIS BY BHB RATING

Age	Prop	Win	Runs	Wins%	£
150+	21%	5	21	23.8%	0.43
130..149	13%	3	75	4.0%	-0.71
120..129	4%	1	15	6.7%	-0.67
110..119	0%	0	13	0.0%	-1.00
100..109	0%	0	9	0.0%	-1.00
80..99	0%	0	7	0.0%	-1.00
60..79	0%	0	6	0.0%	-1.00
..59	0%	0	1	0.0%	-1.00
Unrated	63%	15	159	9.4%	-0.40

ANALYSIS BY WEIGHT CARRIED

Age	Prop	Win	Runs	Wins%	£
12-01+	0%	0	0	0.0%	0.00
11-8..12-00	8%	2	7	28.6%	-0.07
11-0..11-07	67%	16	212	7.5%	-0.63
10-8..10-13	13%	3	63	4.8%	-0.56
10-0..10-07	13%	3	24	12.5%	0.60
..9-13	0%	0	0	0.0%	0.00

ANALYSIS BY DAYS SINCE LAST RUN

Age	Prop	Win	Runs	Wins%	£
1..7	4%	1	7	14.3%	-0.78
8..14	4%	1	18	5.6%	-0.83
15..28	29%	7	95	7.4%	-0.55
29..60	25%	6	88	6.8%	-0.60
61..100	8%	2	33	6.1%	-0.56
101+	25%	6	56	10.7%	-0.38
Unraced	4%	1	9	11.1%	1.33

ANALYSIS BY TODAY'S STARTING PRICE

Age	Prop	Win	Runs	Wins%	£
Odds On	4%	1	1	100.0%	0.57
Ev-2/1	21%	5	13	38.5%	0.00
9/4-4/1	29%	7	25	28.0%	0.15
9/2-6/1	8%	2	23	8.7%	-0.39
13/2-10/1	29%	7	60	11.7%	-0.02
11/1-16/1	4%	1	44	2.3%	-0.66
18/1-33/1	4%	1	62	1.6%	-0.66
40/1+	0%	0	78	0.0%	-1.00

ANALYSIS BY STARTING PRICE LAST TIME

Age	Prop	Win	Runs	Wins%	£
Odds On	21%	5	36	13.9%	0.03
Ev-2/1	13%	3	46	6.5%	-0.74
9/4-4/1	21%	5	50	10.0%	-0.66
9/2-6/1	8%	2	28	7.1%	-0.50
13/2-10/1	8%	2	50	4.0%	-0.78
11/1-16/1	21%	5	34	14.7%	-0.13
18/1-33/1	4%	1	33	3.0%	-0.70
40/1+	0%	0	20	0.0%	-1.00
Unraced	4%	1	9	11.1%	1.33

ANALYSIS BY DISTANCE BEATEN LAST TIME

Age	Prop	Win	Runs	Wins%	£
..-10 lgh	21%	5	30	16.7%	-0.06
-10..0	29%	7	59	11.9%	-0.45
0.1..2	13%	3	24	12.5%	-0.43
2.1..5	4%	1	19	5.3%	-0.53
5.1..10	4%	1	14	7.1%	-0.43
10.1..20	8%	2	25	8.0%	-0.73
20.0..30	4%	1	23	4.3%	-0.57
30.1+	13%	3	54	5.6%	-0.56
Not Compl	0%	0	49	0.0%	-1.00
Unraced	4%	1	9	11.1%	1.33

ANALYSIS BY SUCCESS RATE IN LAST 10 RUNS

Age	Prop	Win	Runs	Wins%	£
No Wins	9%	2	49	4.1%	-0.66
1 Win	0%	0	40	0.0%	-1.00
2 Wins	13%	3	53	5.7%	-0.60
3 Wins	22%	5	67	7.5%	-0.54
4 Wins	22%	5	42	11.9%	-0.44
5+ Wins	35%	8	46	17.4%	-0.15

ANALYSIS BY SUCCESS RATE IN LAST 3 RUNS

Age	Prop	Win	Runs	Wins%	£
No Wins	30%	7	113	6.2%	-0.55
1 Win	22%	5	100	5.0%	-0.69
2 Wins	30%	7	66	10.6%	-0.57
3 Wins	17%	4	18	22.2%	0.15

ANALYSIS BY POSITION LAST TIME

Age	Prop	Win	Runs	Wins%	£
Won	50%	12	89	13.5%	-0.32
2nd or 3rd	25%	6	78	7.7%	-0.57
Unplaced	21%	5	81	6.2%	-0.54
Fell,BD,UR	0%	0	20	0.0%	-1.00
Pulled Up	0%	0	29	0.0%	-1.00
Ref/RanOut	0%	0	0	0.0%	0.00
CO/SlipUp	0%	0	0	0.0%	0.00
Unraced	4%	1	9	11.1%	1.33

OTHER FACTORS (WINS-RUNS, £)

Course Winner:	8-51	-£0.31
Distance Winner:	13-154	-£0.57
Going Winner:	15-164	-£0.64
Beaten Favourite:	1-29	-£0.76
BHA Top Rated:	5-20	£0.22
Absolute Favourites:	9-22	£0.23

Race Profiles

Novices' Chases (class 1..3): up to 7 days off the track

ANALYSIS BY AGE

Age	Prop	Win	Runs	Wins%	£
3yo	0%	0	0	0.0%	0.00
4yo	13%	4	17	23.5%	-0.22
5yo	27%	8	40	20.0%	-0.32
6yo	30%	9	66	13.6%	0.70
7yo	10%	3	51	5.9%	-0.85
8yo	10%	3	32	9.4%	-0.77
9yo	7%	2	17	11.8%	-0.66
10yo	3%	1	17	5.9%	-0.62
11yo	0%	0	6	0.0%	-1.00
12yo+	0%	0	1	0.0%	-1.00

ANALYSIS BY BHB RATING

Age	Prop	Win	Runs	Wins%	£
150+	0%	0	0	0.0%	0.00
130..149	20%	6	16	37.5%	0.09
120..129	13%	4	22	18.2%	-0.61
110..119	17%	5	13	38.5%	0.76
100..109	3%	1	12	8.3%	-0.46
80..99	0%	0	24	0.0%	-1.00
60..79	0%	0	18	0.0%	-1.00
..59	0%	0	0	0.0%	0.00
Unrated	47%	14	142	9.9%	-0.12

ANALYSIS BY WEIGHT CARRIED

Age	Prop	Win	Runs	Wins%	£
12-01+	0%	0	0	0.0%	0.00
11-8..12-00	17%	5	21	23.8%	-0.46
11-0..11-07	47%	14	103	13.6%	-0.03
10-8..10-13	23%	7	79	8.9%	-0.59
10-0..10-07	13%	4	43	9.3%	-0.18
..9-13	0%	0	1	0.0%	-1.00

ANALYSIS BY DAYS SINCE LAST RUN

Age	Prop	Win	Runs	Wins%	£
1..7	57%	17	162	10.5%	-0.66
8..14	0%	0	0	0.0%	0.00
15..28	0%	0	0	0.0%	0.00
29..60	0%	0	0	0.0%	0.00
61..100	0%	0	0	0.0%	0.00
101+	0%	0	0	0.0%	0.00
Unraced	43%	13	85	15.3%	0.47

ANALYSIS BY TODAY'S STARTING PRICE

Age	Prop	Win	Runs	Wins%	£
Odds On	30%	9	16	56.3%	-0.17
Ev-2/1	27%	8	19	42.1%	0.05
9/4-4/1	23%	7	37	18.9%	-0.25
9/2-6/1	10%	3	15	20.0%	0.37
13/2-10/1	3%	1	23	4.3%	-0.57
11/1-16/1	0%	0	31	0.0%	-1.00
18/1-33/1	3%	1	28	3.6%	-0.25
40/1+	3%	1	78	1.3%	-0.14

ANALYSIS BY STARTING PRICE LAST TIME

Age	Prop	Win	Runs	Wins%	£
Odds On	17%	5	9	55.6%	0.27
Ev-2/1	7%	2	16	12.5%	-0.59
9/4-4/1	13%	4	18	22.2%	-0.12
9/2-6/1	7%	2	18	11.1%	-0.77
13/2-10/1	3%	1	23	4.3%	-0.89
11/1-16/1	7%	2	24	8.3%	-0.56
18/1-33/1	3%	1	15	6.7%	-0.77
40/1+	0%	0	39	0.0%	-1.00
Unraced	43%	13	85	15.3%	0.47

ANALYSIS BY DISTANCE BEATEN LAST TIME

Age	Prop	Win	Runs	Wins%	£
..-10 lgh	13%	4	10	40.0%	0.85
-10..0	17%	5	19	26.3%	-0.15
0.1..2	3%	1	6	16.7%	-0.74
2.1..5	0%	0	10	0.0%	-1.00
5.1..10	10%	3	9	33.3%	-0.41
10.1..20	3%	1	16	6.3%	-0.75
20.0..30	3%	1	9	11.1%	-0.72
30.1+	0%	0	32	0.0%	-1.00
Not Compl	7%	2	51	3.9%	-0.87
Unraced	43%	13	85	15.3%	0.47

ANALYSIS BY SUCCESS RATE IN LAST 10 RUNS

Age	Prop	Win	Runs	Wins%	£
No Wins	6%	1	59	1.7%	-0.93
1 Win	24%	4	36	11.1%	-0.45
2 Wins	29%	5	31	16.1%	-0.54
3 Wins	12%	2	18	11.1%	-0.74
4 Wins	24%	4	12	33.3%	-0.14
5+ Wins	6%	1	6	16.7%	-0.74

ANALYSIS BY SUCCESS RATE IN LAST 3 RUNS

Age	Prop	Win	Runs	Wins%	£
No Wins	18%	3	103	2.9%	-0.92
1 Win	53%	9	43	20.9%	-0.26
2 Wins	29%	5	15	33.3%	-0.04
3 Wins	0%	0	1	0.0%	-1.00

ANALYSIS BY POSITION LAST TIME

Age	Prop	Win	Runs	Wins%	£
Won	30%	9	29	31.0%	0.20
2nd or 3rd	17%	5	35	14.3%	-0.69
Unplaced	3%	1	47	2.1%	-0.95
Fell,BD,UR	3%	1	26	3.8%	-0.88
Pulled Up	3%	1	24	4.2%	-0.85
Ref/RanOut	0%	0	1	0.0%	-1.00
CO/SlipUp	0%	0	0	0.0%	0.00
Unraced	43%	13	85	15.3%	0.47

OTHER FACTORS (WINS-RUNS, £)

Course Winner:	2-17	-£0.67
Distance Winner:	7-53	-£0.67
Going Winner:	14-65	-£0.30
Beaten Favourite:	0-4	-£1.00
7-Day Winners:	9-29	£0.20
BHA Top Rated:	6-26	-£0.51
Absolute Favourites:	13-27	-£0.16

Novices' Chases (class 1..3)

Novices' Chases (class 1..3): 100+ days off the track

ANALYSIS BY AGE

Age	Prop	Win	Runs	Wins%	£
3yo	0%	0	0	0.0%	0.00
4yo	5%	7	22	31.8%	-0.26
5yo	18%	25	118	21.2%	-0.10
6yo	37%	52	219	23.7%	-0.17
7yo	26%	37	199	18.6%	-0.06
8yo	9%	13	111	11.7%	-0.49
9yo	4%	6	61	9.8%	-0.65
10yo	1%	2	18	11.1%	-0.15
11yo	0%	0	8	0.0%	-1.00
12yo+	0%	0	5	0.0%	-1.00

ANALYSIS BY BHB RATING

Age	Prop	Win	Runs	Wins%	£
150+	0%	0	1	0.0%	-1.00
130..149	6%	9	37	24.3%	-0.15
120..129	6%	9	31	29.0%	0.66
110..119	2%	3	61	4.9%	-0.64
100..109	1%	1	26	3.8%	-0.54
80..99	0%	0	27	0.0%	-1.00
60..79	0%	0	17	0.0%	-1.00
..59	0%	0	5	0.0%	-1.00
Unrated	85%	120	556	21.6%	-0.16

ANALYSIS BY WEIGHT CARRIED

Age	Prop	Win	Runs	Wins%	£
12-01+	0%	0	0	0.0%	0.00
11-8..12-00	6%	8	28	28.6%	0.61
11-0..11-07	66%	94	443	21.2%	-0.10
10-8..10-13	20%	29	219	13.2%	-0.51
10-0..10-07	7%	10	70	14.3%	-0.55
..9-13	1%	1	1	100.0%	2.75

ANALYSIS BY DAYS SINCE LAST RUN

Age	Prop	Win	Runs	Wins%	£
1..7	0%	0	0	0.0%	0.00
8..14	0%	0	0	0.0%	0.00
15..28	0%	0	0	0.0%	0.00
29..60	0%	0	0	0.0%	0.00
61..100	1%	1	5	20.0%	-0.52
101+	99%	141	756	18.7%	-0.23
Unraced	0%	0	0	0.0%	0.00

ANALYSIS BY TODAY'S STARTING PRICE

Age	Prop	Win	Runs	Wins%	£
Odds On	36%	51	61	83.6%	0.33
Ev-2/1	23%	32	79	40.5%	0.03
9/4-4/1	27%	38	132	28.8%	0.17
9/2-6/1	4%	5	50	10.0%	-0.39
13/2-10/1	6%	8	111	7.2%	-0.32
11/1-16/1	5%	7	84	8.3%	0.12
18/1-33/1	0%	0	92	0.0%	-1.00
40/1+	1%	1	152	0.7%	-0.56

ANALYSIS BY STARTING PRICE LAST TIME

Age	Prop	Win	Runs	Wins%	£
Odds On	17%	24	50	48.0%	0.98
Ev-2/1	11%	16	76	21.1%	-0.31
9/4-4/1	17%	24	111	21.6%	-0.44
9/2-6/1	10%	14	83	16.9%	-0.41
13/2-10/1	20%	28	138	20.3%	-0.29
11/1-16/1	13%	19	101	18.8%	-0.15
18/1-33/1	6%	9	111	8.1%	-0.70
40/1+	6%	8	91	8.8%	0.15
Unraced	0%	0	0	0.0%	0.00

ANALYSIS BY DISTANCE BEATEN LAST TIME

Age	Prop	Win	Runs	Wins%	£
..-10 lgh	6%	9	32	28.1%	-0.23
-10..0	16%	23	93	24.7%	-0.06
0.1..2	10%	14	34	41.2%	0.38
2.1..5	6%	9	41	22.0%	-0.36
5.1..10	11%	15	65	23.1%	-0.49
10.1..20	8%	12	87	13.8%	-0.52
20.0..30	11%	16	79	20.3%	-0.30
30.1+	19%	27	192	14.1%	-0.33
Not Compl	12%	17	138	12.3%	0.01
Unraced	0%	0	0	0.0%	0.00

ANALYSIS BY SUCCESS RATE IN LAST 10 RUNS

Age	Prop	Win	Runs	Wins%	£
No Wins	8%	11	193	5.7%	-0.45
1 Win	27%	38	204	18.6%	-0.06
2 Wins	24%	34	162	21.0%	-0.17
3 Wins	20%	29	115	25.2%	-0.23
4 Wins	13%	18	64	28.1%	-0.43
5+ Wins	8%	12	23	52.2%	0.12

ANALYSIS BY SUCCESS RATE IN LAST 3 RUNS

Age	Prop	Win	Runs	Wins%	£
No Wins	39%	56	409	13.7%	-0.30
1 Win	44%	62	262	23.7%	-0.10
2 Wins	13%	19	78	24.4%	-0.37
3 Wins	4%	5	12	41.7%	-0.02

ANALYSIS BY POSITION LAST TIME

Age	Prop	Win	Runs	Wins%	£
Won	23%	32	125	25.6%	-0.10
2nd or 3rd	26%	37	157	23.6%	-0.26
Unplaced	39%	56	341	16.4%	-0.37
Fell,BD,UR	1%	1	18	5.6%	-0.88
Pulled Up	11%	15	119	12.6%	0.09
Ref/RanOut	0%	0	0	0.0%	0.00
CO/SlipUp	1%	1	1	100.0%	6.00
Unraced	0%	0	0	0.0%	0.00

OTHER FACTORS (WINS-RUNS, £)

Course Winner:	34-122	-£0.23
Distance Winner:	71-281	-£0.20
Going Winner:	83-317	-£0.15
Beaten Favourite:	25-70	£0.15
BHA Top Rated:	12-52	-£0.46
Absolute Favourites:	73-112	£0.23

Race Profiles

Novices' Chases (class 4..6)

ANALYSIS BY AGE

Age	Prop	Win	Runs	Wins%	£
3yo	0%	0	0	0.0%	0.00
4yo	3%	25	122	20.5%	-0.21
5yo	14%	142	942	15.1%	-0.21
6yo	31%	305	1868	16.3%	-0.22
7yo	29%	290	1964	14.8%	-0.32
8yo	14%	138	1205	11.5%	-0.47
9yo	7%	68	641	10.6%	-0.51
10yo	2%	15	268	5.6%	-0.64
11yo	1%	8	100	8.0%	-0.23
12yo+	0%	0	39	0.0%	-1.00

ANALYSIS BY BHB RATING

Age	Prop	Win	Runs	Wins%	£
150+	0%	1	1	100.0%	0.33
130..149	4%	36	84	42.9%	0.07
120..129	10%	96	325	29.5%	0.13
110..119	16%	160	853	18.8%	-0.19
100..109	14%	134	817	16.4%	-0.09
80..99	3%	34	754	4.5%	-0.57
60..79	1%	10	523	1.9%	-0.52
..59	0%	1	73	1.4%	-0.60
Unrated	52%	519	3719	14.0%	-0.39

ANALYSIS BY WEIGHT CARRIED

Age	Prop	Win	Runs	Wins%	£
12-01+	0%	0	1	0.0%	-1.00
11-8..12-00	4%	36	144	25.0%	0.31
11-0..11-07	66%	652	3895	16.7%	-0.25
10-8..10-13	21%	213	2054	10.4%	-0.48
10-0..10-07	9%	89	1016	8.8%	-0.45
..9-13	0%	1	39	2.6%	-0.95

ANALYSIS BY DAYS SINCE LAST RUN

Age	Prop	Win	Runs	Wins%	£
1..7	4%	43	321	13.4%	-0.46
8..14	13%	130	1155	11.3%	-0.43
15..28	32%	319	2069	15.4%	-0.22
29..60	22%	221	1546	14.3%	-0.36
61..100	7%	66	442	14.9%	-0.20
101+	20%	203	1457	13.9%	-0.37
Unraced	1%	9	159	5.7%	-0.66

ANALYSIS BY TODAY'S STARTING PRICE

Age	Prop	Win	Runs	Wins%	£
Odds On	23%	226	367	61.6%	-0.02
Ev-2/1	25%	246	695	35.4%	-0.11
9/4-4/1	29%	288	1146	25.1%	0.01
9/2-6/1	9%	89	615	14.5%	-0.12
13/2-10/1	8%	75	899	8.3%	-0.26
11/1-16/1	4%	41	825	5.0%	-0.28
18/1-33/1	2%	22	1016	2.2%	-0.45
40/1+	0%	4	1586	0.3%	-0.84

ANALYSIS BY STARTING PRICE LAST TIME

Age	Prop	Win	Runs	Wins%	£
Odds On	6%	57	160	35.6%	-0.13
Ev-2/1	13%	127	439	28.9%	-0.10
9/4-4/1	22%	220	971	22.7%	-0.14
9/2-6/1	12%	118	660	17.9%	-0.37
13/2-10/1	16%	161	1131	14.2%	-0.33
11/1-16/1	15%	150	1125	13.3%	-0.29
18/1-33/1	11%	108	1218	8.9%	-0.36
40/1+	4%	41	1286	3.2%	-0.54
Unraced	1%	9	159	5.7%	-0.66

ANALYSIS BY DISTANCE BEATEN LAST TIME

Age	Prop	Win	Runs	Wins%	£
..-10 lgh	4%	36	106	34.0%	-0.03
-10..0	10%	104	359	29.0%	-0.09
0.1..2	7%	73	335	21.8%	-0.21
2.1..5	10%	101	381	26.5%	-0.15
5.1..10	11%	107	553	19.3%	-0.26
10.1..20	18%	175	935	18.7%	-0.14
20.0..30	10%	99	730	13.6%	-0.32
30.1+	15%	152	1899	8.0%	-0.36
Not Compl	14%	135	1692	8.0%	-0.55
Unraced	1%	9	159	5.7%	-0.66

ANALYSIS BY SUCCESS RATE IN LAST 10 RUNS

Age	Prop	Win	Runs	Wins%	£
No Wins	19%	186	3090	6.0%	-0.50
1 Win	29%	283	1845	15.3%	-0.27
2 Wins	29%	284	1295	21.9%	-0.13
3 Wins	16%	156	555	28.1%	-0.14
4 Wins	6%	55	166	33.1%	-0.08
5+ Wins	2%	18	39	46.2%	0.10

ANALYSIS BY SUCCESS RATE IN LAST 3 RUNS

Age	Prop	Win	Runs	Wins%	£
No Wins	61%	603	5423	11.1%	-0.37
1 Win	31%	301	1303	23.1%	-0.18
2 Wins	7%	72	247	29.1%	-0.19
3 Wins	1%	6	17	35.3%	-0.11

ANALYSIS BY POSITION LAST TIME

Age	Prop	Win	Runs	Wins%	£
Won	14%	140	465	30.1%	-0.07
2nd or 3rd	36%	358	1732	20.7%	-0.20
Unplaced	35%	350	3112	11.2%	-0.32
Fell,BD,UR	6%	58	552	10.5%	-0.46
Pulled Up	8%	76	1107	6.9%	-0.58
Ref/RanOut	0%	0	20	0.0%	-1.00
CO/SlipUp	0%	0	2	0.0%	-1.00
Unraced	1%	9	159	5.7%	-0.66

OTHER FACTORS (WINS-RUNS, £)

Course Winner:	183-813	-£0.17
Distance Winner:	373-1771	-£0.15
Going Winner:	437-2066	-£0.19
Beaten Favourite:	131-508	-£0.17
7-Day Winners:	10-324	-£0.26
BHA Top Rated:	187-803	-£0.08
Absolute Favourites:	425-936	-£0.05

TRAINERS (WINS-RUNS, £)

C C Bealby 3-24 £0.10; J A B Old 6-35 £0.06; C J Mann 19-61 £0.03; D E Cantillon 4-11 £0.11; P R Webber 5-52 £0.01; M Scudamore 3-20 £0.00.

Novices' Chases (class 4..6)

Novices' Chases (class 4..6): 2m to 2m3f

ANALYSIS BY AGE
Age	Prop	Win	Runs	Wins%	£
3yo	0%	0	0	0.0%	0.00
4yo	4%	12	70	17.1%	-0.42
5yo	17%	52	390	13.3%	-0.26
6yo	33%	100	613	16.3%	-0.19
7yo	30%	92	584	15.8%	-0.32
8yo	9%	29	305	9.5%	-0.54
9yo	5%	14	157	8.9%	-0.59
10yo	3%	8	68	11.8%	-0.42
11yo	0%	0	14	0.0%	-1.00
12yo+	0%	0	11	0.0%	-1.00

ANALYSIS BY BHB RATING
Age	Prop	Win	Runs	Wins%	£
150+	0%	0	0	0.0%	0.00
130..149	3%	10	17	58.8%	0.52
120..129	7%	22	99	22.2%	0.29
110..119	16%	48	263	18.3%	-0.22
100..109	13%	41	251	16.3%	-0.03
80..99	2%	6	200	3.0%	-0.71
60..79	0%	1	170	0.6%	-0.88
..59	0%	0	21	0.0%	-1.00
Unrated	58%	179	1191	15.0%	-0.34

ANALYSIS BY WEIGHT CARRIED
Age	Prop	Win	Runs	Wins%	£
12-01+	0%	0	0	0.0%	0.00
11-8..12-00	4%	13	66	19.7%	0.76
11-0..11-07	64%	198	1167	17.0%	-0.24
10-8..10-13	21%	65	646	10.1%	-0.52
10-0..10-07	10%	31	319	9.7%	-0.52
..9-13	0%	0	14	0.0%	-1.00

ANALYSIS BY DAYS SINCE LAST RUN
Age	Prop	Win	Runs	Wins%	£
1..7	6%	18	97	18.6%	-0.25
8..14	11%	33	345	9.6%	-0.50
15..28	33%	102	649	15.7%	-0.12
29..60	21%	66	515	12.8%	-0.39
61..100	7%	21	147	14.3%	-0.42
101+	21%	66	430	15.3%	-0.45
Unraced	0%	1	29	3.4%	-0.55

ANALYSIS BY TODAY'S STARTING PRICE
Age	Prop	Win	Runs	Wins%	£
Odds On	23%	70	119	58.8%	-0.07
Ev-2/1	25%	77	211	36.5%	-0.10
9/4-4/1	29%	89	355	25.1%	0.02
9/2-6/1	9%	27	182	14.8%	-0.09
13/2-10/1	7%	22	285	7.7%	-0.32
11/1-16/1	5%	15	236	6.4%	-0.11
18/1-33/1	2%	6	326	1.8%	-0.48
40/1+	0%	1	498	0.2%	-0.87

ANALYSIS BY STARTING PRICE LAST TIME
Age	Prop	Win	Runs	Wins%	£
Odds On	6%	19	55	34.5%	-0.25
Ev-2/1	12%	36	133	27.1%	-0.18
9/4-4/1	21%	65	299	21.7%	-0.21
9/2-6/1	9%	29	211	13.7%	-0.47
13/2-10/1	18%	55	377	14.6%	-0.32
11/1-16/1	15%	47	350	13.4%	-0.35
18/1-33/1	13%	40	366	10.9%	-0.28
40/1+	5%	15	392	3.8%	-0.47
Unraced	0%	1	29	3.4%	-0.55

ANALYSIS BY DISTANCE BEATEN LAST TIME
Age	Prop	Win	Runs	Wins%	£
..-10 lgh	5%	14	28	50.0%	0.22
-10..0	10%	30	97	30.9%	-0.04
0.1..2	7%	20	109	18.3%	-0.40
2.1..5	8%	26	113	23.0%	-0.25
5.1..10	9%	28	193	14.5%	-0.38
10.1..20	19%	58	322	18.0%	-0.02
20.0..30	12%	36	251	14.3%	-0.33
30.1+	18%	55	604	9.1%	-0.43
Not Compl	13%	39	466	8.4%	-0.51
Unraced	0%	1	29	3.4%	-0.55

ANALYSIS BY SUCCESS RATE IN LAST 10 RUNS
Age	Prop	Win	Runs	Wins%	£
No Wins	17%	53	933	5.7%	-0.61
1 Win	31%	94	599	15.7%	-0.15
2 Wins	27%	83	417	19.9%	-0.14
3 Wins	16%	50	168	29.8%	-0.12
4 Wins	6%	19	52	36.5%	-0.01
5+ Wins	2%	7	14	50.0%	0.23

ANALYSIS BY SUCCESS RATE IN LAST 3 RUNS
Age	Prop	Win	Runs	Wins%	£
No Wins	61%	188	1713	11.0%	-0.38
1 Win	30%	91	380	23.9%	-0.15
2 Wins	8%	24	84	28.6%	-0.19
3 Wins	1%	3	6	50.0%	-0.16

ANALYSIS BY POSITION LAST TIME
Age	Prop	Win	Runs	Wins%	£
Won	14%	44	124	35.5%	0.02
2nd or 3rd	32%	97	533	18.2%	-0.27
Unplaced	41%	126	1062	11.9%	-0.33
Fell,BD,UR	6%	18	159	11.3%	-0.29
Pulled Up	7%	21	297	7.1%	-0.60
Ref/RanOut	0%	0	8	0.0%	-1.00
CO/SlipUp	0%	0	0	0.0%	0.00
Unraced	0%	1	29	3.4%	-0.55

OTHER FACTORS (WINS-RUNS, £)
Course Winner:	67-265	-£0.04
Distance Winner:	175-849	-£0.09
Going Winner:	142-675	-£0.15
Beaten Favourite:	37-164	-£0.29
7-Day Winners:	6-10	£0.14
BHA Top Rated:	46-241	-£0.23
Absolute Favourites:	130-292	-£0.10

Race Profiles

Novices' Chases (class 4..6): 2m4f to 2m7f

ANALYSIS BY AGE

Age	Prop	Win	Runs	Wins%	£
3yo	0%	0	0	0.0%	0.00
4yo	3%	11	47	23.4%	-0.20
5yo	16%	66	418	15.8%	-0.26
6yo	35%	148	831	17.8%	-0.15
7yo	26%	108	820	13.2%	-0.28
8yo	13%	53	513	10.3%	-0.47
9yo	6%	24	278	8.6%	-0.57
10yo	1%	5	108	4.6%	-0.52
11yo	1%	3	47	6.4%	-0.41
12yo+	0%	0	16	0.0%	-1.00

ANALYSIS BY BHB RATING

Age	Prop	Win	Runs	Wins%	£
150+	0%	1	1	100.0%	0.33
130..149	3%	12	33	36.4%	-0.03
120..129	10%	40	138	29.0%	-0.10
110..119	16%	66	372	17.7%	-0.18
100..109	13%	56	343	16.3%	-0.07
80..99	4%	17	335	5.1%	-0.45
60..79	1%	6	213	2.8%	-0.13
..59	0%	0	32	0.0%	-1.00
Unrated	53%	220	1611	13.7%	-0.41

ANALYSIS BY WEIGHT CARRIED

Age	Prop	Win	Runs	Wins%	£
12-01+	0%	0	1	0.0%	-1.00
11-8..12-00	5%	19	68	27.9%	-0.12
11-0..11-07	62%	261	1604	16.3%	-0.19
10-8..10-13	23%	97	931	10.4%	-0.47
10-0..10-07	10%	40	458	8.7%	-0.45
..9-13	0%	1	16	6.3%	-0.88

ANALYSIS BY DAYS SINCE LAST RUN

Age	Prop	Win	Runs	Wins%	£
1..7	4%	16	137	11.7%	-0.57
8..14	15%	61	532	11.5%	-0.39
15..28	33%	138	881	15.7%	-0.23
29..60	22%	93	637	14.6%	-0.38
61..100	5%	22	174	12.6%	-0.05
101+	20%	82	651	12.6%	-0.31
Unraced	1%	6	66	9.1%	-0.47

ANALYSIS BY TODAY'S STARTING PRICE

Age	Prop	Win	Runs	Wins%	£
Odds On	22%	91	146	62.3%	0.00
Ev-2/1	26%	108	303	35.6%	-0.08
9/4-4/1	28%	116	476	24.4%	-0.02
9/2-6/1	10%	41	275	14.9%	-0.10
13/2-10/1	8%	33	382	8.6%	-0.23
11/1-16/1	4%	16	381	4.2%	-0.37
18/1-33/1	2%	10	446	2.2%	-0.46
40/1+	1%	3	669	0.4%	-0.71

ANALYSIS BY STARTING PRICE LAST TIME

Age	Prop	Win	Runs	Wins%	£
Odds On	6%	27	69	39.1%	-0.05
Ev-2/1	15%	62	198	31.3%	-0.10
9/4-4/1	21%	87	413	21.1%	-0.18
9/2-6/1	13%	53	273	19.4%	-0.35
13/2-10/1	.16%	65	491	13.2%	-0.34
11/1-16/1	15%	63	473	13.3%	-0.23
18/1-33/1	10%	40	547	7.3%	-0.36
40/1+	4%	15	548	2.7%	-0.50
Unraced	1%	6	66	9.1%	-0.47

ANALYSIS BY DISTANCE BEATEN LAST TIME

Age	Prop	Win	Runs	Wins%	£
..-10 lgh	4%	15	51	29.4%	-0.30
-10..0	12%	50	180	27.8%	-0.13
0.1..2	8%	34	133	25.6%	0.06
2.1..5	12%	51	174	29.3%	0.00
5.1..10	11%	47	231	20.3%	-0.27
10.1..20	16%	65	404	16.1%	-0.34
20.0..30	9%	37	304	12.2%	-0.27
30.1+	15%	62	806	7.7%	-0.24
Not Compl	12%	51	729	7.0%	-0.59
Unraced	1%	6	66	9.1%	-0.47

ANALYSIS BY SUCCESS RATE IN LAST 10 RUNS

Age	Prop	Win	Runs	Wins%	£
No Wins	19%	80	1285	6.2%	-0.38
1 Win	28%	114	830	13.7%	-0.37
2 Wins	30%	124	569	21.8%	-0.18
3 Wins	16%	66	243	27.2%	-0.14
4 Wins	5%	22	70	31.4%	-0.13
5+ Wins	1%	6	15	40.0%	-0.15

ANALYSIS BY SUCCESS RATE IN LAST 3 RUNS

Age	Prop	Win	Runs	Wins%	£
No Wins	60%	249	2291	10.9%	-0.32
1 Win	32%	132	609	21.7%	-0.28
2 Wins	7%	28	102	27.5%	-0.28
3 Wins	1%	3	10	30.0%	0.01

ANALYSIS BY POSITION LAST TIME

Age	Prop	Win	Runs	Wins%	£
Won	16%	65	232	28.0%	-0.17
2nd or 3rd	37%	156	728	21.4%	-0.14
Unplaced	34%	141	1326	10.6%	-0.28
Fell,BD,UR	5%	20	236	8.5%	-0.63
Pulled Up	7%	30	483	6.2%	-0.57
Ref/RanOut	0%	0	6	0.0%	-1.00
CO/SlipUp	0%	0	1	0.0%	-1.00
Unraced	1%	6	66	9.1%	-0.47

OTHER FACTORS (WINS-RUNS, £)

Course Winner:	68-343	-£0.30
Distance Winner:	129-648	-£0.25
Going Winner:	179-895	-£0.24
Beaten Favourite:	56-201	-£0.05
7-Day Winners:	3-10	-£0.54
BHA Top Rated:	81-337	£0.00
Absolute Favourites:	170-391	-£0.08

Novices' Chases (class 4..6)

Novices' Chases (class 4..6): 3m+

ANALYSIS BY AGE

Age	Prop	Win	Runs	Wins%	£
3yo	0%	0	0	0.0%	0.00
4yo	1%	2	5	40.0%	2.70
5yo	9%	24	134	17.9%	0.05
6yo	21%	57	424	13.4%	-0.40
7yo	34%	90	560	16.1%	-0.36
8yo	21%	56	387	14.5%	-0.42
9yo	11%	30	206	14.6%	-0.36
10yo	1%	2	92	2.2%	-0.94
11yo	2%	5	39	12.8%	0.27
12yo+	0%	0	12	0.0%	-1.00

ANALYSIS BY BHB RATING

Age	Prop	Win	Runs	Wins%	£
150+	0%	0	0	0.0%	0.00
130..149	5%	14	34	41.2%	-0.05
120..129	13%	34	88	38.6%	0.30
110..119	17%	46	218	21.1%	-0.18
100..109	14%	37	223	16.6%	-0.21
80..99	4%	11	219	5.0%	-0.64
60..79	1%	3	140	2.1%	-0.68
..59	0%	1	20	5.0%	0.45
Unrated	45%	120	917	13.1%	-0.42

ANALYSIS BY WEIGHT CARRIED

Age	Prop	Win	Runs	Wins%	£
12-01+	0%	0	0	0.0%	0.00
11-8..12-00	2%	4	10	40.0%	0.28
11-0..11-07	73%	193	1124	17.2%	-0.34
10-8..10-13	19%	51	477	10.7%	-0.44
10-0..10-07	7%	18	239	7.5%	-0.35
..9-13	0%	0	9	0.0%	-1.00

ANALYSIS BY DAYS SINCE LAST RUN

Age	Prop	Win	Runs	Wins%	£
1..7	3%	9	87	10.3%	-0.51
8..14	14%	36	278	12.9%	-0.42
15..28	30%	79	539	14.7%	-0.34
29..60	23%	62	394	15.7%	-0.30
61..100	9%	23	121	19.0%	-0.13
101+	21%	55	376	14.6%	-0.37
Unraced	1%	2	64	3.1%	-0.89

ANALYSIS BY TODAY'S STARTING PRICE

Age	Prop	Win	Runs	Wins%	£
Odds On	24%	65	102	63.7%	0.02
Ev-2/1	23%	61	181	33.7%	-0.16
9/4-4/1	31%	83	315	26.3%	0.05
9/2-6/1	8%	21	158	13.3%	-0.18
13/2-10/1	8%	20	232	8.6%	-0.24
11/1-16/1	4%	10	208	4.8%	-0.31
18/1-33/1	2%	6	244	2.5%	-0.41
40/1+	0%	0	419	0.0%	-1.00

ANALYSIS BY STARTING PRICE LAST TIME

Age	Prop	Win	Runs	Wins%	£
Odds On	4%	11	36	30.6%	-0.09
Ev-2/1	11%	29	108	26.9%	-0.03
9/4-4/1	26%	68	259	26.3%	-0.01
9/2-6/1	14%	36	176	20.5%	-0.28
13/2-10/1	15%	41	263	15.6%	-0.30
11/1-16/1	15%	40	302	13.2%	-0.34
18/1-33/1	11%	28	305	9.2%	-0.46
40/1+	4%	11	346	3.2%	-0.70
Unraced	1%	2	64	3.1%	-0.89

ANALYSIS BY DISTANCE BEATEN LAST TIME

Age	Prop	Win	Runs	Wins%	£
..-10 lgh	3%	7	27	25.9%	0.22
-10..0	9%	24	82	29.3%	-0.04
0.1..2	7%	19	93	20.4%	-0.38
2.1..5	9%	24	94	25.5%	-0.28
5.1..10	12%	32	129	24.8%	-0.06
10.1..20	20%	52	209	24.9%	0.06
20.0..30	10%	26	175	14.9%	-0.38
30.1+	13%	35	489	7.2%	-0.49
Not Compl	17%	45	497	9.1%	-0.53
Unraced	1%	2	64	3.1%	-0.89

ANALYSIS BY SUCCESS RATE IN LAST 10 RUNS

Age	Prop	Win	Runs	Wins%	£
No Wins	20%	53	872	6.1%	-0.55
1 Win	28%	75	416	18.0%	-0.24
2 Wins	29%	77	309	24.9%	-0.04
3 Wins	15%	40	144	27.8%	-0.18
4 Wins	5%	14	44	31.8%	-0.09
5+ Wins	2%	5	10	50.0%	0.31

ANALYSIS BY SUCCESS RATE IN LAST 3 RUNS

Age	Prop	Win	Runs	Wins%	£
No Wins	63%	166	1419	11.7%	-0.43
1 Win	30%	78	314	24.8%	-0.04
2 Wins	8%	20	61	32.8%	-0.03
3 Wins	0%	0	1	0.0%	-1.00

ANALYSIS BY POSITION LAST TIME

Age	Prop	Win	Runs	Wins%	£
Won	12%	31	109	28.4%	0.02
2nd or 3rd	39%	105	471	22.3%	-0.20
Unplaced	31%	83	724	11.5%	-0.38
Fell,BD,UR	8%	20	157	12.7%	-0.36
Pulled Up	9%	25	327	7.6%	-0.59
Ref/RanOut	0%	0	6	0.0%	-1.00
CO/SlipUp	0%	0	1	0.0%	-1.00
Unraced	1%	2	64	3.1%	-0.89

OTHER FACTORS (WINS-RUNS, £)

Course Winner:	48-205	-£0.11
Distance Winner:	69-274	-£0.10
Going Winner:	116-496	-£0.14
Beaten Favourite:	38-143	-£0.22
7-Day Winners:	1-4	-£0.58
BHA Top Rated:	60-225	-£0.04
Absolute Favourites:	125-253	£0.04

Race Profiles

Novices' Chases (class 4..6): 2 to 5 runners

ANALYSIS BY AGE

Age	Prop	Win	Runs	Wins%	£
3yo	0%	0	0	0.0%	0.00
4yo	2%	6	19	31.6%	-0.34
5yo	13%	37	154	24.0%	-0.40
6yo	26%	71	309	23.0%	-0.28
7yo	33%	91	346	26.3%	0.02
8yo	15%	42	196	21.4%	-0.46
9yo	8%	22	122	18.0%	-0.45
10yo	2%	6	41	14.6%	0.10
11yo	1%	2	20	10.0%	-0.35
12yo+	0%	0	4	0.0%	-1.00

ANALYSIS BY BHB RATING

Age	Prop	Win	Runs	Wins%	£
150+	0%	1	1	100.0%	0.33
130..149	8%	22	37	59.5%	0.24
120..129	11%	31	83	37.3%	-0.10
110..119	20%	56	204	27.5%	-0.06
100..109	12%	32	138	23.2%	-0.24
80..99	2%	5	129	3.9%	-0.76
60..79	1%	4	92	4.3%	-0.36
..59	0%	0	17	0.0%	-1.00
Unrated	45%	126	510	24.7%	-0.20

ANALYSIS BY WEIGHT CARRIED

Age	Prop	Win	Runs	Wins%	£
12-01+	0%	0	1	0.0%	-1.00
11-8..12-00	5%	15	41	36.6%	-0.29
11-0..11-07	64%	177	653	27.1%	-0.08
10-8..10-13	23%	63	338	18.6%	-0.36
10-0..10-07	8%	21	174	12.1%	-0.60
..9-13	0%	1	4	25.0%	-0.52

ANALYSIS BY DAYS SINCE LAST RUN

Age	Prop	Win	Runs	Wins%	£
1..7	5%	14	68	20.6%	-0.40
8..14	16%	44	223	19.7%	-0.39
15..28	30%	83	355	23.4%	-0.24
29..60	25%	69	259	26.6%	-0.16
61..100	6%	16	83	19.3%	0.09
101+	18%	49	209	23.4%	-0.26
Unraced	1%	2	14	14.3%	-0.62

ANALYSIS BY TODAY'S STARTING PRICE

Age	Prop	Win	Runs	Wins%	£
Odds On	39%	107	177	60.5%	-0.06
Ev-2/1	30%	84	212	39.6%	-0.01
9/4-4/1	22%	61	229	26.6%	0.07
9/2-6/1	3%	9	89	10.1%	-0.40
13/2-10/1	4%	10	129	7.8%	-0.35
11/1-16/1	1%	3	129	2.3%	-0.69
18/1-33/1	1%	2	124	1.6%	-0.49
40/1+	0%	1	122	0.8%	-0.58

ANALYSIS BY STARTING PRICE LAST TIME

Age	Prop	Win	Runs	Wins%	£
Odds On	9%	24	48	50.0%	0.18
Ev-2/1	15%	41	100	41.0%	0.03
9/4-4/1	23%	65	186	34.9%	-0.08
9/2-6/1	10%	29	118	24.6%	-0.21
13/2-10/1	14%	39	183	21.3%	-0.40
11/1-16/1	13%	35	187	18.7%	-0.41
18/1-33/1	13%	35	198	17.7%	0.10
40/1+	3%	7	177	4.0%	-0.73
Unraced	1%	2	14	14.3%	-0.62

ANALYSIS BY DISTANCE BEATEN LAST TIME

Age	Prop	Win	Runs	Wins%	£
..-10 lgh	5%	15	38	39.5%	-0.23
-10..0	12%	34	79	43.0%	0.01
0.1..2	5%	14	62	22.6%	-0.49
2.1..5	9%	24	68	35.3%	-0.17
5.1..10	10%	27	110	24.5%	-0.28
10.1..20	16%	45	143	31.5%	-0.02
20.0..30	10%	28	112	25.0%	-0.15
30.1+	16%	45	324	13.9%	-0.32
Not Compl	16%	43	261	16.5%	-0.32
Unraced	1%	2	14	14.3%	-0.62

ANALYSIS BY SUCCESS RATE IN LAST 10 RUNS

Age	Prop	Win	Runs	Wins%	£
No Wins	18%	50	459	10.9%	-0.33
1 Win	25%	68	319	21.3%	-0.30
2 Wins	30%	83	249	33.3%	-0.16
3 Wins	19%	51	117	43.6%	0.03
4 Wins	6%	17	39	43.6%	-0.07
5+ Wins	2%	6	14	42.9%	-0.31

ANALYSIS BY SUCCESS RATE IN LAST 3 RUNS

Age	Prop	Win	Runs	Wins%	£
No Wins	56%	154	865	17.8%	-0.29
1 Win	35%	95	272	34.9%	-0.11
2 Wins	9%	24	55	43.6%	-0.10
3 Wins	1%	2	5	40.0%	-0.36

ANALYSIS BY POSITION LAST TIME

Age	Prop	Win	Runs	Wins%	£
Won	10%	49	118	41.5%	-0.08
2nd or 3rd	35%	96	346	27.7%	-0.23
Unplaced	31%	87	472	18.4%	-0.24
Fell,BD,UR	6%	16	93	17.2%	-0.16
Pulled Up	10%	27	166	16.3%	-0.40
Ref/RanOut	0%	0	2	0.0%	-1.00
CO/SlipUp	0%	0	0	0.0%	0.00
Unraced	1%	2	14	14.3%	-0.62

OTHER FACTORS (WINS-RUNS, £)

Course Winner:	54-155	-£0.05
Distance Winner:	112-349	-£0.16
Going Winner:	130-397	-£0.09
Beaten Favourite:	32-92	-£0.13
7-Day Winners:	4-9	-£0.30
BHA Top Rated:	64-204	-£0.12
Absolute Favourites:	150-264	£0.01

Novices' Chases (class 4..6)

Novices' Chases (class 4..6): 6 to 10 runners

ANALYSIS BY AGE

Age	Prop	Win	Runs	Wins%	£
3yo	0%	0	0	0.0%	0.00
4yo	3%	16	77	20.8%	-0.16
5yo	15%	90	602	15.0%	-0.14
6yo	32%	190	1150	16.5%	-0.19
7yo	28%	164	1221	13.4%	-0.41
8yo	14%	82	787	10.4%	-0.43
9yo	6%	37	386	9.6%	-0.49
10yo	2%	9	176	5.1%	-0.71
11yo	1%	6	67	9.0%	-0.04
12yo+	0%	0	28	0.0%	-1.00

ANALYSIS BY BHB RATING

Age	Prop	Win	Runs	Wins%	£
150+	0%	0	0	0.0%	0.00
130..149	2%	13	42	31.0%	-0.04
120..129	10%	57	198	28.8%	0.12
110..119	14%	86	520	16.5%	-0.25
100..109	14%	83	530	15.7%	-0.06
80..99	4%	23	486	4.7%	-0.54
60..79	1%	5	332	1.5%	-0.73
..59	0%	1	45	2.2%	-0.36
Unrated	55%	326	2341	13.9%	-0.36

ANALYSIS BY WEIGHT CARRIED

Age	Prop	Win	Runs	Wins%	£
12-01+	0%	0	0	0.0%	0.00
11-8..12-00	3%	16	83	19.3%	0.18
11-0..11-07	66%	392	2449	16.0%	-0.24
10-8..10-13	21%	126	1295	9.7%	-0.45
10-0..10-07	10%	60	640	9.4%	-0.49
..9-13	0%	0	27	0.0%	-1.00

ANALYSIS BY DAYS SINCE LAST RUN

Age	Prop	Win	Runs	Wins%	£
1..7	4%	22	192	11.5%	-0.49
8..14	12%	71	741	9.6%	-0.46
15..28	34%	203	1303	15.6%	-0.20
29..60	22%	129	982	13.1%	-0.35
61..100	7%	40	278	14.4%	-0.25
101+	21%	123	905	13.6%	-0.36
Unraced	1%	6	93	6.5%	-0.61

ANALYSIS BY TODAY'S STARTING PRICE

Age	Prop	Win	Runs	Wins%	£
Odds On	19%	111	179	62.0%	0.00
Ev-2/1	24%	142	428	33.2%	-0.16
9/4-4/1	31%	184	735	25.0%	0.01
9/2-6/1	10%	62	405	15.3%	-0.06
13/2-10/1	8%	47	570	8.2%	-0.28
11/1-16/1	5%	31	521	6.0%	-0.14
18/1-33/1	3%	15	669	2.2%	-0.46
40/1+	0%	2	987	0.2%	-0.89

ANALYSIS BY STARTING PRICE LAST TIME

Age	Prop	Win	Runs	Wins%	£
Odds On	5%	29	93	31.2%	-0.22
Ev-2/1	13%	77	267	28.8%	-0.04
9/4-4/1	22%	129	618	20.9%	-0.17
9/2-6/1	11%	68	412	16.5%	-0.39
13/2-10/1	17%	101	693	14.6%	-0.30
11/1-16/1	16%	93	707	13.2%	-0.28
18/1-33/1	11%	64	785	8.2%	-0.35
40/1+	5%	27	826	3.3%	-0.58
Unraced	1%	6	93	6.5%	-0.61

ANALYSIS BY DISTANCE BEATEN LAST TIME

Age	Prop	Win	Runs	Wins%	£
..-10 lgh	3%	17	60	28.3%	-0.13
-10..0	10%	59	215	27.4%	-0.03
0.1..2	8%	46	211	21.8%	-0.16
2.1..5	11%	63	244	25.8%	-0.24
5.1..10	11%	66	348	19.0%	-0.27
10.1..20	18%	109	604	18.0%	-0.20
20.0..30	9%	54	453	11.9%	-0.39
30.1+	16%	94	1187	7.9%	-0.34
Not Compl	13%	80	1079	7.4%	-0.51
Unraced	1%	6	93	6.5%	-0.61

ANALYSIS BY SUCCESS RATE IN LAST 10 RUNS

Age	Prop	Win	Runs	Wins%	£
No Wins	20%	118	1969	6.0%	-0.52
1 Win	29%	172	1167	14.7%	-0.25
2 Wins	28%	162	802	20.2%	-0.12
3 Wins	15%	89	338	26.3%	-0.16
4 Wins	6%	36	104	34.6%	0.07
5+ Wins	2%	11	21	52.4%	0.51

ANALYSIS BY SUCCESS RATE IN LAST 3 RUNS

Age	Prop	Win	Runs	Wins%	£
No Wins	64%	374	3442	10.9%	-0.37
1 Win	29%	169	805	21.0%	-0.18
2 Wins	7%	41	142	28.9%	-0.11
3 Wins	1%	4	12	33.3%	-0.01

ANALYSIS BY POSITION LAST TIME

Age	Prop	Win	Runs	Wins%	£
Won	13%	76	274	27.7%	-0.05
2nd or 3rd	37%	218	1086	20.1%	-0.19
Unplaced	36%	214	1970	10.9%	-0.35
Fell,BD,UR	6%	38	349	10.9%	-0.42
Pulled Up	7%	42	708	5.9%	-0.53
Ref/RanOut	0%	0	14	0.0%	-1.00
CO/SlipUp	0%	0	0	0.0%	0.00
Unraced	1%	6	93	6.5%	-0.61

OTHER FACTORS (WINS-RUNS, £)

Course Winner:	107-508	-£0.14
Distance Winner:	221-1108	-£0.14
Going Winner:	255-1309	-£0.19
Beaten Favourite:	82-320	-£0.17
7-Day Winners:	6-15	-£0.24
BHA Top Rated:	111-500	-£0.01
Absolute Favourites:	235-559	-£0.09

Race Profiles

Novices' Chases (class 4..6): 11 runners or more

ANALYSIS BY AGE

Age	Prop	Win	Runs	Wins%	£
3yo	0%	0	0	0.0%	0.00
4yo	3%	3	26	11.5%	-0.26
5yo	13%	15	186	8.1%	-0.30
6yo	37%	44	409	10.8%	-0.26
7yo	29%	35	397	8.8%	-0.32
8yo	12%	14	222	6.3%	-0.66
9yo	8%	9	133	6.8%	-0.63
10yo	0%	0	51	0.0%	-1.00
11yo	0%	0	13	0.0%	-1.00
12yo+	0%	0	7	0.0%	-1.00

ANALYSIS BY BHB RATING

Age	Prop	Win	Runs	Wins%	£
150+	0%	0	0	0.0%	0.00
130..149	1%	1	5	20.0%	-0.20
120..129	7%	8	44	18.2%	0.57
110..119	15%	18	129	14.0%	-0.15
100..109	16%	19	149	12.8%	-0.08
80..99	5%	6	139	4.3%	-0.51
60..79	1%	1	99	1.0%	0.02
..59	0%	0	11	0.0%	-1.00
Unrated	56%	67	868	7.7%	-0.59

ANALYSIS BY WEIGHT CARRIED

Age	Prop	Win	Runs	Wins%	£
12-01+	0%	0	0	0.0%	0.00
11-8..12-00	4%	5	20	25.0%	2.10
11-0..11-07	69%	83	793	10.5%	-0.40
10-8..10-13	20%	24	421	5.7%	-0.65
10-0..10-07	7%	8	202	4.0%	-0.18
..9-13	0%	0	8	0.0%	-1.00

ANALYSIS BY DAYS SINCE LAST RUN

Age	Prop	Win	Runs	Wins%	£
1..7	6%	7	61	11.5%	-0.41
8..14	13%	15	191	7.9%	-0.34
15..28	28%	33	411	8.0%	-0.29
29..60	19%	23	305	7.5%	-0.57
61..100	8%	10	81	12.3%	-0.30
101+	26%	31	343	9.0%	-0.43
Unraced	1%	1	52	1.9%	-0.75

ANALYSIS BY TODAY'S STARTING PRICE

Age	Prop	Win	Runs	Wins%	£
Odds On	7%	8	11	72.7%	0.28
Ev-2/1	17%	20	55	36.4%	-0.09
9/4-4/1	36%	43	182	23.6%	-0.04
9/2-6/1	15%	18	121	14.9%	-0.09
13/2-10/1	15%	18	200	9.0%	-0.16
11/1-16/1	6%	7	175	4.0%	-0.41
18/1-33/1	4%	5	223	2.2%	-0.42
40/1+	1%	1	477	0.2%	-0.79

ANALYSIS BY STARTING PRICE LAST TIME

Age	Prop	Win	Runs	Wins%	£
Odds On	3%	4	19	21.1%	-0.49
Ev-2/1	8%	9	72	12.5%	-0.54
9/4-4/1	22%	26	167	15.6%	-0.14
9/2-6/1	18%	21	130	16.2%	-0.42
13/2-10/1	18%	21	255	8.2%	-0.36
11/1-16/1	18%	22	231	9.5%	-0.26
18/1-33/1	8%	9	235	3.8%	-0.80
40/1+	6%	7	283	2.5%	-0.33
Unraced	1%	1	52	1.9%	-0.75

ANALYSIS BY DISTANCE BEATEN LAST TIME

Age	Prop	Win	Runs	Wins%	£
..-10 lgh	3%	4	8	50.0%	1.68
-10..0	9%	11	65	16.9%	-0.39
0.1..2	11%	13	62	21.0%	-0.11
2.1..5	12%	14	69	20.3%	0.23
5.1..10	12%	14	95	14.7%	-0.21
10.1..20	18%	21	188	11.2%	-0.05
20.0..30	14%	17	165	10.3%	-0.23
30.1+	11%	13	388	3.4%	-0.48
Not Compl	10%	12	352	3.4%	-0.85
Unraced	1%	1	52	1.9%	-0.75

ANALYSIS BY SUCCESS RATE IN LAST 10 RUNS

Age	Prop	Win	Runs	Wins%	£
No Wins	15%	18	662	2.7%	-0.55
1 Win	36%	43	359	12.0%	-0.29
2 Wins	33%	39	244	16.0%	-0.15
3 Wins	13%	16	100	16.0%	-0.30
4 Wins	2%	2	23	8.7%	-0.78
5+ Wins	1%	1	4	25.0%	-0.58

ANALYSIS BY SUCCESS RATE IN LAST 3 RUNS

Age	Prop	Win	Runs	Wins%	£
No Wins	63%	75	1116	6.7%	-0.42
1 Win	31%	37	226	16.4%	-0.27
2 Wins	6%	7	50	14.0%	-0.52
3 Wins	0%	0	0	0.0%	0.00

ANALYSIS BY POSITION LAST TIME

Age	Prop	Win	Runs	Wins%	£
Won	13%	15	73	20.5%	-0.16
2nd or 3rd	37%	44	300	14.7%	-0.17
Unplaced	41%	49	670	7.3%	-0.29
Fell,BD,UR	3%	4	110	3.6%	-0.83
Pulled Up	6%	7	233	3.0%	-0.87
Ref/RanOut	0%	0	4	0.0%	-1.00
CO/SlipUp	0%	0	2	0.0%	-1.00
Unraced	1%	1	52	1.9%	-0.75

OTHER FACTORS (WINS-RUNS, £)

Course Winner:	22-150	-£0.41
Distance Winner:	40-314	-£0.20
Going Winner:	52-360	-£0.27
Beaten Favourite:	17-96	-£0.24
BHA Top Rated:	12-99	-£0.32
Absolute Favourites:	40-113	-£0.01

Novices' Chases (class 4..6)

Novices' Chases (class 4..6): up to 7 days off the track

ANALYSIS BY AGE

Age	Prop	Win	Runs	Wins%	£
3yo	0%	0	0	0.0%	0.00
4yo	0%	0	11	0.0%	-1.00
5yo	17%	9	60	15.0%	-0.36
6yo	23%	12	119	10.1%	-0.44
7yo	38%	20	132	15.2%	-0.42
8yo	10%	5	69	7.2%	-0.78
9yo	8%	4	49	8.2%	-0.69
10yo	0%	0	21	0.0%	-1.00
11yo	4%	2	12	16.7%	0.48
12yo+	0%	0	7	0.0%	-1.00

ANALYSIS BY BHB RATING

Age	Prop	Win	Runs	Wins%	£
150+	0%	0	0	0.0%	0.00
130..149	6%	3	3	100.0%	0.49
120..129	6%	3	8	37.5%	0.18
110..119	19%	10	39	25.6%	0.54
100..109	12%	6	38	15.8%	-0.29
80..99	10%	5	59	8.5%	-0.58
60..79	4%	2	51	3.9%	-0.56
..59	0%	0	6	0.0%	-1.00
Unrated	44%	23	276	8.3%	-0.70

ANALYSIS BY WEIGHT CARRIED

Age	Prop	Win	Runs	Wins%	£
12-01+	0%	0	0	0.0%	0.00
11-8..12-00	6%	3	11	27.3%	-0.59
11-0..11-07	69%	36	237	15.2%	-0.39
10-8..10-13	15%	8	142	5.6%	-0.65
10-0..10-07	10%	5	88	5.7%	-0.66
..9-13	0%	0	2	0.0%	-1.00

ANALYSIS BY DAYS SINCE LAST RUN

Age	Prop	Win	Runs	Wins%	£
1..7	83%	43	321	13.4%	-0.46
8..14	0%	0	0	0.0%	0.00
15..28	0%	0	0	0.0%	0.00
29..60	0%	0	0	0.0%	0.00
61..100	0%	0	0	0.0%	0.00
101+	0%	0	0	0.0%	0.00
Unraced	17%	9	159	5.7%	-0.66

ANALYSIS BY TODAY'S STARTING PRICE

Age	Prop	Win	Runs	Wins%	£
Odds On	33%	17	22	77.3%	0.23
Ev-2/1	27%	14	30	46.7%	0.15
9/4-4/1	17%	9	50	18.0%	-0.30
9/2-6/1	6%	3	25	12.0%	-0.32
13/2-10/1	6%	3	55	5.5%	-0.44
11/1-16/1	12%	6	61	9.8%	0.39
18/1-33/1	0%	0	78	0.0%	-1.00
40/1+	0%	0	159	0.0%	-1.00

ANALYSIS BY STARTING PRICE LAST TIME

Age	Prop	Win	Runs	Wins%	£
Odds On	10%	5	9	55.6%	-0.13
Ev-2/1	10%	5	17	29.4%	0.29
9/4-4/1	19%	10	34	29.4%	-0.22
9/2-6/1	13%	7	35	20.0%	-0.07
13/2-10/1	19%	10	49	20.4%	-0.08
11/1-16/1	10%	5	48	10.4%	-0.50
18/1-33/1	2%	1	58	1.7%	-0.71
40/1+	0%	0	71	0.0%	-1.00
Unraced	17%	9	159	5.7%	-0.66

ANALYSIS BY DISTANCE BEATEN LAST TIME

Age	Prop	Win	Runs	Wins%	£
..-10 lgh	12%	6	12	50.0%	-0.20
-10..0	8%	4	12	33.3%	-0.32
0.1..2	13%	7	19	36.8%	1.98
2.1..5	6%	3	14	21.4%	-0.57
5.1..10	10%	5	23	21.7%	-0.30
10.1..20	10%	5	28	17.9%	-0.26
20.0..30	4%	2	28	7.1%	-0.77
30.1+	4%	2	72	2.8%	-0.92
Not Compl	17%	9	113	8.0%	-0.60
Unraced	17%	9	159	5.7%	-0.66

ANALYSIS BY SUCCESS RATE IN LAST 10 RUNS

Age	Prop	Win	Runs	Wins%	£
No Wins	23%	10	176	5.7%	-0.65
1 Win	26%	11	74	14.9%	-0.25
2 Wins	21%	9	39	23.1%	-0.16
3 Wins	21%	9	24	37.5%	-0.29
4 Wins	5%	2	6	33.3%	-0.23
5+ Wins	5%	2	2	100.0%	0.42

ANALYSIS BY SUCCESS RATE IN LAST 3 RUNS

Age	Prop	Win	Runs	Wins%	£
No Wins	56%	24	255	9.4%	-0.53
1 Win	33%	14	55	25.5%	-0.16
2 Wins	12%	5	11	45.5%	-0.20
3 Wins	0%	0	0	0.0%	0.00

ANALYSIS BY POSITION LAST TIME

Age	Prop	Win	Runs	Wins%	£
Won	19%	10	24	41.7%	-0.26
2nd or 3rd	38%	20	80	25.0%	0.16
Unplaced	8%	4	104	3.8%	-0.82
Fell,BD,UR	8%	4	51	7.8%	-0.77
Pulled Up	10%	5	61	8.2%	-0.45
Ref/RanOut	0%	0	1	0.0%	-1.00
CO/SlipUp	0%	0	0	0.0%	0.00
Unraced	17%	9	159	5.7%	-0.66

OTHER FACTORS (WINS-RUNS, £)

Course Winner:	9-34	-£0.26
Distance Winner:	16-65	-£0.35
Going Winner:	20-87	-£0.42
Beaten Favourite:	5-19	£0.33
7-Day Winners:	10-24	-£0.26
BHA Top Rated:	11-42	-£0.10
Absolute Favourites:	29-47	£0.22

Race Profiles

Novices' Chases (class 4..6): 100+ days off the track

ANALYSIS BY AGE

Age	Prop	Win	Runs	Wins%	£
3yo	0%	0	0	0.0%	0.00
4yo	5%	10	30	33.3%	0.09
5yo	17%	34	205	16.6%	-0.32
6yo	30%	61	369	16.5%	-0.24
7yo	27%	55	395	13.9%	-0.40
8yo	15%	30	256	11.7%	-0.40
9yo	4%	9	122	7.4%	-0.69
10yo	2%	4	60	6.7%	-0.30
11yo	0%	1	17	5.9%	-0.41
12yo+	0%	0	11	0.0%	-1.00

ANALYSIS BY BHB RATING

Age	Prop	Win	Runs	Wins%	£
150+	0%	0	0	0.0%	0.00
130..149	1%	2	7	28.6%	-0.41
120..129	3%	7	29	24.1%	-0.09
110..119	8%	17	119	14.3%	-0.12
100..109	8%	17	106	16.0%	-0.27
80..99	1%	3	91	3.3%	-0.60
60..79	0%	1	55	1.8%	-0.47
..59	0%	0	12	0.0%	-1.00
Unrated	77%	157	1046	15.0%	-0.37

ANALYSIS BY WEIGHT CARRIED

Age	Prop	Win	Runs	Wins%	£
12-01+	0%	0	0	0.0%	0.00
11-8..12-00	0%	1	8	12.5%	-0.63
11-0..11-07	76%	156	934	16.7%	-0.26
10-8..10-13	14%	29	354	8.2%	-0.52
10-0..10-07	8%	17	161	10.6%	-0.57
..9-13	0%	1	8	12.5%	-0.76

ANALYSIS BY DAYS SINCE LAST RUN

Age	Prop	Win	Runs	Wins%	£
1..7	0%	0	0	0.0%	0.00
8..14	0%	0	0	0.0%	0.00
15..28	0%	0	0	0.0%	0.00
29..60	0%	0	0	0.0%	0.00
61..100	0%	1	8	12.5%	0.00
101+	100%	203	1457	13.9%	-0.37
Unraced	0%	0	0	0.0%	0.00

ANALYSIS BY TODAY'S STARTING PRICE

Age	Prop	Win	Runs	Wins%	£
Odds On	20%	40	59	67.8%	0.08
Ev-2/1	27%	55	137	40.1%	-0.01
9/4-4/1	31%	64	243	26.3%	0.05
9/2-6/1	8%	17	117	14.5%	-0.09
13/2-10/1	7%	15	186	8.1%	-0.30
11/1-16/1	4%	8	153	5.2%	-0.23
18/1-33/1	2%	5	237	2.1%	-0.49
40/1+	0%	0	333	0.0%	-1.00

ANALYSIS BY STARTING PRICE LAST TIME

Age	Prop	Win	Runs	Wins%	£
Odds On	5%	11	42	26.2%	-0.39
Ev-2/1	15%	31	93	33.3%	0.33
9/4-4/1	16%	33	204	16.2%	-0.19
9/2-6/1	13%	26	145	17.9%	-0.44
13/2-10/1	18%	37	233	15.9%	-0.25
11/1-16/1	14%	29	256	11.3%	-0.38
18/1-33/1	14%	28	240	11.7%	-0.40
40/1+	4%	9	252	3.6%	-0.76
Unraced	0%	0	0	0.0%	0.00

ANALYSIS BY DISTANCE BEATEN LAST TIME

Age	Prop	Win	Runs	Wins%	£
..-10 lgh	3%	7	19	36.8%	0.34
-10..0	16%	32	105	30.5%	-0.04
0.1..2	4%	8	39	20.5%	0.02
2.1..5	6%	13	68	19.1%	0.00
5.1..10	8%	16	101	15.8%	-0.50
10.1..20	18%	36	185	19.5%	-0.10
20.0..30	8%	16	154	10.4%	-0.54
30.1+	21%	43	419	10.3%	-0.39
Not Compl	16%	33	375	8.8%	-0.59
Unraced	0%	0	0	0.0%	0.00

ANALYSIS BY SUCCESS RATE IN LAST 10 RUNS

Age	Prop	Win	Runs	Wins%	£
No Wins	13%	26	587	4.4%	-0.58
1 Win	25%	50	364	13.7%	-0.29
2 Wins	31%	63	318	19.8%	-0.22
3 Wins	19%	38	142	26.8%	-0.27
4 Wins	9%	18	40	45.0%	0.27
5+ Wins	4%	9	14	64.3%	0.64

ANALYSIS BY SUCCESS RATE IN LAST 3 RUNS

Age	Prop	Win	Runs	Wins%	£
No Wins	50%	101	1016	9.9%	-0.43
1 Win	36%	74	338	21.9%	-0.19
2 Wins	13%	26	103	25.2%	-0.26
3 Wins	1%	3	8	37.5%	0.07

ANALYSIS BY POSITION LAST TIME

Age	Prop	Win	Runs	Wins%	£
Won	19%	39	124	31.5%	0.02
2nd or 3rd	21%	43	252	17.1%	-0.25
Unplaced	44%	89	721	12.3%	-0.35
Fell,BD,UR	4%	8	69	11.6%	-0.53
Pulled Up	12%	25	297	8.4%	-0.60
Ref/RanOut	0%	0	2	0.0%	-1.00
CO/SlipUp	0%	0	0	0.0%	0.00
Unraced	0%	0	0	0.0%	0.00

OTHER FACTORS (WINS-RUNS, £)

Course Winner:	35-164	-£0.20
Distance Winner:	82-388	-£0.28
Going Winner:	97-428	-£0.10
Beaten Favourite:	23-117	-£0.21
BHA Top Rated:	14-101	-£0.25
Absolute Favourites:	92-195	£0.03

Maiden Chases

ANALYSIS BY AGE

Age	Prop	Win	Runs	Wins%	£
3yo	0%	0	0	0.0%	0.00
4yo	6%	4	11	36.4%	0.17
5yo	10%	7	102	6.9%	-0.80
6yo	35%	24	170	14.1%	-0.29
7yo	30%	21	177	11.9%	-0.26
8yo	13%	9	97	9.3%	-0.59
9yo	3%	2	31	6.5%	0.14
10yo	3%	2	12	16.7%	-0.13
11yo	0%	0	6	0.0%	-1.00
12yo+	0%	0	1	0.0%	-1.00

ANALYSIS BY BHB RATING

Age	Prop	Win	Runs	Wins%	£
150+	0%	0	0	0.0%	0.00
130..149	0%	0	0	0.0%	0.00
120..129	3%	2	5	40.0%	-0.19
110..119	17%	12	28	42.9%	0.63
100..109	13%	9	49	18.4%	-0.08
80..99	25%	17	105	16.2%	-0.14
60..79	3%	2	81	2.5%	-0.44
..59	0%	0	10	0.0%	-1.00
Unrated	39%	27	329	8.2%	-0.57

ANALYSIS BY WEIGHT CARRIED

Age	Prop	Win	Runs	Wins%	£
12-01+	0%	0	0	0.0%	0.00
11-8..12-00	0%	0	0	0.0%	0.00
11-0..11-07	65%	45	358	12.6%	-0.37
10-8..10-13	23%	16	141	11.3%	-0.18
10-0..10-07	12%	8	105	7.6%	-0.72
..9-13	0%	0	3	0.0%	-1.00

ANALYSIS BY DAYS SINCE LAST RUN

Age	Prop	Win	Runs	Wins%	£
1..7	6%	4	23	17.4%	0.31
8..14	19%	13	96	13.5%	0.04
15..28	26%	18	156	11.5%	-0.57
29..60	28%	19	143	13.3%	-0.35
61..100	6%	4	41	9.8%	-0.76
101+	13%	9	119	7.6%	-0.52
Unraced	3%	2	29	6.9%	-0.55

ANALYSIS BY TODAY'S STARTING PRICE

Age	Prop	Win	Runs	Wins%	£
Odds On	16%	11	17	64.7%	0.02
Ev-2/1	20%	14	44	31.8%	-0.21
9/4-4/1	32%	22	88	25.0%	-0.05
9/2-6/1	10%	7	49	14.3%	-0.10
13/2-10/1	13%	9	83	10.8%	0.00
11/1-16/1	7%	5	75	6.7%	-0.03
18/1-33/1	1%	1	110	0.9%	-0.69
40/1+	0%	0	141	0.0%	-1.00

ANALYSIS BY STARTING PRICE LAST TIME

Age	Prop	Win	Runs	Wins%	£
Odds On	0%	0	0	0.0%	0.00
Ev-2/1	9%	6	14	42.9%	0.83
9/4-4/1	16%	11	62	17.7%	-0.38
9/2-6/1	13%	9	48	18.8%	-0.45
13/2-10/1	22%	15	78	19.2%	0.02
11/1-16/1	16%	11	95	11.6%	-0.30
18/1-33/1	14%	10	124	8.1%	-0.29
40/1+	7%	5	157	3.2%	-0.80
Unraced	3%	2	29	6.9%	-0.55

ANALYSIS BY DISTANCE BEATEN LAST TIME

Age	Prop	Win	Runs	Wins%	£
..-10 lgh	0%	0	0	0.0%	0.00
-10..0	0%	0	0	0.0%	0.00
0.1..2	1%	1	17	5.9%	-0.79
2.1..5	25%	17	34	50.0%	0.62
5.1..10	12%	8	33	24.2%	-0.43
10.1..20	13%	9	64	14.1%	-0.43
20.0..30	14%	10	62	16.1%	-0.02
30.1+	17%	12	194	6.2%	-0.55
Not Compl	14%	10	174	5.7%	-0.46
Unraced	3%	2	29	6.9%	-0.55

ANALYSIS BY SUCCESS RATE IN LAST 10 RUNS

Age	Prop	Win	Runs	Wins%	£
No Wins	93%	62	550	11.3%	-0.41
1 Win	7%	5	25	20.0%	0.38
2 Wins	0%	0	3	0.0%	-1.00
3 Wins	0%	0	0	0.0%	0.00
4 Wins	0%	0	0	0.0%	0.00
5+ Wins	0%	0	0	0.0%	0.00

ANALYSIS BY SUCCESS RATE IN LAST 3 RUNS

Age	Prop	Win	Runs	Wins%	£
No Wins	99%	66	573	11.5%	-0.40
1 Win	1%	1	5	20.0%	2.00
2 Wins	0%	0	0	0.0%	0.00
3 Wins	0%	0	0	0.0%	0.00

ANALYSIS BY POSITION LAST TIME

Age	Prop	Win	Runs	Wins%	£
Won	0%	0	0	0.0%	0.00
2nd or 3rd	48%	33	125	26.4%	0.03
Unplaced	35%	24	279	8.6%	-0.52
Fell,BD,UR	4%	3	52	5.8%	-0.76
Pulled Up	10%	7	119	5.9%	-0.31
Ref/RanOut	0%	0	0	0.0%	0.00
CO/SlipUp	0%	0	3	0.0%	-1.00
Unraced	3%	2	29	6.9%	-0.55

OTHER FACTORS (WINS-RUNS, £)

Course Winner:	0-1	-£1.00
Distance Winner:	2-5	-£0.38
Going Winner:	1-7	-£0.76
Beaten Favourite:	6-22	£0.14
BHA Top Rated:	17-58	-£0.08
Absolute Favourites:	24-60	-£0.13

Race Profiles

Maiden Chases: 2m to 2m3f

ANALYSIS BY AGE

Age	Prop	Win	Runs	Wins%	£
3yo	0%	0	0	0.0%	0.00
4yo	13%	3	7	42.9%	0.58
5yo	9%	2	47	4.3%	-0.90
6yo	35%	8	54	14.8%	-0.36
7yo	22%	5	50	10.0%	-0.66
8yo	9%	2	25	8.0%	-0.82
9yo	4%	1	11	9.1%	-0.87
10yo	9%	2	2	100.0%	4.25
11yo	0%	0	0	0.0%	0.00
12yo+	0%	0	0	0.0%	0.00

ANALYSIS BY BHB RATING

Age	Prop	Win	Runs	Wins%	£
150+	0%	0	0	0.0%	0.00
130..149	0%	0	0	0.0%	0.00
120..129	0%	0	1	0.0%	-1.00
110..119	22%	5	11	45.5%	0.33
100..109	22%	5	18	27.8%	-0.26
80..99	26%	6	40	15.0%	-0.24
60..79	0%	0	30	0.0%	-1.00
..59	0%	0	2	0.0%	-1.00
Unrated	30%	7	94	7.4%	-0.73

ANALYSIS BY WEIGHT CARRIED

Age	Prop	Win	Runs	Wins%	£
12-01+	0%	0	0	0.0%	0.00
11-8..12-00	0%	0	0	0.0%	0.00
11-0..11-07	65%	15	114	13.2%	-0.56
10-8..10-13	22%	5	41	12.2%	-0.41
10-0..10-07	13%	3	39	7.7%	-0.77
..9-13	0%	0	2	0.0%	-1.00

ANALYSIS BY DAYS SINCE LAST RUN

Age	Prop	Win	Runs	Wins%	£
1..7	9%	2	10	20.0%	-0.39
8..14	17%	4	31	12.9%	-0.63
15..28	26%	6	48	12.5%	-0.53
29..60	39%	9	48	18.8%	-0.16
61..100	9%	2	17	11.8%	-0.80
101+	0%	0	35	0.0%	-1.00
Unraced	0%	0	7	0.0%	-1.00

ANALYSIS BY TODAY'S STARTING PRICE

Age	Prop	Win	Runs	Wins%	£
Odds On	26%	6	7	85.7%	0.36
Ev-2/1	13%	3	14	21.4%	-0.48
9/4-4/1	39%	9	28	32.1%	0.20
9/2-6/1	17%	4	15	26.7%	0.63
13/2-10/1	4%	1	24	4.2%	-0.63
11/1-16/1	0%	0	22	0.0%	-1.00
18/1-33/1	0%	0	36	0.0%	-1.00
40/1+	0%	0	50	0.0%	-1.00

ANALYSIS BY STARTING PRICE LAST TIME

Age	Prop	Win	Runs	Wins%	£
Odds On	0%	0	0	0.0%	0.00
Ev-2/1	9%	2	7	28.6%	-0.26
9/4-4/1	17%	4	18	22.2%	-0.23
9/2-6/1	30%	7	16	43.8%	0.27
13/2-10/1	9%	2	26	7.7%	-0.42
11/1-16/1	4%	1	30	3.3%	-0.78
18/1-33/1	22%	5	40	12.5%	-0.59
40/1+	9%	2	52	3.8%	-0.88
Unraced	0%	0	7	0.0%	-1.00

ANALYSIS BY DISTANCE BEATEN LAST TIME

Age	Prop	Win	Runs	Wins%	£
..-10 lgh	0%	0	0	0.0%	0.00
-10..0	0%	0	0	0.0%	0.00
0.1..2	0%	0	6	0.0%	-1.00
2.1..5	26%	6	12	50.0%	0.83
5.1..10	22%	5	14	35.7%	-0.34
10.1..20	13%	3	24	12.5%	-0.65
20.0..30	30%	7	25	28.0%	0.17
30.1+	0%	0	54	0.0%	-1.00
Not Compl	9%	2	54	3.7%	-0.72
Unraced	0%	0	7	0.0%	-1.00

ANALYSIS BY SUCCESS RATE IN LAST 10 RUNS

Age	Prop	Win	Runs	Wins%	£
No Wins	96%	22	185	11.9%	-0.56
1 Win	4%	1	2	50.0%	-0.17
2 Wins	0%	0	2	0.0%	-1.00
3 Wins	0%	0	0	0.0%	0.00
4 Wins	0%	0	0	0.0%	0.00
5+ Wins	0%	0	0	0.0%	0.00

ANALYSIS BY SUCCESS RATE IN LAST 3 RUNS

Age	Prop	Win	Runs	Wins%	£
No Wins	100%	23	189	12.2%	-0.56
1 Win	0%	0	0	0.0%	0.00
2 Wins	0%	0	0	0.0%	0.00
3 Wins	0%	0	0	0.0%	0.00

ANALYSIS BY POSITION LAST TIME

Age	Prop	Win	Runs	Wins%	£
Won	0%	0	0	0.0%	0.00
2nd or 3rd	48%	11	39	28.2%	-0.22
Unplaced	43%	10	96	10.4%	-0.60
Fell,BD,UR	4%	1	20	5.0%	-0.70
Pulled Up	4%	1	33	3.0%	-0.73
Ref/RanOut	0%	0	0	0.0%	0.00
CO/SlipUp	0%	0	1	0.0%	-1.00
Unraced	0%	0	7	0.0%	-1.00

OTHER FACTORS (WINS-RUNS, £)

Distance Winner:	2-5	-£0.38
Going Winner:	1-3	-£0.44
Beaten Favourite:	2-9	-£0.50
BHA Top Rated:	7-20	-£0.17
Absolute Favourites:	9-20	-£0.13

Maiden Chases

Maiden Chases: 2m4f to 2m7f

ANALYSIS BY AGE

Age	Prop	Win	Runs	Wins%	£
3yo	0%	0	0	0.0%	0.00
4yo	4%	1	4	25.0%	-0.54
5yo	9%	2	27	7.4%	-0.68
6yo	35%	8	58	13.8%	-0.24
7yo	30%	7	54	13.0%	-0.25
8yo	17%	4	38	10.5%	-0.58
9yo	4%	1	10	10.0%	2.40
10yo	0%	0	4	0.0%	-1.00
11yo	0%	0	5	0.0%	-1.00
12yo+	0%	0	0	0.0%	0.00

ANALYSIS BY BHB RATING

Age	Prop	Win	Runs	Wins%	£
150+	0%	0	0	0.0%	0.00
130..149	0%	0	0	0.0%	0.00
120..129	4%	1	1	100.0%	0.57
110..119	9%	2	9	22.2%	-0.15
100..109	13%	3	14	21.4%	0.19
80..99	17%	4	31	12.9%	-0.25
60..79	9%	2	22	9.1%	1.05
..59	0%	0	5	0.0%	-1.00
Unrated	48%	11	118	9.3%	-0.56

ANALYSIS BY WEIGHT CARRIED

Age	Prop	Win	Runs	Wins%	£
12-01+	0%	0	0	0.0%	0.00
11-8..12-00	0%	0	0	0.0%	0.00
11-0..11-07	61%	14	116	12.1%	-0.36
10-8..10-13	26%	6	46	13.0%	0.37
10-0..10-07	13%	3	37	8.1%	-0.77
..9-13	0%	0	1	0.0%	-1.00

ANALYSIS BY DAYS SINCE LAST RUN

Age	Prop	Win	Runs	Wins%	£
1..7	4%	1	9	11.1%	0.22
8..14	17%	4	30	13.3%	0.99
15..28	30%	7	50	14.0%	-0.42
29..60	17%	4	38	10.5%	-0.68
61..100	4%	1	11	9.1%	-0.81
101+	22%	5	50	10.0%	-0.46
Unraced	4%	1	12	8.3%	-0.58

ANALYSIS BY TODAY'S STARTING PRICE

Age	Prop	Win	Runs	Wins%	£
Odds On	13%	3	4	75.0%	0.26
Ev-2/1	22%	5	19	26.3%	-0.32
9/4-4/1	30%	7	30	23.3%	-0.04
9/2-6/1	9%	2	14	14.3%	-0.07
13/2-10/1	17%	4	27	14.8%	0.44
11/1-16/1	4%	1	28	3.6%	-0.54
18/1-33/1	4%	1	37	2.7%	-0.08
40/1+	0%	0	41	0.0%	-1.00

ANALYSIS BY STARTING PRICE LAST TIME

Age	Prop	Win	Runs	Wins%	£
Odds On	0%	0	0	0.0%	0.00
Ev-2/1	4%	1	3	33.3%	-0.39
9/4-4/1	17%	4	18	22.2%	-0.14
9/2-6/1	4%	1	13	7.7%	-0.79
13/2-10/1	17%	4	29	13.8%	-0.65
11/1-16/1	22%	5	30	16.7%	-0.15
18/1-33/1	17%	4	45	8.9%	0.33
40/1+	13%	3	50	6.0%	-0.49
Unraced	4%	1	12	8.3%	-0.58

ANALYSIS BY DISTANCE BEATEN LAST TIME

Age	Prop	Win	Runs	Wins%	£
..-10 lgh	0%	0	0	0.0%	0.00
-10..0	0%	0	0	0.0%	0.00
0.1..2	0%	0	5	0.0%	-1.00
2.1..5	17%	4	10	40.0%	-0.12
5.1..10	9%	2	9	22.2%	-0.11
10.1..20	13%	3	20	15.0%	0.00
20.0..30	9%	2	22	9.1%	-0.24
30.1+	26%	6	59	10.2%	-0.44
Not Compl	22%	5	63	7.9%	-0.14
Unraced	4%	1	12	8.3%	-0.58

ANALYSIS BY SUCCESS RATE IN LAST 10 RUNS

Age	Prop	Win	Runs	Wins%	£
No Wins	91%	20	179	11.2%	-0.24
1 Win	9%	2	8	25.0%	-0.41
2 Wins	0%	0	1	0.0%	-1.00
3 Wins	0%	0	0	0.0%	0.00
4 Wins	0%	0	0	0.0%	0.00
5+ Wins	0%	0	0	0.0%	0.00

ANALYSIS BY SUCCESS RATE IN LAST 3 RUNS

Age	Prop	Win	Runs	Wins%	£
No Wins	100%	22	184	12.0%	-0.24
1 Win	0%	0	4	0.0%	-1.00
2 Wins	0%	0	0	0.0%	0.00
3 Wins	0%	0	0	0.0%	0.00

ANALYSIS BY POSITION LAST TIME

Age	Prop	Win	Runs	Wins%	£
Won	0%	0	0	0.0%	0.00
2nd or 3rd	35%	8	33	24.2%	-0.13
Unplaced	39%	9	92	9.8%	-0.37
Fell,BD,UR	9%	2	19	10.5%	-0.65
Pulled Up	13%	3	42	7.1%	0.13
Ref/RanOut	0%	0	0	0.0%	0.00
CO/SlipUp	0%	0	2	0.0%	-1.00
Unraced	4%	1	12	8.3%	-0.58

OTHER FACTORS (WINS-RUNS, £)

Course Winner:	0-1	-£1.00
Going Winner:	0-1	-£1.00
Beaten Favourite:	1-5	-£0.63
BHA Top Rated:	4-19	-£0.48
Absolute Favourites:	8-19	£0.01

Race Profiles

Maiden Chases: 3m+

ANALYSIS BY AGE

Age	Prop	Win	Runs	Wins%	£
3yo	0%	0	0	0.0%	0.00
4yo	0%	0	0	0.0%	0.00
5yo	13%	3	28	10.7%	-0.75
6yo	35%	8	58	13.8%	-0.30
7yo	39%	9	73	12.3%	0.01
8yo	13%	3	34	8.8%	-0.44
9yo	0%	0	10	0.0%	-1.00
10yo	0%	0	6	0.0%	-1.00
11yo	0%	0	1	0.0%	-1.00
12yo+	0%	0	1	0.0%	-1.00

ANALYSIS BY BHB RATING

Age	Prop	Win	Runs	Wins%	£
150+	0%	0	0	0.0%	0.00
130..149	0%	0	0	0.0%	0.00
120..129	4%	1	3	33.3%	-0.17
110..119	22%	5	8	62.5%	1.91
100..109	4%	1	17	5.9%	-0.12
80..99	30%	7	34	20.6%	0.08
60..79	0%	0	29	0.0%	-1.00
..59	0%	0	3	0.0%	-1.00
Unrated	39%	9	117	7.7%	-0.47

ANALYSIS BY WEIGHT CARRIED

Age	Prop	Win	Runs	Wins%	£
12-01+	0%	0	0	0.0%	0.00
11-8..12-00	0%	0	0	0.0%	0.00
11-0..11-07	70%	16	128	12.5%	-0.22
10-8..10-13	22%	5	54	9.3%	-0.47
10-0..10-07	9%	2	29	6.9%	-0.59
..9-13	0%	0	0	0.0%	0.00

ANALYSIS BY DAYS SINCE LAST RUN

Age	Prop	Win	Runs	Wins%	£
1..7	4%	1	4	25.0%	2.25
8..14	22%	5	35	14.3%	-0.18
15..28	22%	5	58	8.6%	-0.73
29..60	26%	6	57	10.5%	-0.29
61..100	4%	1	13	7.7%	-0.67
101+	17%	4	34	11.8%	-0.12
Unraced	4%	1	10	10.0%	-0.20

ANALYSIS BY TODAY'S STARTING PRICE

Age	Prop	Win	Runs	Wins%	£
Odds On	9%	2	6	33.3%	-0.53
Ev-2/1	26%	6	11	54.5%	0.33
9/4-4/1	26%	6	30	20.0%	-0.29
9/2-6/1	4%	1	20	5.0%	-0.68
13/2-10/1	17%	4	32	12.5%	0.09
11/1-16/1	17%	4	25	16.0%	1.40
18/1-33/1	0%	0	37	0.0%	-1.00
40/1+	0%	0	50	0.0%	-1.00

ANALYSIS BY STARTING PRICE LAST TIME

Age	Prop	Win	Runs	Wins%	£
Odds On	0%	0	0	0.0%	0.00
Ev-2/1	13%	3	4	75.0%	3.66
9/4-4/1	13%	3	26	11.5%	-0.63
9/2-6/1	4%	1	19	5.3%	-0.83
13/2-10/1	39%	9	23	39.1%	1.38
11/1-16/1	22%	5	35	14.3%	0.00
18/1-33/1	4%	1	39	2.6%	-0.72
40/1+	0%	0	55	0.0%	-1.00
Unraced	4%	1	10	10.0%	-0.20

ANALYSIS BY DISTANCE BEATEN LAST TIME

Age	Prop	Win	Runs	Wins%	£
..-10 lgh	0%	0	0	0.0%	0.00
-10..0	0%	0	0	0.0%	0.00
0.1..2	4%	1	6	16.7%	-0.42
2.1..5	30%	7	12	58.3%	1.03
5.1..10	4%	1	10	10.0%	-0.86
10.1..20	13%	3	20	15.0%	-0.58
20.0..30	4%	1	15	6.7%	0.00
30.1+	26%	6	81	7.4%	-0.33
Not Compl	13%	3	57	5.3%	-0.56
Unraced	4%	1	10	10.0%	-0.20

ANALYSIS BY SUCCESS RATE IN LAST 10 RUNS

Age	Prop	Win	Runs	Wins%	£
No Wins	91%	20	186	10.8%	-0.44
1 Win	9%	2	15	13.3%	0.87
2 Wins	0%	0	0	0.0%	0.00
3 Wins	0%	0	0	0.0%	0.00
4 Wins	0%	0	0	0.0%	0.00
5+ Wins	0%	0	0	0.0%	0.00

ANALYSIS BY SUCCESS RATE IN LAST 3 RUNS

Age	Prop	Win	Runs	Wins%	£
No Wins	95%	21	200	10.5%	-0.41
1 Win	5%	1	1	100.0%	14.00
2 Wins	0%	0	0	0.0%	0.00
3 Wins	0%	0	0	0.0%	0.00

ANALYSIS BY POSITION LAST TIME

Age	Prop	Win	Runs	Wins%	£
Won	0%	0	0	0.0%	0.00
2nd or 3rd	61%	14	53	26.4%	0.32
Unplaced	22%	5	91	5.5%	-0.59
Fell,BD,UR	0%	0	13	0.0%	-1.00
Pulled Up	13%	3	44	6.8%	-0.43
Ref/RanOut	0%	0	0	0.0%	0.00
CO/SlipUp	0%	0	0	0.0%	0.00
Unraced	4%	1	10	10.0%	-0.20

OTHER FACTORS (WINS-RUNS, £)

Going Winner:	0-3	-£1.00
Beaten Favourite:	3-8	£1.33
BHA Top Rated:	6-19	£0.41
Absolute Favourites:	7-21	-£0.25

Maiden Chases

Maiden Chases: 2 to 5 runners

ANALYSIS BY AGE

Age	Prop	Win	Runs	Wins%	£
3yo	0%	0	0	0.0%	0.00
4yo	0%	0	1	0.0%	-1.00
5yo	40%	2	7	28.6%	-0.28
6yo	20%	1	4	25.0%	-0.68
7yo	20%	1	4	25.0%	-0.06
8yo	0%	0	4	0.0%	-1.00
9yo	20%	1	4	25.0%	-0.64
10yo	0%	0	0	0.0%	0.00
11yo	0%	0	0	0.0%	0.00
12yo+	0%	0	0	0.0%	0.00

ANALYSIS BY BHB RATING

Age	Prop	Win	Runs	Wins%	£
150+	0%	0	0	0.0%	0.00
130..149	0%	0	0	0.0%	0.00
120..129	0%	0	0	0.0%	0.00
110..119	0%	0	1	0.0%	-1.00
100..109	40%	2	3	66.7%	-0.09
80..99	40%	2	6	33.3%	0.25
60..79	0%	0	3	0.0%	-1.00
..59	0%	0	1	0.0%	-1.00
Unrated	20%	1	10	10.0%	-0.87

ANALYSIS BY WEIGHT CARRIED

Age	Prop	Win	Runs	Wins%	£
12-01+	0%	0	0	0.0%	0.00
11-8..12-00	0%	0	0	0.0%	0.00
11-0..11-07	60%	3	12	25.0%	-0.46
10-8..10-13	20%	1	6	16.7%	-0.38
10-0..10-07	20%	1	4	25.0%	-0.68
..9-13	0%	0	2	0.0%	-1.00

ANALYSIS BY DAYS SINCE LAST RUN

Age	Prop	Win	Runs	Wins%	£
1..7	0%	0	1	0.0%	-1.00
8..14	60%	3	6	50.0%	0.47
15..28	0%	0	5	0.0%	-1.00
29..60	20%	1	4	25.0%	-0.68
61..100	20%	1	3	33.3%	-0.52
101+	0%	0	4	0.0%	-1.00
Unraced	0%	0	1	0.0%	-1.00

ANALYSIS BY TODAY'S STARTING PRICE

Age	Prop	Win	Runs	Wins%	£
Odds On	60%	3	4	75.0%	0.01
Ev-2/1	0%	0	0	0.0%	0.00
9/4-4/1	40%	2	8	25.0%	-0.06
9/2-6/1	0%	0	1	0.0%	-1.00
13/2-10/1	0%	0	2	0.0%	-1.00
11/1-16/1	0%	0	2	0.0%	-1.00
18/1-33/1	0%	0	4	0.0%	-1.00
40/1+	0%	0	3	0.0%	-1.00

ANALYSIS BY STARTING PRICE LAST TIME

Age	Prop	Win	Runs	Wins%	£
Odds On	0%	0	0	0.0%	0.00
Ev-2/1	0%	0	0	0.0%	0.00
9/4-4/1	20%	1	4	25.0%	-0.06
9/2-6/1	40%	2	3	66.7%	-0.14
13/2-10/1	20%	1	2	50.0%	0.88
11/1-16/1	0%	0	4	0.0%	-1.00
18/1-33/1	20%	1	6	16.7%	-0.76
40/1+	0%	0	4	0.0%	-1.00
Unraced	0%	0	1	0.0%	-1.00

ANALYSIS BY DISTANCE BEATEN LAST TIME

Age	Prop	Win	Runs	Wins%	£
..-10 lgh	0%	0	0	0.0%	0.00
-10..0	0%	0	0	0.0%	0.00
0.1..2	0%	0	1	0.0%	-1.00
2.1..5	40%	2	2	100.0%	1.52
5.1..10	40%	2	2	100.0%	0.36
10.1..20	0%	0	3	0.0%	-1.00
20.0..30	0%	0	4	0.0%	-1.00
30.1+	0%	0	7	0.0%	-1.00
Not Compl	20%	1	4	25.0%	-0.06
Unraced	0%	0	1	0.0%	-1.00

ANALYSIS BY SUCCESS RATE IN LAST 10 RUNS

Age	Prop	Win	Runs	Wins%	£
No Wins	100%	5	23	21.7%	-0.50
1 Win	0%	0	0	0.0%	0.00
2 Wins	0%	0	0	0.0%	0.00
3 Wins	0%	0	0	0.0%	0.00
4 Wins	0%	0	0	0.0%	0.00
5+ Wins	0%	0	0	0.0%	0.00

ANALYSIS BY SUCCESS RATE IN LAST 3 RUNS

Age	Prop	Win	Runs	Wins%	£
No Wins	100%	5	23	21.7%	-0.50
1 Win	0%	0	0	0.0%	0.00
2 Wins	0%	0	0	0.0%	0.00
3 Wins	0%	0	0	0.0%	0.00

ANALYSIS BY POSITION LAST TIME

Age	Prop	Win	Runs	Wins%	£
Won	0%	0	0	0.0%	0.00
2nd or 3rd	60%	3	8	37.5%	-0.19
Unplaced	20%	1	11	9.1%	-0.88
Fell,BD,UR	20%	1	2	50.0%	0.88
Pulled Up	0%	0	1	0.0%	-1.00
Ref/RanOut	0%	0	0	0.0%	0.00
CO/SlipUp	0%	0	1	0.0%	-1.00
Unraced	0%	0	1	0.0%	-1.00

OTHER FACTORS (WINS-RUNS, £)

Distance Winner:	1-1	£0.44
BHA Top Rated:	2-4	-£0.32
Absolute Favourites:	3-4	£0.01

Race Profiles

Maiden Chases: 6 to 10 runners

ANALYSIS BY AGE

Age	Prop	Win	Runs	Wins%	£
3yo	0%	0	0	0.0%	0.00
4yo	8%	4	9	44.4%	0.43
5yo	10%	5	66	7.6%	-0.77
6yo	27%	13	106	12.3%	-0.44
7yo	33%	16	117	13.7%	-0.08
8yo	16%	8	67	11.9%	-0.63
9yo	2%	1	19	5.3%	0.79
10yo	4%	2	10	20.0%	0.05
11yo	0%	0	4	0.0%	-1.00
12yo+	0%	0	0	0.0%	0.00

ANALYSIS BY BHB RATING

Age	Prop	Win	Runs	Wins%	£
150+	0%	0	0	0.0%	0.00
130..149	0%	0	0	0.0%	0.00
120..129	4%	2	5	40.0%	-0.19
110..119	18%	9	22	40.9%	0.67
100..109	12%	6	31	19.4%	0.25
80..99	24%	12	65	18.5%	-0.21
60..79	4%	2	51	3.9%	-0.12
..59	0%	0	7	0.0%	-1.00
Unrated	37%	18	217	8.3%	-0.59

ANALYSIS BY WEIGHT CARRIED

Age	Prop	Win	Runs	Wins%	£
12-01+	0%	0	0	0.0%	0.00
11-8..12-00	0%	0	0	0.0%	0.00
11-0..11-07	59%	29	227	12.8%	-0.40
10-8..10-13	29%	14	95	14.7%	0.10
10-0..10-07	12%	6	75	8.0%	-0.67
..9-13	0%	0	1	0.0%	-1.00

ANALYSIS BY DAYS SINCE LAST RUN

Age	Prop	Win	Runs	Wins%	£
1..7	8%	4	15	26.7%	1.01
8..14	10%	5	56	8.9%	-0.05
15..28	29%	14	98	14.3%	-0.48
29..60	35%	17	98	17.3%	-0.08
61..100	4%	2	31	6.5%	-0.87
101+	12%	6	82	7.3%	-0.61
Unraced	2%	1	18	5.6%	-0.72

ANALYSIS BY TODAY'S STARTING PRICE

Age	Prop	Win	Runs	Wins%	£
Odds On	16%	8	13	61.5%	0.03
Ev-2/1	24%	12	39	30.8%	-0.23
9/4-4/1	29%	14	54	25.9%	0.01
9/2-6/1	10%	5	35	14.3%	-0.10
13/2-10/1	12%	6	51	11.8%	0.11
11/1-16/1	6%	3	54	5.6%	-0.17
18/1-33/1	2%	1	70	1.4%	-0.51
40/1+	0%	0	82	0.0%	-1.00

ANALYSIS BY STARTING PRICE LAST TIME

Age	Prop	Win	Runs	Wins%	£
Odds On	0%	0	0	0.0%	0.00
Ev-2/1	10%	5	12	41.7%	-0.11
9/4-4/1	14%	7	43	16.3%	-0.57
9/2-6/1	10%	5	25	20.0%	-0.31
13/2-10/1	24%	12	51	23.5%	0.35
11/1-16/1	20%	10	68	14.7%	-0.13
18/1-33/1	14%	7	86	8.1%	-0.17
40/1+	4%	2	95	2.1%	-0.86
Unraced	2%	1	18	5.6%	-0.72

ANALYSIS BY DISTANCE BEATEN LAST TIME

Age	Prop	Win	Runs	Wins%	£
..-10 lgh	0%	0	0	0.0%	0.00
-10..0	0%	0	0	0.0%	0.00
0.1..2	2%	1	13	7.7%	-0.73
2.1..5	29%	14	23	60.9%	1.02
5.1..10	8%	4	18	22.2%	-0.45
10.1..20	12%	6	45	13.3%	-0.48
20.0..30	14%	7	44	15.9%	-0.38
30.1+	18%	9	117	7.7%	-0.34
Not Compl	14%	7	120	5.8%	-0.40
Unraced	2%	1	18	5.6%	-0.72

ANALYSIS BY SUCCESS RATE IN LAST 10 RUNS

Age	Prop	Win	Runs	Wins%	£
No Wins	92%	44	359	12.3%	-0.33
1 Win	8%	4	19	21.1%	0.02
2 Wins	0%	0	2	0.0%	-1.00
3 Wins	0%	0	0	0.0%	0.00
4 Wins	0%	0	0	0.0%	0.00
5+ Wins	0%	0	0	0.0%	0.00

ANALYSIS BY SUCCESS RATE IN LAST 3 RUNS

Age	Prop	Win	Runs	Wins%	£
No Wins	100%	48	379	12.7%	-0.31
1 Win	0%	0	1	0.0%	-1.00
2 Wins	0%	0	0	0.0%	0.00
3 Wins	0%	0	0	0.0%	0.00

ANALYSIS BY POSITION LAST TIME

Age	Prop	Win	Runs	Wins%	£
Won	0%	0	0	0.0%	0.00
2nd or 3rd	55%	27	84	32.1%	0.35
Unplaced	29%	14	176	8.0%	-0.58
Fell,BD,UR	4%	2	40	5.0%	-0.78
Pulled Up	10%	5	79	6.3%	-0.20
Ref/RanOut	0%	0	0	0.0%	0.00
CO/SlipUp	0%	0	1	0.0%	-1.00
Unraced	2%	1	18	5.6%	-0.72

OTHER FACTORS (WINS-RUNS, £)

Course Winner:	0-1	-£1.00
Distance Winner:	1-4	-£0.58
Going Winner:	1-5	-£0.67
Beaten Favourite:	5-16	-£0.37
BHA Top Rated:	12-42	£0.00
Absolute Favourites:	17-43	-£0.15

Maiden Chases

Maiden Chases: 11 runners or more

ANALYSIS BY AGE

Age	Prop	Win	Runs	Wins%	£
3yo	0%	0	0	0.0%	0.00
4yo	0%	0	1	0.0%	-1.00
5yo	0%	0	29	0.0%	-1.00
6yo	67%	10	60	16.7%	-0.02
7yo	27%	4	56	7.1%	-0.65
8yo	7%	1	26	3.8%	-0.42
9yo	0%	0	8	0.0%	-1.00
10yo	0%	0	2	0.0%	-1.00
11yo	0%	0	2	0.0%	-1.00
12yo+	0%	0	1	0.0%	-1.00

ANALYSIS BY BHB RATING

Age	Prop	Win	Runs	Wins%	£
150+	0%	0	0	0.0%	0.00
130..149	0%	0	0	0.0%	0.00
120..129	0%	0	0	0.0%	0.00
110..119	20%	3	5	60.0%	0.75
100..109	7%	1	15	6.7%	-0.78
80..99	20%	3	34	8.8%	-0.07
60..79	0%	0	27	0.0%	-1.00
..59	0%	0	2	0.0%	-1.00
Unrated	53%	8	102	7.8%	-0.51

ANALYSIS BY WEIGHT CARRIED

Age	Prop	Win	Runs	Wins%	£
12-01+	0%	0	0	0.0%	0.00
11-8..12-00	0%	0	0	0.0%	0.00
11-0..11-07	87%	13	119	10.9%	-0.30
10-8..10-13	7%	1	40	2.5%	-0.81
10-0..10-07	7%	1	26	3.8%	-0.88
..9-13	0%	0	0	0.0%	0.00

ANALYSIS BY DAYS SINCE LAST RUN

Age	Prop	Win	Runs	Wins%	£
1..7	0%	0	7	0.0%	-1.00
8..14	33%	5	34	14.7%	0.12
15..28	27%	4	53	7.5%	-0.70
29..60	7%	1	41	2.4%	-0.95
61..100	7%	1	7	14.3%	-0.38
101+	20%	3	33	9.1%	-0.23
Unraced	7%	1	10	10.0%	-0.20

ANALYSIS BY TODAY'S STARTING PRICE

Age	Prop	Win	Runs	Wins%	£
Odds On	0%	0	0	0.0%	0.00
Ev-2/1	13%	2	5	40.0%	0.00
9/4-4/1	40%	6	26	23.1%	-0.17
9/2-6/1	13%	2	13	15.4%	-0.04
13/2-10/1	20%	3	30	10.0%	-0.12
11/1-16/1	13%	2	19	10.5%	0.47
18/1-33/1	0%	0	36	0.0%	-1.00
40/1+	0%	0	56	0.0%	-1.00

ANALYSIS BY STARTING PRICE LAST TIME

Age	Prop	Win	Runs	Wins%	£
Odds On	0%	0	0	0.0%	0.00
Ev-2/1	7%	1	2	50.0%	6.50
9/4-4/1	20%	3	15	20.0%	0.10
9/2-6/1	13%	2	20	10.0%	-0.68
13/2-10/1	13%	2	25	8.0%	-0.71
11/1-16/1	7%	1	23	4.3%	-0.67
18/1-33/1	13%	2	32	6.3%	-0.55
40/1+	20%	3	58	5.2%	-0.69
Unraced	7%	1	10	10.0%	-0.20

ANALYSIS BY DISTANCE BEATEN LAST TIME

Age	Prop	Win	Runs	Wins%	£
..-10 lgh	0%	0	0	0.0%	0.00
-10..0	0%	0	0	0.0%	0.00
0.1..2	0%	0	3	0.0%	-1.00
2.1..5	7%	1	9	11.1%	-0.61
5.1..10	13%	2	13	15.4%	-0.54
10.1..20	20%	3	16	18.8%	-0.17
20.0..30	20%	3	14	21.4%	1.39
30.1+	20%	3	70	4.3%	-0.85
Not Compl	13%	2	50	4.0%	-0.63
Unraced	7%	1	10	10.0%	-0.20

ANALYSIS BY SUCCESS RATE IN LAST 10 RUNS

Age	Prop	Win	Runs	Wins%	£
No Wins	93%	13	168	7.7%	-0.58
1 Win	7%	1	6	16.7%	1.50
2 Wins	0%	0	1	0.0%	-1.00
3 Wins	0%	0	0	0.0%	0.00
4 Wins	0%	0	0	0.0%	0.00
5+ Wins	0%	0	0	0.0%	0.00

ANALYSIS BY SUCCESS RATE IN LAST 3 RUNS

Age	Prop	Win	Runs	Wins%	£
No Wins	93%	13	171	7.6%	-0.59
1 Win	7%	1	4	25.0%	2.75
2 Wins	0%	0	0	0.0%	0.00
3 Wins	0%	0	0	0.0%	0.00

ANALYSIS BY POSITION LAST TIME

Age	Prop	Win	Runs	Wins%	£
Won	0%	0	0	0.0%	0.00
2nd or 3rd	20%	3	33	9.1%	-0.72
Unplaced	60%	9	92	9.8%	-0.37
Fell,BD,UR	0%	0	10	0.0%	-1.00
Pulled Up	13%	2	39	5.1%	-0.53
Ref/RanOut	0%	0	0	0.0%	0.00
CO/SlipUp	0%	0	1	0.0%	-1.00
Unraced	7%	1	10	10.0%	-0.20

OTHER FACTORS (WINS-RUNS, £)

Going Winner:	0-2	-£1.00
Beaten Favourite:	1-6	£1.50
BHA Top Rated:	3-12	-£0.29
Absolute Favourites:	4-13	-£0.12

Race Profiles

Maiden Chases: up to 7 days off the track

ANALYSIS BY AGE

Age	Prop	Win	Runs	Wins%	£
3yo	0%	0	0	0.0%	0.00
4yo	17%	1	2	50.0%	0.75
5yo	17%	1	9	11.1%	-0.44
6yo	17%	1	11	9.1%	-0.27
7yo	50%	3	19	15.8%	0.40
8yo	0%	0	7	0.0%	-1.00
9yo	0%	0	2	0.0%	-1.00
10yo	0%	0	1	0.0%	-1.00
11yo	0%	0	1	0.0%	-1.00
12yo+	0%	0	0	0.0%	0.00

ANALYSIS BY BHB RATING

Age	Prop	Win	Runs	Wins%	£
150+	0%	0	0	0.0%	0.00
130..149	0%	0	0	0.0%	0.00
120..129	0%	0	0	0.0%	0.00
110..119	17%	1	1	100.0%	12.00
100..109	0%	0	5	0.0%	-1.00
80..99	33%	2	6	33.3%	0.02
60..79	17%	1	4	25.0%	1.75
..59	0%	0	0	0.0%	0.00
Unrated	33%	2	36	5.6%	-0.64

ANALYSIS BY WEIGHT CARRIED

Age	Prop	Win	Runs	Wins%	£
12-01+	0%	0	0	0.0%	0.00
11-8..12-00	0%	0	0	0.0%	0.00
11-0..11-07	67%	4	35	11.4%	-0.18
10-8..10-13	17%	1	7	14.3%	0.57
10-0..10-07	17%	1	9	11.1%	-0.61
..9-13	0%	0	1	0.0%	-1.00

ANALYSIS BY DAYS SINCE LAST RUN

Age	Prop	Win	Runs	Wins%	£
1..7	67%	4	23	17.4%	0.31
8..14	0%	0	0	0.0%	0.00
15..28	0%	0	0	0.0%	0.00
29..60	0%	0	0	0.0%	0.00
61..100	0%	0	0	0.0%	0.00
101+	0%	0	0	0.0%	0.00
Unraced	33%	2	29	6.9%	-0.55

ANALYSIS BY TODAY'S STARTING PRICE

Age	Prop	Win	Runs	Wins%	£
Odds On	0%	0	0	0.0%	0.00
Ev-2/1	17%	1	2	50.0%	0.31
9/4-4/1	33%	2	6	33.3%	0.42
9/2-6/1	0%	0	4	0.0%	-1.00
13/2-10/1	33%	2	10	20.0%	0.90
11/1-16/1	17%	1	10	10.0%	0.30
18/1-33/1	0%	0	10	0.0%	-1.00
40/1+	0%	0	10	0.0%	-1.00

ANALYSIS BY STARTING PRICE LAST TIME

Age	Prop	Win	Runs	Wins%	£
Odds On	0%	0	0	0.0%	0.00
Ev-2/1	0%	0	0	0.0%	0.00
9/4-4/1	17%	1	3	33.3%	-0.12
9/2-6/1	17%	1	3	33.3%	0.17
13/2-10/1	17%	1	4	25.0%	2.25
11/1-16/1	0%	0	2	0.0%	-1.00
18/1-33/1	17%	1	5	20.0%	1.20
40/1+	0%	0	6	0.0%	-1.00
Unraced	33%	2	29	6.9%	-0.55

ANALYSIS BY DISTANCE BEATEN LAST TIME

Age	Prop	Win	Runs	Wins%	£
..-10 lgh	0%	0	0	0.0%	0.00
-10..0	0%	0	0	0.0%	0.00
0.1..2	0%	0	0	0.0%	0.00
2.1..5	17%	1	3	33.3%	-0.12
5.1..10	0%	0	0	0.0%	0.00
10.1..20	17%	1	2	50.0%	0.75
20.0..30	0%	0	2	0.0%	-1.00
30.1+	33%	2	7	28.6%	2.43
Not Compl	0%	0	9	0.0%	-1.00
Unraced	33%	2	29	6.9%	-0.55

ANALYSIS BY SUCCESS RATE IN LAST 10 RUNS

Age	Prop	Win	Runs	Wins%	£
No Wins	75%	3	22	13.6%	-0.22
1 Win	25%	1	1	100.0%	12.00
2 Wins	0%	0	0	0.0%	0.00
3 Wins	0%	0	0	0.0%	0.00
4 Wins	0%	0	0	0.0%	0.00
5+ Wins	0%	0	0	0.0%	0.00

ANALYSIS BY SUCCESS RATE IN LAST 3 RUNS

Age	Prop	Win	Runs	Wins%	£
No Wins	100%	4	23	17.4%	0.31
1 Win	0%	0	0	0.0%	0.00
2 Wins	0%	0	0	0.0%	0.00
3 Wins	0%	0	0	0.0%	0.00

ANALYSIS BY POSITION LAST TIME

Age	Prop	Win	Runs	Wins%	£
Won	0%	0	0	0.0%	0.00
2nd or 3rd	17%	1	4	25.0%	-0.34
Unplaced	50%	3	10	30.0%	1.75
Fell,BD,UR	0%	0	6	0.0%	-1.00
Pulled Up	0%	0	3	0.0%	-1.00
Ref/RanOut	0%	0	0	0.0%	0.00
CO/SlipUp	0%	0	0	0.0%	0.00
Unraced	33%	2	29	6.9%	-0.55

OTHER FACTORS (WINS-RUNS, £)

Beaten Favourite:	1-1	£1.63
BHA Top Rated:	1-2	£0.75
Absolute Favourites:	0-1	-£1.00

Maiden Chases

Maiden Chases: 100+ days off the track

ANALYSIS BY AGE

Age	Prop	Win	Runs	Wins%	£
3yo	0%	0	0	0.0%	0.00
4yo	0%	0	0	0.0%	0.00
5yo	10%	1	21	4.8%	-0.85
6yo	30%	3	34	8.8%	-0.60
7yo	30%	3	32	9.4%	-0.41
8yo	30%	3	23	13.0%	0.12
9yo	0%	0	7	0.0%	-1.00
10yo	0%	0	3	0.0%	-1.00
11yo	0%	0	1	0.0%	-1.00
12yo+	0%	0	0	0.0%	0.00

ANALYSIS BY BHB RATING

Age	Prop	Win	Runs	Wins%	£
150+	0%	0	0	0.0%	0.00
130..149	0%	0	0	0.0%	0.00
120..129	0%	0	2	0.0%	-1.00
110..119	10%	1	3	33.3%	0.04
100..109	0%	0	6	0.0%	-1.00
80..99	10%	1	13	7.7%	-0.79
60..79	0%	0	13	0.0%	-1.00
..59	0%	0	2	0.0%	-1.00
Unrated	80%	8	82	9.8%	-0.33

ANALYSIS BY WEIGHT CARRIED

Age	Prop	Win	Runs	Wins%	£
12-01+	0%	0	0	0.0%	0.00
11-8..12-00	0%	0	0	0.0%	0.00
11-0..11-07	80%	8	78	10.3%	-0.36
10-8..10-13	10%	1	28	3.6%	-0.90
10-0..10-07	10%	1	15	6.7%	-0.43
..9-13	0%	0	0	0.0%	0.00

ANALYSIS BY DAYS SINCE LAST RUN

Age	Prop	Win	Runs	Wins%	£
1..7	0%	0	0	0.0%	0.00
8..14	0%	0	0	0.0%	0.00
15..28	0%	0	0	0.0%	0.00
29..60	0%	0	0	0.0%	0.00
61..100	10%	1	2	50.0%	1.17
101+	90%	9	119	7.6%	-0.52
Unraced	0%	0	0	0.0%	0.00

ANALYSIS BY TODAY'S STARTING PRICE

Age	Prop	Win	Runs	Wins%	£
Odds On	0%	0	2	0.0%	-1.00
Ev-2/1	10%	1	9	11.1%	-0.69
9/4-4/1	40%	4	13	30.8%	0.07
9/2-6/1	20%	2	7	28.6%	0.86
13/2-10/1	20%	2	22	9.1%	-0.25
11/1-16/1	10%	1	18	5.6%	-0.17
18/1-33/1	0%	0	12	0.0%	-1.00
40/1+	0%	0	38	0.0%	-1.00

ANALYSIS BY STARTING PRICE LAST TIME

Age	Prop	Win	Runs	Wins%	£
Odds On	0%	0	0	0.0%	0.00
Ev-2/1	10%	1	5	20.0%	2.00
9/4-4/1	20%	2	16	12.5%	-0.36
9/2-6/1	10%	1	10	10.0%	-0.72
13/2-10/1	20%	2	15	13.3%	-0.50
11/1-16/1	30%	3	26	11.5%	-0.13
18/1-33/1	0%	0	24	0.0%	-1.00
40/1+	10%	1	25	4.0%	-0.87
Unraced	0%	0	0	0.0%	0.00

ANALYSIS BY DISTANCE BEATEN LAST TIME

Age	Prop	Win	Runs	Wins%	£
..-10 lgh	0%	0	0	0.0%	0.00
-10..0	0%	0	0	0.0%	0.00
0.1..2	0%	0	6	0.0%	-1.00
2.1..5	30%	3	7	42.9%	1.07
5.1..10	0%	0	3	0.0%	-1.00
10.1..20	30%	3	12	25.0%	0.51
20.0..30	10%	1	11	9.1%	0.36
30.1+	30%	3	43	7.0%	-0.68
Not Compl	0%	0	39	0.0%	-1.00
Unraced	0%	0	0	0.0%	0.00

ANALYSIS BY SUCCESS RATE IN LAST 10 RUNS

Age	Prop	Win	Runs	Wins%	£
No Wins	90%	9	115	7.8%	-0.60
1 Win	10%	1	5	20.0%	2.00
2 Wins	0%	0	1	0.0%	-1.00
3 Wins	0%	0	0	0.0%	0.00
4 Wins	0%	0	0	0.0%	0.00
5+ Wins	0%	0	0	0.0%	0.00

ANALYSIS BY SUCCESS RATE IN LAST 3 RUNS

Age	Prop	Win	Runs	Wins%	£
No Wins	90%	9	118	7.6%	-0.61
1 Win	10%	1	3	33.3%	4.00
2 Wins	0%	0	0	0.0%	0.00
3 Wins	0%	0	0	0.0%	0.00

ANALYSIS BY POSITION LAST TIME

Age	Prop	Win	Runs	Wins%	£
Won	0%	0	0	0.0%	0.00
2nd or 3rd	50%	5	25	20.0%	0.03
Unplaced	50%	5	57	8.8%	-0.38
Fell,BD,UR	0%	0	10	0.0%	-1.00
Pulled Up	0%	0	29	0.0%	-1.00
Ref/RanOut	0%	0	0	0.0%	0.00
CO/SlipUp	0%	0	0	0.0%	0.00
Unraced	0%	0	0	0.0%	0.00

OTHER FACTORS (WINS-RUNS, £)

Going Winner:	0-1	-£1.00
Beaten Favourite:	1-5	£2.00
BHA Top Rated:	0-10	-£1.00
Absolute Favourites:	1-12	-£0.77

Race Profiles

Claiming Chases

ANALYSIS BY AGE

Age	Prop	Win	Runs	Wins%	£
3yo	0%	0	0	0.0%	0.00
4yo	0%	0	0	0.0%	0.00
5yo	8%	1	3	33.3%	1.67
6yo	8%	1	2	50.0%	5.50
7yo	25%	3	17	17.6%	-0.39
8yo	25%	3	16	18.8%	-0.48
9yo	17%	2	16	12.5%	0.94
10yo	0%	0	14	0.0%	-1.00
11yo	8%	1	7	14.3%	-0.29
12yo+	8%	1	15	6.7%	-0.70

ANALYSIS BY BHB RATING

Age	Prop	Win	Runs	Wins%	£
150+	0%	0	0	0.0%	0.00
130..149	8%	1	11	9.1%	-0.64
120..129	42%	5	9	55.6%	1.07
110..119	17%	2	15	13.3%	-0.63
100..109	17%	2	12	16.7%	0.75
80..99	0%	0	28	0.0%	-1.00
60..79	8%	1	6	16.7%	2.83
..59	0%	0	0	0.0%	0.00
Unrated	8%	1	9	11.1%	-0.11

ANALYSIS BY WEIGHT CARRIED

Age	Prop	Win	Runs	Wins%	£
12-01+	0%	0	0	0.0%	0.00
11-8..12-00	17%	2	8	25.0%	-0.30
11-0..11-07	42%	5	26	19.2%	-0.32
10-8..10-13	17%	2	27	7.4%	-0.52
10-0..10-07	25%	3	28	10.7%	0.57
..9-13	0%	0	1	0.0%	-1.00

ANALYSIS BY DAYS SINCE LAST RUN

Age	Prop	Win	Runs	Wins%	£
1..7	17%	2	7	28.6%	-0.09
8..14	25%	3	17	17.6%	0.18
15..28	33%	4	26	15.4%	-0.12
29..60	17%	2	16	12.5%	0.64
61..100	0%	0	12	0.0%	-1.00
101+	8%	1	12	8.3%	-0.63
Unraced	0%	0	0	0.0%	0.00

ANALYSIS BY TODAY'S STARTING PRICE

Age	Prop	Win	Runs	Wins%	£
Odds On	0%	0	2	0.0%	-1.00
Ev-2/1	25%	3	9	33.3%	-0.11
9/4-4/1	42%	5	16	31.3%	0.27
9/2-6/1	0%	0	6	0.0%	-1.00
13/2-10/1	17%	2	20	10.0%	-0.20
11/1-16/1	8%	1	13	7.7%	0.00
18/1-33/1	8%	1	14	7.1%	0.64
40/1+	0%	0	10	0.0%	-1.00

ANALYSIS BY STARTING PRICE LAST TIME

Age	Prop	Win	Runs	Wins%	£
Odds On	0%	0	0	0.0%	0.00
Ev-2/1	8%	1	2	50.0%	0.63
9/4-4/1	8%	1	7	14.3%	-0.50
9/2-6/1	17%	2	14	14.3%	-0.58
13/2-10/1	17%	2	20	10.0%	-0.38
11/1-16/1	25%	3	15	20.0%	0.01
18/1-33/1	17%	2	19	10.5%	0.42
40/1+	8%	1	13	7.7%	0.00
Unraced	0%	0	0	0.0%	0.00

ANALYSIS BY DISTANCE BEATEN LAST TIME

Age	Prop	Win	Runs	Wins%	£
..-10 lgh	17%	2	2	100.0%	2.88
-10..0	8%	1	4	25.0%	-0.25
0.1..2	0%	0	3	0.0%	-1.00
2.1..5	0%	0	2	0.0%	-1.00
5.1..10	8%	1	5	20.0%	-0.42
10.1..20	17%	2	12	16.7%	-0.16
20.0..30	8%	1	7	14.3%	-0.43
30.1+	33%	4	24	16.7%	0.65
Not Compl	8%	1	31	3.2%	-0.58
Unraced	0%	0	0	0.0%	0.00

ANALYSIS BY SUCCESS RATE IN LAST 10 RUNS

Age	Prop	Win	Runs	Wins%	£
No Wins	17%	2	35	5.7%	-0.67
1 Win	33%	4	29	13.8%	-0.40
2 Wins	25%	3	17	17.6%	1.31
3 Wins	17%	2	6	33.3%	0.50
4 Wins	8%	1	3	33.3%	0.00
5+ Wins	0%	0	0	0.0%	0.00

ANALYSIS BY SUCCESS RATE IN LAST 3 RUNS

Age	Prop	Win	Runs	Wins%	£
No Wins	67%	8	73	11.0%	-0.12
1 Win	25%	3	15	20.0%	-0.15
2 Wins	8%	1	2	50.0%	0.50
3 Wins	0%	0	0	0.0%	0.00

ANALYSIS BY POSITION LAST TIME

Age	Prop	Win	Runs	Wins%	£
Won	25%	3	6	50.0%	0.79
2nd or 3rd	8%	1	16	6.3%	-0.82
Unplaced	58%	7	37	18.9%	0.45
Fell,BD,UR	0%	0	7	0.0%	-1.00
Pulled Up	8%	1	23	4.3%	-0.43
Ref/RanOut	0%	0	1	0.0%	-1.00
CO/SlipUp	0%	0	0	0.0%	0.00
Unraced	0%	0	0	0.0%	0.00

OTHER FACTORS (WINS-RUNS, £)

Course Winner:	3-19	-£0.39
Distance Winner:	4-29	-£0.47
Going Winner:	7-44	£0.01
Beaten Favourite:	0-2	-£1.00
7-Day Winners:	0-1	-£1.00
BHA Top Rated:	0-7	-£1.00
Absolute Favourites:	1-12	-£0.83

Claiming Chases

Claiming Chases: 2m to 2m3f

ANALYSIS BY AGE

Age	Prop	Win	Runs	Wins%	£
3yo	0%	0	0	0.0%	0.00
4yo	0%	0	0	0.0%	0.00
5yo	0%	0	1	0.0%	-1.00
6yo	0%	0	0	0.0%	0.00
7yo	100%	1	1	100.0%	2.50
8yo	0%	0	0	0.0%	0.00
9yo	0%	0	1	0.0%	-1.00
10yo	0%	0	0	0.0%	0.00
11yo	0%	0	0	0.0%	0.00
12yo+	0%	0	1	0.0%	-1.00

ANALYSIS BY BHB RATING

Age	Prop	Win	Runs	Wins%	£
150+	0%	0	0	0.0%	0.00
130..149	0%	0	1	0.0%	-1.00
120..129	0%	0	0	0.0%	0.00
110..119	100%	1	1	100.0%	2.50
100..109	0%	0	2	0.0%	-1.00
80..99	0%	0	0	0.0%	0.00
60..79	0%	0	0	0.0%	0.00
..59	0%	0	0	0.0%	0.00
Unrated	0%	0	0	0.0%	0.00

ANALYSIS BY WEIGHT CARRIED

Age	Prop	Win	Runs	Wins%	£
12-01+	0%	0	0	0.0%	0.00
11-8..12-00	100%	1	2	50.0%	0.75
11-0..11-07	0%	0	0	0.0%	0.00
10-8..10-13	0%	0	1	0.0%	-1.00
10-0..10-07	0%	0	1	0.0%	-1.00
..9-13	0%	0	0	0.0%	0.00

ANALYSIS BY DAYS SINCE LAST RUN

Age	Prop	Win	Runs	Wins%	£
1..7	100%	1	1	100.0%	2.50
8..14	0%	0	0	0.0%	0.00
15..28	0%	0	2	0.0%	-1.00
29..60	0%	0	1	0.0%	-1.00
61..100	0%	0	0	0.0%	0.00
101+	0%	0	0	0.0%	0.00
Unraced	0%	0	0	0.0%	0.00

ANALYSIS BY TODAY'S STARTING PRICE

Age	Prop	Win	Runs	Wins%	£
Odds On	0%	0	1	0.0%	-1.00
Ev-2/1	0%	0	0	0.0%	0.00
9/4-4/1	100%	1	1	100.0%	2.50
9/2-6/1	0%	0	0	0.0%	0.00
13/2-10/1	0%	0	0	0.0%	0.00
11/1-16/1	0%	0	1	0.0%	-1.00
18/1-33/1	0%	0	1	0.0%	-1.00
40/1+	0%	0	0	0.0%	0.00

ANALYSIS BY STARTING PRICE LAST TIME

Age	Prop	Win	Runs	Wins%	£
Odds On	0%	0	0	0.0%	0.00
Ev-2/1	0%	0	0	0.0%	0.00
9/4-4/1	100%	1	1	100.0%	2.50
9/2-6/1	0%	0	0	0.0%	0.00
13/2-10/1	0%	0	1	0.0%	-1.00
11/1-16/1	0%	0	0	0.0%	0.00
18/1-33/1	0%	0	1	0.0%	-1.00
40/1+	0%	0	1	0.0%	-1.00
Unraced	0%	0	0	0.0%	0.00

ANALYSIS BY DISTANCE BEATEN LAST TIME

Age	Prop	Win	Runs	Wins%	£
..-10 lgh	0%	0	0	0.0%	0.00
-10..0	0%	0	0	0.0%	0.00
0.1..2	0%	0	0	0.0%	0.00
2.1..5	0%	0	0	0.0%	0.00
5.1..10	0%	0	0	0.0%	0.00
10.1..20	0%	0	1	0.0%	-1.00
20.0..30	0%	0	0	0.0%	0.00
30.1+	100%	1	3	33.3%	0.17
Not Compl	0%	0	0	0.0%	0.00
Unraced	0%	0	0	0.0%	0.00

ANALYSIS BY SUCCESS RATE IN LAST 10 RUNS

Age	Prop	Win	Runs	Wins%	£
No Wins	100%	1	3	33.3%	0.17
1 Win	0%	0	1	0.0%	-1.00
2 Wins	0%	0	0	0.0%	0.00
3 Wins	0%	0	0	0.0%	0.00
4 Wins	0%	0	0	0.0%	0.00
5+ Wins	0%	0	0	0.0%	0.00

ANALYSIS BY SUCCESS RATE IN LAST 3 RUNS

Age	Prop	Win	Runs	Wins%	£
No Wins	100%	1	4	25.0%	-0.13
1 Win	0%	0	0	0.0%	0.00
2 Wins	0%	0	0	0.0%	0.00
3 Wins	0%	0	0	0.0%	0.00

ANALYSIS BY POSITION LAST TIME

Age	Prop	Win	Runs	Wins%	£
Won	0%	0	0	0.0%	0.00
2nd or 3rd	0%	0	1	0.0%	-1.00
Unplaced	100%	1	3	33.3%	0.17
Fell,BD,UR	0%	0	0	0.0%	0.00
Pulled Up	0%	0	0	0.0%	0.00
Ref/RanOut	0%	0	0	0.0%	0.00
CO/SlipUp	0%	0	0	0.0%	0.00
Unraced	0%	0	0	0.0%	0.00

OTHER FACTORS (WINS-RUNS, £)

Course Winner:	0-1	-£1.00
Going Winner:	0-2	-£1.00
BHA Top Rated:	0-1	-£1.00
Absolute Favourites:	0-1	-£1.00

Race Profiles

Claiming Chases: 2m4f to 2m7f

ANALYSIS BY AGE

Age	Prop	Win	Runs	Wins%	£
3yo	0%	0	0	0.0%	0.00
4yo	0%	0	0	0.0%	0.00
5yo	25%	1	1	100.0%	7.00
6yo	0%	0	1	0.0%	-1.00
7yo	25%	1	5	20.0%	-0.20
8yo	25%	1	7	14.3%	-0.57
9yo	25%	1	9	11.1%	1.56
10yo	0%	0	8	0.0%	-1.00
11yo	0%	0	2	0.0%	-1.00
12yo+	0%	0	8	0.0%	-1.00

ANALYSIS BY BHB RATING

Age	Prop	Win	Runs	Wins%	£
150+	0%	0	0	0.0%	0.00
130..149	25%	1	3	33.3%	0.33
120..129	25%	1	1	100.0%	2.00
110..119	0%	0	7	0.0%	-1.00
100..109	0%	0	3	0.0%	-1.00
80..99	0%	0	17	0.0%	-1.00
60..79	25%	1	3	33.3%	6.67
..59	0%	0	0	0.0%	0.00
Unrated	25%	1	7	14.3%	0.14

ANALYSIS BY WEIGHT CARRIED

Age	Prop	Win	Runs	Wins%	£
12-01+	0%	0	0	0.0%	0.00
11-8..12-00	0%	0	0	0.0%	0.00
11-0..11-07	50%	2	11	18.2%	-0.36
10-8..10-13	25%	1	15	6.7%	-0.47
10-0..10-07	25%	1	15	6.7%	0.53
..9-13	0%	0	0	0.0%	0.00

ANALYSIS BY DAYS SINCE LAST RUN

Age	Prop	Win	Runs	Wins%	£
1..7	0%	0	2	0.0%	-1.00
8..14	0%	0	7	0.0%	-1.00
15..28	75%	3	12	25.0%	0.25
29..60	25%	1	8	12.5%	1.88
61..100	0%	0	5	0.0%	-1.00
101+	0%	0	7	0.0%	-1.00
Unraced	0%	0	0	0.0%	0.00

ANALYSIS BY TODAY'S STARTING PRICE

Age	Prop	Win	Runs	Wins%	£
Odds On	0%	0	0	0.0%	0.00
Ev-2/1	25%	1	3	33.3%	0.00
9/4-4/1	25%	1	5	20.0%	-0.20
9/2-6/1	0%	0	2	0.0%	-1.00
13/2-10/1	25%	1	12	8.3%	-0.33
11/1-16/1	0%	0	5	0.0%	-1.00
18/1-33/1	25%	1	6	16.7%	2.83
40/1+	0%	0	8	0.0%	-1.00

ANALYSIS BY STARTING PRICE LAST TIME

Age	Prop	Win	Runs	Wins%	£
Odds On	0%	0	0	0.0%	0.00
Ev-2/1	0%	0	0	0.0%	0.00
9/4-4/1	0%	0	6	0.0%	-1.00
9/2-6/1	25%	1	6	16.7%	-0.50
13/2-10/1	0%	0	4	0.0%	-1.00
11/1-16/1	25%	1	8	12.5%	0.00
18/1-33/1	50%	2	10	20.0%	1.70
40/1+	0%	0	7	0.0%	-1.00
Unraced	0%	0	0	0.0%	0.00

ANALYSIS BY DISTANCE BEATEN LAST TIME

Age	Prop	Win	Runs	Wins%	£
..-10 lgh	0%	0	0	0.0%	0.00
-10..0	25%	1	2	50.0%	0.50
0.1..2	0%	0	2	0.0%	-1.00
2.1..5	0%	0	0	0.0%	0.00
5.1..10	0%	0	3	0.0%	-1.00
10.1..20	0%	0	5	0.0%	-1.00
20.0..30	25%	1	5	20.0%	-0.20
30.1+	50%	2	11	18.2%	1.82
Not Compl	0%	0	13	0.0%	-1.00
Unraced	0%	0	0	0.0%	0.00

ANALYSIS BY SUCCESS RATE IN LAST 10 RUNS

Age	Prop	Win	Runs	Wins%	£
No Wins	25%	1	17	5.9%	-0.53
1 Win	0%	0	13	0.0%	-1.00
2 Wins	25%	1	7	14.3%	2.29
3 Wins	25%	1	2	50.0%	1.00
4 Wins	25%	1	2	50.0%	0.50
5+ Wins	0%	0	0	0.0%	0.00

ANALYSIS BY SUCCESS RATE IN LAST 3 RUNS

Age	Prop	Win	Runs	Wins%	£
No Wins	75%	3	35	8.6%	-0.53
1 Win	0%	0	4	0.0%	-1.00
2 Wins	25%	1	2	50.0%	0.50
3 Wins	0%	0	0	0.0%	0.00

ANALYSIS BY POSITION LAST TIME

Age	Prop	Win	Runs	Wins%	£
Won	25%	1	2	50.0%	0.50
2nd or 3rd	0%	0	6	0.0%	-1.00
Unplaced	75%	3	20	15.0%	0.75
Fell,BD,UR	0%	0	4	0.0%	-1.00
Pulled Up	0%	0	8	0.0%	-1.00
Ref/RanOut	0%	0	1	0.0%	-1.00
CO/SlipUp	0%	0	0	0.0%	0.00
Unraced	0%	0	0	0.0%	0.00

OTHER FACTORS (WINS-RUNS, £)

Course Winner:	0-10	-£1.00
Distance Winner:	2-19	-£0.63
Going Winner:	3-24	£0.25
Beaten Favourite:	0-1	-£1.00
BHA Top Rated:	0-3	-£1.00
Absolute Favourites:	0-4	-£1.00

Claiming Chases

Claiming Chases: 3m+

ANALYSIS BY AGE

Age	Prop	Win	Runs	Wins%	£
3yo	0%	0	0	0.0%	0.00
4yo	0%	0	0	0.0%	0.00
5yo	0%	0	1	0.0%	-1.00
6yo	14%	1	1	100.0%	12.00
7yo	14%	1	11	9.1%	-0.74
8yo	29%	2	9	22.2%	-0.41
9yo	14%	1	6	16.7%	0.33
10yo	0%	0	6	0.0%	-1.00
11yo	14%	1	5	20.0%	0.00
12yo+	14%	1	6	16.7%	-0.25

ANALYSIS BY BHB RATING

Age	Prop	Win	Runs	Wins%	£
150+	0%	0	0	0.0%	0.00
130..149	0%	0	7	0.0%	-1.00
120..129	57%	4	8	50.0%	0.95
110..119	14%	1	7	14.3%	-0.70
100..109	29%	2	7	28.6%	2.00
80..99	0%	0	11	0.0%	-1.00
60..79	0%	0	3	0.0%	-1.00
..59	0%	0	0	0.0%	0.00
Unrated	0%	0	2	0.0%	-1.00

ANALYSIS BY WEIGHT CARRIED

Age	Prop	Win	Runs	Wins%	£
12-01+	0%	0	0	0.0%	0.00
11-8..12-00	14%	1	6	16.7%	-0.65
11-0..11-07	43%	3	15	20.0%	-0.29
10-8..10-13	14%	1	11	9.1%	-0.55
10-0..10-07	29%	2	12	16.7%	0.75
..9-13	0%	0	1	0.0%	-1.00

ANALYSIS BY DAYS SINCE LAST RUN

Age	Prop	Win	Runs	Wins%	£
1..7	14%	1	4	25.0%	-0.28
8..14	43%	3	10	30.0%	1.01
15..28	14%	1	12	8.3%	-0.33
29..60	14%	1	7	14.3%	-0.54
61..100	0%	0	7	0.0%	-1.00
101+	14%	1	5	20.0%	-0.10
Unraced	0%	0	0	0.0%	0.00

ANALYSIS BY TODAY'S STARTING PRICE

Age	Prop	Win	Runs	Wins%	£
Odds On	0%	0	1	0.0%	-1.00
Ev-2/1	29%	2	6	33.3%	-0.17
9/4-4/1	43%	3	10	30.0%	0.28
9/2-6/1	0%	0	4	0.0%	-1.00
13/2-10/1	14%	1	8	12.5%	0.00
11/1-16/1	14%	1	7	14.3%	0.86
18/1-33/1	0%	0	7	0.0%	-1.00
40/1+	0%	0	2	0.0%	-1.00

ANALYSIS BY STARTING PRICE LAST TIME

Age	Prop	Win	Runs	Wins%	£
Odds On	0%	0	0	0.0%	0.00
Ev-2/1	14%	1	2	50.0%	0.63
9/4-4/1	0%	0	0	0.0%	0.00
9/2-6/1	14%	1	8	12.5%	-0.64
13/2-10/1	29%	2	15	13.3%	-0.17
11/1-16/1	29%	2	7	28.6%	0.01
18/1-33/1	0%	0	8	0.0%	-1.00
40/1+	14%	1	5	20.0%	1.60
Unraced	0%	0	0	0.0%	0.00

ANALYSIS BY DISTANCE BEATEN LAST TIME

Age	Prop	Win	Runs	Wins%	£
..-10 lgh	29%	2	2	100.0%	2.88
-10..0	0%	0	2	0.0%	-1.00
0.1..2	0%	0	1	0.0%	-1.00
2.1..5	0%	0	2	0.0%	-1.00
5.1..10	14%	1	2	50.0%	0.44
10.1..20	29%	2	6	33.3%	0.68
20.0..30	0%	0	2	0.0%	-1.00
30.1+	14%	1	10	10.0%	-0.50
Not Compl	14%	1	18	5.6%	-0.28
Unraced	0%	0	0	0.0%	0.00

ANALYSIS BY SUCCESS RATE IN LAST 10 RUNS

Age	Prop	Win	Runs	Wins%	£
No Wins	0%	0	15	0.0%	-1.00
1 Win	57%	4	15	26.7%	0.17
2 Wins	29%	2	10	20.0%	0.63
3 Wins	14%	1	4	25.0%	0.25
4 Wins	0%	0	1	0.0%	-1.00
5+ Wins	0%	0	0	0.0%	0.00

ANALYSIS BY SUCCESS RATE IN LAST 3 RUNS

Age	Prop	Win	Runs	Wins%	£
No Wins	57%	4	34	11.8%	-0.24
1 Win	43%	3	11	27.3%	0.16
2 Wins	0%	0	0	0.0%	0.00
3 Wins	0%	0	0	0.0%	0.00

ANALYSIS BY POSITION LAST TIME

Age	Prop	Win	Runs	Wins%	£
Won	29%	2	4	50.0%	0.94
2nd or 3rd	14%	1	9	11.1%	-0.68
Unplaced	43%	3	14	21.4%	0.08
Fell,BD,UR	0%	0	3	0.0%	-1.00
Pulled Up	14%	1	15	6.7%	-0.13
Ref/RanOut	0%	0	0	0.0%	0.00
CO/SlipUp	0%	0	0	0.0%	0.00
Unraced	0%	0	0	0.0%	0.00

OTHER FACTORS (WINS-RUNS, £)

Course Winner:	3-8	£0.45
Distance Winner:	2-10	-£0.17
Going Winner:	4-18	-£0.20
Beaten Favourite:	0-1	-£1.00
7-Day Winners:	0-1	-£1.00
BHA Top Rated:	0-3	-£1.00
Absolute Favourites:	1-7	-£0.70

Race Profiles

Claiming Chases: 2 to 5 runners

ANALYSIS BY AGE

Age	Prop	Win	Runs	Wins%	£
3yo	0%	0	0	0.0%	0.00
4yo	0%	0	0	0.0%	0.00
5yo	0%	0	1	0.0%	-1.00
6yo	0%	0	0	0.0%	0.00
7yo	33%	1	4	25.0%	-0.13
8yo	33%	1	2	50.0%	0.05
9yo	0%	0	3	0.0%	-1.00
10yo	0%	0	0	0.0%	0.00
11yo	0%	0	2	0.0%	-1.00
12yo+	33%	1	2	50.0%	1.25

ANALYSIS BY BHB RATING

Age	Prop	Win	Runs	Wins%	£
150+	0%	0	0	0.0%	0.00
130..149	0%	0	2	0.0%	-1.00
120..129	33%	1	2	50.0%	1.25
110..119	67%	2	5	40.0%	0.12
100..109	0%	0	3	0.0%	-1.00
80..99	0%	0	1	0.0%	-1.00
60..79	0%	0	0	0.0%	0.00
..59	0%	0	0	0.0%	0.00
Unrated	0%	0	1	0.0%	-1.00

ANALYSIS BY WEIGHT CARRIED

Age	Prop	Win	Runs	Wins%	£
12-01+	0%	0	0	0.0%	0.00
11-8..12-00	67%	2	4	50.0%	0.40
11-0..11-07	33%	1	5	20.0%	-0.10
10-8..10-13	0%	0	4	0.0%	-1.00
10-0..10-07	0%	0	1	0.0%	-1.00
..9-13	0%	0	0	0.0%	0.00

ANALYSIS BY DAYS SINCE LAST RUN

Age	Prop	Win	Runs	Wins%	£
1..7	33%	1	1	100.0%	2.50
8..14	33%	1	2	50.0%	0.05
15..28	0%	0	6	0.0%	-1.00
29..60	0%	0	3	0.0%	-1.00
61..100	0%	0	1	0.0%	-1.00
101+	33%	1	1	100.0%	3.50
Unraced	0%	0	0	0.0%	0.00

ANALYSIS BY TODAY'S STARTING PRICE

Age	Prop	Win	Runs	Wins%	£
Odds On	0%	0	1	0.0%	-1.00
Ev-2/1	33%	1	2	50.0%	0.05
9/4-4/1	67%	2	4	50.0%	1.00
9/2-6/1	0%	0	2	0.0%	-1.00
13/2-10/1	0%	0	2	0.0%	-1.00
11/1-16/1	0%	0	1	0.0%	-1.00
18/1-33/1	0%	0	2	0.0%	-1.00
40/1+	0%	0	0	0.0%	0.00

ANALYSIS BY STARTING PRICE LAST TIME

Age	Prop	Win	Runs	Wins%	£
Odds On	0%	0	0	0.0%	0.00
Ev-2/1	0%	0	0	0.0%	0.00
9/4-4/1	33%	1	1	100.0%	2.50
9/2-6/1	0%	0	2	0.0%	-1.00
13/2-10/1	33%	1	4	25.0%	0.13
11/1-16/1	33%	1	2	50.0%	0.05
18/1-33/1	0%	0	4	0.0%	-1.00
40/1+	0%	0	1	0.0%	-1.00
Unraced	0%	0	0	0.0%	0.00

ANALYSIS BY DISTANCE BEATEN LAST TIME

Age	Prop	Win	Runs	Wins%	£
..-10 lgh	33%	1	1	100.0%	3.50
-10..0	0%	0	0	0.0%	0.00
0.1..2	0%	0	0	0.0%	0.00
2.1..5	0%	0	0	0.0%	0.00
5.1..10	0%	0	1	0.0%	-1.00
10.1..20	33%	1	3	33.3%	-0.30
20.0..30	0%	0	1	0.0%	-1.00
30.1+	33%	1	4	25.0%	-0.13
Not Compl	0%	0	4	0.0%	-1.00
Unraced	0%	0	0	0.0%	0.00

ANALYSIS BY SUCCESS RATE IN LAST 10 RUNS

Age	Prop	Win	Runs	Wins%	£
No Wins	33%	1	5	20.0%	-0.30
1 Win	67%	2	5	40.0%	0.32
2 Wins	0%	0	3	0.0%	-1.00
3 Wins	0%	0	1	0.0%	-1.00
4 Wins	0%	0	0	0.0%	0.00
5+ Wins	0%	0	0	0.0%	0.00

ANALYSIS BY SUCCESS RATE IN LAST 3 RUNS

Age	Prop	Win	Runs	Wins%	£
No Wins	67%	2	11	18.2%	-0.49
1 Win	33%	1	3	33.3%	0.50
2 Wins	0%	0	0	0.0%	0.00
3 Wins	0%	0	0	0.0%	0.00

ANALYSIS BY POSITION LAST TIME

Age	Prop	Win	Runs	Wins%	£
Won	33%	1	1	100.0%	3.50
2nd or 3rd	0%	0	3	0.0%	-1.00
Unplaced	67%	2	6	33.3%	-0.07
Fell,BD,UR	0%	0	1	0.0%	-1.00
Pulled Up	0%	0	3	0.0%	-1.00
Ref/RanOut	0%	0	0	0.0%	0.00
CO/SlipUp	0%	0	0	0.0%	0.00
Unraced	0%	0	0	0.0%	0.00

OTHER FACTORS (WINS-RUNS, £)

Course Winner:	2-5	£0.32
Distance Winner:	0-2	-£1.00
Going Winner:	2-7	-£0.06
BHA Top Rated:	0-2	-£1.00
Absolute Favourites:	1-3	-£0.30

Claiming Chases

Claiming Chases: 6 to 10 runners

ANALYSIS BY AGE

Age	Prop	Win	Runs	Wins%	£
3yo	0%	0	0	0.0%	0.00
4yo	0%	0	0	0.0%	0.00
5yo	0%	0	1	0.0%	-1.00
6yo	14%	1	2	50.0%	5.50
7yo	29%	2	10	20.0%	-0.31
8yo	29%	2	10	20.0%	-0.38
9yo	14%	1	7	14.3%	0.14
10yo	0%	0	11	0.0%	-1.00
11yo	14%	1	4	25.0%	0.25
12yo+	0%	0	7	0.0%	-1.00

ANALYSIS BY BHB RATING

Age	Prop	Win	Runs	Wins%	£
150+	0%	0	0	0.0%	0.00
130..149	14%	1	8	12.5%	-0.50
120..129	57%	4	7	57.1%	1.02
110..119	0%	0	6	0.0%	-1.00
100..109	29%	2	8	25.0%	1.63
80..99	0%	0	16	0.0%	-1.00
60..79	0%	0	4	0.0%	-1.00
..59	0%	0	0	0.0%	0.00
Unrated	0%	0	3	0.0%	-1.00

ANALYSIS BY WEIGHT CARRIED

Age	Prop	Win	Runs	Wins%	£
12-01+	0%	0	0	0.0%	0.00
11-8..12-00	0%	0	4	0.0%	-1.00
11-0..11-07	57%	4	16	25.0%	-0.18
10-8..10-13	14%	1	15	6.7%	-0.67
10-0..10-07	29%	2	16	12.5%	0.31
..9-13	0%	0	1	0.0%	-1.00

ANALYSIS BY DAYS SINCE LAST RUN

Age	Prop	Win	Runs	Wins%	£
1..7	14%	1	4	25.0%	-0.28
8..14	29%	2	12	16.7%	0.50
15..28	43%	3	11	27.3%	0.36
29..60	14%	1	8	12.5%	-0.59
61..100	0%	0	10	0.0%	-1.00
101+	0%	0	7	0.0%	-1.00
Unraced	0%	0	0	0.0%	0.00

ANALYSIS BY TODAY'S STARTING PRICE

Age	Prop	Win	Runs	Wins%	£
Odds On	0%	0	1	0.0%	-1.00
Ev-2/1	29%	2	6	33.3%	-0.02
9/4-4/1	43%	3	10	30.0%	0.23
9/2-6/1	0%	0	3	0.0%	-1.00
13/2-10/1	14%	1	9	11.1%	-0.11
11/1-16/1	14%	1	8	12.5%	0.63
18/1-33/1	0%	0	9	0.0%	-1.00
40/1+	0%	0	6	0.0%	-1.00

ANALYSIS BY STARTING PRICE LAST TIME

Age	Prop	Win	Runs	Wins%	£
Odds On	0%	0	0	0.0%	0.00
Ev-2/1	14%	1	2	50.0%	0.63
9/4-4/1	0%	0	1	0.0%	-1.00
9/2-6/1	29%	2	10	20.0%	-0.41
13/2-10/1	14%	1	13	7.7%	-0.38
11/1-16/1	14%	1	9	11.1%	-0.44
18/1-33/1	14%	1	9	11.1%	-0.56
40/1+	14%	1	8	12.5%	0.63
Unraced	0%	0	0	0.0%	0.00

ANALYSIS BY DISTANCE BEATEN LAST TIME

Age	Prop	Win	Runs	Wins%	£
..-10 lgh	14%	1	1	100.0%	2.25
-10..0	14%	1	4	25.0%	-0.25
0.1..2	0%	0	2	0.0%	-1.00
2.1..5	0%	0	2	0.0%	-1.00
5.1..10	14%	1	3	33.3%	-0.04
10.1..20	14%	1	4	25.0%	1.00
20.0..30	14%	1	4	25.0%	0.00
30.1+	14%	1	12	8.3%	-0.58
Not Compl	14%	1	20	5.0%	-0.35
Unraced	0%	0	0	0.0%	0.00

ANALYSIS BY SUCCESS RATE IN LAST 10 RUNS

Age	Prop	Win	Runs	Wins%	£
No Wins	0%	0	19	0.0%	-1.00
1 Win	29%	2	16	12.5%	-0.32
2 Wins	29%	2	10	20.0%	0.63
3 Wins	29%	2	4	50.0%	1.25
4 Wins	14%	1	3	33.3%	0.00
5+ Wins	0%	0	0	0.0%	0.00

ANALYSIS BY SUCCESS RATE IN LAST 3 RUNS

Age	Prop	Win	Runs	Wins%	£
No Wins	57%	4	39	10.3%	-0.29
1 Win	29%	2	11	18.2%	-0.25
2 Wins	14%	1	2	50.0%	0.50
3 Wins	0%	0	0	0.0%	0.00

ANALYSIS BY POSITION LAST TIME

Age	Prop	Win	Runs	Wins%	£
Won	29%	2	5	40.0%	0.25
2nd or 3rd	14%	1	9	11.1%	-0.68
Unplaced	43%	3	18	16.7%	-0.06
Fell,BD,UR	0%	0	5	0.0%	-1.00
Pulled Up	14%	1	15	6.7%	-0.13
Ref/RanOut	0%	0	0	0.0%	0.00
CO/SlipUp	0%	0	0	0.0%	0.00
Unraced	0%	0	0	0.0%	0.00

OTHER FACTORS (WINS-RUNS, £)

Course Winner:	1-7	-£0.29
Distance Winner:	4-17	-£0.10
Going Winner:	4-23	-£0.35
Beaten Favourite:	0-1	-£1.00
7-Day Winners:	0-1	-£1.00
BHA Top Rated:	0-3	-£1.00
Absolute Favourites:	0-7	-£1.00

Race Profiles

Claiming Chases: 11 runners or more

ANALYSIS BY AGE

Age	Prop	Win	Runs	Wins%	£
3yo	0%	0	0	0.0%	0.00
4yo	0%	0	0	0.0%	0.00
5yo	50%	1	1	100.0%	7.00
6yo	0%	0	0	0.0%	0.00
7yo	0%	0	3	0.0%	-1.00
8yo	0%	0	4	0.0%	-1.00
9yo	50%	1	6	16.7%	2.83
10yo	0%	0	3	0.0%	-1.00
11yo	0%	0	1	0.0%	-1.00
12yo+	0%	0	6	0.0%	-1.00

ANALYSIS BY BHB RATING

Age	Prop	Win	Runs	Wins%	£
150+	0%	0	0	0.0%	0.00
130..149	0%	0	1	0.0%	-1.00
120..129	0%	0	0	0.0%	0.00
110..119	0%	0	4	0.0%	-1.00
100..109	0%	0	1	0.0%	-1.00
80..99	0%	0	11	0.0%	-1.00
60..79	50%	1	2	50.0%	10.50
..59	0%	0	0	0.0%	0.00
Unrated	50%	1	5	20.0%	0.60

ANALYSIS BY WEIGHT CARRIED

Age	Prop	Win	Runs	Wins%	£
12-01+	0%	0	0	0.0%	0.00
11-8..12-00	0%	0	0	0.0%	0.00
11-0..11-07	0%	0	5	0.0%	-1.00
10-8..10-13	50%	1	8	12.5%	0.00
10-0..10-07	50%	1	11	9.1%	1.09
..9-13	0%	0	0	0.0%	0.00

ANALYSIS BY DAYS SINCE LAST RUN

Age	Prop	Win	Runs	Wins%	£
1..7	0%	0	2	0.0%	-1.00
8..14	0%	0	3	0.0%	-1.00
15..28	50%	1	9	11.1%	-0.11
29..60	50%	1	5	20.0%	3.60
61..100	0%	0	1	0.0%	-1.00
101+	0%	0	4	0.0%	-1.00
Unraced	0%	0	0	0.0%	0.00

ANALYSIS BY TODAY'S STARTING PRICE

Age	Prop	Win	Runs	Wins%	£
Odds On	0%	0	0	0.0%	0.00
Ev-2/1	0%	0	1	0.0%	-1.00
9/4-4/1	0%	0	2	0.0%	-1.00
9/2-6/1	0%	0	1	0.0%	-1.00
13/2-10/1	50%	1	9	11.1%	-0.11
11/1-16/1	0%	0	4	0.0%	-1.00
18/1-33/1	50%	1	3	33.3%	6.67
40/1+	0%	0	4	0.0%	-1.00

ANALYSIS BY STARTING PRICE LAST TIME

Age	Prop	Win	Runs	Wins%	£
Odds On	0%	0	0	0.0%	0.00
Ev-2/1	0%	0	0	0.0%	0.00
9/4-4/1	0%	0	5	0.0%	-1.00
9/2-6/1	0%	0	2	0.0%	-1.00
13/2-10/1	0%	0	3	0.0%	-1.00
11/1-16/1	50%	1	4	25.0%	1.00
18/1-33/1	50%	1	6	16.7%	2.83
40/1+	0%	0	4	0.0%	-1.00
Unraced	0%	0	0	0.0%	0.00

ANALYSIS BY DISTANCE BEATEN LAST TIME

Age	Prop	Win	Runs	Wins%	£
..-10 lgh	0%	0	0	0.0%	0.00
-10..0	0%	0	0	0.0%	0.00
0.1..2	0%	0	1	0.0%	-1.00
2.1..5	0%	0	0	0.0%	0.00
5.1..10	0%	0	1	0.0%	-1.00
10.1..20	0%	0	5	0.0%	-1.00
20.0..30	0%	0	2	0.0%	-1.00
30.1+	100%	2	8	25.0%	2.88
Not Compl	0%	0	7	0.0%	-1.00
Unraced	0%	0	0	0.0%	0.00

ANALYSIS BY SUCCESS RATE IN LAST 10 RUNS

Age	Prop	Win	Runs	Wins%	£
No Wins	50%	1	11	9.1%	-0.27
1 Win	0%	0	8	0.0%	-1.00
2 Wins	50%	1	4	25.0%	4.75
3 Wins	0%	0	1	0.0%	-1.00
4 Wins	0%	0	0	0.0%	0.00
5+ Wins	0%	0	0	0.0%	0.00

ANALYSIS BY SUCCESS RATE IN LAST 3 RUNS

Age	Prop	Win	Runs	Wins%	£
No Wins	100%	2	23	8.7%	0.35
1 Win	0%	0	1	0.0%	-1.00
2 Wins	0%	0	0	0.0%	0.00
3 Wins	0%	0	0	0.0%	0.00

ANALYSIS BY POSITION LAST TIME

Age	Prop	Win	Runs	Wins%	£
Won	0%	0	0	0.0%	0.00
2nd or 3rd	0%	0	4	0.0%	-1.00
Unplaced	100%	2	13	15.4%	1.38
Fell,BD,UR	0%	0	1	0.0%	-1.00
Pulled Up	0%	0	5	0.0%	-1.00
Ref/RanOut	0%	0	1	0.0%	-1.00
CO/SlipUp	0%	0	0	0.0%	0.00
Unraced	0%	0	0	0.0%	0.00

OTHER FACTORS (WINS-RUNS, £)

Course Winner:	0-7	-£1.00
Distance Winner:	0-10	-£1.00
Going Winner:	1-14	£0.64
Beaten Favourite:	0-1	-£1.00
BHA Top Rated:	0-2	-£1.00
Absolute Favourites:	0-2	-£1.00

Claiming Chases

Claiming Chases: up to 7 days off the track

ANALYSIS BY AGE

Age	Prop	Win	Runs	Wins%	£
3yo	0%	0	0	0.0%	0.00
4yo	0%	0	0	0.0%	0.00
5yo	0%	0	0	0.0%	0.00
6yo	0%	0	0	0.0%	0.00
7yo	100%	2	3	66.7%	1.13
8yo	0%	0	1	0.0%	-1.00
9yo	0%	0	0	0.0%	0.00
10yo	0%	0	1	0.0%	-1.00
11yo	0%	0	0	0.0%	0.00
12yo+	0%	0	2	0.0%	-1.00

ANALYSIS BY BHB RATING

Age	Prop	Win	Runs	Wins%	£
150+	0%	0	0	0.0%	0.00
130..149	0%	0	0	0.0%	0.00
120..129	50%	1	2	50.0%	0.44
110..119	50%	1	1	100.0%	2.50
100..109	0%	0	0	0.0%	0.00
80..99	0%	0	3	0.0%	-1.00
60..79	0%	0	1	0.0%	-1.00
..59	0%	0	0	0.0%	0.00
Unrated	0%	0	0	0.0%	0.00

ANALYSIS BY WEIGHT CARRIED

Age	Prop	Win	Runs	Wins%	£
12-01+	0%	0	0	0.0%	0.00
11-8..12-00	50%	1	1	100.0%	2.50
11-0..11-07	50%	1	2	50.0%	0.44
10-8..10-13	0%	0	1	0.0%	-1.00
10-0..10-07	0%	0	3	0.0%	-1.00
..9-13	0%	0	0	0.0%	0.00

ANALYSIS BY DAYS SINCE LAST RUN

Age	Prop	Win	Runs	Wins%	£
1..7	100%	2	7	28.6%	-0.09
8..14	0%	0	0	0.0%	0.00
15..28	0%	0	0	0.0%	0.00
29..60	0%	0	0	0.0%	0.00
61..100	0%	0	0	0.0%	0.00
101+	0%	0	0	0.0%	0.00
Unraced	0%	0	0	0.0%	0.00

ANALYSIS BY TODAY'S STARTING PRICE

Age	Prop	Win	Runs	Wins%	£
Odds On	0%	0	0	0.0%	0.00
Ev-2/1	50%	1	2	50.0%	0.44
9/4-4/1	50%	1	2	50.0%	0.75
9/2-6/1	0%	0	0	0.0%	0.00
13/2-10/1	0%	0	0	0.0%	0.00
11/1-16/1	0%	0	0	0.0%	0.00
18/1-33/1	0%	0	0	0.0%	0.00
40/1+	0%	0	3	0.0%	-1.00

ANALYSIS BY STARTING PRICE LAST TIME

Age	Prop	Win	Runs	Wins%	£
Odds On	0%	0	0	0.0%	0.00
Ev-2/1	0%	0	1	0.0%	-1.00
9/4-4/1	50%	1	2	50.0%	0.75
9/2-6/1	50%	1	1	100.0%	1.88
13/2-10/1	0%	0	1	0.0%	-1.00
11/1-16/1	0%	0	0	0.0%	0.00
18/1-33/1	0%	0	2	0.0%	-1.00
40/1+	0%	0	0	0.0%	0.00
Unraced	0%	0	0	0.0%	0.00

ANALYSIS BY DISTANCE BEATEN LAST TIME

Age	Prop	Win	Runs	Wins%	£
..-10 lgh	0%	0	0	0.0%	0.00
-10..0	0%	0	1	0.0%	-1.00
0.1..2	0%	0	1	0.0%	-1.00
2.1..5	0%	0	0	0.0%	0.00
5.1..10	50%	1	1	100.0%	1.88
10.1..20	0%	0	0	0.0%	0.00
20.0..30	0%	0	0	0.0%	0.00
30.1+	50%	1	3	33.3%	0.17
Not Compl	0%	0	1	0.0%	-1.00
Unraced	0%	0	0	0.0%	0.00

ANALYSIS BY SUCCESS RATE IN LAST 10 RUNS

Age	Prop	Win	Runs	Wins%	£
No Wins	50%	1	3	33.3%	0.17
1 Win	50%	1	3	33.3%	-0.04
2 Wins	0%	0	1	0.0%	-1.00
3 Wins	0%	0	0	0.0%	0.00
4 Wins	0%	0	0	0.0%	0.00
5+ Wins	0%	0	0	0.0%	0.00

ANALYSIS BY SUCCESS RATE IN LAST 3 RUNS

Age	Prop	Win	Runs	Wins%	£
No Wins	100%	2	6	33.3%	0.06
1 Win	0%	0	1	0.0%	-1.00
2 Wins	0%	0	0	0.0%	0.00
3 Wins	0%	0	0	0.0%	0.00

ANALYSIS BY POSITION LAST TIME

Age	Prop	Win	Runs	Wins%	£
Won	0%	0	1	0.0%	-1.00
2nd or 3rd	50%	1	2	50.0%	0.44
Unplaced	50%	1	3	33.3%	0.17
Fell,BD,UR	0%	0	0	0.0%	0.00
Pulled Up	0%	0	0	0.0%	0.00
Ref/RanOut	0%	0	1	0.0%	-1.00
CO/SlipUp	0%	0	0	0.0%	0.00
Unraced	0%	0	0	0.0%	0.00

OTHER FACTORS (WINS-RUNS, £)

Distance Winner:	0-1	-£1.00
Going Winner:	1-4	-£0.28
Beaten Favourite:	0-1	-£1.00
7-Day Winners:	0-1	-£1.00
Absolute Favourites:	0-2	-£1.00

Race Profiles

Claiming Chases: 100+ days off the track

ANALYSIS BY AGE

Age	Prop	Win	Runs	Wins%	£
3yo	0%	0	0	0.0%	0.00
4yo	0%	0	0	0.0%	0.00
5yo	0%	0	0	0.0%	0.00
6yo	0%	0	0	0.0%	0.00
7yo	0%	0	1	0.0%	-1.00
8yo	0%	0	2	0.0%	-1.00
9yo	0%	0	4	0.0%	-1.00
10yo	0%	0	4	0.0%	-1.00
11yo	0%	0	0	0.0%	0.00
12yo+	100%	1	1	100.0%	3.50

ANALYSIS BY BHB RATING

Age	Prop	Win	Runs	Wins%	£
150+	0%	0	0	0.0%	0.00
130..149	0%	0	1	0.0%	-1.00
120..129	100%	1	1	100.0%	3.50
110..119	0%	0	2	0.0%	-1.00
100..109	0%	0	1	0.0%	-1.00
80..99	0%	0	4	0.0%	-1.00
60..79	0%	0	0	0.0%	0.00
..59	0%	0	0	0.0%	0.00
Unrated	0%	0	3	0.0%	-1.00

ANALYSIS BY WEIGHT CARRIED

Age	Prop	Win	Runs	Wins%	£
12-01+	0%	0	0	0.0%	0.00
11-8..12-00	0%	0	0	0.0%	0.00
11-0..11-07	100%	1	6	16.7%	-0.25
10-8..10-13	0%	0	4	0.0%	-1.00
10-0..10-07	0%	0	2	0.0%	-1.00
..9-13	0%	0	0	0.0%	0.00

ANALYSIS BY DAYS SINCE LAST RUN

Age	Prop	Win	Runs	Wins%	£
1..7	0%	0	0	0.0%	0.00
8..14	0%	0	0	0.0%	0.00
15..28	0%	0	0	0.0%	0.00
29..60	0%	0	0	0.0%	0.00
61..100	0%	0	0	0.0%	0.00
101+	100%	1	12	8.3%	-0.63
Unraced	0%	0	0	0.0%	0.00

ANALYSIS BY TODAY'S STARTING PRICE

Age	Prop	Win	Runs	Wins%	£
Odds On	0%	0	0	0.0%	0.00
Ev-2/1	0%	0	1	0.0%	-1.00
9/4-4/1	100%	1	2	50.0%	1.25
9/2-6/1	0%	0	0	0.0%	0.00
13/2-10/1	0%	0	2	0.0%	-1.00
11/1-16/1	0%	0	3	0.0%	-1.00
18/1-33/1	0%	0	2	0.0%	-1.00
40/1+	0%	0	2	0.0%	-1.00

ANALYSIS BY STARTING PRICE LAST TIME

Age	Prop	Win	Runs	Wins%	£
Odds On	0%	0	0	0.0%	0.00
Ev-2/1	0%	0	0	0.0%	0.00
9/4-4/1	0%	0	0	0.0%	0.00
9/2-6/1	0%	0	1	0.0%	-1.00
13/2-10/1	100%	1	6	16.7%	-0.25
11/1-16/1	0%	0	0	0.0%	0.00
18/1-33/1	0%	0	2	0.0%	-1.00
40/1+	0%	0	3	0.0%	-1.00
Unraced	0%	0	0	0.0%	0.00

ANALYSIS BY DISTANCE BEATEN LAST TIME

Age	Prop	Win	Runs	Wins%	£
..-10 lgh	100%	1	1	100.0%	3.50
-10..0	0%	0	1	0.0%	-1.00
0.1..2	0%	0	1	0.0%	-1.00
2.1..5	0%	0	1	0.0%	-1.00
5.1..10	0%	0	0	0.0%	0.00
10.1..20	0%	0	0	0.0%	0.00
20.0..30	0%	0	1	0.0%	-1.00
30.1+	0%	0	2	0.0%	-1.00
Not Compl	0%	0	5	0.0%	-1.00
Unraced	0%	0	0	0.0%	0.00

ANALYSIS BY SUCCESS RATE IN LAST 10 RUNS

Age	Prop	Win	Runs	Wins%	£
No Wins	0%	0	5	0.0%	-1.00
1 Win	100%	1	5	20.0%	-0.10
2 Wins	0%	0	1	0.0%	-1.00
3 Wins	0%	0	0	0.0%	0.00
4 Wins	0%	0	1	0.0%	-1.00
5+ Wins	0%	0	0	0.0%	0.00

ANALYSIS BY SUCCESS RATE IN LAST 3 RUNS

Age	Prop	Win	Runs	Wins%	£
No Wins	0%	0	10	0.0%	-1.00
1 Win	100%	1	1	100.0%	3.50
2 Wins	0%	0	1	0.0%	-1.00
3 Wins	0%	0	0	0.0%	0.00

ANALYSIS BY POSITION LAST TIME

Age	Prop	Win	Runs	Wins%	£
Won	100%	1	2	50.0%	1.25
2nd or 3rd	0%	0	1	0.0%	-1.00
Unplaced	0%	0	4	0.0%	-1.00
Fell,BD,UR	0%	0	0	0.0%	0.00
Pulled Up	0%	0	5	0.0%	-1.00
Ref/RanOut	0%	0	0	0.0%	0.00
CO/SlipUp	0%	0	0	0.0%	0.00
Unraced	0%	0	0	0.0%	0.00

OTHER FACTORS (WINS-RUNS, £)

Course Winner:	1-4	£0.13
Distance Winner:	0-7	-£1.00
Going Winner:	1-5	-£0.10
BHA Top Rated:	0-1	-£1.00
Absolute Favourites:	0-1	-£1.00

Amateur Chases

ANALYSIS BY AGE

Age	Prop	Win	Runs	Wins%	£
3yo	0%	0	0	0.0%	0.00
4yo	0%	0	0	0.0%	0.00
5yo	0%	0	2	0.0%	-1.00
6yo	19%	3	17	17.6%	0.25
7yo	31%	5	43	11.6%	0.49
8yo	19%	3	35	8.6%	-0.72
9yo	19%	3	37	8.1%	-0.66
10yo	13%	2	25	8.0%	-0.86
11yo	0%	0	13	0.0%	-1.00
12yo+	0%	0	12	0.0%	-1.00

ANALYSIS BY BHB RATING

Age	Prop	Win	Runs	Wins%	£
150+	0%	0	1	0.0%	-1.00
130..149	31%	5	46	10.9%	-0.62
120..129	38%	6	42	14.3%	0.64
110..119	19%	3	18	16.7%	0.08
100..109	6%	1	19	5.3%	-0.84
80..99	0%	0	24	0.0%	-1.00
60..79	0%	0	12	0.0%	-1.00
..59	0%	0	2	0.0%	-1.00
Unrated	6%	1	20	5.0%	-0.89

ANALYSIS BY WEIGHT CARRIED

Age	Prop	Win	Runs	Wins%	£
12-01+	13%	2	10	20.0%	-0.64
11-8..12-00	38%	6	73	8.2%	-0.14
11-0..11-07	50%	8	92	8.7%	-0.51
10-8..10-13	0%	0	7	0.0%	-1.00
10-0..10-07	0%	0	2	0.0%	-1.00
..9-13	0%	0	0	0.0%	0.00

ANALYSIS BY DAYS SINCE LAST RUN

Age	Prop	Win	Runs	Wins%	£
1..7	0%	0	2	0.0%	-1.00
8..14	6%	1	27	3.7%	-0.93
15..28	31%	5	62	8.1%	-0.63
29..60	38%	6	55	10.9%	-0.21
61..100	19%	3	11	27.3%	2.61
101+	6%	1	24	4.2%	-0.85
Unraced	0%	0	3	0.0%	-1.00

ANALYSIS BY TODAY'S STARTING PRICE

Age	Prop	Win	Runs	Wins%	£
Odds On	25%	4	5	80.0%	0.41
Ev-2/1	25%	4	8	50.0%	0.22
9/4-4/1	13%	2	14	14.3%	-0.46
9/2-6/1	0%	0	14	0.0%	-1.00
13/2-10/1	19%	3	19	15.8%	0.37
11/1-16/1	13%	2	37	5.4%	-0.27
18/1-33/1	6%	1	42	2.4%	-0.19
40/1+	0%	0	45	0.0%	-1.00

ANALYSIS BY STARTING PRICE LAST TIME

Age	Prop	Win	Runs	Wins%	£
Odds On	0%	0	2	0.0%	-1.00
Ev-2/1	25%	4	16	25.0%	0.38
9/4-4/1	0%	0	24	0.0%	-1.00
9/2-6/1	25%	4	24	16.7%	-0.12
13/2-10/1	19%	3	35	8.6%	-0.41
11/1-16/1	13%	2	28	7.1%	-0.86
18/1-33/1	19%	3	34	8.8%	0.27
40/1+	0%	0	18	0.0%	-1.00
Unraced	0%	0	3	0.0%	-1.00

ANALYSIS BY DISTANCE BEATEN LAST TIME

Age	Prop	Win	Runs	Wins%	£
..-10 lgh	6%	1	10	10.0%	0.50
-10..0	25%	4	22	18.2%	-0.34
0.1..2	6%	1	7	14.3%	-0.75
2.1..5	13%	2	9	22.2%	-0.17
5.1..10	6%	1	11	9.1%	-0.85
10.1..20	19%	3	29	10.3%	-0.16
20.0..30	6%	1	19	5.3%	-0.91
30.1+	6%	1	42	2.4%	-0.19
Not Compl	13%	2	32	6.3%	-0.66
Unraced	0%	0	3	0.0%	-1.00

ANALYSIS BY SUCCESS RATE IN LAST 10 RUNS

Age	Prop	Win	Runs	Wins%	£
No Wins	6%	1	56	1.8%	-0.97
1 Win	50%	8	50	16.0%	0.09
2 Wins	19%	3	34	8.8%	-0.57
3 Wins	13%	2	28	7.1%	0.29
4 Wins	13%	2	11	18.2%	-0.63
5+ Wins	0%	0	2	0.0%	-1.00

ANALYSIS BY SUCCESS RATE IN LAST 3 RUNS

Age	Prop	Win	Runs	Wins%	£
No Wins	44%	7	106	6.6%	-0.42
1 Win	50%	8	58	13.8%	-0.17
2 Wins	6%	1	17	5.9%	-0.89
3 Wins	0%	0	0	0.0%	0.00

ANALYSIS BY POSITION LAST TIME

Age	Prop	Win	Runs	Wins%	£
Won	31%	5	32	15.6%	-0.08
2nd or 3rd	31%	5	40	12.5%	-0.22
Unplaced	25%	4	77	5.2%	-0.48
Fell,BD,UR	0%	0	6	0.0%	-1.00
Pulled Up	13%	2	26	7.7%	-0.59
Ref/RanOut	0%	0	0	0.0%	0.00
CO/SlipUp	0%	0	0	0.0%	0.00
Unraced	0%	0	3	0.0%	-1.00

OTHER FACTORS (WINS-RUNS, £)

Course Winner:	7-30	£0.77
Distance Winner:	6-33	-£0.30
Going Winner:	10-86	-£0.66
Beaten Favourite:	1-10	-£0.78
BHA Top Rated:	4-13	-£0.46
Absolute Favourites:	9-16	£0.27

Race Profiles

Amateur Chases: 2m4f to 2m7f

ANALYSIS BY AGE

Age	Prop	Win	Runs	Wins%	£
3yo	0%	0	0	0.0%	0.00
4yo	0%	0	0	0.0%	0.00
5yo	0%	0	2	0.0%	-1.00
6yo	0%	0	0	0.0%	0.00
7yo	50%	1	7	14.3%	-0.57
8yo	50%	1	4	25.0%	-0.44
9yo	0%	0	4	0.0%	-1.00
10yo	0%	0	1	0.0%	-1.00
11yo	0%	0	0	0.0%	0.00
12yo+	0%	0	0	0.0%	0.00

ANALYSIS BY BHB RATING

Age	Prop	Win	Runs	Wins%	£
150+	0%	0	0	0.0%	0.00
130..149	0%	0	0	0.0%	0.00
120..129	0%	0	1	0.0%	-1.00
110..119	0%	0	0	0.0%	0.00
100..109	50%	1	3	33.3%	0.00
80..99	0%	0	4	0.0%	-1.00
60..79	0%	0	3	0.0%	-1.00
..59	0%	0	0	0.0%	0.00
Unrated	50%	1	7	14.3%	-0.68

ANALYSIS BY WEIGHT CARRIED

Age	Prop	Win	Runs	Wins%	£
12-01+	0%	0	0	0.0%	0.00
11-8..12-00	0%	0	0	0.0%	0.00
11-0..11-07	100%	2	11	18.2%	-0.52
10-8..10-13	0%	0	5	0.0%	-1.00
10-0..10-07	0%	0	2	0.0%	-1.00
..9-13	0%	0	0	0.0%	0.00

ANALYSIS BY DAYS SINCE LAST RUN

Age	Prop	Win	Runs	Wins%	£
1..7	0%	0	0	0.0%	0.00
8..14	0%	0	2	0.0%	-1.00
15..28	50%	1	6	16.7%	-0.50
29..60	50%	1	5	20.0%	-0.55
61..100	0%	0	1	0.0%	-1.00
101+	0%	0	3	0.0%	-1.00
Unraced	0%	0	1	0.0%	-1.00

ANALYSIS BY TODAY'S STARTING PRICE

Age	Prop	Win	Runs	Wins%	£
Odds On	0%	0	0	0.0%	0.00
Ev-2/1	100%	2	2	100.0%	1.63
9/4-4/1	0%	0	3	0.0%	-1.00
9/2-6/1	0%	0	3	0.0%	-1.00
13/2-10/1	0%	0	0	0.0%	0.00
11/1-16/1	0%	0	2	0.0%	-1.00
18/1-33/1	0%	0	3	0.0%	-1.00
40/1+	0%	0	5	0.0%	-1.00

ANALYSIS BY STARTING PRICE LAST TIME

Age	Prop	Win	Runs	Wins%	£
Odds On	0%	0	0	0.0%	0.00
Ev-2/1	100%	2	3	66.7%	0.75
9/4-4/1	0%	0	1	0.0%	-1.00
9/2-6/1	0%	0	2	0.0%	-1.00
13/2-10/1	0%	0	3	0.0%	-1.00
11/1-16/1	0%	0	2	0.0%	-1.00
18/1-33/1	0%	0	3	0.0%	-1.00
40/1+	0%	0	3	0.0%	-1.00
Unraced	0%	0	1	0.0%	-1.00

ANALYSIS BY DISTANCE BEATEN LAST TIME

Age	Prop	Win	Runs	Wins%	£
..-10 lgh	0%	0	0	0.0%	0.00
-10..0	50%	1	1	100.0%	2.00
0.1..2	0%	0	0	0.0%	0.00
2.1..5	0%	0	0	0.0%	0.00
5.1..10	0%	0	1	0.0%	-1.00
10.1..20	50%	1	4	25.0%	-0.44
20.0..30	0%	0	4	0.0%	-1.00
30.1+	0%	0	5	0.0%	-1.00
Not Compl	0%	0	2	0.0%	-1.00
Unraced	0%	0	1	0.0%	-1.00

ANALYSIS BY SUCCESS RATE IN LAST 10 RUNS

Age	Prop	Win	Runs	Wins%	£
No Wins	0%	0	13	0.0%	-1.00
1 Win	0%	0	0	0.0%	0.00
2 Wins	50%	1	2	50.0%	0.50
3 Wins	50%	1	2	50.0%	0.13
4 Wins	0%	0	0	0.0%	0.00
5+ Wins	0%	0	0	0.0%	0.00

ANALYSIS BY SUCCESS RATE IN LAST 3 RUNS

Age	Prop	Win	Runs	Wins%	£
No Wins	0%	0	14	0.0%	-1.00
1 Win	100%	2	3	66.7%	0.75
2 Wins	0%	0	0	0.0%	0.00
3 Wins	0%	0	0	0.0%	0.00

ANALYSIS BY POSITION LAST TIME

Age	Prop	Win	Runs	Wins%	£
Won	50%	1	1	100.0%	2.00
2nd or 3rd	0%	0	2	0.0%	-1.00
Unplaced	50%	1	12	8.3%	-0.81
Fell,BD,UR	0%	0	0	0.0%	0.00
Pulled Up	0%	0	2	0.0%	-1.00
Ref/RanOut	0%	0	0	0.0%	0.00
CO/SlipUp	0%	0	0	0.0%	0.00
Unraced	0%	0	1	0.0%	-1.00

OTHER FACTORS (WINS-RUNS, £)

Distance Winner:	1-1	£2.00
Going Winner:	1-2	£0.50
Beaten Favourite:	1-2	£0.13
BHA Top Rated:	0-2	-£1.00
Absolute Favourites:	2-2	£1.63

Amateur Chases

Amateur Chases: 3m+

ANALYSIS BY AGE
Age	Prop	Win	Runs	Wins%	£
3yo	0%	0	0	0.0%	0.00
4yo	0%	0	0	0.0%	0.00
5yo	0%	0	0	0.0%	0.00
6yo	21%	3	17	17.6%	0.25
7yo	29%	4	36	11.1%	0.70
8yo	14%	2	31	6.5%	-0.76
9yo	21%	3	33	9.1%	-0.62
10yo	14%	2	24	8.3%	-0.85
11yo	0%	0	13	0.0%	-1.00
12yo+	0%	0	12	0.0%	-1.00

ANALYSIS BY BHB RATING
Age	Prop	Win	Runs	Wins%	£
150+	0%	0	1	0.0%	-1.00
130..149	36%	5	46	10.9%	-0.62
120..129	43%	6	41	14.6%	0.68
110..119	21%	3	18	16.7%	0.08
100..109	0%	0	16	0.0%	-1.00
80..99	0%	0	20	0.0%	-1.00
60..79	0%	0	9	0.0%	-1.00
..59	0%	0	2	0.0%	-1.00
Unrated	0%	0	13	0.0%	-1.00

ANALYSIS BY WEIGHT CARRIED
Age	Prop	Win	Runs	Wins%	£
12-01+	14%	2	10	20.0%	-0.64
11-8..12-00	43%	6	73	8.2%	-0.14
11-0..11-07	43%	6	81	7.4%	-0.51
10-8..10-13	0%	0	2	0.0%	-1.00
10-0..10-07	0%	0	0	0.0%	0.00
..9-13	0%	0	0	0.0%	0.00

ANALYSIS BY DAYS SINCE LAST RUN
Age	Prop	Win	Runs	Wins%	£
1..7	0%	0	2	0.0%	-1.00
8..14	7%	1	25	4.0%	-0.93
15..28	29%	4	56	7.1%	-0.64
29..60	36%	5	50	10.0%	-0.18
61..100	21%	3	10	30.0%	2.97
101+	7%	1	21	4.8%	-0.83
Unraced	0%	0	2	0.0%	-1.00

ANALYSIS BY TODAY'S STARTING PRICE
Age	Prop	Win	Runs	Wins%	£
Odds On	29%	4	5	80.0%	0.41
Ev-2/1	14%	2	6	33.3%	-0.25
9/4-4/1	14%	2	11	18.2%	-0.32
9/2-6/1	0%	0	11	0.0%	-1.00
13/2-10/1	21%	3	19	15.8%	0.37
11/1-16/1	14%	2	35	5.7%	-0.23
18/1-33/1	7%	1	39	2.6%	-0.13
40/1+	0%	0	40	0.0%	-1.00

ANALYSIS BY STARTING PRICE LAST TIME
Age	Prop	Win	Runs	Wins%	£
Odds On	0%	0	2	0.0%	-1.00
Ev-2/1	14%	2	13	15.4%	0.29
9/4-4/1	0%	0	23	0.0%	-1.00
9/2-6/1	29%	4	22	18.2%	-0.04
13/2-10/1	21%	3	32	9.4%	-0.35
11/1-16/1	14%	2	26	7.7%	-0.85
18/1-33/1	21%	3	31	9.7%	0.40
40/1+	0%	0	15	0.0%	-1.00
Unraced	0%	0	2	0.0%	-1.00

ANALYSIS BY DISTANCE BEATEN LAST TIME
Age	Prop	Win	Runs	Wins%	£
..-10 lgh	7%	1	10	10.0%	0.50
-10..0	21%	3	21	14.3%	-0.45
0.1..2	7%	1	7	14.3%	-0.75
2.1..5	14%	2	9	22.2%	-0.17
5.1..10	7%	1	10	10.0%	-0.83
10.1..20	14%	2	25	8.0%	-0.12
20.0..30	7%	1	15	6.7%	-0.88
30.1+	7%	1	37	2.7%	-0.08
Not Compl	14%	2	30	6.7%	-0.64
Unraced	0%	0	2	0.0%	-1.00

ANALYSIS BY SUCCESS RATE IN LAST 10 RUNS
Age	Prop	Win	Runs	Wins%	£
No Wins	7%	1	43	2.3%	-0.96
1 Win	57%	8	50	16.0%	0.09
2 Wins	14%	2	32	6.3%	-0.63
3 Wins	7%	1	26	3.8%	0.31
4 Wins	14%	2	11	18.2%	-0.63
5+ Wins	0%	0	2	0.0%	-1.00

ANALYSIS BY SUCCESS RATE IN LAST 3 RUNS
Age	Prop	Win	Runs	Wins%	£
No Wins	50%	7	92	7.6%	-0.33
1 Win	43%	6	55	10.9%	-0.22
2 Wins	7%	1	17	5.9%	-0.89
3 Wins	0%	0	0	0.0%	0.00

ANALYSIS BY POSITION LAST TIME
Age	Prop	Win	Runs	Wins%	£
Won	29%	4	31	12.9%	-0.14
2nd or 3rd	36%	5	38	13.2%	-0.18
Unplaced	21%	3	65	4.6%	-0.42
Fell,BD,UR	0%	0	6	0.0%	-1.00
Pulled Up	14%	2	24	8.3%	-0.55
Ref/RanOut	0%	0	0	0.0%	0.00
CO/SlipUp	0%	0	0	0.0%	0.00
Unraced	0%	0	2	0.0%	-1.00

OTHER FACTORS (WINS-RUNS, £)
Course Winner:	7-30	£0.77
Distance Winner:	5-32	-£0.37
Going Winner:	9-84	-£0.68
Beaten Favourite:	0-8	-£1.00
BHA Top Rated:	4-11	-£0.36
Absolute Favourites:	7-14	£0.07

Race Profiles

Amateur Chases: 2 to 5 runners

ANALYSIS BY AGE

Age	Prop	Win	Runs	Wins%	£
3yo	0%	0	0	0.0%	0.00
4yo	0%	0	0	0.0%	0.00
5yo	0%	0	0	0.0%	0.00
6yo	0%	0	0	0.0%	0.00
7yo	100%	2	5	40.0%	0.05
8yo	0%	0	1	0.0%	-1.00
9yo	0%	0	0	0.0%	0.00
10yo	0%	0	1	0.0%	-1.00
11yo	0%	0	0	0.0%	0.00
12yo+	0%	0	0	0.0%	0.00

ANALYSIS BY BHB RATING

Age	Prop	Win	Runs	Wins%	£
150+	0%	0	0	0.0%	0.00
130..149	50%	1	2	50.0%	0.13
120..129	0%	0	0	0.0%	0.00
110..119	0%	0	0	0.0%	0.00
100..109	50%	1	3	33.3%	0.00
80..99	0%	0	1	0.0%	-1.00
60..79	0%	0	0	0.0%	0.00
..59	0%	0	0	0.0%	0.00
Unrated	0%	0	1	0.0%	-1.00

ANALYSIS BY WEIGHT CARRIED

Age	Prop	Win	Runs	Wins%	£
12-01+	0%	0	0	0.0%	0.00
11-8..12-00	0%	0	2	0.0%	-1.00
11-0..11-07	100%	2	4	50.0%	0.31
10-8..10-13	0%	0	1	0.0%	-1.00
10-0..10-07	0%	0	0	0.0%	0.00
..9-13	0%	0	0	0.0%	0.00

ANALYSIS BY DAYS SINCE LAST RUN

Age	Prop	Win	Runs	Wins%	£
1..7	0%	0	0	0.0%	0.00
8..14	0%	0	2	0.0%	-1.00
15..28	50%	1	1	100.0%	2.00
29..60	50%	1	3	33.3%	-0.25
61..100	0%	0	0	0.0%	0.00
101+	0%	0	1	0.0%	-1.00
Unraced	0%	0	0	0.0%	0.00

ANALYSIS BY TODAY'S STARTING PRICE

Age	Prop	Win	Runs	Wins%	£
Odds On	0%	0	0	0.0%	0.00
Ev-2/1	100%	2	3	66.7%	0.75
9/4-4/1	0%	0	4	0.0%	-1.00
9/2-6/1	0%	0	0	0.0%	0.00
13/2-10/1	0%	0	0	0.0%	0.00
11/1-16/1	0%	0	0	0.0%	0.00
18/1-33/1	0%	0	0	0.0%	0.00
40/1+	0%	0	0	0.0%	0.00

ANALYSIS BY STARTING PRICE LAST TIME

Age	Prop	Win	Runs	Wins%	£
Odds On	0%	0	0	0.0%	0.00
Ev-2/1	50%	1	1	100.0%	2.00
9/4-4/1	0%	0	1	0.0%	-1.00
9/2-6/1	0%	0	1	0.0%	-1.00
13/2-10/1	0%	0	2	0.0%	-1.00
11/1-16/1	50%	1	1	100.0%	1.25
18/1-33/1	0%	0	1	0.0%	-1.00
40/1+	0%	0	0	0.0%	0.00
Unraced	0%	0	0	0.0%	0.00

ANALYSIS BY DISTANCE BEATEN LAST TIME

Age	Prop	Win	Runs	Wins%	£
..-10 lgh	0%	0	0	0.0%	0.00
-10..0	100%	2	2	100.0%	1.63
0.1..2	0%	0	0	0.0%	0.00
2.1..5	0%	0	0	0.0%	0.00
5.1..10	0%	0	1	0.0%	-1.00
10.1..20	0%	0	2	0.0%	-1.00
20.0..30	0%	0	1	0.0%	-1.00
30.1+	0%	0	0	0.0%	0.00
Not Compl	0%	0	1	0.0%	-1.00
Unraced	0%	0	0	0.0%	0.00

ANALYSIS BY SUCCESS RATE IN LAST 10 RUNS

Age	Prop	Win	Runs	Wins%	£
No Wins	0%	0	2	0.0%	-1.00
1 Win	0%	0	0	0.0%	0.00
2 Wins	50%	1	2	50.0%	0.50
3 Wins	0%	0	1	0.0%	-1.00
4 Wins	50%	1	2	50.0%	0.13
5+ Wins	0%	0	0	0.0%	0.00

ANALYSIS BY SUCCESS RATE IN LAST 3 RUNS

Age	Prop	Win	Runs	Wins%	£
No Wins	0%	0	3	0.0%	-1.00
1 Win	100%	2	3	66.7%	0.75
2 Wins	0%	0	1	0.0%	-1.00
3 Wins	0%	0	0	0.0%	0.00

ANALYSIS BY POSITION LAST TIME

Age	Prop	Win	Runs	Wins%	£
Won	100%	2	2	100.0%	1.63
2nd or 3rd	0%	0	3	0.0%	-1.00
Unplaced	0%	0	1	0.0%	-1.00
Fell,BD,UR	0%	0	0	0.0%	0.00
Pulled Up	0%	0	1	0.0%	-1.00
Ref/RanOut	0%	0	0	0.0%	0.00
CO/SlipUp	0%	0	0	0.0%	0.00
Unraced	0%	0	0	0.0%	0.00

OTHER FACTORS (WINS-RUNS, £)

Course Winner:	1-2	£0.13
Distance Winner:	2-2	£1.63
Going Winner:	2-4	£0.31
BHA Top Rated:	0-1	-£1.00
Absolute Favourites:	2-2	£1.63

Amateur Chases

Amateur Chases: 6 to 10 runners

ANALYSIS BY AGE

Age	Prop	Win	Runs	Wins%	£
3yo	0%	0	0	0.0%	0.00
4yo	0%	0	0	0.0%	0.00
5yo	0%	0	0	0.0%	0.00
6yo	0%	0	0	0.0%	0.00
7yo	0%	0	4	0.0%	-1.00
8yo	20%	1	8	12.5%	-0.56
9yo	60%	3	9	33.3%	0.38
10yo	20%	1	8	12.5%	-0.78
11yo	0%	0	7	0.0%	-1.00
12yo+	0%	0	3	0.0%	-1.00

ANALYSIS BY BHB RATING

Age	Prop	Win	Runs	Wins%	£
150+	0%	0	0	0.0%	0.00
130..149	20%	1	2	50.0%	-0.17
120..129	40%	2	9	22.2%	-0.56
110..119	40%	2	5	40.0%	1.40
100..109	0%	0	8	0.0%	-1.00
80..99	0%	0	9	0.0%	-1.00
60..79	0%	0	5	0.0%	-1.00
..59	0%	0	1	0.0%	-1.00
Unrated	0%	0	0	0.0%	0.00

ANALYSIS BY WEIGHT CARRIED

Age	Prop	Win	Runs	Wins%	£
12-01+	0%	0	4	0.0%	-1.00
11-8..12-00	60%	3	15	20.0%	-0.17
11-0..11-07	40%	2	19	10.5%	-0.72
10-8..10-13	0%	0	1	0.0%	-1.00
10-0..10-07	0%	0	0	0.0%	0.00
..9-13	0%	0	0	0.0%	0.00

ANALYSIS BY DAYS SINCE LAST RUN

Age	Prop	Win	Runs	Wins%	£
1..7	0%	0	2	0.0%	-1.00
8..14	0%	0	6	0.0%	-1.00
15..28	60%	3	10	30.0%	0.25
29..60	0%	0	7	0.0%	-1.00
61..100	20%	1	3	33.3%	-0.44
101+	20%	1	11	9.1%	-0.68
Unraced	0%	0	0	0.0%	0.00

ANALYSIS BY TODAY'S STARTING PRICE

Age	Prop	Win	Runs	Wins%	£
Odds On	40%	2	3	66.7%	0.13
Ev-2/1	20%	1	2	50.0%	0.13
9/4-4/1	20%	1	5	20.0%	-0.30
9/2-6/1	0%	0	4	0.0%	-1.00
13/2-10/1	20%	1	2	50.0%	3.25
11/1-16/1	0%	0	10	0.0%	-1.00
18/1-33/1	0%	0	7	0.0%	-1.00
40/1+	0%	0	6	0.0%	-1.00

ANALYSIS BY STARTING PRICE LAST TIME

Age	Prop	Win	Runs	Wins%	£
Odds On	0%	0	0	0.0%	0.00
Ev-2/1	0%	0	1	0.0%	-1.00
9/4-4/1	0%	0	3	0.0%	-1.00
9/2-6/1	40%	2	3	66.7%	0.72
13/2-10/1	40%	2	6	33.3%	0.79
11/1-16/1	20%	1	9	11.1%	-0.81
18/1-33/1	0%	0	9	0.0%	-1.00
40/1+	0%	0	8	0.0%	-1.00
Unraced	0%	0	0	0.0%	0.00

ANALYSIS BY DISTANCE BEATEN LAST TIME

Age	Prop	Win	Runs	Wins%	£
..-10 lgh	0%	0	1	0.0%	-1.00
-10..0	0%	0	1	0.0%	-1.00
0.1..2	20%	1	2	50.0%	-0.14
2.1..5	20%	1	2	50.0%	0.75
5.1..10	20%	1	3	33.3%	-0.44
10.1..20	0%	0	5	0.0%	-1.00
20.0..30	0%	0	4	0.0%	-1.00
30.1+	0%	0	10	0.0%	-1.00
Not Compl	40%	2	11	18.2%	-0.02
Unraced	0%	0	0	0.0%	0.00

ANALYSIS BY SUCCESS RATE IN LAST 10 RUNS

Age	Prop	Win	Runs	Wins%	£
No Wins	20%	1	14	7.1%	-0.88
1 Win	60%	3	14	21.4%	0.02
2 Wins	20%	1	7	14.3%	-0.75
3 Wins	0%	0	4	0.0%	-1.00
4 Wins	0%	0	0	0.0%	0.00
5+ Wins	0%	0	0	0.0%	0.00

ANALYSIS BY SUCCESS RATE IN LAST 3 RUNS

Age	Prop	Win	Runs	Wins%	£
No Wins	80%	4	31	12.9%	-0.50
1 Win	20%	1	6	16.7%	-0.63
2 Wins	0%	0	2	0.0%	-1.00
3 Wins	0%	0	0	0.0%	0.00

ANALYSIS BY POSITION LAST TIME

Age	Prop	Win	Runs	Wins%	£
Won	0%	0	2	0.0%	-1.00
2nd or 3rd	40%	2	7	28.6%	-0.25
Unplaced	20%	1	19	5.3%	-0.91
Fell,BD,UR	0%	0	1	0.0%	-1.00
Pulled Up	40%	2	10	20.0%	0.07
Ref/RanOut	0%	0	0	0.0%	0.00
CO/SlipUp	0%	0	0	0.0%	0.00
Unraced	0%	0	0	0.0%	0.00

OTHER FACTORS (WINS-RUNS, £)

Course Winner:	1-7	-£0.75
Distance Winner:	2-12	£0.00
Going Winner:	4-19	-£0.52
BHA Top Rated:	2-3	£0.13
Absolute Favourites:	4-5	£0.83

Race Profiles

Amateur Chases: 11 runners or more

ANALYSIS BY AGE

Age	Prop	Win	Runs	Wins%	£
3yo	0%	0	0	0.0%	0.00
4yo	0%	0	0	0.0%	0.00
5yo	0%	0	2	0.0%	-1.00
6yo	33%	3	17	17.6%	0.25
7yo	33%	3	34	8.8%	0.74
8yo	22%	2	26	7.7%	-0.76
9yo	0%	0	28	0.0%	-1.00
10yo	11%	1	16	6.3%	-0.89
11yo	0%	0	6	0.0%	-1.00
12yo+	0%	0	9	0.0%	-1.00

ANALYSIS BY BHB RATING

Age	Prop	Win	Runs	Wins%	£
150+	0%	0	1	0.0%	-1.00
130..149	33%	3	42	7.1%	-0.68
120..129	44%	4	33	12.1%	0.97
110..119	11%	1	13	7.7%	-0.42
100..109	0%	0	8	0.0%	-1.00
80..99	0%	0	14	0.0%	-1.00
60..79	0%	0	7	0.0%	-1.00
..59	0%	0	1	0.0%	-1.00
Unrated	11%	1	19	5.3%	-0.88

ANALYSIS BY WEIGHT CARRIED

Age	Prop	Win	Runs	Wins%	£
12-01+	22%	2	6	33.3%	-0.40
11-8..12-00	33%	3	56	5.4%	-0.11
11-0..11-07	44%	4	69	5.8%	-0.50
10-8..10-13	0%	0	5	0.0%	-1.00
10-0..10-07	0%	0	2	0.0%	-1.00
..9-13	0%	0	0	0.0%	0.00

ANALYSIS BY DAYS SINCE LAST RUN

Age	Prop	Win	Runs	Wins%	£
1..7	0%	0	0	0.0%	0.00
8..14	11%	1	19	5.3%	-0.90
15..28	11%	1	51	2.0%	-0.85
29..60	56%	5	45	11.1%	-0.09
61..100	22%	2	8	25.0%	3.75
101+	0%	0	12	0.0%	-1.00
Unraced	0%	0	3	0.0%	-1.00

ANALYSIS BY TODAY'S STARTING PRICE

Age	Prop	Win	Runs	Wins%	£
Odds On	22%	2	2	100.0%	0.82
Ev-2/1	11%	1	3	33.3%	-0.25
9/4-4/1	11%	1	5	20.0%	-0.20
9/2-6/1	0%	0	10	0.0%	-1.00
13/2-10/1	22%	2	17	11.8%	0.03
11/1-16/1	22%	2	27	7.4%	0.00
18/1-33/1	11%	1	35	2.9%	-0.03
40/1+	0%	0	39	0.0%	-1.00

ANALYSIS BY STARTING PRICE LAST TIME

Age	Prop	Win	Runs	Wins%	£
Odds On	0%	0	2	0.0%	-1.00
Ev-2/1	33%	3	14	21.4%	0.36
9/4-4/1	0%	0	20	0.0%	-1.00
9/2-6/1	22%	2	20	10.0%	-0.20
13/2-10/1	11%	1	27	3.7%	-0.63
11/1-16/1	0%	0	18	0.0%	-1.00
18/1-33/1	33%	3	24	12.5%	0.80
40/1+	0%	0	10	0.0%	-1.00
Unraced	0%	0	3	0.0%	-1.00

ANALYSIS BY DISTANCE BEATEN LAST TIME

Age	Prop	Win	Runs	Wins%	£
..-10 lgh	11%	1	9	11.1%	0.67
-10..0	22%	2	19	10.5%	-0.51
0.1..2	0%	0	5	0.0%	-1.00
2.1..5	11%	1	7	14.3%	-0.43
5.1..10	0%	0	7	0.0%	-1.00
10.1..20	33%	3	22	13.6%	0.10
20.0..30	11%	1	14	7.1%	-0.87
30.1+	11%	1	32	3.1%	0.06
Not Compl	0%	0	20	0.0%	-1.00
Unraced	0%	0	3	0.0%	-1.00

ANALYSIS BY SUCCESS RATE IN LAST 10 RUNS

Age	Prop	Win	Runs	Wins%	£
No Wins	0%	0	40	0.0%	-1.00
1 Win	56%	5	36	13.9%	0.12
2 Wins	11%	1	25	4.0%	-0.60
3 Wins	22%	2	23	8.7%	0.58
4 Wins	11%	1	9	11.1%	-0.80
5+ Wins	0%	0	2	0.0%	-1.00

ANALYSIS BY SUCCESS RATE IN LAST 3 RUNS

Age	Prop	Win	Runs	Wins%	£
No Wins	33%	3	72	4.2%	-0.36
1 Win	56%	5	49	10.2%	-0.17
2 Wins	11%	1	14	7.1%	-0.87
3 Wins	0%	0	0	0.0%	0.00

ANALYSIS BY POSITION LAST TIME

Age	Prop	Win	Runs	Wins%	£
Won	33%	3	28	10.7%	-0.13
2nd or 3rd	33%	3	30	10.0%	-0.13
Unplaced	33%	3	57	5.3%	-0.33
Fell,BD,UR	0%	0	5	0.0%	-1.00
Pulled Up	0%	0	15	0.0%	-1.00
Ref/RanOut	0%	0	0	0.0%	0.00
CO/SlipUp	0%	0	0	0.0%	0.00
Unraced	0%	0	3	0.0%	-1.00

OTHER FACTORS (WINS-RUNS, £)

Course Winner:	5-21	£1.34
Distance Winner:	2-19	-£0.69
Going Winner:	4-63	-£0.76
Beaten Favourite:	1-10	-£0.78
BHA Top Rated:	2-9	-£0.60
Absolute Favourites:	3-9	-£0.35

Amateur Chases

Amateur Chases: up to 7 days off the track

ANALYSIS BY AGE

Age	Prop	Win	Runs	Wins%	£
3yo	-	0	0	0.0%	0.00
4yo	-	0	0	0.0%	0.00
5yo	-	0	0	0.0%	0.00
6yo	-	0	1	0.0%	-1.00
7yo	-	0	1	0.0%	-1.00
8yo	-	0	0	0.0%	0.00
9yo	-	0	3	0.0%	-1.00
10yo	-	0	0	0.0%	0.00
11yo	-	0	0	0.0%	0.00
12yo+	-	0	0	0.0%	0.00

ANALYSIS BY BHB RATING

Age	Prop	Win	Runs	Wins%	£
150+	-	0	0	0.0%	0.00
130..149	-	0	0	0.0%	0.00
120..129	-	0	0	0.0%	0.00
110..119	-	0	0	0.0%	0.00
100..109	-	0	1	0.0%	-1.00
80..99	-	0	0	0.0%	0.00
60..79	-	0	1	0.0%	-1.00
..59	-	0	0	0.0%	0.00
Unrated	-	0	3	0.0%	-1.00

ANALYSIS BY WEIGHT CARRIED

Age	Prop	Win	Runs	Wins%	£
12-01+	-	0	1	0.0%	-1.00
11-8..12-00	-	0	2	0.0%	-1.00
11-0..11-07	-	0	1	0.0%	-1.00
10-8..10-13	-	0	0	0.0%	0.00
10-0..10-07	-	0	1	0.0%	-1.00
..9-13	-	0	0	0.0%	0.00

ANALYSIS BY DAYS SINCE LAST RUN

Age	Prop	Win	Runs	Wins%	£
1..7	-	0	2	0.0%	-1.00
8..14	-	0	0	0.0%	0.00
15..28	-	0	0	0.0%	0.00
29..60	-	0	0	0.0%	0.00
61..100	-	0	0	0.0%	0.00
101+	-	0	0	0.0%	0.00
Unraced	-	0	3	0.0%	-1.00

ANALYSIS BY TODAY'S STARTING PRICE

Age	Prop	Win	Runs	Wins%	£
Odds On	-	0	0	0.0%	0.00
Ev-2/1	-	0	0	0.0%	0.00
9/4-4/1	-	0	0	0.0%	0.00
9/2-6/1	-	0	0	0.0%	0.00
13/2-10/1	-	0	1	0.0%	-1.00
11/1-16/1	-	0	0	0.0%	0.00
18/1-33/1	-	0	2	0.0%	-1.00
40/1+	-	0	2	0.0%	-1.00

ANALYSIS BY STARTING PRICE LAST TIME

Age	Prop	Win	Runs	Wins%	£
Odds On	-	0	0	0.0%	0.00
Ev-2/1	-	0	0	0.0%	0.00
9/4-4/1	-	0	0	0.0%	0.00
9/2-6/1	-	0	0	0.0%	0.00
13/2-10/1	-	0	0	0.0%	0.00
11/1-16/1	-	0	0	0.0%	0.00
18/1-33/1	-	0	1	0.0%	-1.00
40/1+	-	0	1	0.0%	-1.00
Unraced	-	0	3	0.0%	-1.00

ANALYSIS BY DISTANCE BEATEN LAST TIME

Age	Prop	Win	Runs	Wins%	£
..-10 lgh	-	0	0	0.0%	0.00
-10..0	-	0	0	0.0%	0.00
0.1..2	-	0	0	0.0%	0.00
2.1..5	-	0	0	0.0%	0.00
5.1..10	-	0	0	0.0%	0.00
10.1..20	-	0	0	0.0%	0.00
20.0..30	-	0	1	0.0%	-1.00
30.1+	-	0	0	0.0%	0.00
Not Compl	-	0	1	0.0%	-1.00
Unraced	-	0	3	0.0%	-1.00

ANALYSIS BY SUCCESS RATE IN LAST 10 RUNS

Age	Prop	Win	Runs	Wins%	£
No Wins	-	0	1	0.0%	-1.00
1 Win	-	0	1	0.0%	-1.00
2 Wins	-	0	0	0.0%	0.00
3 Wins	-	0	0	0.0%	0.00
4 Wins	-	0	0	0.0%	0.00
5+ Wins	-	0	0	0.0%	0.00

ANALYSIS BY SUCCESS RATE IN LAST 3 RUNS

Age	Prop	Win	Runs	Wins%	£
No Wins	-	0	2	0.0%	-1.00
1 Win	-	0	0	0.0%	0.00
2 Wins	-	0	0	0.0%	0.00
3 Wins	-	0	0	0.0%	0.00

ANALYSIS BY POSITION LAST TIME

Age	Prop	Win	Runs	Wins%	£
Won	-	0	0	0.0%	0.00
2nd or 3rd	-	0	0	0.0%	0.00
Unplaced	-	0	1	0.0%	-1.00
Fell,BD,UR	-	0	0	0.0%	0.00
Pulled Up	-	0	1	0.0%	-1.00
Ref/RanOut	-	0	0	0.0%	0.00
CO/SlipUp	-	0	0	0.0%	0.00
Unraced	-	0	3	0.0%	-1.00

OTHER FACTORS (WINS-RUNS, £)

Distance Winner:	0-1	-£1.00
Going Winner:	0-1	-£1.00

Race Profiles

Amateur Chases: 100+ days off the track

ANALYSIS BY AGE

Age	Prop	Win	Runs	Wins%	£
3yo	0%	0	0	0.0%	0.00
4yo	0%	0	0	0.0%	0.00
5yo	0%	0	0	0.0%	0.00
6yo	0%	0	1	0.0%	-1.00
7yo	0%	0	0	0.0%	0.00
8yo	100%	1	5	20.0%	-0.30
9yo	0%	0	3	0.0%	-1.00
10yo	0%	0	6	0.0%	-1.00
11yo	0%	0	4	0.0%	-1.00
12yo+	0%	0	5	0.0%	-1.00

ANALYSIS BY BHB RATING

Age	Prop	Win	Runs	Wins%	£
150+	0%	0	0	0.0%	0.00
130..149	0%	0	2	0.0%	-1.00
120..129	0%	0	2	0.0%	-1.00
110..119	100%	1	5	20.0%	-0.30
100..109	0%	0	1	0.0%	-1.00
80..99	0%	0	8	0.0%	-1.00
60..79	0%	0	2	0.0%	-1.00
..59	0%	0	1	0.0%	-1.00
Unrated	0%	0	3	0.0%	-1.00

ANALYSIS BY WEIGHT CARRIED

Age	Prop	Win	Runs	Wins%	£
12-01+	0%	0	1	0.0%	-1.00
11-8..12-00	0%	0	5	0.0%	-1.00
11-0..11-07	100%	1	15	6.7%	-0.77
10-8..10-13	0%	0	2	0.0%	-1.00
10-0..10-07	0%	0	1	0.0%	-1.00
..9-13	0%	0	0	0.0%	0.00

ANALYSIS BY DAYS SINCE LAST RUN

Age	Prop	Win	Runs	Wins%	£
1..7	0%	0	0	0.0%	0.00
8..14	0%	0	0	0.0%	0.00
15..28	0%	0	0	0.0%	0.00
29..60	0%	0	0	0.0%	0.00
61..100	0%	0	0	0.0%	0.00
101+	100%	1	24	4.2%	-0.85
Unraced	0%	0	0	0.0%	0.00

ANALYSIS BY TODAY'S STARTING PRICE

Age	Prop	Win	Runs	Wins%	£
Odds On	0%	0	0	0.0%	0.00
Ev-2/1	0%	0	1	0.0%	-1.00
9/4-4/1	100%	1	3	33.3%	0.17
9/2-6/1	0%	0	1	0.0%	-1.00
13/2-10/1	0%	0	1	0.0%	-1.00
11/1-16/1	0%	0	5	0.0%	-1.00
18/1-33/1	0%	0	5	0.0%	-1.00
40/1+	0%	0	8	0.0%	-1.00

ANALYSIS BY STARTING PRICE LAST TIME

Age	Prop	Win	Runs	Wins%	£
Odds On	0%	0	0	0.0%	0.00
Ev-2/1	0%	0	0	0.0%	0.00
9/4-4/1	0%	0	2	0.0%	-1.00
9/2-6/1	100%	1	2	50.0%	0.75
13/2-10/1	0%	0	3	0.0%	-1.00
11/1-16/1	0%	0	6	0.0%	-1.00
18/1-33/1	0%	0	9	0.0%	-1.00
40/1+	0%	0	2	0.0%	-1.00
Unraced	0%	0	0	0.0%	0.00

ANALYSIS BY DISTANCE BEATEN LAST TIME

Age	Prop	Win	Runs	Wins%	£
..-10 lgh	0%	0	0	0.0%	0.00
-10..0	0%	0	1	0.0%	-1.00
0.1..2	0%	0	0	0.0%	0.00
2.1..5	100%	1	3	33.3%	0.17
5.1..10	0%	0	1	0.0%	-1.00
10.1..20	0%	0	6	0.0%	-1.00
20.0..30	0%	0	5	0.0%	-1.00
30.1+	0%	0	5	0.0%	-1.00
Not Compl	0%	0	3	0.0%	-1.00
Unraced	0%	0	0	0.0%	0.00

ANALYSIS BY SUCCESS RATE IN LAST 10 RUNS

Age	Prop	Win	Runs	Wins%	£
No Wins	0%	0	14	0.0%	-1.00
1 Win	100%	1	3	33.3%	0.17
2 Wins	0%	0	5	0.0%	-1.00
3 Wins	0%	0	2	0.0%	-1.00
4 Wins	0%	0	0	0.0%	0.00
5+ Wins	0%	0	0	0.0%	0.00

ANALYSIS BY SUCCESS RATE IN LAST 3 RUNS

Age	Prop	Win	Runs	Wins%	£
No Wins	100%	1	20	5.0%	-0.82
1 Win	0%	0	4	0.0%	-1.00
2 Wins	0%	0	0	0.0%	0.00
3 Wins	0%	0	0	0.0%	0.00

ANALYSIS BY POSITION LAST TIME

Age	Prop	Win	Runs	Wins%	£
Won	0%	0	1	0.0%	-1.00
2nd or 3rd	100%	1	5	20.0%	-0.30
Unplaced	0%	0	15	0.0%	-1.00
Fell,BD,UR	0%	0	1	0.0%	-1.00
Pulled Up	0%	0	2	0.0%	-1.00
Ref/RanOut	0%	0	0	0.0%	0.00
CO/SlipUp	0%	0	0	0.0%	0.00
Unraced	0%	0	0	0.0%	0.00

OTHER FACTORS (WINS-RUNS, £)

Course Winner:	0-4	-£1.00
Distance Winner:	1-6	-£0.42
Going Winner:	1-10	-£0.65
BHA Top Rated:	0-3	-£1.00
Absolute Favourites:	1-2	£0.75

Conditions Chases (class 1..3)

ANALYSIS BY AGE

Age	Prop	Win	Runs	Wins%	£
3yo	0%	0	0	0.0%	0.00
4yo	0%	0	3	0.0%	-1.00
5yo	8%	11	40	27.5%	-0.15
6yo	15%	21	100	21.0%	-0.40
7yo	22%	31	185	16.8%	-0.38
8yo	26%	36	243	14.8%	-0.09
9yo	16%	22	209	10.5%	-0.18
10yo	8%	11	142	7.7%	-0.28
11yo	2%	3	66	4.5%	-0.48
12yo+	3%	4	46	8.7%	-0.59

ANALYSIS BY BHB RATING

Age	Prop	Win	Runs	Wins%	£
150+	61%	85	496	17.1%	-0.11
130..149	24%	34	266	12.8%	-0.24
120..129	1%	2	54	3.7%	-0.71
110..119	0%	0	34	0.0%	-1.00
100..109	1%	1	13	7.7%	-0.27
80..99	0%	0	24	0.0%	-1.00
60..79	0%	0	8	0.0%	-1.00
..59	0%	0	0	0.0%	0.00
Unrated	12%	17	139	12.2%	-0.36

ANALYSIS BY WEIGHT CARRIED

Age	Prop	Win	Runs	Wins%	£
12-01+	1%	1	1	100.0%	1.38
11-8..12-00	38%	53	429	12.4%	-0.37
11-0..11-07	55%	77	538	14.3%	-0.22
10-8..10-13	5%	7	57	12.3%	-0.04
10-0..10-07	1%	1	9	11.1%	0.06
..9-13	0%	0	0	0.0%	0.00

ANALYSIS BY DAYS SINCE LAST RUN

Age	Prop	Win	Runs	Wins%	£
1..7	1%	1	29	3.4%	-0.81
8..14	3%	4	75	5.3%	-0.60
15..28	34%	47	328	14.3%	-0.16
29..60	33%	46	284	16.2%	-0.15
61..100	7%	10	66	15.2%	-0.15
101+	22%	30	237	12.7%	-0.40
Unraced	1%	1	15	6.7%	-0.57

ANALYSIS BY TODAY'S STARTING PRICE

Age	Prop	Win	Runs	Wins%	£
Odds On	20%	28	53	52.8%	-0.20
Ev-2/1	22%	31	84	36.9%	-0.07
9/4-4/1	22%	31	146	21.2%	-0.17
9/2-6/1	13%	18	96	18.8%	0.16
13/2-10/1	12%	17	161	10.6%	0.00
11/1-16/1	8%	11	157	7.0%	0.03
18/1-33/1	2%	3	173	1.7%	-0.53
40/1+	0%	0	164	0.0%	-1.00

ANALYSIS BY STARTING PRICE LAST TIME

Age	Prop	Win	Runs	Wins%	£
Odds On	16%	22	73	30.1%	-0.22
Ev-2/1	11%	15	93	16.1%	-0.39
9/4-4/1	22%	31	188	16.5%	-0.11
9/2-6/1	12%	16	125	12.8%	-0.37
13/2-10/1	15%	21	194	10.8%	-0.36
11/1-16/1	13%	18	165	10.9%	-0.21
18/1-33/1	10%	14	128	10.9%	0.05
40/1+	1%	1	53	1.9%	-0.95
Unraced	1%	1	15	6.7%	-0.57

ANALYSIS BY DISTANCE BEATEN LAST TIME

Age	Prop	Win	Runs	Wins%	£
..-10 lgh	7%	10	56	17.9%	-0.56
-10..0	24%	34	167	20.4%	0.01
0.1..2	8%	11	66	16.7%	-0.17
2.1..5	9%	12	72	16.7%	-0.21
5.1..10	9%	12	87	13.8%	-0.07
10.1..20	12%	17	141	12.1%	-0.48
20.0..30	6%	8	85	9.4%	-0.64
30.1+	12%	16	179	8.9%	-0.31
Not Compl	13%	18	166	10.8%	-0.18
Unraced	1%	1	15	6.7%	-0.57

ANALYSIS BY SUCCESS RATE IN LAST 10 RUNS

Age	Prop	Win	Runs	Wins%	£
No Wins	4%	5	100	5.0%	-0.36
1 Win	16%	22	212	10.4%	-0.32
2 Wins	12%	17	190	8.9%	-0.36
3 Wins	20%	27	184	14.7%	-0.39
4 Wins	20%	28	165	17.0%	0.02
5+ Wins	28%	39	168	23.2%	-0.16

ANALYSIS BY SUCCESS RATE IN LAST 3 RUNS

Age	Prop	Win	Runs	Wins%	£
No Wins	33%	45	491	9.2%	-0.35
1 Win	40%	55	342	16.1%	-0.15
2 Wins	22%	31	162	19.1%	-0.22
3 Wins	5%	7	24	29.2%	-0.47

ANALYSIS BY POSITION LAST TIME

Age	Prop	Win	Runs	Wins%	£
Won	32%	44	224	19.6%	-0.14
2nd or 3rd	27%	38	271	14.0%	-0.23
Unplaced	27%	38	359	10.6%	-0.41
Fell,BD,UR	6%	9	79	11.4%	-0.34
Pulled Up	6%	9	82	11.0%	0.03
Ref/RanOut	0%	0	4	0.0%	-1.00
CO/SlipUp	0%	0	0	0.0%	0.00
Unraced	1%	1	15	6.7%	-0.57

OTHER FACTORS (WINS-RUNS, £)

Course Winner:	64-354	-£0.13
Distance Winner:	86-578	-£0.34
Going Winner:	116-757	-£0.20
Beaten Favourite:	18-98	-£0.36
7-Day Winners:	0-4	-£1.00
BHA Top Rated:	42-118	-£0.01
Absolute Favourites:	51-128	-£0.21

Race Profiles

Conditions Chases (class 1..3): 2m to 2m3f

ANALYSIS BY AGE

Age	Prop	Win	Runs	Wins%	£
3yo	0%	0	0	0.0%	0.00
4yo	0%	0	1	0.0%	-1.00
5yo	20%	8	21	38.1%	0.09
6yo	18%	7	41	17.1%	-0.56
7yo	20%	8	50	16.0%	-0.38
8yo	25%	10	64	15.6%	0.37
9yo	15%	6	43	14.0%	-0.11
10yo	3%	1	30	3.3%	-0.88
11yo	0%	0	11	0.0%	-1.00
12yo+	0%	0	2	0.0%	-1.00

ANALYSIS BY BHB RATING

Age	Prop	Win	Runs	Wins%	£
150+	68%	27	149	18.1%	-0.19
130..149	18%	7	62	11.3%	-0.29
120..129	0%	0	4	0.0%	-1.00
110..119	0%	0	1	0.0%	-1.00
100..109	3%	1	4	25.0%	1.38
80..99	0%	0	6	0.0%	-1.00
60..79	0%	0	4	0.0%	-1.00
..59	0%	0	0	0.0%	0.00
Unrated	13%	5	33	15.2%	-0.16

ANALYSIS BY WEIGHT CARRIED

Age	Prop	Win	Runs	Wins%	£
12-01+	0%	0	0	0.0%	0.00
11-8..12-00	25%	10	72	13.9%	-0.24
11-0..11-07	70%	28	188	14.9%	-0.28
10-8..10-13	3%	1	1	100.0%	1.25
10-0..10-07	3%	1	2	50.0%	3.75
..9-13	0%	0	0	0.0%	0.00

ANALYSIS BY DAYS SINCE LAST RUN

Age	Prop	Win	Runs	Wins%	£
1..7	3%	1	13	7.7%	-0.58
8..14	5%	2	25	8.0%	-0.54
15..28	28%	11	83	13.3%	-0.20
29..60	43%	17	80	21.3%	0.10
61..100	3%	1	10	10.0%	-0.84
101+	20%	8	47	17.0%	-0.37
Unraced	0%	0	5	0.0%	-1.00

ANALYSIS BY TODAY'S STARTING PRICE

Age	Prop	Win	Runs	Wins%	£
Odds On	20%	8	17	47.1%	-0.32
Ev-2/1	20%	8	23	34.8%	-0.15
9/4-4/1	28%	11	44	25.0%	-0.07
9/2-6/1	10%	4	25	16.0%	-0.04
13/2-10/1	15%	6	38	15.8%	0.54
11/1-16/1	8%	3	44	6.8%	0.07
18/1-33/1	0%	0	36	0.0%	-1.00
40/1+	0%	0	36	0.0%	-1.00

ANALYSIS BY STARTING PRICE LAST TIME

Age	Prop	Win	Runs	Wins%	£
Odds On	15%	6	24	25.0%	-0.41
Ev-2/1	13%	5	31	16.1%	-0.30
9/4-4/1	25%	10	58	17.2%	-0.47
9/2-6/1	8%	3	26	11.5%	-0.03
13/2-10/1	10%	4	42	9.5%	-0.54
11/1-16/1	18%	7	43	16.3%	0.07
18/1-33/1	10%	4	26	15.4%	0.61
40/1+	3%	1	8	12.5%	-0.64
Unraced	0%	0	5	0.0%	-1.00

ANALYSIS BY DISTANCE BEATEN LAST TIME

Age	Prop	Win	Runs	Wins%	£
..-10 lgh	10%	4	19	21.1%	-0.66
-10..0	28%	11	38	28.9%	0.83
0.1..2	10%	4	15	26.7%	0.22
2.1..5	13%	5	23	21.7%	-0.04
5.1..10	10%	4	26	15.4%	-0.54
10.1..20	10%	4	45	8.9%	-0.64
20.0..30	3%	1	20	5.0%	-0.68
30.1+	5%	2	38	5.3%	-0.85
Not Compl	13%	5	34	14.7%	0.34
Unraced	0%	0	5	0.0%	-1.00

ANALYSIS BY SUCCESS RATE IN LAST 10 RUNS

Age	Prop	Win	Runs	Wins%	£
No Wins	5%	2	21	9.5%	0.26
1 Win	23%	9	47	19.1%	-0.26
2 Wins	18%	7	44	15.9%	-0.11
3 Wins	18%	7	54	13.0%	-0.42
4 Wins	15%	6	50	12.0%	-0.38
5+ Wins	23%	9	42	21.4%	-0.08

ANALYSIS BY SUCCESS RATE IN LAST 3 RUNS

Age	Prop	Win	Runs	Wins%	£
No Wins	40%	16	122	13.1%	-0.16
1 Win	33%	13	93	14.0%	-0.42
2 Wins	28%	11	39	28.2%	0.17
3 Wins	0%	0	4	0.0%	-1.00

ANALYSIS BY POSITION LAST TIME

Age	Prop	Win	Runs	Wins%	£
Won	38%	15	57	26.3%	0.33
2nd or 3rd	40%	16	83	19.3%	-0.21
Unplaced	10%	4	84	4.8%	-0.82
Fell,BD,UR	8%	3	24	12.5%	0.15
Pulled Up	5%	2	9	22.2%	1.00
Ref/RanOut	0%	0	1	0.0%	-1.00
CO/SlipUp	0%	0	0	0.0%	0.00
Unraced	0%	0	5	0.0%	-1.00

OTHER FACTORS (WINS-RUNS, £)

Course Winner:	17-91	-£0.24
Distance Winner:	28-202	-£0.35
Going Winner:	35-199	-£0.15
Beaten Favourite:	4-38	-£0.79
7-Day Winners:	0-4	-£1.00
BHA Top Rated:	12-34	£0.02
Absolute Favourites:	14-37	-£0.27

Conditions Chases (class 1..3): 2m4f to 2m7f

ANALYSIS BY AGE
Age	Prop	Win	Runs	Wins%	£
3yo	0%	0	0	0.0%	0.00
4yo	0%	0	1	0.0%	-1.00
5yo	3%	1	11	9.1%	-0.73
6yo	18%	7	28	25.0%	-0.15
7yo	21%	8	41	19.5%	-0.49
8yo	29%	11	64	17.2%	-0.16
9yo	18%	7	60	11.7%	-0.04
10yo	8%	3	33	9.1%	-0.54
11yo	0%	0	11	0.0%	-1.00
12yo+	3%	1	7	14.3%	-0.07

ANALYSIS BY BHB RATING
Age	Prop	Win	Runs	Wins%	£
150+	58%	22	129	17.1%	-0.20
130..149	32%	12	72	16.7%	-0.27
120..129	0%	0	13	0.0%	-1.00
110..119	0%	0	5	0.0%	-1.00
100..109	0%	0	2	0.0%	-1.00
80..99	0%	0	3	0.0%	-1.00
60..79	0%	0	0	0.0%	0.00
..59	0%	0	0	0.0%	0.00
Unrated	11%	4	32	12.5%	-0.22

ANALYSIS BY WEIGHT CARRIED
Age	Prop	Win	Runs	Wins%	£
12-01+	0%	0	0	0.0%	0.00
11-8..12-00	32%	12	97	12.4%	-0.16
11-0..11-07	63%	24	142	16.9%	-0.34
10-8..10-13	5%	2	12	16.7%	-0.55
10-0..10-07	0%	0	5	0.0%	-1.00
..9-13	0%	0	0	0.0%	0.00

ANALYSIS BY DAYS SINCE LAST RUN
Age	Prop	Win	Runs	Wins%	£
1..7	0%	0	6	0.0%	-1.00
8..14	5%	2	17	11.8%	0.09
15..28	37%	14	90	15.6%	-0.22
29..60	29%	11	64	17.2%	-0.10
61..100	8%	3	23	13.0%	-0.28
101+	21%	8	56	14.3%	-0.67
Unraced	0%	0	0	0.0%	0.00

ANALYSIS BY TODAY'S STARTING PRICE
Age	Prop	Win	Runs	Wins%	£
Odds On	24%	9	17	52.9%	-0.19
Ev-2/1	21%	8	20	40.0%	0.01
9/4-4/1	24%	9	46	19.6%	-0.18
9/2-6/1	16%	6	22	27.3%	0.68
13/2-10/1	8%	3	43	7.0%	-0.33
11/1-16/1	8%	3	42	7.1%	0.02
18/1-33/1	0%	0	38	0.0%	-1.00
40/1+	0%	0	28	0.0%	-1.00

ANALYSIS BY STARTING PRICE LAST TIME
Age	Prop	Win	Runs	Wins%	£
Odds On	11%	4	11	36.4%	-0.22
Ev-2/1	11%	4	29	13.8%	-0.37
9/4-4/1	34%	13	47	27.7%	0.29
9/2-6/1	21%	8	35	22.9%	0.08
13/2-10/1	13%	5	45	11.1%	-0.10
11/1-16/1	11%	4	43	9.3%	-0.65
18/1-33/1	0%	0	32	0.0%	-1.00
40/1+	0%	0	14	0.0%	-1.00
Unraced	0%	0	0	0.0%	0.00

ANALYSIS BY DISTANCE BEATEN LAST TIME
Age	Prop	Win	Runs	Wins%	£
..-10 lgh	3%	1	10	10.0%	-0.86
-10..0	24%	9	45	20.0%	-0.04
0.1..2	11%	4	13	30.8%	0.68
2.1..5	5%	2	16	12.5%	-0.41
5.1..10	11%	4	19	21.1%	-0.31
10.1..20	16%	6	42	14.3%	-0.17
20.0..30	8%	3	21	14.3%	-0.56
30.1+	11%	4	43	9.3%	-0.38
Not Compl	13%	5	47	10.6%	-0.55
Unraced	0%	0	0	0.0%	0.00

ANALYSIS BY SUCCESS RATE IN LAST 10 RUNS
Age	Prop	Win	Runs	Wins%	£
No Wins	5%	2	16	12.5%	-0.50
1 Win	18%	7	59	11.9%	-0.25
2 Wins	13%	5	56	8.9%	-0.28
3 Wins	24%	9	52	17.3%	-0.32
4 Wins	16%	6	36	16.7%	-0.52
5+ Wins	24%	9	37	24.3%	-0.04

ANALYSIS BY SUCCESS RATE IN LAST 3 RUNS
Age	Prop	Win	Runs	Wins%	£
No Wins	34%	13	116	11.2%	-0.35
1 Win	50%	19	90	21.1%	-0.05
2 Wins	16%	6	48	12.5%	-0.57
3 Wins	0%	0	2	0.0%	-1.00

ANALYSIS BY POSITION LAST TIME
Age	Prop	Win	Runs	Wins%	£
Won	26%	10	55	18.2%	-0.19
2nd or 3rd	29%	11	67	16.4%	-0.10
Unplaced	32%	12	87	13.8%	-0.37
Fell,BD,UR	8%	3	25	12.0%	-0.62
Pulled Up	5%	2	21	9.5%	-0.43
Ref/RanOut	0%	0	1	0.0%	-1.00
CO/SlipUp	0%	0	0	0.0%	0.00
Unraced	0%	0	0	0.0%	0.00

OTHER FACTORS (WINS-RUNS, £)
Course Winner:	19-85	-£0.03
Distance Winner:	25-143	-£0.17
Going Winner:	30-185	-£0.25
Beaten Favourite:	9-20	£0.85
BHA Top Rated:	10-31	-£0.18
Absolute Favourites:	14-35	-£0.28

Race Profiles

Conditions Chases (class 1..3): 3m+

ANALYSIS BY AGE

Age	Prop	Win	Runs	Wins%	£
3yo	0%	0	0	0.0%	0.00
4yo	0%	0	1	0.0%	-1.00
5yo	3%	2	8	25.0%	0.00
6yo	11%	7	31	22.6%	-0.42
7yo	25%	15	94	16.0%	-0.33
8yo	25%	15	115	13.0%	-0.30
9yo	15%	9	106	8.5%	-0.28
10yo	11%	7	79	8.9%	0.04
11yo	5%	3	44	6.8%	-0.23
12yo+	5%	3	37	8.1%	-0.67

ANALYSIS BY BHB RATING

Age	Prop	Win	Runs	Wins%	£
150+	59%	36	218	16.5%	0.00
130..149	25%	15	132	11.4%	-0.21
120..129	3%	2	37	5.4%	-0.58
110..119	0%	0	28	0.0%	-1.00
100..109	0%	0	7	0.0%	-1.00
80..99	0%	0	15	0.0%	-1.00
60..79	0%	0	4	0.0%	-1.00
..59	0%	0	0	0.0%	0.00
Unrated	13%	8	74	10.8%	-0.51

ANALYSIS BY WEIGHT CARRIED

Age	Prop	Win	Runs	Wins%	£
12-01+	2%	1	1	100.0%	1.38
11-8..12-00	51%	31	260	11.9%	-0.48
11-0..11-07	41%	25	208	12.0%	-0.09
10-8..10-13	7%	4	44	9.1%	0.07
10-0..10-07	0%	0	2	0.0%	-1.00
..9-13	0%	0	0	0.0%	0.00

ANALYSIS BY DAYS SINCE LAST RUN

Age	Prop	Win	Runs	Wins%	£
1..7	0%	0	10	0.0%	-1.00
8..14	0%	0	33	0.0%	-1.00
15..28	36%	22	155	14.2%	-0.10
29..60	30%	18	140	12.9%	-0.32
61..100	10%	6	33	18.2%	0.16
101+	23%	14	134	10.4%	-0.29
Unraced	2%	1	10	10.0%	-0.35

ANALYSIS BY TODAY'S STARTING PRICE

Age	Prop	Win	Runs	Wins%	£
Odds On	18%	11	19	57.9%	-0.11
Ev-2/1	25%	15	41	36.6%	-0.07
9/4-4/1	18%	11	56	19.6%	-0.26
9/2-6/1	13%	8	49	16.3%	0.03
13/2-10/1	13%	8	80	10.0%	-0.09
11/1-16/1	8%	5	71	7.0%	0.01
18/1-33/1	5%	3	99	3.0%	-0.17
40/1+	0%	0	100	0.0%	-1.00

ANALYSIS BY STARTING PRICE LAST TIME

Age	Prop	Win	Runs	Wins%	£
Odds On	20%	12	38	31.6%	-0.09
Ev-2/1	10%	6	33	18.2%	-0.49
9/4-4/1	13%	8	83	9.6%	-0.09
9/2-6/1	8%	5	64	7.8%	-0.76
13/2-10/1	20%	12	107	11.2%	-0.41
11/1-16/1	11%	7	79	8.9%	-0.13
18/1-33/1	16%	10	70	14.3%	0.32
40/1+	0%	0	31	0.0%	-1.00
Unraced	2%	1	10	10.0%	-0.35

ANALYSIS BY DISTANCE BEATEN LAST TIME

Age	Prop	Win	Runs	Wins%	£
..-10 lgh	8%	5	27	18.5%	-0.38
-10..0	23%	14	84	16.7%	-0.34
0.1..2	5%	3	38	7.9%	-0.62
2.1..5	8%	5	33	15.2%	-0.23
5.1..10	7%	4	42	9.5%	0.34
10.1..20	11%	7	54	13.0%	-0.57
20.0..30	7%	4	44	9.1%	-0.66
30.1+	16%	10	98	10.2%	-0.07
Not Compl	13%	8	85	9.4%	-0.18
Unraced	2%	1	10	10.0%	-0.35

ANALYSIS BY SUCCESS RATE IN LAST 10 RUNS

Age	Prop	Win	Runs	Wins%	£
No Wins	2%	1	63	1.6%	-0.54
1 Win	10%	6	106	5.7%	-0.38
2 Wins	8%	5	90	5.6%	-0.54
3 Wins	18%	11	78	14.1%	-0.43
4 Wins	27%	16	79	20.3%	0.52
5+ Wins	35%	21	89	23.6%	-0.25

ANALYSIS BY SUCCESS RATE IN LAST 3 RUNS

Age	Prop	Win	Runs	Wins%	£
No Wins	27%	16	253	6.3%	-0.44
1 Win	38%	23	159	14.5%	-0.04
2 Wins	23%	14	75	18.7%	-0.20
3 Wins	12%	7	18	38.9%	-0.29

ANALYSIS BY POSITION LAST TIME

Age	Prop	Win	Runs	Wins%	£
Won	31%	19	112	17.0%	-0.36
2nd or 3rd	18%	11	121	9.1%	-0.31
Unplaced	36%	22	188	11.7%	-0.24
Fell,BD,UR	5%	3	30	10.0%	-0.49
Pulled Up	8%	5	52	9.6%	0.05
Ref/RanOut	0%	0	2	0.0%	-1.00
CO/SlipUp	0%	0	0	0.0%	0.00
Unraced	2%	1	10	10.0%	-0.35

OTHER FACTORS (WINS-RUNS, £)

Course Winner:	28-178	-£0.12
Distance Winner:	33-233	-£0.44
Going Winner:	51-373	-£0.21
Beaten Favourite:	5-40	-£0.56
BHA Top Rated:	20-53	£0.07
Absolute Favourites:	23-56	-£0.13

Conditions Chases (class 1..3)

Conditions Chases (class 1..3): 2 to 5 runners

ANALYSIS BY AGE

Age	Prop	Win	Runs	Wins%	£
3yo	0%	0	0	0.0%	0.00
4yo	0%	0	1	0.0%	-1.00
5yo	10%	5	12	41.7%	0.09
6yo	15%	7	27	25.9%	-0.40
7yo	35%	17	54	31.5%	-0.08
8yo	25%	12	51	23.5%	-0.17
9yo	6%	3	41	7.3%	-0.45
10yo	2%	1	16	6.3%	-0.38
11yo	6%	3	7	42.9%	3.86
12yo+	0%	0	2	0.0%	-1.00

ANALYSIS BY BHB RATING

Age	Prop	Win	Runs	Wins%	£
150+	54%	26	85	30.6%	-0.12
130..149	31%	15	71	21.1%	0.10
120..129	4%	2	14	14.3%	0.11
110..119	0%	0	6	0.0%	-1.00
100..109	2%	1	4	25.0%	1.38
80..99	0%	0	6	0.0%	-1.00
60..79	0%	0	2	0.0%	-1.00
..59	0%	0	0	0.0%	0.00
Unrated	8%	4	23	17.4%	-0.59

ANALYSIS BY WEIGHT CARRIED

Age	Prop	Win	Runs	Wins%	£
12-01+	0%	0	0	0.0%	0.00
11-8..12-00	27%	13	42	31.0%	-0.03
11-0..11-07	60%	29	146	19.9%	-0.21
10-8..10-13	10%	5	20	25.0%	0.12
10-0..10-07	2%	1	3	33.3%	2.17
..9-13	0%	0	0	0.0%	0.00

ANALYSIS BY DAYS SINCE LAST RUN

Age	Prop	Win	Runs	Wins%	£
1..7	0%	0	9	0.0%	-1.00
8..14	0%	0	16	0.0%	-1.00
15..28	40%	19	70	27.1%	0.05
29..60	31%	15	46	32.6%	0.71
61..100	4%	2	6	33.3%	-0.15
101+	25%	12	61	19.7%	-0.50
Unraced	0%	0	3	0.0%	-1.00

ANALYSIS BY TODAY'S STARTING PRICE

Age	Prop	Win	Runs	Wins%	£
Odds On	29%	14	22	63.6%	-0.09
Ev-2/1	33%	16	40	40.0%	0.00
9/4-4/1	17%	8	49	16.3%	-0.41
9/2-6/1	6%	3	20	15.0%	-0.07
13/2-10/1	13%	6	31	19.4%	0.98
11/1-16/1	0%	0	21	0.0%	-1.00
18/1-33/1	2%	1	18	5.6%	0.06
40/1+	0%	0	10	0.0%	-1.00

ANALYSIS BY STARTING PRICE LAST TIME

Age	Prop	Win	Runs	Wins%	£
Odds On	10%	5	15	33.3%	-0.48
Ev-2/1	10%	5	20	25.0%	-0.24
9/4-4/1	23%	11	38	28.9%	-0.22
9/2-6/1	15%	7	23	30.4%	-0.16
13/2-10/1	17%	8	44	18.2%	-0.25
11/1-16/1	17%	8	35	22.9%	0.36
18/1-33/1	6%	3	22	13.6%	0.48
40/1+	2%	1	11	9.1%	-0.74
Unraced	0%	0	3	0.0%	-1.00

ANALYSIS BY DISTANCE BEATEN LAST TIME

Age	Prop	Win	Runs	Wins%	£
..-10 lgh	2%	1	6	16.7%	-0.79
-10..0	27%	13	33	39.4%	0.14
0.1..2	8%	4	17	23.5%	-0.39
2.1..5	10%	5	13	38.5%	0.50
5.1..10	10%	5	23	21.7%	-0.48
10.1..20	15%	7	25	28.0%	-0.13
20.0..30	8%	4	20	20.0%	-0.24
30.1+	6%	3	35	8.6%	-0.09
Not Compl	13%	6	36	16.7%	0.07
Unraced	0%	0	3	0.0%	-1.00

ANALYSIS BY SUCCESS RATE IN LAST 10 RUNS

Age	Prop	Win	Runs	Wins%	£
No Wins	2%	1	17	5.9%	-0.44
1 Win	21%	10	47	21.3%	0.41
2 Wins	6%	3	32	9.4%	-0.55
3 Wins	25%	12	41	29.3%	-0.13
4 Wins	21%	10	41	24.4%	-0.22
5+ Wins	25%	12	30	40.0%	0.00

ANALYSIS BY SUCCESS RATE IN LAST 3 RUNS

Age	Prop	Win	Runs	Wins%	£
No Wins	40%	19	94	20.2%	0.20
1 Win	33%	16	79	20.3%	-0.42
2 Wins	23%	11	33	33.3%	-0.19
3 Wins	4%	2	2	100.0%	0.38

ANALYSIS BY POSITION LAST TIME

Age	Prop	Win	Runs	Wins%	£
Won	29%	14	40	35.0%	-0.03
2nd or 3rd	31%	15	63	23.8%	-0.20
Unplaced	27%	13	69	18.8%	-0.12
Fell,BD,UR	6%	3	19	15.8%	-0.43
Pulled Up	6%	3	17	17.6%	0.62
Ref/RanOut	0%	0	0	0.0%	0.00
CO/SlipUp	0%	0	0	0.0%	0.00
Unraced	0%	0	3	0.0%	-1.00

OTHER FACTORS (WINS-RUNS, £)

Course Winner:	19-64	£0.09
Distance Winner:	29-124	-£0.19
Going Winner:	38-141	£0.09
Beaten Favourite:	5-20	-£0.43
7-Day Winners:	0-1	-£1.00
BHA Top Rated:	18-44	-£0.04
Absolute Favourites:	23-43	-£0.04

Race Profiles

Conditions Chases (class 1..3): 6 to 10 runners

ANALYSIS BY AGE

Age	Prop	Win	Runs	Wins%	£
3yo	0%	0	0	0.0%	0.00
4yo	0%	0	2	0.0%	-1.00
5yo	9%	6	27	22.2%	-0.23
6yo	19%	13	59	22.0%	-0.29
7yo	16%	11	86	12.8%	-0.45
8yo	30%	21	125	16.8%	0.23
9yo	16%	11	100	11.0%	-0.37
10yo	10%	7	74	9.5%	0.08
11yo	0%	0	35	0.0%	-1.00
12yo+	1%	1	13	7.7%	-0.50

ANALYSIS BY BHB RATING

Age	Prop	Win	Runs	Wins%	£
150+	69%	48	290	16.6%	0.07
130..149	23%	16	138	11.6%	-0.40
120..129	0%	0	15	0.0%	-1.00
110..119	0%	0	5	0.0%	-1.00
100..109	0%	0	3	0.0%	-1.00
80..99	0%	0	10	0.0%	-1.00
60..79	0%	0	5	0.0%	-1.00
..59	0%	0	0	0.0%	0.00
Unrated	9%	6	55	10.9%	-0.63

ANALYSIS BY WEIGHT CARRIED

Age	Prop	Win	Runs	Wins%	£
12-01+	1%	1	1	100.0%	1.38
11-8..12-00	33%	23	176	13.1%	-0.31
11-0..11-07	64%	45	326	13.8%	-0.12
10-8..10-13	1%	1	12	8.3%	-0.71
10-0..10-07	0%	0	6	0.0%	-1.00
..9-13	0%	0	0	0.0%	0.00

ANALYSIS BY DAYS SINCE LAST RUN

Age	Prop	Win	Runs	Wins%	£
1..7	0%	0	13	0.0%	-1.00
8..14	4%	3	41	7.3%	-0.64
15..28	27%	19	158	12.0%	-0.06
29..60	37%	26	162	16.0%	-0.16
61..100	7%	5	32	15.6%	0.00
101+	24%	17	114	14.9%	-0.27
Unraced	0%	0	1	0.0%	-1.00

ANALYSIS BY TODAY'S STARTING PRICE

Age	Prop	Win	Runs	Wins%	£
Odds On	16%	11	26	42.3%	-0.32
Ev-2/1	17%	12	38	31.6%	-0.20
9/4-4/1	29%	20	79	25.3%	0.01
9/2-6/1	14%	10	58	17.2%	0.09
13/2-10/1	11%	8	85	9.4%	-0.14
11/1-16/1	11%	8	76	10.5%	0.51
18/1-33/1	1%	1	89	1.1%	-0.62
40/1+	0%	0	70	0.0%	-1.00

ANALYSIS BY STARTING PRICE LAST TIME

Age	Prop	Win	Runs	Wins%	£
Odds On	16%	11	31	35.5%	0.05
Ev-2/1	14%	10	48	20.8%	-0.13
9/4-4/1	23%	16	94	17.0%	0.09
9/2-6/1	10%	7	65	10.8%	-0.42
13/2-10/1	16%	11	102	10.8%	-0.34
11/1-16/1	10%	7	85	8.2%	-0.50
18/1-33/1	11%	8	70	11.4%	0.28
40/1+	0%	0	25	0.0%	-1.00
Unraced	0%	0	1	0.0%	-1.00

ANALYSIS BY DISTANCE BEATEN LAST TIME

Age	Prop	Win	Runs	Wins%	£
..-10 lgh	9%	6	31	19.4%	-0.57
-10..0	21%	15	85	17.6%	0.08
0.1..2	9%	6	28	21.4%	0.04
2.1..5	7%	5	36	13.9%	-0.35
5.1..10	9%	6	39	15.4%	0.67
10.1..20	13%	9	85	10.6%	-0.56
20.0..30	4%	3	37	8.1%	-0.63
30.1+	11%	8	87	9.2%	-0.52
Not Compl	17%	12	92	13.0%	0.07
Unraced	0%	0	1	0.0%	-1.00

ANALYSIS BY SUCCESS RATE IN LAST 10 RUNS

Age	Prop	Win	Runs	Wins%	£
No Wins	4%	3	44	6.8%	-0.43
1 Win	10%	7	98	7.1%	-0.58
2 Wins	17%	12	100	12.0%	-0.17
3 Wins	19%	13	99	13.1%	-0.45
4 Wins	21%	15	89	16.9%	0.35
5+ Wins	29%	20	90	22.2%	0.00

ANALYSIS BY SUCCESS RATE IN LAST 3 RUNS

Age	Prop	Win	Runs	Wins%	£
No Wins	29%	20	249	8.0%	-0.48
1 Win	44%	31	175	17.7%	0.10
2 Wins	24%	17	84	20.2%	0.07
3 Wins	3%	2	12	16.7%	-0.76

ANALYSIS BY POSITION LAST TIME

Age	Prop	Win	Runs	Wins%	£
Won	30%	21	116	18.1%	-0.09
2nd or 3rd	26%	18	129	14.0%	-0.14
Unplaced	27%	19	183	10.4%	-0.45
Fell,BD,UR	9%	6	39	15.4%	0.06
Pulled Up	9%	6	50	12.0%	0.14
Ref/RanOut	0%	0	3	0.0%	-1.00
CO/SlipUp	0%	0	0	0.0%	0.00
Unraced	0%	0	1	0.0%	-1.00

OTHER FACTORS (WINS-RUNS, £)

Course Winner:	32-180	-£0.04
Distance Winner:	43-324	-£0.38
Going Winner:	61-402	-£0.12
Beaten Favourite:	13-53	-£0.03
7-Day Winners:	0-3	-£1.00
BHA Top Rated:	20-55	£0.09
Absolute Favourites:	22-67	-£0.29

Conditions Chases (class 1..3)

Conditions Chases (class 1..3): 11 runners or more

ANALYSIS BY AGE

Age	Prop	Win	Runs	Wins%	£
3yo	0%	0	0	0.0%	0.00
4yo	0%	0	0	0.0%	0.00
5yo	0%	0	1	0.0%	-1.00
6yo	5%	1	14	7.1%	-0.90
7yo	14%	3	45	6.7%	-0.62
8yo	14%	3	67	4.5%	-0.62
9yo	38%	8	68	11.8%	0.27
10yo	14%	3	52	5.8%	-0.78
11yo	0%	0	24	0.0%	-1.00
12yo+	14%	3	31	9.7%	-0.60

ANALYSIS BY BHB RATING

Age	Prop	Win	Runs	Wins%	£
150+	52%	11	121	9.1%	-0.55
130..149	14%	3	57	5.3%	-0.29
120..129	0%	0	25	0.0%	-1.00
110..119	0%	0	23	0.0%	-1.00
100..109	0%	0	6	0.0%	-1.00
80..99	0%	0	8	0.0%	-1.00
60..79	0%	0	1	0.0%	-1.00
..59	0%	0	0	0.0%	0.00
Unrated	33%	7	61	11.5%	-0.03

ANALYSIS BY WEIGHT CARRIED

Age	Prop	Win	Runs	Wins%	£
12-01+	0%	0	0	0.0%	0.00
11-8..12-00	81%	17	211	8.1%	-0.48
11-0..11-07	14%	3	66	4.5%	-0.76
10-8..10-13	5%	1	25	4.0%	0.16
10-0..10-07	0%	0	0	0.0%	0.00
..9-13	0%	0	0	0.0%	0.00

ANALYSIS BY DAYS SINCE LAST RUN

Age	Prop	Win	Runs	Wins%	£
1..7	5%	1	7	14.3%	-0.21
8..14	5%	1	18	5.6%	-0.17
15..28	43%	9	100	9.0%	-0.46
29..60	24%	5	76	6.6%	-0.66
61..100	14%	3	28	10.7%	-0.31
101+	5%	1	62	1.6%	-0.53
Unraced	5%	1	11	9.1%	-0.41

ANALYSIS BY TODAY'S STARTING PRICE

Age	Prop	Win	Runs	Wins%	£
Odds On	14%	3	5	60.0%	-0.07
Ev-2/1	14%	3	6	50.0%	0.27
9/4-4/1	14%	3	18	16.7%	-0.37
9/2-6/1	24%	5	18	27.8%	0.64
13/2-10/1	14%	3	45	6.7%	-0.43
11/1-16/1	14%	3	60	5.0%	-0.22
18/1-33/1	5%	1	66	1.5%	-0.56
40/1+	0%	0	84	0.0%	-1.00

ANALYSIS BY STARTING PRICE LAST TIME

Age	Prop	Win	Runs	Wins%	£
Odds On	29%	6	27	22.2%	-0.38
Ev-2/1	0%	0	25	0.0%	-1.00
9/4-4/1	19%	4	56	7.1%	-0.38
9/2-6/1	10%	2	37	5.4%	-0.42
13/2-10/1	10%	2	48	4.2%	-0.52
11/1-16/1	14%	3	45	6.7%	-0.12
18/1-33/1	14%	3	36	8.3%	-0.66
40/1+	0%	0	17	0.0%	-1.00
Unraced	5%	1	11	9.1%	-0.41

ANALYSIS BY DISTANCE BEATEN LAST TIME

Age	Prop	Win	Runs	Wins%	£
..-10 lgh	14%	3	19	15.8%	-0.47
-10..0	29%	6	49	12.2%	-0.21
0.1..2	5%	1	21	4.8%	-0.29
2.1..5	10%	2	23	8.7%	-0.39
5.1..10	5%	1	25	4.0%	-0.83
10.1..20	5%	1	31	3.2%	-0.52
20.0..30	5%	1	28	3.6%	-0.94
30.1+	24%	5	57	8.8%	-0.13
Not Compl	0%	0	38	0.0%	-1.00
Unraced	5%	1	11	9.1%	-0.41

ANALYSIS BY SUCCESS RATE IN LAST 10 RUNS

Age	Prop	Win	Runs	Wins%	£
No Wins	5%	1	39	2.6%	-0.26
1 Win	25%	5	67	7.5%	-0.45
2 Wins	10%	2	58	3.4%	-0.59
3 Wins	10%	2	44	4.5%	-0.53
4 Wins	15%	3	35	8.6%	-0.54
5+ Wins	35%	7	48	14.6%	-0.55

ANALYSIS BY SUCCESS RATE IN LAST 3 RUNS

Age	Prop	Win	Runs	Wins%	£
No Wins	30%	6	148	4.1%	-0.47
1 Win	40%	8	88	9.1%	-0.40
2 Wins	15%	3	45	6.7%	-0.79
3 Wins	15%	3	10	30.0%	-0.29

ANALYSIS BY POSITION LAST TIME

Age	Prop	Win	Runs	Wins%	£
Won	43%	9	68	13.2%	-0.28
2nd or 3rd	24%	5	79	6.3%	-0.39
Unplaced	29%	6	107	5.6%	-0.52
Fell,BD,UR	0%	0	21	0.0%	-1.00
Pulled Up	0%	0	15	0.0%	-1.00
Ref/RanOut	0%	0	1	0.0%	-1.00
CO/SlipUp	0%	0	0	0.0%	0.00
Unraced	5%	1	11	9.1%	-0.41

OTHER FACTORS (WINS-RUNS, £)

Course Winner:	13-110	-£0.41
Distance Winner:	14-130	-£0.39
Going Winner:	17-214	-£0.55
Beaten Favourite:	0-25	-£1.00
BHA Top Rated:	4-19	-£0.23
Absolute Favourites:	6-18	-£0.32

Race Profiles

Conditions Chases (class 1..3): up to 7 days off the track

ANALYSIS BY AGE

Age	Prop	Win	Runs	Wins%	£
3yo	0%	0	0	0.0%	0.00
4yo	0%	0	1	0.0%	-1.00
5yo	0%	0	1	0.0%	-1.00
6yo	0%	0	4	0.0%	-1.00
7yo	50%	1	9	11.1%	-0.28
8yo	50%	1	10	10.0%	-0.45
9yo	0%	0	7	0.0%	-1.00
10yo	0%	0	7	0.0%	-1.00
11yo	0%	0	3	0.0%	-1.00
12yo+	0%	0	2	0.0%	-1.00

ANALYSIS BY BHB RATING

Age	Prop	Win	Runs	Wins%	£
150+	50%	1	9	11.1%	-0.39
130..149	0%	0	10	0.0%	-1.00
120..129	0%	0	3	0.0%	-1.00
110..119	0%	0	3	0.0%	-1.00
100..109	0%	0	0	0.0%	0.00
80..99	0%	0	2	0.0%	-1.00
60..79	0%	0	3	0.0%	-1.00
..59	0%	0	0	0.0%	0.00
Unrated	50%	1	14	7.1%	-0.54

ANALYSIS BY WEIGHT CARRIED

Age	Prop	Win	Runs	Wins%	£
12-01+	0%	0	0	0.0%	0.00
11-8..12-00	50%	1	9	11.1%	-0.28
11-0..11-07	50%	1	33	3.0%	-0.83
10-8..10-13	0%	0	2	0.0%	-1.00
10-0..10-07	0%	0	0	0.0%	0.00
..9-13	0%	0	0	0.0%	0.00

ANALYSIS BY DAYS SINCE LAST RUN

Age	Prop	Win	Runs	Wins%	£
1..7	50%	1	29	3.4%	-0.81
8..14	0%	0	0	0.0%	0.00
15..28	0%	0	0	0.0%	0.00
29..60	0%	0	0	0.0%	0.00
61..100	0%	0	0	0.0%	0.00
101+	0%	0	0	0.0%	0.00
Unraced	50%	1	15	6.7%	-0.57

ANALYSIS BY TODAY'S STARTING PRICE

Age	Prop	Win	Runs	Wins%	£
Odds On	0%	0	1	0.0%	-1.00
Ev-2/1	0%	0	2	0.0%	-1.00
9/4-4/1	0%	0	3	0.0%	-1.00
9/2-6/1	100%	2	3	66.7%	3.00
13/2-10/1	0%	0	5	0.0%	-1.00
11/1-16/1	0%	0	7	0.0%	-1.00
18/1-33/1	0%	0	8	0.0%	-1.00
40/1+	0%	0	15	0.0%	-1.00

ANALYSIS BY STARTING PRICE LAST TIME

Age	Prop	Win	Runs	Wins%	£
Odds On	0%	0	0	0.0%	0.00
Ev-2/1	0%	0	1	0.0%	-1.00
9/4-4/1	50%	1	7	14.3%	-0.21
9/2-6/1	0%	0	2	0.0%	-1.00
13/2-10/1	0%	0	6	0.0%	-1.00
11/1-16/1	0%	0	5	0.0%	-1.00
18/1-33/1	0%	0	4	0.0%	-1.00
40/1+	0%	0	4	0.0%	-1.00
Unraced	50%	1	15	6.7%	-0.57

ANALYSIS BY DISTANCE BEATEN LAST TIME

Age	Prop	Win	Runs	Wins%	£
..-10 lgh	0%	0	4	0.0%	-1.00
-10..0	0%	0	0	0.0%	0.00
0.1..2	0%	0	1	0.0%	-1.00
2.1..5	50%	1	5	20.0%	0.10
5.1..10	0%	0	2	0.0%	-1.00
10.1..20	0%	0	2	0.0%	-1.00
20.0..30	0%	0	3	0.0%	-1.00
30.1+	0%	0	7	0.0%	-1.00
Not Compl	0%	0	5	0.0%	-1.00
Unraced	50%	1	15	6.7%	-0.57

ANALYSIS BY SUCCESS RATE IN LAST 10 RUNS

Age	Prop	Win	Runs	Wins%	£
No Wins	0%	0	7	0.0%	-1.00
1 Win	100%	1	8	12.5%	-0.31
2 Wins	0%	0	5	0.0%	-1.00
3 Wins	0%	0	4	0.0%	-1.00
4 Wins	0%	0	2	0.0%	-1.00
5+ Wins	0%	0	3	0.0%	-1.00

ANALYSIS BY SUCCESS RATE IN LAST 3 RUNS

Age	Prop	Win	Runs	Wins%	£
No Wins	100%	1	18	5.6%	-0.69
1 Win	0%	0	9	0.0%	-1.00
2 Wins	0%	0	2	0.0%	-1.00
3 Wins	0%	0	0	0.0%	0.00

ANALYSIS BY POSITION LAST TIME

Age	Prop	Win	Runs	Wins%	£
Won	0%	0	4	0.0%	-1.00
2nd or 3rd	50%	1	9	11.1%	-0.39
Unplaced	0%	0	11	0.0%	-1.00
Fell,BD,UR	0%	0	1	0.0%	-1.00
Pulled Up	0%	0	3	0.0%	-1.00
Ref/RanOut	0%	0	1	0.0%	-1.00
CO/SlipUp	0%	0	0	0.0%	0.00
Unraced	50%	1	15	6.7%	-0.57

OTHER FACTORS (WINS-RUNS, £)

Course Winner:	0-9	-£1.00
Distance Winner:	1-11	-£0.50
Going Winner:	1-19	-£0.71
7-Day Winners:	0-4	-£1.00
BHA Top Rated:	0-2	-£1.00
Absolute Favourites:	0-4	-£1.00

Conditions Chases (class 1..3)

Conditions Chases (class 1..3): 100+ days off the track

ANALYSIS BY AGE

Age	Prop	Win	Runs	Wins%	£
3yo	0%	0	0	0.0%	0.00
4yo	0%	0	0	0.0%	0.00
5yo	6%	2	12	16.7%	-0.77
6yo	13%	4	20	20.0%	-0.33
7yo	29%	9	41	22.0%	-0.36
8yo	32%	10	58	17.2%	-0.24
9yo	16%	5	49	10.2%	0.14
10yo	3%	1	26	3.8%	-0.86
11yo	0%	0	17	0.0%	-1.00
12yo+	0%	0	15	0.0%	-1.00

ANALYSIS BY BHB RATING

Age	Prop	Win	Runs	Wins%	£
150+	48%	15	85	17.6%	-0.23
130..149	29%	9	78	11.5%	-0.25
120..129	3%	1	16	6.3%	-0.72
110..119	0%	0	12	0.0%	-1.00
100..109	0%	0	1	0.0%	-1.00
80..99	0%	0	2	0.0%	-1.00
60..79	0%	0	1	0.0%	-1.00
..59	0%	0	0	0.0%	0.00
Unrated	19%	6	43	14.0%	-0.58

ANALYSIS BY WEIGHT CARRIED

Age	Prop	Win	Runs	Wins%	£
12-01+	0%	0	0	0.0%	0.00
11-8..12-00	29%	9	88	10.2%	-0.67
11-0..11-07	65%	20	129	15.5%	-0.34
10-8..10-13	6%	2	19	10.5%	0.71
10-0..10-07	0%	0	2	0.0%	-1.00
..9-13	0%	0	0	0.0%	0.00

ANALYSIS BY DAYS SINCE LAST RUN

Age	Prop	Win	Runs	Wins%	£
1..7	0%	0	0	0.0%	0.00
8..14	0%	0	0	0.0%	0.00
15..28	0%	0	0	0.0%	0.00
29..60	0%	0	0	0.0%	0.00
61..100	3%	1	1	100.0%	2.50
101+	97%	30	237	12.7%	-0.40
Unraced	0%	0	0	0.0%	0.00

ANALYSIS BY TODAY'S STARTING PRICE

Age	Prop	Win	Runs	Wins%	£
Odds On	23%	7	14	50.0%	-0.30
Ev-2/1	16%	5	17	29.4%	-0.21
9/4-4/1	42%	13	46	28.3%	0.09
9/2-6/1	10%	3	16	18.8%	0.19
13/2-10/1	3%	1	31	3.2%	-0.74
11/1-16/1	3%	1	30	3.3%	-0.43
18/1-33/1	3%	1	42	2.4%	-0.31
40/1+	0%	0	42	0.0%	-1.00

ANALYSIS BY STARTING PRICE LAST TIME

Age	Prop	Win	Runs	Wins%	£
Odds On	10%	3	15	20.0%	-0.57
Ev-2/1	13%	4	16	25.0%	-0.20
9/4-4/1	23%	7	42	16.7%	-0.39
9/2-6/1	13%	4	32	12.5%	-0.55
13/2-10/1	10%	3	46	6.5%	-0.83
11/1-16/1	19%	6	46	13.0%	0.07
18/1-33/1	10%	3	30	10.0%	-0.09
40/1+	3%	1	11	9.1%	-0.74
Unraced	0%	0	0	0.0%	0.00

ANALYSIS BY DISTANCE BEATEN LAST TIME

Age	Prop	Win	Runs	Wins%	£
..-10 lgh	6%	2	12	16.7%	-0.50
-10..0	29%	9	37	24.3%	-0.14
0.1..2	6%	2	11	18.2%	-0.53
2.1..5	3%	1	9	11.1%	-0.68
5.1..10	3%	1	14	7.1%	-0.73
10.1..20	13%	4	32	12.5%	-0.74
20.0..30	10%	3	21	14.3%	-0.42
30.1+	13%	4	44	9.1%	-0.10
Not Compl	16%	5	58	8.6%	-0.38
Unraced	0%	0	0	0.0%	0.00

ANALYSIS BY SUCCESS RATE IN LAST 10 RUNS

Age	Prop	Win	Runs	Wins%	£
No Wins	3%	1	31	3.2%	-0.06
1 Win	10%	3	54	5.6%	-0.81
2 Wins	6%	2	31	6.5%	-0.63
3 Wins	32%	10	54	18.5%	-0.40
4 Wins	19%	6	34	17.6%	-0.32
5+ Wins	29%	9	34	26.5%	0.18

ANALYSIS BY SUCCESS RATE IN LAST 3 RUNS

Age	Prop	Win	Runs	Wins%	£
No Wins	42%	13	118	11.0%	-0.37
1 Win	32%	10	77	13.0%	-0.38
2 Wins	26%	8	37	21.6%	-0.33
3 Wins	0%	0	6	0.0%	-1.00

ANALYSIS BY POSITION LAST TIME

Age	Prop	Win	Runs	Wins%	£
Won	35%	11	49	22.4%	-0.23
2nd or 3rd	16%	5	49	10.2%	-0.73
Unplaced	32%	10	82	12.2%	-0.28
Fell,BD,UR	6%	2	21	9.5%	-0.61
Pulled Up	10%	3	36	8.3%	-0.22
Ref/RanOut	0%	0	1	0.0%	-1.00
CO/SlipUp	0%	0	0	0.0%	0.00
Unraced	0%	0	0	0.0%	0.00

OTHER FACTORS (WINS-RUNS, £)

Course Winner:	13-79	-£0.34
Distance Winner:	20-125	-£0.56
Going Winner:	25-167	-£0.38
Beaten Favourite:	2-21	-£0.80
BHA Top Rated:	10-30	£0.10
Absolute Favourites:	11-29	-£0.22

Race Profiles

Conditions Chases (class 4..6)

ANALYSIS BY AGE

Age	Prop	Win	Runs	Wins%	£
3yo	0%	0	0	0.0%	0.00
4yo	0%	0	1	0.0%	-1.00
5yo	3%	1	19	5.3%	-0.32
6yo	21%	8	49	16.3%	-0.25
7yo	26%	10	71	14.1%	-0.22
8yo	18%	7	71	9.9%	0.04
9yo	23%	9	60	15.0%	1.23
10yo	8%	3	41	7.3%	-0.49
11yo	0%	0	21	0.0%	-1.00
12yo+	3%	1	27	3.7%	-0.65

ANALYSIS BY BHB RATING

Age	Prop	Win	Runs	Wins%	£
150+	0%	0	0	0.0%	0.00
130..149	0%	0	1	0.0%	-1.00
120..129	3%	1	2	50.0%	1.17
110..119	3%	1	10	10.0%	-0.60
100..109	5%	2	7	28.6%	1.64
80..99	72%	28	220	12.7%	-0.09
60..79	13%	5	101	5.0%	0.09
..59	0%	0	7	0.0%	-1.00
Unrated	5%	2	12	16.7%	-0.51

ANALYSIS BY WEIGHT CARRIED

Age	Prop	Win	Runs	Wins%	£
12-01+	0%	0	1	0.0%	-1.00
11-8..12-00	0%	0	3	0.0%	-1.00
11-0..11-07	36%	14	127	11.0%	-0.10
10-8..10-13	44%	17	148	11.5%	0.13
10-0..10-07	21%	8	81	9.9%	-0.24
..9-13	0%	0	0	0.0%	0.00

ANALYSIS BY DAYS SINCE LAST RUN

Age	Prop	Win	Runs	Wins%	£
1..7	18%	7	41	17.1%	0.44
8..14	21%	8	80	10.0%	-0.25
15..28	28%	11	102	10.8%	0.29
29..60	21%	8	64	12.5%	0.04
61..100	0%	0	9	0.0%	-1.00
101+	13%	5	63	7.9%	-0.59
Unraced	0%	0	1	0.0%	-1.00

ANALYSIS BY TODAY'S STARTING PRICE

Age	Prop	Win	Runs	Wins%	£
Odds On	3%	1	4	25.0%	-0.52
Ev-2/1	13%	5	19	26.3%	-0.32
9/4-4/1	23%	9	56	16.1%	-0.38
9/2-6/1	18%	7	42	16.7%	-0.02
13/2-10/1	23%	9	71	12.7%	0.08
11/1-16/1	13%	5	57	8.8%	0.21
18/1-33/1	5%	2	64	3.1%	-0.38
40/1+	3%	1	47	2.1%	0.43

ANALYSIS BY STARTING PRICE LAST TIME

Age	Prop	Win	Runs	Wins%	£
Odds On	0%	0	2	0.0%	-1.00
Ev-2/1	10%	4	10	40.0%	0.18
9/4-4/1	23%	9	34	26.5%	0.61
9/2-6/1	8%	3	37	8.1%	-0.50
13/2-10/1	31%	12	83	14.5%	0.00
11/1-16/1	18%	7	68	10.3%	0.20
18/1-33/1	8%	3	73	4.1%	-0.64
40/1+	3%	1	52	1.9%	0.29
Unraced	0%	0	1	0.0%	-1.00

ANALYSIS BY DISTANCE BEATEN LAST TIME

Age	Prop	Win	Runs	Wins%	£
..-10 lgh	3%	1	6	16.7%	-0.28
-10..0	8%	3	27	11.1%	-0.62
0.1..2	3%	1	11	9.1%	0.18
2.1..5	5%	2	18	11.1%	-0.46
5.1..10	13%	5	23	21.7%	0.13
10.1..20	15%	6	51	11.8%	-0.29
20.0..30	13%	5	39	12.8%	-0.01
30.1+	13%	5	98	5.1%	-0.50
Not Compl	28%	11	86	12.8%	0.82
Unraced	0%	0	1	0.0%	-1.00

ANALYSIS BY SUCCESS RATE IN LAST 10 RUNS

Age	Prop	Win	Runs	Wins%	£
No Wins	41%	16	180	8.9%	0.20
1 Win	38%	15	124	12.1%	-0.36
2 Wins	15%	6	43	14.0%	-0.46
3 Wins	5%	2	10	20.0%	1.55
4 Wins	0%	0	2	0.0%	-1.00
5+ Wins	0%	0	0	0.0%	0.00

ANALYSIS BY SUCCESS RATE IN LAST 3 RUNS

Age	Prop	Win	Runs	Wins%	£
No Wins	72%	28	277	10.1%	0.07
1 Win	23%	9	73	12.3%	-0.45
2 Wins	5%	2	9	22.2%	-0.27
3 Wins	0%	0	0	0.0%	0.00

ANALYSIS BY POSITION LAST TIME

Age	Prop	Win	Runs	Wins%	£
Won	10%	4	33	12.1%	-0.56
2nd or 3rd	28%	11	65	16.9%	0.17
Unplaced	33%	13	176	7.4%	-0.45
Fell,BD,UR	13%	5	23	21.7%	0.37
Pulled Up	13%	5	61	8.2%	0.93
Ref/RanOut	3%	1	1	100.0%	6.50
CO/SlipUp	0%	0	0	0.0%	0.00
Unraced	0%	0	1	0.0%	-1.00

OTHER FACTORS (WINS-RUNS, £)

Course Winner:	6-60	-£0.25
Distance Winner:	11-95	-£0.05
Going Winner:	9-115	-£0.55
Beaten Favourite:	4-12	£0.14
7-Day Winners:	1-6	-£0.65
BHA Top Rated:	6-40	-£0.31
Absolute Favourites:	9-35	-£0.26

Conditions Chases (class 4..6)

Conditions Chases (class 4..6): 2m to 2m3f

ANALYSIS BY AGE
Age	Prop	Win	Runs	Wins%	£
3yo	0%	0	0	0.0%	0.00
4yo	0%	0	0	0.0%	0.00
5yo	0%	0	4	0.0%	-1.00
6yo	14%	1	6	16.7%	-0.28
7yo	0%	0	13	0.0%	-1.00
8yo	43%	3	13	23.1%	2.42
9yo	29%	2	15	13.3%	-0.13
10yo	14%	1	7	14.3%	0.14
11yo	0%	0	2	0.0%	-1.00
12yo+	0%	0	3	0.0%	-1.00

ANALYSIS BY BHB RATING
Age	Prop	Win	Runs	Wins%	£
150+	0%	0	0	0.0%	0.00
130..149	0%	0	1	0.0%	-1.00
120..129	14%	1	1	100.0%	3.33
110..119	0%	0	3	0.0%	-1.00
100..109	14%	1	3	33.3%	1.17
80..99	57%	4	37	10.8%	0.14
60..79	14%	1	11	9.1%	0.55
..59	0%	0	2	0.0%	-1.00
Unrated	0%	0	5	0.0%	-1.00

ANALYSIS BY WEIGHT CARRIED
Age	Prop	Win	Runs	Wins%	£
12-01+	0%	0	1	0.0%	-1.00
11-8..12-00	0%	0	1	0.0%	-1.00
11-0..11-07	43%	3	29	10.3%	0.46
10-8..10-13	43%	3	22	13.6%	-0.11
10-0..10-07	14%	1	10	10.0%	-0.20
..9-13	0%	0	0	0.0%	0.00

ANALYSIS BY DAYS SINCE LAST RUN
Age	Prop	Win	Runs	Wins%	£
1..7	43%	3	13	23.1%	0.69
8..14	0%	0	11	0.0%	-1.00
15..28	29%	2	15	13.3%	0.77
29..60	29%	2	9	22.2%	1.37
61..100	0%	0	3	0.0%	-1.00
101+	0%	0	11	0.0%	-1.00
Unraced	0%	0	1	0.0%	-1.00

ANALYSIS BY TODAY'S STARTING PRICE
Age	Prop	Win	Runs	Wins%	£
Odds On	0%	0	1	0.0%	-1.00
Ev-2/1	0%	0	1	0.0%	-1.00
9/4-4/1	14%	1	13	7.7%	-0.67
9/2-6/1	29%	2	8	25.0%	0.50
13/2-10/1	29%	2	10	20.0%	0.55
11/1-16/1	14%	1	7	14.3%	1.43
18/1-33/1	14%	1	16	6.3%	0.31
40/1+	0%	0	7	0.0%	-1.00

ANALYSIS BY STARTING PRICE LAST TIME
Age	Prop	Win	Runs	Wins%	£
Odds On	0%	0	0	0.0%	0.00
Ev-2/1	14%	1	4	25.0%	0.08
9/4-4/1	29%	2	6	33.3%	3.08
9/2-6/1	0%	0	6	0.0%	-1.00
13/2-10/1	43%	3	16	18.8%	1.16
11/1-16/1	14%	1	10	10.0%	-0.35
18/1-33/1	0%	0	12	0.0%	-1.00
40/1+	0%	0	8	0.0%	-1.00
Unraced	0%	0	1	0.0%	-1.00

ANALYSIS BY DISTANCE BEATEN LAST TIME
Age	Prop	Win	Runs	Wins%	£
..-10 lgh	14%	1	1	100.0%	3.33
-10..0	0%	0	6	0.0%	-1.00
0.1..2	0%	0	3	0.0%	-1.00
2.1..5	0%	0	2	0.0%	-1.00
5.1..10	14%	1	4	25.0%	0.63
10.1..20	14%	1	9	11.1%	-0.11
20.0..30	14%	1	6	16.7%	2.50
30.1+	0%	0	18	0.0%	-1.00
Not Compl	43%	3	13	23.1%	1.31
Unraced	0%	0	1	0.0%	-1.00

ANALYSIS BY SUCCESS RATE IN LAST 10 RUNS
Age	Prop	Win	Runs	Wins%	£
No Wins	14%	1	29	3.4%	-0.41
1 Win	57%	4	20	20.0%	0.38
2 Wins	14%	1	10	10.0%	-0.57
3 Wins	14%	1	2	50.0%	9.50
4 Wins	0%	0	1	0.0%	-1.00
5+ Wins	0%	0	0	0.0%	0.00

ANALYSIS BY SUCCESS RATE IN LAST 3 RUNS
Age	Prop	Win	Runs	Wins%	£
No Wins	57%	4	46	8.7%	0.09
1 Win	43%	3	13	23.1%	0.53
2 Wins	0%	0	3	0.0%	-1.00
3 Wins	0%	0	0	0.0%	0.00

ANALYSIS BY POSITION LAST TIME
Age	Prop	Win	Runs	Wins%	£
Won	14%	1	7	14.3%	-0.38
2nd or 3rd	14%	1	9	11.1%	-0.28
Unplaced	29%	2	34	5.9%	-0.15
Fell,BD,UR	14%	1	3	33.3%	0.83
Pulled Up	14%	1	8	12.5%	1.13
Ref/RanOut	14%	1	1	100.0%	6.50
CO/SlipUp	0%	0	0	0.0%	0.00
Unraced	0%	0	1	0.0%	-1.00

OTHER FACTORS (WINS-RUNS, £)
Course Winner:	1-11	-£0.50
Distance Winner:	4-26	£0.47
Going Winner:	1-22	-£0.75
Beaten Favourite:	0-3	-£1.00
7-Day Winners:	0-1	-£1.00
BHA Top Rated:	2-7	£0.76
Absolute Favourites:	0-7	-£1.00

Race Profiles

Conditions Chases (class 4..6): 2m4f to 2m7f

ANALYSIS BY AGE

Age	Prop	Win	Runs	Wins%	£
3yo	0%	0	0	0.0%	0.00
4yo	0%	0	0	0.0%	0.00
5yo	6%	1	12	8.3%	0.08
6yo	19%	3	21	14.3%	-0.44
7yo	38%	6	29	20.7%	0.31
8yo	6%	1	28	3.6%	-0.89
9yo	25%	4	22	18.2%	0.78
10yo	6%	1	16	6.3%	-0.53
11yo	0%	0	11	0.0%	-1.00
12yo+	0%	0	12	0.0%	-1.00

ANALYSIS BY BHB RATING

Age	Prop	Win	Runs	Wins%	£
150+	0%	0	0	0.0%	0.00
130..149	0%	0	0	0.0%	0.00
120..129	0%	0	0	0.0%	0.00
110..119	0%	0	0	0.0%	0.00
100..109	0%	0	1	0.0%	-1.00
80..99	94%	15	102	14.7%	-0.03
60..79	6%	1	46	2.2%	-0.72
..59	0%	0	2	0.0%	-1.00
Unrated	0%	0	0	0.0%	0.00

ANALYSIS BY WEIGHT CARRIED

Age	Prop	Win	Runs	Wins%	£
12-01+	0%	0	0	0.0%	0.00
11-8..12-00	0%	0	0	0.0%	0.00
11-0..11-07	38%	6	47	12.8%	0.01
10-8..10-13	44%	7	67	10.4%	-0.38
10-0..10-07	19%	3	37	8.1%	-0.37
..9-13	0%	0	0	0.0%	0.00

ANALYSIS BY DAYS SINCE LAST RUN

Age	Prop	Win	Runs	Wins%	£
1..7	6%	1	13	7.7%	0.46
8..14	13%	2	31	6.5%	-0.40
15..28	31%	5	48	10.4%	-0.58
29..60	31%	5	30	16.7%	0.20
61..100	0%	0	3	0.0%	-1.00
101+	19%	3	26	11.5%	-0.29
Unraced	0%	0	0	0.0%	0.00

ANALYSIS BY TODAY'S STARTING PRICE

Age	Prop	Win	Runs	Wins%	£
Odds On	0%	0	1	0.0%	-1.00
Ev-2/1	19%	3	9	33.3%	-0.10
9/4-4/1	31%	5	23	21.7%	-0.18
9/2-6/1	13%	2	17	11.8%	-0.29
13/2-10/1	19%	3	25	12.0%	0.06
11/1-16/1	13%	2	27	7.4%	0.04
18/1-33/1	6%	1	26	3.8%	-0.27
40/1+	0%	0	23	0.0%	-1.00

ANALYSIS BY STARTING PRICE LAST TIME

Age	Prop	Win	Runs	Wins%	£
Odds On	0%	0	0	0.0%	0.00
Ev-2/1	6%	1	4	25.0%	-0.13
9/4-4/1	19%	3	13	23.1%	0.12
9/2-6/1	0%	0	12	0.0%	-1.00
13/2-10/1	44%	7	39	17.9%	-0.14
11/1-16/1	19%	3	24	12.5%	0.79
18/1-33/1	13%	2	32	6.3%	-0.44
40/1+	0%	0	27	0.0%	-1.00
Unraced	0%	0	0	0.0%	0.00

ANALYSIS BY DISTANCE BEATEN LAST TIME

Age	Prop	Win	Runs	Wins%	£
..-10 lgh	0%	0	1	0.0%	-1.00
-10..0	0%	0	8	0.0%	-1.00
0.1..2	6%	1	3	33.3%	3.33
2.1..5	6%	1	9	11.1%	-0.58
5.1..10	19%	3	11	27.3%	0.40
10.1..20	13%	2	25	8.0%	-0.72
20.0..30	13%	2	19	10.5%	-0.67
30.1+	13%	2	38	5.3%	-0.49
Not Compl	31%	5	37	13.5%	0.28
Unraced	0%	0	0	0.0%	0.00

ANALYSIS BY SUCCESS RATE IN LAST 10 RUNS

Age	Prop	Win	Runs	Wins%	£
No Wins	50%	8	79	10.1%	0.02
1 Win	44%	7	53	13.2%	-0.48
2 Wins	0%	0	16	0.0%	-1.00
3 Wins	6%	1	3	33.3%	0.50
4 Wins	0%	0	0	0.0%	0.00
5+ Wins	0%	0	0	0.0%	0.00

ANALYSIS BY SUCCESS RATE IN LAST 3 RUNS

Age	Prop	Win	Runs	Wins%	£
No Wins	75%	12	124	9.7%	-0.21
1 Win	19%	3	25	12.0%	-0.60
2 Wins	6%	1	2	50.0%	1.25
3 Wins	0%	0	0	0.0%	0.00

ANALYSIS BY POSITION LAST TIME

Age	Prop	Win	Runs	Wins%	£
Won	0%	0	9	0.0%	-1.00
2nd or 3rd	31%	5	32	15.6%	0.03
Unplaced	38%	6	73	8.2%	-0.56
Fell,BD,UR	13%	2	9	22.2%	0.56
Pulled Up	19%	3	28	10.7%	0.20
Ref/RanOut	0%	0	0	0.0%	0.00
CO/SlipUp	0%	0	0	0.0%	0.00
Unraced	0%	0	0	0.0%	0.00

OTHER FACTORS (WINS-RUNS, £)

Course Winner:	1-15	£0.27
Distance Winner:	3-34	-£0.16
Going Winner:	2-45	-£0.77
Beaten Favourite:	2-4	£0.56
7-Day Winners:	0-2	-£1.00
BHA Top Rated:	4-17	-£0.10
Absolute Favourites:	5-15	£0.03

Conditions Chases (class 4..6)

Conditions Chases (class 4..6): 3m+

ANALYSIS BY AGE

Age	Prop	Win	Runs	Wins%	£
3yo	0%	0	0	0.0%	0.00
4yo	0%	0	1	0.0%	-1.00
5yo	0%	0	3	0.0%	-1.00
6yo	25%	4	22	18.2%	-0.06
7yo	25%	4	29	13.8%	-0.39
8yo	19%	3	30	10.0%	-0.12
9yo	19%	3	23	13.0%	2.55
10yo	6%	1	18	5.6%	-0.69
11yo	0%	0	8	0.0%	-1.00
12yo+	6%	1	12	8.3%	-0.21

ANALYSIS BY BHB RATING

Age	Prop	Win	Runs	Wins%	£
150+	0%	0	0	0.0%	0.00
130..149	0%	0	0	0.0%	0.00
120..129	0%	0	1	0.0%	-1.00
110..119	6%	1	7	14.3%	-0.43
100..109	6%	1	3	33.3%	3.00
80..99	56%	9	81	11.1%	-0.27
60..79	19%	3	44	6.8%	0.83
..59	0%	0	3	0.0%	-1.00
Unrated	13%	2	7	28.6%	-0.16

ANALYSIS BY WEIGHT CARRIED

Age	Prop	Win	Runs	Wins%	£
12-01+	0%	0	0	0.0%	0.00
11-8..12-00	0%	0	2	0.0%	-1.00
11-0..11-07	31%	5	51	9.8%	-0.53
10-8..10-13	44%	7	59	11.9%	0.81
10-0..10-07	25%	4	34	11.8%	-0.10
..9-13	0%	0	0	0.0%	0.00

ANALYSIS BY DAYS SINCE LAST RUN

Age	Prop	Win	Runs	Wins%	£
1..7	19%	3	15	20.0%	0.21
8..14	38%	6	38	15.8%	0.09
15..28	25%	4	39	10.3%	1.18
29..60	6%	1	25	4.0%	-0.62
61..100	0%	0	3	0.0%	-1.00
101+	13%	2	26	7.7%	-0.71
Unraced	0%	0	0	0.0%	0.00

ANALYSIS BY TODAY'S STARTING PRICE

Age	Prop	Win	Runs	Wins%	£
Odds On	6%	1	2	50.0%	-0.04
Ev-2/1	13%	2	9	22.2%	-0.47
9/4-4/1	19%	3	20	15.0%	-0.41
9/2-6/1	19%	3	17	17.6%	0.00
13/2-10/1	25%	4	36	11.1%	-0.03
11/1-16/1	13%	2	23	8.7%	0.04
18/1-33/1	0%	0	22	0.0%	-1.00
40/1+	6%	1	17	5.9%	2.94

ANALYSIS BY STARTING PRICE LAST TIME

Age	Prop	Win	Runs	Wins%	£
Odds On	0%	0	2	0.0%	-1.00
Ev-2/1	13%	2	2	100.0%	1.01
9/4-4/1	25%	4	15	26.7%	0.06
9/2-6/1	19%	3	19	15.8%	-0.03
13/2-10/1	13%	2	28	7.1%	-0.45
11/1-16/1	19%	3	34	8.8%	-0.06
18/1-33/1	6%	1	29	3.4%	-0.71
40/1+	6%	1	17	5.9%	2.94
Unraced	0%	0	0	0.0%	0.00

ANALYSIS BY DISTANCE BEATEN LAST TIME

Age	Prop	Win	Runs	Wins%	£
..-10 lgh	0%	0	4	0.0%	-1.00
-10..0	19%	3	13	23.1%	-0.21
0.1..2	0%	0	5	0.0%	-1.00
2.1..5	6%	1	7	14.3%	-0.14
5.1..10	6%	1	8	12.5%	-0.50
10.1..20	19%	3	17	17.6%	0.25
20.0..30	13%	2	14	14.3%	-0.18
30.1+	19%	3	42	7.1%	-0.30
Not Compl	19%	3	36	8.3%	1.19
Unraced	0%	0	0	0.0%	0.00

ANALYSIS BY SUCCESS RATE IN LAST 10 RUNS

Age	Prop	Win	Runs	Wins%	£
No Wins	44%	7	72	9.7%	0.64
1 Win	25%	4	51	7.8%	-0.52
2 Wins	31%	5	17	29.4%	0.12
3 Wins	0%	0	5	0.0%	-1.00
4 Wins	0%	0	1	0.0%	-1.00
5+ Wins	0%	0	0	0.0%	0.00

ANALYSIS BY SUCCESS RATE IN LAST 3 RUNS

Age	Prop	Win	Runs	Wins%	£
No Wins	75%	12	107	11.2%	0.39
1 Win	19%	3	35	8.6%	-0.71
2 Wins	6%	1	4	25.0%	-0.47
3 Wins	0%	0	0	0.0%	0.00

ANALYSIS BY POSITION LAST TIME

Age	Prop	Win	Runs	Wins%	£
Won	19%	3	17	17.6%	-0.40
2nd or 3rd	31%	5	24	20.8%	0.52
Unplaced	31%	5	69	7.2%	-0.48
Fell,BD,UR	13%	2	11	18.2%	0.09
Pulled Up	6%	1	25	4.0%	1.68
Ref/RanOut	0%	0	0	0.0%	0.00
CO/SlipUp	0%	0	0	0.0%	0.00
Unraced	0%	0	0	0.0%	0.00

OTHER FACTORS (WINS-RUNS, £)

Course Winner:	4-34	-£0.39
Distance Winner:	4-35	-£0.34
Going Winner:	6-48	-£0.26
Beaten Favourite:	2-5	£0.48
7-Day Winners:	1-3	-£0.30
BHA Top Rated:	0-16	-£1.00
Absolute Favourites:	4-13	-£0.20

Race Profiles

Conditions Chases (class 4..6): 2 to 5 runners

ANALYSIS BY AGE

Age	Prop	Win	Runs	Wins%	£
3yo	0%	0	0	0.0%	0.00
4yo	0%	0	0	0.0%	0.00
5yo	0%	0	1	0.0%	-1.00
6yo	0%	0	3	0.0%	-1.00
7yo	75%	3	8	37.5%	0.74
8yo	0%	0	4	0.0%	-1.00
9yo	25%	1	1	100.0%	18.00
10yo	0%	0	1	0.0%	-1.00
11yo	0%	0	0	0.0%	0.00
12yo+	0%	0	1	0.0%	-1.00

ANALYSIS BY BHB RATING

Age	Prop	Win	Runs	Wins%	£
150+	0%	0	0	0.0%	0.00
130..149	0%	0	0	0.0%	0.00
120..129	0%	0	1	0.0%	-1.00
110..119	25%	1	3	33.3%	0.33
100..109	0%	0	0	0.0%	0.00
80..99	25%	1	7	14.3%	1.71
60..79	25%	1	4	25.0%	1.00
..59	0%	0	0	0.0%	0.00
Unrated	25%	1	4	25.0%	-0.52

ANALYSIS BY WEIGHT CARRIED

Age	Prop	Win	Runs	Wins%	£
12-01+	0%	0	0	0.0%	0.00
11-8..12-00	0%	0	0	0.0%	0.00
11-0..11-07	50%	2	14	14.3%	0.49
10-8..10-13	25%	1	1	100.0%	7.00
10-0..10-07	25%	1	4	25.0%	0.00
..9-13	0%	0	0	0.0%	0.00

ANALYSIS BY DAYS SINCE LAST RUN

Age	Prop	Win	Runs	Wins%	£
1..7	25%	1	4	25.0%	3.75
8..14	0%	0	1	0.0%	-1.00
15..28	50%	2	7	28.6%	0.71
29..60	0%	0	3	0.0%	-1.00
61..100	0%	0	2	0.0%	-1.00
101+	25%	1	2	50.0%	-0.04
Unraced	0%	0	0	0.0%	0.00

ANALYSIS BY TODAY'S STARTING PRICE

Age	Prop	Win	Runs	Wins%	£
Odds On	25%	1	2	50.0%	-0.04
Ev-2/1	0%	0	5	0.0%	-1.00
9/4-4/1	25%	1	3	33.3%	0.33
9/2-6/1	0%	0	0	0.0%	0.00
13/2-10/1	25%	1	3	33.3%	1.67
11/1-16/1	0%	0	1	0.0%	-1.00
18/1-33/1	25%	1	3	33.3%	5.33
40/1+	0%	0	2	0.0%	-1.00

ANALYSIS BY STARTING PRICE LAST TIME

Age	Prop	Win	Runs	Wins%	£
Odds On	0%	0	0	0.0%	0.00
Ev-2/1	25%	1	2	50.0%	-0.04
9/4-4/1	25%	1	3	33.3%	0.33
9/2-6/1	0%	0	5	0.0%	-1.00
13/2-10/1	0%	0	1	0.0%	-1.00
11/1-16/1	50%	2	3	66.7%	8.00
18/1-33/1	0%	0	3	0.0%	-1.00
40/1+	0%	0	2	0.0%	-1.00
Unraced	0%	0	0	0.0%	0.00

ANALYSIS BY DISTANCE BEATEN LAST TIME

Age	Prop	Win	Runs	Wins%	£
..-10 lgh	0%	0	1	0.0%	-1.00
-10..0	0%	0	0	0.0%	0.00
0.1..2	0%	0	0	0.0%	0.00
2.1..5	0%	0	1	0.0%	-1.00
5.1..10	25%	1	4	25.0%	0.00
10.1..20	0%	0	2	0.0%	-1.00
20.0..30	25%	1	2	50.0%	-0.04
30.1+	0%	0	3	0.0%	-1.00
Not Compl	50%	2	6	33.3%	3.50
Unraced	0%	0	0	0.0%	0.00

ANALYSIS BY SUCCESS RATE IN LAST 10 RUNS

Age	Prop	Win	Runs	Wins%	£
No Wins	50%	2	9	22.2%	2.00
1 Win	25%	1	5	20.0%	-0.20
2 Wins	25%	1	4	25.0%	-0.52
3 Wins	0%	0	1	0.0%	-1.00
4 Wins	0%	0	0	0.0%	0.00
5+ Wins	0%	0	0	0.0%	0.00

ANALYSIS BY SUCCESS RATE IN LAST 3 RUNS

Age	Prop	Win	Runs	Wins%	£
No Wins	75%	3	11	27.3%	1.82
1 Win	25%	1	7	14.3%	-0.73
2 Wins	0%	0	1	0.0%	-1.00
3 Wins	0%	0	0	0.0%	0.00

ANALYSIS BY POSITION LAST TIME

Age	Prop	Win	Runs	Wins%	£
Won	0%	0	1	0.0%	-1.00
2nd or 3rd	25%	1	6	16.7%	-0.33
Unplaced	25%	1	6	16.7%	-0.68
Fell,BD,UR	25%	1	2	50.0%	3.00
Pulled Up	25%	1	4	25.0%	3.75
Ref/RanOut	0%	0	0	0.0%	0.00
CO/SlipUp	0%	0	0	0.0%	0.00
Unraced	0%	0	0	0.0%	0.00

OTHER FACTORS (WINS-RUNS, £)

Course Winner:	1-2	£8.50
Distance Winner:	1-3	£5.33
Going Winner:	0-3	-£1.00
Beaten Favourite:	1-2	-£0.04
7-Day Winners:	0-1	-£1.00
BHA Top Rated:	0-5	-£1.00
Absolute Favourites:	1-4	-£0.52

Conditions Chases (class 4..6)

Conditions Chases (class 4..6): 6 to 10 runners

ANALYSIS BY AGE

Age	Prop	Win	Runs	Wins%	£
3yo	0%	0	0	0.0%	0.00
4yo	0%	0	0	0.0%	0.00
5yo	4%	1	14	7.1%	-0.07
6yo	26%	6	26	23.1%	-0.15
7yo	17%	4	32	12.5%	-0.27
8yo	22%	5	37	13.5%	0.61
9yo	22%	5	28	17.9%	2.27
10yo	9%	2	25	8.0%	-0.48
11yo	0%	0	12	0.0%	-1.00
12yo+	0%	0	13	0.0%	-1.00

ANALYSIS BY BHB RATING

Age	Prop	Win	Runs	Wins%	£
150+	0%	0	0	0.0%	0.00
130..149	0%	0	1	0.0%	-1.00
120..129	4%	1	1	100.0%	3.33
110..119	0%	0	7	0.0%	-1.00
100..109	9%	2	7	28.6%	1.64
80..99	65%	15	114	13.2%	-0.18
60..79	17%	4	44	9.1%	1.33
..59	0%	0	5	0.0%	-1.00
Unrated	4%	1	8	12.5%	-0.50

ANALYSIS BY WEIGHT CARRIED

Age	Prop	Win	Runs	Wins%	£
12-01+	0%	0	1	0.0%	-1.00
11-8..12-00	0%	0	3	0.0%	-1.00
11-0..11-07	43%	10	79	12.7%	0.04
10-8..10-13	48%	11	74	14.9%	0.56
10-0..10-07	9%	2	30	6.7%	-0.17
..9-13	0%	0	0	0.0%	0.00

ANALYSIS BY DAYS SINCE LAST RUN

Age	Prop	Win	Runs	Wins%	£
1..7	22%	5	21	23.8%	0.53
8..14	22%	5	44	11.4%	-0.10
15..28	30%	7	57	12.3%	0.90
29..60	13%	3	27	11.1%	-0.11
61..100	0%	0	3	0.0%	-1.00
101+	13%	3	34	8.8%	-0.46
Unraced	0%	0	1	0.0%	-1.00

ANALYSIS BY TODAY'S STARTING PRICE

Age	Prop	Win	Runs	Wins%	£
Odds On	0%	0	2	0.0%	-1.00
Ev-2/1	17%	4	8	50.0%	0.28
9/4-4/1	30%	7	45	15.6%	-0.40
9/2-6/1	13%	3	26	11.5%	-0.33
13/2-10/1	13%	3	31	9.7%	-0.16
11/1-16/1	17%	4	23	17.4%	1.35
18/1-33/1	4%	1	30	3.3%	-0.30
40/1+	4%	1	22	4.5%	2.05

ANALYSIS BY STARTING PRICE LAST TIME

Age	Prop	Win	Runs	Wins%	£
Odds On	0%	0	2	0.0%	-1.00
Ev-2/1	13%	3	6	50.0%	0.65
9/4-4/1	22%	5	19	26.3%	0.92
9/2-6/1	4%	1	18	5.6%	-0.78
13/2-10/1	30%	7	48	14.6%	0.00
11/1-16/1	22%	5	32	15.6%	0.70
18/1-33/1	4%	1	35	2.9%	-0.91
40/1+	4%	1	26	3.8%	1.58
Unraced	0%	0	1	0.0%	-1.00

ANALYSIS BY DISTANCE BEATEN LAST TIME

Age	Prop	Win	Runs	Wins%	£
..-10 lgh	4%	1	3	33.3%	0.44
-10..0	4%	1	13	7.7%	-0.84
0.1..2	4%	1	10	10.0%	0.30
2.1..5	0%	0	7	0.0%	-1.00
5.1..10	17%	4	16	25.0%	0.37
10.1..20	22%	5	28	17.9%	0.01
20.0..30	13%	3	20	15.0%	0.36
30.1+	9%	2	42	4.8%	-0.61
Not Compl	26%	6	47	12.8%	1.33
Unraced	0%	0	1	0.0%	-1.00

ANALYSIS BY SUCCESS RATE IN LAST 10 RUNS

Age	Prop	Win	Runs	Wins%	£
No Wins	39%	9	86	10.5%	0.70
1 Win	35%	8	67	11.9%	-0.48
2 Wins	17%	4	24	16.7%	-0.34
3 Wins	9%	2	8	25.0%	2.19
4 Wins	0%	0	1	0.0%	-1.00
5+ Wins	0%	0	0	0.0%	0.00

ANALYSIS BY SUCCESS RATE IN LAST 3 RUNS

Age	Prop	Win	Runs	Wins%	£
No Wins	70%	16	141	11.3%	0.38
1 Win	22%	5	40	12.5%	-0.45
2 Wins	9%	2	5	40.0%	0.32
3 Wins	0%	0	0	0.0%	0.00

ANALYSIS BY POSITION LAST TIME

Age	Prop	Win	Runs	Wins%	£
Won	9%	2	16	12.5%	-0.60
2nd or 3rd	30%	7	39	17.9%	0.37
Unplaced	35%	8	85	9.4%	-0.37
Fell,BD,UR	13%	3	14	21.4%	0.29
Pulled Up	9%	2	31	6.5%	1.71
Ref/RanOut	4%	1	1	100.0%	6.50
CO/SlipUp	0%	0	0	0.0%	0.00
Unraced	0%	0	1	0.0%	-1.00

OTHER FACTORS (WINS-RUNS, £)

Course Winner:	2-29	-£0.67
Distance Winner:	5-53	-£0.22
Going Winner:	5-62	-£0.56
Beaten Favourite:	3-8	£0.47
7-Day Winners:	1-2	£0.05
BHA Top Rated:	5-21	-£0.06
Absolute Favourites:	7-21	£0.01

Race Profiles

Conditions Chases (class 4..6): 11 runners or more

ANALYSIS BY AGE

Age	Prop	Win	Runs	Wins%	£
3yo	0%	0	0	0.0%	0.00
4yo	0%	0	1	0.0%	-1.00
5yo	0%	0	4	0.0%	-1.00
6yo	17%	2	20	10.0%	-0.28
7yo	25%	3	31	9.7%	-0.41
8yo	17%	2	30	6.7%	-0.52
9yo	25%	3	31	9.7%	-0.25
10yo	8%	1	15	6.7%	-0.47
11yo	0%	0	9	0.0%	-1.00
12yo+	8%	1	13	7.7%	-0.27

ANALYSIS BY BHB RATING

Age	Prop	Win	Runs	Wins%	£
150+	0%	0	0	0.0%	0.00
130..149	0%	0	0	0.0%	0.00
120..129	0%	0	0	0.0%	0.00
110..119	0%	0	0	0.0%	0.00
100..109	0%	0	0	0.0%	0.00
80..99	100%	12	99	12.1%	-0.11
60..79	0%	0	53	0.0%	-1.00
..59	0%	0	2	0.0%	-1.00
Unrated	0%	0	0	0.0%	0.00

ANALYSIS BY WEIGHT CARRIED

Age	Prop	Win	Runs	Wins%	£
12-01+	0%	0	0	0.0%	0.00
11-8..12-00	0%	0	0	0.0%	0.00
11-0..11-07	17%	2	34	5.9%	-0.69
10-8..10-13	42%	5	73	6.8%	-0.39
10-0..10-07	42%	5	47	10.6%	-0.30
..9-13	0%	0	0	0.0%	0.00

ANALYSIS BY DAYS SINCE LAST RUN

Age	Prop	Win	Runs	Wins%	£
1..7	8%	1	16	6.3%	-0.50
8..14	25%	3	35	8.6%	-0.42
15..28	17%	2	38	5.3%	-0.70
29..60	42%	5	34	14.7%	0.26
61..100	0%	0	4	0.0%	-1.00
101+	8%	1	27	3.7%	-0.80
Unraced	0%	0	0	0.0%	0.00

ANALYSIS BY TODAY'S STARTING PRICE

Age	Prop	Win	Runs	Wins%	£
Odds On	0%	0	0	0.0%	0.00
Ev-2/1	8%	1	6	16.7%	-0.56
9/4-4/1	8%	1	8	12.5%	-0.53
9/2-6/1	33%	4	16	25.0%	0.47
13/2-10/1	42%	5	37	13.5%	0.16
11/1-16/1	8%	1	33	3.0%	-0.55
18/1-33/1	0%	0	31	0.0%	-1.00
40/1+	0%	0	23	0.0%	-1.00

ANALYSIS BY STARTING PRICE LAST TIME

Age	Prop	Win	Runs	Wins%	£
Odds On	0%	0	0	0.0%	0.00
Ev-2/1	0%	0	2	0.0%	-1.00
9/4-4/1	25%	3	12	25.0%	0.20
9/2-6/1	17%	2	14	14.3%	0.04
13/2-10/1	42%	5	34	14.7%	0.04
11/1-16/1	0%	0	33	0.0%	-1.00
18/1-33/1	17%	2	35	5.7%	-0.33
40/1+	0%	0	24	0.0%	-1.00
Unraced	0%	0	0	0.0%	0.00

ANALYSIS BY DISTANCE BEATEN LAST TIME

Age	Prop	Win	Runs	Wins%	£
..-10 lgh	0%	0	2	0.0%	-1.00
-10..0	17%	2	14	14.3%	-0.42
0.1..2	0%	0	1	0.0%	-1.00
2.1..5	17%	2	10	20.0%	-0.03
5.1..10	0%	0	3	0.0%	-1.00
10.1..20	8%	1	21	4.8%	-0.62
20.0..30	8%	1	17	5.9%	-0.44
30.1+	25%	3	53	5.7%	-0.39
Not Compl	25%	3	33	9.1%	-0.39
Unraced	0%	0	0	0.0%	0.00

ANALYSIS BY SUCCESS RATE IN LAST 10 RUNS

Age	Prop	Win	Runs	Wins%	£
No Wins	42%	5	85	5.9%	-0.51
1 Win	50%	6	52	11.5%	-0.22
2 Wins	8%	1	15	6.7%	-0.63
3 Wins	0%	0	1	0.0%	-1.00
4 Wins	0%	0	1	0.0%	-1.00
5+ Wins	0%	0	0	0.0%	0.00

ANALYSIS BY SUCCESS RATE IN LAST 3 RUNS

Age	Prop	Win	Runs	Wins%	£
No Wins	75%	9	125	7.2%	-0.43
1 Win	25%	3	26	11.5%	-0.38
2 Wins	0%	0	3	0.0%	-1.00
3 Wins	0%	0	0	0.0%	0.00

ANALYSIS BY POSITION LAST TIME

Age	Prop	Win	Runs	Wins%	£
Won	17%	2	16	12.5%	-0.49
2nd or 3rd	25%	3	20	15.0%	-0.06
Unplaced	33%	4	85	4.7%	-0.52
Fell,BD,UR	8%	1	7	14.3%	-0.21
Pulled Up	17%	2	26	7.7%	-0.44
Ref/RanOut	0%	0	0	0.0%	0.00
CO/SlipUp	0%	0	0	0.0%	0.00
Unraced	0%	0	0	0.0%	0.00

OTHER FACTORS (WINS-RUNS, £)

Course Winner:	3-29	-£0.43
Distance Winner:	5-39	-£0.24
Going Winner:	4-50	-£0.52
Beaten Favourite:	0-2	-£1.00
7-Day Winners:	0-3	-£1.00
BHA Top Rated:	1-14	-£0.43
Absolute Favourites:	1-10	-£0.74

Conditions Chases (class 4..6)

Conditions Chases (class 4..6): up to 7 days off the track

ANALYSIS BY AGE
Age	Prop	Win	Runs	Wins%	£
3yo	0%	0	0	0.0%	0.00
4yo	0%	0	0	0.0%	0.00
5yo	0%	0	2	0.0%	-1.00
6yo	29%	2	7	28.6%	-0.13
7yo	0%	0	5	0.0%	-1.00
8yo	14%	1	10	10.0%	-0.35
9yo	43%	3	11	27.3%	2.50
10yo	14%	1	4	25.0%	1.00
11yo	0%	0	2	0.0%	-1.00
12yo+	0%	0	1	0.0%	-1.00

ANALYSIS BY BHB RATING
Age	Prop	Win	Runs	Wins%	£
150+	0%	0	0	0.0%	0.00
130..149	0%	0	0	0.0%	0.00
120..129	0%	0	0	0.0%	0.00
110..119	0%	0	1	0.0%	-1.00
100..109	29%	2	3	66.7%	5.17
80..99	57%	4	24	16.7%	0.53
60..79	0%	0	11	0.0%	-1.00
..59	0%	0	0	0.0%	0.00
Unrated	14%	1	3	33.3%	0.33

ANALYSIS BY WEIGHT CARRIED
Age	Prop	Win	Runs	Wins%	£
12-01+	0%	0	0	0.0%	0.00
11-8..12-00	0%	0	0	0.0%	0.00
11-0..11-07	29%	2	15	13.3%	0.41
10-8..10-13	43%	3	14	21.4%	0.29
10-0..10-07	29%	2	13	15.4%	0.54
..9-13	0%	0	0	0.0%	0.00

ANALYSIS BY DAYS SINCE LAST RUN
Age	Prop	Win	Runs	Wins%	£
1..7	100%	7	41	17.1%	0.44
8..14	0%	0	0	0.0%	0.00
15..28	0%	0	0	0.0%	0.00
29..60	0%	0	0	0.0%	0.00
61..100	0%	0	0	0.0%	0.00
101+	0%	0	0	0.0%	0.00
Unraced	0%	0	1	0.0%	-1.00

ANALYSIS BY TODAY'S STARTING PRICE
Age	Prop	Win	Runs	Wins%	£
Odds On	0%	0	2	0.0%	-1.00
Ev-2/1	14%	1	3	33.3%	-0.30
9/4-4/1	14%	1	5	20.0%	-0.20
9/2-6/1	14%	1	4	25.0%	0.63
13/2-10/1	29%	2	9	22.2%	0.72
11/1-16/1	14%	1	7	14.3%	0.71
18/1-33/1	14%	1	8	12.5%	1.38
40/1+	0%	0	4	0.0%	-1.00

ANALYSIS BY STARTING PRICE LAST TIME
Age	Prop	Win	Runs	Wins%	£
Odds On	0%	0	0	0.0%	0.00
Ev-2/1	14%	1	2	50.0%	0.05
9/4-4/1	14%	1	4	25.0%	0.88
9/2-6/1	14%	1	8	12.5%	-0.50
13/2-10/1	14%	1	6	16.7%	0.33
11/1-16/1	43%	3	6	50.0%	5.25
18/1-33/1	0%	0	7	0.0%	-1.00
40/1+	0%	0	8	0.0%	-1.00
Unraced	0%	0	1	0.0%	-1.00

ANALYSIS BY DISTANCE BEATEN LAST TIME
Age	Prop	Win	Runs	Wins%	£
..-10 lgh	0%	0	2	0.0%	-1.00
-10..0	14%	1	4	25.0%	-0.47
0.1..2	0%	0	2	0.0%	-1.00
2.1..5	0%	0	3	0.0%	-1.00
5.1..10	14%	1	3	33.3%	1.17
10.1..20	14%	1	5	20.0%	0.60
20.0..30	0%	0	4	0.0%	-1.00
30.1+	14%	1	8	12.5%	0.50
Not Compl	43%	3	10	30.0%	2.05
Unraced	0%	0	1	0.0%	-1.00

ANALYSIS BY SUCCESS RATE IN LAST 10 RUNS
Age	Prop	Win	Runs	Wins%	£
No Wins	29%	2	21	9.5%	0.48
1 Win	43%	3	11	27.3%	1.00
2 Wins	29%	2	8	25.0%	-0.24
3 Wins	0%	0	0	0.0%	0.00
4 Wins	0%	0	1	0.0%	-1.00
5+ Wins	0%	0	0	0.0%	0.00

ANALYSIS BY SUCCESS RATE IN LAST 3 RUNS
Age	Prop	Win	Runs	Wins%	£
No Wins	57%	4	31	12.9%	0.34
1 Win	29%	2	8	25.0%	0.94
2 Wins	14%	1	2	50.0%	0.05
3 Wins	0%	0	0	0.0%	0.00

ANALYSIS BY POSITION LAST TIME
Age	Prop	Win	Runs	Wins%	£
Won	14%	1	6	16.7%	-0.65
2nd or 3rd	14%	1	7	14.3%	-0.07
Unplaced	29%	2	18	11.1%	0.11
Fell,BD,UR	14%	1	3	33.3%	0.33
Pulled Up	14%	1	6	16.7%	2.17
Ref/RanOut	14%	1	1	100.0%	6.50
CO/SlipUp	0%	0	0	0.0%	0.00
Unraced	0%	0	1	0.0%	-1.00

OTHER FACTORS (WINS-RUNS, £)
Course Winner:	2-7	£2.29
Distance Winner:	2-8	£2.31
Going Winner:	3-11	£0.65
Beaten Favourite:	0-1	-£1.00
7-Day Winners:	1-6	-£0.65
BHA Top Rated:	1-5	£0.60
Absolute Favourites:	1-7	-£0.70

Race Profiles

Conditions Chases (class 4..6): 100+ days off the track

ANALYSIS BY AGE

Age	Prop	Win	Runs	Wins%	£
3yo	0%	0	0	0.0%	0.00
4yo	0%	0	0	0.0%	0.00
5yo	0%	0	1	0.0%	-1.00
6yo	20%	1	9	11.1%	-0.50
7yo	40%	2	11	18.2%	0.17
8yo	40%	2	10	20.0%	-0.15
9yo	0%	0	10	0.0%	-1.00
10yo	0%	0	10	0.0%	-1.00
11yo	0%	0	6	0.0%	-1.00
12yo+	0%	0	7	0.0%	-1.00

ANALYSIS BY BHB RATING

Age	Prop	Win	Runs	Wins%	£
150+	0%	0	0	0.0%	0.00
130..149	0%	0	0	0.0%	0.00
120..129	0%	0	0	0.0%	0.00
110..119	0%	0	2	0.0%	-1.00
100..109	0%	0	1	0.0%	-1.00
80..99	80%	4	39	10.3%	-0.38
60..79	0%	0	17	0.0%	-1.00
..59	0%	0	2	0.0%	-1.00
Unrated	20%	1	3	33.3%	-0.36

ANALYSIS BY WEIGHT CARRIED

Age	Prop	Win	Runs	Wins%	£
12-01+	0%	0	0	0.0%	0.00
11-8..12-00	0%	0	0	0.0%	0.00
11-0..11-07	40%	2	24	8.3%	-0.46
10-8..10-13	60%	3	29	10.3%	-0.55
10-0..10-07	0%	0	11	0.0%	-1.00
..9-13	0%	0	0	0.0%	0.00

ANALYSIS BY DAYS SINCE LAST RUN

Age	Prop	Win	Runs	Wins%	£
1..7	0%	0	0	0.0%	0.00
8..14	0%	0	0	0.0%	0.00
15..28	0%	0	0	0.0%	0.00
29..60	0%	0	0	0.0%	0.00
61..100	0%	0	1	0.0%	-1.00
101+	100%	5	63	7.9%	-0.59
Unraced	0%	0	0	0.0%	0.00

ANALYSIS BY TODAY'S STARTING PRICE

Age	Prop	Win	Runs	Wins%	£
Odds On	20%	1	1	100.0%	0.91
Ev-2/1	20%	1	3	33.3%	0.00
9/4-4/1	20%	1	4	25.0%	0.13
9/2-6/1	20%	1	9	11.1%	-0.39
13/2-10/1	20%	1	13	7.7%	-0.15
11/1-16/1	0%	0	9	0.0%	-1.00
18/1-33/1	0%	0	16	0.0%	-1.00
40/1+	0%	0	9	0.0%	-1.00

ANALYSIS BY STARTING PRICE LAST TIME

Age	Prop	Win	Runs	Wins%	£
Odds On	0%	0	1	0.0%	-1.00
Ev-2/1	20%	1	2	50.0%	-0.04
9/4-4/1	0%	0	5	0.0%	-1.00
9/2-6/1	20%	1	5	20.0%	0.10
13/2-10/1	20%	1	18	5.6%	-0.75
11/1-16/1	20%	1	15	6.7%	-0.27
18/1-33/1	20%	1	11	9.1%	-0.73
40/1+	0%	0	7	0.0%	-1.00
Unraced	0%	0	0	0.0%	0.00

ANALYSIS BY DISTANCE BEATEN LAST TIME

Age	Prop	Win	Runs	Wins%	£
..-10 lgh	0%	0	0	0.0%	0.00
-10..0	20%	1	3	33.3%	0.83
0.1..2	0%	0	4	0.0%	-1.00
2.1..5	0%	0	2	0.0%	-1.00
5.1..10	0%	0	2	0.0%	-1.00
10.1..20	0%	0	6	0.0%	-1.00
20.0..30	20%	1	4	25.0%	-0.52
30.1+	20%	1	23	4.3%	-0.80
Not Compl	40%	2	20	10.0%	-0.30
Unraced	0%	0	0	0.0%	0.00

ANALYSIS BY SUCCESS RATE IN LAST 10 RUNS

Age	Prop	Win	Runs	Wins%	£
No Wins	20%	1	33	3.0%	-0.67
1 Win	20%	1	18	5.6%	-0.83
2 Wins	40%	2	11	18.2%	-0.33
3 Wins	20%	1	2	50.0%	1.25
4 Wins	0%	0	0	0.0%	0.00
5+ Wins	0%	0	0	0.0%	0.00

ANALYSIS BY SUCCESS RATE IN LAST 3 RUNS

Age	Prop	Win	Runs	Wins%	£
No Wins	40%	2	50	4.0%	-0.72
1 Win	40%	2	13	15.4%	-0.43
2 Wins	20%	1	1	100.0%	3.50
3 Wins	0%	0	0	0.0%	0.00

ANALYSIS BY POSITION LAST TIME

Age	Prop	Win	Runs	Wins%	£
Won	20%	1	3	33.3%	0.83
2nd or 3rd	0%	0	8	0.0%	-1.00
Unplaced	40%	2	33	6.1%	-0.81
Fell,BD,UR	40%	2	9	22.2%	0.56
Pulled Up	0%	0	11	0.0%	-1.00
Ref/RanOut	0%	0	0	0.0%	0.00
CO/SlipUp	0%	0	0	0.0%	0.00
Unraced	0%	0	0	0.0%	0.00

OTHER FACTORS (WINS-RUNS, £)

Course Winner:	0-10	-£1.00
Distance Winner:	2-19	-£0.55
Going Winner:	0-13	-£1.00
Beaten Favourite:	1-4	-£0.52
BHA Top Rated:	2-6	£0.25
Absolute Favourites:	2-5	-£0.02

Novices' Handicap Chases

ANALYSIS BY AGE

Age	Prop	Win	Runs	Wins%	£
3yo	0%	0	0	0.0%	0.00
4yo	2%	18	95	18.9%	0.08
5yo	8%	60	670	9.0%	-0.36
6yo	26%	187	1588	11.8%	-0.15
7yo	29%	208	1738	12.0%	-0.16
8yo	21%	156	1309	11.9%	-0.15
9yo	10%	70	685	10.2%	-0.05
10yo	3%	23	294	7.8%	-0.42
11yo	1%	5	86	5.8%	-0.20
12yo+	0%	1	31	3.2%	-0.58

ANALYSIS BY BHB RATING

Age	Prop	Win	Runs	Wins%	£
130..149	2%	16	167	9.6%	-0.28
120..129	6%	47	331	14.2%	-0.11
110..119	12%	84	643	13.1%	0.00
100..109	19%	140	1226	11.4%	-0.24
80..99	48%	353	3047	11.6%	-0.11
60..79	12%	88	1079	8.2%	-0.37
..59	0%	0	1	0.0%	-1.00
Unrated	0%	0	2	0.0%	-1.00

ANALYSIS BY WEIGHT CARRIED

Age	Prop	Win	Runs	Wins%	£
12-01+	0%	2	5	40.0%	0.13
11-8..12-00	24%	174	1305	13.3%	-0.16
11-0..11-07	31%	229	2023	11.3%	-0.17
10-8..10-13	19%	141	1257	11.2%	-0.10
10-0..10-07	19%	139	1370	10.1%	-0.25
..9-13	6%	43	536	8.0%	-0.23

ANALYSIS BY DAYS SINCE LAST RUN

Age	Prop	Win	Runs	Wins%	£
1..7	7%	52	322	16.1%	-0.14
8..14	20%	147	1257	11.7%	-0.21
15..28	34%	247	2161	11.4%	-0.18
29..60	21%	153	1473	10.4%	-0.18
61..100	6%	42	392	10.7%	-0.08
101+	11%	82	875	9.4%	-0.16
Unraced	1%	5	16	31.3%	0.37

ANALYSIS BY TODAY'S STARTING PRICE

Age	Prop	Win	Runs	Wins%	£
Odds On	3%	21	40	52.5%	-0.11
Ev-2/1	13%	98	283	34.6%	-0.10
9/4-4/1	31%	228	1057	21.6%	-0.09
9/2-6/1	20%	143	902	15.9%	-0.03
13/2-10/1	18%	131	1521	8.6%	-0.22
11/1-16/1	10%	71	1222	5.8%	-0.15
18/1-33/1	5%	33	1045	3.2%	-0.18
40/1+	0%	3	426	0.7%	-0.66

ANALYSIS BY STARTING PRICE LAST TIME

Age	Prop	Win	Runs	Wins%	£
Odds On	3%	19	82	23.2%	-0.07
Ev-2/1	8%	57	324	17.6%	-0.15
9/4-4/1	21%	150	975	15.4%	-0.11
9/2-6/1	15%	112	825	13.6%	-0.17
13/2-10/1	25%	179	1364	13.1%	-0.15
11/1-16/1	16%	113	1181	9.6%	-0.10
18/1-33/1	9%	63	1038	6.1%	-0.25
40/1+	4%	30	691	4.3%	-0.39
Unraced	1%	5	16	31.3%	0.37

ANALYSIS BY DISTANCE BEATEN LAST TIME

Age	Prop	Win	Runs	Wins%	£
..-10 lgh	4%	30	147	20.4%	-0.25
-10..0	15%	111	610	18.2%	-0.23
0.1..2	7%	54	316	17.1%	-0.01
2.1..5	7%	50	329	15.2%	-0.01
5.1..10	10%	76	506	15.0%	-0.10
10.1..20	16%	115	893	12.9%	-0.08
20.0..30	10%	74	725	10.2%	-0.12
30.1+	15%	108	1590	6.8%	-0.33
Not Compl	14%	105	1364	7.7%	-0.17
Unraced	1%	5	16	31.3%	0.37

ANALYSIS BY SUCCESS RATE IN LAST 10 RUNS

Age	Prop	Win	Runs	Wins%	£
No Wins	43%	313	3351	9.3%	-0.18
1 Win	33%	238	1898	12.5%	-0.20
2 Wins	14%	101	806	12.5%	-0.21
3 Wins	7%	48	311	15.4%	-0.11
4 Wins	2%	18	82	22.0%	0.22
5+ Wins	1%	5	32	15.6%	0.59

ANALYSIS BY SUCCESS RATE IN LAST 3 RUNS

Age	Prop	Win	Runs	Wins%	£
No Wins	65%	468	4795	9.8%	-0.16
1 Win	29%	208	1434	14.5%	-0.24
2 Wins	6%	41	232	17.7%	-0.03
3 Wins	1%	6	19	31.6%	-0.35

ANALYSIS BY POSITION LAST TIME

Age	Prop	Win	Runs	Wins%	£
Won	19%	141	758	18.6%	-0.24
2nd or 3rd	32%	231	1529	15.1%	-0.05
Unplaced	34%	246	2832	8.7%	-0.24
Fell,BD,UR	7%	51	469	10.9%	0.10
Pulled Up	7%	51	865	5.9%	-0.32
Ref/RanOut	0%	2	23	8.7%	-0.54
CO/SlipUp	0%	1	4	25.0%	4.25
Unraced	1%	5	16	31.3%	0.37

OTHER FACTORS (WINS-RUNS, £)

Course Winner:	91-616	-£0.25
Distance Winner:	200-1394	-£0.17
Going Winner:	228-1628	-£0.12
Beaten Favourite:	61-437	-£0.29
7-Day Winners:	26-69	£0.11
Absolute Favourites:	191-652	-£0.09

TRAINERS (WINS-RUNS, £)

J Wade 6-28 £0.14; N G Richards 5-39 £0.10; N W Alexander 4-20 £0.17; C L Tizzard 10-64 £0.05; Miss Suzy Smith 3-12 £0.27; N J Henderson 9-61 £0.03; D J Wintle 3-20 £0.08; R H Mrs S Alner 3-23 £0.05; Evan Williams 18-130 £0.01; Mrs T J Hill 3-17 £0.03.

Race Profiles

Novices' Handicap Chases: 2m to 2m3f

ANALYSIS BY AGE

Age	Prop	Win	Runs	Wins%	£
3yo	0%	0	0	0.0%	0.00
4yo	4%	9	48	18.8%	-0.26
5yo	10%	22	275	8.0%	-0.52
6yo	32%	71	525	13.5%	-0.13
7yo	27%	61	447	13.6%	-0.06
8yo	18%	41	300	13.7%	-0.23
9yo	6%	14	181	7.7%	-0.67
10yo	3%	6	67	9.0%	-0.49
11yo	0%	0	17	0.0%	-1.00
12yo+	0%	0	5	0.0%	-1.00

ANALYSIS BY BHB RATING

Age	Prop	Win	Runs	Wins%	£
150+	0%	0	0	0.0%	0.00
130..149	1%	3	15	20.0%	-0.27
120..129	5%	12	48	25.0%	-0.09
110..119	6%	13	115	11.3%	-0.54
100..109	20%	45	333	13.5%	-0.25
80..99	54%	120	992	12.1%	-0.19
60..79	14%	31	361	8.6%	-0.44
..59	0%	0	0	0.0%	0.00
Unrated	0%	0	1	0.0%	-1.00

ANALYSIS BY WEIGHT CARRIED

Age	Prop	Win	Runs	Wins%	£
12-01+	0%	1	3	33.3%	-0.04
11-8..12-00	27%	60	376	16.0%	-0.24
11-0..11-07	32%	72	569	12.7%	-0.15
10-8..10-13	17%	37	354	10.5%	-0.31
10-0..10-07	18%	40	394	10.2%	-0.37
..9-13	6%	14	169	8.3%	-0.41

ANALYSIS BY DAYS SINCE LAST RUN

Age	Prop	Win	Runs	Wins%	£
1..7	8%	17	111	15.3%	-0.37
8..14	22%	50	378	13.2%	-0.11
15..28	29%	64	598	10.7%	-0.32
29..60	21%	47	398	11.8%	-0.43
61..100	8%	18	116	15.5%	0.13
101+	12%	26	259	10.0%	-0.27
Unraced	1%	2	5	40.0%	0.50

ANALYSIS BY TODAY'S STARTING PRICE

Age	Prop	Win	Runs	Wins%	£
Odds On	4%	8	16	50.0%	-0.11
Ev-2/1	20%	44	108	40.7%	0.04
9/4-4/1	35%	78	320	24.4%	0.00
9/2-6/1	21%	47	270	17.4%	0.05
13/2-10/1	13%	29	425	6.8%	-0.38
11/1-16/1	5%	11	292	3.8%	-0.42
18/1-33/1	3%	6	303	2.0%	-0.50
40/1+	0%	1	131	0.8%	-0.61

ANALYSIS BY STARTING PRICE LAST TIME

Age	Prop	Win	Runs	Wins%	£
Odds On	3%	7	18	38.9%	0.30
Ev-2/1	8%	17	76	22.4%	-0.21
9/4-4/1	20%	44	231	19.0%	-0.27
9/2-6/1	13%	29	226	12.8%	-0.31
13/2-10/1	25%	57	375	15.2%	-0.15
11/1-16/1	17%	37	356	10.4%	-0.12
18/1-33/1	9%	21	326	6.4%	-0.29
40/1+	4%	10	252	4.0%	-0.66
Unraced	1%	2	5	40.0%	0.50

ANALYSIS BY DISTANCE BEATEN LAST TIME

Age	Prop	Win	Runs	Wins%	£
..-10 lgh	3%	7	25	28.0%	-0.26
-10..0	16%	35	139	25.2%	-0.10
0.1..2	8%	19	87	21.8%	-0.08
2.1..5	8%	17	98	17.3%	0.14
5.1..10	10%	22	140	15.7%	-0.23
10.1..20	18%	41	281	14.6%	-0.25
20.0..30	9%	21	227	9.3%	-0.37
30.1+	15%	34	491	6.9%	-0.46
Not Compl	12%	26	372	7.0%	-0.21
Unraced	1%	2	5	40.0%	0.50

ANALYSIS BY SUCCESS RATE IN LAST 10 RUNS

Age	Prop	Win	Runs	Wins%	£
No Wins	49%	108	1113	9.7%	-0.24
1 Win	30%	67	505	13.3%	-0.38
2 Wins	11%	24	174	13.8%	-0.33
3 Wins	7%	15	53	28.3%	-0.06
4 Wins	3%	6	12	50.0%	0.87
5+ Wins	1%	2	3	66.7%	2.30

ANALYSIS BY SUCCESS RATE IN LAST 3 RUNS

Age	Prop	Win	Runs	Wins%	£
No Wins	67%	149	1486	10.0%	-0.27
1 Win	27%	59	328	18.0%	-0.30
2 Wins	5%	12	40	30.0%	0.07
3 Wins	1%	2	6	33.3%	-0.41

ANALYSIS BY POSITION LAST TIME

Age	Prop	Win	Runs	Wins%	£
Won	19%	42	164	25.6%	-0.13
2nd or 3rd	33%	75	413	18.2%	-0.10
Unplaced	35%	79	912	8.7%	-0.40
Fell,BD,UR	5%	11	142	7.7%	-0.09
Pulled Up	6%	14	225	6.2%	-0.36
Ref/RanOut	0%	0	3	0.0%	-1.00
CO/SlipUp	0%	1	1	100.0%	20.00
Unraced	1%	2	5	40.0%	0.50

OTHER FACTORS (WINS-RUNS, £)

Course Winner:	31-159	-£0.26
Distance Winner:	67-474	-£0.32
Going Winner:	72-414	-£0.21
Beaten Favourite:	21-110	-£0.21
7-Day Winners:	8-20	£0.09
Absolute Favourites:	79-204	£0.19

Novices' Handicap Chases

Novices' Handicap Chases: 2m4f to 2m7f

ANALYSIS BY AGE

Age	Prop	Win	Runs	Wins%	£
3yo	0%	0	0	0.0%	0.00
4yo	2%	7	36	19.4%	0.24
5yo	9%	28	286	9.8%	-0.31
6yo	22%	70	675	10.4%	-0.29
7yo	28%	89	798	11.2%	-0.23
8yo	23%	71	626	11.3%	-0.08
9yo	12%	38	316	12.0%	0.23
10yo	3%	8	120	6.7%	-0.41
11yo	1%	2	40	5.0%	0.10
12yo+	0%	1	22	4.5%	-0.41

ANALYSIS BY BHB RATING

Age	Prop	Win	Runs	Wins%	£
150+	0%	0	0	0.0%	0.00
130..149	4%	13	138	9.4%	-0.20
120..129	7%	21	208	10.1%	-0.27
110..119	14%	44	361	12.2%	-0.08
100..109	24%	74	566	13.1%	-0.07
80..99	42%	133	1250	10.6%	-0.15
60..79	9%	29	395	7.3%	-0.36
..59	0%	0	0	0.0%	0.00
Unrated	0%	0	1	0.0%	-1.00

ANALYSIS BY WEIGHT CARRIED

Age	Prop	Win	Runs	Wins%	£
12-01+	0%	0	1	0.0%	-1.00
11-8..12-00	23%	73	582	12.5%	-0.18
11-0..11-07	33%	104	928	11.2%	-0.17
10-8..10-13	21%	67	561	11.9%	0.10
10-0..10-07	17%	52	618	8.4%	-0.41
..9-13	6%	18	229	7.9%	-0.11

ANALYSIS BY DAYS SINCE LAST RUN

Age	Prop	Win	Runs	Wins%	£
1..7	8%	24	144	16.7%	0.20
8..14	20%	64	545	11.7%	-0.23
15..28	31%	98	964	10.2%	-0.26
29..60	22%	70	678	10.3%	-0.07
61..100	5%	17	186	9.1%	-0.14
101+	12%	39	393	9.9%	-0.17
Unraced	1%	2	9	22.2%	0.28

ANALYSIS BY TODAY'S STARTING PRICE

Age	Prop	Win	Runs	Wins%	£
Odds On	3%	10	17	58.8%	-0.03
Ev-2/1	10%	32	108	29.6%	-0.20
9/4-4/1	29%	91	457	19.9%	-0.15
9/2-6/1	18%	56	392	14.3%	-0.11
13/2-10/1	24%	75	685	10.9%	-0.01
11/1-16/1	11%	33	585	5.6%	-0.21
18/1-33/1	5%	16	496	3.2%	-0.17
40/1+	0%	1	179	0.6%	-0.77

ANALYSIS BY STARTING PRICE LAST TIME

Age	Prop	Win	Runs	Wins%	£
Odds On	3%	9	49	18.4%	-0.09
Ev-2/1	10%	30	171	17.5%	-0.10
9/4-4/1	22%	68	475	14.3%	0.07
9/2-6/1	15%	46	368	12.5%	-0.22
13/2-10/1	22%	70	623	11.2%	-0.25
11/1-16/1	14%	45	518	8.7%	-0.28
18/1-33/1	10%	32	439	7.3%	-0.09
40/1+	4%	12	267	4.5%	-0.28
Unraced	1%	2	9	22.2%	0.28

ANALYSIS BY DISTANCE BEATEN LAST TIME

Age	Prop	Win	Runs	Wins%	£
..-10 lgh	6%	18	84	21.4%	-0.06
-10..0	15%	46	314	14.6%	-0.32
0.1..2	6%	19	150	12.7%	-0.23
2.1..5	6%	20	150	13.3%	-0.14
5.1..10	10%	31	234	13.2%	-0.14
10.1..20	15%	46	394	11.7%	-0.08
20.0..30	11%	33	321	10.3%	-0.02
30.1+	16%	51	665	7.7%	-0.24
Not Compl	15%	48	598	8.0%	-0.17
Unraced	1%	2	9	22.2%	0.28

ANALYSIS BY SUCCESS RATE IN LAST 10 RUNS

Age	Prop	Win	Runs	Wins%	£
No Wins	40%	126	1352	9.3%	-0.16
1 Win	35%	108	873	12.4%	-0.10
2 Wins	14%	45	417	10.8%	-0.42
3 Wins	8%	24	189	12.7%	-0.06
4 Wins	2%	6	53	11.3%	-0.21
5+ Wins	1%	3	26	11.5%	0.57

ANALYSIS BY SUCCESS RATE IN LAST 3 RUNS

Age	Prop	Win	Runs	Wins%	£
No Wins	64%	201	2043	9.8%	-0.12
1 Win	28%	88	719	12.2%	-0.32
2 Wins	7%	21	141	14.9%	-0.12
3 Wins	1%	2	7	28.6%	-0.44

ANALYSIS BY POSITION LAST TIME

Age	Prop	Win	Runs	Wins%	£
Won	20%	64	399	16.0%	-0.27
2nd or 3rd	28%	88	714	12.3%	-0.09
Unplaced	36%	112	1200	9.3%	-0.18
Fell,BD,UR	8%	26	206	12.6%	0.20
Pulled Up	7%	21	375	5.6%	-0.35
Ref/RanOut	0%	1	14	7.1%	-0.50
CO/SlipUp	0%	0	2	0.0%	-1.00
Unraced	1%	2	9	22.2%	0.28

OTHER FACTORS (WINS-RUNS, £)

Course Winner:	38-293	-£0.28
Distance Winner:	94-626	-£0.07
Going Winner:	94-799	-£0.17
Beaten Favourite:	25-203	-£0.29
7-Day Winners:	10-29	£0.18
Absolute Favourites:	67-280	-£0.25

Race Profiles

Novices' Handicap Chases: 3m+

ANALYSIS BY AGE

Age	Prop	Win	Runs	Wins%	£
3yo	0%	0	0	0.0%	0.00
4yo	1%	2	11	18.2%	1.00
5yo	5%	10	109	9.2%	-0.09
6yo	24%	46	388	11.9%	0.07
7yo	31%	58	493	11.8%	-0.14
8yo	23%	44	383	11.5%	-0.20
9yo	9%	18	188	9.6%	0.05
10yo	5%	9	107	8.4%	-0.38
11yo	2%	3	29	10.3%	-0.16
12yo+	0%	0	4	0.0%	-1.00

ANALYSIS BY BHB RATING

Age	Prop	Win	Runs	Wins%	£
150+	0%	0	0	0.0%	0.00
130..149	0%	0	14	0.0%	-1.00
120..129	7%	14	75	18.7%	0.33
110..119	14%	27	167	16.2%	0.55
100..109	11%	21	327	6.4%	-0.53
80..99	53%	100	805	12.4%	0.03
60..79	15%	28	323	8.7%	-0.32
..59	0%	0	1	0.0%	-1.00
Unrated	0%	0	0	0.0%	0.00

ANALYSIS BY WEIGHT CARRIED

Age	Prop	Win	Runs	Wins%	£
12-01+	1%	1	1	100.0%	1.75
11-8..12-00	22%	41	347	11.8%	-0.02
11-0..11-07	28%	53	526	10.1%	-0.17
10-8..10-13	19%	37	342	10.8%	-0.24
10-0..10-07	25%	47	358	13.1%	0.15
..9-13	6%	11	138	8.0%	-0.22

ANALYSIS BY DAYS SINCE LAST RUN

Age	Prop	Win	Runs	Wins%	£
1..7	6%	11	67	16.4%	-0.50
8..14	17%	33	334	9.9%	-0.28
15..28	45%	85	599	14.2%	0.08
29..60	19%	36	397	9.1%	-0.11
61..100	4%	7	90	7.8%	-0.25
101+	9%	17	223	7.6%	-0.03
Unraced	1%	1	2	50.0%	0.44

ANALYSIS BY TODAY'S STARTING PRICE

Age	Prop	Win	Runs	Wins%	£
Odds On	2%	3	7	42.9%	-0.26
Ev-2/1	12%	22	67	32.8%	-0.17
9/4-4/1	31%	59	280	21.1%	-0.10
9/2-6/1	21%	40	240	16.7%	0.01
13/2-10/1	14%	27	411	6.6%	-0.39
11/1-16/1	14%	27	345	7.8%	0.17
18/1-33/1	6%	11	246	4.5%	0.21
40/1+	1%	1	116	0.9%	-0.56

ANALYSIS BY STARTING PRICE LAST TIME

Age	Prop	Win	Runs	Wins%	£
Odds On	2%	3	15	20.0%	-0.48
Ev-2/1	5%	10	77	13.0%	-0.19
9/4-4/1	20%	38	269	14.1%	-0.29
9/2-6/1	19%	37	231	16.0%	0.05
13/2-10/1	27%	52	366	14.2%	0.03
11/1-16/1	16%	31	307	10.1%	0.25
18/1-33/1	5%	10	273	3.7%	-0.45
40/1+	4%	8	172	4.7%	-0.16
Unraced	1%	1	2	50.0%	0.44

ANALYSIS BY DISTANCE BEATEN LAST TIME

Age	Prop	Win	Runs	Wins%	£
..-10 lgh	3%	5	38	13.2%	-0.65
-10..0	16%	30	157	19.1%	-0.17
0.1..2	8%	16	79	20.3%	0.48
2.1..5	7%	13	81	16.0%	0.05
5.1..10	12%	23	132	17.4%	0.10
10.1..20	15%	28	218	12.8%	0.13
20.0..30	11%	20	177	11.3%	0.02
30.1+	12%	23	434	5.3%	-0.32
Not Compl	16%	31	394	7.9%	-0.13
Unraced	1%	1	2	50.0%	0.44

ANALYSIS BY SUCCESS RATE IN LAST 10 RUNS

Age	Prop	Win	Runs	Wins%	£
No Wins	42%	79	886	8.9%	-0.12
1 Win	33%	63	520	12.1%	-0.21
2 Wins	17%	32	215	14.9%	0.30
3 Wins	5%	9	69	13.0%	-0.32
4 Wins	3%	6	17	35.3%	1.10
5+ Wins	0%	0	3	0.0%	-1.00

ANALYSIS BY SUCCESS RATE IN LAST 3 RUNS

Age	Prop	Win	Runs	Wins%	£
No Wins	62%	118	1266	9.3%	-0.11
1 Win	32%	61	387	15.8%	-0.04
2 Wins	4%	8	51	15.7%	0.13
3 Wins	1%	2	6	33.3%	-0.20

ANALYSIS BY POSITION LAST TIME

Age	Prop	Win	Runs	Wins%	£
Won	18%	35	195	17.9%	-0.26
2nd or 3rd	36%	68	402	16.9%	0.09
Unplaced	29%	55	720	7.6%	-0.12
Fell,BD,UR	7%	14	121	11.6%	0.14
Pulled Up	8%	16	265	6.0%	-0.24
Ref/RanOut	1%	1	6	16.7%	-0.42
CO/SlipUp	0%	0	1	0.0%	-1.00
Unraced	1%	1	2	50.0%	0.44

OTHER FACTORS (WINS-RUNS, £)

Course Winner:	22-164	-£0.20
Distance Winner:	39-294	-£0.12
Going Winner:	62-415	£0.06
Beaten Favourite:	15-124	-£0.37
7-Day Winners:	8-20	£0.01
Absolute Favourites:	45-168	-£0.14

Novices' Handicap Chases

Novices' Handicap Chases: 2 to 5 runners

ANALYSIS BY AGE

Age	Prop	Win	Runs	Wins%	£
3yo	0%	0	0	0.0%	0.00
4yo	3%	3	6	50.0%	0.21
5yo	6%	6	57	10.5%	-0.56
6yo	31%	29	111	26.1%	0.24
7yo	32%	30	115	26.1%	0.06
8yo	11%	10	73	13.7%	-0.21
9yo	9%	8	39	20.5%	-0.29
10yo	8%	7	15	46.7%	0.82
11yo	0%	0	4	0.0%	-1.00
12yo+	0%	0	1	0.0%	-1.00

ANALYSIS BY BHB RATING

Age	Prop	Win	Runs	Wins%	£
150+	0%	0	0	0.0%	0.00
130..149	4%	4	14	28.6%	0.00
120..129	6%	6	32	18.8%	-0.29
110..119	24%	22	81	27.2%	0.06
100..109	24%	22	103	21.4%	-0.01
80..99	39%	36	153	23.5%	0.12
60..79	3%	3	38	7.9%	-0.75
..59	0%	0	0	0.0%	0.00
Unrated	0%	0	0	0.0%	0.00

ANALYSIS BY WEIGHT CARRIED

Age	Prop	Win	Runs	Wins%	£
12-01+	0%	0	0	0.0%	0.00
11-8..12-00	30%	28	114	24.6%	0.06
11-0..11-07	32%	30	127	23.6%	0.11
10-8..10-13	22%	20	66	30.3%	0.37
10-0..10-07	12%	11	90	12.2%	-0.59
..9-13	4%	4	24	16.7%	-0.32

ANALYSIS BY DAYS SINCE LAST RUN

Age	Prop	Win	Runs	Wins%	£
1..7	8%	7	34	20.6%	-0.32
8..14	23%	21	94	22.3%	-0.09
15..28	41%	38	144	26.4%	0.30
29..60	19%	18	87	20.7%	-0.20
61..100	2%	2	23	8.7%	-0.76
101+	8%	7	38	18.4%	-0.11
Unraced	0%	0	1	0.0%	-1.00

ANALYSIS BY TODAY'S STARTING PRICE

Age	Prop	Win	Runs	Wins%	£
Odds On	12%	11	20	55.0%	-0.07
Ev-2/1	29%	27	84	32.1%	-0.17
9/4-4/1	37%	34	145	23.4%	-0.03
9/2-6/1	12%	11	57	19.3%	0.19
13/2-10/1	9%	8	58	13.8%	0.34
11/1-16/1	2%	2	36	5.6%	-0.17
18/1-33/1	0%	0	15	0.0%	-1.00
40/1+	0%	0	6	0.0%	-1.00

ANALYSIS BY STARTING PRICE LAST TIME

Age	Prop	Win	Runs	Wins%	£
Odds On	4%	4	7	57.1%	0.42
Ev-2/1	12%	11	36	30.6%	0.26
9/4-4/1	27%	25	82	30.5%	0.02
9/2-6/1	14%	13	64	20.3%	-0.30
13/2-10/1	24%	22	90	24.4%	0.21
11/1-16/1	12%	11	57	19.3%	0.11
18/1-33/1	5%	5	56	8.9%	-0.31
40/1+	2%	2	28	7.1%	-0.63
Unraced	0%	0	1	0.0%	-1.00

ANALYSIS BY DISTANCE BEATEN LAST TIME

Age	Prop	Win	Runs	Wins%	£
..-10 lgh	4%	4	10	40.0%	0.26
-10..0	25%	23	61	37.7%	0.15
0.1..2	9%	8	28	28.6%	-0.08
2.1..5	3%	3	36	8.3%	-0.57
5.1..10	11%	10	31	32.3%	0.39
10.1..20	17%	16	58	27.6%	0.07
20.0..30	9%	8	42	19.0%	-0.11
30.1+	13%	12	94	12.8%	-0.21
Not Compl	10%	9	60	15.0%	0.07
Unraced	0%	0	1	0.0%	-1.00

ANALYSIS BY SUCCESS RATE IN LAST 10 RUNS

Age	Prop	Win	Runs	Wins%	£
No Wins	29%	27	163	16.6%	-0.03
1 Win	39%	36	136	26.5%	0.10
2 Wins	15%	14	65	21.5%	-0.28
3 Wins	13%	12	41	29.3%	-0.10
4 Wins	3%	3	11	27.3%	0.16
5+ Wins	1%	1	4	25.0%	-0.52

ANALYSIS BY SUCCESS RATE IN LAST 3 RUNS

Age	Prop	Win	Runs	Wins%	£
No Wins	49%	46	262	17.6%	-0.06
1 Win	38%	35	129	27.1%	-0.06
2 Wins	11%	10	24	41.7%	0.41
3 Wins	2%	2	5	40.0%	-0.32

ANALYSIS BY POSITION LAST TIME

Age	Prop	Win	Runs	Wins%	£
Won	29%	27	71	38.0%	0.17
2nd or 3rd	33%	31	121	25.6%	-0.02
Unplaced	28%	26	168	15.5%	-0.17
Fell,BD,UR	5%	5	27	18.5%	0.16
Pulled Up	4%	4	33	12.1%	0.00
Ref/RanOut	0%	0	0	0.0%	0.00
CO/SlipUp	0%	0	0	0.0%	0.00
Unraced	0%	0	1	0.0%	-1.00

OTHER FACTORS (WINS-RUNS, £)

Course Winner:	20-61	£0.10
Distance Winner:	33-138	-£0.22
Going Winner:	35-130	£0.04
Beaten Favourite:	10-36	-£0.10
7-Day Winners:	3-12	-£0.10
Absolute Favourites:	33-84	-£0.11

Race Profiles

Novices' Handicap Chases: 6 to 10 runners

ANALYSIS BY AGE

Age	Prop	Win	Runs	Wins%	£
3yo	0%	0	0	0.0%	0.00
4yo	2%	9	52	17.3%	0.12
5yo	9%	37	341	10.9%	-0.25
6yo	23%	101	866	11.7%	-0.16
7yo	30%	131	953	13.7%	-0.05
8yo	24%	102	717	14.2%	-0.04
9yo	9%	39	353	11.0%	-0.02
10yo	2%	9	149	6.0%	-0.46
11yo	1%	3	41	7.3%	-0.26
12yo+	0%	1	15	6.7%	-0.13

ANALYSIS BY BHB RATING

Age	Prop	Win	Runs	Wins%	£
150+	0%	0	0	0.0%	0.00
130..149	1%	4	47	8.5%	-0.47
120..129	8%	34	208	16.3%	0.02
110..119	10%	45	384	11.7%	-0.10
100..109	20%	88	745	11.8%	-0.22
80..99	50%	217	1582	13.7%	0.03
60..79	10%	44	519	8.5%	-0.40
..59	0%	0	1	0.0%	-1.00
Unrated	0%	0	1	0.0%	-1.00

ANALYSIS BY WEIGHT CARRIED

Age	Prop	Win	Runs	Wins%	£
12-01+	0%	1	3	33.3%	-0.04
11-8..12-00	24%	103	750	13.7%	-0.20
11-0..11-07	32%	140	1038	13.5%	-0.01
10-8..10-13	19%	84	673	12.5%	0.06
10-0..10-07	18%	76	717	10.6%	-0.29
..9-13	6%	28	306	9.2%	-0.16

ANALYSIS BY DAYS SINCE LAST RUN

Age	Prop	Win	Runs	Wins%	£
1..7	8%	34	177	19.2%	0.19
8..14	20%	86	729	11.8%	-0.17
15..28	33%	143	1129	12.7%	-0.17
29..60	21%	90	754	11.9%	-0.11
61..100	5%	21	196	10.7%	-0.25
101+	13%	56	493	11.4%	0.05
Unraced	0%	2	9	22.2%	0.22

ANALYSIS BY TODAY'S STARTING PRICE

Age	Prop	Win	Runs	Wins%	£
Odds On	2%	8	17	47.1%	-0.19
Ev-2/1	13%	58	163	35.6%	-0.08
9/4-4/1	33%	143	704	20.3%	-0.15
9/2-6/1	21%	91	573	15.9%	-0.03
13/2-10/1	17%	75	859	8.7%	-0.22
11/1-16/1	8%	36	615	5.9%	-0.15
18/1-33/1	5%	20	426	4.7%	0.26
40/1+	0%	1	130	0.8%	-0.61

ANALYSIS BY STARTING PRICE LAST TIME

Age	Prop	Win	Runs	Wins%	£
Odds On	2%	8	42	19.0%	-0.51
Ev-2/1	8%	34	181	18.8%	-0.21
9/4-4/1	19%	83	527	15.7%	-0.05
9/2-6/1	17%	73	472	15.5%	-0.06
13/2-10/1	23%	100	738	13.6%	-0.17
11/1-16/1	17%	72	636	11.3%	0.04
18/1-33/1	9%	39	540	7.2%	-0.28
40/1+	5%	21	342	6.1%	-0.07
Unraced	0%	2	9	22.2%	0.22

ANALYSIS BY DISTANCE BEATEN LAST TIME

Age	Prop	Win	Runs	Wins%	£
..-10 lgh	5%	21	91	23.1%	-0.14
-10..0	13%	58	345	16.8%	-0.33
0.1..2	7%	30	169	17.8%	-0.09
2.1..5	6%	28	165	17.0%	-0.08
5.1..10	10%	45	275	16.4%	0.02
10.1..20	15%	63	491	12.8%	-0.15
20.0..30	11%	46	383	12.0%	0.00
30.1+	16%	67	826	8.1%	-0.21
Not Compl	17%	72	733	9.8%	0.02
Unraced	0%	2	9	22.2%	0.22

ANALYSIS BY SUCCESS RATE IN LAST 10 RUNS

Age	Prop	Win	Runs	Wins%	£
No Wins	43%	184	1708	10.8%	-0.07
1 Win	33%	143	1072	13.3%	-0.17
2 Wins	15%	64	470	13.6%	-0.25
3 Wins	6%	24	178	13.5%	-0.17
4 Wins	3%	12	37	32.4%	0.73
5+ Wins	1%	3	13	23.1%	2.62

ANALYSIS BY SUCCESS RATE IN LAST 3 RUNS

Age	Prop	Win	Runs	Wins%	£
No Wins	66%	284	2517	11.3%	-0.07
1 Win	29%	124	831	14.9%	-0.22
2 Wins	4%	19	119	16.0%	-0.14
3 Wins	1%	3	11	27.3%	-0.45

ANALYSIS BY POSITION LAST TIME

Age	Prop	Win	Runs	Wins%	£
Won	18%	79	436	18.1%	-0.29
2nd or 3rd	30%	131	819	16.0%	-0.02
Unplaced	34%	148	1490	9.9%	-0.17
Fell,BD,UR	8%	35	261	13.4%	0.29
Pulled Up	8%	35	457	7.7%	-0.17
Ref/RanOut	0%	1	12	8.3%	-0.42
CO/SlipUp	0%	1	3	33.3%	6.00
Unraced	0%	2	9	22.2%	0.22

OTHER FACTORS (WINS-RUNS, £)

Course Winner:	54-363	-£0.26
Distance Winner:	125-806	-£0.14
Going Winner:	139-912	-£0.10
Beaten Favourite:	38-235	-£0.19
7-Day Winners:	18-37	£0.42
Absolute Favourites:	107-393	-£0.18

TRAINERS (WINS-RUNS, £)

Mrs S J Smith 7-50 £0.05; R H Alner 8-31 £0.04; B G Powell 5-36 £0.03; P Winkworth 3-11 £0.05.

Novices' Handicap Chases

Novices' Handicap Chases: 11 runners or more

ANALYSIS BY AGE

Age	Prop	Win	Runs	Wins%	£
3yo	0%	0	0	0.0%	0.00
4yo	3%	6	37	16.2%	0.00
5yo	8%	17	272	6.3%	-0.46
6yo	28%	57	611	9.3%	-0.22
7yo	23%	47	670	7.0%	-0.34
8yo	22%	44	519	8.5%	-0.29
9yo	11%	23	293	7.8%	-0.06
10yo	3%	7	130	5.4%	-0.52
11yo	1%	2	41	4.9%	-0.07
12yo+	0%	0	15	0.0%	-1.00

ANALYSIS BY BHB RATING

Age	Prop	Win	Runs	Wins%	£
150+	0%	0	0	0.0%	0.00
130..149	4%	8	106	7.5%	-0.23
120..129	3%	7	91	7.7%	-0.34
110..119	8%	17	178	9.6%	0.17
100..109	15%	30	378	7.9%	-0.35
80..99	49%	100	1312	7.6%	-0.31
60..79	20%	41	522	7.9%	-0.32
..59	0%	0	0	0.0%	0.00
Unrated	0%	0	1	0.0%	-1.00

ANALYSIS BY WEIGHT CARRIED

Age	Prop	Win	Runs	Wins%	£
12-01+	0%	1	2	50.0%	0.38
11-8..12-00	21%	43	441	9.8%	-0.13
11-0..11-07	29%	59	858	6.9%	-0.39
10-8..10-13	18%	37	518	7.1%	-0.38
10-0..10-07	26%	52	563	9.2%	-0.15
..9-13	5%	11	206	5.3%	-0.33

ANALYSIS BY DAYS SINCE LAST RUN

Age	Prop	Win	Runs	Wins%	£
1..7	5%	11	111	9.9%	-0.62
8..14	20%	40	434	9.2%	-0.30
15..28	33%	66	888	7.4%	-0.28
29..60	22%	45	632	7.1%	-0.26
61..100	9%	19	173	11.0%	0.19
101+	9%	19	344	5.5%	-0.47
Unraced	1%	3	6	50.0%	0.81

ANALYSIS BY TODAY'S STARTING PRICE

Age	Prop	Win	Runs	Wins%	£
Odds On	1%	2	3	66.7%	0.17
Ev-2/1	6%	13	36	36.1%	-0.04
9/4-4/1	25%	51	208	24.5%	0.05
9/2-6/1	20%	41	272	15.1%	-0.09
13/2-10/1	24%	48	604	7.9%	-0.27
11/1-16/1	16%	33	571	5.8%	-0.15
18/1-33/1	6%	13	604	2.2%	-0.46
40/1+	1%	2	290	0.7%	-0.68

ANALYSIS BY STARTING PRICE LAST TIME

Age	Prop	Win	Runs	Wins%	£
Odds On	3%	7	33	21.2%	0.37
Ev-2/1	6%	12	107	11.2%	-0.18
9/4-4/1	21%	42	366	11.5%	-0.23
9/2-6/1	13%	26	289	9.0%	-0.32
13/2-10/1	28%	57	536	10.6%	-0.18
11/1-16/1	15%	30	488	6.1%	-0.30
18/1-33/1	9%	19	442	4.3%	-0.20
40/1+	3%	7	321	2.2%	-0.70
Unraced	1%	3	6	50.0%	0.81

ANALYSIS BY DISTANCE BEATEN LAST TIME

Age	Prop	Win	Runs	Wins%	£
..-10 lgh	2%	5	46	10.9%	-0.57
-10..0	15%	30	204	14.7%	-0.19
0.1..2	8%	16	119	13.4%	0.11
2.1..5	9%	19	128	14.8%	0.24
5.1..10	10%	21	200	10.5%	-0.34
10.1..20	18%	36	344	10.5%	-0.01
20.0..30	10%	20	300	6.7%	-0.27
30.1+	14%	29	670	4.3%	-0.48
Not Compl	12%	24	571	4.2%	-0.43
Unraced	1%	3	6	50.0%	0.81

ANALYSIS BY SUCCESS RATE IN LAST 10 RUNS

Age	Prop	Win	Runs	Wins%	£
No Wins	51%	102	1480	6.9%	-0.32
1 Win	30%	59	690	8.6%	-0.31
2 Wins	12%	23	271	8.5%	-0.12
3 Wins	6%	12	92	13.0%	-0.02
4 Wins	2%	3	34	8.8%	-0.31
5+ Wins	1%	1	15	6.7%	-0.88

ANALYSIS BY SUCCESS RATE IN LAST 3 RUNS

Age	Prop	Win	Runs	Wins%	£
No Wins	69%	138	2016	6.8%	-0.29
1 Win	25%	49	474	10.3%	-0.32
2 Wins	6%	12	89	13.5%	-0.01
3 Wins	1%	1	3	33.3%	-0.04

ANALYSIS BY POSITION LAST TIME

Age	Prop	Win	Runs	Wins%	£
Won	17%	35	251	13.9%	-0.26
2nd or 3rd	34%	69	589	11.7%	-0.10
Unplaced	35%	72	1174	6.1%	-0.32
Fell,BD,UR	5%	11	181	6.1%	-0.19
Pulled Up	6%	12	375	3.2%	-0.53
Ref/RanOut	0%	1	11	9.1%	-0.68
CO/SlipUp	0%	0	1	0.0%	-1.00
Unraced	1%	3	6	50.0%	0.81

OTHER FACTORS (WINS-RUNS, £)

Course Winner:	17-192	-£0.35
Distance Winner:	42-450	-£0.20
Going Winner:	54-586	-£0.18
Beaten Favourite:	13-166	-£0.48
7-Day Winners:	5-20	-£0.35
Absolute Favourites:	51-175	£0.14

Race Profiles

Novices' Handicap Chases: up to 7 days off the track

ANALYSIS BY AGE

Age	Prop	Win	Runs	Wins%	£
3yo	0%	0	0	0.0%	0.00
4yo	7%	4	12	33.3%	0.31
5yo	9%	5	35	14.3%	-0.23
6yo	21%	12	83	14.5%	-0.48
7yo	28%	16	74	21.6%	0.10
8yo	19%	11	65	16.9%	0.06
9yo	12%	7	45	15.6%	0.22
10yo	2%	1	15	6.7%	-0.89
11yo	2%	1	4	25.0%	0.25
12yo+	0%	0	5	0.0%	-1.00

ANALYSIS BY BHB RATING

Age	Prop	Win	Runs	Wins%	£
150+	0%	0	0	0.0%	0.00
130..149	0%	0	7	0.0%	-1.00
120..129	11%	6	14	42.9%	2.71
110..119	4%	2	26	7.7%	-0.50
100..109	19%	11	44	25.0%	0.10
80..99	58%	33	176	18.8%	-0.19
60..79	9%	5	71	7.0%	-0.43
..59	0%	0	0	0.0%	0.00
Unrated	0%	0	0	0.0%	0.00

ANALYSIS BY WEIGHT CARRIED

Age	Prop	Win	Runs	Wins%	£
12-01+	2%	1	2	50.0%	0.44
11-8..12-00	25%	14	63	22.2%	-0.20
11-0..11-07	23%	13	81	16.0%	0.29
10-8..10-13	18%	10	76	13.2%	-0.50
10-0..10-07	26%	15	80	18.8%	-0.11
..9-13	7%	4	36	11.1%	-0.14

ANALYSIS BY DAYS SINCE LAST RUN

Age	Prop	Win	Runs	Wins%	£
1..7	91%	52	322	16.1%	-0.14
8..14	0%	0	0	0.0%	0.00
15..28	0%	0	0	0.0%	0.00
29..60	0%	0	0	0.0%	0.00
61..100	0%	0	0	0.0%	0.00
101+	0%	0	0	0.0%	0.00
Unraced	9%	5	16	31.3%	0.37

ANALYSIS BY TODAY'S STARTING PRICE

Age	Prop	Win	Runs	Wins%	£
Odds On	12%	7	15	46.7%	-0.23
Ev-2/1	33%	19	34	55.9%	0.41
9/4-4/1	25%	14	72	19.4%	-0.19
9/2-6/1	16%	9	47	19.1%	0.15
13/2-10/1	5%	3	58	5.2%	-0.53
11/1-16/1	5%	3	53	5.7%	-0.23
18/1-33/1	4%	2	43	4.7%	0.33
40/1+	0%	0	16	0.0%	-1.00

ANALYSIS BY STARTING PRICE LAST TIME

Age	Prop	Win	Runs	Wins%	£
Odds On	11%	6	11	54.5%	0.12
Ev-2/1	5%	3	18	16.7%	-0.49
9/4-4/1	16%	9	48	18.8%	0.23
9/2-6/1	16%	9	45	20.0%	-0.38
13/2-10/1	23%	13	67	19.4%	-0.03
11/1-16/1	16%	9	54	16.7%	0.23
18/1-33/1	4%	2	43	4.7%	-0.71
40/1+	2%	1	36	2.8%	-0.36
Unraced	9%	5	16	31.3%	0.37

ANALYSIS BY DISTANCE BEATEN LAST TIME

Age	Prop	Win	Runs	Wins%	£
..-10 lgh	16%	9	22	40.9%	0.10
-10..0	30%	17	47	36.2%	0.11
0.1..2	9%	5	15	33.3%	0.57
2.1..5	2%	1	15	6.7%	-0.63
5.1..10	7%	4	26	15.4%	1.18
10.1..20	7%	4	35	11.4%	-0.51
20.0..30	5%	3	26	11.5%	0.21
30.1+	5%	3	55	5.5%	-0.66
Not Compl	11%	6	81	7.4%	-0.43
Unraced	9%	5	16	31.3%	0.37

ANALYSIS BY SUCCESS RATE IN LAST 10 RUNS

Age	Prop	Win	Runs	Wins%	£
No Wins	29%	15	167	9.0%	-0.27
1 Win	50%	26	95	27.4%	-0.03
2 Wins	4%	2	32	6.3%	-0.81
3 Wins	8%	4	16	25.0%	-0.33
4 Wins	6%	3	9	33.3%	-0.01
5+ Wins	4%	2	3	66.7%	10.94

ANALYSIS BY SUCCESS RATE IN LAST 3 RUNS

Age	Prop	Win	Runs	Wins%	£
No Wins	37%	19	213	8.9%	-0.37
1 Win	44%	23	85	27.1%	-0.02
2 Wins	13%	7	19	36.8%	1.68
3 Wins	6%	3	5	60.0%	0.40

ANALYSIS BY POSITION LAST TIME

Age	Prop	Win	Runs	Wins%	£
Won	46%	26	69	37.7%	0.11
2nd or 3rd	23%	13	81	16.0%	0.27
Unplaced	12%	7	91	7.7%	-0.45
Fell,BD,UR	7%	4	38	10.5%	-0.43
Pulled Up	4%	2	38	5.3%	-0.36
Ref/RanOut	0%	0	4	0.0%	-1.00
CO/SlipUp	0%	0	1	0.0%	-1.00
Unraced	9%	5	16	31.3%	0.37

OTHER FACTORS (WINS-RUNS, £)

Course Winner:	6-27	£0.13
Distance Winner:	23-78	£0.15
Going Winner:	25-96	£0.35
Beaten Favourite:	2-17	-£0.79
7-Day Winners:	26-69	£0.11
Absolute Favourites:	30-72	£0.05

Novices' Handicap Chases

Novices' Handicap Chases: 100+ days off the track

ANALYSIS BY AGE

Age	Prop	Win	Runs	Wins%	£
3yo	0%	0	0	0.0%	0.00
4yo	4%	3	17	17.6%	-0.45
5yo	7%	6	101	5.9%	-0.63
6yo	30%	25	221	11.3%	0.33
7yo	34%	28	226	12.4%	-0.08
8yo	16%	13	157	8.3%	-0.34
9yo	9%	7	93	7.5%	-0.12
10yo	0%	0	46	0.0%	-1.00
11yo	0%	0	10	0.0%	-1.00
12yo+	0%	0	9	0.0%	-1.00

ANALYSIS BY BHB RATING

Age	Prop	Win	Runs	Wins%	£
150+	0%	0	0	0.0%	0.00
130..149	0%	0	7	0.0%	-1.00
120..129	2%	2	27	7.4%	-0.74
110..119	16%	13	77	16.9%	0.77
100..109	18%	15	182	8.2%	-0.56
80..99	48%	39	422	9.2%	-0.04
60..79	16%	13	165	7.9%	-0.39
..59	0%	0	0	0.0%	0.00
Unrated	0%	0	0	0.0%	0.00

ANALYSIS BY WEIGHT CARRIED

Age	Prop	Win	Runs	Wins%	£
12-01+	0%	0	0	0.0%	0.00
11-8..12-00	22%	18	182	9.9%	-0.32
11-0..11-07	35%	29	293	9.9%	-0.13
10-8..10-13	21%	17	160	10.6%	0.37
10-0..10-07	20%	16	187	8.6%	-0.40
..9-13	2%	2	58	3.4%	-0.60

ANALYSIS BY DAYS SINCE LAST RUN

Age	Prop	Win	Runs	Wins%	£
1..7	0%	0	0	0.0%	0.00
8..14	0%	0	0	0.0%	0.00
15..28	0%	0	0	0.0%	0.00
29..60	0%	0	0	0.0%	0.00
61..100	0%	0	5	0.0%	-1.00
101+	100%	82	875	9.4%	-0.16
Unraced	0%	0	0	0.0%	0.00

ANALYSIS BY TODAY'S STARTING PRICE

Age	Prop	Win	Runs	Wins%	£
Odds On	1%	1	2	50.0%	-0.04
Ev-2/1	7%	6	16	37.5%	-0.05
9/4-4/1	29%	24	101	23.8%	0.01
9/2-6/1	20%	16	106	15.1%	-0.09
13/2-10/1	21%	17	227	7.5%	-0.32
11/1-16/1	12%	10	177	5.6%	-0.16
18/1-33/1	10%	8	167	4.8%	0.28
40/1+	0%	0	84	0.0%	-1.00

ANALYSIS BY STARTING PRICE LAST TIME

Age	Prop	Win	Runs	Wins%	£
Odds On	2%	2	9	22.2%	0.00
Ev-2/1	6%	5	43	11.6%	-0.25
9/4-4/1	17%	14	120	11.7%	-0.31
9/2-6/1	15%	12	99	12.1%	0.11
13/2-10/1	18%	15	155	9.7%	-0.21
11/1-16/1	24%	20	187	10.7%	0.06
18/1-33/1	12%	10	157	6.4%	-0.34
40/1+	5%	4	110	3.6%	-0.34
Unraced	0%	0	0	0.0%	0.00

ANALYSIS BY DISTANCE BEATEN LAST TIME

Age	Prop	Win	Runs	Wins%	£
..-10 lgh	0%	0	6	0.0%	-1.00
-10..0	4%	3	34	8.8%	-0.60
0.1..2	1%	1	32	3.1%	-0.84
2.1..5	4%	3	32	9.4%	-0.42
5.1..10	5%	4	50	8.0%	-0.34
10.1..20	20%	16	109	14.7%	-0.08
20.0..30	21%	17	108	15.7%	0.55
30.1+	22%	18	269	6.7%	-0.26
Not Compl	24%	20	240	8.3%	-0.19
Unraced	0%	0	0	0.0%	0.00

ANALYSIS BY SUCCESS RATE IN LAST 10 RUNS

Age	Prop	Win	Runs	Wins%	£
No Wins	61%	50	547	9.1%	-0.11
1 Win	28%	23	232	9.9%	-0.34
2 Wins	10%	8	76	10.5%	0.17
3 Wins	1%	1	20	5.0%	-0.70
4 Wins	0%	0	5	0.0%	-1.00
5+ Wins	0%	0	0	0.0%	0.00

ANALYSIS BY SUCCESS RATE IN LAST 3 RUNS

Age	Prop	Win	Runs	Wins%	£
No Wins	85%	70	746	9.4%	-0.14
1 Win	13%	11	115	9.6%	-0.45
2 Wins	1%	1	19	5.3%	0.37
3 Wins	0%	0	0	0.0%	0.00

ANALYSIS BY POSITION LAST TIME

Age	Prop	Win	Runs	Wins%	£
Won	4%	3	40	7.5%	-0.66
2nd or 3rd	17%	14	146	9.6%	-0.29
Unplaced	55%	45	455	9.9%	-0.08
Fell,BD,UR	6%	5	44	11.4%	-0.38
Pulled Up	18%	15	195	7.7%	-0.14
Ref/RanOut	0%	0	0	0.0%	0.00
CO/SlipUp	0%	0	0	0.0%	0.00
Unraced	0%	0	0	0.0%	0.00

OTHER FACTORS (WINS-RUNS, £)

Course Winner:	6-54	-£0.52
Distance Winner:	10-133	-£0.47
Going Winner:	15-152	-£0.23
Beaten Favourite:	10-73	-£0.30
Absolute Favourites:	17-45	£0.27

Race Profiles

Selling Handicap Chases

ANALYSIS BY AGE

Age	Prop	Win	Runs	Wins%	£
3yo	0%	0	0	0.0%	0.00
4yo	0%	0	2	0.0%	-1.00
5yo	0%	0	14	0.0%	-1.00
6yo	3%	1	26	3.8%	-0.86
7yo	13%	5	60	8.3%	-0.48
8yo	3%	1	60	1.7%	-0.95
9yo	32%	12	74	16.2%	0.13
10yo	24%	9	49	18.4%	0.31
11yo	16%	6	63	9.5%	-0.19
12yo+	11%	4	40	10.0%	-0.30

ANALYSIS BY BHB RATING

Age	Prop	Win	Runs	Wins%	£
150+	0%	0	0	0.0%	0.00
130..149	0%	0	0	0.0%	0.00
120..129	0%	0	0	0.0%	0.00
110..119	0%	0	0	0.0%	0.00
100..109	0%	0	0	0.0%	0.00
80..99	32%	12	133	9.0%	-0.50
60..79	63%	24	248	9.7%	-0.26
..59	5%	2	7	28.6%	0.86
Unrated	0%	0	0	0.0%	0.00

ANALYSIS BY WEIGHT CARRIED

Age	Prop	Win	Runs	Wins%	£
12-01+	0%	0	0	0.0%	0.00
11-8..12-00	16%	6	65	9.2%	-0.52
11-0..11-07	26%	10	103	9.7%	-0.39
10-8..10-13	18%	7	75	9.3%	-0.29
10-0..10-07	24%	9	99	9.1%	-0.40
..9-13	16%	6	46	13.0%	0.24

ANALYSIS BY DAYS SINCE LAST RUN

Age	Prop	Win	Runs	Wins%	£
1..7	8%	3	29	10.3%	-0.61
8..14	24%	9	88	10.2%	-0.22
15..28	29%	11	121	9.1%	-0.45
29..60	13%	5	72	6.9%	-0.66
61..100	8%	3	19	15.8%	0.47
101+	18%	7	59	11.9%	0.10
Unraced	0%	0	0	0.0%	0.00

ANALYSIS BY TODAY'S STARTING PRICE

Age	Prop	Win	Runs	Wins%	£
Odds On	0%	0	0	0.0%	0.00
Ev-2/1	5%	2	8	25.0%	-0.34
9/4-4/1	42%	16	49	32.7%	0.39
9/2-6/1	16%	6	60	10.0%	-0.37
13/2-10/1	29%	11	108	10.2%	-0.12
11/1-16/1	3%	1	76	1.3%	-0.83
18/1-33/1	5%	2	62	3.2%	-0.27
40/1+	0%	0	25	0.0%	-1.00

ANALYSIS BY STARTING PRICE LAST TIME

Age	Prop	Win	Runs	Wins%	£
Odds On	0%	0	0	0.0%	0.00
Ev-2/1	3%	1	5	20.0%	0.00
9/4-4/1	16%	6	22	27.3%	0.01
9/2-6/1	18%	7	36	19.4%	-0.05
13/2-10/1	13%	5	73	6.8%	-0.46
11/1-16/1	29%	11	79	13.9%	0.14
18/1-33/1	8%	3	93	3.2%	-0.80
40/1+	13%	5	80	6.3%	-0.31
Unraced	0%	0	0	0.0%	0.00

ANALYSIS BY DISTANCE BEATEN LAST TIME

Age	Prop	Win	Runs	Wins%	£
..-10 lgh	3%	1	2	50.0%	0.13
-10..0	3%	1	10	10.0%	-0.10
0.1..2	0%	0	5	0.0%	-1.00
2.1..5	3%	1	7	14.3%	0.43
5.1..10	11%	4	20	20.0%	0.04
10.1..20	18%	7	44	15.9%	-0.05
20.0..30	13%	5	49	10.2%	-0.55
30.1+	26%	10	133	7.5%	-0.47
Not Compl	24%	9	118	7.6%	-0.26
Unraced	0%	0	0	0.0%	0.00

ANALYSIS BY SUCCESS RATE IN LAST 10 RUNS

Age	Prop	Win	Runs	Wins%	£
No Wins	63%	24	262	9.2%	-0.37
1 Win	29%	11	110	10.0%	-0.34
2 Wins	8%	3	16	18.8%	0.58
3 Wins	0%	0	0	0.0%	0.00
4 Wins	0%	0	0	0.0%	0.00
5+ Wins	0%	0	0	0.0%	0.00

ANALYSIS BY SUCCESS RATE IN LAST 3 RUNS

Age	Prop	Win	Runs	Wins%	£
No Wins	82%	31	354	8.8%	-0.36
1 Win	16%	6	33	18.2%	-0.02
2 Wins	3%	1	1	100.0%	3.00
3 Wins	0%	0	0	0.0%	0.00

ANALYSIS BY POSITION LAST TIME

Age	Prop	Win	Runs	Wins%	£
Won	5%	2	12	16.7%	-0.06
2nd or 3rd	26%	10	59	16.9%	0.01
Unplaced	45%	17	199	8.5%	-0.47
Fell,BD,UR	5%	2	29	6.9%	-0.59
Pulled Up	18%	7	86	8.1%	-0.12
Ref/RanOut	0%	0	3	0.0%	-1.00
CO/SlipUp	0%	0	0	0.0%	0.00
Unraced	0%	0	0	0.0%	0.00

OTHER FACTORS (WINS-RUNS, £)

Course Winner:	7-37	£1.19
Distance Winner:	7-64	-£0.14
Going Winner:	15-122	-£0.33
Beaten Favourite:	3-8	£0.72
7-Day Winners:	1-4	-£0.44
Absolute Favourites:	12-31	£0.55

Selling Handicap Chases

Selling Handicap Chases: 2m to 2m3f

ANALYSIS BY AGE

Age	Prop	Win	Runs	Wins%	£
3yo	0%	0	0	0.0%	0.00
4yo	0%	0	2	0.0%	-1.00
5yo	0%	0	8	0.0%	-1.00
6yo	0%	0	15	0.0%	-1.00
7yo	14%	3	32	9.4%	-0.52
8yo	5%	1	38	2.6%	-0.92
9yo	32%	7	36	19.4%	0.44
10yo	27%	6	26	23.1%	-0.03
11yo	9%	2	32	6.3%	-0.64
12yo+	14%	3	17	17.6%	0.06

ANALYSIS BY BHB RATING

Age	Prop	Win	Runs	Wins%	£
150+	0%	0	0	0.0%	0.00
130..149	0%	0	0	0.0%	0.00
120..129	0%	0	0	0.0%	0.00
110..119	0%	0	0	0.0%	0.00
100..109	0%	0	0	0.0%	0.00
80..99	41%	9	75	12.0%	-0.34
60..79	55%	12	126	9.5%	-0.45
..59	5%	1	5	20.0%	0.10
Unrated	0%	0	0	0.0%	0.00

ANALYSIS BY WEIGHT CARRIED

Age	Prop	Win	Runs	Wins%	£
12-01+	0%	0	0	0.0%	0.00
11-8..12-00	23%	5	41	12.2%	-0.40
11-0..11-07	41%	9	60	15.0%	0.02
10-8..10-13	9%	2	35	5.7%	-0.74
10-0..10-07	14%	3	44	6.8%	-0.63
..9-13	14%	3	26	11.5%	-0.47

ANALYSIS BY DAYS SINCE LAST RUN

Age	Prop	Win	Runs	Wins%	£
1..7	9%	2	19	10.5%	-0.53
8..14	14%	3	38	7.9%	-0.46
15..28	36%	8	63	12.7%	-0.28
29..60	18%	4	46	8.7%	-0.55
61..100	9%	2	10	20.0%	-0.10
101+	14%	3	30	10.0%	-0.32
Unraced	0%	0	0	0.0%	0.00

ANALYSIS BY TODAY'S STARTING PRICE

Age	Prop	Win	Runs	Wins%	£
Odds On	0%	0	0	0.0%	0.00
Ev-2/1	5%	1	6	16.7%	-0.50
9/4-4/1	64%	14	34	41.2%	0.75
9/2-6/1	5%	1	31	3.2%	-0.82
13/2-10/1	23%	5	58	8.6%	-0.24
11/1-16/1	5%	1	34	2.9%	-0.62
18/1-33/1	0%	0	31	0.0%	-1.00
40/1+	0%	0	12	0.0%	-1.00

ANALYSIS BY STARTING PRICE LAST TIME

Age	Prop	Win	Runs	Wins%	£
Odds On	0%	0	0	0.0%	0.00
Ev-2/1	5%	1	3	33.3%	0.67
9/4-4/1	23%	5	14	35.7%	0.43
9/2-6/1	23%	5	16	31.3%	0.23
13/2-10/1	14%	3	37	8.1%	-0.34
11/1-16/1	23%	5	42	11.9%	-0.18
18/1-33/1	0%	0	47	0.0%	-1.00
40/1+	14%	3	47	6.4%	-0.54
Unraced	0%	0	0	0.0%	0.00

ANALYSIS BY DISTANCE BEATEN LAST TIME

Age	Prop	Win	Runs	Wins%	£
..-10 lgh	0%	0	0	0.0%	0.00
-10..0	0%	0	7	0.0%	-1.00
0.1..2	0%	0	2	0.0%	-1.00
2.1..5	0%	0	6	0.0%	-1.00
5.1..10	9%	2	12	16.7%	-0.40
10.1..20	32%	7	26	26.9%	0.62
20.0..30	14%	3	28	10.7%	-0.58
30.1+	32%	7	74	9.5%	-0.34
Not Compl	14%	3	51	5.9%	-0.70
Unraced	0%	0	0	0.0%	0.00

ANALYSIS BY SUCCESS RATE IN LAST 10 RUNS

Age	Prop	Win	Runs	Wins%	£
No Wins	73%	16	144	11.1%	-0.36
1 Win	23%	5	52	9.6%	-0.43
2 Wins	5%	1	10	10.0%	-0.60
3 Wins	0%	0	0	0.0%	0.00
4 Wins	0%	0	0	0.0%	0.00
5+ Wins	0%	0	0	0.0%	0.00

ANALYSIS BY SUCCESS RATE IN LAST 3 RUNS

Age	Prop	Win	Runs	Wins%	£
No Wins	82%	18	185	9.7%	-0.42
1 Win	14%	3	20	15.0%	-0.35
2 Wins	5%	1	1	100.0%	3.00
3 Wins	0%	0	0	0.0%	0.00

ANALYSIS BY POSITION LAST TIME

Age	Prop	Win	Runs	Wins%	£
Won	0%	0	7	0.0%	-1.00
2nd or 3rd	32%	7	35	20.0%	0.03
Unplaced	55%	12	113	10.6%	-0.35
Fell,BD,UR	5%	1	17	5.9%	-0.71
Pulled Up	9%	2	33	6.1%	-0.68
Ref/RanOut	0%	0	1	0.0%	-1.00
CO/SlipUp	0%	0	0	0.0%	0.00
Unraced	0%	0	0	0.0%	0.00

OTHER FACTORS (WINS-RUNS, £)

Course Winner:	0-18	-£1.00
Distance Winner:	2-21	-£0.64
Going Winner:	11-69	-£0.20
Beaten Favourite:	3-4	£2.44
7-Day Winners:	0-2	-£1.00
Absolute Favourites:	8-17	£0.85

Race Profiles

Selling Handicap Chases: 2m4f to 2m7f

ANALYSIS BY AGE

Age	Prop	Win	Runs	Wins%	£
3yo	0%	0	0	0.0%	0.00
4yo	0%	0	0	0.0%	0.00
5yo	0%	0	6	0.0%	-1.00
6yo	0%	0	6	0.0%	-1.00
7yo	9%	1	21	4.8%	-0.60
8yo	0%	0	16	0.0%	-1.00
9yo	27%	3	23	13.0%	-0.32
10yo	27%	3	17	17.6%	1.29
11yo	36%	4	23	17.4%	0.72
12yo+	0%	0	12	0.0%	-1.00

ANALYSIS BY BHB RATING

Age	Prop	Win	Runs	Wins%	£
150+	0%	0	0	0.0%	0.00
130..149	0%	0	0	0.0%	0.00
120..129	0%	0	0	0.0%	0.00
110..119	0%	0	0	0.0%	0.00
100..109	0%	0	0	0.0%	0.00
80..99	27%	3	34	8.8%	-0.49
60..79	73%	8	89	9.0%	-0.04
..59	0%	0	1	0.0%	-1.00
Unrated	0%	0	0	0.0%	0.00

ANALYSIS BY WEIGHT CARRIED

Age	Prop	Win	Runs	Wins%	£
12-01+	0%	0	0	0.0%	0.00
11-8..12-00	9%	1	17	5.9%	-0.62
11-0..11-07	9%	1	26	3.8%	-0.91
10-8..10-13	36%	4	29	13.8%	0.40
10-0..10-07	36%	4	40	10.0%	-0.31
..9-13	9%	1	12	8.3%	1.17

ANALYSIS BY DAYS SINCE LAST RUN

Age	Prop	Win	Runs	Wins%	£
1..7	9%	1	7	14.3%	-0.68
8..14	27%	3	34	8.8%	-0.28
15..28	18%	2	40	5.0%	-0.69
29..60	0%	0	18	0.0%	-1.00
61..100	9%	1	4	25.0%	3.75
101+	36%	4	21	19.0%	1.12
Unraced	0%	0	0	0.0%	0.00

ANALYSIS BY TODAY'S STARTING PRICE

Age	Prop	Win	Runs	Wins%	£
Odds On	0%	0	0	0.0%	0.00
Ev-2/1	9%	1	2	50.0%	0.13
9/4-4/1	9%	1	10	10.0%	-0.50
9/2-6/1	36%	4	20	20.0%	0.30
13/2-10/1	27%	3	33	9.1%	-0.26
11/1-16/1	0%	0	29	0.0%	-1.00
18/1-33/1	18%	2	21	9.5%	1.14
40/1+	0%	0	9	0.0%	-1.00

ANALYSIS BY STARTING PRICE LAST TIME

Age	Prop	Win	Runs	Wins%	£
Odds On	0%	0	0	0.0%	0.00
Ev-2/1	0%	0	2	0.0%	-1.00
9/4-4/1	9%	1	5	20.0%	-0.55
9/2-6/1	9%	1	12	8.3%	-0.54
13/2-10/1	18%	2	21	9.5%	-0.26
11/1-16/1	45%	5	25	20.0%	0.82
18/1-33/1	9%	1	34	2.9%	-0.76
40/1+	9%	1	25	4.0%	0.04
Unraced	0%	0	0	0.0%	0.00

ANALYSIS BY DISTANCE BEATEN LAST TIME

Age	Prop	Win	Runs	Wins%	£
..-10 lgh	9%	1	2	50.0%	0.13
-10..0	0%	0	1	0.0%	-1.00
0.1..2	0%	0	1	0.0%	-1.00
2.1..5	0%	0	0	0.0%	0.00
5.1..10	18%	2	4	50.0%	2.38
10.1..20	0%	0	11	0.0%	-1.00
20.0..30	0%	0	11	0.0%	-1.00
30.1+	18%	2	43	4.7%	-0.65
Not Compl	55%	6	51	11.8%	0.41
Unraced	0%	0	0	0.0%	0.00

ANALYSIS BY SUCCESS RATE IN LAST 10 RUNS

Age	Prop	Win	Runs	Wins%	£
No Wins	36%	4	81	4.9%	-0.42
1 Win	45%	5	38	13.2%	-0.09
2 Wins	18%	2	5	40.0%	3.25
3 Wins	0%	0	0	0.0%	0.00
4 Wins	0%	0	0	0.0%	0.00
5+ Wins	0%	0	0	0.0%	0.00

ANALYSIS BY SUCCESS RATE IN LAST 3 RUNS

Age	Prop	Win	Runs	Wins%	£
No Wins	82%	9	115	7.8%	-0.20
1 Win	18%	2	9	22.2%	0.14
2 Wins	0%	0	0	0.0%	0.00
3 Wins	0%	0	0	0.0%	0.00

ANALYSIS BY POSITION LAST TIME

Age	Prop	Win	Runs	Wins%	£
Won	9%	1	3	33.3%	-0.25
2nd or 3rd	18%	2	16	12.5%	-0.16
Unplaced	18%	2	54	3.7%	-0.72
Fell,BD,UR	9%	1	9	11.1%	-0.22
Pulled Up	45%	5	40	12.5%	0.63
Ref/RanOut	0%	0	2	0.0%	-1.00
CO/SlipUp	0%	0	0	0.0%	0.00
Unraced	0%	0	0	0.0%	0.00

OTHER FACTORS (WINS-RUNS, £)

Course Winner:	5-13	£4.04
Distance Winner:	4-30	£0.25
Going Winner:	3-34	-£0.49
Beaten Favourite:	0-3	-£1.00
7-Day Winners:	1-2	£0.13
Absolute Favourites:	3-10	£0.28

Selling Handicap Chases

Selling Handicap Chases: 3m+

ANALYSIS BY AGE
Age	Prop	Win	Runs	Wins%	£
3yo	0%	0	0	0.0%	0.00
4yo	0%	0	0	0.0%	0.00
5yo	0%	0	0	0.0%	0.00
6yo	20%	1	5	20.0%	-0.25
7yo	20%	1	7	14.3%	0.07
8yo	0%	0	6	0.0%	-1.00
9yo	40%	2	15	13.3%	0.03
10yo	0%	0	6	0.0%	-1.00
11yo	0%	0	8	0.0%	-1.00
12yo+	20%	1	11	9.1%	-0.09

ANALYSIS BY BHB RATING
Age	Prop	Win	Runs	Wins%	£
150+	0%	0	0	0.0%	0.00
130..149	0%	0	0	0.0%	0.00
120..129	0%	0	0	0.0%	0.00
110..119	0%	0	0	0.0%	0.00
100..109	0%	0	0	0.0%	0.00
80..99	0%	0	24	0.0%	-1.00
60..79	80%	4	33	12.1%	-0.11
..59	20%	1	1	100.0%	6.50
Unrated	0%	0	0	0.0%	0.00

ANALYSIS BY WEIGHT CARRIED
Age	Prop	Win	Runs	Wins%	£
12-01+	0%	0	0	0.0%	0.00
11-8..12-00	0%	0	7	0.0%	-1.00
11-0..11-07	0%	0	17	0.0%	-1.00
10-8..10-13	20%	1	11	9.1%	-0.66
10-0..10-07	40%	2	15	13.3%	0.03
..9-13	40%	2	8	25.0%	1.19

ANALYSIS BY DAYS SINCE LAST RUN
Age	Prop	Win	Runs	Wins%	£
1..7	0%	0	3	0.0%	-1.00
8..14	60%	3	16	18.8%	0.50
15..28	20%	1	18	5.6%	-0.50
29..60	20%	1	8	12.5%	-0.53
61..100	0%	0	5	0.0%	-1.00
101+	0%	0	8	0.0%	-1.00
Unraced	0%	0	0	0.0%	0.00

ANALYSIS BY TODAY'S STARTING PRICE
Age	Prop	Win	Runs	Wins%	£
Odds On	0%	0	0	0.0%	0.00
Ev-2/1	0%	0	0	0.0%	0.00
9/4-4/1	20%	1	5	20.0%	-0.25
9/2-6/1	20%	1	9	11.1%	-0.28
13/2-10/1	60%	3	17	17.6%	0.56
11/1-16/1	0%	0	13	0.0%	-1.00
18/1-33/1	0%	0	10	0.0%	-1.00
40/1+	0%	0	4	0.0%	-1.00

ANALYSIS BY STARTING PRICE LAST TIME
Age	Prop	Win	Runs	Wins%	£
Odds On	0%	0	0	0.0%	0.00
Ev-2/1	0%	0	0	0.0%	0.00
9/4-4/1	0%	0	3	0.0%	-1.00
9/2-6/1	20%	1	8	12.5%	0.13
13/2-10/1	0%	0	15	0.0%	-1.00
11/1-16/1	20%	1	12	8.3%	-0.17
18/1-33/1	40%	2	12	16.7%	-0.15
40/1+	20%	1	8	12.5%	-0.06
Unraced	0%	0	0	0.0%	0.00

ANALYSIS BY DISTANCE BEATEN LAST TIME
Age	Prop	Win	Runs	Wins%	£
..-10 lgh	0%	0	0	0.0%	0.00
-10..0	20%	1	2	50.0%	3.50
0.1..2	0%	0	2	0.0%	-1.00
2.1..5	20%	1	1	100.0%	9.00
5.1..10	0%	0	4	0.0%	-1.00
10.1..20	0%	0	7	0.0%	-1.00
20.0..30	40%	2	10	20.0%	0.03
30.1+	20%	1	16	6.3%	-0.53
Not Compl	0%	0	16	0.0%	-1.00
Unraced	0%	0	0	0.0%	0.00

ANALYSIS BY SUCCESS RATE IN LAST 10 RUNS
Age	Prop	Win	Runs	Wins%	£
No Wins	80%	4	37	10.8%	-0.25
1 Win	20%	1	20	5.0%	-0.55
2 Wins	0%	0	1	0.0%	-1.00
3 Wins	0%	0	0	0.0%	0.00
4 Wins	0%	0	0	0.0%	0.00
5+ Wins	0%	0	0	0.0%	0.00

ANALYSIS BY SUCCESS RATE IN LAST 3 RUNS
Age	Prop	Win	Runs	Wins%	£
No Wins	80%	4	54	7.4%	-0.49
1 Win	20%	1	4	25.0%	1.25
2 Wins	0%	0	0	0.0%	0.00
3 Wins	0%	0	0	0.0%	0.00

ANALYSIS BY POSITION LAST TIME
Age	Prop	Win	Runs	Wins%	£
Won	20%	1	2	50.0%	3.50
2nd or 3rd	20%	1	8	12.5%	0.25
Unplaced	60%	3	32	9.4%	-0.45
Fell,BD,UR	0%	0	3	0.0%	-1.00
Pulled Up	0%	0	13	0.0%	-1.00
Ref/RanOut	0%	0	0	0.0%	0.00
CO/SlipUp	0%	0	0	0.0%	0.00
Unraced	0%	0	0	0.0%	0.00

OTHER FACTORS (WINS-RUNS, £)
Course Winner:	2-6	£1.58
Distance Winner:	1-13	-£0.23
Going Winner:	1-19	-£0.53
Beaten Favourite:	0-1	-£1.00
Absolute Favourites:	1-4	-£0.06

Race Profiles

Selling Handicap Chases: 2 to 5 runners

ANALYSIS BY AGE
Age	Prop	Win	Runs	Wins%	£
3yo	0%	0	0	0.0%	0.00
4yo	0%	0	0	0.0%	0.00
5yo	0%	0	0	0.0%	0.00
6yo	0%	0	0	0.0%	0.00
7yo	50%	1	3	33.3%	0.33
8yo	0%	0	2	0.0%	-1.00
9yo	0%	0	0	0.0%	0.00
10yo	0%	0	1	0.0%	-1.00
11yo	0%	0	0	0.0%	0.00
12yo+	50%	1	3	33.3%	0.67

ANALYSIS BY BHB RATING
Age	Prop	Win	Runs	Wins%	£
150+	0%	0	0	0.0%	0.00
130..149	0%	0	0	0.0%	0.00
120..129	0%	0	0	0.0%	0.00
110..119	0%	0	0	0.0%	0.00
100..109	0%	0	0	0.0%	0.00
80..99	50%	1	3	33.3%	0.67
60..79	50%	1	6	16.7%	-0.33
..59	0%	0	0	0.0%	0.00
Unrated	0%	0	0	0.0%	0.00

ANALYSIS BY WEIGHT CARRIED
Age	Prop	Win	Runs	Wins%	£
12-01+	0%	0	0	0.0%	0.00
11-8..12-00	50%	1	3	33.3%	0.67
11-0..11-07	50%	1	1	100.0%	3.00
10-8..10-13	0%	0	1	0.0%	-1.00
10-0..10-07	0%	0	2	0.0%	-1.00
..9-13	0%	0	2	0.0%	-1.00

ANALYSIS BY DAYS SINCE LAST RUN
Age	Prop	Win	Runs	Wins%	£
1..7	0%	0	1	0.0%	-1.00
8..14	50%	1	2	50.0%	1.00
15..28	50%	1	2	50.0%	1.50
29..60	0%	0	2	0.0%	-1.00
61..100	0%	0	0	0.0%	0.00
101+	0%	0	2	0.0%	-1.00
Unraced	0%	0	0	0.0%	0.00

ANALYSIS BY TODAY'S STARTING PRICE
Age	Prop	Win	Runs	Wins%	£
Odds On	0%	0	0	0.0%	0.00
Ev-2/1	0%	0	4	0.0%	-1.00
9/4-4/1	100%	2	2	100.0%	3.50
9/2-6/1	0%	0	2	0.0%	-1.00
13/2-10/1	0%	0	0	0.0%	0.00
11/1-16/1	0%	0	0	0.0%	0.00
18/1-33/1	0%	0	1	0.0%	-1.00
40/1+	0%	0	0	0.0%	0.00

ANALYSIS BY STARTING PRICE LAST TIME
Age	Prop	Win	Runs	Wins%	£
Odds On	0%	0	0	0.0%	0.00
Ev-2/1	50%	1	1	100.0%	4.00
9/4-4/1	0%	0	0	0.0%	0.00
9/2-6/1	50%	1	1	100.0%	3.00
13/2-10/1	0%	0	4	0.0%	-1.00
11/1-16/1	0%	0	0	0.0%	0.00
18/1-33/1	0%	0	1	0.0%	-1.00
40/1+	0%	0	2	0.0%	-1.00
Unraced	0%	0	0	0.0%	0.00

ANALYSIS BY DISTANCE BEATEN LAST TIME
Age	Prop	Win	Runs	Wins%	£
..-10 lgh	0%	0	0	0.0%	0.00
-10..0	0%	0	1	0.0%	-1.00
0.1..2	0%	0	0	0.0%	0.00
2.1..5	0%	0	1	0.0%	-1.00
5.1..10	0%	0	0	0.0%	0.00
10.1..20	50%	1	1	100.0%	4.00
20.0..30	0%	0	1	0.0%	-1.00
30.1+	50%	1	4	25.0%	0.00
Not Compl	0%	0	1	0.0%	-1.00
Unraced	0%	0	0	0.0%	0.00

ANALYSIS BY SUCCESS RATE IN LAST 10 RUNS
Age	Prop	Win	Runs	Wins%	£
No Wins	0%	0	3	0.0%	-1.00
1 Win	100%	2	5	40.0%	0.80
2 Wins	0%	0	1	0.0%	-1.00
3 Wins	0%	0	0	0.0%	0.00
4 Wins	0%	0	0	0.0%	0.00
5+ Wins	0%	0	0	0.0%	0.00

ANALYSIS BY SUCCESS RATE IN LAST 3 RUNS
Age	Prop	Win	Runs	Wins%	£
No Wins	0%	0	5	0.0%	-1.00
1 Win	100%	2	4	50.0%	1.25
2 Wins	0%	0	0	0.0%	0.00
3 Wins	0%	0	0	0.0%	0.00

ANALYSIS BY POSITION LAST TIME
Age	Prop	Win	Runs	Wins%	£
Won	0%	0	1	0.0%	-1.00
2nd or 3rd	50%	1	2	50.0%	1.50
Unplaced	50%	1	5	20.0%	-0.20
Fell,BD,UR	0%	0	0	0.0%	0.00
Pulled Up	0%	0	1	0.0%	-1.00
Ref/RanOut	0%	0	0	0.0%	0.00
CO/SlipUp	0%	0	0	0.0%	0.00
Unraced	0%	0	0	0.0%	0.00

OTHER FACTORS (WINS-RUNS, £)
Course Winner:	0-1	-£1.00
Distance Winner:	0-2	-£1.00
Going Winner:	0-2	-£1.00
Beaten Favourite:	1-1	£4.00
Absolute Favourites:	0-1	-£1.00

Selling Handicap Chases

Selling Handicap Chases: 6 to 10 runners

ANALYSIS BY AGE

Age	Prop	Win	Runs	Wins%	£
3yo	0%	0	0	0.0%	0.00
4yo	0%	0	1	0.0%	-1.00
5yo	0%	0	4	0.0%	-1.00
6yo	6%	1	9	11.1%	-0.58
7yo	17%	3	22	13.6%	-0.15
8yo	6%	1	23	4.3%	-0.87
9yo	22%	4	35	11.4%	-0.41
10yo	22%	4	17	23.5%	1.29
11yo	17%	3	21	14.3%	-0.10
12yo+	11%	2	12	16.7%	0.08

ANALYSIS BY BHB RATING

Age	Prop	Win	Runs	Wins%	£
150+	0%	0	0	0.0%	0.00
130..149	0%	0	0	0.0%	0.00
120..129	0%	0	0	0.0%	0.00
110..119	0%	0	0	0.0%	0.00
100..109	0%	0	0	0.0%	0.00
80..99	22%	4	47	8.5%	-0.52
60..79	67%	12	92	13.0%	-0.11
..59	11%	2	5	40.0%	1.60
Unrated	0%	0	0	0.0%	0.00

ANALYSIS BY WEIGHT CARRIED

Age	Prop	Win	Runs	Wins%	£
12-01+	0%	0	0	0.0%	0.00
11-8..12-00	11%	2	23	8.7%	-0.54
11-0..11-07	22%	4	40	10.0%	-0.50
10-8..10-13	17%	3	29	10.3%	-0.46
10-0..10-07	22%	4	35	11.4%	-0.33
..9-13	28%	5	17	29.4%	1.78

ANALYSIS BY DAYS SINCE LAST RUN

Age	Prop	Win	Runs	Wins%	£
1..7	11%	2	16	12.5%	-0.44
8..14	17%	3	36	8.3%	-0.36
15..28	22%	4	43	9.3%	-0.64
29..60	22%	4	27	14.8%	-0.24
61..100	6%	1	4	25.0%	0.25
101+	22%	4	18	22.2%	1.44
Unraced	0%	0	0	0.0%	0.00

ANALYSIS BY TODAY'S STARTING PRICE

Age	Prop	Win	Runs	Wins%	£
Odds On	0%	0	0	0.0%	0.00
Ev-2/1	6%	1	2	50.0%	0.50
9/4-4/1	50%	9	36	25.0%	0.03
9/2-6/1	17%	3	27	11.1%	-0.30
13/2-10/1	22%	4	41	9.8%	-0.22
11/1-16/1	0%	0	23	0.0%	-1.00
18/1-33/1	6%	1	12	8.3%	1.17
40/1+	0%	0	3	0.0%	-1.00

ANALYSIS BY STARTING PRICE LAST TIME

Age	Prop	Win	Runs	Wins%	£
Odds On	0%	0	0	0.0%	0.00
Ev-2/1	0%	0	3	0.0%	-1.00
9/4-4/1	22%	4	11	36.4%	0.45
9/2-6/1	11%	2	10	20.0%	-0.25
13/2-10/1	17%	3	29	10.3%	-0.37
11/1-16/1	28%	5	22	22.7%	0.48
18/1-33/1	6%	1	35	2.9%	-0.89
40/1+	17%	3	34	8.8%	0.15
Unraced	0%	0	0	0.0%	0.00

ANALYSIS BY DISTANCE BEATEN LAST TIME

Age	Prop	Win	Runs	Wins%	£
..-10 lgh	0%	0	0	0.0%	0.00
-10..0	0%	0	3	0.0%	-1.00
0.1..2	0%	0	0	0.0%	0.00
2.1..5	0%	0	4	0.0%	-1.00
5.1..10	17%	3	9	33.3%	0.69
10.1..20	22%	4	16	25.0%	0.28
20.0..30	17%	3	23	13.0%	-0.49
30.1+	22%	4	51	7.8%	-0.49
Not Compl	22%	4	38	10.5%	0.14
Unraced	0%	0	0	0.0%	0.00

ANALYSIS BY SUCCESS RATE IN LAST 10 RUNS

Age	Prop	Win	Runs	Wins%	£
No Wins	78%	14	95	14.7%	-0.04
1 Win	22%	4	43	9.3%	-0.41
2 Wins	0%	0	6	0.0%	-1.00
3 Wins	0%	0	0	0.0%	0.00
4 Wins	0%	0	0	0.0%	0.00
5+ Wins	0%	0	0	0.0%	0.00

ANALYSIS BY SUCCESS RATE IN LAST 3 RUNS

Age	Prop	Win	Runs	Wins%	£
No Wins	94%	17	132	12.9%	-0.14
1 Win	6%	1	12	8.3%	-0.67
2 Wins	0%	0	0	0.0%	0.00
3 Wins	0%	0	0	0.0%	0.00

ANALYSIS BY POSITION LAST TIME

Age	Prop	Win	Runs	Wins%	£
Won	0%	0	3	0.0%	-1.00
2nd or 3rd	33%	6	27	22.2%	0.11
Unplaced	44%	8	76	10.5%	-0.43
Fell,BD,UR	6%	1	9	11.1%	-0.44
Pulled Up	17%	3	27	11.1%	0.43
Ref/RanOut	0%	0	2	0.0%	-1.00
CO/SlipUp	0%	0	0	0.0%	0.00
Unraced	0%	0	0	0.0%	0.00

OTHER FACTORS (WINS-RUNS, £)

Course Winner:	2-16	£1.06
Distance Winner:	4-20	£0.05
Going Winner:	7-36	£0.05
Beaten Favourite:	1-2	£1.50
7-Day Winners:	0-1	-£1.00
Absolute Favourites:	5-14	£0.29

Race Profiles

Selling Handicap Chases : 11 runners or more

ANALYSIS BY AGE

Age	Prop	Win	Runs	Wins%	£
3yo	0%	0	0	0.0%	0.00
4yo	0%	0	1	0.0%	-1.00
5yo	0%	0	10	0.0%	-1.00
6yo	0%	0	17	0.0%	-1.00
7yo	6%	1	35	2.9%	-0.76
8yo	0%	0	35	0.0%	-1.00
9yo	44%	8	39	20.5%	0.61
10yo	28%	5	31	16.1%	-0.19
11yo	17%	3	42	7.1%	-0.24
12yo+	6%	1	25	4.0%	-0.60

ANALYSIS BY BHB RATING

Age	Prop	Win	Runs	Wins%	£
150+	0%	0	0	0.0%	0.00
130..149	0%	0	0	0.0%	0.00
120..129	0%	0	0	0.0%	0.00
110..119	0%	0	0	0.0%	0.00
100..109	0%	0	0	0.0%	0.00
80..99	39%	7	83	8.4%	-0.52
60..79	61%	11	150	7.3%	-0.34
..59	0%	0	2	0.0%	-1.00
Unrated	0%	0	0	0.0%	0.00

ANALYSIS BY WEIGHT CARRIED

Age	Prop	Win	Runs	Wins%	£
12-01+	0%	0	0	0.0%	0.00
11-8..12-00	17%	3	39	7.7%	-0.60
11-0..11-07	28%	5	62	8.1%	-0.37
10-8..10-13	22%	4	45	8.9%	-0.17
10-0..10-07	28%	5	62	8.1%	-0.42
..9-13	6%	1	27	3.7%	-0.63

ANALYSIS BY DAYS SINCE LAST RUN

Age	Prop	Win	Runs	Wins%	£
1..7	6%	1	12	8.3%	-0.81
8..14	28%	5	50	10.0%	-0.16
15..28	33%	6	76	7.9%	-0.39
29..60	6%	1	43	2.3%	-0.91
61..100	11%	2	15	13.3%	0.53
101+	17%	3	39	7.7%	-0.46
Unraced	0%	0	0	0.0%	0.00

ANALYSIS BY TODAY'S STARTING PRICE

Age	Prop	Win	Runs	Wins%	£
Odds On	0%	0	0	0.0%	0.00
Ev-2/1	6%	1	2	50.0%	0.13
9/4-4/1	28%	5	11	45.5%	1.02
9/2-6/1	17%	3	31	9.7%	-0.39
13/2-10/1	39%	7	67	10.4%	-0.06
11/1-16/1	6%	1	53	1.9%	-0.75
18/1-33/1	6%	1	49	2.0%	-0.61
40/1+	0%	0	22	0.0%	-1.00

ANALYSIS BY STARTING PRICE LAST TIME

Age	Prop	Win	Runs	Wins%	£
Odds On	0%	0	0	0.0%	0.00
Ev-2/1	0%	0	1	0.0%	-1.00
9/4-4/1	11%	2	11	18.2%	-0.43
9/2-6/1	22%	4	25	16.0%	-0.09
13/2-10/1	11%	2	40	5.0%	-0.46
11/1-16/1	33%	6	57	10.5%	0.01
18/1-33/1	11%	2	57	3.5%	-0.75
40/1+	11%	2	44	4.5%	-0.64
Unraced	0%	0	0	0.0%	0.00

ANALYSIS BY DISTANCE BEATEN LAST TIME

Age	Prop	Win	Runs	Wins%	£
..-10 lgh	6%	1	2	50.0%	0.13
-10..0	6%	1	6	16.7%	0.50
0.1..2	0%	0	5	0.0%	-1.00
2.1..5	6%	1	2	50.0%	4.00
5.1..10	6%	1	11	9.1%	-0.50
10.1..20	11%	2	27	7.4%	-0.39
20.0..30	11%	2	25	8.0%	-0.59
30.1+	28%	5	78	6.4%	-0.47
Not Compl	28%	5	79	6.3%	-0.44
Unraced	0%	0	0	0.0%	0.00

ANALYSIS BY SUCCESS RATE IN LAST 10 RUNS

Age	Prop	Win	Runs	Wins%	£
No Wins	56%	10	164	6.1%	-0.54
1 Win	28%	5	62	8.1%	-0.38
2 Wins	17%	3	9	33.3%	1.81
3 Wins	0%	0	0	0.0%	0.00
4 Wins	0%	0	0	0.0%	0.00
5+ Wins	0%	0	0	0.0%	0.00

ANALYSIS BY SUCCESS RATE IN LAST 3 RUNS

Age	Prop	Win	Runs	Wins%	£
No Wins	78%	14	217	6.5%	-0.47
1 Win	17%	3	17	17.6%	0.13
2 Wins	6%	1	1	100.0%	3.00
3 Wins	0%	0	0	0.0%	0.00

ANALYSIS BY POSITION LAST TIME

Age	Prop	Win	Runs	Wins%	£
Won	11%	2	8	25.0%	0.41
2nd or 3rd	17%	3	30	10.0%	-0.18
Unplaced	44%	8	118	6.8%	-0.50
Fell,BD,UR	6%	1	20	5.0%	-0.65
Pulled Up	22%	4	58	6.9%	-0.36
Ref/RanOut	0%	0	1	0.0%	-1.00
CO/SlipUp	0%	0	0	0.0%	0.00
Unraced	0%	0	0	0.0%	0.00

OTHER FACTORS (WINS-RUNS, £)

Course Winner:	5-20	£1.40
Distance Winner:	3-42	-£0.19
Going Winner:	8-84	-£0.48
Beaten Favourite:	1-5	-£0.25
7-Day Winners:	1-3	-£0.25
Absolute Favourites:	7-16	£0.88

Selling Handicap Chases

Selling Handicap Chases: up to 7 days off the track

ANALYSIS BY AGE
Age	Prop	Win	Runs	Wins%	£
3yo	0%	0	0	0.0%	0.00
4yo	0%	0	1	0.0%	-1.00
5yo	0%	0	1	0.0%	-1.00
6yo	0%	0	0	0.0%	0.00
7yo	0%	0	3	0.0%	-1.00
8yo	0%	0	4	0.0%	-1.00
9yo	67%	2	10	20.0%	-0.23
10yo	33%	1	3	33.3%	0.17
11yo	0%	0	3	0.0%	-1.00
12yo+	0%	0	4	0.0%	-1.00

ANALYSIS BY BHB RATING
Age	Prop	Win	Runs	Wins%	£
150+	0%	0	0	0.0%	0.00
130..149	0%	0	0	0.0%	0.00
120..129	0%	0	0	0.0%	0.00
110..119	0%	0	0	0.0%	0.00
100..109	0%	0	0	0.0%	0.00
80..99	33%	1	12	8.3%	-0.81
60..79	33%	1	16	6.3%	-0.78
..59	33%	1	1	100.0%	4.50
Unrated	0%	0	0	0.0%	0.00

ANALYSIS BY WEIGHT CARRIED
Age	Prop	Win	Runs	Wins%	£
12-01+	0%	0	0	0.0%	0.00
11-8..12-00	0%	0	4	0.0%	-1.00
11-0..11-07	67%	2	10	20.0%	-0.42
10-8..10-13	0%	0	6	0.0%	-1.00
10-0..10-07	0%	0	8	0.0%	-1.00
..9-13	33%	1	1	100.0%	4.50

ANALYSIS BY DAYS SINCE LAST RUN
Age	Prop	Win	Runs	Wins%	£
1..7	100%	3	29	10.3%	-0.61
8..14	0%	0	0	0.0%	0.00
15..28	0%	0	0	0.0%	0.00
29..60	0%	0	0	0.0%	0.00
61..100	0%	0	0	0.0%	0.00
101+	0%	0	0	0.0%	0.00
Unraced	0%	0	0	0.0%	0.00

ANALYSIS BY TODAY'S STARTING PRICE
Age	Prop	Win	Runs	Wins%	£
Odds On	0%	0	0	0.0%	0.00
Ev-2/1	33%	1	3	33.3%	-0.25
9/4-4/1	33%	1	6	16.7%	-0.42
9/2-6/1	33%	1	6	16.7%	-0.08
13/2-10/1	0%	0	6	0.0%	-1.00
11/1-16/1	0%	0	4	0.0%	-1.00
18/1-33/1	0%	0	4	0.0%	-1.00
40/1+	0%	0	0	0.0%	0.00

ANALYSIS BY STARTING PRICE LAST TIME
Age	Prop	Win	Runs	Wins%	£
Odds On	0%	0	0	0.0%	0.00
Ev-2/1	0%	0	1	0.0%	-1.00
9/4-4/1	33%	1	3	33.3%	-0.25
9/2-6/1	33%	1	2	50.0%	0.75
13/2-10/1	0%	0	6	0.0%	-1.00
11/1-16/1	0%	0	6	0.0%	-1.00
18/1-33/1	0%	0	2	0.0%	-1.00
40/1+	33%	1	9	11.1%	-0.39
Unraced	0%	0	0	0.0%	0.00

ANALYSIS BY DISTANCE BEATEN LAST TIME
Age	Prop	Win	Runs	Wins%	£
..-10 lgh	33%	1	2	50.0%	0.13
-10..0	0%	0	2	0.0%	-1.00
0.1..2	0%	0	0	0.0%	0.00
2.1..5	0%	0	2	0.0%	-1.00
5.1..10	33%	1	4	25.0%	-0.13
10.1..20	0%	0	3	0.0%	-1.00
20.0..30	0%	0	3	0.0%	-1.00
30.1+	0%	0	8	0.0%	-1.00
Not Compl	33%	1	5	20.0%	0.10
Unraced	0%	0	0	0.0%	0.00

ANALYSIS BY SUCCESS RATE IN LAST 10 RUNS
Age	Prop	Win	Runs	Wins%	£
No Wins	67%	2	14	14.3%	-0.36
1 Win	0%	0	13	0.0%	-1.00
2 Wins	33%	1	2	50.0%	0.13
3 Wins	0%	0	0	0.0%	0.00
4 Wins	0%	0	0	0.0%	0.00
5+ Wins	0%	0	0	0.0%	0.00

ANALYSIS BY SUCCESS RATE IN LAST 3 RUNS
Age	Prop	Win	Runs	Wins%	£
No Wins	67%	2	23	8.7%	-0.61
1 Win	33%	1	6	16.7%	-0.63
2 Wins	0%	0	0	0.0%	0.00
3 Wins	0%	0	0	0.0%	0.00

ANALYSIS BY POSITION LAST TIME
Age	Prop	Win	Runs	Wins%	£
Won	33%	1	4	25.0%	-0.44
2nd or 3rd	33%	1	7	14.3%	-0.50
Unplaced	0%	0	13	0.0%	-1.00
Fell,BD,UR	0%	0	1	0.0%	-1.00
Pulled Up	33%	1	3	33.3%	0.83
Ref/RanOut	0%	0	1	0.0%	-1.00
CO/SlipUp	0%	0	0	0.0%	0.00
Unraced	0%	0	0	0.0%	0.00

OTHER FACTORS (WINS-RUNS, £)
Course Winner:	0-4	-£1.00
Distance Winner:	1-4	-£0.13
Going Winner:	3-15	-£0.25
7-Day Winners:	1-4	-£0.44
Absolute Favourites:	2-3	£0.92

Race Profiles

Selling Handicap Chases: 100+ days off the track

ANALYSIS BY AGE

Age	Prop	Win	Runs	Wins%	£
3yo	0%	0	0	0.0%	0.00
4yo	0%	0	0	0.0%	0.00
5yo	0%	0	1	0.0%	-1.00
6yo	0%	0	2	0.0%	-1.00
7yo	0%	0	9	0.0%	-1.00
8yo	0%	0	9	0.0%	-1.00
9yo	43%	3	11	27.3%	1.05
10yo	43%	3	10	30.0%	2.55
11yo	14%	1	13	7.7%	-0.46
12yo+	0%	0	4	0.0%	-1.00

ANALYSIS BY BHB RATING

Age	Prop	Win	Runs	Wins%	£
150+	0%	0	0	0.0%	0.00
130..149	0%	0	0	0.0%	0.00
120..129	0%	0	0	0.0%	0.00
110..119	0%	0	0	0.0%	0.00
100..109	0%	0	0	0.0%	0.00
80..99	14%	1	9	11.1%	-0.28
60..79	86%	6	49	12.2%	0.19
..59	0%	0	1	0.0%	-1.00
Unrated	0%	0	0	0.0%	0.00

ANALYSIS BY WEIGHT CARRIED

Age	Prop	Win	Runs	Wins%	£
12-01+	0%	0	0	0.0%	0.00
11-8..12-00	14%	1	6	16.7%	0.08
11-0..11-07	14%	1	12	8.3%	-0.08
10-8..10-13	29%	2	10	20.0%	0.08
10-0..10-07	14%	1	19	5.3%	-0.63
..9-13	29%	2	12	16.7%	1.54

ANALYSIS BY DAYS SINCE LAST RUN

Age	Prop	Win	Runs	Wins%	£
1..7	0%	0	0	0.0%	0.00
8..14	0%	0	0	0.0%	0.00
15..28	0%	0	0	0.0%	0.00
29..60	0%	0	0	0.0%	0.00
61..100	0%	0	0	0.0%	0.00
101+	100%	7	59	11.9%	0.10
Unraced	0%	0	0	0.0%	0.00

ANALYSIS BY TODAY'S STARTING PRICE

Age	Prop	Win	Runs	Wins%	£
Odds On	0%	0	0	0.0%	0.00
Ev-2/1	0%	0	0	0.0%	0.00
9/4-4/1	43%	3	7	42.9%	1.07
9/2-6/1	29%	2	9	22.2%	0.50
13/2-10/1	14%	1	12	8.3%	-0.08
11/1-16/1	0%	0	10	0.0%	-1.00
18/1-33/1	14%	1	15	6.7%	0.73
40/1+	0%	0	6	0.0%	-1.00

ANALYSIS BY STARTING PRICE LAST TIME

Age	Prop	Win	Runs	Wins%	£
Odds On	0%	0	0	0.0%	0.00
Ev-2/1	0%	0	0	0.0%	0.00
9/4-4/1	0%	0	2	0.0%	-1.00
9/2-6/1	0%	0	4	0.0%	-1.00
13/2-10/1	14%	1	10	10.0%	-0.30
11/1-16/1	43%	3	13	23.1%	0.23
18/1-33/1	0%	0	16	0.0%	-1.00
40/1+	43%	3	14	21.4%	2.00
Unraced	0%	0	0	0.0%	0.00

ANALYSIS BY DISTANCE BEATEN LAST TIME

Age	Prop	Win	Runs	Wins%	£
..-10 lgh	0%	0	0	0.0%	0.00
-10..0	0%	0	0	0.0%	0.00
0.1..2	0%	0	0	0.0%	0.00
2.1..5	0%	0	0	0.0%	0.00
5.1..10	0%	0	2	0.0%	-1.00
10.1..20	0%	0	3	0.0%	-1.00
20.0..30	0%	0	6	0.0%	-1.00
30.1+	43%	3	19	15.8%	0.16
Not Compl	57%	4	29	13.8%	0.48
Unraced	0%	0	0	0.0%	0.00

ANALYSIS BY SUCCESS RATE IN LAST 10 RUNS

Age	Prop	Win	Runs	Wins%	£
No Wins	57%	4	44	9.1%	0.06
1 Win	43%	3	15	20.0%	0.23
2 Wins	0%	0	0	0.0%	0.00
3 Wins	0%	0	0	0.0%	0.00
4 Wins	0%	0	0	0.0%	0.00
5+ Wins	0%	0	0	0.0%	0.00

ANALYSIS BY SUCCESS RATE IN LAST 3 RUNS

Age	Prop	Win	Runs	Wins%	£
No Wins	100%	7	57	12.3%	0.14
1 Win	0%	0	2	0.0%	-1.00
2 Wins	0%	0	0	0.0%	0.00
3 Wins	0%	0	0	0.0%	0.00

ANALYSIS BY POSITION LAST TIME

Age	Prop	Win	Runs	Wins%	£
Won	0%	0	0	0.0%	0.00
2nd or 3rd	0%	0	5	0.0%	-1.00
Unplaced	43%	3	25	12.0%	-0.12
Fell,BD,UR	0%	0	5	0.0%	-1.00
Pulled Up	57%	4	23	17.4%	0.87
Ref/RanOut	0%	0	1	0.0%	-1.00
CO/SlipUp	0%	0	0	0.0%	0.00
Unraced	0%	0	0	0.0%	0.00

OTHER FACTORS (WINS-RUNS, £)

Course Winner:	2-7	£3.71
Distance Winner:	3-12	£0.54
Going Winner:	2-17	-£0.29
Absolute Favourites:	2-3	£2.33

Handicap Chases (class 1..3)

ANALYSIS BY AGE

Age	Prop	Win	Runs	Wins%	£
3yo	0%	0	0	0.0%	0.00
4yo	0%	2	28	7.1%	-0.39
5yo	4%	55	422	13.0%	-0.22
6yo	12%	169	1342	12.6%	-0.17
7yo	22%	305	2569	11.9%	-0.14
8yo	24%	334	3085	10.8%	-0.14
9yo	18%	256	2736	9.4%	-0.13
10yo	11%	155	1950	7.9%	-0.24
11yo	6%	80	1077	7.4%	-0.18
12yo+	2%	33	581	5.7%	-0.36

ANALYSIS BY BHB RATING

Age	Prop	Win	Runs	Wins%	£
150+	3%	35	435	8.0%	-0.27
130..149	23%	318	3927	8.1%	-0.20
120..129	28%	395	3626	10.9%	-0.12
110..119	28%	395	3544	11.1%	-0.18
100..109	14%	191	1683	11.3%	-0.16
80..99	4%	55	575	9.6%	-0.20

ANALYSIS BY WEIGHT CARRIED

Age	Prop	Win	Runs	Wins%	£
12-01+	0%	1	5	20.0%	-0.10
11-8..12-00	22%	306	2631	11.6%	-0.18
11-0..11-07	33%	465	4376	10.6%	-0.18
10-8..10-13	20%	275	2931	9.4%	-0.23
10-0..10-07	20%	284	3098	9.2%	-0.11
..9-13	4%	58	749	7.7%	-0.07

ANALYSIS BY DAYS SINCE LAST RUN

Age	Prop	Win	Runs	Wins%	£
1..7	5%	67	479	14.0%	-0.12
8..14	17%	230	1824	12.6%	-0.09
15..28	34%	474	4710	10.1%	-0.19
29..60	23%	319	3571	8.9%	-0.20
61..100	6%	87	877	9.9%	-0.19
101+	15%	207	2293	9.0%	-0.15
Unraced	0%	5	36	13.9%	0.37

ANALYSIS BY TODAY'S STARTING PRICE

Age	Prop	Win	Runs	Wins%	£
Odds On	2%	22	39	56.4%	-0.01
Ev-2/1	9%	122	364	33.5%	-0.11
9/4-4/1	29%	403	1920	21.0%	-0.12
9/2-6/1	18%	244	1898	12.9%	-0.20
13/2-10/1	24%	338	3440	9.8%	-0.12
11/1-16/1	13%	179	2885	6.2%	-0.11
18/1-33/1	5%	74	2360	3.1%	-0.22
40/1+	1%	7	884	0.8%	-0.51

ANALYSIS BY STARTING PRICE LAST TIME

Age	Prop	Win	Runs	Wins%	£
Odds On	2%	33	224	14.7%	-0.23
Ev-2/1	9%	129	718	18.0%	0.08
9/4-4/1	20%	275	2255	12.2%	-0.19
9/2-6/1	17%	235	1981	11.9%	-0.08
13/2-10/1	23%	313	3227	9.7%	-0.18
11/1-16/1	15%	207	2636	7.9%	-0.26
18/1-33/1	11%	152	1988	7.6%	-0.12
40/1+	3%	40	725	5.5%	-0.36
Unraced	0%	5	36	13.9%	0.37

ANALYSIS BY DISTANCE BEATEN LAST TIME

Age	Prop	Win	Runs	Wins%	£
..-10 lgh	4%	60	407	14.7%	-0.14
-10..0	18%	253	1807	14.0%	-0.11
0.1..2	7%	101	788	12.8%	-0.22
2.1..5	8%	110	875	12.6%	-0.02
5.1..10	10%	136	1207	11.3%	-0.17
10.1..20	15%	215	2054	10.5%	-0.15
20.0..30	8%	115	1390	8.3%	-0.27
30.1+	14%	192	2657	7.2%	-0.19
Not Compl	15%	202	2569	7.9%	-0.19
Unraced	0%	5	36	13.9%	0.37

ANALYSIS BY SUCCESS RATE IN LAST 10 RUNS

Age	Prop	Win	Runs	Wins%	£
No Wins	12%	161	1796	9.0%	-0.13
1 Win	29%	404	4109	9.8%	-0.11
2 Wins	31%	429	4127	10.4%	-0.20
3 Wins	18%	247	2430	10.2%	-0.21
4 Wins	7%	99	947	10.5%	-0.23
5+ Wins	3%	44	345	12.8%	-0.27

ANALYSIS BY SUCCESS RATE IN LAST 3 RUNS

Age	Prop	Win	Runs	Wins%	£
No Wins	53%	727	8003	9.1%	-0.18
1 Win	36%	495	4511	11.0%	-0.15
2 Wins	10%	145	1126	12.9%	-0.21
3 Wins	1%	17	114	14.9%	-0.11

ANALYSIS BY POSITION LAST TIME

Age	Prop	Win	Runs	Wins%	£
Won	23%	313	2215	14.1%	-0.12
2nd or 3rd	29%	406	3296	12.3%	-0.11
Unplaced	33%	463	5682	8.1%	-0.21
Fell,BD,UR	6%	88	921	9.6%	-0.22
Pulled Up	8%	112	1608	7.0%	-0.17
Ref/RanOut	0%	1	19	5.3%	-0.32
CO/SlipUp	0%	1	13	7.7%	-0.58
Unraced	0%	5	36	13.9%	0.37

OTHER FACTORS (WINS-RUNS, £)

Course Winner: 397-3720 -£0.70
Distance Winner: 696-6286 -£0.16
Going Winner: 877-8800 -£0.17
Beaten Favourite: 149-1053 -£0.07
7-Day Winners: 23-98 £0.04
Absolute Favourites: 309-1215 -£0.12

TRAINERS (WINS-RUNS, £)

B Ellison 3-15 £0.68; J L Spearing 8-62 £0.13; Miss P Robson 3-25 £0.32; Miss E C Lavelle 23-140 £0.05; C C Bealby 4-49 £0.11; M Bradstock 4-46 £0.12; Miss H C Knight 15-111 £0.05; G A Charlton 3-15 £0.27; P Monteith 14-119 £0.03; T D Easterby 12-95 £0.03; V R A Dartnall 6-53 £0.06.

Race Profiles

Handicap Chases (class 1..3): 2m to 2m3f

ANALYSIS BY AGE

Age	Prop	Win	Runs	Wins%	£
3yo	0%	0	0	0.0%	0.00
4yo	0%	1	6	16.7%	-0.33
5yo	6%	20	140	14.3%	-0.26
6yo	17%	53	352	15.1%	-0.22
7yo	23%	73	570	12.8%	-0.12
8yo	26%	81	611	13.3%	-0.04
9yo	16%	51	468	10.9%	-0.17
10yo	7%	22	264	8.3%	-0.31
11yo	3%	9	148	6.1%	-0.36
12yo+	2%	6	63	9.5%	0.03

ANALYSIS BY BHB RATING

Age	Prop	Win	Runs	Wins%	£
150+	2%	7	76	9.2%	-0.33
130..149	23%	73	718	10.2%	-0.24
120..129	27%	86	659	13.1%	-0.11
110..119	32%	102	702	14.5%	-0.03
100..109	11%	35	335	10.4%	-0.33
80..99	4%	13	132	9.8%	-0.18
60..79	0%	0	0	0.0%	0.00
..59	0%	0	0	0.0%	0.00
Unrated	0%	0	0	0.0%	0.00

ANALYSIS BY WEIGHT CARRIED

Age	Prop	Win	Runs	Wins%	£
12-01+	0%	0	1	0.0%	-1.00
11-8..12-00	22%	69	569	12.1%	-0.17
11-0..11-07	37%	117	813	14.4%	-0.13
10-8..10-13	21%	65	561	11.6%	-0.20
10-0..10-07	16%	52	552	9.4%	-0.19
..9-13	4%	13	126	10.3%	-0.08

ANALYSIS BY DAYS SINCE LAST RUN

Age	Prop	Win	Runs	Wins%	£
1..7	7%	21	127	16.5%	0.02
8..14	15%	48	374	12.8%	-0.25
15..28	34%	108	870	12.4%	-0.18
29..60	20%	64	625	10.2%	-0.21
61..100	4%	13	161	8.1%	-0.39
101+	19%	61	456	13.4%	0.05
Unraced	0%	1	9	11.1%	-0.28

ANALYSIS BY TODAY'S STARTING PRICE

Age	Prop	Win	Runs	Wins%	£
Odds On	2%	6	15	40.0%	-0.32
Ev-2/1	13%	41	113	36.3%	-0.05
9/4-4/1	31%	97	489	19.8%	-0.18
9/2-6/1	18%	58	401	14.5%	-0.10
13/2-10/1	24%	75	694	10.8%	-0.03
11/1-16/1	9%	29	487	6.0%	-0.14
18/1-33/1	3%	10	325	3.1%	-0.30
40/1+	0%	0	98	0.0%	-1.00

ANALYSIS BY STARTING PRICE LAST TIME

Age	Prop	Win	Runs	Wins%	£
Odds On	2%	6	43	14.0%	-0.38
Ev-2/1	11%	36	164	22.0%	0.18
9/4-4/1	25%	80	465	17.2%	-0.03
9/2-6/1	14%	43	373	11.5%	-0.20
13/2-10/1	21%	65	635	10.2%	-0.20
11/1-16/1	12%	39	475	8.2%	-0.32
18/1-33/1	12%	39	345	11.3%	-0.08
40/1+	2%	7	113	6.2%	-0.36
Unraced	0%	1	9	11.1%	-0.28

ANALYSIS BY DISTANCE BEATEN LAST TIME

Age	Prop	Win	Runs	Wins%	£
...-10 lgh	4%	12	68	17.6%	-0.18
-10..0	19%	60	358	16.8%	-0.12
0.1..2	9%	27	163	16.6%	-0.05
2.1..5	8%	26	192	13.5%	-0.17
5.1..10	11%	34	267	12.7%	-0.26
10.1..20	14%	45	412	10.9%	-0.21
20.0..30	10%	31	304	10.2%	-0.20
30.1+	11%	34	457	7.4%	-0.28
Not Compl	15%	46	392	11.7%	0.06
Unraced	0%	1	9	11.1%	-0.28

ANALYSIS BY SUCCESS RATE IN LAST 10 RUNS

Age	Prop	Win	Runs	Wins%	£
No Wins	12%	39	359	10.9%	-0.17
1 Win	30%	95	812	11.7%	-0.11
2 Wins	31%	99	757	13.1%	-0.14
3 Wins	18%	57	447	12.8%	-0.16
4 Wins	6%	18	182	9.9%	-0.43
5+ Wins	2%	7	56	12.5%	-0.29

ANALYSIS BY SUCCESS RATE IN LAST 3 RUNS

Age	Prop	Win	Runs	Wins%	£
No Wins	50%	159	1478	10.8%	-0.18
1 Win	36%	113	895	12.6%	-0.17
2 Wins	11%	36	207	17.4%	0.02
3 Wins	2%	7	33	21.2%	-0.06

ANALYSIS BY POSITION LAST TIME

Age	Prop	Win	Runs	Wins%	£
Won	23%	72	426	16.9%	-0.13
2nd or 3rd	30%	95	667	14.2%	-0.16
Unplaced	32%	102	1131	9.0%	-0.25
Fell,BD,UR	6%	20	166	12.0%	-0.10
Pulled Up	8%	25	219	11.4%	0.18
Ref/RanOut	0%	0	2	0.0%	-1.00
CO/SlipUp	0%	1	2	50.0%	1.75
Unraced	0%	1	9	11.1%	-0.28

OTHER FACTORS (WINS-RUNS, £)

Course Winner:	84-614	-£0.03
Distance Winner:	212-1743	-£0.16
Going Winner:	196-1643	-£0.16
Beaten Favourite:	37-196	£0.13
7-Day Winners:	4-21	-£0.43
Absolute Favourites:	75-277	-£0.15

Handicap Chases (class 1..3)

Handicap Chases (class 1..3): 2m4f to 2m7f

ANALYSIS BY AGE

Age	Prop	Win	Runs	Wins%	£
3yo	0%	0	0	0.0%	0.00
4yo	0%	0	12	0.0%	-1.00
5yo	4%	19	161	11.8%	-0.27
6yo	13%	55	446	12.3%	-0.28
7yo	24%	104	851	12.2%	-0.20
8yo	23%	100	939	10.6%	-0.10
9yo	18%	77	803	9.6%	-0.21
10yo	12%	54	599	9.0%	-0.23
11yo	6%	26	303	8.6%	0.14
12yo+	1%	4	135	3.0%	-0.73

ANALYSIS BY BHB RATING

Age	Prop	Win	Runs	Wins%	£
150+	2%	8	111	7.2%	-0.44
130..149	23%	103	1141	9.0%	-0.26
120..129	30%	131	1165	11.2%	-0.07
110..119	30%	130	1185	11.0%	-0.22
100..109	13%	59	498	11.8%	-0.05
80..99	2%	8	149	5.4%	-0.68
60..79	0%	0	0	0.0%	0.00
..59	0%	0	0	0.0%	0.00
Unrated	0%	0	0	0.0%	0.00

ANALYSIS BY WEIGHT CARRIED

Age	Prop	Win	Runs	Wins%	£
12-01+	0%	0	2	0.0%	-1.00
11-8..12-00	23%	100	882	11.3%	-0.26
11-0..11-07	34%	151	1392	10.8%	-0.24
10-8..10-13	20%	89	870	10.2%	-0.12
10-0..10-07	20%	89	915	9.7%	-0.10
..9-13	2%	10	188	5.3%	-0.30

ANALYSIS BY DAYS SINCE LAST RUN

Age	Prop	Win	Runs	Wins%	£
1..7	6%	26	157	16.6%	0.05
8..14	19%	83	589	14.1%	-0.04
15..28	31%	134	1399	9.6%	-0.26
29..60	19%	85	1024	8.3%	-0.39
61..100	9%	38	290	13.1%	0.12
101+	16%	71	774	9.2%	-0.10
Unraced	0%	2	16	12.5%	0.50

ANALYSIS BY TODAY'S STARTING PRICE

Age	Prop	Win	Runs	Wins%	£
Odds On	2%	10	11	90.9%	0.61
Ev-2/1	9%	39	115	33.9%	-0.11
9/4-4/1	34%	148	664	22.3%	-0.07
9/2-6/1	15%	67	578	11.6%	-0.28
13/2-10/1	21%	94	1006	9.3%	-0.17
11/1-16/1	14%	62	878	7.1%	0.02
18/1-33/1	4%	17	729	2.3%	-0.43
40/1+	0%	2	268	0.7%	-0.50

ANALYSIS BY STARTING PRICE LAST TIME

Age	Prop	Win	Runs	Wins%	£
Odds On	3%	12	77	15.6%	-0.36
Ev-2/1	9%	38	247	15.4%	-0.14
9/4-4/1	22%	95	708	13.4%	-0.05
9/2-6/1	15%	65	620	10.5%	-0.22
13/2-10/1	22%	96	976	9.8%	-0.21
11/1-16/1	15%	66	785	8.4%	-0.23
18/1-33/1	13%	55	590	9.3%	-0.12
40/1+	2%	10	230	4.3%	-0.57
Unraced	0%	2	16	12.5%	0.50

ANALYSIS BY DISTANCE BEATEN LAST TIME

Age	Prop	Win	Runs	Wins%	£
..-10 lgh	4%	19	124	15.3%	-0.33
-10..0	18%	78	564	13.8%	-0.12
0.1..2	6%	27	218	12.4%	-0.39
2.1..5	8%	36	270	13.3%	-0.27
5.1..10	9%	38	385	9.9%	-0.25
10.1..20	17%	75	676	11.1%	0.01
20.0..30	10%	42	434	9.7%	-0.15
30.1+	14%	62	850	7.3%	-0.31
Not Compl	14%	60	712	8.4%	-0.18
Unraced	0%	2	16	12.5%	0.50

ANALYSIS BY SUCCESS RATE IN LAST 10 RUNS

Age	Prop	Win	Runs	Wins%	£
No Wins	13%	58	530	10.9%	0.01
1 Win	29%	127	1293	9.8%	-0.20
2 Wins	28%	122	1279	9.5%	-0.27
3 Wins	18%	80	723	11.1%	-0.17
4 Wins	8%	33	296	11.1%	-0.19
5+ Wins	4%	17	112	15.2%	-0.33

ANALYSIS BY SUCCESS RATE IN LAST 3 RUNS

Age	Prop	Win	Runs	Wins%	£
No Wins	52%	227	2490	9.1%	-0.21
1 Win	35%	155	1364	11.4%	-0.17
2 Wins	11%	49	348	14.1%	-0.21
3 Wins	1%	6	31	19.4%	0.21

ANALYSIS BY POSITION LAST TIME

Age	Prop	Win	Runs	Wins%	£
Won	22%	97	688	14.1%	-0.16
2nd or 3rd	30%	132	1014	13.0%	-0.10
Unplaced	34%	148	1819	8.1%	-0.26
Fell,BD,UR	6%	28	274	10.2%	-0.29
Pulled Up	7%	32	430	7.4%	-0.10
Ref/RanOut	0%	0	7	0.0%	-1.00
CO/SlipUp	0%	0	1	0.0%	-1.00
Unraced	0%	2	16	12.5%	0.50

OTHER FACTORS (WINS-RUNS, £)

Course Winner:	123-1166	-£0.27
Distance Winner:	228-2078	-£0.18
Going Winner:	270-2709	-£0.21
Beaten Favourite:	49-346	-£0.13
7-Day Winners:	11-43	£0.20
Absolute Favourites:	115-391	-£0.01

Race Profiles

Handicap Chases (class 1..3): 3m+

ANALYSIS BY AGE

Age	Prop	Win	Runs	Wins%	£
3yo	0%	0	0	0.0%	0.00
4yo	0%	1	10	10.0%	0.30
5yo	3%	16	121	13.2%	-0.10
6yo	10%	61	544	11.2%	-0.04
7yo	20%	128	1148	11.1%	-0.10
8yo	24%	153	1535	10.0%	-0.20
9yo	20%	128	1465	8.7%	-0.07
10yo	12%	79	1087	7.3%	-0.22
11yo	7%	45	626	7.2%	-0.29
12yo+	4%	23	383	6.0%	-0.29

ANALYSIS BY BHB RATING

Age	Prop	Win	Runs	Wins%	£
150+	3%	20	248	8.1%	-0.19
130..149	22%	142	2068	6.9%	-0.14
120..129	28%	178	1802	9.9%	-0.15
110..119	26%	163	1657	9.8%	-0.22
100..109	15%	97	850	11.4%	-0.15
80..99	5%	34	294	11.6%	0.03

ANALYSIS BY WEIGHT CARRIED

Age	Prop	Win	Runs	Wins%	£
12-01+	0%	1	2	50.0%	1.25
11-8..12-00	22%	137	1180	11.6%	-0.13
11-0..11-07	31%	197	2171	9.1%	-0.16
10-8..10-13	19%	121	1500	8.1%	-0.30
10-0..10-07	23%	143	1631	8.8%	-0.10
..9-13	6%	35	435	8.0%	0.03

ANALYSIS BY DAYS SINCE LAST RUN

Age	Prop	Win	Runs	Wins%	£
1..7	3%	20	195	10.3%	-0.34
8..14	16%	99	861	11.5%	-0.05
15..28	37%	232	2441	9.5%	-0.15
29..60	27%	170	1922	8.8%	-0.10
61..100	6%	36	426	8.5%	-0.33
101+	12%	75	1063	7.1%	-0.26
Unraced	0%	2	11	18.2%	0.72

ANALYSIS BY TODAY'S STARTING PRICE

Age	Prop	Win	Runs	Wins%	£
Odds On	1%	6	13	46.2%	-0.18
Ev-2/1	7%	42	136	30.9%	-0.16
9/4-4/1	25%	158	767	20.6%	-0.13
9/2-6/1	19%	119	919	12.9%	-0.20
13/2-10/1	27%	169	1740	9.7%	-0.12
11/1-16/1	14%	88	1520	5.8%	-0.17
18/1-33/1	7%	47	1306	3.6%	-0.08
40/1+	1%	5	518	1.0%	-0.42

ANALYSIS BY STARTING PRICE LAST TIME

Age	Prop	Win	Runs	Wins%	£
Odds On	2%	15	104	14.4%	-0.06
Ev-2/1	9%	55	307	17.9%	0.21
9/4-4/1	16%	100	1082	9.2%	-0.35
9/2-6/1	20%	127	988	12.9%	0.06
13/2-10/1	24%	152	1616	9.4%	-0.16
11/1-16/1	16%	102	1376	7.4%	-0.26
18/1-33/1	9%	58	1053	5.5%	-0.13
40/1+	4%	23	382	6.0%	-0.23
Unraced	0%	2	11	18.2%	0.72

ANALYSIS BY DISTANCE BEATEN LAST TIME

Age	Prop	Win	Runs	Wins%	£
..-10 lgh	5%	29	215	13.5%	-0.01
-10..0	18%	115	885	13.0%	-0.10
0.1..2	7%	47	407	11.5%	-0.20
2.1..5	8%	48	413	11.6%	0.22
5.1..10	10%	64	555	11.5%	-0.07
10.1..20	15%	95	966	9.8%	-0.23
20.0..30	7%	42	652	6.4%	-0.39
30.1+	15%	96	1350	7.1%	-0.08
Not Compl	15%	96	1465	6.6%	-0.26
Unraced	0%	2	11	18.2%	0.72

ANALYSIS BY SUCCESS RATE IN LAST 10 RUNS

Age	Prop	Win	Runs	Wins%	£
No Wins	10%	64	907	7.1%	-0.20
1 Win	29%	182	2004	9.1%	-0.06
2 Wins	33%	208	2091	9.9%	-0.17
3 Wins	17%	110	1260	8.7%	-0.25
4 Wins	8%	48	469	10.2%	-0.18
5+ Wins	3%	20	177	11.3%	-0.23

ANALYSIS BY SUCCESS RATE IN LAST 3 RUNS

Age	Prop	Win	Runs	Wins%	£
No Wins	54%	341	4035	8.5%	-0.16
1 Win	36%	227	2252	10.1%	-0.12
2 Wins	9%	60	571	10.5%	-0.30
3 Wins	1%	4	50	8.0%	-0.35

ANALYSIS BY POSITION LAST TIME

Age	Prop	Win	Runs	Wins%	£
Won	23%	144	1101	13.1%	-0.09
2nd or 3rd	28%	179	1615	11.1%	-0.10
Unplaced	34%	213	2732	7.8%	-0.17
Fell,BD,UR	6%	40	481	8.3%	-0.21
Pulled Up	9%	55	959	5.7%	-0.28
Ref/RanOut	0%	1	10	10.0%	0.30
CO/SlipUp	0%	0	10	0.0%	-1.00
Unraced	0%	2	11	18.2%	0.72

OTHER FACTORS (WINS-RUNS, £)

Course Winner:	190-1940	-£0.17
Distance Winner:	256-2465	-£0.16
Going Winner:	411-4448	-£0.16
Beaten Favourite:	63-511	-£0.10
7-Day Winners:	8-34	£0.12
Absolute Favourites:	119-547	-£0.17

TRAINERS (WINS-RUNS, £)

D McCain Jnr 16-94 £0.19; Ian Williams 8-42 £0.19; R Lee 3-31 £0.26; N P Mulholland 4-18 £0.39; J J Quinn 4-38 £0.16; R H Buckler 7-72 £0.08; J M Jefferson 5-42 £0.10; O Sherwood 6-61 £0.07; K G Reveley 10-90 £0.02; V R A Dartnall 4-45 £0.01.

Handicap Chases (class 1..3)

Handicap Chases (class 1..3): 2 to 5 runners

ANALYSIS BY AGE
Age	Prop	Win	Runs	Wins%	£
3yo	0%	0	0	0.0%	0.00
4yo	0%	0	1	0.0%	-1.00
5yo	3%	4	21	19.0%	-0.55
6yo	11%	16	77	20.8%	-0.41
7yo	24%	34	136	25.0%	-0.16
8yo	24%	34	131	26.0%	-0.08
9yo	20%	29	139	20.9%	-0.15
10yo	12%	17	89	19.1%	0.15
11yo	4%	6	35	17.1%	-0.18
12yo+	3%	4	27	14.8%	0.17

ANALYSIS BY BHB RATING
Age	Prop	Win	Runs	Wins%	£
150+	1%	2	18	11.1%	-0.71
130..149	15%	22	95	23.2%	0.04
120..129	33%	47	173	27.2%	0.10
110..119	31%	45	227	19.8%	-0.23
100..109	15%	21	101	20.8%	-0.28
80..99	5%	7	42	16.7%	-0.36
60..79	0%	0	0	0.0%	0.00
..59	0%	0	0	0.0%	0.00
Unrated	0%	0	0	0.0%	0.00

ANALYSIS BY WEIGHT CARRIED
Age	Prop	Win	Runs	Wins%	£
12-01+	0%	0	0	0.0%	0.00
11-8..12-00	31%	44	195	22.6%	-0.14
11-0..11-07	35%	50	209	23.9%	-0.17
10-8..10-13	17%	24	97	24.7%	0.10
10-0..10-07	14%	20	116	17.2%	-0.38
..9-13	4%	6	39	15.4%	0.29

ANALYSIS BY DAYS SINCE LAST RUN
Age	Prop	Win	Runs	Wins%	£
1..7	10%	15	48	31.3%	0.24
8..14	26%	38	139	27.3%	-0.12
15..28	29%	42	195	21.5%	-0.03
29..60	14%	20	136	14.7%	-0.45
61..100	6%	9	35	25.7%	0.27
101+	13%	19	99	19.2%	-0.23
Unraced	1%	1	4	25.0%	-0.52

ANALYSIS BY TODAY'S STARTING PRICE
Age	Prop	Win	Puns	Wins%	£
Odds On	11%	16	25	64.0%	0.14
Ev-2/1	35%	51	135	37.8%	-0.01
9/4-4/1	38%	55	235	23.4%	-0.08
9/2-6/1	8%	12	101	11.9%	-0.30
13/2-10/1	5%	7	93	7.5%	-0.38
11/1-16/1	1%	2	41	4.9%	-0.29
18/1-33/1	1%	1	20	5.0%	0.70
40/1+	0%	0	6	0.0%	-1.00

ANALYSIS BY STARTING PRICE LAST TIME
Age	Prop	Win	Runs	Wins%	£
Odds On	2%	3	11	27.3%	-0.18
Ev-2/1	8%	12	41	29.3%	-0.22
9/4-4/1	22%	32	114	28.1%	-0.17
9/2-6/1	20%	29	106	27.4%	0.29
13/2-10/1	21%	30	150	20.0%	-0.22
11/1-16/1	15%	21	117	17.9%	-0.31
18/1-33/1	8%	11	72	15.3%	-0.15
40/1+	3%	5	41	12.2%	-0.10
Unraced	1%	1	4	25.0%	-0.52

ANALYSIS BY DISTANCE BEATEN LAST TIME
Age	Prop	Win	Runs	Wins%	£
..-10 lgh	4%	6	21	28.6%	-0.26
-10..0	19%	27	87	31.0%	-0.12
0.1..2	10%	15	36	41.7%	0.45
2.1..5	9%	13	48	27.1%	-0.25
5.1..10	8%	12	61	19.7%	-0.39
10.1..20	12%	17	91	18.7%	-0.29
20.0..30	8%	11	66	16.7%	-0.23
30.1+	17%	24	128	18.8%	0.10
Not Compl	13%	18	114	15.8%	-0.18
Unraced	1%	1	4	25.0%	-0.52

ANALYSIS BY SUCCESS RATE IN LAST 10 RUNS
Age	Prop	Win	Runs	Wins%	£
No Wins	12%	17	93	18.3%	-0.31
1 Win	27%	38	212	17.9%	-0.19
2 Wins	35%	50	176	28.4%	0.22
3 Wins	17%	25	113	22.1%	-0.23
4 Wins	5%	7	41	17.1%	-0.58
5+ Wins	4%	6	17	35.3%	-0.22

ANALYSIS BY SUCCESS RATE IN LAST 3 RUNS
Age	Prop	Win	Runs	Wins%	£
No Wins	50%	71	375	18.9%	-0.20
1 Win	38%	54	219	24.7%	-0.02
2 Wins	12%	17	52	32.7%	0.00
3 Wins	1%	1	6	16.7%	-0.73

ANALYSIS BY POSITION LAST TIME
Age	Prop	Win	Runs	Wins%	£
Won	23%	33	108	30.6%	-0.15
2nd or 3rd	35%	51	184	27.7%	-0.07
Unplaced	28%	41	246	16.7%	-0.14
Fell,BD,UR	9%	13	54	24.1%	0.39
Pulled Up	3%	5	60	8.3%	-0.70
Ref/RanOut	0%	0	0	0.0%	0.00
CO/SlipUp	0%	0	0	0.0%	0.00
Unraced	1%	1	4	25.0%	-0.52

OTHER FACTORS (WINS-RUNS, £)
Course Winner:	53-197	-£0.13
Distance Winner:	89-357	£0.05
Going Winner:	87-378	-£0.10
Beaten Favourite:	15-45	£0.22
7-Day Winners:	3-7	£0.37
Absolute Favourites:	59-133	£0.06

Race Profiles

Handicap Chases (class 1..3): 6 to 10 runners

ANALYSIS BY AGE

Age	Prop	Win	Runs	Wins%	£
3yo	0%	0	0	0.0%	0.00
4yo	0%	2	18	11.1%	-0.06
5yo	4%	31	215	14.4%	-0.33
6yo	13%	96	595	16.1%	-0.13
7yo	22%	167	1131	14.8%	-0.04
8yo	24%	178	1403	12.7%	-0.14
9yo	18%	135	1164	11.6%	-0.08
10yo	10%	78	775	10.1%	-0.27
11yo	6%	48	453	10.6%	-0.05
12yo+	2%	16	244	6.6%	-0.40

ANALYSIS BY BHB RATING

Age	Prop	Win	Runs	Wins%	£
150+	1%	11	96	11.5%	-0.28
130..149	17%	124	1010	12.3%	-0.21
120..129	28%	211	1639	12.9%	-0.12
110..119	33%	248	1941	12.8%	-0.12
100..109	16%	121	958	12.6%	-0.12
80..99	5%	36	354	10.2%	-0.16

ANALYSIS BY WEIGHT CARRIED

Age	Prop	Win	Runs	Wins%	£
12-01+	0%	1	5	20.0%	-0.10
11-8..12-00	23%	174	1347	12.9%	-0.11
11-0..11-07	35%	265	2004	13.2%	-0.13
10-8..10-13	19%	141	1174	12.0%	-0.20
10-0..10-07	19%	141	1160	12.2%	-0.10
..9-13	4%	29	308	9.4%	-0.21

ANALYSIS BY DAYS SINCE LAST RUN

Age	Prop	Win	Runs	Wins%	£
1..7	4%	31	241	12.9%	-0.28
8..14	17%	124	886	14.0%	-0.13
15..28	37%	279	2107	13.2%	-0.12
29..60	21%	159	1380	11.5%	-0.18
61..100	7%	50	353	14.2%	0.07
101+	14%	106	1017	10.4%	-0.16
Unraced	0%	2	14	14.3%	0.39

ANALYSIS BY TODAY'S STARTING PRICE

Age	Prop	Win	Runs	Wins%	£
Odds On	1%	5	11	45.5%	-0.24
Ev-2/1	8%	63	197	32.0%	-0.14
9/4-4/1	37%	279	1304	21.4%	-0.10
9/2-6/1	20%	153	1129	13.6%	-0.15
13/2-10/1	22%	164	1650	9.9%	-0.11
11/1-16/1	10%	72	1036	6.9%	-0.01
18/1-33/1	2%	14	565	2.5%	-0.41
40/1+	0%	1	106	0.9%	-0.61

ANALYSIS BY STARTING PRICE LAST TIME

Age	Prop	Win	Runs	Wins%	£
Odds On	2%	18	79	22.8%	0.01
Ev-2/1	9%	67	336	19.9%	0.03
9/4-4/1	21%	154	1033	14.9%	-0.20
9/2-6/1	17%	130	902	14.4%	-0.05
13/2-10/1	21%	161	1428	11.3%	-0.22
11/1-16/1	15%	113	1120	10.1%	-0.17
18/1-33/1	12%	88	806	10.9%	0.04
40/1+	2%	18	280	6.4%	-0.38
Unraced	0%	2	14	14.3%	0.39

ANALYSIS BY DISTANCE BEATEN LAST TIME

Age	Prop	Win	Runs	Wins%	£
..-10 lgh	4%	33	178	18.5%	-0.07
-10..0	17%	127	761	16.7%	-0.12
0.1..2	7%	52	318	16.4%	-0.22
2.1..5	8%	61	383	15.9%	-0.06
5.1..10	9%	71	525	13.5%	-0.23
10.1..20	15%	114	913	12.5%	-0.22
20.0..30	9%	69	620	11.1%	-0.15
30.1+	14%	105	1185	8.9%	-0.10
Not Compl	16%	117	1101	10.6%	-0.09
Unraced	0%	2	14	14.3%	0.39

ANALYSIS BY SUCCESS RATE IN LAST 10 RUNS

Age	Prop	Win	Runs	Wins%	£
No Wins	12%	91	814	11.2%	-0.16
1 Win	30%	221	1910	11.6%	-0.18
2 Wins	32%	243	1825	13.3%	-0.10
3 Wins	18%	134	981	13.7%	-0.05
4 Wins	6%	44	343	12.8%	-0.29
5+ Wins	2%	16	111	14.4%	-0.15

ANALYSIS BY SUCCESS RATE IN LAST 3 RUNS

Age	Prop	Win	Runs	Wins%	£
No Wins	53%	395	3564	11.1%	-0.17
1 Win	36%	272	1913	14.2%	-0.07
2 Wins	10%	74	461	16.1%	-0.11
3 Wins	1%	8	46	17.4%	-0.32

ANALYSIS BY POSITION LAST TIME

Age	Prop	Win	Runs	Wins%	£
Won	21%	160	940	17.0%	-0.11
2nd or 3rd	28%	210	1461	14.4%	-0.20
Unplaced	35%	262	2483	10.6%	-0.13
Fell,BD,UR	6%	48	406	11.8%	-0.14
Pulled Up	9%	67	676	9.9%	-0.06
Ref/RanOut	0%	1	11	9.1%	0.18
CO/SlipUp	0%	1	7	14.3%	-0.21
Unraced	0%	2	14	14.3%	0.39

OTHER FACTORS (WINS-RUNS, £)

Course Winner:	207-1681	-£0.16
Distance Winner:	392-3030	-£0.12
Going Winner:	471-3693	-£0.11
Beaten Favourite:	82-459	-£0.01
7-Day Winners:	12-53	-£0.12
Absolute Favourites:	179-659	-£0.07

TRAINERS (WINS-RUNS, £)

A W Carroll 5-23 £0.41; J P L Ewart 4-16 £0.44; C R Egerton 4-11 £0.61; J M Jefferson 11-73 £0.08; N J Henderson 16-73 £0.08; M Sheppard 4-33 £0.13; Miss H C Knight 9-51 £0.08; R C Guest 7-53 £0.08; M Todhunter 7-54 £0.06; G L Moore 10-72 £0.04; A King 15-109 £0.03.

Handicap Chases (class 1..3)

Handicap Chases (class 1..3): 11 runners or more

ANALYSIS BY AGE

Age	Prop	Win	Runs	Wins%	£
3yo	0%	0	0	0.0%	0.00
4yo	0%	0	9	0.0%	-1.00
5yo	4%	20	186	10.8%	-0.06
6yo	12%	57	670	8.5%	-0.17
7yo	21%	104	1302	8.0%	-0.22
8yo	25%	122	1551	7.9%	-0.14
9yo	19%	92	1433	6.4%	-0.16
10yo	12%	60	1086	5.5%	-0.25
11yo	5%	26	589	4.4%	-0.28
12yo+	3%	13	310	4.2%	-0.38

ANALYSIS BY BHB RATING

Age	Prop	Win	Runs	Wins%	£
150+	4%	22	321	6.9%	-0.25
130..149	35%	172	2822	6.1%	-0.20
120..129	28%	137	1814	7.6%	-0.14
110..119	21%	102	1376	7.4%	-0.26
100..109	10%	49	624	7.9%	-0.19
80..99	2%	12	179	6.7%	-0.24
60..79	0%	0	0	0.0%	0.00
..59	0%	0	0	0.0%	0.00
Unrated	0%	0	0	0.0%	0.00

ANALYSIS BY WEIGHT CARRIED

Age	Prop	Win	Runs	Wins%	£
12-01+	0%	0	0	0.0%	0.00
11-8..12-00	18%	88	1089	8.1%	-0.27
11-0..11-07	30%	150	2163	6.9%	-0.22
10-8..10-13	22%	110	1660	6.6%	-0.27
10-0..10-07	25%	123	1822	6.8%	-0.11
..9-13	5%	23	402	5.7%	0.00

ANALYSIS BY DAYS SINCE LAST RUN

Age	Prop	Win	Runs	Wins%	£
1..7	4%	21	190	11.1%	0.00
8..14	14%	68	799	8.5%	-0.04
15..28	31%	153	2408	6.4%	-0.26
29..60	28%	140	2055	6.8%	-0.20
61..100	6%	28	489	5.7%	-0.41
101+	17%	82	1177	7.0%	-0.13
Unraced	0%	2	18	11.1%	0.56

ANALYSIS BY TODAY'S STARTING PRICE

Age	Prop	Win	Runs	Wins%	£
Odds On	0%	1	3	33.3%	-0.40
Ev-2/1	2%	8	32	25.0%	-0.34
9/4-4/1	14%	69	381	18.1%	-0.21
9/2-6/1	16%	79	668	11.8%	-0.27
13/2-10/1	34%	167	1697	9.8%	-0.11
11/1-16/1	21%	105	1308	5.8%	-0.16
18/1-33/1	12%	59	1775	3.3%	-0.17
40/1+	1%	6	772	0.8%	-0.49

ANALYSIS BY STARTING PRICE LAST TIME

Age	Prop	Win	Runs	Wins%	£
Odds On	2%	12	34	9.0%	-0.37
Ev-2/1	10%	50	341	14.7%	0.18
9/4-4/1	18%	89	1108	8.0%	-0.18
9/2-6/1	15%	76	973	7.8%	-0.15
13/2-10/1	25%	122	1649	7.4%	-0.15
11/1-16/1	15%	73	1399	5.2%	-0.33
18/1-33/1	11%	53	1110	4.8%	-0.23
40/1+	3%	17	404	4.2%	-0.37
Unraced	0%	2	18	11.1%	0.56

ANALYSIS BY DISTANCE BEATEN LAST TIME

Age	Prop	Win	Runs	Wins%	£
..-10 lgh	4%	21	208	10.1%	-0.18
-10..0	20%	99	959	10.3%	-0.11
0.1..2	7%	34	434	7.8%	-0.28
2.1..5	7%	36	444	8.1%	0.04
5.1..10	11%	53	621	8.5%	-0.10
10.1..20	17%	84	1050	8.0%	-0.08
20.0..30	7%	35	704	5.0%	-0.39
30.1+	13%	63	1344	4.7%	-0.30
Not Compl	14%	67	1354	4.9%	-0.28
Unraced	0%	2	18	11.1%	0.56

ANALYSIS BY SUCCESS RATE IN LAST 10 RUNS

Age	Prop	Win	Runs	Wins%	£
No Wins	11%	53	889	6.0%	-0.09
1 Win	29%	145	1987	7.3%	-0.04
2 Wins	28%	136	2126	6.4%	-0.32
3 Wins	18%	88	1336	6.6%	-0.33
4 Wins	10%	48	563	8.5%	-0.17
5+ Wins	4%	22	217	10.1%	-0.34

ANALYSIS BY SUCCESS RATE IN LAST 3 RUNS

Age	Prop	Win	Runs	Wins%	£
No Wins	53%	261	4064	6.4%	-0.18
1 Win	34%	169	2379	7.1%	-0.22
2 Wins	11%	54	613	8.8%	-0.30
3 Wins	2%	8	62	12.9%	0.10

ANALYSIS BY POSITION LAST TIME

Age	Prop	Win	Runs	Wins%	£
Won	24%	120	1167	10.3%	-0.12
2nd or 3rd	29%	145	1651	8.8%	-0.04
Unplaced	32%	160	2953	5.4%	-0.29
Fell,BD,UR	5%	27	461	5.9%	-0.36
Pulled Up	8%	40	872	4.6%	-0.22
Ref/RanOut	0%	0	8	0.0%	-1.00
CO/SlipUp	0%	0	6	0.0%	-1.00
Unraced	0%	2	18	11.1%	0.56

OTHER FACTORS (WINS-RUNS, £)

Course Winner:	137-1842	-£0.20
Distance Winner:	215-2899	-£0.24
Going Winner:	319-4729	-£0.23
Beaten Favourite:	52-549	-£0.14
7-Day Winners:	8-38	£0.19
Absolute Favourites:	71-423	-£0.25

Race Profiles

Handicap Chases (class 1..3): up to 7 days off the track

ANALYSIS BY AGE

Age	Prop	Win	Runs	Wins%	£
3yo	0%	0	0	0.0%	0.00
4yo	0%	0	3	0.0%	-1.00
5yo	7%	5	38	13.2%	-0.14
6yo	18%	13	55	23.6%	0.00
7yo	19%	14	78	17.9%	0.07
8yo	24%	17	111	15.3%	-0.02
9yo	15%	11	98	11.2%	0.06
10yo	8%	6	65	9.2%	-0.22
11yo	4%	3	47	6.4%	-0.68
12yo+	4%	3	20	15.0%	0.17

ANALYSIS BY BHB RATING

Age	Prop	Win	Runs	Wins%	£
150+	0%	0	9	0.0%	-1.00
130..149	19%	14	107	13.1%	-0.03
120..129	21%	15	129	11.6%	-0.06
110..119	32%	23	134	17.2%	-0.07
100..109	21%	15	98	15.3%	-0.03
80..99	7%	5	38	13.2%	-0.24
60..79	0%	0	0	0.0%	0.00
..59	0%	0	0	0.0%	0.00
Unrated	0%	0	0	0.0%	0.00

ANALYSIS BY WEIGHT CARRIED

Age	Prop	Win	Runs	Wins%	£
12-01+	0%	0	3	0.0%	-1.00
11-8..12-00	10%	7	70	10.0%	-0.38
11-0..11-07	42%	30	164	18.3%	-0.14
10-8..10-13	17%	12	92	13.0%	-0.11
10-0..10-07	28%	20	134	14.9%	0.37
..9-13	4%	3	52	5.8%	-0.56

ANALYSIS BY DAYS SINCE LAST RUN

Age	Prop	Win	Runs	Wins%	£
1..7	93%	67	479	14.0%	-0.12
8..14	0%	0	0	0.0%	0.00
15..28	0%	0	0	0.0%	0.00
29..60	0%	0	0	0.0%	0.00
61..100	0%	0	0	0.0%	0.00
101+	0%	0	0	0.0%	0.00
Unraced	7%	5	36	13.9%	0.37

ANALYSIS BY TODAY'S STARTING PRICE

Age	Prop	Win	Runs	Wins%	£
Odds On	8%	6	12	50.0%	-0.17
Ev-2/1	15%	11	27	40.7%	0.01
9/4-4/1	33%	24	102	23.5%	-0.05
9/2-6/1	13%	9	60	15.0%	-0.05
13/2-10/1	15%	11	95	11.6%	0.02
11/1-16/1	13%	9	82	11.0%	0.63
18/1-33/1	3%	2	95	2.1%	-0.53
40/1+	0%	0	42	0.0%	-1.00

ANALYSIS BY STARTING PRICE LAST TIME

Age	Prop	Win	Runs	Wins%	£
Odds On	3%	2	4	50.0%	0.80
Ev-2/1	19%	14	30	46.7%	0.49
9/4-4/1	18%	13	74	17.6%	-0.04
9/2-6/1	8%	6	60	10.0%	-0.06
13/2-10/1	26%	19	116	16.4%	0.17
11/1-16/1	6%	4	88	4.5%	-0.55
18/1-33/1	11%	8	75	10.7%	-0.15
40/1+	1%	1	32	3.1%	-0.88
Unraced	7%	5	36	13.9%	0.37

ANALYSIS BY DISTANCE BEATEN LAST TIME

Age	Prop	Win	Runs	Wins%	£
..-10 lgh	10%	7	31	22.6%	-0.30
-10..0	22%	16	67	23.9%	0.19
0.1..2	11%	8	33	24.2%	-0.10
2.1..5	4%	3	26	11.5%	-0.12
5.1..10	10%	7	38	18.4%	-0.24
10.1..20	13%	9	56	16.1%	-0.02
20.0..30	6%	4	37	10.8%	0.28
30.1+	7%	5	70	7.1%	-0.06
Not Compl	11%	8	121	6.6%	-0.40
Unraced	7%	5	36	13.9%	0.37

ANALYSIS BY SUCCESS RATE IN LAST 10 RUNS

Age	Prop	Win	Runs	Wins%	£
No Wins	12%	8	85	9.4%	-0.30
1 Win	36%	24	166	14.5%	-0.09
2 Wins	25%	17	120	14.2%	0.13
3 Wins	13%	9	67	13.4%	-0.33
4 Wins	6%	4	26	15.4%	-0.56
5+ Wins	7%	5	15	33.3%	0.35

ANALYSIS BY SUCCESS RATE IN LAST 3 RUNS

Age	Prop	Win	Runs	Wins%	£
No Wins	37%	25	288	8.7%	-0.33
1 Win	42%	28	143	19.6%	0.24
2 Wins	18%	12	37	32.4%	0.36
3 Wins	3%	2	11	18.2%	-0.67

ANALYSIS BY POSITION LAST TIME

Age	Prop	Win	Runs	Wins%	£
Won	32%	23	98	23.5%	0.04
2nd or 3rd	29%	21	100	21.0%	0.12
Unplaced	21%	15	160	9.4%	-0.14
Fell,BD,UR	7%	5	66	7.6%	-0.29
Pulled Up	4%	3	54	5.6%	-0.52
Ref/RanOut	0%	0	1	0.0%	-1.00
CO/SlipUp	0%	0	0	0.0%	0.00
Unraced	7%	5	36	13.9%	0.37

OTHER FACTORS (WINS-RUNS, £)

Course Winner:	15-122	-£0.02
Distance Winner:	30-216	-£0.19
Going Winner:	47-320	£0.00
Beaten Favourite:	7-23	£0.22
7-Day Winners:	23-98	£0.04
Absolute Favourites:	21-75	-£0.30

Handicap Chases (class 1..3)

Handicap Chases (class 1..3): 100+ days off the track

ANALYSIS BY AGE
Age	Prop	Win	Runs	Wins%	£
3yo	0%	0	0	0.0%	0.00
4yo	0%	0	2	0.0%	-1.00
5yo	3%	7	66	10.6%	-0.33
6yo	11%	23	245	9.4%	-0.27
7yo	21%	43	442	9.7%	-0.31
8yo	22%	47	491	9.6%	-0.02
9yo	21%	43	474	9.1%	-0.15
10yo	15%	31	320	9.7%	0.00
11yo	5%	10	171	5.8%	0.05
12yo+	2%	5	94	5.3%	-0.19

ANALYSIS BY BHB RATING
Age	Prop	Win	Runs	Wins%	£
150+	7%	15	117	12.8%	0.12
130..149	26%	55	728	7.6%	-0.26
120..129	26%	55	609	9.0%	-0.23
110..119	26%	55	564	9.8%	-0.12
100..109	11%	24	219	11.0%	0.44
80..99	2%	5	68	7.4%	-0.42
60..79	0%	0	0	0.0%	0.00
..59	0%	0	0	0.0%	0.00
Unrated	0%	0	0	0.0%	0.00

ANALYSIS BY WEIGHT CARRIED
Age	Prop	Win	Runs	Wins%	£
12-01+	0%	0	0	0.0%	0.00
11-8..12-00	32%	66	547	12.1%	-0.05
11-0..11-07	28%	59	773	7.6%	-0.29
10-8..10-13	18%	38	457	8.3%	-0.31
10-0..10-07	19%	40	445	9.0%	0.10
..9-13	3%	6	83	7.2%	0.43

ANALYSIS BY DAYS SINCE LAST RUN
Age	Prop	Win	Runs	Wins%	£
1..7	0%	0	0	0.0%	0.00
8..14	0%	0	0	0.0%	0.00
15..28	0%	0	0	0.0%	0.00
29..60	0%	0	0	0.0%	0.00
61..100	1%	2	12	16.7%	1.33
101+	99%	207	2293	9.0%	-0.15
Unraced	0%	0	0	0.0%	0.00

ANALYSIS BY TODAY'S STARTING PRICE
Age	Prop	Win	Runs	Wins%	£
Odds On	0%	1	4	25.0%	-0.55
Ev-2/1	8%	17	43	39.5%	0.07
9/4-4/1	22%	45	254	17.7%	-0.26
9/2-6/1	17%	35	302	11.6%	-0.29
13/2-10/1	30%	62	573	10.8%	0.00
11/1-16/1	15%	32	545	5.9%	-0.15
18/1-33/1	7%	15	421	3.6%	-0.10
40/1+	1%	2	163	1.2%	-0.28

ANALYSIS BY STARTING PRICE LAST TIME
Age	Prop	Win	Runs	Wins%	£
Odds On	3%	7	55	12.7%	-0.20
Ev-2/1	9%	19	143	13.3%	0.06
9/4-4/1	21%	43	420	10.2%	-0.23
9/2-6/1	16%	33	313	10.5%	0.06
13/2-10/1	18%	38	503	7.6%	-0.28
11/1-16/1	17%	35	432	8.1%	-0.21
18/1-33/1	13%	28	304	9.2%	0.17
40/1+	3%	6	135	4.4%	-0.42
Unraced	0%	0	0	0.0%	0.00

ANALYSIS BY DISTANCE BEATEN LAST TIME
Age	Prop	Win	Runs	Wins%	£
..-10 lgh	2%	5	58	8.6%	-0.04
-10..0	13%	27	284	9.5%	-0.20
0.1..2	4%	8	89	9.0%	-0.41
2.1..5	5%	11	102	10.8%	-0.19
5.1..10	8%	16	160	10.0%	-0.04
10.1..20	10%	21	300	7.0%	-0.50
20.0..30	9%	19	197	9.6%	-0.29
30.1+	21%	43	490	8.8%	0.00
Not Compl	28%	59	625	9.4%	0.02
Unraced	0%	0	0	0.0%	0.00

ANALYSIS BY SUCCESS RATE IN LAST 10 RUNS
Age	Prop	Win	Runs	Wins%	£
No Wins	8%	16	221	7.2%	0.17
1 Win	27%	56	619	9.0%	-0.17
2 Wins	34%	71	715	9.9%	-0.06
3 Wins	19%	39	470	8.3%	-0.28
4 Wins	8%	17	188	9.0%	-0.16
5+ Wins	5%	10	92	10.9%	-0.46

ANALYSIS BY SUCCESS RATE IN LAST 3 RUNS
Age	Prop	Win	Runs	Wins%	£
No Wins	52%	108	1210	8.9%	-0.14
1 Win	36%	76	830	9.2%	-0.12
2 Wins	10%	21	243	8.6%	-0.19
3 Wins	2%	4	22	18.2%	-0.20

ANALYSIS BY POSITION LAST TIME
Age	Prop	Win	Runs	Wins%	£
Won	15%	32	342	9.4%	-0.17
2nd or 3rd	21%	43	427	10.1%	-0.23
Unplaced	36%	75	914	8.2%	-0.19
Fell,BD,UR	11%	22	173	12.7%	0.11
Pulled Up	18%	37	443	8.4%	0.00
Ref/RanOut	0%	0	5	0.0%	-1.00
CO/SlipUp	0%	0	1	0.0%	-1.00
Unraced	0%	0	0	0.0%	0.00

OTHER FACTORS (WINS-RUNS, £)
Course Winner:	61-627 -£0.27
Distance Winner:	107-1161 -£0.21
Going Winner:	126-1493 -£0.22
Beaten Favourite:	29-229 -£0.01
Absolute Favourites:	38-164 -£0.17

Race Profiles

Handicap Chases (class 4..6)

ANALYSIS BY AGE

Age	Prop	Win	Runs	Wins%	£
3yo	0%	0	0	0.0%	0.00
4yo	1%	14	102	13.7%	0.09
5yo	4%	88	885	9.9%	-0.28
6yo	15%	313	2378	13.2%	-0.01
7yo	20%	407	3517	11.6%	-0.18
8yo	23%	473	3849	12.3%	-0.09
9yo	16%	327	3394	9.6%	-0.19
10yo	11%	223	2496	8.9%	-0.24
11yo	6%	114	1564	7.3%	-0.29
12yo+	4%	87	1340	6.5%	-0.30

ANALYSIS BY BHB RATING

Age	Prop	Win	Runs	Wins%	£
120..129	1%	15	109	13.8%	-0.21
110..119	11%	215	1565	13.7%	-0.12
100..109	21%	427	3965	10.8%	-0.26
80..99	51%	1036	9840	10.5%	-0.17
60..79	17%	349	3997	8.7%	-0.11
..59	0%	4	47	8.5%	1.03
Unrated	0%	0	2	0.0%	-1.00

ANALYSIS BY WEIGHT CARRIED

Age	Prop	Win	Runs	Wins%	£
12-01+	0%	7	32	21.9%	-0.33
11-8..12-00	24%	482	4034	11.9%	-0.17
11-0..11-07	32%	650	6170	10.5%	-0.23
10-8..10-13	18%	374	3653	10.2%	-0.18
10-0..10-07	20%	406	3992	10.2%	-0.12
..9-13	6%	127	1644	7.7%	-0.09

ANALYSIS BY DAYS SINCE LAST RUN

Age	Prop	Win	Runs	Wins%	£
1..7	8%	161	1158	13.9%	-0.25
8..14	19%	393	3721	10.6%	-0.19
15..28	33%	671	6392	10.5%	-0.19
29..60	21%	436	4306	10.1%	-0.16
61..100	5%	96	1078	8.9%	0.05
101+	14%	288	2854	10.1%	-0.17
Unraced	0%	1	16	6.3%	-0.83

ANALYSIS BY TODAY'S STARTING PRICE

Age	Prop	Win	Runs	Wins%	£
Odds On	2%	37	61	60.7%	0.05
Ev-2/1	11%	224	587	38.2%	0.00
9/4-4/1	30%	606	2886	21.0%	-0.13
9/2-6/1	19%	395	2840	13.9%	-0.14
13/2-10/1	23%	475	4867	9.8%	-0.12
11/1-16/1	10%	196	3851	5.1%	-0.27
18/1-33/1	4%	91	3254	2.8%	-0.30
40/1+	1%	22	1179	1.9%	0.00

ANALYSIS BY STARTING PRICE LAST TIME

Age	Prop	Win	Runs	Wins%	£
Odds On	1%	18	73	24.7%	-0.15
Ev-2/1	6%	122	596	20.5%	-0.18
9/4-4/1	22%	445	2726	16.3%	-0.14
9/2-6/1	16%	327	2652	12.3%	-0.25
13/2-10/1	23%	470	4574	10.3%	-0.22
11/1-16/1	17%	352	3713	9.5%	-0.09
18/1-33/1	11%	225	3395	6.6%	-0.18
40/1+	4%	86	1780	4.8%	-0.13
Unraced	0%	1	16	6.3%	-0.83

ANALYSIS BY DISTANCE BEATEN LAST TIME

Age	Prop	Win	Runs	Wins%	£
..-10 lgh	4%	86	315	27.3%	0.01
-10..0	13%	268	1400	19.1%	-0.13
0.1..2	6%	127	885	14.4%	-0.25
2.1..5	7%	142	976	14.5%	-0.14
5.1..10	10%	206	1522	13.5%	-0.22
10.1..20	16%	333	2779	12.0%	-0.14
20.0..30	12%	249	2266	11.0%	-0.09
30.1+	16%	331	4939	6.7%	-0.19
Not Compl	15%	303	4427	6.8%	-0.21
Unraced	0%	1	16	6.3%	-0.83

ANALYSIS BY SUCCESS RATE IN LAST 10 RUNS

Age	Prop	Win	Runs	Wins%	£
No Wins	35%	708	8214	8.6%	-0.19
1 Win	38%	782	6900	11.3%	-0.13
2 Wins	20%	403	3265	12.3%	-0.18
3 Wins	6%	118	887	13.3%	-0.27
4 Wins	1%	28	207	13.5%	-0.35
5+ Wins	0%	6	36	16.7%	-0.24

ANALYSIS BY SUCCESS RATE IN LAST 3 RUNS

Age	Prop	Win	Runs	Wins%	£
No Wins	67%	1377	15026	9.2%	-0.17
1 Win	28%	563	3916	14.4%	-0.14
2 Wins	5%	95	525	18.1%	-0.29
3 Wins	0%	10	42	23.8%	-0.33

ANALYSIS BY POSITION LAST TIME

Age	Prop	Win	Runs	Wins%	£
Won	17%	354	1713	20.7%	-0.11
2nd or 3rd	30%	612	4332	14.1%	-0.16
Unplaced	38%	777	9051	8.6%	-0.17
Fell,BD,UR	5%	97	1211	8.0%	-0.29
Pulled Up	10%	200	3133	6.4%	-0.18
Ref/RanOut	0%	4	54	7.4%	-0.03
CO/SlipUp	0%	1	15	6.7%	-0.71
Unraced	0%	1	16	6.3%	-0.83

OTHER FACTORS (WINS-RUNS, £)

Course Winner:	470-3997	-£0.15
Distance Winner:	795-6983	-£0.19
Going Winner:	857-8016	-£0.22
Beaten Favourite:	194-1234	-£0.14
7-Day Winners:	66-195	£0.11
Absolute Favourites:	529-1797	-£0.03

TRAINERS (WINS-RUNS, £)

G R I Smyly 3-16 £1.72; W K Goldsworthy 3-26 £1.04; M Bradstock 4-18 £1.50; D E Cantillon 4-14 £1.89; D McCain 6-23 £1.13; Miss E C Lavelle 19-90 £0.29; Mrs A M Thorpe 17-71 £0.34; G J Smith 5-36 £0.61; A Crook 6-45 £0.48; W Davies 4-27 £0.70; Mrs Caroline Keevil 7-24 £0.78; J I A Charlton 3-17 £1.07; Mrs H Dalton 7-34 £0.53; Mrs A M Woodrow 4-22 £0.80; A C Whillans 7-41 £0.43; S J Marshall 3-26 £0.65; A Fleming 6-11 £1.50; J C Haynes 4-55 £0.29; P F Nicholls 14-56 £0.26; C P Morlock 3-17 £0.85.

Handicap Chases (class 4..6)

Handicap Chases (class 4..6): 2m to 2m3f

ANALYSIS BY AGE

Age	Prop	Win	Runs	Wins%	£
3yo	0%	0	0	0.0%	0.00
4yo	1%	8	55	14.5%	0.27
5yo	7%	40	363	11.0%	-0.29
6yo	22%	123	805	15.3%	-0.03
7yo	18%	104	959	10.8%	-0.29
8yo	21%	116	984	11.8%	-0.17
9yo	14%	79	820	9.6%	-0.18
10yo	9%	49	488	10.0%	-0.16
11yo	5%	28	325	8.6%	-0.18
12yo+	3%	17	239	7.1%	-0.06

ANALYSIS BY BHB RATING

Age	Prop	Win	Runs	Wins%	£
120..129	1%	5	28	17.9%	0.06
110..119	13%	74	410	18.0%	-0.02
100..109	21%	120	1041	11.5%	-0.31
80..99	49%	279	2580	10.8%	-0.17
60..79	15%	85	971	8.8%	-0.07
..59	0%	1	7	14.3%	-0.50
Unrated	0%	0	1	0.0%	-1.00

ANALYSIS BY WEIGHT CARRIED

Age	Prop	Win	Runs	Wins%	£
12-01+	0%	2	7	28.6%	-0.11
11-8..12-00	25%	139	1098	12.7%	-0.14
11-0..11-07	36%	204	1588	12.8%	-0.12
10-8..10-13	16%	89	934	9.5%	-0.24
10-0..10-07	19%	109	1037	10.5%	-0.10
..9-13	4%	21	374	5.6%	-0.46

ANALYSIS BY DAYS SINCE LAST RUN

Age	Prop	Win	Runs	Wins%	£
1..7	9%	52	361	14.4%	-0.25
8..14	21%	120	1016	11.8%	-0.15
15..28	29%	166	1537	10.8%	-0.24
29..60	21%	121	1109	10.9%	-0.13
61..100	5%	26	287	9.1%	-0.17
101+	14%	78	722	10.8%	-0.06
Unraced	0%	1	6	16.7%	-0.54

ANALYSIS BY TODAY'S STARTING PRICE

Age	Prop	Win	Runs	Wins%	£
Odds On	3%	17	24	70.8%	0.21
Ev-2/1	12%	65	197	33.0%	-0.13
9/4-4/1	31%	173	837	20.7%	-0.14
9/2-6/1	21%	116	739	15.7%	-0.04
13/2-10/1	21%	121	1205	10.0%	-0.09
11/1-16/1	7%	42	952	4.4%	-0.38
18/1-33/1	5%	26	786	3.3%	-0.16
40/1+	1%	4	298	1.3%	-0.28

ANALYSIS BY STARTING PRICE LAST TIME

Age	Prop	Win	Runs	Wins%	£
Odds On	1%	5	23	21.7%	-0.44
Ev-2/1	6%	33	163	20.2%	-0.09
9/4-4/1	23%	131	748	17.5%	-0.16
9/2-6/1	18%	101	677	14.9%	-0.18
13/2-10/1	18%	104	1070	9.7%	-0.32
11/1-16/1	17%	95	933	10.2%	-0.08
18/1-33/1	12%	66	900	7.3%	-0.16
40/1+	5%	28	518	5.4%	-0.06
Unraced	0%	1	6	16.7%	-0.54

ANALYSIS BY DISTANCE BEATEN LAST TIME

Age	Prop	Win	Runs	Wins%	£
..-10 lgh	3%	18	74	24.3%	-0.11
-10..0	16%	89	359	24.8%	-0.01
0.1..2	6%	33	243	13.6%	-0.32
2.1..5	8%	43	282	15.2%	-0.15
5.1..10	11%	62	440	14.1%	-0.22
10.1..20	18%	101	780	12.9%	-0.10
20.0..30	12%	67	632	10.6%	-0.17
30.1+	15%	82	1228	6.7%	-0.23
Not Compl	12%	68	994	6.8%	-0.16
Unraced	0%	1	6	16.7%	-0.54

ANALYSIS BY SUCCESS RATE IN LAST 10 RUNS

Age	Prop	Win	Runs	Wins%	£
No Wins	37%	210	2306	9.1%	-0.15
1 Win	36%	203	1693	12.0%	-0.19
2 Wins	19%	107	767	14.0%	-0.16
3 Wins	6%	35	203	17.2%	-0.21
4 Wins	1%	7	59	11.9%	-0.51
5+ Wins	0%	1	4	25.0%	0.08

ANALYSIS BY SUCCESS RATE IN LAST 3 RUNS

Age	Prop	Win	Runs	Wins%	£
No Wins	65%	367	3935	9.3%	-0.17
1 Win	29%	165	950	17.4%	-0.14
2 Wins	5%	30	140	21.4%	-0.18
3 Wins	0%	1	7	14.3%	-0.66

ANALYSIS BY POSITION LAST TIME

Age	Prop	Win	Runs	Wins%	£
Won	19%	107	432	24.8%	-0.02
2nd or 3rd	30%	170	1153	14.7%	-0.17
Unplaced	39%	219	2457	8.9%	-0.20
Fell,BD,UR	4%	22	309	7.1%	-0.41
Pulled Up	8%	43	665	6.5%	-0.04
Ref/RanOut	0%	1	13	7.7%	-0.46
CO/SlipUp	0%	1	3	33.3%	0.44
Unraced	0%	1	6	16.7%	-0.54

OTHER FACTORS (WINS-RUNS, £)

Course Winner:	105-912	-£0.19
Distance Winner:	284-2320	-£0.15
Going Winner:	245-1975	-£0.16
Beaten Favourite:	48-302	-£0.16
7-Day Winners:	21-56	-£0.06
Absolute Favourites:	143-505	-£0.13

TRAINERS (WINS-RUNS, £)

C J Down 3-14 £0.50; Miss E C Lavelle 5-20 £0.29; D A Rees 3-15 £0.37; R Ford 3-25 £0.22; C Grant 3-24 £0.22; Miss S E Forster 5-30 £0.15; J L Spearing 5-34 £0.12; Miss Lucinda V Russe 15-78 £0.05; Dr R D P Newland 7-39 £0.10; N J Hawke 3-17 £0.13; Tim Vaughan 6-34 £0.03; A King 6-21 £0.04; R H Alner 4-23 £0.03.

Race Profiles

Handicap Chases (class 4..6): 2m4f to 2m7f

ANALYSIS BY AGE

Age	Prop	Win	Runs	Wins%	£
3yo	0%	0	0	0.0%	0.00
4yo	1%	6	37	16.2%	0.11
5yo	5%	31	314	9.9%	-0.22
6yo	15%	102	772	13.2%	0.11
7yo	20%	134	1151	11.6%	-0.22
8yo	22%	145	1251	11.6%	-0.11
9yo	17%	113	1112	10.2%	-0.17
10yo	12%	78	826	9.4%	-0.17
11yo	5%	34	481	7.1%	-0.23
12yo+	4%	25	371	6.7%	-0.36

ANALYSIS BY BHB RATING

Age	Prop	Win	Runs	Wins%	£
120..129	1%	5	35	14.3%	-0.07
110..119	10%	65	541	12.0%	-0.24
100..109	22%	146	1350	10.8%	-0.17
80..99	51%	343	3171	10.8%	-0.17
60..79	16%	107	1200	8.9%	-0.05
..59	0%	2	17	11.8%	1.41
Unrated	0%	0	1	0.0%	-1.00

ANALYSIS BY WEIGHT CARRIED

Age	Prop	Win	Runs	Wins%	£
12-01+	0%	2	13	15.4%	-0.59
11-8..12-00	24%	163	1379	11.8%	-0.13
11-0..11-07	31%	207	2053	10.1%	-0.27
10-8..10-13	19%	130	1200	10.8%	-0.18
10-0..10-07	19%	127	1208	10.5%	-0.05
..9-13	6%	39	462	8.4%	0.12

ANALYSIS BY DAYS SINCE LAST RUN

Age	Prop	Win	Runs	Wins%	£
1..7	9%	57	350	16.3%	-0.17
8..14	19%	125	1182	10.6%	-0.25
15..28	33%	219	2025	10.8%	-0.15
29..60	18%	118	1349	8.7%	-0.22
61..100	5%	32	351	9.1%	0.24
101+	18%	117	1051	11.1%	-0.07
Unraced	0%	0	7	0.0%	-1.00

ANALYSIS BY TODAY'S STARTING PRICE

Age	Prop	Win	Runs	Wins%	£
Odds On	2%	15	27	55.6%	-0.03
Ev-2/1	11%	74	202	36.6%	-0.04
9/4-4/1	31%	204	937	21.8%	-0.10
9/2-6/1	16%	109	910	12.0%	-0.25
13/2-10/1	24%	160	1567	10.2%	-0.08
11/1-16/1	10%	70	1227	5.7%	-0.17
18/1-33/1	4%	26	1060	2.5%	-0.40
40/1+	1%	10	385	2.6%	0.35

ANALYSIS BY STARTING PRICE LAST TIME

Age	Prop	Win	Runs	Wins%	£
Odds On	1%	8	27	29.6%	0.15
Ev-2/1	7%	48	205	23.4%	-0.18
9/4-4/1	22%	145	877	16.5%	-0.11
9/2-6/1	14%	96	817	11.8%	-0.22
13/2-10/1	23%	155	1539	10.1%	-0.23
11/1-16/1	19%	129	1193	10.8%	0.05
18/1-33/1	10%	67	1103	6.1%	-0.15
40/1+	3%	20	547	3.7%	-0.31
Unraced	0%	0	7	0.0%	-1.00

ANALYSIS BY DISTANCE BEATEN LAST TIME

Age	Prop	Win	Runs	Wins%	£
..-10 lgh	4%	30	92	32.6%	0.29
-10..0	12%	83	445	18.7%	-0.22
0.1..2	6%	40	273	14.7%	-0.20
2.1..5	7%	44	301	14.6%	-0.13
5.1..10	11%	71	482	14.7%	-0.20
10.1..20	16%	108	929	11.6%	-0.13
20.0..30	12%	78	745	10.5%	-0.06
30.1+	16%	106	1640	6.5%	-0.21
Not Compl	16%	108	1401	7.7%	-0.12
Unraced	0%	0	7	0.0%	-1.00

ANALYSIS BY SUCCESS RATE IN LAST 10 RUNS

Age	Prop	Win	Runs	Wins%	£
No Wins	36%	240	2680	9.0%	-0.16
1 Win	39%	261	2242	11.6%	-0.07
2 Wins	17%	116	1030	11.3%	-0.27
3 Wins	6%	39	282	13.8%	-0.22
4 Wins	2%	11	65	16.9%	-0.34
5+ Wins	0%	1	9	11.1%	-0.74

ANALYSIS BY SUCCESS RATE IN LAST 3 RUNS

Age	Prop	Win	Runs	Wins%	£
No Wins	69%	463	4914	9.4%	-0.13
1 Win	25%	169	1226	13.8%	-0.20
2 Wins	4%	29	147	19.7%	-0.31
3 Wins	1%	7	21	33.3%	-0.12

ANALYSIS BY POSITION LAST TIME

Age	Prop	Win	Runs	Wins%	£
Won	17%	113	538	21.0%	-0.13
2nd or 3rd	30%	199	1365	14.6%	-0.13
Unplaced	37%	248	3007	8.2%	-0.18
Fell,BD,UR	5%	34	385	8.8%	-0.18
Pulled Up	11%	71	995	7.1%	-0.12
Ref/RanOut	0%	3	15	20.0%	2.03
CO/SlipUp	0%	0	3	0.0%	-1.00
Unraced	0%	0	7	0.0%	-1.00

OTHER FACTORS (WINS-RUNS, £)

Course Winner:	174-1339	-£0.05
Distance Winner:	237-2100	-£0.21
Going Winner:	282-2617	-£0.20
Beaten Favourite:	66-404	-£0.08
7-Day Winners:	27-73	£0.26
Absolute Favourites:	183-576	£0.05

TRAINERS (WINS-RUNS, £)

P F Nicholls 5-16 £0.81; K Bishop 4-29 £0.41; M Keighley 4-17 £0.71; N A Twiston-Davies 15-71 £0.17; M Bradstock 3-12 £0.99; N B King 4-22 £0.44; D McCain Jnr 4-18 £0.50; P Beaumont 3-23 £0.39; N J Gifford 9-40 £0.19; J M Jefferson 4-31 £0.24; Mrs E Slack 6-46 £0.14; R Ford 4-31 £0.21; S Gollings 4-22 £0.30; R Lee 5-59 £0.09; Mrs L Wadham 3-14 £0.38; P Monteith 3-26 £0.17; C Grant 3-16 £0.23; R H Alner 6-38 £0.09; Nick Williams 5-31 £0.08; Evan Williams 14-77 £0.03.

Handicap Chases (class 4..6)

Handicap Chases (class 4..6): 3m+

ANALYSIS BY AGE

Age	Prop	Win	Runs	Wins%	£
3yo	0%	0	0	0.0%	0.00
4yo	0%	0	10	0.0%	-1.00
5yo	2%	17	208	8.2%	-0.37
6yo	11%	88	801	11.0%	-0.11
7yo	21%	169	1407	12.0%	-0.08
8yo	26%	212	1614	13.1%	-0.03
9yo	17%	135	1462	9.2%	-0.20
10yo	12%	96	1182	8.1%	-0.32
11yo	6%	52	758	6.9%	-0.38
12yo+	6%	45	730	6.2%	-0.34

ANALYSIS BY BHB RATING

Age	Prop	Win	Runs	Wins%	£
120..129	1%	5	46	10.9%	-0.49
110..119	9%	76	614	12.4%	-0.08
100..109	20%	161	1574	10.2%	-0.31
80..99	51%	414	4089	10.1%	-0.17
60..79	19%	157	1826	8.6%	-0.18
..59	0%	1	23	4.3%	1.22
Unrated	0%	0	0	0.0%	0.00

ANALYSIS BY WEIGHT CARRIED

Age	Prop	Win	Runs	Wins%	£
12-01+	0%	3	12	25.0%	-0.19
11-8..12-00	22%	180	1557	11.6%	-0.23
11-0..11-07	29%	239	2529	9.5%	-0.26
10-8..10-13	19%	155	1519	10.2%	-0.14
10-0..10-07	21%	170	1747	9.7%	-0.18
..9-13	8%	67	808	8.3%	-0.04

ANALYSIS BY DAYS SINCE LAST RUN

Age	Prop	Win	Runs	Wins%	£
1..7	6%	52	447	11.6%	-0.32
8..14	18%	148	1523	9.7%	-0.17
15..28	35%	286	2830	10.1%	-0.20
29..60	24%	197	1848	10.7%	-0.14
61..100	5%	38	440	8.6%	0.06
101+	11%	93	1081	8.6%	-0.35
Unraced	0%	0	3	0.0%	-1.00

ANALYSIS BY TODAY'S STARTING PRICE

Age	Prop	Win	Runs	Wins%	£
Odds On	1%	5	10	50.0%	-0.11
Ev-2/1	10%	85	188	45.2%	0.19
9/4-4/1	28%	229	1112	20.6%	-0.14
9/2-6/1	21%	170	1191	14.3%	-0.12
13/2-10/1	24%	194	2095	9.3%	-0.16
11/1-16/1	10%	84	1672	5.0%	-0.29
18/1-33/1	5%	39	1408	2.8%	-0.29
40/1+	1%	8	496	1.6%	-0.10

ANALYSIS BY STARTING PRICE LAST TIME

Age	Prop	Win	Runs	Wins%	£
Odds On	1%	5	23	21.7%	-0.23
Ev-2/1	5%	41	228	18.0%	-0.24
9/4-4/1	21%	169	1101	15.3%	-0.16
9/2-6/1	16%	130	1158	11.2%	-0.30
13/2-10/1	26%	211	1965	10.7%	-0.16
11/1-16/1	16%	128	1587	8.1%	-0.20
18/1-33/1	11%	92	1392	6.6%	-0.22
40/1+	5%	38	715	5.3%	-0.04
Unraced	0%	0	3	0.0%	-1.00

ANALYSIS BY DISTANCE BEATEN LAST TIME

Age	Prop	Win	Runs	Wins%	£
..-10 lgh	5%	38	149	25.5%	-0.11
-10..0	12%	96	596	16.1%	-0.15
0.1..2	7%	54	369	14.6%	-0.24
2.1..5	7%	55	393	14.0%	-0.14
5.1..10	9%	73	600	12.2%	-0.24
10.1..20	15%	124	1070	11.6%	-0.17
20.0..30	13%	104	889	11.7%	-0.06
30.1+	18%	143	2071	6.9%	-0.15
Not Compl	16%	127	2032	6.3%	-0.30
Unraced	0%	0	3	0.0%	-1.00

ANALYSIS BY SUCCESS RATE IN LAST 10 RUNS

Age	Prop	Win	Runs	Wins%	£
No Wins	32%	258	3228	8.0%	-0.24
1 Win	39%	318	2965	10.7%	-0.15
2 Wins	22%	180	1468	12.3%	-0.12
3 Wins	5%	44	402	10.9%	-0.34
4 Wins	1%	10	83	12.0%	-0.24
5+ Wins	0%	4	23	17.4%	-0.11

ANALYSIS BY SUCCESS RATE IN LAST 3 RUNS

Age	Prop	Win	Runs	Wins%	£
No Wins	67%	547	6177	8.9%	-0.21
1 Win	28%	229	1740	13.2%	-0.10
2 Wins	4%	36	238	15.1%	-0.34
3 Wins	0%	2	14	14.3%	-0.48

ANALYSIS BY POSITION LAST TIME

Age	Prop	Win	Runs	Wins%	£
Won	16%	134	743	18.0%	-0.14
2nd or 3rd	30%	243	1814	13.4%	-0.19
Unplaced	38%	310	3587	8.6%	-0.14
Fell,BD,UR	5%	41	517	7.9%	-0.29
Pulled Up	11%	86	1473	5.8%	-0.29
Ref/RanOut	0%	0	26	0.0%	-1.00
CO/SlipUp	0%	0	9	0.0%	-1.00
Unraced	0%	0	3	0.0%	-1.00

OTHER FACTORS (WINS-RUNS, £)

Course Winner:	191-1746	-£0.20
Distance Winner:	274-2563	-£0.20
Going Winner:	330-3424	-£0.26
Beaten Favourite:	80-528	-£0.19
7-Day Winners:	18-66	£0.10
Absolute Favourites:	203-716	-£0.02

TRAINERS (WINS-RUNS, £)

R Lee 12-94 £0.15; Mrs A Hamilton 4-14 £0.99; R J Hodges 5-35 £0.35; D P Keane 4-24 £0.44; V R A Dartnall 4-20 £0.51; Mrs Caroline Bailey 5-28 £0.30; Nick Williams 4-31 £0.26; A King 4-33 £0.23; Jim Best 4-20 £0.38; Mrs S C Bradburne 9-75 £0.10; A M Hales 4-21 £0.33; Andrew Turnell 7-57 £0.11; Mrs A M Thorpe 5-20 £0.31; O Sherwood 10-51 £0.12; Mrs S Wall 3-19 £0.32; C T Pogson 3-19 £0.24; J Wade 10-62 £0.06; Miss Suzy Smith 7-59 £0.06; T D Walford 5-19 £0.15; J G Cann 3-14 £0.19.

Race Profiles

Handicap Chases (class 4..6): 2 to 5 runners

ANALYSIS BY AGE

Age	Prop	Win	Runs	Wins%	£
3yo	0%	0	0	0.0%	0.00
4yo	1%	2	5	40.0%	-0.20
5yo	5%	7	34	20.6%	-0.35
6yo	11%	16	82	19.5%	-0.39
7yo	19%	28	123	22.8%	-0.09
8yo	23%	34	132	25.8%	0.38
9yo	22%	33	139	23.7%	-0.01
10yo	9%	13	91	14.3%	-0.40
11yo	7%	10	50	20.0%	-0.04
12yo+	5%	8	41	19.5%	-0.35

ANALYSIS BY BHB RATING

Age	Prop	Win	Runs	Wins%	£
150+	0%	0	0	0.0%	0.00
130..149	0%	0	0	0.0%	0.00
120..129	1%	2	8	25.0%	-0.20
110..119	16%	24	97	24.7%	0.04
100..109	30%	45	236	19.1%	-0.23
80..99	45%	68	298	22.8%	-0.01
60..79	8%	12	58	20.7%	-0.08
..59	0%	0	0	0.0%	0.00
Unrated	0%	0	0	0.0%	0.00

ANALYSIS BY WEIGHT CARRIED

Age	Prop	Win	Runs	Wins%	£
12-01+	0%	0	2	0.0%	-1.00
11-8..12-00	27%	41	200	20.5%	-0.20
11-0..11-07	34%	52	226	23.0%	-0.12
10-8..10-13	13%	20	109	18.3%	-0.03
10-0..10-07	20%	30	123	24.4%	0.13
..9-13	5%	8	37	21.6%	-0.16

ANALYSIS BY DAYS SINCE LAST RUN

Age	Prop	Win	Runs	Wins%	£
1..7	7%	10	51	19.6%	0.01
8..14	26%	40	173	23.1%	-0.20
15..28	29%	44	225	19.6%	-0.22
29..60	19%	28	123	22.8%	-0.15
61..100	6%	9	33	27.3%	0.31
101+	13%	19	91	20.9%	0.33
Unraced	1%	1	1	100.0%	1.75

ANALYSIS BY TODAY'S STARTING PRICE

Age	Prop	Win	Runs	Wins%	£
Odds On	7%	11	27	40.7%	-0.29
Ev-2/1	34%	51	128	39.8%	0.03
9/4-4/1	39%	59	253	23.3%	-0.09
9/2-6/1	13%	19	102	18.6%	0.16
13/2-10/1	5%	7	109	6.4%	-0.40
11/1-16/1	2%	3	53	5.7%	-0.30
18/1-33/1	1%	1	19	5.3%	0.79
40/1+	0%	0	6	0.0%	-1.00

ANALYSIS BY STARTING PRICE LAST TIME

Age	Prop	Win	Runs	Wins%	£
Odds On	1%	2	4	50.0%	0.52
Ev-2/1	5%	7	41	17.1%	-0.59
9/4-4/1	29%	44	135	32.6%	-0.04
9/2-6/1	19%	29	104	27.9%	0.08
13/2-10/1	21%	32	143	22.4%	0.07
11/1-16/1	13%	20	121	16.5%	-0.16
18/1-33/1	9%	13	100	13.0%	-0.33
40/1+	2%	3	48	6.3%	-0.02
Unraced	1%	1	1	100.0%	1.75

ANALYSIS BY DISTANCE BEATEN LAST TIME

Age	Prop	Win	Runs	Wins%	£
..-10 lgh	4%	6	22	27.3%	-0.42
-10..0	19%	29	76	38.2%	0.07
0.1..2	7%	10	38	26.3%	-0.15
2.1..5	5%	7	27	25.9%	-0.27
5.1..10	11%	17	59	28.8%	0.02
10.1..20	13%	20	90	22.2%	0.14
20.0..30	13%	20	95	21.1%	-0.11
30.1+	14%	21	166	12.7%	-0.29
Not Compl	13%	20	123	16.3%	0.00
Unraced	1%	1	1	100.0%	1.75

ANALYSIS BY SUCCESS RATE IN LAST 10 RUNS

Age	Prop	Win	Runs	Wins%	£
No Wins	27%	40	219	18.3%	-0.19
1 Win	35%	52	246	21.1%	-0.06
2 Wins	24%	36	154	23.4%	-0.03
3 Wins	11%	17	57	29.8%	0.08
4 Wins	3%	5	17	29.4%	-0.29
5+ Wins	0%	0	3	0.0%	-1.00

ANALYSIS BY SUCCESS RATE IN LAST 3 RUNS

Age	Prop	Win	Runs	Wins%	£
No Wins	61%	92	481	19.1%	-0.06
1 Win	30%	45	177	25.4%	-0.18
2 Wins	7%	11	35	31.4%	-0.14
3 Wins	1%	2	3	66.7%	0.46

ANALYSIS BY POSITION LAST TIME

Age	Prop	Win	Runs	Wins%	£
Won	23%	35	98	35.7%	-0.04
2nd or 3rd	28%	43	162	26.5%	-0.09
Unplaced	34%	52	313	16.6%	-0.14
Fell,BD,UR	7%	11	39	28.2%	0.11
Pulled Up	5%	8	82	9.8%	-0.09
Ref/RanOut	0%	0	0	0.0%	0.00
CO/SlipUp	1%	1	2	50.0%	1.17
Unraced	1%	1	1	100.0%	1.75

OTHER FACTORS (WINS-RUNS, £)

Course Winner:	36-176	-£0.21
Distance Winner:	77-352	-£0.11
Going Winner:	66-313	-£0.19
Beaten Favourite:	8-57	-£0.60
7-Day Winners:	4-11	-£0.06
Absolute Favourites:	51-137	-£0.11

Handicap Chases (class 4..6)

Handicap Chases (class 4..6): 6 to 10 runners

ANALYSIS BY AGE
Age	Prop	Win	Runs	Wins%	£
3yo	0%	0	0	0.0%	0.00
4yo	1%	7	55	12.7%	-0.19
5yo	4%	51	461	11.1%	-0.25
6yo	16%	191	1164	16.4%	0.02
7yo	20%	230	1715	13.4%	-0.19
8yo	23%	266	1898	14.0%	-0.17
9yo	15%	182	1640	11.1%	-0.19
10yo	12%	139	1208	11.5%	-0.12
11yo	5%	60	768	7.8%	-0.39
12yo+	4%	49	620	7.9%	-0.34

ANALYSIS BY BHB RATING
Age	Prop	Win	Runs	Wins%	£
120..129	1%	9	64	14.1%	-0.30
110..119	12%	143	945	15.1%	-0.11
100..109	25%	290	2362	12.3%	-0.21
80..99	50%	586	4719	12.4%	-0.18
60..79	12%	146	1434	10.2%	-0.18
..59	0%	1	5	20.0%	-0.30
Unrated	0%	0	0	0.0%	0.00

ANALYSIS BY WEIGHT CARRIED
Age	Prop	Win	Runs	Wins%	£
12-01+	0%	5	17	29.4%	-0.02
11-8..12-00	26%	310	2125	14.6%	-0.08
11-0..11-07	32%	380	2940	12.9%	-0.20
10-8..10-13	18%	209	1765	11.8%	-0.21
10-0..10-07	17%	205	1921	10.7%	-0.24
..9-13	6%	66	761	8.7%	-0.16

ANALYSIS BY DAYS SINCE LAST RUN
Age	Prop	Win	Runs	Wins%	£
1..7	9%	102	606	16.8%	-0.19
8..14	20%	239	1912	12.5%	-0.21
15..28	33%	393	3155	12.5%	-0.19
29..60	20%	230	1946	11.8%	-0.20
61..100	4%	44	463	9.5%	0.00
101+	14%	167	1438	11.6%	-0.14
Unraced	0%	0	9	0.0%	-1.00

ANALYSIS BY TODAY'S STARTING PRICE
Age	Prop	Win	Runs	Wins%	£
Odds On	2%	22	29	75.9%	0.31
Ev-2/1	12%	144	359	40.1%	0.06
9/4-4/1	36%	423	1986	21.3%	-0.12
9/2-6/1	20%	235	1658	14.2%	-0.13
13/2-10/1	20%	232	2473	9.4%	-0.16
11/1-16/1	7%	83	1617	5.1%	-0.27
18/1-33/1	3%	34	1121	3.0%	-0.26
40/1+	0%	2	286	0.7%	-0.68

ANALYSIS BY STARTING PRICE LAST TIME
Age	Prop	Win	Runs	Wins%	£
Odds On	1%	16	47	34.0%	0.18
Ev-2/1	7%	77	324	23.8%	-0.09
9/4-4/1	23%	269	1464	18.4%	-0.10
9/2-6/1	17%	194	1343	14.4%	-0.18
13/2-10/1	23%	267	2242	11.9%	-0.22
11/1-16/1	16%	186	1756	10.6%	-0.14
18/1-33/1	10%	120	1604	7.5%	-0.30
40/1+	4%	46	740	6.2%	-0.11
Unraced	0%	0	9	0.0%	-1.00

ANALYSIS BY DISTANCE BEATEN LAST TIME
Age	Prop	Win	Runs	Wins%	£
..-10 Igh	5%	59	181	32.6%	0.15
-10..0	14%	168	745	22.6%	-0.05
0.1..2	7%	78	491	15.9%	-0.23
2.1..5	8%	95	517	18.4%	-0.05
5.1..10	11%	126	780	16.2%	-0.16
10.1..20	15%	180	1410	12.8%	-0.16
20.0..30	11%	134	1092	12.3%	-0.09
30.1+	15%	180	2264	8.0%	-0.21
Not Compl	13%	155	2040	7.6%	-0.32
Unraced	0%	0	9	0.0%	-1.00

ANALYSIS BY SUCCESS RATE IN LAST 10 RUNS
Age	Prop	Win	Runs	Wins%	£
No Wins	32%	371	3586	10.3%	-0.19
1 Win	39%	457	3542	12.9%	-0.15
2 Wins	21%	247	1733	14.3%	-0.19
3 Wins	7%	77	502	15.3%	-0.22
4 Wins	2%	18	130	13.8%	-0.29
5+ Wins	0%	5	27	18.5%	-0.18

ANALYSIS BY SUCCESS RATE IN LAST 3 RUNS
Age	Prop	Win	Runs	Wins%	£
No Wins	64%	750	7132	10.5%	-0.21
1 Win	30%	353	2065	17.1%	-0.08
2 Wins	5%	64	295	21.7%	-0.14
3 Wins	1%	8	28	28.6%	-0.15

ANALYSIS BY POSITION LAST TIME
Age	Prop	Win	Runs	Wins%	£
Won	19%	227	926	24.5%	-0.01
2nd or 3rd	31%	369	2245	16.4%	-0.12
Unplaced	36%	425	4318	9.8%	-0.18
Fell,BD,UR	4%	48	574	8.4%	-0.36
Pulled Up	9%	103	1424	7.2%	-0.32
Ref/RanOut	0%	3	25	12.0%	0.82
CO/SlipUp	0%	0	8	0.0%	-1.00
Unraced	0%	0	9	0.0%	-1.00

OTHER FACTORS (WINS-RUNS, £)
Course Winner:	291-2134	-£0.13
Distance Winner:	482-3739	-£0.18
Going Winner:	536-4204	-£0.18
Beaten Favourite:	112-642	-£0.11
7-Day Winners:	45-120	£0.11
Absolute Favourites:	345-1041	£0.05

TRAINERS (WINS-RUNS, £)
C J Down 4-18 £0.69; P C Haslam 3-15 £0.83; A J Lidderdale 3-10 £1.20; Mrs H Dalton 5-23 £0.48; A E Jones 6-30 £0.35; Mark Gillard 3-15 £0.70; A J Whiting 4-23 £0.39; J M Jefferson 10-56 £0.16; K C Bailey 12-67 £0.13; S C Burrough 3-25 £0.34; Mrs S J Smith 27-165 £0.05; Mrs A Hamilton 4-17 £0.43; P Beaumont 3-35 £0.20; L Lungo 5-27 £0.23; P F Nicholls 9-31 £0.19; B J M Ryall 4-28 £0.17; Mrs L Williamson 5-70 £0.07; Mrs Caroline Bailey 8-39 £0.10; Mrs P Robeson 4-14 £0.27; N J Gifford 7-41 £0.08.

Race Profiles

Handicap Chases (class 4..6): 11 runners or more

ANALYSIS BY AGE

Age	Prop	Win	Runs	Wins%	£
3yo	0%	0	0	0.0%	0.00
4yo	1%	5	42	11.9%	0.49
5yo	4%	30	390	7.7%	-0.32
6yo	15%	106	1132	9.4%	-0.01
7yo	21%	149	1679	8.9%	-0.18
8yo	24%	173	1819	9.5%	-0.05
9yo	16%	112	1615	6.9%	-0.20
10yo	10%	71	1197	5.9%	-0.35
11yo	6%	44	746	5.9%	-0.21
12yo+	4%	30	679	4.4%	-0.25

ANALYSIS BY BHB RATING

Age	Prop	Win	Runs	Wins%	£
120..129	1%	4	37	10.8%	-0.07
110..119	7%	48	523	9.2%	-0.18
100..109	13%	92	1367	6.7%	-0.34
80..99	53%	382	4823	7.9%	-0.18
60..79	27%	191	2505	7.6%	-0.08
..59	0%	3	42	7.1%	1.19
Unrated	0%	0	2	0.0%	-1.00

ANALYSIS BY WEIGHT CARRIED

Age	Prop	Win	Runs	Wins%	£
12-01+	0%	2	13	15.4%	-0.64
11-8..12-00	18%	131	1709	7.7%	-0.28
11-0..11-07	30%	218	3004	7.3%	-0.26
10-8..10-13	20%	145	1779	8.2%	-0.15
10-0..10-07	24%	171	1948	8.8%	-0.02
..9-13	7%	53	846	6.3%	-0.02

ANALYSIS BY DAYS SINCE LAST RUN

Age	Prop	Win	Runs	Wins%	£
1..7	7%	49	501	9.8%	-0.34
8..14	16%	114	1636	7.0%	-0.17
15..28	33%	234	3012	7.8%	-0.19
29..60	25%	178	2237	8.0%	-0.13
61..100	6%	43	582	7.4%	0.09
101+	14%	102	1325	7.7%	-0.24
Unraced	0%	0	6	0.0%	-1.00

ANALYSIS BY TODAY'S STARTING PRICE

Age	Prop	Win	Runs	Wins%	£
Odds On	1%	4	5	80.0%	0.40
Ev-2/1	4%	29	100	29.0%	-0.23
9/4-4/1	17%	124	647	19.2%	-0.18
9/2-6/1	20%	141	1080	13.1%	-0.19
13/2-10/1	33%	236	2285	10.3%	-0.06
11/1-16/1	15%	110	2181	5.0%	-0.28
18/1-33/1	8%	56	2114	2.6%	-0.33
40/1+	3%	20	887	2.3%	0.22

ANALYSIS BY STARTING PRICE LAST TIME

Age	Prop	Win	Runs	Wins%	£
Odds On	0%	0	22	0.0%	-1.00
Ev-2/1	5%	38	231	16.5%	-0.23
9/4-4/1	18%	132	1127	11.7%	-0.22
9/2-6/1	14%	104	1205	8.6%	-0.35
13/2-10/1	24%	171	2189	7.8%	-0.23
11/1-16/1	20%	146	1836	8.0%	-0.03
18/1-33/1	13%	92	1691	5.4%	-0.06
40/1+	5%	37	992	3.7%	-0.14
Unraced	0%	0	6	0.0%	-1.00

ANALYSIS BY DISTANCE BEATEN LAST TIME

Age	Prop	Win	Runs	Wins%	£
..-10 lgh	3%	21	112	18.8%	-0.14
-10..0	10%	71	579	12.3%	-0.28
0.1..2	5%	39	356	11.0%	-0.29
2.1..5	6%	40	432	9.3%	-0.25
5.1..10	9%	63	683	9.2%	-0.31
10.1..20	18%	133	1279	10.4%	-0.13
20.0..30	13%	95	1079	8.8%	-0.09
30.1+	18%	130	2509	5.2%	-0.17
Not Compl	18%	128	2264	5.7%	-0.13
Unraced	0%	0	6	0.0%	-1.00

ANALYSIS BY SUCCESS RATE IN LAST 10 RUNS

Age	Prop	Win	Runs	Wins%	£
No Wins	41%	297	4409	6.7%	-0.18
1 Win	38%	273	3112	8.8%	-0.12
2 Wins	17%	120	1378	8.7%	-0.18
3 Wins	3%	24	328	7.3%	-0.42
4 Wins	1%	5	60	8.3%	-0.49
5+ Wins	0%	1	6	16.7%	-0.17

ANALYSIS BY SUCCESS RATE IN LAST 3 RUNS

Age	Prop	Win	Runs	Wins%	£
No Wins	74%	535	7413	7.2%	-0.15
1 Win	23%	165	1674	9.9%	-0.21
2 Wins	3%	20	195	10.3%	-0.54
3 Wins	0%	0	11	0.0%	-1.00

ANALYSIS BY POSITION LAST TIME

Age	Prop	Win	Runs	Wins%	£
Won	13%	92	689	13.4%	-0.25
2nd or 3rd	28%	200	1925	10.4%	-0.22
Unplaced	42%	300	4420	6.8%	-0.16
Fell,BD,UR	5%	38	598	6.4%	-0.24
Pulled Up	12%	89	1627	5.5%	-0.07
Ref/RanOut	0%	1	29	3.4%	-0.76
CO/SlipUp	0%	0	5	0.0%	-1.00
Unraced	0%	0	6	0.0%	-1.00

OTHER FACTORS (WINS-RUNS, £)

Course Winner:	143-1687	-£0.16
Distance Winner:	236-2892	-£0.20
Going Winner:	255-3499	-£0.26
Beaten Favourite:	74-535	-£0.14
7-Day Winners:	17-64	£0.14
Absolute Favourites:	133-619	-£0.15

TRAINERS (WINS-RUNS, £)

B J Llewellyn 4-18 £1.33; J A B Old 5-35 £0.66; Mrs L Wadham 4-15 £1.43; C J Mann 6-35 £0.56; G J Smith 3-20 £0.90; H D Daly 8-45 £0.39; Miss Lucinda V Russe 14-113 £0.15; Mrs Caroline Keevil 4-14 £1.13; R T Phillips 4-70 £0.21; W Davies 3-19 £0.79; C L Tizzard 10-82 £0.18; Heather Dalton 4-36 £0.36; P D Evans 4-15 £0.87; R H Buckler 6-56 £0.21; Andrew Turnell 7-53 £0.22; Evan Williams 21-140 £0.08; M Mullineaux 3-33 £0.30; Jim Best 3-14 £0.68; P F Nicholls 4-22 £0.41; T D Easterby 3-22 £0.41.

Handicap Chases (class 4..6)

Handicap Chases (class 4..6): up to 7 days off the track

ANALYSIS BY AGE

Age	Prop	Win	Runs	Wins%	£
3yo	0%	0	0	0.0%	0.00
4yo	2%	3	16	18.8%	-0.52
5yo	4%	7	75	9.3%	-0.55
6yo	15%	25	141	17.7%	-0.17
7yo	12%	20	194	10.3%	-0.49
8yo	26%	42	241	17.4%	-0.09
9yo	17%	27	194	13.9%	-0.19
10yo	15%	25	153	16.3%	0.02
11yo	5%	8	88	9.1%	-0.32
12yo+	3%	5	72	6.9%	-0.66

ANALYSIS BY BHB RATING

Age	Prop	Win	Runs	Wins%	£
150+	0%	0	0	0.0%	0.00
130..149	0%	0	0	0.0%	0.00
120..129	1%	2	7	28.6%	-0.05
110..119	10%	17	73	23.3%	0.14
100..109	16%	26	201	12.9%	-0.23
80..99	56%	90	598	15.1%	-0.25
60..79	17%	27	294	9.2%	-0.40
..59	0%	0	1	0.0%	-1.00
Unrated	0%	0	0	0.0%	0.00

ANALYSIS BY WEIGHT CARRIED

Age	Prop	Win	Runs	Wins%	£
12-01+	2%	4	10	40.0%	0.38
11-8..12-00	22%	35	196	17.9%	0.09
11-0..11-07	25%	41	328	12.5%	-0.41
10-8..10-13	19%	31	214	14.5%	-0.38
10-0..10-07	22%	36	288	12.5%	-0.29
..9-13	9%	15	138	10.9%	-0.19

ANALYSIS BY DAYS SINCE LAST RUN

Age	Prop	Win	Runs	Wins%	£
1..7	99%	161	1158	13.9%	-0.25
8..14	0%	0	0	0.0%	0.00
15..28	0%	0	0	0.0%	0.00
29..60	0%	0	0	0.0%	0.00
61..100	0%	0	0	0.0%	0.00
101+	0%	0	0	0.0%	0.00
Unraced	1%	1	16	6.3%	-0.83

ANALYSIS BY TODAY'S STARTING PRICE

Age	Prop	Win	Runs	Wins%	£
Odds On	9%	14	21	66.7%	0.16
Ev-2/1	24%	39	102	38.2%	-0.02
9/4-4/1	31%	51	214	23.8%	-0.03
9/2-6/1	13%	21	165	12.7%	-0.23
13/2-10/1	19%	30	236	12.7%	0.19
11/1-16/1	2%	3	180	1.7%	-0.79
18/1-33/1	2%	4	181	2.2%	-0.48
40/1+	0%	0	75	0.0%	-1.00

ANALYSIS BY STARTING PRICE LAST TIME

Age	Prop	Win	Runs	Wins%	£
Odds On	2%	4	9	44.4%	0.15
Ev-2/1	12%	19	51	37.3%	0.18
9/4-4/1	27%	44	179	24.6%	-0.01
9/2-6/1	17%	28	162	17.3%	-0.10
13/2-10/1	20%	32	259	12.4%	-0.29
11/1-16/1	10%	17	189	9.0%	-0.27
18/1-33/1	7%	11	197	5.6%	-0.47
40/1+	4%	6	112	5.4%	-0.57
Unraced	1%	1	16	6.3%	-0.83

ANALYSIS BY DISTANCE BEATEN LAST TIME

Age	Prop	Win	Runs	Wins%	£
..-10 lgh	14%	22	58	37.9%	0.07
-10..0	27%	44	137	32.1%	0.13
0.1..2	10%	16	68	23.5%	-0.11
2.1..5	3%	5	69	7.2%	-0.70
5.1..10	9%	15	78	19.2%	-0.07
10.1..20	11%	18	137	13.1%	-0.11
20.0..30	6%	10	92	10.9%	-0.12
30.1+	7%	11	236	4.7%	-0.50
Not Compl	12%	20	283	7.1%	-0.38
Unraced	1%	1	16	6.3%	-0.83

ANALYSIS BY SUCCESS RATE IN LAST 10 RUNS

Age	Prop	Win	Runs	Wins%	£
No Wins	27%	44	494	8.9%	-0.36
1 Win	39%	62	424	14.6%	-0.26
2 Wins	19%	31	162	19.1%	-0.15
3 Wins	10%	16	52	30.8%	0.41
4 Wins	5%	8	22	36.4%	0.31
5+ Wins	0%	0	4	0.0%	-1.00

ANALYSIS BY SUCCESS RATE IN LAST 3 RUNS

Age	Prop	Win	Runs	Wins%	£
No Wins	48%	77	819	9.4%	-0.36
1 Win	39%	63	282	22.3%	-0.01
2 Wins	11%	17	47	36.2%	0.21
3 Wins	2%	4	10	40.0%	-0.12

ANALYSIS BY POSITION LAST TIME

Age	Prop	Win	Runs	Wins%	£
Won	41%	66	195	33.8%	0.11
2nd or 3rd	28%	45	262	17.2%	-0.16
Unplaced	19%	30	418	7.2%	-0.39
Fell,BD,UR	6%	10	116	8.6%	-0.42
Pulled Up	5%	8	160	5.0%	-0.48
Ref/RanOut	1%	2	7	28.6%	2.50
CO/SlipUp	0%	0	0	0.0%	0.00
Unraced	1%	1	16	6.3%	-0.83

OTHER FACTORS (WINS-RUNS, £)

Course Winner:	38-234	-£0.19
Distance Winner:	75-446	-£0.01
Going Winner:	82-553	-£0.25
Beaten Favourite:	14-59	-£0.03
7-Day Winners:	66-195	£0.11
Absolute Favourites:	73-215	-£0.05

Race Profiles

Handicap Chases (class 4..6): 100+ days off the track

ANALYSIS BY AGE

Age	Prop	Win	Runs	Wins%	£
3yo	0%	0	0	0.0%	0.00
4yo	0%	1	14	7.1%	-0.32
5yo	4%	11	113	9.7%	-0.28
6yo	16%	47	337	13.9%	0.11
7yo	21%	61	532	11.5%	-0.28
8yo	23%	68	555	12.3%	-0.08
9yo	21%	60	488	12.3%	0.29
10yo	8%	24	377	6.4%	-0.34
11yo	4%	12	236	5.1%	-0.58
12yo+	2%	7	221	3.2%	-0.71

ANALYSIS BY BHB RATING

Age	Prop	Win	Runs	Wins%	£
150+	0%	0	0	0.0%	0.00
130..149	0%	0	0	0.0%	0.00
120..129	1%	2	27	7.4%	-0.55
110..119	14%	40	288	13.9%	-0.14
100..109	22%	63	646	9.8%	-0.23
80..99	47%	136	1375	9.9%	-0.17
60..79	17%	49	531	9.2%	-0.14
..59	0%	1	6	16.7%	4.67
Unrated	0%	0	0	0.0%	0.00

ANALYSIS BY WEIGHT CARRIED

Age	Prop	Win	Runs	Wins%	£
12-01+	0%	0	0	0.0%	0.00
11-8..12-00	31%	91	705	12.9%	-0.11
11-0..11-07	27%	78	890	8.8%	-0.32
10-8..10-13	20%	57	547	10.4%	-0.04
10-0..10-07	17%	50	548	9.1%	-0.18
..9-13	5%	15	183	8.2%	0.00

ANALYSIS BY DAYS SINCE LAST RUN

Age	Prop	Win	Runs	Wins%	£
1..7	0%	0	0	0.0%	0.00
8..14	0%	0	0	0.0%	0.00
15..28	0%	0	0	0.0%	0.00
29..60	0%	0	0	0.0%	0.00
61..100	1%	3	19	15.8%	0.53
101+	99%	288	2854	10.1%	-0.17
Unraced	0%	0	0	0.0%	0.00

ANALYSIS BY TODAY'S STARTING PRICE

Age	Prop	Win	Runs	Wins%	£
Odds On	0%	1	1	100.0%	0.80
Ev-2/1	10%	29	57	50.9%	0.34
9/4-4/1	30%	86	340	25.3%	0.05
9/2-6/1	20%	59	349	16.9%	0.05
13/2-10/1	23%	68	686	9.9%	-0.08
11/1-16/1	10%	30	633	4.7%	-0.34
18/1-33/1	5%	15	606	2.5%	-0.33
40/1+	1%	3	201	1.5%	-0.34

ANALYSIS BY STARTING PRICE LAST TIME

Age	Prop	Win	Runs	Wins%	£
Odds On	1%	3	19	15.8%	-0.27
Ev-2/1	5%	14	119	11.8%	-0.55
9/4-4/1	23%	68	453	15.0%	-0.07
9/2-6/1	12%	36	393	9.2%	-0.34
13/2-10/1	27%	78	668	11.7%	-0.08
11/1-16/1	19%	54	544	9.9%	-0.01
18/1-33/1	9%	27	443	6.1%	-0.27
40/1+	4%	11	234	4.7%	-0.30
Unraced	0%	0	0	0.0%	0.00

ANALYSIS BY DISTANCE BEATEN LAST TIME

Age	Prop	Win	Runs	Wins%	£
..-10 lgh	2%	6	38	15.8%	-0.40
-10..0	8%	22	172	12.8%	-0.24
0.1..2	4%	11	81	13.6%	-0.24
2.1..5	5%	16	97	16.5%	0.05
5.1..10	9%	26	174	14.9%	-0.20
10.1..20	14%	41	331	12.4%	-0.24
20.0..30	11%	31	332	9.3%	-0.34
30.1+	23%	67	772	8.7%	-0.18
Not Compl	24%	71	876	8.1%	-0.05
Unraced	0%	0	0	0.0%	0.00

ANALYSIS BY SUCCESS RATE IN LAST 10 RUNS

Age	Prop	Win	Runs	Wins%	£
No Wins	34%	99	1077	9.2%	-0.13
1 Win	37%	108	1016	10.6%	-0.17
2 Wins	20%	57	555	10.3%	-0.21
3 Wins	7%	21	173	12.1%	-0.19
4 Wins	2%	5	45	11.1%	-0.48
5+ Wins	0%	1	7	14.3%	-0.38

ANALYSIS BY SUCCESS RATE IN LAST 3 RUNS

Age	Prop	Win	Runs	Wins%	£
No Wins	71%	207	2110	9.8%	-0.12
1 Win	25%	74	667	11.1%	-0.28
2 Wins	3%	10	93	10.8%	-0.38
3 Wins	0%	0	3	0.0%	-1.00

ANALYSIS BY POSITION LAST TIME

Age	Prop	Win	Runs	Wins%	£
Won	10%	28	210	13.3%	-0.27
2nd or 3rd	21%	61	446	13.7%	-0.21
Unplaced	45%	132	1348	9.8%	-0.21
Fell,BD,UR	5%	15	139	10.8%	0.21
Pulled Up	19%	55	717	7.7%	-0.09
Ref/RanOut	0%	0	11	0.0%	-1.00
CO/SlipUp	0%	0	2	0.0%	-1.00
Unraced	0%	0	0	0.0%	0.00

OTHER FACTORS (WINS-RUNS, £)

Course Winner:	51-573	-£0.27
Distance Winner:	98-1049	-£0.25
Going Winner:	121-1175	-£0.19
Beaten Favourite:	41-235	-£0.09
Absolute Favourites:	72-197	£0.28

Hunter Chases

ANALYSIS BY AGE

Age	Prop	Win	Runs	Wins%	£
3yo-4yo	0%	0	0	0.0%	0.00
5yo	0%	1	29	3.4%	-0.89
6yo	3%	16	197	8.1%	-0.48
7yo	13%	67	513	13.1%	-0.12
8yo	16%	84	825	10.2%	-0.36
9yo	20%	108	957	11.3%	-0.10
10yo	18%	98	941	10.4%	-0.37
11yo	13%	70	758	9.2%	-0.43
12yo+	17%	91	994	9.2%	-0.48

ANALYSIS BY BHB RATING

Age	Prop	Win	Runs	Wins%	£
150+	0%	0	3	0.0%	-1.00
130..149	5%	27	108	25.0%	-0.29
120..129	9%	48	234	20.5%	-0.15
110..119	10%	56	366	15.3%	-0.15
100..109	11%	57	388	14.7%	-0.28
80..99	7%	39	645	6.0%	-0.53
60..79	2%	9	297	3.0%	-0.62
..59	0%	0	30	0.0%	-1.00
Unrated	56%	299	3143	9.5%	-0.30

ANALYSIS BY WEIGHT CARRIED

Age	Prop	Win	Runs	Wins%	£
12-01+	16%	85	425	20.0%	-0.15
11-8..12-00	48%	257	2205	11.7%	-0.26
11-0..11-07	33%	174	2382	7.3%	-0.42
10-8..10-13	2%	13	137	9.5%	-0.47
10-0..10-07	1%	5	64	7.8%	-0.55
..9-13	0%	1	1	100.0%	16.00

ANALYSIS BY DAYS SINCE LAST RUN

Age	Prop	Win	Runs	Wins%	£
1..7	4%	21	128	16.4%	-0.04
8..14	17%	91	655	13.9%	-0.18
15..28	21%	112	957	11.7%	-0.36
29..60	14%	73	588	12.4%	-0.33
61..100	1%	7	130	5.4%	-0.50
101+	38%	201	2397	8.4%	-0.38
Unraced	6%	30	359	8.4%	-0.22

ANALYSIS BY TODAY'S STARTING PRICE

Age	Prop	Win	Runs	Wins%	£
Odds On	13%	67	110	60.9%	-0.01
Ev-2/1	21%	114	289	39.4%	0.01
9/4-4/1	29%	156	677	23.0%	-0.05
9/2-6/1	9%	49	423	11.6%	-0.28
13/2-10/1	13%	68	792	8.6%	-0.24
11/1-16/1	10%	52	849	6.1%	-0.12
18/1-33/1	5%	25	1069	2.3%	-0.43
40/1+	1%	4	1005	0.4%	-0.82

ANALYSIS BY STARTING PRICE LAST TIME

Age	Prop	Win	Runs	Wins%	£
Odds On	4%	22	88	25.0%	-0.15
Ev-2/1	11%	58	234	24.8%	-0.03
9/4-4/1	18%	98	584	16.8%	-0.15
9/2-6/1	11%	59	474	12.4%	-0.30
13/2-10/1	16%	85	868	9.8%	-0.33
11/1-16/1	11%	60	850	7.1%	-0.48
18/1-33/1	15%	81	973	8.3%	-0.26
40/1+	8%	42	784	5.4%	-0.57
Unraced	6%	30	359	8.4%	-0.22

ANALYSIS BY DISTANCE BEATEN LAST TIME

Age	Prop	Win	Runs	Wins%	£
..-10 lgh	5%	28	130	21.5%	-0.34
-10..0	12%	64	342	18.7%	-0.11
0.1..2	6%	33	202	16.3%	-0.32
2.1..5	6%	30	214	14.0%	-0.43
5.1..10	7%	40	282	14.2%	-0.18
10.1..20	11%	59	540	10.9%	-0.33
20.0..30	10%	52	478	10.9%	-0.19
30.1+	15%	79	1224	6.5%	-0.45
Not Compl	22%	120	1443	8.3%	-0.38
Unraced	6%	30	359	8.4%	-0.22

ANALYSIS BY SUCCESS RATE IN LAST 10 RUNS

Age	Prop	Win	Runs	Wins%	£
No Wins	36%	182	2422	7.5%	-0.43
1 Win	28%	140	1343	10.4%	-0.31
2 Wins	20%	101	627	16.1%	-0.20
3 Wins	10%	52	307	16.9%	-0.07
4 Wins	4%	21	123	17.1%	-0.33
5+ Wins	2%	9	33	27.3%	-0.27

ANALYSIS BY SUCCESS RATE IN LAST 3 RUNS

Age	Prop	Win	Runs	Wins%	£
No Wins	63%	318	3705	8.6%	-0.38
1 Win	29%	146	956	15.3%	-0.24
2 Wins	8%	39	177	22.0%	-0.07
3 Wins	0%	2	17	11.8%	-0.59

ANALYSIS BY POSITION LAST TIME

Age	Prop	Win	Runs	Wins%	£
Won	17%	92	473	19.5%	-0.18
2nd or 3rd	27%	146	1007	14.5%	-0.23
Unplaced	28%	148	1946	7.6%	-0.41
Fell,BD,UR	10%	51	422	12.1%	-0.10
Pulled Up	13%	67	988	6.8%	-0.49
Ref/RanOut	0%	1	16	6.3%	-0.84
CO/SlipUp	0%	0	3	0.0%	-1.00
Unraced	6%	30	359	8.4%	-0.22

OTHER FACTORS (WINS-RUNS, £)

Course Winner:	96-637	-£0.31
Distance Winner:	161-1141	-£0.25
Going Winner:	212-1681	-£0.31
Beaten Favourite:	49-246	-£0.09
7-Day Winners:	5-17	£0.14
BHA Top Rated:	94-422	-£0.23
Absolute Favourites:	197-486	-£0.01

TRAINERS (WINS-RUNS, £)

T R George 3-13 £0.08; Mrs O Bush 4-24 £0.02; Mrs V S Jackson 5-14 £0.03; J Wade 4-10 £0.04.

Race Profiles

Hunter Chases: 2m to 2m3f

ANALYSIS BY AGE

Age	Prop	Win	Runs	Wins%	£
3yo	0%	0	0	0.0%	0.00
4yo	0%	0	0	0.0%	0.00
5yo	3%	1	3	33.3%	0.08
6yo	0%	0	14	0.0%	-1.00
7yo	23%	7	49	14.3%	0.30
8yo	10%	3	49	6.1%	-0.44
9yo	10%	3	78	3.8%	-0.85
10yo	32%	10	67	14.9%	-0.40
11yo	6%	2	44	4.5%	-0.68
12yo+	16%	5	49	10.2%	0.11

ANALYSIS BY BHB RATING

Age	Prop	Win	Runs	Wins%	£
150+	0%	0	1	0.0%	-1.00
130..149	0%	0	2	0.0%	-1.00
120..129	13%	4	8	50.0%	0.24
110..119	10%	3	16	18.8%	-0.49
100..109	6%	2	24	8.3%	-0.68
80..99	10%	3	49	6.1%	-0.40
60..79	6%	2	27	7.4%	0.93
..59	0%	0	0	0.0%	0.00
Unrated	55%	17	226	7.5%	-0.53

ANALYSIS BY WEIGHT CARRIED

Age	Prop	Win	Runs	Wins%	£
12-01+	16%	5	27	18.5%	-0.52
11-8..12-00	52%	16	132	12.1%	-0.16
11-0..11-07	32%	10	190	5.3%	-0.52
10-8..10-13	0%	0	4	0.0%	-1.00
10-0..10-07	0%	0	0	0.0%	0.00
..9-13	0%	0	0	0.0%	0.00

ANALYSIS BY DAYS SINCE LAST RUN

Age	Prop	Win	Runs	Wins%	£
1..7	3%	1	15	6.7%	-0.70
8..14	39%	12	63	19.0%	-0.13
15..28	23%	7	70	10.0%	-0.18
29..60	10%	3	43	7.0%	-0.70
61..100	0%	0	9	0.0%	-1.00
101+	26%	8	139	5.8%	-0.39
Unraced	0%	0	14	0.0%	-1.00

ANALYSIS BY TODAY'S STARTING PRICE

Age	Prop	Win	Runs	Wins%	£
Odds On	13%	4	7	57.1%	-0.08
Ev-2/1	16%	5	12	41.7%	0.07
9/4-4/1	32%	10	42	23.8%	-0.07
9/2-6/1	10%	3	24	12.5%	-0.27
13/2-10/1	13%	4	45	8.9%	-0.21
11/1-16/1	6%	2	59	3.4%	-0.49
18/1-33/1	10%	3	74	4.1%	-0.01
40/1+	0%	0	90	0.0%	-1.00

ANALYSIS BY STARTING PRICE LAST TIME

Age	Prop	Win	Runs	Wins%	£
Odds On	3%	1	2	50.0%	-0.42
Ev-2/1	10%	3	12	25.0%	-0.39
9/4-4/1	16%	5	39	12.8%	0.22
9/2-6/1	13%	4	34	11.8%	-0.49
13/2-10/1	26%	8	66	12.1%	-0.16
11/1-16/1	6%	2	49	4.1%	-0.47
18/1-33/1	16%	5	56	8.9%	-0.50
40/1+	10%	3	81	3.7%	-0.61
Unraced	0%	0	14	0.0%	-1.00

ANALYSIS BY DISTANCE BEATEN LAST TIME

Age	Prop	Win	Runs	Wins%	£
..-10 lgh	0%	0	4	0.0%	-1.00
-10..0	26%	8	25	32.0%	0.41
0.1..2	3%	1	8	12.5%	-0.53
2.1..5	0%	0	12	0.0%	-1.00
5.1..10	6%	2	18	11.1%	-0.42
10.1..20	19%	6	34	17.6%	-0.15
20.0..30	13%	4	34	11.8%	-0.15
30.1+	10%	3	89	3.4%	-0.55
Not Compl	23%	7	115	6.1%	-0.42
Unraced	0%	0	14	0.0%	-1.00

ANALYSIS BY SUCCESS RATE IN LAST 10 RUNS

Age	Prop	Win	Runs	Wins%	£
No Wins	35%	11	169	6.5%	-0.39
1 Win	29%	9	115	7.8%	-0.54
2 Wins	26%	8	42	19.0%	-0.01
3 Wins	10%	3	10	30.0%	0.60
4 Wins	0%	0	3	0.0%	-1.00
5+ Wins	0%	0	0	0.0%	0.00

ANALYSIS BY SUCCESS RATE IN LAST 3 RUNS

Age	Prop	Win	Runs	Wins%	£
No Wins	65%	20	271	7.4%	-0.39
1 Win	23%	7	59	11.9%	-0.54
2 Wins	13%	4	9	44.4%	1.38
3 Wins	0%	0	0	0.0%	0.00

ANALYSIS BY POSITION LAST TIME

Age	Prop	Win	Runs	Wins%	£
Won	26%	8	29	27.6%	0.22
2nd or 3rd	32%	10	56	17.9%	-0.24
Unplaced	19%	6	139	4.3%	-0.50
Fell,BD,UR	10%	3	31	9.7%	-0.66
Pulled Up	10%	3	82	3.7%	-0.34
Ref/RanOut	3%	1	2	50.0%	0.25
CO/SlipUp	0%	0	0	0.0%	0.00
Unraced	0%	0	14	0.0%	-1.00

OTHER FACTORS (WINS-RUNS, £)

Course Winner:	4-26	-£0.38
Distance Winner:	6-63	-£0.76
Going Winner:	12-119	-£0.36
Beaten Favourite:	2-13	-£0.37
7-Day Winners:	0-1	-£1.00
BHA Top Rated:	5-24	-£0.43
Absolute Favourites:	13-29	£0.15

Hunter Chases

Hunter Chases: 2m4f to 2m7f

ANALYSIS BY AGE

Age	Prop	Win	Runs	Wins%	£
3yo	0%	0	0	0.0%	0.00
4yo	0%	0	0	0.0%	0.00
5yo	0%	0	16	0.0%	-1.00
6yo	4%	8	98	8.2%	-0.33
7yo	15%	29	216	13.4%	-0.04
8yo	16%	31	323	9.6%	-0.32
9yo	22%	43	371	11.6%	0.06
10yo	16%	32	375	8.5%	-0.40
11yo	10%	20	267	7.5%	-0.63
12yo+	17%	33	357	9.2%	-0.42

ANALYSIS BY BHB RATING

Age	Prop	Win	Runs	Wins%	£
150+	0%	0	1	0.0%	-1.00
130..149	6%	11	46	23.9%	-0.28
120..129	7%	14	94	14.9%	-0.55
110..119	12%	23	132	17.4%	0.32
100..109	12%	23	142	16.2%	-0.10
80..99	9%	17	242	7.0%	-0.34
60..79	1%	1	102	1.0%	-0.90
..59	0%	0	7	0.0%	-1.00
Unrated	55%	107	1257	8.5%	-0.31

ANALYSIS BY WEIGHT CARRIED

Age	Prop	Win	Runs	Wins%	£
12-01+	15%	29	143	20.3%	-0.07
11-8..12-00	47%	92	834	11.0%	-0.23
11-0..11-07	33%	65	947	6.9%	-0.41
10-8..10-13	3%	6	59	10.2%	-0.29
10-0..10-07	2%	3	39	7.7%	-0.55
..9-13	1%	1	1	100.0%	16.00

ANALYSIS BY DAYS SINCE LAST RUN

Age	Prop	Win	Runs	Wins%	£
1..7	5%	10	46	21.7%	0.18
8..14	15%	29	225	12.9%	0.08
15..28	19%	37	368	10.1%	-0.42
29..60	15%	30	221	13.6%	-0.30
61..100	2%	3	47	6.4%	-0.47
101+	37%	73	975	7.5%	-0.39
Unraced	7%	14	141	9.9%	-0.08

ANALYSIS BY TODAY'S STARTING PRICE

Age	Prop	Win	Runs	Wins%	£
Odds On	11%	22	41	53.7%	-0.13
Ev-2/1	22%	44	108	40.7%	0.01
9/4-4/1	23%	46	244	18.9%	-0.22
9/2-6/1	12%	23	144	16.0%	-0.03
13/2-10/1	13%	26	299	8.7%	-0.21
11/1-16/1	11%	22	322	6.8%	0.00
18/1-33/1	6%	11	415	2.7%	-0.33
40/1+	1%	2	450	0.4%	-0.77

ANALYSIS BY STARTING PRICE LAST TIME

Age	Prop	Win	Runs	Wins%	£
Odds On	3%	5	25	20.0%	-0.60
Ev-2/1	10%	19	78	24.4%	-0.14
9/4-4/1	16%	32	199	16.1%	-0.15
9/2-6/1	10%	20	171	11.7%	-0.51
13/2-10/1	16%	32	323	9.9%	-0.13
11/1-16/1	13%	26	339	7.7%	-0.47
18/1-33/1	18%	35	409	8.6%	-0.09
40/1+	7%	13	338	3.8%	-0.64
Unraced	7%	14	141	9.9%	-0.08

ANALYSIS BY DISTANCE BEATEN LAST TIME

Age	Prop	Win	Runs	Wins%	£
...-10 lgh	6%	12	47	25.5%	-0.26
-10..0	10%	20	114	17.5%	-0.04
0.1..2	5%	10	56	17.9%	0.14
2.1..5	4%	7	73	9.6%	-0.75
5.1..10	7%	13	98	13.3%	0.02
10.1..20	12%	23	211	10.9%	-0.22
20.0..30	9%	17	202	8.4%	-0.41
30.1+	16%	32	517	6.2%	-0.39
Not Compl	24%	48	564	8.5%	-0.37
Unraced	7%	14	141	9.9%	-0.08

ANALYSIS BY SUCCESS RATE IN LAST 10 RUNS

Age	Prop	Win	Runs	Wins%	£
No Wins	37%	67	999	6.7%	-0.39
1 Win	27%	49	495	9.9%	-0.26
2 Wins	21%	39	240	16.3%	-0.17
3 Wins	9%	16	93	17.2%	-0.21
4 Wins	4%	8	40	20.0%	-0.07
5+ Wins	2%	3	15	20.0%	-0.63

ANALYSIS BY SUCCESS RATE IN LAST 3 RUNS

Age	Prop	Win	Runs	Wins%	£
No Wins	60%	110	1477	7.4%	-0.37
1 Win	33%	60	337	17.8%	-0.12
2 Wins	5%	10	61	16.4%	-0.25
3 Wins	1%	2	7	28.6%	-0.01

ANALYSIS BY POSITION LAST TIME

Age	Prop	Win	Runs	Wins%	£
Won	16%	32	162	19.8%	-0.11
2nd or 3rd	22%	44	350	12.6%	-0.12
Unplaced	30%	58	813	7.1%	-0.41
Fell,BD,UR	11%	21	151	13.9%	0.16
Pulled Up	14%	27	400	6.8%	-0.55
Ref/RanOut	0%	0	5	0.0%	-1.00
CO/SlipUp	0%	0	1	0.0%	-1.00
Unraced	7%	14	141	9.9%	-0.08

OTHER FACTORS (WINS-RUNS, £)

Course Winner:	43-244	£0.07
Distance Winner:	58-429	-£0.10
Going Winner:	79-648	-£0.26
Beaten Favourite:	14-78	-£0.06
7-Day Winners:	2-6	-£0.22
BHA Top Rated:	35-149	-£0.13
Absolute Favourites:	69-181	-£0.11

Race Profiles

Hunter Chases: 3m+

ANALYSIS BY AGE

Age	Prop	Win	Runs	Wins%	£
3yo	0%	0	0	0.0%	0.00
4yo	0%	0	0	0.0%	0.00
5yo	0%	0	10	0.0%	-1.00
6yo	3%	8	85	9.4%	-0.58
7yo	10%	31	248	12.5%	-0.28
8yo	16%	50	453	11.0%	-0.38
9yo	20%	62	508	12.2%	-0.09
10yo	18%	56	499	11.2%	-0.34
11yo	16%	48	447	10.7%	-0.28
12yo+	17%	53	588	9.0%	-0.57

ANALYSIS BY BHB RATING

Age	Prop	Win	Runs	Wins%	£
150+	0%	0	1	0.0%	-1.00
130..149	5%	16	60	26.7%	-0.27
120..129	10%	30	132	22.7%	0.11
110..119	10%	30	218	13.8%	-0.41
100..109	10%	32	222	14.4%	-0.35
80..99	6%	19	354	5.4%	-0.68
60..79	2%	6	168	3.6%	-0.70
..59	0%	0	23	0.0%	-1.00
Unrated	57%	175	1660	10.5%	-0.26

ANALYSIS BY WEIGHT CARRIED

Age	Prop	Win	Runs	Wins%	£
12-01+	17%	51	255	20.0%	-0.16
11-8..12-00	48%	149	1239	12.0%	-0.29
11-0..11-07	32%	99	1245	8.0%	-0.41
10-8..11-13	2%	7	74	9.5%	-0.58
10-0..10-07	1%	2	25	8.0%	-0.54
..9-13	0%	0	0	0.0%	0.00

ANALYSIS BY DAYS SINCE LAST RUN

Age	Prop	Win	Runs	Wins%	£
1..7	3%	10	67	14.9%	-0.04
8..14	16%	50	367	13.6%	-0.34
15..28	22%	68	519	13.1%	-0.35
29..60	13%	40	324	12.3%	-0.31
61..100	1%	4	74	5.4%	-0.46
101+	39%	120	1283	9.4%	-0.38
Unraced	5%	16	204	7.8%	-0.26

ANALYSIS BY TODAY'S STARTING PRICE

Age	Prop	Win	Runs	Wins%	£
Odds On	13%	41	62	66.1%	0.08
Ev-2/1	21%	65	169	38.5%	0.00
9/4-4/1	32%	100	391	25.6%	0.06
9/2-6/1	7%	23	255	9.0%	-0.43
13/2-10/1	12%	38	448	8.5%	-0.26
11/1-16/1	9%	28	468	6.0%	-0.16
18/1-33/1	4%	11	580	1.9%	-0.55
40/1+	1%	2	465	0.4%	-0.82

ANALYSIS BY STARTING PRICE LAST TIME

Age	Prop	Win	Runs	Wins%	£
Odds On	5%	16	61	26.2%	0.04
Ev-2/1	12%	36	144	25.0%	0.05
9/4-4/1	20%	61	346	17.6%	-0.19
9/2-6/1	11%	35	269	13.0%	-0.13
13/2-10/1	15%	45	479	9.4%	-0.49
11/1-16/1	10%	32	462	6.9%	-0.50
18/1-33/1	13%	41	508	8.1%	-0.37
40/1+	8%	26	365	7.1%	-0.49
Unraced	5%	16	204	7.8%	-0.26

ANALYSIS BY DISTANCE BEATEN LAST TIME

Age	Prop	Win	Runs	Wins%	£
..-10 lgh	5%	16	79	20.3%	-0.35
-10..0	12%	36	203	17.7%	-0.21
0.1..2	7%	22	138	15.9%	-0.50
2.1..5	7%	23	129	17.8%	-0.20
5.1..10	8%	25	166	15.1%	-0.27
10.1..20	10%	30	295	10.2%	-0.43
20.0..30	10%	31	242	12.8%	-0.01
30.1+	14%	44	618	7.1%	-0.48
Not Compl	21%	65	764	8.5%	-0.38
Unraced	5%	16	204	7.8%	-0.26

ANALYSIS BY SUCCESS RATE IN LAST 10 RUNS

Age	Prop	Win	Runs	Wins%	£
No Wins	36%	104	1254	8.3%	-0.46
1 Win	28%	82	733	11.2%	-0.31
2 Wins	18%	54	345	15.7%	-0.24
3 Wins	11%	33	204	16.2%	-0.03
4 Wins	4%	13	80	16.3%	-0.44
5+ Wins	2%	6	18	33.3%	0.03

ANALYSIS BY SUCCESS RATE IN LAST 3 RUNS

Age	Prop	Win	Runs	Wins%	£
No Wins	64%	188	1957	9.6%	-0.38
1 Win	27%	79	560	14.1%	-0.28
2 Wins	9%	25	107	23.4%	-0.09
3 Wins	0%	0	10	0.0%	-1.00

ANALYSIS BY POSITION LAST TIME

Age	Prop	Win	Runs	Wins%	£
Won	17%	52	282	18.4%	-0.25
2nd or 3rd	30%	92	601	15.3%	-0.29
Unplaced	27%	84	994	8.5%	-0.39
Fell,BD,UR	9%	27	240	11.3%	-0.18
Pulled Up	12%	37	506	7.3%	-0.47
Ref/RanOut	0%	0	9	0.0%	-1.00
CO/SlipUp	0%	0	2	0.0%	-1.00
Unraced	5%	16	204	7.8%	-0.26

OTHER FACTORS (WINS-RUNS, £)

Course Winner:	49-367	-£0.56
Distance Winner:	97-649	-£0.29
Going Winner:	121-914	-£0.34
Beaten Favourite:	33-155	-£0.08
7-Day Winners:	3-10	£0.47
BHA Top Rated:	54-249	-£0.27
Absolute Favourites:	115-276	£0.03

Hunter Chases

Hunter Chases: 2 to 5 runners

ANALYSIS BY AGE

Age	Prop	Win	Runs	Wins%	£
3yo	0%	0	0	0.0%	0.00
4yo	0%	0	0	0.0%	0.00
5yo	0%	0	2	0.0%	-1.00
6yo	5%	2	5	40.0%	0.07
7yo	8%	3	18	16.7%	-0.63
8yo	8%	3	25	12.0%	-0.47
9yo	23%	9	26	34.6%	0.43
10yo	21%	8	32	25.0%	-0.29
11yo	13%	5	31	16.1%	-0.44
12yo+	23%	9	39	23.1%	-0.41

ANALYSIS BY BHB RATING

Age	Prop	Win	Runs	Wins%	£
150+	0%	0	0	0.0%	0.00
130..149	3%	1	6	16.7%	-0.71
120..129	10%	4	10	40.0%	-0.24
110..119	18%	7	16	43.8%	0.22
100..109	13%	5	21	23.8%	-0.44
80..99	0%	0	17	0.0%	-1.00
60..79	3%	1	7	14.3%	-0.66
..59	0%	0	0	0.0%	0.00
Unrated	54%	21	101	20.8%	-0.18

ANALYSIS BY WEIGHT CARRIED

Age	Prop	Win	Runs	Wins%	£
12-01+	18%	7	21	33.3%	0.25
11-8..12-00	54%	21	69	30.4%	-0.23
11-0..11-07	28%	11	83	13.3%	-0.44
10-8..10-13	0%	0	4	0.0%	-1.00
10-0..10-07	0%	0	1	0.0%	-1.00
..9-13	0%	0	0	0.0%	0.00

ANALYSIS BY DAYS SINCE LAST RUN

Age	Prop	Win	Runs	Wins%	£
1..7	3%	1	4	25.0%	-0.58
8..14	15%	6	22	27.3%	-0.08
15..28	26%	10	29	34.5%	-0.26
29..60	15%	6	15	40.0%	1.12
61..100	0%	0	4	0.0%	-1.00
101+	41%	16	97	16.5%	-0.48
Unraced	0%	0	7	0.0%	-1.00

ANALYSIS BY TODAY'S STARTING PRICE

Age	Prop	Win	Runs	Wins%	£
Odds On	31%	12	17	70.6%	0.16
Ev-2/1	38%	15	35	42.9%	0.05
9/4-4/1	21%	8	37	21.6%	-0.09
9/2-6/1	5%	2	16	12.5%	-0.28
13/2-10/1	3%	1	31	3.2%	-0.69
11/1-16/1	3%	1	23	4.3%	-0.35
18/1-33/1	0%	0	15	0.0%	-1.00
40/1+	0%	0	4	0.0%	-1.00

ANALYSIS BY STARTING PRICE LAST TIME

Age	Prop	Win	Runs	Wins%	£
Odds On	5%	2	2	100.0%	4.58
Ev-2/1	21%	8	15	53.3%	0.27
9/4-4/1	10%	4	13	30.8%	0.29
9/2-6/1	13%	5	25	20.0%	-0.44
13/2-10/1	8%	3	32	9.4%	-0.74
11/1-16/1	5%	2	30	6.7%	-0.74
18/1-33/1	26%	10	36	27.8%	0.00
40/1+	13%	5	18	27.8%	-0.29
Unraced	0%	0	7	0.0%	-1.00

ANALYSIS BY DISTANCE BEATEN LAST TIME

Age	Prop	Win	Runs	Wins%	£
..-10 lgh	10%	4	5	80.0%	0.52
-10..0	10%	4	9	44.4%	1.05
0.1..2	3%	1	3	33.3%	-0.33
2.1..5	8%	3	6	50.0%	0.11
5.1..10	3%	1	11	9.1%	-0.80
10.1..20	8%	3	19	15.8%	0.19
20.0..30	13%	5	19	26.3%	-0.09
30.1+	21%	8	47	17.0%	-0.61
Not Compl	26%	10	52	19.2%	-0.41
Unraced	0%	0	7	0.0%	-1.00

ANALYSIS BY SUCCESS RATE IN LAST 10 RUNS

Age	Prop	Win	Runs	Wins%	£
No Wins	36%	14	71	19.7%	-0.28
1 Win	26%	10	49	20.4%	-0.40
2 Wins	28%	11	34	32.4%	0.11
3 Wins	5%	2	9	22.2%	-0.54
4 Wins	5%	2	7	28.6%	-0.55
5+ Wins	0%	0	1	0.0%	-1.00

ANALYSIS BY SUCCESS RATE IN LAST 3 RUNS

Age	Prop	Win	Runs	Wins%	£
No Wins	59%	23	125	18.4%	-0.41
1 Win	31%	12	39	30.8%	0.12
2 Wins	10%	4	6	66.7%	0.45
3 Wins	0%	0	1	0.0%	-1.00

ANALYSIS BY POSITION LAST TIME

Age	Prop	Win	Runs	Wins%	£
Won	21%	8	14	57.1%	0.86
2nd or 3rd	23%	9	33	27.3%	0.16
Unplaced	31%	12	72	16.7%	-0.57
Fell,BD,UR	8%	3	18	16.7%	-0.45
Pulled Up	18%	7	34	20.6%	-0.38
Ref/RanOut	0%	0	0	0.0%	0.00
CO/SlipUp	0%	0	0	0.0%	0.00
Unraced	0%	0	7	0.0%	-1.00

OTHER FACTORS (WINS-RUNS, £)

Course Winner:	5-18	£0.08
Distance Winner:	10-48	-£0.49
Going Winner:	18-64	-£0.20
Beaten Favourite:	3-10	-£0.36
7-Day Winners:	1-1	£0.67
BHA Top Rated:	11-28	-£0.16
Absolute Favourites:	23-37	£0.23

Race Profiles

Hunter Chases: 6 to 10 runners

ANALYSIS BY AGE

Age	Prop	Win	Runs	Wins%	£
3yo	0%	0	0	0.0%	0.00
4yo	0%	0	0	0.0%	0.00
5yo	0%	1	18	5.6%	-0.82
6yo	3%	8	82	9.8%	-0.34
7yo	11%	35	215	16.3%	-0.25
8yo	14%	44	369	11.9%	-0.36
9yo	21%	64	430	14.9%	-0.16
10yo	21%	64	448	14.3%	-0.18
11yo	13%	40	380	10.5%	-0.33
12yo+	16%	50	474	10.5%	-0.53

ANALYSIS BY BHB RATING

Age	Prop	Win	Runs	Wins%	£
150+	0%	0	2	0.0%	-1.00
130..149	7%	20	56	35.7%	-0.23
120..129	10%	30	125	24.0%	-0.20
110..119	11%	35	177	19.8%	-0.15
100..109	11%	34	193	17.6%	-0.24
80..99	8%	24	311	7.7%	-0.53
60..79	2%	5	122	4.1%	-0.60
..59	0%	0	20	0.0%	-1.00
Unrated	52%	158	1410	11.2%	-0.28

ANALYSIS BY WEIGHT CARRIED

Age	Prop	Win	Runs	Wins%	£
12-01+	16%	49	232	21.1%	-0.16
11-8..12-00	47%	143	941	15.2%	-0.28
11-0..11-07	33%	101	1127	9.0%	-0.37
10-8..10-13	3%	10	76	13.2%	-0.34
10-0..10-07	1%	2	39	5.1%	-0.68
..9-13	0%	1	1	100.0%	16.00

ANALYSIS BY DAYS SINCE LAST RUN

Age	Prop	Win	Runs	Wins%	£
1..7	4%	12	65	18.5%	0.04
8..14	16%	50	309	16.2%	-0.32
15..28	22%	67	419	16.0%	-0.29
29..60	12%	37	237	15.6%	-0.27
61..100	2%	5	63	7.9%	-0.12
101+	39%	119	1163	10.2%	-0.38
Unraced	5%	16	160	10.0%	-0.20

ANALYSIS BY TODAY'S STARTING PRICE

Age	Prop	Win	Runs	Wins%	£
Odds On	15%	45	73	61.6%	0.00
Ev-2/1	25%	77	191	40.3%	0.02
9/4-4/1	29%	90	384	23.4%	-0.04
9/2-6/1	8%	25	226	11.1%	-0.33
13/2-10/1	11%	34	408	8.3%	-0.27
11/1-16/1	9%	29	394	7.4%	0.03
18/1-33/1	2%	5	467	1.1%	-0.73
40/1+	0%	1	273	0.4%	-0.85

ANALYSIS BY STARTING PRICE LAST TIME

Age	Prop	Win	Runs	Wins%	£
Odds On	5%	14	48	29.2%	-0.32
Ev-2/1	10%	30	99	30.3%	-0.01
9/4-4/1	20%	60	290	20.7%	-0.15
9/2-6/1	10%	31	230	13.5%	-0.18
13/2-10/1	18%	54	400	13.5%	-0.33
11/1-16/1	11%	34	394	8.6%	-0.40
18/1-33/1	13%	40	430	9.3%	-0.39
40/1+	9%	27	365	7.4%	-0.45
Unraced	5%	16	160	10.0%	-0.20

ANALYSIS BY DISTANCE BEATEN LAST TIME

Age	Prop	Win	Runs	Wins%	£
..-10 lgh	6%	17	57	29.8%	-0.24
-10..0	10%	32	153	20.9%	-0.25
0.1..2	6%	19	93	20.4%	-0.40
2.1..5	6%	19	107	17.8%	-0.39
5.1..10	7%	22	138	15.9%	-0.24
10.1..20	13%	39	256	15.2%	-0.08
20.0..30	9%	28	225	12.4%	-0.40
30.1+	15%	45	549	8.2%	-0.38
Not Compl	23%	69	678	10.2%	-0.36
Unraced	5%	16	160	10.0%	-0.20

ANALYSIS BY SUCCESS RATE IN LAST 10 RUNS

Age	Prop	Win	Runs	Wins%	£
No Wins	34%	98	1055	9.3%	-0.41
1 Win	29%	85	669	12.7%	-0.33
2 Wins	20%	59	291	20.3%	-0.03
3 Wins	9%	27	163	16.6%	-0.27
4 Wins	5%	14	65	21.5%	-0.36
5+ Wins	2%	7	13	53.8%	0.32

ANALYSIS BY SUCCESS RATE IN LAST 3 RUNS

Age	Prop	Win	Runs	Wins%	£
No Wins	63%	184	1698	10.8%	-0.37
1 Win	29%	85	477	17.8%	-0.21
2 Wins	7%	20	73	27.4%	0.10
3 Wins	0%	1	8	12.5%	-0.38

ANALYSIS BY POSITION LAST TIME

Age	Prop	Win	Runs	Wins%	£
Won	16%	49	211	23.2%	-0.25
2nd or 3rd	27%	84	478	17.6%	-0.28
Unplaced	29%	89	894	10.0%	-0.33
Fell,BD,UR	9%	27	190	14.2%	-0.22
Pulled Up	13%	40	472	8.5%	-0.42
Ref/RanOut	0%	1	9	11.1%	-0.72
CO/SlipUp	0%	0	2	0.0%	-1.00
Unraced	5%	16	160	10.0%	-0.20

OTHER FACTORS (WINS-RUNS, £)

Course Winner:	63-329	-£0.32
Distance Winner:	101-606	-£0.29
Going Winner:	125-784	-£0.29
Beaten Favourite:	27-128	-£0.24
7-Day Winners:	2-5	£0.33
BHA Top Rated:	60-237	-£0.12
Absolute Favourites:	119-282	-£0.04

Hunter Chases

Hunter Chases: 11 runners or more

ANALYSIS BY AGE

Age	Prop	Win	Runs	Wins%	£
3yo	0%	0	0	0.0%	0.00
4yo	0%	0	0	0.0%	0.00
5yo	0%	0	9	0.0%	-1.00
6yo	3%	6	110	5.5%	-0.61
7yo	15%	29	280	10.4%	0.01
8yo	19%	37	431	8.6%	-0.36
9yo	18%	35	501	7.0%	-0.07
10yo	14%	26	461	5.6%	-0.56
11yo	13%	25	347	7.2%	-0.53
12yo+	17%	32	481	6.7%	-0.44

ANALYSIS BY BHB RATING

Age	Prop	Win	Runs	Wins%	£
150+	0%	0	1	0.0%	-1.00
130..149	3%	6	46	13.0%	-0.29
120..129	7%	14	99	14.1%	-0.07
110..119	7%	14	173	8.1%	-0.19
100..109	9%	18	174	10.3%	-0.31
80..99	8%	15	317	4.7%	-0.51
60..79	2%	3	168	1.8%	-0.63
..59	0%	0	10	0.0%	-1.00
Unrated	63%	120	1632	7.4%	-0.32

ANALYSIS BY WEIGHT CARRIED

Age	Prop	Win	Runs	Wins%	£
12-01+	15%	29	172	16.9%	-0.19
11-8..12-00	49%	93	1195	7.8%	-0.25
11-0..11-07	33%	62	1172	5.3%	-0.47
10-8..10-13	2%	3	57	5.3%	-0.61
10-0..10-07	2%	3	24	12.5%	-0.31
..9-13	0%	0	0	0.0%	0.00

ANALYSIS BY DAYS SINCE LAST RUN

Age	Prop	Win	Runs	Wins%	£
1..7	4%	8	59	13.6%	-0.08
8..14	18%	35	324	10.8%	-0.05
15..28	18%	35	509	6.9%	-0.43
29..60	16%	30	336	8.9%	-0.44
61..100	1%	2	63	3.2%	-0.86
101+	35%	66	1137	5.8%	-0.38
Unraced	7%	14	192	7.3%	-0.21

ANALYSIS BY TODAY'S STARTING PRICE

Age	Prop	Win	Runs	Wins%	£
Odds On	5%	10	20	50.0%	-0.16
Ev-2/1	12%	22	63	34.9%	-0.07
9/4-4/1	31%	58	256	22.7%	-0.06
9/2-6/1	12%	22	181	12.2%	-0.22
13/2-10/1	17%	33	353	9.3%	-0.17
11/1-16/1	12%	22	432	5.1%	-0.25
18/1-33/1	11%	20	587	3.4%	-0.17
40/1+	2%	3	728	0.4%	-0.80

ANALYSIS BY STARTING PRICE LAST TIME

Age	Prop	Win	Runs	Wins%	£
Odds On	3%	6	38	15.8%	-0.18
Ev-2/1	11%	20	120	16.7%	-0.09
9/4-4/1	18%	34	281	12.1%	-0.18
9/2-6/1	12%	23	219	10.5%	-0.40
13/2-10/1	15%	28	436	6.4%	-0.30
11/1-16/1	13%	24	426	5.6%	-0.54
18/1-33/1	16%	31	507	6.1%	-0.17
40/1+	5%	10	401	2.5%	-0.69
Unraced	7%	14	192	7.3%	-0.21

ANALYSIS BY DISTANCE BEATEN LAST TIME

Age	Prop	Win	Runs	Wins%	£
..-10 lgh	4%	7	68	10.3%	-0.49
-10..0	15%	28	180	15.6%	-0.05
0.1..2	7%	13	106	12.3%	-0.25
2.1..5	4%	8	101	7.9%	-0.51
5.1..10	9%	17	133	12.8%	-0.06
10.1..20	9%	17	265	6.4%	-0.61
20.0..30	10%	19	234	8.1%	0.01
30.1+	14%	26	628	4.1%	-0.49
Not Compl	22%	41	713	5.8%	-0.39
Unraced	7%	14	192	7.3%	-0.21

ANALYSIS BY SUCCESS RATE IN LAST 10 RUNS

Age	Prop	Win	Runs	Wins%	£
No Wins	40%	70	1296	5.4%	-0.45
1 Win	26%	45	625	7.2%	-0.29
2 Wins	18%	31	302	10.3%	-0.39
3 Wins	13%	23	135	17.0%	0.20
4 Wins	3%	5	51	9.8%	-0.27
5+ Wins	1%	2	19	10.5%	-0.64

ANALYSIS BY SUCCESS RATE IN LAST 3 RUNS

Age	Prop	Win	Runs	Wins%	£
No Wins	63%	111	1882	5.9%	-0.38
1 Win	28%	49	440	11.1%	-0.31
2 Wins	9%	15	98	15.3%	-0.23
3 Wins	1%	1	8	12.5%	-0.76

ANALYSIS BY POSITION LAST TIME

Age	Prop	Win	Runs	Wins%	£
Won	18%	35	248	14.1%	-0.17
2nd or 3rd	28%	53	496	10.7%	-0.21
Unplaced	25%	47	980	4.8%	-0.47
Fell,BD,UR	11%	21	214	9.8%	0.04
Pulled Up	11%	20	482	4.1%	-0.56
Ref/RanOut	0%	0	7	0.0%	-1.00
CO/SlipUp	0%	0	1	0.0%	-1.00
Unraced	7%	14	192	7.3%	-0.21

OTHER FACTORS (WINS-RUNS, £)

Course Winner:	28-290	-£0.33
Distance Winner:	50-487	-£0.16
Going Winner:	69-833	-£0.34
Beaten Favourite:	19-108	£0.13
7-Day Winners:	2-11	£0.00
BHA Top Rated:	23-157	-£0.41
Absolute Favourites:	55-167	-£0.02

Race Profiles

Hunter Chases: up to 7 days off the track

ANALYSIS BY AGE

Age	Prop	Win	Runs	Wins%	£
3yo	0%	0	0	0.0%	0.00
4yo	0%	0	0	0.0%	0.00
5yo	0%	0	8	0.0%	-1.00
6yo	10%	5	58	8.6%	-0.28
7yo	24%	12	108	11.1%	-0.04
8yo	18%	9	107	8.4%	-0.38
9yo	20%	10	79	12.7%	0.05
10yo	10%	5	55	9.1%	-0.22
11yo	10%	5	35	14.3%	-0.22
12yo+	10%	5	37	13.5%	0.05

ANALYSIS BY BHB RATING

Age	Prop	Win	Runs	Wins%	£
150+	0%	0	0	0.0%	0.00
130..149	2%	1	5	20.0%	-0.56
120..129	6%	3	6	50.0%	0.89
110..119	8%	4	15	26.7%	0.94
100..109	4%	2	8	25.0%	-0.08
80..99	4%	2	20	10.0%	-0.38
60..79	0%	0	9	0.0%	-1.00
..59	0%	0	1	0.0%	-1.00
Unrated	76%	39	423	9.2%	-0.19

ANALYSIS BY WEIGHT CARRIED

Age	Prop	Win	Runs	Wins%	£
12-01+	12%	6	21	28.6%	0.53
11-8..12-00	41%	21	187	11.2%	-0.15
11-0..11-07	43%	22	253	8.7%	-0.26
10-8..10-13	2%	1	20	5.0%	0.05
10-0..10-07	2%	1	6	16.7%	-0.33
..9-13	0%	0	0	0.0%	0.00

ANALYSIS BY DAYS SINCE LAST RUN

Age	Prop	Win	Runs	Wins%	£
1..7	41%	21	128	16.4%	-0.04
8..14	0%	0	0	0.0%	0.00
15..28	0%	0	0	0.0%	0.00
29..60	0%	0	0	0.0%	0.00
61..100	0%	0	0	0.0%	0.00
101+	0%	0	0	0.0%	0.00
Unraced	59%	30	359	8.4%	-0.22

ANALYSIS BY TODAY'S STARTING PRICE

Age	Prop	Win	Runs	Wins%	£
Odds On	12%	6	10	60.0%	0.01
Ev-2/1	18%	9	24	37.5%	-0.05
9/4-4/1	22%	11	51	21.6%	-0.08
9/2-6/1	8%	4	30	13.3%	-0.18
13/2-10/1	18%	9	80	11.3%	0.04
11/1-16/1	16%	8	98	8.2%	0.16
18/1-33/1	6%	3	102	2.9%	-0.40
40/1+	2%	1	92	1.1%	-0.55

ANALYSIS BY STARTING PRICE LAST TIME

Age	Prop	Win	Runs	Wins%	£
Odds On	6%	3	6	50.0%	0.89
Ev-2/1	4%	2	6	33.3%	-0.24
9/4-4/1	12%	6	13	46.2%	1.70
9/2-6/1	4%	2	9	22.2%	-0.17
13/2-10/1	2%	1	18	5.6%	-0.78
11/1-16/1	8%	4	24	16.7%	0.46
18/1-33/1	4%	2	29	6.9%	-0.84
40/1+	2%	1	23	4.3%	-0.09
Unraced	59%	30	359	8.4%	-0.22

ANALYSIS BY DISTANCE BEATEN LAST TIME

Age	Prop	Win	Runs	Wins%	£
..-10 lgh	4%	2	6	33.3%	0.61
-10..0	6%	3	11	27.3%	-0.12
0.1..2	4%	2	7	28.6%	-0.25
2.1..5	2%	1	4	25.0%	-0.06
5.1..10	10%	5	8	62.5%	3.31
10.1..20	0%	0	12	0.0%	-1.00
20.0..30	4%	2	17	11.8%	-0.62
30.1+	4%	2	25	8.0%	-0.36
Not Compl	8%	4	38	10.5%	0.00
Unraced	59%	30	359	8.4%	-0.22

ANALYSIS BY SUCCESS RATE IN LAST 10 RUNS

Age	Prop	Win	Runs	Wins%	£
No Wins	19%	4	60	6.7%	-0.03
1 Win	33%	7	33	21.2%	-0.20
2 Wins	38%	8	19	42.1%	0.50
3 Wins	5%	1	11	9.1%	-0.27
4 Wins	0%	0	3	0.0%	-1.00
5+ Wins	5%	1	2	50.0%	-0.17

ANALYSIS BY SUCCESS RATE IN LAST 3 RUNS

Age	Prop	Win	Runs	Wins%	£
No Wins	48%	10	92	10.9%	-0.12
1 Win	38%	8	28	28.6%	0.07
2 Wins	14%	3	8	37.5%	0.58
3 Wins	0%	0	0	0.0%	0.00

ANALYSIS BY POSITION LAST TIME

Age	Prop	Win	Runs	Wins%	£
Won	10%	5	17	29.4%	0.14
2nd or 3rd	14%	7	28	25.0%	0.42
Unplaced	10%	5	45	11.1%	-0.42
Fell,BD,UR	6%	3	22	13.6%	-0.23
Pulled Up	2%	1	16	6.3%	0.31
Ref/RanOut	0%	0	0	0.0%	0.00
CO/SlipUp	0%	0	0	0.0%	0.00
Unraced	59%	30	359	8.4%	-0.22

OTHER FACTORS (WINS-RUNS, £)

Course Winner:	6-15	£0.39
Distance Winner:	9-29	£0.65
Going Winner:	13-50	£0.41
Beaten Favourite:	3-5	£1.28
7-Day Winners:	5-17	£0.14
BHA Top Rated:	6-17	£1.35
Absolute Favourites:	17-43	-£0.02

Hunter Chases

Hunter Chases: 100+ days off the track

ANALYSIS BY AGE

Age	Prop	Win	Runs	Wins%	£
3yo	0%	0	0	0.0%	0.00
4yo	0%	0	0	0.0%	0.00
5yo	0%	0	14	0.0%	-1.00
6yo	3%	6	80	7.5%	-0.64
7yo	12%	25	190	13.2%	-0.12
8yo	17%	34	356	9.6%	-0.28
9yo	19%	38	440	8.6%	-0.21
10yo	17%	35	437	8.0%	-0.42
11yo	12%	25	378	6.6%	-0.55
12yo+	19%	38	502	7.6%	-0.49

ANALYSIS BY BHB RATING

Age	Prop	Win	Runs	Wins%	£
150+	0%	0	1	0.0%	-1.00
130..149	6%	12	45	26.7%	-0.07
120..129	6%	12	80	15.0%	-0.04
110..119	6%	12	110	10.9%	-0.10
100..109	7%	14	117	12.0%	-0.23
80..99	4%	8	217	3.7%	-0.75
60..79	1%	3	129	2.3%	-0.73
..59	0%	0	16	0.0%	-1.00
Unrated	70%	140	1682	8.3%	-0.36

ANALYSIS BY WEIGHT CARRIED

Age	Prop	Win	Runs	Wins%	£
12-01+	11%	22	157	14.0%	-0.21
11-8..12-00	48%	97	954	10.2%	-0.32
11-0..11-07	40%	80	1211	6.6%	-0.42
10-8..10-13	1%	2	64	3.1%	-0.92
10-0..10-07	0%	0	11	0.0%	-1.00
..9-13	0%	0	0	0.0%	0.00

ANALYSIS BY DAYS SINCE LAST RUN

Age	Prop	Win	Runs	Wins%	£
1..7	0%	0	0	0.0%	0.00
8..14	0%	0	0	0.0%	0.00
15..28	0%	0	0	0.0%	0.00
29..60	0%	0	0	0.0%	0.00
61..100	0%	0	0	0.0%	0.00
101+	100%	201	2397	8.4%	-0.38
Unraced	0%	0	0	0.0%	0.00

ANALYSIS BY TODAY'S STARTING PRICE

Age	Prop	Win	Runs	Wins%	£
Odds On	5%	11	22	50.0%	-0.21
Ev-2/1	23%	46	100	46.0%	0.18
9/4-4/1	27%	55	257	21.4%	-0.14
9/2-6/1	11%	23	177	13.0%	-0.18
13/2-10/1	15%	30	362	8.3%	-0.27
11/1-16/1	10%	21	387	5.4%	-0.25
18/1-33/1	6%	13	561	2.3%	-0.42
40/1+	1%	2	531	0.4%	-0.83

ANALYSIS BY STARTING PRICE LAST TIME

Age	Prop	Win	Runs	Wins%	£
Odds On	3%	6	29	20.7%	-0.15
Ev-2/1	7%	14	80	17.5%	-0.04
9/4-4/1	13%	26	248	10.5%	-0.25
9/2-6/1	10%	20	245	8.2%	-0.49
13/2-10/1	20%	41	454	9.0%	-0.38
11/1-16/1	12%	24	465	5.2%	-0.61
18/1-33/1	22%	45	493	9.1%	-0.11
40/1+	12%	25	383	6.5%	-0.56
Unraced	0%	0	0	0.0%	0.00

ANALYSIS BY DISTANCE BEATEN LAST TIME

Age	Prop	Win	Runs	Wins%	£
..-10 lgh	2%	4	35	11.4%	-0.75
-10..0	5%	11	99	11.1%	-0.34
0.1..2	4%	9	62	14.5%	-0.33
2.1..5	5%	10	72	13.9%	-0.30
5.1..10	4%	8	129	6.2%	-0.61
10.1..20	10%	20	249	8.0%	-0.41
20.0..30	11%	23	245	9.4%	-0.17
30.1+	25%	50	684	7.3%	-0.39
Not Compl	33%	66	822	8.0%	-0.40
Unraced	0%	0	0	0.0%	0.00

ANALYSIS BY SUCCESS RATE IN LAST 10 RUNS

Age	Prop	Win	Runs	Wins%	£
No Wins	49%	98	1355	7.2%	-0.45
1 Win	26%	53	614	8.6%	-0.36
2 Wins	12%	24	261	9.2%	-0.38
3 Wins	8%	16	115	13.9%	0.04
4 Wins	4%	8	44	18.2%	0.17
5+ Wins	1%	2	8	25.0%	0.17

ANALYSIS BY SUCCESS RATE IN LAST 3 RUNS

Age	Prop	Win	Runs	Wins%	£
No Wins	78%	156	1970	7.9%	-0.39
1 Win	17%	35	361	9.7%	-0.41
2 Wins	4%	9	57	15.8%	-0.14
3 Wins	0%	1	9	11.1%	-0.44

ANALYSIS BY POSITION LAST TIME

Age	Prop	Win	Runs	Wins%	£
Won	7%	15	135	11.1%	-0.45
2nd or 3rd	17%	35	356	9.8%	-0.44
Unplaced	43%	86	1095	7.9%	-0.34
Fell,BD,UR	10%	20	169	11.8%	0.00
Pulled Up	22%	45	635	7.1%	-0.50
Ref/RanOut	0%	0	6	0.0%	-1.00
CO/SlipUp	0%	0	1	0.0%	-1.00
Unraced	0%	0	0	0.0%	0.00

OTHER FACTORS (WINS-RUNS, £)

Course Winner:	27-276	-£0.33
Distance Winner:	53-492	-£0.14
Going Winner:	70-719	-£0.33
Beaten Favourite:	21-118	£0.08
BHA Top Rated:	23-141	-£0.31
Absolute Favourites:	60-148	£0.03

Race Profiles

National Hunt Flat Races

ANALYSIS BY AGE

Age	Prop	Win	Runs	Wins%	£
3yo	0%	1	8	12.5%	0.63
4yo	44%	517	5539	9.3%	-0.28
5yo	41%	482	5994	8.0%	-0.34
6yo	14%	163	2512	6.5%	-0.33
7yo	0%	1	20	5.0%	-0.55
8yo+	0%	0	0	0.0%	0.00

ANALYSIS BY BHB RATING

Age	Prop	Win	Runs	Wins%	£
130..149	0%	1	5	20.0%	0.10
120..129	0%	1	41	2.4%	0.00
110..119	0%	4	76	5.3%	0.36
100..109	0%	2	34	5.9%	-0.07
80..99	0%	0	6	0.0%	-1.00
60..79	0%	0	0	0.0%	0.00
..59	0%	0	0	0.0%	0.00
Unrated	99%	1156	13911	8.3%	-0.32

ANALYSIS BY WEIGHT CARRIED

Age	Prop	Win	Runs	Wins%	£
12-01+	0%	0	0	0.0%	0.00
11-8..12-00	4%	45	255	17.6%	-0.24
11-0..11-07	46%	540	5433	9.9%	-0.26
10-8..10-13	33%	379	4936	7.7%	-0.33
10-0..10-07	16%	191	3181	6.0%	-0.38
..9-13	1%	9	268	3.4%	-0.53

ANALYSIS BY DAYS SINCE LAST RUN

Age	Prop	Win	Runs	Wins%	£
1..7	1%	7	98	7.1%	-0.60
8..14	4%	41	581	7.1%	-0.56
15..28	14%	165	2041	8.1%	-0.37
29..60	17%	203	2232	9.1%	-0.32
61..100	7%	79	891	8.9%	-0.31
101+	13%	157	1946	8.1%	-0.30
Unraced	44%	512	6284	8.1%	-0.28

ANALYSIS BY TODAY'S STARTING PRICE

Age	Prop	Win	Runs	Wins%	£
Odds On	9%	101	201	50.2%	-0.18
Ev-2/1	18%	205	605	33.9%	-0.13
9/4-4/1	29%	339	1486	22.8%	-0.07
9/2-6/1	12%	144	1008	14.3%	-0.13
13/2-10/1	14%	165	1877	8.8%	-0.21
11/1-16/1	9%	106	2020	5.2%	-0.21
18/1-33/1	7%	82	3117	2.6%	-0.32
40/1+	2%	22	3759	0.6%	-0.62

ANALYSIS BY STARTING PRICE LAST TIME

Age	Prop	Win	Runs	Wins%	£
Odds On	2%	27	119	22.7%	0.04
Ev-2/1	5%	64	332	19.3%	-0.32
9/4-4/1	12%	140	823	17.0%	-0.03
9/2-6/1	6%	72	584	12.3%	-0.23
13/2-10/1	11%	127	1111	11.4%	-0.16
11/1-16/1	7%	78	1126	6.9%	-0.37
18/1-33/1	9%	103	1812	5.7%	-0.34
40/1+	4%	41	1882	2.2%	-0.67
Unraced	44%	512	6284	8.1%	-0.28

ANALYSIS BY DISTANCE BEATEN LAST TIME

Age	Prop	Win	Runs	Wins%	£
..-10 lgh	2%	27	95	28.4%	0.13
-10..0	11%	126	722	17.5%	-0.03
0.1..2	7%	86	469	18.3%	-0.26
2.1..5	7%	76	532	14.3%	-0.15
5.1..10	9%	103	875	11.8%	-0.22
10.1..20	11%	123	1495	8.2%	-0.37
20.0..30	4%	44	994	4.4%	-0.50
30.1+	5%	59	2417	2.4%	-0.52
Not Compl	1%	8	190	4.2%	-0.08
Unraced	44%	512	6284	8.1%	-0.28

ANALYSIS BY SUCCESS RATE IN LAST 10 RUNS

Age	Prop	Win	Runs	Wins%	£
No Wins	69%	451	6659	6.8%	-0.41
1 Win	28%	180	986	18.3%	0.02
2 Wins	2%	16	130	12.3%	-0.20
3 Wins	1%	4	13	30.8%	-0.09
4 Wins	0%	1	1	100.0%	2.50
5+ Wins	0%	0	0	0.0%	0.00

ANALYSIS BY SUCCESS RATE IN LAST 3 RUNS

Age	Prop	Win	Runs	Wins%	£
No Wins	69%	451	6666	6.8%	-0.41
1 Win	28%	180	992	18.1%	0.01
2 Wins	2%	16	119	13.4%	-0.13
3 Wins	1%	5	12	41.7%	0.28

ANALYSIS BY POSITION LAST TIME

Age	Prop	Win	Runs	Wins%	£
Won	13%	153	816	18.8%	-0.01
2nd or 3rd	19%	223	1557	14.3%	-0.28
Unplaced	23%	268	5229	5.1%	-0.44
Fell,BD,UR	0%	3	42	7.1%	1.74
Pulled Up	0%	1	99	1.0%	-0.87
Ref/RanOut	0%	3	34	8.8%	-0.63
CO/SlipUp	0%	1	12	8.3%	1.83
Unraced	44%	512	6284	8.1%	-0.28

OTHER FACTORS (WINS-RUNS, £)

Course Winner:	38-144	-£0.24
Distance Winner:	116-619	-£0.20
Going Winner:	58-327	-£0.16
Beaten Favourite:	63-364	-£0.26
7-Day Winners:	0-4	-£1.00
Absolute Favourites:	375-1094	-£0.11

TRAINERS (WINS-RUNS, £)

Mrs L B Normile 3-73 £0.29; D E Pipe 19-80 £0.23; P D Evans 3-29 £0.60; S Pike 3-14 £1.11; A G Newcombe 3-24 £0.52; N J Henderson 77-262 £0.05; Miss Rebecca Curtis 10-27 £0.45; N J Gifford 12-58 £0.20; Andrew Turnell 4-30 £0.37; C E Longsdon 3-56 £0.16; J A B Old 6-65 £0.12; P D Niven 5-39 £0.15; W S Kittow 3-20 £0.20; J J Lambe 6-34 £0.11; Karen McLintock 7-36 £0.09; S R B Crawford 3-13 £0.21; Jean-Rene Auvray 3-21 £0.12; Carl Llewellyn 19-113 £0.02; V R A Dartnall 12-64 £0.03; Mrs L Wadham 5-47 £0.04.

National Hunt Flat Races

National Hunt Flat Races: 2m to 2m3f

ANALYSIS BY AGE
Age	Prop	Win	Runs	Wins%	£
3yo	0%	1	8	12.5%	0.63
4yo	44%	498	5361	9.3%	-0.28
5yo	42%	471	5349	8.1%	-0.34
6yo	14%	161	2466	6.5%	-0.32
7yo	0%	1	20	5.0%	-0.55
8yo+	0%	0	0	0.0%	0.00

ANALYSIS BY BHB RATING
Age	Prop	Win	Runs	Wins%	£
130..149	0%	1	5	20.0%	0.10
120..129	0%	1	41	2.4%	0.00
110..119	0%	4	76	5.3%	0.36
100..109	0%	2	34	5.9%	-0.07
80..99	0%	0	6	0.0%	-1.00
60..79	0%	0	0	0.0%	0.00
..59	0%	0	0	0.0%	0.00
Unrated	99%	1124	13542	8.3%	-0.32

ANALYSIS BY WEIGHT CARRIED
Age	Prop	Win	Runs	Wins%	£
12-01+	0%	0	0	0.0%	0.00
11-8..12-00	4%	45	254	17.7%	-0.24
11-0..11-07	47%	528	5329	9.9%	-0.26
10-8..10-13	33%	370	4831	7.7%	-0.33
10-0..10-07	16%	181	3049	5.9%	-0.38
..9-13	1%	8	241	3.3%	-0.50

ANALYSIS BY DAYS SINCE LAST RUN
Age	Prop	Win	Runs	Wins%	£
1..7	1%	7	95	7.4%	-0.59
8..14	4%	40	565	7.1%	-0.56
15..28	14%	162	1990	8.1%	-0.36
29..60	17%	196	2175	9.0%	-0.32
61..100	7%	74	868	8.5%	-0.32
101+	14%	153	1898	8.1%	-0.29
Unraced	44%	500	6113	8.2%	-0.27

ANALYSIS BY TODAY'S STARTING PRICE
Age	Prop	Win	Runs	Wins%	£
Odds On	9%	99	196	50.5%	-0.17
Ev-2/1	17%	192	584	32.9%	-0.15
9/4-4/1	30%	334	1448	23.1%	-0.06
9/2-6/1	12%	138	979	14.1%	-0.14
13/2-10/1	14%	164	1831	9.0%	-0.19
11/1-16/1	9%	102	1963	5.2%	-0.22
18/1-33/1	7%	81	3036	2.7%	-0.31
40/1+	2%	22	3667	0.6%	-0.61

ANALYSIS BY STARTING PRICE LAST TIME
Age	Prop	Win	Runs	Wins%	£
Odds On	2%	27	118	22.9%	0.05
Ev-2/1	5%	60	323	18.6%	-0.34
9/4-4/1	12%	137	808	17.0%	-0.03
9/2-6/1	6%	70	571	12.3%	-0.23
13/2-10/1	11%	122	1092	11.2%	-0.18
11/1-16/1	6%	73	1098	6.6%	-0.37
18/1-33/1	9%	102	1759	5.8%	-0.32
40/1+	4%	41	1822	2.3%	-0.65
Unraced	44%	500	6113	8.2%	-0.27

ANALYSIS BY DISTANCE BEATEN LAST TIME
Age	Prop	Win	Runs	Wins%	£
..-10 lgh	2%	26	93	28.0%	0.14
-10..0	11%	120	708	16.9%	-0.05
0.1..2	7%	84	464	18.1%	-0.29
2.1..5	7%	74	524	14.1%	-0.15
5.1..10	9%	102	859	11.9%	-0.20
10.1..20	10%	118	1460	8.1%	-0.37
20.0..30	4%	44	977	4.5%	-0.49
30.1+	5%	56	2325	2.4%	-0.51
Not Compl	1%	8	181	4.4%	-0.04
Unraced	44%	500	6113	8.2%	-0.27

ANALYSIS BY SUCCESS RATE IN LAST 10 RUNS
Age	Prop	Win	Runs	Wins%	£
No Wins	69%	438	6478	6.8%	-0.40
1 Win	27%	173	969	17.9%	0.01
2 Wins	3%	16	130	12.3%	-0.20
3 Wins	1%	4	13	30.8%	-0.09
4 Wins	0%	1	1	100.0%	2.50
5+ Wins	0%	0	0	0.0%	0.00

ANALYSIS BY SUCCESS RATE IN LAST 3 RUNS
Age	Prop	Win	Runs	Wins%	£
No Wins	69%	438	6485	6.8%	-0.40
1 Win	27%	173	975	17.7%	0.01
2 Wins	3%	16	119	13.4%	-0.13
3 Wins	1%	5	12	41.7%	0.28

ANALYSIS BY POSITION LAST TIME
Age	Prop	Win	Runs	Wins%	£
Won	13%	146	800	18.3%	-0.02
2nd or 3rd	19%	216	1538	14.0%	-0.29
Unplaced	23%	262	5075	5.2%	-0.42
Fell,BD,UR	0%	3	40	7.5%	1.88
Pulled Up	0%	1	95	1.1%	-0.86
Ref/RanOut	0%	3	31	9.7%	-0.60
CO/SlipUp	0%	1	12	8.3%	1.83
Unraced	44%	500	6113	8.2%	-0.27

OTHER FACTORS (WINS-RUNS, £)
Course Winner:	37-141	-£0.27
Distance Winner:	114-614	-£0.22
Going Winner:	56-321	-£0.16
Beaten Favourite:	59-354	-£0.28
7-Day Winners:	0-4	-£1.00
Absolute Favourites:	360-1063	-£0.12

TRAINERS (WINS-RUNS, £)
G M Moore 11-78 £0.26; P D Evans 3-26 £0.79; D E Pipe 19-78 £0.26; S Pike 3-14 £1.11; Andrew Turnell 4-26 £0.58; N J Henderson 74-255 £0.05; Miss Rebecca Curtis 10-27 £0.45; J A B Old 6-63 £0.16; P D Niven 5-39 £0.15; Carl Llewellyn 18-107 £0.06; W S Kittow 3-20 £0.20; J J Lambe 6-34 £0.11; Karen McLintock 7-36 £0.09; V R A Dartnall 12-63 £0.05; Mrs L Wadham 5-46 £0.06; S R B Crawford 3-13 £0.21; Gordon Elliott 6-15 £0.07; D W P Arbuthnot 5-30 £0.03; T P Tate 4-28 £0.03;

Race Profiles

National Hunt Flat Races: 2 to 5 runners

M Keighley 4-34 £0.01.

ANALYSIS BY AGE

Age	Prop	Win	Runs	Wins%	£
3yo	0%	0	0	0.0%	0.00
4yo	58%	15	47	31.9%	-0.06
5yo	38%	10	52	19.2%	-0.51
6yo	4%	1	20	5.0%	-0.89
7yo	0%	0	0	0.0%	0.00
8yo	0%	0	0	0.0%	0.00
9yo	0%	0	0	0.0%	0.00
10yo	0%	0	0	0.0%	0.00
11yo	0%	0	0	0.0%	0.00
12yo+	0%	0	0	0.0%	0.00

ANALYSIS BY BHB RATING

Age	Prop	Win	Runs	Wins%	£
150+	0%	0	0	0.0%	0.00
130..149	0%	0	0	0.0%	0.00
120..129	0%	0	0	0.0%	0.00
110..119	0%	0	0	0.0%	0.00
100..109	0%	0	0	0.0%	0.00
80..99	0%	0	0	0.0%	0.00
60..79	0%	0	0	0.0%	0.00
..59	0%	0	0	0.0%	0.00
Unrated	100%	26	119	21.8%	-0.40

ANALYSIS BY WEIGHT CARRIED

Age	Prop	Win	Runs	Wins%	£
12-01+	0%	0	0	0.0%	0.00
11-8..12-00	0%	0	1	0.0%	-1.00
11-0..11-07	35%	9	41	22.0%	-0.50
10-8..10-13	50%	13	50	26.0%	-0.27
10-0..10-07	15%	4	25	16.0%	-0.41
..9-13	0%	0	2	0.0%	-1.00

ANALYSIS BY DAYS SINCE LAST RUN

Age	Prop	Win	Runs	Wins%	£
1..7	0%	0	4	0.0%	-1.00
8..14	8%	2	10	20.0%	-0.67
15..28	23%	6	25	24.0%	-0.45
29..60	12%	3	12	25.0%	-0.32
61..100	0%	0	2	0.0%	-1.00
101+	15%	4	17	23.5%	-0.59
Unraced	42%	11	49	22.4%	-0.19

ANALYSIS BY TODAY'S STARTING PRICE

Age	Prop	Win	Runs	Wins%	£
Odds On	42%	11	14	78.6%	0.11
Ev-2/1	23%	6	18	33.3%	-0.23
9/4-4/1	31%	8	27	29.6%	0.23
9/2-6/1	0%	0	8	0.0%	-1.00
13/2-10/1	4%	1	14	7.1%	-0.36
11/1-16/1	0%	0	20	0.0%	-1.00
18/1-33/1	0%	0	14	0.0%	-1.00
40/1+	0%	0	4	0.0%	-1.00

ANALYSIS BY STARTING PRICE LAST TIME

Age	Prop	Win	Runs	Wins%	£
Odds On	4%	1	1	100.0%	0.13
Ev-2/1	4%	1	1	100.0%	1.25
9/4-4/1	8%	2	9	22.2%	-0.74
9/2-6/1	12%	3	6	50.0%	0.21
13/2-10/1	8%	2	8	25.0%	-0.65
11/1-16/1	8%	2	7	28.6%	-0.43
18/1-33/1	15%	4	23	17.4%	-0.46
40/1+	0%	0	15	0.0%	-1.00
Unraced	42%	11	49	22.4%	-0.19

ANALYSIS BY DISTANCE BEATEN LAST TIME

Age	Prop	Win	Runs	Wins%	£
..-10 lgh	8%	2	2	100.0%	0.13
-10..0	15%	4	7	57.1%	0.26
0.1..2	4%	1	4	25.0%	-0.67
2.1..5	0%	0	1	0.0%	-1.00
5.1..10	15%	4	12	33.3%	-0.14
10.1..20	15%	4	21	19.0%	-0.55
20.0..30	0%	0	5	0.0%	-1.00
30.1+	0%	0	15	0.0%	-1.00
Not Compl	0%	0	3	0.0%	-1.00
Unraced	42%	11	49	22.4%	-0.19

ANALYSIS BY SUCCESS RATE IN LAST 10 RUNS

Age	Prop	Win	Runs	Wins%	£
No Wins	53%	8	58	13.8%	-0.68
1 Win	40%	6	10	60.0%	0.24
2 Wins	7%	1	2	50.0%	-0.44
3 Wins	0%	0	0	0.0%	0.00
4 Wins	0%	0	0	0.0%	0.00
5+ Wins	0%	0	0	0.0%	0.00

ANALYSIS BY SUCCESS RATE IN LAST 3 RUNS

Age	Prop	Win	Runs	Wins%	£
No Wins	53%	8	59	13.6%	-0.69
1 Win	40%	6	10	60.0%	0.24
2 Wins	7%	1	1	100.0%	0.13
3 Wins	0%	0	0	0.0%	0.00

ANALYSIS BY POSITION LAST TIME

Age	Prop	Win	Runs	Wins%	£
Won	23%	6	9	66.7%	0.23
2nd or 3rd	8%	2	17	11.8%	-0.84
Unplaced	27%	7	41	17.1%	-0.55
Fell,BD,UR	0%	0	0	0.0%	0.00
Pulled Up	0%	0	2	0.0%	-1.00
Ref/RanOut	0%	0	1	0.0%	-1.00
CO/SlipUp	0%	0	0	0.0%	0.00
Unraced	42%	11	49	22.4%	-0.19

OTHER FACTORS (WINS-RUNS, £)

Course Winner:	2-4	-£0.36
Distance Winner:	3-7	-£0.38
Going Winner:	1-3	-£0.62
Beaten Favourite:	1-1	£1.25
Absolute Favourites:	15-26	-£0.06

National Hunt Flat Races

National Hunt Flat Races: 6 to 10 runners

ANALYSIS BY AGE
Age	Prop	Win	Runs	Wins%	£
3yo	0%	0	0	0.0%	0.00
4yo	40%	141	1146	12.3%	-0.32
5yo	44%	155	1299	11.9%	-0.29
6yo	15%	54	541	10.0%	-0.36
7yo	0%	0	4	0.0%	-1.00
8yo	0%	0	0	0.0%	0.00
9yo	0%	0	0	0.0%	0.00
10yo	0%	0	0	0.0%	0.00
11yo	0%	0	0	0.0%	0.00
12yo+	0%	0	0	0.0%	0.00

ANALYSIS BY BHB RATING
Age	Prop	Win	Runs	Wins%	£
150+	0%	0	0	0.0%	0.00
130..149	0%	0	0	0.0%	0.00
120..129	0%	0	0	0.0%	0.00
110..119	0%	0	0	0.0%	0.00
100..109	0%	0	0	0.0%	0.00
80..99	0%	0	0	0.0%	0.00
60..79	0%	0	0	0.0%	0.00
..59	0%	0	0	0.0%	0.00
Unrated	100%	350	2990	11.7%	-0.32

ANALYSIS BY WEIGHT CARRIED
Age	Prop	Win	Runs	Wins%	£
12-01+	0%	0	0	0.0%	0.00
11-8..12-00	5%	17	72	23.6%	-0.32
11-0..11-07	47%	163	1135	14.4%	-0.28
10-8..10-13	32%	112	1016	11.0%	-0.29
10-0..10-07	16%	55	714	7.7%	-0.41
..9-13	1%	3	53	5.7%	-0.34

ANALYSIS BY DAYS SINCE LAST RUN
Age	Prop	Win	Runs	Wins%	£
1..7	1%	3	21	14.3%	-0.32
8..14	4%	15	153	9.8%	-0.50
15..28	15%	54	438	12.3%	-0.36
29..60	18%	63	492	12.8%	-0.36
61..100	7%	25	177	14.1%	-0.21
101+	13%	46	419	11.0%	-0.19
Unraced	41%	144	1290	11.2%	-0.32

ANALYSIS BY TODAY'S STARTING PRICE
Age	Prop	Win	Runs	Wins%	£
Odds On	12%	41	90	45.6%	-0.26
Ev-2/1	25%	87	222	39.2%	0.02
9/4-4/1	31%	109	456	23.9%	-0.04
9/2-6/1	11%	38	257	14.8%	-0.10
13/2-10/1	12%	41	425	9.6%	-0.13
11/1-16/1	4%	15	463	3.2%	-0.52
18/1-33/1	5%	17	623	2.7%	-0.36
40/1+	1%	2	454	0.4%	-0.80

ANALYSIS BY STARTING PRICE LAST TIME
Age	Prop	Win	Runs	Wins%	£
Odds On	2%	7	18	38.9%	0.23
Ev-2/1	7%	23	73	31.5%	-0.03
9/4-4/1	12%	41	172	23.8%	0.03
9/2-6/1	7%	26	126	20.6%	-0.25
13/2-10/1	11%	40	263	15.2%	-0.40
11/1-16/1	7%	25	229	10.9%	-0.42
18/1-33/1	8%	29	392	7.4%	-0.21
40/1+	4%	15	427	3.5%	-0.52
Unraced	41%	144	1290	11.2%	-0.32

ANALYSIS BY DISTANCE BEATEN LAST TIME
Age	Prop	Win	Runs	Wins%	£
..-10 lgh	3%	9	20	45.0%	-0.10
-10..0	13%	44	156	28.2%	0.00
0.1..2	7%	23	94	24.5%	-0.21
2.1..5	7%	24	119	20.2%	-0.15
5.1..10	9%	30	183	16.4%	-0.20
10.1..20	13%	47	350	13.4%	-0.32
20.0..30	3%	12	216	5.6%	-0.51
30.1+	5%	17	523	3.3%	-0.37
Not Compl	0%	0	39	0.0%	-1.00
Unraced	41%	144	1290	11.2%	-0.32

ANALYSIS BY SUCCESS RATE IN LAST 10 RUNS
Age	Prop	Win	Runs	Wins%	£
No Wins	70%	144	1480	9.7%	-0.35
1 Win	29%	59	204	28.9%	-0.06
2 Wins	1%	3	15	20.0%	-0.32
3 Wins	0%	0	1	0.0%	-1.00
4 Wins	0%	0	0	0.0%	0.00
5+ Wins	0%	0	0	0.0%	0.00

ANALYSIS BY SUCCESS RATE IN LAST 3 RUNS
Age	Prop	Win	Runs	Wins%	£
No Wins	70%	144	1481	9.7%	-0.35
1 Win	29%	59	204	28.9%	-0.06
2 Wins	1%	3	14	21.4%	-0.28
3 Wins	0%	0	1	0.0%	-1.00

ANALYSIS BY POSITION LAST TIME
Age	Prop	Win	Runs	Wins%	£
Won	15%	53	175	30.3%	0.00
2nd or 3rd	21%	75	336	22.3%	-0.19
Unplaced	22%	78	1150	6.8%	-0.37
Fell,BD,UR	0%	0	4	0.0%	-1.00
Pulled Up	0%	0	23	0.0%	-1.00
Ref/RanOut	0%	0	7	0.0%	-1.00
CO/SlipUp	0%	0	5	0.0%	-1.00
Unraced	41%	144	1290	11.2%	-0.32

OTHER FACTORS (WINS-RUNS, £)
Course Winner:	17-42	-£0.03
Distance Winner:	39-132	-£0.04
Going Winner:	16-72	-£0.29
Beaten Favourite:	16-79	-£0.03
7-Day Winners:	0-1	-£1.00
Absolute Favourites:	132-329	-£0.03

Race Profiles

National Hunt Flat Races: 11 runners or more

ANALYSIS BY AGE

Age	Prop	Win	Runs	Wins%	£
3yo	0%	1	8	12.5%	0.63
4yo	46%	361	4346	8.3%	-0.28
5yo	40%	317	4643	6.8%	-0.35
6yo	14%	108	1951	5.5%	-0.32
7yo	0%	1	16	6.3%	-0.44
8yo+	0%	0	0	0.0%	0.00

ANALYSIS BY BHB RATING

Age	Prop	Win	Runs	Wins%	£
130..149	0%	1	5	20.0%	0.10
120..129	0%	1	41	2.4%	0.00
110..119	1%	4	76	5.3%	0.36
100..109	0%	2	34	5.9%	-0.07
80..99	0%	0	6	0.0%	-1.00
60..79	0%	0	0	0.0%	0.00
..59	0%	0	0	0.0%	0.00
Unrated	99%	780	10802	7.2%	-0.32

ANALYSIS BY WEIGHT CARRIED

Age	Prop	Win	Runs	Wins%	£
11-8..12-00	4%	28	182	15.4%	-0.21
11-0..11-07	47%	368	4257	8.6%	-0.25
10-8..10-13	32%	254	3870	6.6%	-0.34
10-0..10-07	17%	132	2442	5.4%	-0.37
..9-13	1%	6	213	2.8%	-0.57

ANALYSIS BY DAYS SINCE LAST RUN

Age	Prop	Win	Runs	Wins%	£
1..7	1%	4	73	5.5%	-0.66
8..14	3%	24	418	5.7%	-0.58
15..28	13%	105	1578	6.7%	-0.38
29..60	17%	137	1728	7.9%	-0.31
61..100	7%	54	712	7.6%	-0.34
101+	14%	107	1510	7.1%	-0.33
Unraced	45%	357	4945	7.2%	-0.27

ANALYSIS BY TODAY'S STARTING PRICE

Age	Prop	Win	Runs	Wins%	£
Odds On	6%	49	97	50.5%	-0.14
Ev-2/1	14%	112	365	30.7%	-0.21
9/4-4/1	28%	222	1003	22.1%	-0.09
9/2-6/1	13%	106	743	14.3%	-0.13
13/2-10/1	16%	123	1438	8.6%	-0.23
11/1-16/1	12%	91	1537	5.9%	-0.10
18/1-33/1	8%	65	2480	2.6%	-0.30
40/1+	3%	20	3301	0.6%	-0.59

ANALYSIS BY STARTING PRICE LAST TIME

Age	Prop	Win	Runs	Wins%	£
Odds On	2%	19	100	19.0%	0.01
Ev-2/1	5%	40	258	15.5%	-0.41
9/4-4/1	12%	97	642	15.1%	-0.04
9/2-6/1	5%	43	452	9.5%	-0.23
13/2-10/1	11%	85	840	10.1%	-0.09
11/1-16/1	6%	51	890	5.7%	-0.35
18/1-33/1	9%	70	1397	5.0%	-0.37
40/1+	3%	26	1440	1.8%	-0.71
Unraced	45%	357	4945	7.2%	-0.27

ANALYSIS BY DISTANCE BEATEN LAST TIME

Age	Prop	Win	Runs	Wins%	£
..-10 lgh	2%	16	73	21.9%	0.20
-10..0	10%	78	559	14.0%	-0.04
0.1..2	8%	62	371	16.7%	-0.27
2.1..5	7%	52	412	12.6%	-0.15
5.1..10	9%	69	680	10.1%	-0.22
10.1..20	9%	72	1124	6.4%	-0.38
20.0..30	4%	32	773	4.1%	-0.50
30.1+	5%	42	1879	2.2%	-0.56
Not Compl	1%	8	148	5.4%	0.18
Unraced	45%	357	4945	7.2%	-0.27

ANALYSIS BY SUCCESS RATE IN LAST 10 RUNS

Age	Prop	Win	Runs	Wins%	£
No Wins	69%	299	5121	5.8%	-0.42
1 Win	27%	115	772	14.9%	0.04
2 Wins	3%	12	113	10.6%	-0.18
3 Wins	1%	4	12	33.3%	-0.01
4 Wins	0%	1	1	100.0%	2.50
5+ Wins	0%	0	0	0.0%	0.00

ANALYSIS BY SUCCESS RATE IN LAST 3 RUNS

Age	Prop	Win	Runs	Wins%	£
No Wins	69%	299	5126	5.8%	-0.42
1 Win	27%	115	778	14.8%	0.03
2 Wins	3%	12	104	11.5%	-0.11
3 Wins	1%	5	11	45.5%	0.40

ANALYSIS BY POSITION LAST TIME

Age	Prop	Win	Runs	Wins%	£
Won	12%	94	632	14.9%	-0.02
2nd or 3rd	19%	146	1204	12.1%	-0.29
Unplaced	23%	183	4038	4.5%	-0.45
Fell,BD,UR	0%	3	38	7.9%	2.03
Pulled Up	0%	1	74	1.4%	-0.82
Ref/RanOut	0%	3	26	11.5%	-0.52
CO/SlipUp	0%	1	7	14.3%	3.86
Unraced	45%	357	4945	7.2%	-0.27

OTHER FACTORS (WINS-RUNS, £)

Course Winner:	19-98	-£0.33
Distance Winner:	74-480	-£0.25
Going Winner:	41-252	-£0.11
Beaten Favourite:	46-284	-£0.25
7-Day Winners:	0-3	-£1.00
Absolute Favourites:	228-739	-£0.15

TRAINERS (WINS-RUNS, £)

G A Charlton 5-64 £0.15; Miss Rebecca Curtis 7-20 £0.45; Jean-Rene Auvray 3-15 £0.57; A C Whillans 3-40 £0.20; V R A Dartnall 8-47 £0.15; G A Swinbank 38-154 £0.03; Karen McLintock 5-27 £0.14; T P Tate 3-21 £0.18; George Baker 4-28 £0.13; Mrs L Wadham 3-39 £0.09; P R Webber 9-119 £0.03; M Keighley 3-28 £0.09; N J Henderson 53-214 £0.01; P J Hobbs 20-139 £0.00.

National Hunt Flat Races

National Hunt Flat Races: up to 7 days off the track

ANALYSIS BY AGE
Age	Prop	Win	Runs	Wins%	£
3yo	0%	1	8	12.5%	0.63
4yo	52%	270	2301	9.6%	-0.22
5yo	38%	198	2579	7.7%	-0.28
6yo	9%	49	986	5.0%	-0.47
7yo	0%	1	8	12.5%	0.13
8yo	0%	0	0	0.0%	0.00
9yo	0%	0	0	0.0%	0.00
10yo	0%	0	0	0.0%	0.00
11yo	0%	0	0	0.0%	0.00
12yo+	0%	0	0	0.0%	0.00

ANALYSIS BY BHB RATING
Age	Prop	Win	Runs	Wins%	£
150+	0%	0	0	0.0%	0.00
130..149	0%	0	0	0.0%	0.00
120..129	0%	0	0	0.0%	0.00
110..119	0%	0	0	0.0%	0.00
100..109	0%	0	0	0.0%	0.00
80..99	0%	0	0	0.0%	0.00
60..79	0%	0	0	0.0%	0.00
..59	0%	0	0	0.0%	0.00
Unrated	100%	519	6382	8.1%	-0.28

ANALYSIS BY WEIGHT CARRIED
Age	Prop	Win	Runs	Wins%	£
12-01+	0%	0	0	0.0%	0.00
11-8..12-00	0%	1	17	5.9%	-0.78
11-0..11-07	40%	206	2329	8.8%	-0.33
10-8..10-13	38%	198	2368	8.4%	-0.27
10-0..10-07	21%	111	1538	7.2%	-0.19
..9-13	1%	3	130	2.3%	-0.73

ANALYSIS BY DAYS SINCE LAST RUN
Age	Prop	Win	Runs	Wins%	£
1..7	1%	7	98	7.1%	-0.60
8..14	0%	0	0	0.0%	0.00
15..28	0%	0	0	0.0%	0.00
29..60	0%	0	0	0.0%	0.00
61..100	0%	0	0	0.0%	0.00
101+	0%	0	0	0.0%	0.00
Unraced	99%	512	6284	8.1%	-0.28

ANALYSIS BY TODAY'S STARTING PRICE
Age	Prop	Win	Runs	Wins%	£
Odds On	7%	35	65	53.8%	-0.08
Ev-2/1	15%	78	208	37.5%	-0.02
9/4-4/1	30%	154	599	25.7%	0.06
9/2-6/1	14%	71	442	16.1%	-0.01
13/2-10/1	15%	79	830	9.5%	-0.13
11/1-16/1	10%	50	971	5.1%	-0.21
18/1-33/1	8%	43	1599	2.7%	-0.31
40/1+	2%	9	1668	0.5%	-0.60

ANALYSIS BY STARTING PRICE LAST TIME
Age	Prop	Win	Runs	Wins%	£
Odds On	0%	0	1	0.0%	-1.00
Ev-2/1	0%	1	4	25.0%	-0.57
9/4-4/1	0%	1	8	12.5%	-0.13
9/2-6/1	0%	0	1	0.0%	-1.00
13/2-10/1	1%	3	11	27.3%	0.09
11/1-16/1	0%	1	12	8.3%	-0.50
18/1-33/1	0%	0	22	0.0%	-1.00
40/1+	0%	1	39	2.6%	-0.69
Unraced	99%	512	6284	8.1%	-0.28

ANALYSIS BY DISTANCE BEATEN LAST TIME
Age	Prop	Win	Runs	Wins%	£
..-10 lgh	0%	0	0	0.0%	0.00
-10..0	0%	0	4	0.0%	-1.00
0.1..2	0%	0	1	0.0%	-1.00
2.1..5	0%	2	5	40.0%	1.95
5.1..10	0%	1	5	20.0%	-0.25
10.1..20	0%	1	18	5.6%	-0.69
20.0..30	0%	1	3	33.3%	1.00
30.1+	0%	0	38	0.0%	-1.00
Not Compl	0%	2	24	8.3%	-0.64
Unraced	99%	512	6284	8.1%	-0.28

ANALYSIS BY SUCCESS RATE IN LAST 10 RUNS
Age	Prop	Win	Runs	Wins%	£
No Wins	86%	6	91	6.6%	-0.59
1 Win	14%	1	7	14.3%	-0.75
2 Wins	0%	0	0	0.0%	0.00
3 Wins	0%	0	0	0.0%	0.00
4 Wins	0%	0	0	0.0%	0.00
5+ Wins	0%	0	0	0.0%	0.00

ANALYSIS BY SUCCESS RATE IN LAST 3 RUNS
Age	Prop	Win	Runs	Wins%	£
No Wins	86%	6	91	6.6%	-0.59
1 Win	14%	1	7	14.3%	-0.75
2 Wins	0%	0	0	0.0%	0.00
3 Wins	0%	0	0	0.0%	0.00

ANALYSIS BY POSITION LAST TIME
Age	Prop	Win	Runs	Wins%	£
Won	0%	0	4	0.0%	-1.00
2nd or 3rd	0%	2	9	22.2%	-0.08
Unplaced	1%	3	61	4.9%	-0.64
Fell,BD,UR	0%	0	5	0.0%	-1.00
Pulled Up	0%	0	12	0.0%	-1.00
Ref/RanOut	0%	2	5	40.0%	0.75
CO/SlipUp	0%	0	2	0.0%	-1.00
Unraced	99%	512	6284	8.1%	-0.28

OTHER FACTORS (WINS-RUNS, £)
Course Winner:	0-1	-£1.00
Distance Winner:	1-5	-£0.65
Going Winner:	1-3	-£0.42
Beaten Favourite:	0-3	-£1.00
7-Day Winners:	0-4	-£1.00
Absolute Favourites:	145-398	-£0.02

TRAINERS (WINS-RUNS, £)
R H York 3-15 £0.43; P D Niven 4-20 £0.20; P J Hobbs 12-82 £0.04.

Race Profiles

National Hunt Flat Races: 100+ days off the track

ANALYSIS BY AGE

Age	Prop	Win	Runs	Wins%	£
3yo	0%	0	0	0.0%	0.00
4yo	31%	50	600	8.3%	-0.45
5yo	45%	72	841	8.6%	-0.29
6yo	24%	38	507	7.5%	-0.12
7yo	0%	0	4	0.0%	-1.00
8yo	0%	0	0	0.0%	0.00
9yo	0%	0	0	0.0%	0.00
10yo	0%	0	0	0.0%	0.00
11yo	0%	0	0	0.0%	0.00
12yo+	0%	0	0	0.0%	0.00

ANALYSIS BY BHB RATING

Age	Prop	Win	Runs	Wins%	£
150+	0%	0	0	0.0%	0.00
130..149	0%	0	1	0.0%	-1.00
120..129	0%	0	6	0.0%	-1.00
110..119	0%	0	11	0.0%	-1.00
100..109	1%	1	9	11.1%	-0.39
80..99	0%	0	1	0.0%	-1.00
60..79	0%	0	0	0.0%	0.00
..59	0%	0	0	0.0%	0.00
Unrated	99%	159	1924	8.3%	-0.29

ANALYSIS BY WEIGHT CARRIED

Age	Prop	Win	Runs	Wins%	£
12-01+	0%	0	0	0.0%	0.00
11-8..12-00	6%	9	64	14.1%	-0.16
11-0..11-07	59%	95	896	10.6%	-0.17
10-8..10-13	26%	41	649	6.3%	-0.39
10-0..10-07	8%	13	331	3.9%	-0.60
..9-13	1%	2	12	16.7%	2.03

ANALYSIS BY DAYS SINCE LAST RUN

Age	Prop	Win	Runs	Wins%	£
1..7	0%	0	0	0.0%	0.00
8..14	0%	0	0	0.0%	0.00
15..28	0%	0	0	0.0%	0.00
29..60	0%	0	0	0.0%	0.00
61..100	2%	3	6	50.0%	1.01
101+	98%	157	1946	8.1%	-0.30
Unraced	0%	0	0	0.0%	0.00

ANALYSIS BY TODAY'S STARTING PRICE

Age	Prop	Win	Runs	Wins%	£
Odds On	6%	10	23	43.5%	-0.31
Ev-2/1	19%	31	89	34.8%	-0.14
9/4-4/1	24%	39	177	22.0%	-0.14
9/2-6/1	16%	25	143	17.5%	0.06
13/2-10/1	13%	21	273	7.7%	-0.33
11/1-16/1	11%	18	276	6.5%	-0.01
18/1-33/1	8%	12	403	3.0%	-0.24
40/1+	3%	4	568	0.7%	-0.63

ANALYSIS BY STARTING PRICE LAST TIME

Age	Prop	Win	Runs	Wins%	£
Odds On	4%	7	32	21.9%	0.26
Ev-2/1	12%	19	89	21.3%	-0.23
9/4-4/1	18%	28	194	14.4%	-0.28
9/2-6/1	11%	17	159	10.7%	-0.25
13/2-10/1	17%	27	266	10.2%	-0.14
11/1-16/1	13%	20	286	7.0%	-0.29
18/1-33/1	18%	29	452	6.4%	-0.21
40/1+	8%	13	474	2.7%	-0.55
Unraced	0%	0	0	0.0%	0.00

ANALYSIS BY DISTANCE BEATEN LAST TIME

Age	Prop	Win	Runs	Wins%	£
..-10 lgh	4%	7	18	38.9%	0.18
-10..0	14%	22	164	13.4%	-0.38
0.1..2	9%	15	93	16.1%	-0.39
2.1..5	11%	17	116	14.7%	-0.10
5.1..10	12%	19	170	11.2%	-0.37
10.1..20	21%	33	341	9.7%	-0.27
20.0..30	10%	16	252	6.3%	-0.28
30.1+	19%	31	734	4.2%	-0.25
Not Compl	0%	0	64	0.0%	-1.00
Unraced	0%	0	0	0.0%	0.00

ANALYSIS BY SUCCESS RATE IN LAST 10 RUNS

Age	Prop	Win	Runs	Wins%	£
No Wins	72%	115	1688	6.8%	-0.33
1 Win	26%	41	231	17.7%	0.00
2 Wins	2%	3	30	10.0%	-0.80
3 Wins	1%	1	3	33.3%	1.17
4 Wins	0%	0	0	0.0%	0.00
5+ Wins	0%	0	0	0.0%	0.00

ANALYSIS BY SUCCESS RATE IN LAST 3 RUNS

Age	Prop	Win	Runs	Wins%	£
No Wins	72%	115	1692	6.8%	-0.33
1 Win	26%	41	234	17.5%	-0.02
2 Wins	2%	3	24	12.5%	-0.75
3 Wins	1%	1	2	50.0%	2.25

ANALYSIS BY POSITION LAST TIME

Age	Prop	Win	Runs	Wins%	£
Won	18%	29	181	16.0%	-0.32
2nd or 3rd	26%	42	331	12.7%	-0.38
Unplaced	56%	89	1378	6.5%	-0.24
Fell,BD,UR	0%	0	10	0.0%	-1.00
Pulled Up	0%	0	40	0.0%	-1.00
Ref/RanOut	0%	0	11	0.0%	-1.00
CO/SlipUp	0%	0	1	0.0%	-1.00
Unraced	0%	0	0	0.0%	0.00

OTHER FACTORS (WINS-RUNS, £)

Course Winner:	8-33	-£0.16
Distance Winner:	23-151	-£0.32
Going Winner:	14-72	-£0.09
Beaten Favourite:	22-112	£0.10
Absolute Favourites:	52-147	-£0.10